Marriages of Albemarle County

and

Charlottesville, Virginia

1781 - 1929

William L. Norford

Southern Historical Press, Inc.
Greenville, South Carolina

Please direct all correspondence and book orders to:
SOUTHERN HISTORICAL PRESS, Inc.
PO Box 1267
Greenville, SC   29602-1267

Originally printed: Charlottesville, VA. 1956
Copyright 1956 by: William L. Norford
ISBN #978-1-63914-124-1
Printed in the United States of America

Table of Contents

*

PUBLISHER'S NOTE

Both the value and the limitations of this index will be readily apparent to the user. The publishers have attempted simply to reproduce accurately a manuscript as it stands, with all its vagaries of arrangement and spelling. Duplicate entries have been omitted when they are in fact identical, but they have been retained when they show spelling, date, or name variation, even though they obviously refer to the same marriage. Those interested in resolving the inconsistency of duplicate entries, or in verifying any of the marriages recorded in this index, have the materials before them to undertake a search in the Albemarle Court records for the original marriage bond or license. For comments on both the history of the Albemarle marriage records and for some comment on the nature of the errors arising in the process of their arrangement and copying, the reader is referred to two articles in the *Papers of the Albemarle County Historical Society,* in Vol. 6, p. 4-53 and in Vol. 9, p. 42-75.

Albemarle County, Virginia

Marriages of 1781 - 1929

A - Z

A

1781

Allen, John and Jane Tandy, Aug. 15th.
Aldridge, John and Mary Riley, Aug. 4th.

1785

Anderson, Edmund and Jane Lewis, May 18th.

1786

Allen, William and Elizabeth Mahew, April 19th.
Alphin, Zeanlan and Letty Clarkson, June 8th.

1788

Austen, Henry and Nancy Watts, Jan. 2nd.

1789

Appleberry, Abslolm and Nancy Brown, Dec. 24th.

1791

Appleberry, John and Elizabeth Thurmond, March 22nd.
Austin, Samuel and Gatty Catterton Dec. 2nd.

1792

Alexander, Hugh and Polly Bailey, Nov. 8th.

1793

Alexander, William and Betsy Smith, Dec. 12th.

1795

Allen, Richard and Polly Minor, Nov. 17th.
Alexander, John and Jean Alexander, Jan. 2nd.

1798

Allen, Hancock and Elizabeth Davis, Dec. 12th.

1799

Adcock, William and Nancy McGehee, March 3rd.
Austin, William and Edith Dickinson, Dec. 20th.

1801

Allen, Micajah and Elizabeth Boswell, Oct. 21st.
Austin, Samuel and Elizabeth Johnson, Oct. 31st.

1802

Anderson, Jasper and Susanna Cole, Jan. 29th.

1803

Anderson, William and Nancy Farrar, Nov. 25th.
Askew, John and Mary Faris, Dec. 12th.
Alexander, William and Anna Bibbins, Jan. 3rd.
Andrews, Campbell and Sarah McFall, Jan. 23rd.

1806

Ammonet, Thomas and Jane Clarkson, Dec. 11th.

1807

Austin, John and Enina Burrus, Dec. 23rd.
Anderson, Edmund and Fanny Moore, Nov. 31st.
Adams, Thomas and Nancy Goolsby, May 6th.

1808

Anderson, Robert and Maria Shelton, Nov. 8th.

1810

Alexander, Reubin and Sarah Smith, July 23rd.

1812

Austin, Elkanah Davis and Susanna Trevilian, Dec. 1st.

1813

Anderson, William and Elizabeth Ann Leake, June 14th.
Anderson, Edmund and Ann Cole, June 13th.

1815

Austin, Obediah and Sarah W. Birckhead, Jan. 12th.

1816

Amos, John S. and Mary Shiflett, July 31st.
Abell, John L. and Liddy Rolls—
Atkinson, James and Lucy W. Field, Dec. 17th.

1817

Anderson, Nathaniel and Mildred Moon, Dec. 7th.

1819

Anderson, Lewis and Sophia Pettet, Nov. 1st.

1820

Austin, Garnett and Nancy P. Wilkinson, Feb. 6th.

1822

Abell, Caleb S. and Jane Black, Nov. 21st.
Alexander, Joseph and Elizabeth Barksdale, Dec. 12th.
Appling, Austen M. and June W. Johnson, Nov. 7th.

1823

Abell, Joseph W. and Caroline Martin, Sept. 11th.

1824

Alexander, Andrew and Malinda Grayson, April 5th.

1825

Atkins, John and Elizabeth McAllister, Oct. 15th.

1827

Akers, William T. and Mary E. F. Winebarger, Dec. 25th.

1829

Anderson, David and Mary W. Dutch March 25th.

1830

Abney, William A. and Virginia S. Kinsolving, Feb. 20th.

Austin, Renelda W. and M. H. Watts, Feb. 9th.

Alford, Charles and Agnes Langford, Nov. 2nd.

1831

Abell, Richard S. and Emily Martin, Feb. 7th.

Austin, Henry and H. Dickerson, Jan. 26th.

Anderson, Meriwether S. and Lucy S. Harper, June 16th.

Anderson, Meriwether S. and E. M. Leitch, Dec. 22nd.

Adams, Samuel G. and Maria J. Gilmer, Dec. 22nd.

1832

Alexander, James and Rebecca Ann Wills, Dec. 20th.

Alvin, John W. and Eliza Ann Emmerson, Dec. 20th.

Anderson, Dabney M. and Elizabeth S. Barrett, July 5th.

1833

Amos, Robert A. and Judith Taylor, Feb. 4th.

1835

Ancil, Robert and Harriet Boswell, May 12th.

Atkins, Albert A. W. and Mary A. Lindsay, Jan. 5th.

1836

Anderson, Richard G. and S. A. E. Yates, Oct. 26th.

1837

Austen, John T. and Nancy Wilhoit, Jan. 22nd.

Abell, Alex F. and Ann J. McLeord, Dec. 14th.

1838

Allen, William and Sarah A. Humphrey, April 18th.

Austin, Eli and Harriet Wood, Dec. 10th.

1839

Abell, Uriel H. and Lucy A. Brown, Sept. 19th.

1840

Antrim, John T. and Margaret Wayland, June 25th.

Ash, John H. and Frances W. Maupin, Oct. 27th.

1842

Amos, James S. and Mary Ann Pace, Aug. 25th.

1843

Anderson, John B. and Mary E. Norris, May 16th.

Anderson, Gedian and Martha S. Morris, July 5th.

1844

Allen, John R. and Susan Marr, May 2nd.

Abell, Benjamin F. Elizabeth W. Grayson, April 27th.

Anderson, Archibald B. and C. B. Buckner, Sept. 4th.

Alexander, William S. and S. A. Maxwell, Nov. 4th.

Austin, Eli and Harriet Walton, Nov. 16th.

Allen, Orville and Sarah Ann Davis, Dec. 17th.

1845

Arnold, Cornelius and Mary Garland, Jan. 23rd.

Abott, J. Rolls and S. E. Dunkum, July 4th.

Allen, James and Mary F. Starkes, Aug. 5th.

Ancill, Thomas W. and M. H. Moon, Dec. 2nd.

1846

Anderson, John W. and Sarah Jane Rodes, Jan. 2nd.

Ammonett, Benjamin F. and Martha E. Brown, July 14th.

Alexander, James G. and Semary E. Oaks, Aug. 20th.

1848

Ayres W. S. and E. S. Brown, Sept. 6th.

1849

Abell, Caleb and Julia Ann Maupin, April 2d.

Abell, Caleb S. and Mildred C. Lobbin, Sept. 6th.

1850

Anderson, Zebulon M. and Georgianna Saunders, Nov. 28th.

1851

Adams, James A. and Ellen Pace, Oct. 20th.

Anderson, and Crack (Free Negroes) June 25th.

1852

Austin, Henry O. and M. C. Barksdale, May 26th.

1854

Adams, Charles and Ann Vest, Oct. 19th.

Antrim, Charles W. and Sarah S. Brown, Sept. 26th.

1855

Ambroselli, Jo. and Cor. Widderfield, July 22nd.
Ambroselli, Joseph and Carnelia Middifield, July 20th.
Ancell, Jno. E. and Martha M. Herndon, Jan. 7th.
Anall, John S. and Martha M. Hamdon, Jan. 1st.
Anderson, J. N. and H. V. Watson, Nov. 28th.

1856

Abell, Benjamin and L. S. Martin, Oct. 6th.
Abell, Benj. and Sallie S. Martin Oct. 28th.
Abell, Caleb and Maria O. Garland March 3rd.
Abell, Jas. W. and Julia A. Wheeler, Nov. 3rd.

1857

Abell, Caleb and Maria O. Garland, Feb. 18th.
Abell, Joshia W. and Juliand Wheeler, Nov 2nd.

1859

Abell, Theopholus and Eliza Caroline Powers, Jan. 24th.
Abell, Theopkilas and Eliza C. Owens Jan. 25th.
Ambroselli, Jno. B. and A. F. Eubank, Dec. 20th.
Anderson, Joseph W. and Susan W. Morris, Jan. 30th.
Adams, Thompson and Gabriella Goodwin, Jan. 18th.
Ambroselli, John B. and Amelia F. Eubank, Dec. 11th.

1860

Anderson, Edward G. and Jane M. Randolph, Nov. 8th.
Anderson, Peter E. and Lucy A. Hyde, Jan. 18th.
Anderson, P. E. and Lucy A. Hyde, June 18th.
Auchincloss, Henry B. and Mary Cabell, Dec. 4th.

1861

Anderson, Charles K. and Mary B. Rodes, Nov. 5th.
Andrews, John S. and Ore R. Moon, Nov. 22nd.
Andrew, Jno. S. and Ora R. Moon Nov. 28th.
Austin, William T. and Sarah A. Wood, Feb. 2nd.
Austin, Wm. F. and Sarah A. Wood, Feb. 7th.

1862

Allen, Jno. J. and Susan Dudley, March 14th.
Alexander, Jno. and Ella C. Winsbisk, July 10th.
Adams, E. R. and Susan J. Johns, Feb. 4th.

1863

Allen, David W. and Helen T. Ross, Dec. 8th.
Abbott, Wm. R. and Lucy R. Minor, Oct. 7th.
Apperson, Samuel H. and Maria S. Gentry, Dec. 24th.

1864

Austin, Wm. H. H. and Chastean E. S. Wood, Feb. 2nd.
Ames, Chas. B. and Eva Bailey, Oct. 20th.
Ambler, Edward and Mary Ellen Taylor, Dec. 22nd.

1865

Anderson, Jno. R. and Ann C. Woody, Nov. 2nd.
Anderson, John R. and Ann C. Woody, Oct. 30th.

1866

Apperson, James and Ophelia Rivercomb, Nov. 8th.
Apperson, James and Ophelia Rivercomb, Oct. 29th.
Armstrong, John and Sally Clements, Dec. 20th.
Armstrong, Jno. and Sally Clements, Dec. 18th.
Atkins, Jas. H. and Mary A. Webb, Jan. 21st.
Atkins, James H. and Mary Ann Webb, Jan. 20th.

1867

Anderson, Jno. and Caroline Coleman, Jan. 12th.
Angel, Nelson S. and Mary J. Spencer, June 13th.
Armstrong, W. and Cynthia A. Hunter, Aug. 19th.

1868

Attz, John J. and Mary F. Wells, Oct. 6th.

1869

Amiss, J. S. and Sarah A. Mallory, Sept. 23rd.
Arnitt, Wm. A. and Susan M. Moon, Dec. 23rd.

1872

Applebury, D. J. and M. J. Houchens, Dec. 17th.
Antrim, C. W. and Emilie H. Brown, Dec. 12th.

1873

Allen, Robert H. and May R. Carter, Jan. 8th.

1874

Ayres, Geo. C. and Maria E. Payne, May 20th.
Allen, Robt. J. and Alice M. Craddock, Aug. 3rd.
Alexander, Jno. D. and Ella C. Webb, Aug 12th.

1876

Ayres, Wm. C. and Lucie D. Shaler, Jan. 25th.

1877

Alexander, Jas. G. and Edmonia C. Barksdale, Jan. 23rd.
Austin, Wm. G. and Lucy A. Patterson, Feb. 12th.
Allen, Edw. J. and Ann E. Rhodes, Dec. 24th.

1879

Alexander, John H. F. and Mollie E. Baber, Jan. 7th.

Adams, John T. and Bettie A. Thomas, Dec. 17th.

Anderson, Samuel L. and Susan J. Carter, Dec. 13th.

1880

Atkins, Wm. W. and Susan Sprouse, Feb. 14th.

1882

Andrews, Julian M. B. and Edmonia O. Bell, Oct. 25th.

1883

Adams, Patrick Henry and Ann Eliz. Smith, June 14th.

Austin, James W. and Sallie J. Austin, Oct. 18th.

Alexander, Joseph H. and Melinda Jones Dollins, Nov. 28th.

1885

Allin, Martin H. and Lizzie P. Walker, Feb. 26th.

Addison, Arthur D. and Minnie S. Chewning, Aug. 5th.

Armistead, Wm. M. and Helen M. Lewis, Dec. 6th.

1886

Alvis, Geo. H. and Mary W. May, April 28th.

Antrim, H. T. and Jennie A. Smith, Aug. 4th.

Abell, Creed W. and Cornelia A. Rea, Sept. 22nd.

1888

Atkinson, B. W. and C. R. Randolph, Jan. 9th.

Andrew, F. E. and Fanny E. Sutherland, Nov. 30th.

Adams, J. R. and Nettie Martin, Dec. 19th.

1889

Akens, J. W. and M. E. Fatwell, Aug. 14th.

Anderson, L. C. and E. M. Barnette, Oct. 30th.

Anderson, R. H. and R. B. Hughes, Oct. 10th.

1890

Allen, E. B. and Joe E. Wise, June 18th.

Addison, W. E. and Va. C. Harrison, Oct. 22nd.

1891

Anderson, Dan and H. Simpson, Nov. 23rd.

Abell, J. L. and L. L. Porterfield, April 13th.

1892

Avery, H. G. and M. L. Smitherson, Oct. 10th.

1893

Abell, J. E. and M. L. Rea, Oct. 2nd.

Armstrong, Wm. and Ida F. Bashaw, Dec. 22nd.

1894

Austin, Abe and Alice A. Simmons, April 3rd.

Amiss, Jo. E. and Emma J. Baltimore, Aug. 25th.

Amos, A. J. and Ella Harlow, Dec. 8th.

1895

Adams, John and Nancy Gibson, Sept. 25th.

1896

Austin, Alex C. and M. L. Donald, July 7th.

Adams, H. H. and H. M. Harlowe, Sept. 4th.

Anderson, C. W. and M. A. Smith, Nov. 17th.

1897

Amiss, Lewis G. and Ida A. Grubbs, Feb. 17th.

Adams, Berkeley D. and Marie Prunear, Oct. 6th.

Armstrong, E. H. and Cora A. Carroll, Oct. 8th.

1898

Abell, J. C. and M. L. Martin, Dec. 19th.

Anderson, J. B. and E. S. Thomas, April 1st.

1899

Allen, A. J. and S. G. Madison, March 13th.

Amiss, Wm. H. and Maggie V. Rhodes, Jan. 12th.

Atkins, John and Sarah Holly, March 6th.

1900

Anderson, J. W. and Lulie R. Marchant, Sept. 18th.

Allen, Geo. L. and M. M. Brown, Dec. 17th.

Alexander, F. E. and T. R. Fretwell, Dec. 26th.

1901

Andrews, D. G. and Mary Purvis, July 10th.

Armistead, W. B. and H. M. Hughes, July 16th.

1902

Abell, A. P. and Julia A. Ward, Jan. 22nd.

Abell, Benj. C. and Delia S. Clark, April 12th.

Amos, A. J. and Katie Gillispie, Sept. 8th.

1903

Adkins, Wm. and Willie Scruggs, May 4th.

1904

Austin, Eddie B. and Maud A. Davis, March 28th.

Alexander, John I. and Birtha E. Layman, April 27th.

Alexander, C. N. and Maud D. Layman, April 27th.

1905

Alphis, Joseph and Ruby Lillian Edwards, Aug. 22nd.

Armentrout, James William and Mattie Brenice Bruffy, Jan. 16th.
Atkins, A. J. and Sarah E. Scruggs, May 19th.
Austin, Charles B. and Lena P. Mask, Dec. 1st.

1906

Andes, John Kline and Mada Eleanor Norford, Sept. 20th.
Apperson, E. R. and Lula T. Robertson, Dec. 24th.

1907

Adkins, Emmet and Lizzie Edwards, Dec. 22nd.

1908

Abbott, Elisher and Lucy A. Crickerberger, July 2nd.
Argenbright, Cornelius C. G. and Nellie Caldwell, Sept. 3rd.
Allen, Robert L. and Maude R. Scruggs, Nov. 18th.

1909

Allen, Rev. Joseph T. and Annie M. Payne, April 20th.
Alley, Ortho H. and Roberta A. Wood, Oct. 15th.
Armentrout, Alfred and Agnes L. Haeberle, Oct. 25th.

1910

Austin, Lilban and Mandella Hensley, July 3rd.
Ast, Joseph P. and Hattie B. Timberlake, Nov. 15th.
Appirson, John Wm. and Annie E. James, Nov. 30th.

1911

Adams, Robert Edw. L. and Lelia Powell, April 20th.
Anderson, William B. and Lelia M. Critzer, Dec. 7th.
Adcock, John F. and Lula M. Kirby, Dec. 23rd.
Adams, Guy and Myrtie Ballard, Dec. 26th.
Arbogast, Jno. Pall and Essie P. Bruffy, Dec. 31st.

1912

Ash, John F. and Minnie E. Gibson, March 24th.
Anderson, John J. and Sallie A. Johnson, Dec. 17th.

1913

Austin, Clarence A and Emmie F. Garrison, Jan. 9th.
Alexander, Eaerett C. and Lottie A. Wood, March 5th.
Austin, Levi L. and Carry T. Shifflett, Aug. 27th.

1914

Allen, John W. and Ada C. Maupin. Dec. 19th.

Angus, Claude L. and Lillian Reynolds, Jan. 28th.

1915

Arnette, Charles E. and Mrs. Daisy Clements, April 28th.
Anderson, H. H. and Hausie Truslow, Aug. 30th.
Anderson, Thomas Bruce and Mabel Keller Lane, Nov. 18th.

1916

Ayers, John and Nora Dowell, March 20th.
Allen, Patrick H. and Gracie E. Hackett, April 22nd.
Austin, George E. and Ethel F. Shiflett, Dec. 28th.

1917

Allen, John E. and Grace Stooks, Jan. 4th.
Alexander, Frederic M. and Lucille C. Burgess, July 28th.
Anderson, R. D. and Constance Bainbridge, Oct. 20th.
Allen, John L. and Martha R. Boswell, Dec. 3rd.

1918

Anderson, John E. and Bertha N. Gibson, March 6th.

1919

Adams, Cary Lewis and Fannie E. Wade, May 12th.
Ash, Clarence S. and Cora Hatcher, June 15th.
Allen, Robert F. and Flossie Fatwell, Sept. 13th.

1920

Adams, James R. and Daisy Blout Sandridge, May 12th.
Adock, Bennie G. and Zenora Johnson, Aug. 18th.
Abell, Joshua Earl and Amy Bertha Lamb, Nov. 10th.
Abell, Aubrey L. and Lena T. Ragland, Dec. 23rd.

1922

Anderson, James C. and Katherine Syosbane, July 4th.
Abbott, George M. and Romane Ubil, Sept. 19th.
Allen, Charles F. and Minnie E. Napier, Oct. 21st.

1923

Adams, James E. and Mary P. Wade, Feb. 1st.
Alexander, Aston C. and Roberta L. Wood, Feb. 24th.
Adams, Ordway S. and Ruth E. Bedell, Sept. 1st.

1924

Allen, Kidd W. and Rachel V. Via, April 17th.

Andes, Charles C. and Ella F. Batten, Aug. 14th.

Addington, Hobart M. and Maude P. Eppard, Sept. 17th.

Amos, Howard and Sweetie Beasley, Oct. 2nd.

Austin, Lilburn O. and Vera M. Garrison, Oct. 4th.

Allen, Richard D. and Irene Barksdale, Nov. 22nd.

1925

Adcock, Cleveland E. and Mattie L. Harris, May 8th.

Arbogast, Reigart H. and Blanche Biggers, Nov. 29th.

Atkins, Bradford and Vertie Shiflett, April 11th.

Atkins, James A. and Lessie M. Shiflett, June 6th.

1926

Abell, Hugh S. and Ruby S. Hoston, Dec. 20th.

Allen, Lewis P. and Alma Maupin, Dec. 25th.

Allen, Thomas D. and Edna B. Wright, Jan. 13th.

Amos, Andrew J. and Willie M. Amos, Jan. 17th.

Armstrong, Charles A. and Ruth May Manuel, Feb. 1st.

Armstrong, Donald L. and Willie Marie Woodward, Feb. 20th.

Anderson, Charlie C. and Meta S. Dinges, Dec. 18th.

1927

Adams, Kenneth and Sally Moon, Oct. 14th.

Addington, Clyde S. and Bonnie G. Templeton, Oct. 29th.

Allen, Willie C. and Eveline A. Critzer, Sept. 1st.

Armstrong, Norman H. and Vivian E. Hackett, Aug. 4th.

Atkinson, Edward N. and Nellie V. Booz, Oct. 1st.

Austin, Griffith and Alice Long, Feb. 2nd.

1928

Allen, Lewis T. and Merry R. Barksdale, May 24th.

Anderson, John and Margaret Dameron, July 2nd.

1929

Ashby, John T. and Mirian G. Haden, Feb. 27th.

Ashbury, Howard H. and Emilie Caroline Stroham, Nov. 29th.

Arnett, Charles E. and Sally B. Moneymaker, Dec. 27th.

B

1783

Bailey, Elisha and Hannah Gay, Dec. 11th.

Broodhead, Jonathan and Exoney Eastin—

1784

Brown, Elliott and Lucy Shelton, May 25th.

Barksdale, Jonathan and Lucy Rogers, Nov. 11th.

1785

Britt, Obadiah and Sarah Wheeler, Feb. 10th.

Boyd, William and Rebekah Maxwell, April 4th.

Barnett, Charles and Lucy Bowles, Sept. 7th.

Barrett, James and Catharine Maury, Sept. 29th

Breedlove, William and Mary Watts, Oct. 19th.

Burch, Samuel and Mary Kerr, Oct. 16th.

1786

Bailey, John and Elizabeth Britt, Aug. 5th.

Ballord, Richard and Elizabeth—April 26th.

Benge, Cotton and Mary Spenser, April 24th.

Bethel, James and Ann Staton, Dec. 20th.

Bethel, John and Janey Farrar, Oct. 23rd.

Birch, Joseph and Mary Rodes, Nov. 26th.

Bowen, John and Mary Hail, April 13th.

Burch, John and Jane Epperson, Jan. 17th.

Burrus, Charles and Susannah Ballard, Oct. 23rd.

1787

Bacon, William and Nancy Huckstep, Dec. 19th.

Berry, George and Sarah Clark, Dec. 21st.

Booth, George and Elizabeth Shiflet, Dec. 8th.

Bowles, Nathan and Milly Dawson, Dec. 14th.

Bullen, Luke and Judith Abney, March 13th

Burruss, John and Anna Ferguson, March 8th.

Burruss, Walter and Mary Lively, May 1st.

Bryan John and Elizabeth Robinson, March 22nd.

1788

Barksdale, Samuel and Polly Hamner, March 4th.

Bell, Robert and Jean Roberts Richardson, Dec. 18th.

Brown, Brightberry and Luca Thompson, Jan. 2nd.

Burford, William and Sarah Appleberry, Jan. 10th.

1789

Beaber, George and Rachel Dowell, May 30th.

Bell, Roger and Caty Brockman, Dec. 25th.

Boswell, John and Jenny Hinsley, Dec. 23rd.

Breedlove, Richard and Milley Watts, Dec. 23rd.

1790

Ballard, James and Ann Rodes, May 10th.

Bowling, Jonathan and Susannah Wood, Nov. 17th.

Brockman, Samuel and Anna Sims, Jan. 14th.

Busby, James and Elizabeth Shackelford, March 4th.
Butler, Griffen and Martha Bowles, Oct. 24th.

1791

Bailey, Charles and Patience Buster, Jan. 10th.
Blain, Alexander and Ales Blain, Jan. 11th.
Branham, John and Susannah Branham, April 16th.
Breedlove, Martin and Elizabeth Carr, Dec. 19th.
Brown, Travis and Elizabeth Carver, Jan. 8th.
Brumwell, Thomas and Judah Bullin, Oct. 31st.
Broke, Richard and Mary Goin, Jan. 3rd.
Bunger, Nicholas and Susannah Harris, Nov. 2nd.
Burch, Richard and Lucy Barksdale, Aug. 24th.
Burruss, Charles and Jean Owens, Nov. 11th.

1792

Beaver, Jesse and Polly Berry, Dec. 12th.
Bishop, Isaac and Elizabeth Hunter, May 2nd.
Burrus, Thomas and Dicey Cardin, Dec. 17th.

1793

Baber, Killis and Lidia Humphrey, Dec. 3rd.
Barksdale, Samuel and Jemima Wingfield, March 28th.
Battles, Robert and Nancy Bowls, Dec. 12th.
Bowman, Ralph and Mary Irwin, May 9th.
Burgess, William and Margaret Austin, Sept. 3rd.

1794

Bailey, John and Mildred Hall, April 2nd.
Barksdale, Archilles and Ann Shelton, Nov. 11th.
Berry, Jacob and Nancy Kyle, Nov. 27th.
Borden, John and Mary Denton, Nov 25th.
Boswell, William and Marget Marshall, Dec. 31st.
Boulware, Reuben and Mary Bell, Dec. 11th.

1795

Ballard, William and Mary Snow, March 4th.
Breedlove, Cornelius and Jane Beck, Dec. 17th.
Brown, Benjamin and Sarah E. W. Lewis, Nov. 5th.

1796

Blades, John C. and Polly Bibb Key, May 12th.

1797

Britt, Archelus and Elizabeth Britt, Dec. 21st.
Burruss, Nelson and Lucy Duke, Dec. 24th.

1798

Boian, James and Elizabeth Fortune, July 23rd.
Broadus, Richard and Polly Mahone, Feb. 12th.
Brown, Meriwether and Elizabeth Gillaspy, Oct. 1st.
Bryant, Henry and Elizabeth Moon, Jan. 19th.

1799

Boston, James and Nancy Hill, Aug. 8th.

Bullock, Janius and Lucy Dowell, March 11th.

1801

Bailey, Lewis and Lucy Mallory, Nov. 17th.
Bailey, William and Lucy Bailey, May 18th.
Beck, Reuben and Nancy Fitch, Dec. 28th.
Bowman, Gilbert and Sally Elson, Oct. 21st.
Brown, Reuben D. and Lucy T. Brown, Dec. 7th.
Butler, Richard and Catharine Butler, Feb. 20th.

1802

Ballard, James and Fanney German, May 31st.
Becks, Charles and Milley England, March 15th.
Bell, James and Sally Smithson, Oct. 6th.
Brown, Bernard and Mira Maupin, Jan. 18th.
Bryant, David and Polley Crank, Jan. 22nd.

1803

Bailey, William and Kezia Cook, Jan. 2nd.
Bise, John and Elizabeth Grymes, Dec. 29th.
Borden, William and Nancy Nelley, Oct. 28th.
Boswell, Matthew and Nancy Marr, Nov. 23rd.
Branham, James W. and Polly Lewis, April 9th.
Breedlove, Nathan and Elizabeth Burch, Aug. 16th.
Brooks, John and Sally H. Snead, April 19th.
Burks, John and Lucy Price, Dec. 5th.
Burrus, Joshua and Patsy Lively, Dec. 1st.

1804

Bailey, Harry and Judith Thomas, Feb. 13th.
Ballinger, William and Anna Sharp, Oct. 15th.
Barksdale, Nelson and Jane Lewis, Feb. 8th.
Bibb, Minor and Susannah Carr, Nov. 30th.
Broadhead, William and Nancy Carver, Dec. 12th.
Brown, David and Lucy Davis, July 25th.
Brown, Elijah and Patsy Key, Nov. 5th.
Brown, Tarlton and Lucy Dandridge, March 1st.

1805

Bacon, Richard and Judith Bacon, Dec. 10th.
Bailey, James and Nancy Mallery, May 6th.
Banks, Gerald and Ann Davis, Jan. 16th.
Bibb, John and Ann Allen, Dec. 24th.
Ball, John and Susannah Hensley, Dec. 7th.
Biggers, Joshia and Nancy Padgett, Dec. 16th.
Bise, Eleazar and Lucy Homan, Jan. 9th.
Brockman, James and Nancy Harris, Dec. 18th.
Bunch, Dandridge and Jane Jameson, March 11th.
Burruss, Dickerson and Rachel Fraley, Jan. 1st.
Burruss, Jacob and Nancy Thomason, July 16th.
Burruss, Thomas and Rachel Fraley, Jan. 3rd.

1806

Baber, William and Sally Grymes, Jan. 7th.
Broadhead, Thomas and Lucy Carver, Dec. 18th.

Brockman, William and Lucy Brockman, Feb. 5th.

1807

Bailey, James and Betsy Mapie, Nov. 28th.
Ballard, David and Elizabeth Thompson—
Ballew, Soloman and Philadelphia Davis, Aug. 1st.
Bates, Robert and Elizabeth Perry, May 11th.
Bise, John and Elizabeth Jones, Dec. 6th.
Blain, John and Delia Rice, Sept. 11th.
Bradshaw, Gedian and Jarusha Thacker, Feb. 17th.
Brock, John and Nancy Tyree, Jan. 18th.
Brock, William and Milly Tyree, Jan. 5th.
Brown, Thomas H. and Milly Brown, Sept. 30th.
Burrus, Jormer and Polly Thompson, Jan. 9th.
Butler, James and Susan Ropon, Dec. 10th.

1808

Bailey, Merideth and Elizabeth Thacker, May 20th.
Bandhead, Charles S. and Ann C. Randolph, Sept. 19th.
Beazly, Cornelius and Patsy Carr, Oct. 3rd.
Bowler, Marvin and Sally Cook, May 26th.
Brooks, Robert and Elizabeth Hays, April—
Brown, Anderson and Susan Woodson, June 3rd.
Burruss, Dickerson and Sarah Snow, Dec. 27th.
Buster, John and Ela Gillum, March 30th.

1809

Bailey, Merideth and Elizabeth Thacker, Nov. 29th.
Bailey, John and Polly Goodwin, Dec. 7th.
Ballard, William and Sally Jarman, Feb. 6th.
Bashaw, Daniel and Elizabeth Irvin, Dec. 25th.
Bankhead, Charles S. and Ann C. Randolph, 30th.
Black, William and Matilda Rowe, Dec. 21st.
Brown, Beze G. and Elizabeth Michie, Jan. 10th.
Bruce, Daniel and Betsy Wyant, Oct. 30th.
Buckner, Henry and Polly Ballew, Nov. 25th.
Burch, William and Polly Burton, May 25th.

1810

Ballard, Garland and Susan Phillips, May 11th.
Brown, Beverly A. and Sarah Brown, Dec. 29th.
Brown, William W. and Mary Harris, April 21st.

1811

Bacon, James and Martha Bacon, March 6th.
Bailey, William and Lucy Carter, Nov. 5th.
Ballew, John and Ann McCord, Feb. 1st.
Bartly, George and Catharine Kublings, Aug. 5th.
Bates, Roland and Jane Boyd, April 4th.
Beady, Richard and Patsy Johnson, April 9th.
Bennett, John and Elizabeth Dudley, March 7th.

Black, James and Catharine Black, April 2nd.
Bowen, Ephran and Lucy Gillaspie, Dec. 12th.
Boyd, James and Jane Rice, Sept. 2nd.
Boyd, William and Ann Pemberton, May 27th.
Buckner, Archibald and Fanny Durrett, June 18th.
Burks, David J. and Betsy Porter, Dec. 3rd.
Burnly— and Sally Wood, April 4th.

1812

Baker, Joseph and Nancy Moore, Jan. 25th.
Ballard, Wilson and Fanny Austin, Dec. 7th.
Beckett, Bland and Polly Hall, Oct. 12th.
Beedon, James and Elizabeth Dowell, March 17th.
Bernard, Joseph and Sally Thomas, Feb. 10th.
Blairlabell, Edward and Harriet F. Monroe, April 9th.

1813

Barksdale, Hudson C. and Lucinda Head, Sept. 4th.
Barksdale, Hudson and Sally Wood, April 5th.
Barksdale, Nathan and Elizabeth Rogers, Feb. 2nd.
Barley, Ansil and Frances Bailey, Feb. 2nd.
Blaydes, Walker J. and Mary Carr, Feb. 17th.
Brockman, Sims and Patsy Dickinson, Dec. 22nd.
Brown, Charles and Mary Brown, March 31st.
Burton, Thomas and Frances Ballard, June 15th.

1814

Bailey, Joshua and Nancy Day, March 10th.
Baker, Greensberry and Perrlina Wade, Nov. 11th.
Beck, Richard M. and Jemima Rea, Dec. 28th.
Beddow, William and Maria Long, July 18th.
Billups, Thomas and Ann Cleveland, March 21st.
Bolling, John and Ann Wallace, May 2nd.
Boothe, William and Dolly Wingfield, Feb. 21st.
Brown, William and Susannah Fretwell, Jan. 3rd.
Burgess, William and Sally Freeman, Dec. 8th.

1815

Bailey, Temple and Dolly Smith, Nov. 6th.
Brown, Mathew O. and Elizabeth Townly, Aug. 18th.
Burton, James and Catharine Goodridge, May 1st.

1816

Bailey, Daniel Mayo and Lucy Jane Watson, Nov. 4th.
Bailey, Carlton and Malinda Wheeler, Dec. 12th.
Barksdale, John H. and Mary G. Burchhead, July 25th.
Bibb, David and Nancy Worth, Dec. 31st.
Birkhead, Thomas and Mildred Dollins, Dec. 2nd.

Bishop, Samuel and Sarah Via, Feb. 19th.
Browning, Francis and Mildred Dollins, Dec. 12th.
Burks, John and Martha Bragg, May 8th.
Burruss, Henry and Lucy Johnston, Dec. 19th.

1817

Barnett, James and Sophia Hughes, Jan. 16th.
Beaseley, James and Elizabeth L. Mills, Nov. 9th.
Bickett, William and Polley Hundley, Jan. 20th.
Broadhead, Achillis and Mary W. Carr, Nov. 21st.
Brockman, John and Merria Watson, March 3rd.
Brown, Benjamin H. and Judith Fretwell, Dec. 23rd.
Brown, Ira B. and Frances J. Mullins, Feb. 6th.

1818

Baber, William and Elizabeth Baber, Dec. 22nd.
Bimgardner, William and Mildred Durrett, Oct. 14th.
Brooks, James and Susan Speace, Jan. 5th.
Brown, William and Ann Morrison, Sept. 6th.

1819

Bailes, John and Anna Rea, Jan. 7th.
Bernard, Thomas and Catherine Dettor, Oct. 2nd.
Britt, William and Anne Barnett, Oct. 27th.
Bruce, Eli and Nancy Rhoades, March 30th.
Burnley, Seth and Nancy Goodman, March 17th.
Burnsides, John and Polley Dudley, Jan. 14th.
Burton, William and Mary Johnson, June 26th.
Burruss, Walter and Lucy P. Shikell, April 1st.

1820

Bails, John and Anna Rea, Jan. 7th
Bibb, William A. and Sarah Branham, Dec. 20th.
Bishop, John T. and Mary Ann Jeffries, Feb. 11th.
Bowles, Peter F. and Lucy Bowles, Oct. 19th.
Britt, George and Elizabeth Wood, Nov. 9th.
Brown, Edmund and Theodoser Mickie, Nov. 7th.
Beckett, Winston and Ann Browning, Aug. 29th.

1821

Bailey, Samuel and Jane M. Baily, July 2nd.
Baily, Wilson and Nancy Moore, Nov. 15th
Bales, William and Maria Goodman, Sept. 6th.
Barksdale, William G. and Mira Wood, Sept. 6th.
Barksdale, Rice G. and Elizabeth S. White, Nov. 15th.
Battles, Elijah and Nancy Farrar, April 24th.

Battles, Robert Jr. and Mary Farrar, Jan. 1st.
Beddo, Thomas and Lucy Day, Aug. 2nd.
Boyd, John and Mary S. Cobbs, Jan. 1st.
Brown, Elijah and Maria T. Gordon, Sept. 8th.

1822

Baily, Parks and Frances Wheeler, Oct. 16th.
Bagby, Thomas and Catharine Maury, Aug. 13th.
Barnett, James and Nancy Martin, Jan. 30th.
Barnett, William and Susannah Dudly, Feb. 28th.
Bell, John F. and Catherine Bowcoke, June 13th.
Bellamy, Elisha and Polly Carver, Oct. 17th.
Bias, David and Nancy Munday, Oct. 17.
Blackley, Reuben and Patsy Walker, Aug. 5th
Bragg, John and Elizabeth Jones, Feb. 14th.
Brockman, Bluford and Elizabeth Catterton, Dec. 17th.
Brown, Bernice and Patsy M. Garrison, Dec. 23rd.

1823

Barksdale, Nathan and Mary Clarkson, July 8th.
Branham, Johnett and Mary T. Louden, March 11th.
Branham, Lyman and Mary A. Townley, Feb. 6th.
Brockman, Joseph and Sarah Shiflett, April 26th.
Brown, Clifton and Sally J. Brown, Jan. 30th.
Brown, Nelson and Martha Yancey, Oct. 9th.
Bryant, Charles and Polly Snow, March 24th.

1824

Barnett, Charles and Sally Langford, March 3rd.
Bishop, Reuben and Maria Lively, March 2nd.
Black, James and Roseana Merrett, Oct. 11th.
Bowen, James and Jane Martin, Feb. —
Brown, Garland and Patsey Ballard, Sept. 23rd.
Brown, Matthew D. and Adaline Harris, Feb. 19th.
Brown, Mordica and Sarah Shiflett, July 21st.
Browning, William H. Polly Browning, Feb. 25th.

1825

Balthis, George and Sarah Ann Day, Feb. 3rd.
Batten, George and Nancy Perry, Dec. 13th.
Battles, Robert and M. A. R. Butler, April 28th.
Bingham, George and Priscilla Ross, June 8th.
Blain, Samuel and Almira B. Morrison, March 22nd.
Bowen, Reuben and Nancy Drumheller, Dec. 17th.
Brown, Wilson and Lucinda Thurmond, Oct. 12th.

1826

Barrett, Charles and Mildred Gentry, June 12th

Beache, William J. and Sarah Dolson, Aug. 22nd.

Brandes, William and Elizabeth Kinsolving, July 6th.

Branham, Nimrod, Jr. and Sarah A. F. Goss, Nov. 22nd.

Brockman, Robert and Sarah Brockman, Feb. 16th.

Burton, Thomas and Dicey Reynolds, March 10th.

1827

Bailey, Charles and Patsy Shoap, May 14th.

Barksdale, Jonathan and Martha Appleberry, Jan. 16th.

Bishop, John and Lucy Bishop, Jan.—

Bohannon, Thomas J. and Selina Ballard, Dec. 26th.

1828

Bakes, Martin and Martha Ann Shelton, Feb. 20th.

Bartly, Oliver and Maria Riley, May 26th.

Bise, John and Nancy Pleasants, March 4th.

Bowen, William and Peachy Wash, March 19th.

Bryant, Spotswood and Susan Hudson, Oct. 21st.

Burgess, Robert and Amanda Burruss, May 26th.

1829

Baily, Charles W. and Elizabeth A. Coleman, Jan. 30th.

Baily, James H. and Mary C. Harp, Feb. 26th.

Blain, James and Elizabeth Hays, Sept. 3rd.

Bradford, William A. and E. S. M. Clarkson, Feb. 21st.

Brigham, Charles and Mary Jane Day, Sept. 14th.

Brown, Garland and Virginia Beard, Jan. 24th.

Brown, Benely and Mary Ann Sandridge, April 23rd.

Browning, Elisha C. and Martha A. Gentry, Dec. 12th.

Brown, Matthew and Casandia Hall, Nov. 2nd.

Brown, William T. and M. A. M. Jarman, Jan. 5th.

Butler, Addison and Mary Martin, Nov. 2nd.

1830

Ballard, Thomas and Lucy B. Duke, Nov. 18th.

Beck, Jesse and Mary Roathwell, Jan. 2nd.

Bragg, Galbot and E. S. Ragland, Aug. 5th.

Brockman, Thomas and Mary Gillaspy, July 15th.

Brown, George T. and Amanda Brown, Nov. 18th.

1831

Bouliware, Alex and Polly Jackson, Nov. 9th.

Boyers, Alexander and Mary Ann Cooper, May 25th.

Brockman, William and Judith Bailey, Nov. 7th.

Burne, George P. and Eliza H. C. Gray, July 28th.

Burruss, Charles and Agness Keaton, Sept. 5th.

Burton, Hudson and A. M. Garland, Aug. 2nd.

1832

Bankhead, John W. and Elizabeth P. Christian, Nov. 3rd.

Birkhead, Francis and Emily Wood, Jan. 21st.

Bowen, John and Letty Thacker, Oct. 31st.

Brown, John D. and Maria Brady, March 8th.

Butler, Carry and Evelina Gowing, Jan. 24th.

1833

Bailey, Rice and Amanda Wingfield, April 30th.

Bailey, Thomas R. and Ann Eliza Brand, Dec. 24th.

Baker, Noah and Susan Gowing, Sept. 19th.

Barksdale, Achilles M. and Lucy J. Kinsolving, Dec. 25th

Beirne, Andrew Jr. and Eleanor Maria Gray, Dec. 24th.

Bethel, Samuel and Martha Carter, March 14th.

Bethel, Nelson and Mrs. Harriett Drumheller, Jan. 25th.

Bishop, Charles and Mary Ann Jones, July 13th.

Blades, James S. and Francis Harris, May 22nd.

Boatwright, Henry and Posey Moon, Nov. 17th.

Brockman, James and Jane Marshall, June 3rd.

Brown, Nelson and Malinda A. Wheat, Nov. 9th.

Brown, Thomas H. and Lucy Goodman, March 28th.

Bryant, William C. and Mary J. Via, Dec. 19th.

1834

Bailey, Meredith and Mary Dodson, Dec. 29th.

Ballard, John B. and Ann N. Johnson, May 8th.

Bell, William and Oelila Wood, May 2nd.

Bowhware, Walker and Eliza A. Herrin, Dec. 22nd.

Bradford, C. Alexander S. and M. W. Clarkson, Oct. 4th.

Burch, David and Patsy Hurt, May 15th.

Burges, John and Elizabeth Geomnia, July 7th.

1835

Baber, Thomas and Sarah J. McLean, Jan. 26th.

Balsey, Samuel and Eliza Payne, Dec. 21st.

Barcher, Archabald and Martha Hughes, Dec. 22nd.

Beck, Jarrell and Julia A. Breedlove, Jan. 24th.

Bishop, Francis and Lucy J. Kirby, Dec. 30th.

Blackwell, William B. and M. E. Sims, Aug. 13th.

Blain, William W. and Ann M. Turner, Feb. 4th.

Brand, David and S. I. Watson, June 8th.

Britton, Thomas J. and Claripa Garrett, Oct. 16th.

Brown, John G. and Frances B. Rodes, Dec. 8th.

Burnley, William and Emily Baldwin, May 12th.

1836

Ballard, Ira J. and Elizabeth Brown, Oct. 24th.

Beard, Marcus and Catherne Beard, Feb. 17th.

Bibb, William and Sarah J. Hudson, Feb. 1st.

Bobinett, Allen W. and Lucy King, Dec. 30th.

Brockman, Font D. and Lucy Ficklin, Sept. 12th.

Brown, Lewis A. and Isabella Ballard, Nov. 3rd.

Bruffey, Strother and Susan Hurt, March 7th.

1837

Ballard, William J. and Sarah C. Blackwell, Nov. 21st

Beard, John S. and Mary Harp, May 13th.

Beck, Andrew and Sarah Merrett, Jan. 23rd.

Birkhead, William and Mary Peyton, Nov. 15th.

Branham, Anderson and Edith Wood, Feb. 16th.

Bridy, Jese and Milly Field, March 20th

Bruce, Snoden B. and Lina Shiflett, April 30th

Bruce, Souden and Anselina Wood, Jan. 30th.

Burnley, James F. and Ann E. Burnley, April 11th

Burnley, William R. and C. D. Davis, July 20th

Bryant, John H. and P. M. Garland, June 2nd

1838

Ballew, William and Elizabeth Thurston, Dec. 7th.

Barton, Alfred S. and Nancy A. D. Payne, Dec. 24th

Black, James W. and Lucy J. Thurmond, April 2nd

Branham, James M. and Elizabeth Davis, Nov. 26th

1839

Bailey, Woodcliffe and Evetina B. Foster, April 3rd.

Ballard, Thomas M. Sarah A. Via, Dec. 2nd

Ballew, John and Barbara Fisher, Feb. 7th

Becks, William N. and Nancy Golding, April 8th

Blankenburg, C. G. and H. Sugfield, Nov. 14th

Blaydes, Micajah C. and Frances Jeffries, Dec. 11th

Branham, Hyman and Mary E. Clarkson, July 18th

Britt, William and Polly Bruffy, May 22nd

Brockman, Charles J. and Margaret T. Cobbs, Feb. 26th

Brown, Benjamin T. and S. A. M. Richards, Oct. 23rd

Brown, Elijah T. and Ann Wood, Nov. 19th

Brown, William H. and Catharine A. Brown, Oct. 12th

Burnley, Samuel G. and Martha C. Burnley, May 16th

1840

Bailey, John F. and Sarah Wheeler, March 21st

Barnett, Miles and Sarah Martin, Aug. 11th

Barrett, John Y. and Sarah Winn, Sept. 8th

Bass, Robert and Ellen Pace, June 8th

Baxton, Joseph F. and Susan E. Rogers, March 31st

Bennett, Unah P. and Nancy Harper, Jan. 1st

Blake, George S. and A. R. Harlow, Nov. 26th

Boatwright, R. L. and Margaret Bear, July 3rd

Brockenbrough, J. N. and M. E. White, Nov. 11th

Bunch, James and F. E. Hughes, Nov. 12th

Bunch, Reuben and Mary Dudley, March 2nd

Bunch, Reuben F. and Mary Faris, March 24th

Burch, John and Lucinda E. Gay, Jan. 6th

Burkhead, Granville and Lucy Ann Rodes, Jan. 16th

1841

Ballard, John A. and Mary A. Via, Nov. 1st

Barnett, James and Louisa Johnson, Sept. 15th

Bass, John and Jane Pace, Dec. 23rd

Bragg, Joseph and Mildred P. Moon, Jan. 16th

Bragg, Thomas and Catharine S. Gregory, Oct. 2nd

Bruce, Charles and Fanny R. Walton, Aug. 11th

Burnett, Horatio and Elizabeth Stargell, March 7th

Burns, James S. and Margaret Davis, Nov. 22nd

1842

Bailey, John and Sarah Mildred Rothwell, Oct. 6th

Baily, Burwell S. and Sarah Jane Powell, April 4th

Ballard, Willis H. and Eliza Jane Rogers, Nov. 21st

Berrington, Samuel and Martha A. Detter, Aug. 13th

Brown, Edwin B. and Elizabeth M. Thompson, Nov. 7th

Brown, William A. and Julia Ann Elsom, Oct. 20th

1843

Bailey, Charles S. and Elizabeth F. Wood, Feb. 17th

Ballard, William C. and Nancy C. Via, Jan. 2nd

Beazley, John S. and Virginia F. Davis, Dec. 14th

Beck, James R. and Eveline Heron, March 2nd

Bellamy, Reuben W. and Frances Carver, June 27th

Brockman, Fountain D. and Sarah Langhorne, April 5th

Brown, Andrew J. and Betty S. Minor, July 14th

Brown, George E. W. and Lucenthia A. Pettit, Feb. 6th

Brown, Burlington D. and Mary Ann Harris, Jan. 11th

Buford, Albert G. and Mary E. Warwick, March 4th

Burns, Robert H. and Frances E. Blackwell, Sept. 4th

1844

Bailey, Samuel M. and N. C. Drumheller, Nov. 4th

Ball, Stephen and Marinda Broadhead, Jan. 9th

Bates, Edwin J. and Charlotte D. Carr, Dec. 11th

Beard, Thomas E. and Jermel A. Dwandle, Feb. 7th

Belleman, Archelus and Elvira Sprouce, Oct. 3rd

Brent, George W. and Cornelia D. Wood, Dec. 16th

Brown, George B. and H. E. Golding, July 30th

1845

Baber, George E. and M. A. Dunn, Nov. 6th

Barnett, William T. and Lucy Jane Wood, Jan. 14th

Battles, Joseph and Elizabeth A. Pleasants, Dec. 31st

Bowen, John and Susan Tooley, Aug. 12th

Burgess, Charles T. and Elizabeth Hudson, Feb. 13th

Burgess, William J. and Martha Williams, Jan. 23rd

Bryant, Mathew and M. J. Boyd, July 5th

Burton, William C. and M. J. Harris, March 8th

1846

Bacon, Phillip E. and Mary A. Gillette, Sept. 29th

Ballard, Chester and Mary S. Dunkum, June 13th

Barksdale, Orlando B. and Elizabeth E. Austin, Feb. 17th

Barnett, William and Catherine Bishop, Nov. 18th

Baylor, John R. and Anne Bowen, Jan. 5th

Bills, John H. and Lucy A. Wood, Oct. 29th

Brockman, F. D. and Mary A. Terrell, Dec. 16th

Brown, Charles S. and Ann C. Carr, Jan. 14th

Brown, John A. and Columbia E. Brown, Sept. 12th

1847

Beddow, Nathaniel and Sarah A. Marshall, Sept. 2nd

Bethel, William and Ann R. McCue, Jan. 15th

Brockman, Tazewell and Sarah Salmon, Nov. 16th

Brockman, Tandy B. and Jane Simms, Dec. 23rd

Brown, William B. and Elizabeth C. Smith, March 27th

Bunch, David E. and F. A. Dobbs, Jan. 11th

Bunch, Francis and Elizabeth Hart, Jan. 20th

Burnett, Phillo J. and M. J. Moon, May 11th

1848

Beaber, David and M. A. Shaffer, Nov. 2nd

Bishop, Shadwick and Caroline Manly, April 3rd

Boaz, Henry J. and Mary Ann Wood, Oct. 10th

Briggs, G. W. and Mary Wind, June 27th

Brown, John R. and Candess Hall, Oct. 31st

Brown, J. Maury and Cara Harris, May 23rd

Buck, J. J. and M. A. Morris, Aug. 7th

1849

Bailey, James W. and Mary A. Thomas, Nov. 26th

Bates, Poland H. and Susan Wood, Oct. 30th

Batten, William and Elvina Bishop, March 13th

Battles, Frederick and Jane Martin, March 16th

Bing, John and Sophia J. Hudson, Dec. 26th

Bolton, Lindsay C. and Catherine Drumheller, May 23rd

Boon, Jeffrey and Whitehunt, Jan. 16th

Broadhead, Fleming and Mary Clive, Aug. 6th

Brockman, Walter D. and Ann Ferguson, Jan. 4th

Bruffy, Samuel and Anne E. Johnson, Sept. 2nd

Burford, Nelson C. and Sarah E. Farris, March 23rd

1850

Baber, James H. and Sarah J. Powell, July 17th

Barnett, Allen and Susan Barnett, Feb. 4th

Bishop, William and Anne Pace, Jan. 13th

Blaydes, John J. and Mary E. Jeffries, Dec. 6th

Boaz, William D. and Cornelia Harris, May 15th

Bowyer, James T. and Rutha Wood, Jan. 11th

Bragg, James M. and Joana M. Johnson, Dec. 18th

Branden, John A. and Maria C. Harrison, Nov. 12th

Bransford, Owen and Sarah E. Trice, Nov 13th

Brown, Benjamin J. and Margarine E. Garth, Feb. 28th

Brown, George D. and Mary J. Johnson, Feb. 6th

Bruce, Arthur M. and Susan Pitts, May 8th

Bunk, William and Sarah Morris, Sept. 24th

1851

Baber, William R. and Sarah Dollins, Nov. 15th

Barger, Thomas C. and Nancy Carr, Sept. 12th

Barger, Ira H. and Sarah J. Lindsay, Feb. 26th

Barksdale, James S. and Mildred J. Fry, Oct. 5th

Barksdale, Isaac R. and Isaetta L. Hudson, Dec. 10th

Bell, H. H. and M. C. Henderson, Nov. 27th

Bibb, John R. and Lucy J. Foster, April 15th

Bowles, Edward and Mary Farrar, April 30th

Branham, Dana and Elizabeth Johnson, July 21st

Brown, S. W. and Mary E. Mallory, Oct. 2nd

Bruffy, Shopler and Willie A. Morris, March 11th

Bunkum, Thomas G. and Ann E. Lewis, May 17th

Burnley, James H. and Mildred J. Bowcock, Nov. 3rd

1852

Bacon, Richard E. and Rebecca Seay, Jan. 5th

Baker, John T. and Susan A. Omohundro, March 18th

Booker, Samuel J. and S. I. Perkins, Aug. 2nd

Boothe, William and Sarah Lane, Jan. 6th

Branham, John S. and Annie E. Bailey, Nov. 23rd

Bremond, Lewis and Martha Quinne, Nov. 15th

Brown, William T. and Lucy A. Ashlier, Nov. 18th

Bruffy, John and E. B. B. Morris, Dec. 14th

Bunch, Downey A. and Catharine Bruffy, Dec. 2nd

Butler, William J. and Sarah Snow, Aug. 9th

1853

Bailes, William S. and Mary E. McLain, Jan. 20th

Bailey, John P. and Mary May, Aug. 29th

Beddoe, Nashville and Elizabeth A. Gardner, Dec. 15th

Bowie, Walter and Gillie A. Jones, Nov. 3rd

Bowles, Miles and Mary A. Spurs, Nov. 29th

Brown, Benjamin F. and Mary Pritchett, Nov. 13th

Bunch, Anderson H. and Elizabeth J. Dudley, Oct. 18th

1854

Baber, James and Martha Graves, Dec. 24th.

Bankhead, William S. and Elizabeth B. Garth, June 20th

Barnett, David and Jane A. Maupin, Jan. 26th

Beal, Samuel H. and Mary E. Tyler, Dec. 19th

Beck, William and Hardenia P. Terrell, Nov. 28th

Boatwright, John G. and Pattie P. Phillips, May, 25th

Bowen, William and Mary Morris, May 11th

Bowman, Thomas E. and Elizabeth I. Railey, Oct. 24th

Brand, William W. and Elizabeth A. Davis, Jan. 18th

Britt, Lindsay W. and C. M. Wingfield, June 4th

Brockman, James P. and Elizabeth Flynt, Dec. 21st

Buck, David W. and Elizabeth A. Allen, Dec. 24th

Bunton, James M. and Virginia West, Nov. 28th

Bowen, William and May Morris, May 11th

Bowman, Thos. E. and Eliz. J. Railey, Oct. 11th

1855

Bacon, James T. and Susan S. Lewis, Nov. 15th

Bailey, John A. and G. Marshall, May 30th

Battles, William W. and Nancy Farrow, Dec. 18th

Birkhead, Joseph and E. Wood, Nov. 22nd

Birkhead, Nehemiah and Mary Pritchett, Aug. 16th

Birkhead, Samuel and Adeline Durrett, Aug. 25th

Bishop, James and Mildred P. Moseley, Dec. 3rd

Boswell, Washington and S. S. Carrington, June 17th

Bowen, George M. and Eliza M. Bowen, June 30th

Bowles, Miles and Georgianna Cooper, Dec. 22nd

Boyd, Austin P. and Martha J. Alexander, June 19th

Bruce, Henry and Frances Shiflett, Jan. 15th

Bacon, James T. and Susan S. Lewis, March 15th

Bruce, Harry and Frances Shiflett, Jan. 15th

Battles, Wm. W. and Nancy Farrow, Dec. 19th

Bowles, Miles and Georgiania "?", Dec. 24th

Birckhead, Jos. and Elvira Wood, Nov. 28th

Bishop, James and Mildred P. Mosby, Dec. 6th

Barnett, Cl. David and Jane A. Maupin, Jan. 18th

Brand, Wm. W. and Eliz A. Davis, Jan. 26th

Boutwright, Jno. G. and Pattie P. Phillips, May 23rd

1856

Bailey, Henry A. and Jane F. Devinney, March 27th

Barksdale, John H. and Martha C. Dunkum, Nov. 17th

Bellamy, Francis and Henly Sprouse, March 23rd

Blackford, Charles M. and Susan L. Cotston, Feb. 19th

Brown, Abron G. and Sally T. Johnson, Dec. 19th

Brown, Clifton and Elizabeth D. Brown, May 18th

Buck, Fleming N. and Arithelia E. Wheat, Jan. 7th

Bantey, Henry A. and Jane F. Dwinning, March 27th

Brady, Benj. H. and Mary E. Brady, Dec. 28th

1857

Barnett, Anderson and Mary F. Gibson, Jan. 8th

Bibb, William E. and Mollie J. Brown, July 7th

Birkhead, James G. and Elizabeth Jarrell, Dec. 23rd

Bishop, Lewis and Mary A. McRae, March 4th

Buckley, Thomas and Patrick McNamarah, Jan. 10th

Burton, George W. and Carharine H. Brown, Jan. 24th

1858

Baber, Richard S. and Sarah E. Garrison, March 4th

Baber, William and Lizett Critzer, May 3rd

Bailey, Richard and Elizabeth Norris, Aug 28th

Beagle, Theodore F. and Sarah F. Houchens, Nov. 13th

Beaver, Samuel and Martha Lupton, Dec. 23rd

Bishop, Joseph and Fanny M. Grath, Sept. 25th

Bishop, William O. and Nancy Wood, Aug. 9th

Bowyer, David G. and Louisa A. Turpin, Sept. 9th

Bradley, Charles S. and Charlotte A. Saunders, Aug. 11th

Brockman, Birtley and Martha J. Edwards, Jan. 4th

Brown, J. Thompson and Mary M. Southal, April 15th

Bruffy, Samuel and Jane Talley, Aug. 21st

Bush, John D. and Martha C. Taylor, Feb. 24th

Baber, Rich. S. and Sarah E. Garrison, March 11th

Bush, Jno. D. and Martha C. Taylor, Feb. 24th

Birkhead, Jas. G. and Elizabeth Jarrall, Jan. 14th

Baber, Wm. and Lizette Critzer, May 6th

Brown, Jno. T. and Mary M. Southall, April 15th

Brockman, Bully and Martha J. Edwards, Jan. 14th

Bishop, Joseph and Fanny McGoath, Sept. 29th

Bear, Harvey and Frances J. Bear, June 22nd

Bishop, Wm. O. and Nancy Wood, Aug. 12th

Baber, Samuel and Martha Lupton, Dec. 23rd

Braithwaite, Jacob R. and Arabella H. Graves, Dec. 21st

Bailey, Richd. and Elizabeth Norris, Aug. 29th

1859

Baber, John H. and George Eller Garrison, Feb. 17th

Bailes, John T. and Amanda Baber, March 25th

Bailey, George and Cynthia Gillaspie, March 1st

Battles, Noah and Martha J. Farrar, Jan. 19th.

Bishop, Eli W. and Mary F. Burgess, Feb. 14th

Blackwell, James M. and Elizabeth Batton, Jan. 20th

Braton, James D. and Eliza J. Hawkins, July 16th

Broadus, John A. and Charlotte E. Sinclair, Jan. 3rd

Browning, Jonathan and Elvina D. P. Moon, Aug. 1st

Butler, William C. and Mary F. Woods, Dec. 20th

Baber, Jno. H. and George Eller Garrison, Feb. 24th

Battles, Noah and Martha J. Farrar, Jan. 20th

Bishop, Eli W. and Mary F. Burgess, Feb. 17th

Broadus, Jno. A. and Charlotte E. Sinclair, Jan. 4th

Blackwell, Jas. M. and Eliz. Batton, Jan. 25th

Bailes, Jno. T. and Amanda E. Baber, March 29th

Braton, Jas. D. and Eliza J. Hawkins, July 21st

1860

Bowen, Miles and Jane Battles, Aug 1st

Bragg, Robert S. and Ellen J. Haislip, July 21st

Brown, Thomas W. and Martha F. Via, Dec 3rd

Butler, Washington B. and Lucy Wood, July 10th

Brown, Thos. W. and Martha F. Via, Dec. 13th

Bragg, Robert S. and Jane E. Haislip, July 25th

Bowles, Miles and Jane Battles, Aug. 7th

1861

Brown, Wm. G. and Rosila Clarke, Feb. 12th

Breffy, James and Isabella Wingfield, March 10th

Berry, Wm. F. and Lucy J. Madison, March 15th

Butler, W. B. and Lucy Wood, July 3rd

Balloney, Reuben W. and Sarah J. Stevens, April 29th

Berry, William F. and Lucy Jane Madison, Feb. 26th

Birkhead, Richard and Mildred E. Garton, Feb. 22nd

Bowinson, James H. and Semonia G. Martin, Dec. 31st

Boyd, James R. and Semonia G. Martin, Dec. 31st

Brown, Thomas H. and Sallie J. Keyton, July 10th

Brown, William G. and Rosila Clarke, Feb. 1st

Bruffy, James and Isabella Wingfield, March 4th

Bowman, Jas. H. and Lemonia G. Martin, Dec. 31st

1862

Brereton, Richard and Mary Jane Byers, Nov. 20th

Bronough, Francis S. and Nannie P. Carr, Oct. 1st

Bailey, Luther R. and Mary Ellen Crank, July 10th

Brown, Henry J. and Sarah E. Bruffy, Sept. 19th

Brown, Richard and Eliz. Brown, May 24th

Bruffy, Strother and Anne Lane, May 8th

Burton, Hudson and Amanda M. Ward, Oct. 9th

Bailey, Geo. Wm. and Susan M. Garrett, Jan. 15th

1863

Brown, James M. and Mary Nimmo, July 21st

Brigess, Jas. D. and Cornellia F. Wood, June 9th

Byers, D. H. and Matilda J. Salmon, May 28th

1864

Bugg, Samuel S. and Mollie E. Johnson, March 27th

Burgess, Jno. M. and Sarah A. Mayo, March 9th

Blair, Jno. T. and Mattie M. Wade, Jan. 13th

Britt, Wm. and Mourning Bishop, Jan. 2nd

Birkhead, N. F. and Cornelia Cox, Dec. 29th

1865

Bailey, James H. and June A. Reynolds, Dec. 19th

Ballew, John Thomas and Amanda J. Mc-Cauley, April 11th

Bailey, S. W. and Elvira Wingfield, Nov. 5th

Barksdale, R. T. and Clementine Day, Sept. 3rd

Bass, William E. and Mary F. Crenshaw, April 16th

Bocock, N. F. and O. R. Garitt, Jan. 20th

Bowen, George A. and Lucy J. Via, Jan. 26th

Boyd, Charles and Charlotte J. Duncan, Nov. 23rd

Bruce, Arthur M. and Mary A. Johnson, Dec. 18th

Bunton, Clifton G. and Ello Mayo Dec. 28th

Burgess, R. M. and Willie A. Gillispie, July 17th

Busonger, Anthony and Nancy E. Bishop, Jan. 16th

Bailey, James H. and Jane A. Reynolds, Dec. 21st

Bruce, Luther M. and Mary A. Johnson, Dec. 21st

Boyd, Chas. and C. J. Duncan, Nov. 23rd

Burgess, Ro. M. and W. A. Gillaspie, Aug. 8th

Ballew, Jno. T. and A. J. McCauley, Apr. 19th

Bowler, Geo. A. and Lucy M. Via, Jan. 26th

Bowcock, N. F. and O. R. Gautt, Jan. 31st

Busonger, A. and Nancy E. Bishop, Jan. 16th

Brown, Bezl. G. and Nancy Ballard, Nov. 21st

1866

Beckham, James M. and Julia Flannagin, Sept. 4th

Birch, Sylvania A. and Elizabeth W. Manning, Sept. 12th

Bishop, William and Sarah M. Shackelford, Jan. 11th

Blackwell, R. B. and Columbia E. Maupin, April 23rd

Brown, John and Caroline Southal, Oct. 13th

Burton, Addison W. and Susan R. Farrar —

Burnley, W. H. and Emma C. Dyson, July 9th

Burnley, James F. and A. J. B. Vest, Oct. 3rd

Brown, William H. and Nancy Hawkins, April 2nd

Bailey, O. L. and Martha E. Wood, Dec. 20th

Bowman, F. H. and Rosalee P. Benson, Nov. 22nd

Broadhead, Jonathan and Exoney Eastin —

Brown, Chas. B. and Jennie N. Cobbs, Dec. 20th

Bass, Wm. E. and Mary F. Crenshaw, Apr. 19th

Brown, Wm. H. and Nancy Hawkins, April 3rd

Bishop, Wm. and Sarah N. Shackleford, Jan. 11th

Blackwell, R. B. and C. S. Maupin, May 2nd

Burnley, W. H. and Emma C. Dyson, July 17th

Birch, Sylvanur and Eliz. W. Manning, Sept. 13th

Burnley, Jas. F. and Amanda J. B. Vest, Oct. 3rd

Barksdale, Reuben T. and Clementine Day, Sept. 20th

Bickham, Jno. M. and Julia M. Flannagan, Sept. 15th

Bowyer, Geo. J. and Bettie A. Wood, Nov. 12th

Battles, Reuben and Mariah Spennier, Dec. 18th

Brown, Spotwood and Lucy Chatman, Oct. 20th

Biroman, Francis H. and Rosa Lee F. Bensen, Nov. 21st

1867

Bragg, James Y. and Ella V. Fitz, Jan. 24th

Bolton, Hamilton and Susan Alexander, Dec. 24th

Bunch, Wm. R. and Lucy M. Sinco, Nov. 5th

Bryan, J. R. and Marg R. Minor, Feb. 19th

Bailey, S. W. and Elovia L. Wingfield, Mar. 6th

Bruce, Robt. W. and Eliz. M. Wood, Aug. 1st

Barnett, Jas. A. and Rhoda Parish, May 6th

Brown, Jas. W. and Mary J. Wood, Apr. 4th

Blackey, Lewis and Milly Walker, Dec. 17th

Belton, Hamilton and Susan Alexander, Dec. 23rd

Bruce, Robert W. and Eliz. M. Wood, July 27th

Bannister, Wm. and Sally Woodson, Nov. 4th

Berkley, Robert and Susannah Jackson, Dec. 3rd

1868

Baker, Samuel and Louisa McIntire, Jan. 1st
Boyd, Robt. N. and Catilda A. F. Wood, Jan. 6th
Bellamy, John and Mary F. Calvert, Feb. 5th
Bear, Wm. D. and Lucy E. Riley, Feb. 17th
Bailey, Francis M. and Eliz. E. Coleman, Mar. 7th
Brown, R. C. and Rose E. Wood, Mar. 12th
Bridgewater, Wm. N. and Mary P. Bailey, Mar. 30th
Briggs, Willis and Cynthia A. Banks, Apr. 11th
Bryant, James and Cornelia Goings, Apr. 25th
Brown, Ben and Caroline Danbas, May 16th
Bowin, Marian and Mary K. Jarman, July 11th
Brown, Robt. C. and Rose E. Wood, Mar. 19th
Bear, Wm. D. and Lucy E. Riley, Feb. 21st
Beach, Thos. and Isabellaret Stevens, Jan. 16th
Baker, Samuel and Louisia McIntire, Jan. 2nd
Bishop, Adolphur and Ann Watson, Mar. 29th
Bailey, M. G. and Marg. Baber, Mar. 17th
Barnett, Chas. M. and Sarah J. Gibson, Nov. 19th
Brown, Richard T. and S. M. Sandridge, Dec. 15th
Boothe, G. W. and E. M. Johnson, Nov. 17th
Bell, Wm. H. and Catherine V. Brand, Dec. 31st
Bryant, Jerry and Martha Maupin, June 1st

1869

Burgess, Wm. J. and Agnes E. Briggs, Feb. 25th
Baber Wm. and Elizabeth Vest, —
Bibb, James D. and Zestirall A. Woodson, Mar. 16th
Burwell, Josiah and Elizabeth Burnett, Apr. 11th
Branford, Cornelius and Annie Jones, Apr. 1st
Bryand, Albert and Judy Joenson, Mar. 15th
Bryan, Juex and Ang. Emette Dinwiddie, May 24th
Beazley, Simon and Hester B. Whittoen, July 3rd
Brown, John and Synthia Jordan, Aug. 27th
Bailey, Chas. L. and Jane E. Taylor, Oct. 28th
Booker, G. E. and Fanny Eubank, Nov. 9th
Blake, W. N. and Mary S. Moss, Nov. 22nd
Benson, Chas. P. and Nannie Southall, Nov. 30th
Brown, Wm. J. and Martha L. Briggs, Dec. 16th
Burnley, Alex and Sally J. Mozer, Dec. 21st
Bill, Eamuna and Maline A. Scott, —

1870

Burkhead, Edw. and Sally M. Abhurston, Jan. 13th
Binglar, H. A. and M. E. Gates, Jan. 27th
Bowles, J. and Lucy Holmes, Mar. 26th
Balz, Henry and Mary Hartman, Apr. 7th
Beck, Andrew B. and M. M. Browning, Sept. 29th

Bashaw, G. N. and A. E. Melton, Sept. 29th
Brown, Albert and Martha Lewis, Dec. 29th
Barksdale, Jas. J. and Ann L. Tomblin, Feb. 24th

1871

Brown, Thomas and Lydia Thompson, Feb. 4th
Bowen, J. Walter and Martha H. Amner, Feb. 23rd
Barnett, Joshua and Susan A. Dudley, Feb. 27th
Booth, M. L. and Mary S. Dobbins, Mar. 9th
Blackburne, J. S. and Susan B. Taylor, June 27th
Bramham, John W. and Susan J. Jones, July 13th
Bashaw, Wm. S. and Jennie Omohundro, July 19th
Bruce, John and Henrietta Powell, July 23rd
Bunch, Lewis W. and Sarah A. Craddock, July 23rd
Beasley, W. L. and Annie E. Gilham, July 13th
Barnes, Theodore and Alice S. Toole, Sept. 4th
Ballard, Burwell T. and Sarah S. Via, Oct. 15th
Buclett, James B. and Mary Morton Woods, Nov. 9th
Bowman, James S. and Mary E. Hawkins, Nov. 16th
Bragg, James H. and Nannie J. Baber, Nov. 16th
Bunch, John A. and Sarah Eliz. Hughes, Sept. 28th

1872

Birckhead, Thomas and Cary A. Etherton, Jan. 4th
Bishop, Lewis and Eliz. McKnight, Feb. 15th
Bruffey, Wm. and Elizabeth Sprouse, Apr. 1st
Bruffey, Thomas J. and Martha Smith, Oct. 31st
Brooks, George W. and Mary A. Minter, Oct. 13th
Breekin, Alex C. and Martha E. Leitch, Oct. 23rd
Ballard, Ira L. and Martha W. Via, Nov. 11th
Burgess, R. S. and S. M. Geemene, Dec. 17th
Bramham, Nimrod and Fannie C. Carter, July 10th

1873

Bibb, A. P. and M. E. Leitch, Feb. 12th
Brown, E. M. K. and S. R. Tilman, Mar. 24th
Bruce, Loudan and Amanda S. Farrer, July 5th
Becks, John N. and Cornelia Madison, July 24th
Bruffey, Wm. W. and Lucy Hicks, Nov. 4th
Bate, Alex and Julia M. Leeds, Nov. 17th
Brown, Wm. Geo. and Luberuce E. Wood, Nov. 6th
Bronaugh, J. W. and M. D. Minoe, Jan. 16th
Burgess, Jas. A. and Henrietta Gianning, Oct. 25th

1874

Barnett, Ed. and Jane Schackleford, Jan. 1st
Bolton, Chas. S. and Emaline Sutherland, Jan. 27th
Bing, Jno. C. and Susan A. Burrus, Feb. 9th
Bellew, Geo. R. and Mary W. Rice, Feb. 17th
Baber, Henry E. and Lucy R. Rogers, Mar. 31st
Bedden, Jas. N. and Va. M. Marshall, Apr. 1st
Black, Nicholas M. and Gabrilla C. Gentry, May 18th
Baber, Henry E. and Kate Wise, June 8th
Bolton, Benj. and Anne Meeks, June 13th
Brown, Geo. W. and Pocahuntus Mayo, July 2nd
Bingham, Allen W. and Maggie Smith, Aug. 8th
Beddow, Bernard and Columbia L. Bruce, Sept. 5th
Blake, Jacob H. and Ann E. Moore, Oct. 10th
Barbour, Joe and Flora Johnson, Oct. 15th
Burgess, Benj. F. and Bettie Gillespie, Nov. 4th
Birckhead, Thos. M. and Ellen McCauley, Dec. 2nd
Blake, Jno. L. Bettie E. Harlowe, Dec. 24th
Boyd, Jas. H. and Sallie E. Duke, June 20th
Bruffey, Alonza F. and Martha J. Dudley, Jan. 10th

1875

Ballard, Wm. S. and Ida M. Etherton, Jan. 7th
Baltimore, Geo. J. and E. F. Tilman, Mar. 27th
Bruce, Thos. F. and Marg. T. Mahanes, Apr. 5th
Bolton, Jno. H. and Nancy F. Dunn, Nov. 15th
Boykin, Elias M. and Lucy C. Cooke, Nov. 25th
Bragg, Horatio C. Annie S. Spencer, Dec. 13th
Bailey, Jas. T. and Lavenia H. Gilbert, Dec. 18th
Brown, Wm. G. and Bettie C. McAllister, Dec. 22nd
Baker, Chas. and Ann E. Gardner, Dec. 25th
Barnett, Sidney and Annie C. Wheeler, Oct. 11th
Batton, Jno. H. and Nancy F. Dunn, Nov. 15th
Ballard, Willis P. and Sarah L. Powell, Sept. 13th

1876

Boothe, Jno. F. and Kate A. Burgess, Jan. 18th
Bruce, Jno. W. and George Emma Wood, Jan. 24th
Batten, Walker J. and Mary F. Rossen, Feb. 9th
Brown, Willie N. and Ida H. Ashlin, Feb. 17th
Bunch, Wm. W. and Mary J. Dudley, Mar. 6th
Ballew, Jas. A. and Lucy J. Brown, Apr. 17th

Bailey, Jno. H. and Sarah E. Jones, Apr. 17th
Branton, J. P. and Mary J. Gilmore, Apr. 18th
Barnett, Lewis J. and Susan H. Bishop, May 18th
Bishop, David H. and Mildred C. Fielding, July 3rd
Baber, Wm. J. and Cornelia S. Bailey, Oct. 23rd
Burgess, Jas. W. and Emma F. Pleasants, Oct. 28th
Brown, James P. and Lucetta C. Wood, Nov. 13th
Baber, J. W. and Emma S. Eubank, Dec. 9th
Blackwell, Jas. S. and Martha A. Luck, Dec. 23rd
Biggers, Geo. R. and Mary E. Drumright, Jan. 25th

1877

Bruce, Olmon and Virginia C. Sprinkle, Jan. 21st
Black, Samuel and Martha W. Rogers, Feb. 8th
Ballard, Crozett and Molly A. Powell, Mar. 21st
Burgess, Jno. W. and Nancy Pace, Apr. 5th
Baber, Cornelius L. and Martha F. Humphreys, Apr. 13th
Baltimore, Jno. B. and Martha A. Lilly, Apr. 14th
Broadhead, Wm. F. and Betty G. Fray, May 28th
Brown, A. J. and Sallie E. Ross, July 23rd
Boland, John and Sarah Gooch, Oct. 20th
Brent, Wm. E. and Fannie W. Manning, Nov. 12th
Burton, Benj. L. and Margaret J. Humphrey, Nov 1st
Bailey, Wm. H. and Mollie S. Gibson, Nov. 22nd
Brown, Woods G. and Emma B. Wood, Dec. 14th
Blake, Geo. S. and Mary L. Kirby, Dec. 22nd
Bellomy, S. J., and Mary Seccella, Dec. 26th
Brown, Virgil A. and Addie R. Chapman, Oct. 1st

1878

Batton, Wm. D. and Mary E. Dunn, Mar. 4th
Baber, Elisha C. and Julia N. Foster, Mar. 8th
Burnley, Jno. G. and Nella B. Burnley, May 29th
Bishop, A. G. and M. A. Scantling, June 3rd
Blue, John L. and Ida V. Woodson, Aug. 2nd
Bryant, Jas. G. O. and Sally E. Coleman, Dec. 20th
Beattie, Robt. F. and Mildred A. Dolin, June 17th
Bailey, T. W. and Lutie A. Pettit, Oct. 21st
Bailey, James L. and Drucella C. Ward, Nov. 10th
Brooks, John E. and Susannah E. Ward, Dec. 12th

1879

Brown, Jefferson R. and Frances A. Carter, Jan. 4th

Ballard, Andrew C. and Lucy S. Jones, Jan. 20th

Barnett, Robert and Mary A. Garner, Feb. 13th

Brown, Jesse O. and Bettie D. August, Oct. 23rd

Bolton, George F. and Cora C. Garland, Nov. 10th

Bowen, Silas and Mary Alice Ross, Nov. 20th

Burgess, Andrew J. and Sallie E. Dunn, Nov. 29th

Blackwell, Jas. A. and Emily A. Burton, Dec. 15th

Buckanan, H. Littlebery and Mrs. Bettie Buckanan, Dec. 19th

Ballard, Chas. F. and Cornelia E. Jones, Dec. 20th

Bishop, Chas. H. and Sarah F. Ricks, Dec. 22nd

Brown, Samuel P. and Julia D. Carr, Dec. 26th

Bramham, Jas. M. and Annie L. Page, Nov. 13th

Bragg, John F. and Sallie J. Lincon, Dec. 4th

1880

Breeding, Memoah and Ella J. Shifflett, Nov. 9th

Bayby, George N. and C. H. Durham, Nov. 17th

Burford, P. D. and Billie Eubank, June 9th

Butler, Wm. D. and Mary A. Morrison, June 10th

Baber, Jacob F. and Willie H. Baber, Sept. 13th

Breeden, Joel W. and Susan M. Johnson, Nov. 26th

Buckley, Calvin V. and Cora Twyman, Oct. 7th

Bayor, Thomas C. and Mary E. Rothwell, Nov. 18th

Bragg, James R. and Ada H. Mann, Nov. 20th

Bickers, James B. and Eliz. A. Gibson, Dec. 23rd

1881

Bryant, Jack and Julia Brooks, Feb. 3rd

Brown, Wm. P. and Ann Rives, Feb. 28th

Bruce, George and Lucy Mildred Walton, Mar. 16th

Birckhead, James G. and Mary L. E. Marshall, Sept. 8th

Black, Robt. L. and Mollie L. Hoy, Oct. 5th

Burnley, Chas. H. and Lucyle Burnley, Oct. 11th

Brookin, Walter R. and Mollie F. Rothwell, Oct. 31st

Black, Nicholas and Fannie Shepherd, Nov. 7th

Burton, John M. and Ella W. Berry, Nov. 22nd

Bibb, John L. and Ellen Geanni, Dec. 29th

Byumn, Benj. F. and Virginia Atkinson, Dec. 30th

Ballard, Jermiah and Laura S. Ballard, Nov. 23rd

1882

Behrenett, Thos. G. and Mary E. Bonsall, Jan. 26th

Bunch, Reuben G. and Mary W. McKenzie, Mar. 1st

Baber, Henry and Matilda J. Thomas, Mar. 30th

Blackwell, John and Lizzie Miller, Apr. 18th

Baleman, John S. and Frances A. Foster, May 17th

Black, William P. and Sally M. Tyler, May 21st

Barnett, Jas. O. and Mary Ann Marsh, May 25th

Brown, Lucian and Fanny A. Michie, June 19th

Benson, Charles P. and Henrietta G. Budd, Sept. 30th

Brockman, James R. and Molly Wilkerson, Oct. 5th

Brand, Charles N. and Ella B. Goode, Nov. 1st

Bibb, James H. L. B. and Elizabeth J. Wood, Nov. 4th

Bledsoe, John and Lucy M. Carver, Dec. 1st

Berry, Thomas W. and Sevilla Maupin, Dec. 25th

Bagby, George N. and Mary E. Barnett, Dec. 25th

1883

Bradley, George L. F. and Sarah Jane Edwards, Jan. 6th

Brown, Emmett E. and Sukey Mary Brown, Jan. 10th

Behrnett, T. G. and Lizzie H. Marshall, June 29th

Bruffy, Rufus C. and Emma F. Ragland, Sept. 2nd

Bishop, Chas. Edward and Annie E. Beddow, Oct. 4th

Burton, George L. and Alice Mayo, Nov. 4th

Ballard, Andrew C. and Nancy Fry, Nov. 8th

Bunch, James E. and Rosa Lee Dudley, Nov. 8th

1884

Bledso, Geo. W. and Josephine Daniels, Dec. 23rd

Burchans, Robert F. and Lottie F. Marshall, Dec. 26th

Briggs, David K. and Mary J. Barker, Feb. 7th

Bowen, Jas. Wm. and Mary Sipes, Mar. 17th

Baer, Soloman and Lena Lavine, Apr. 2nd

Breeden, Geo. Wash. and Martha Emily McCauley, July 24th

Berry, J. H. and Elizabeth A. Madison, Sept. 16th

Bowler, James H. and Alice B. Bullock, Oct. 11th

Blakey, James and Bessie Bell Boucock, Oct. 21st

Bowyer, Theophiler and Martha J. Gooderryer, Oct. 29th

1885

Bragg, Wm. Benj. and Ellen Baltimore, Apr. 9th

Bunch, Charles E. and Nettie Ann Chisholm, June 25th

Batton, Wesley G. and Cassie J. Gaugh, Sept. 19th

Barnett, Sidney and Katie Mix, Oct. 6th

Broadhead, Fleming and Margaret A. Terrell, Oct. 15th

Brown, Henry Baker and Lizzie C. Garnett, Oct. 13th

Barksdale, Jno. T. and Dolly Ann Gilbert, Oct. 21st

Brooks, Wm. Albert and Sallie B. Powers, Nov. 11th

Bryant, Wm. H. and Sarah L. Goodman, Nov. 12th

Birckhead, Robt. Lee and Lucy West, Nov. 22nd

Buton, Charles and Alice Quarles, Dec. 31st

Bishop, Henry J. and Josephine Lilly, Dec. 31st

1886

Branham, Jno. H. and L. J. Carroll, Jan. 10th

Bishop, John W. and Willie A. Smith, Jan. 18th

Bowyer, Geo. J. and Augusta B. Hecker, Mar. 19th

Baber, Wm. H. and Nancy J. Powell, May 2nd

Ballard, Willis P. and Willie Ann Austin, May 5th

Barnett, Wm. and Sally F. Davis, May 19th

Blair, Archibald and Mary F. Wright, Aug. 1st

Bruce, Samuel E. and Mattie F. Wright, Aug. 5th

Butler, Lee Davis and Florence N. Payne, Sept. 2nd

Bowen, Silas C. and Hetty M. McCauley, Sept. 23rd

Bunch, Thos. B. and Mary L. Glass, Sept. 28th

Brown, R. Julian and Mattie L. Hamner, Dec. 8th

Bruffey, Burnett W. and Ella J. Giddings, Dec. 16th

Brown, Wm. and Maria Kinny, Dec. 25th

Burnett, Henry and Nellie Nelson, Dec. 25th

Bruce, Jas. F. and Alice C. Wood, Aug. 26th

1887

Blackwell, Francis M. and Margaret A. Dudley, Feb. 17th

Burnett, Geo. H. and Annie Walstrum, Mar. 24th

Bussenger, Henry J. and Lucy Ann Sullivan, May 12th

Bowen, Samuel and Susan Shiflett, Aug. 8th

Blackwell, Wm. J. and H. R. Peaco, Sept. 3rd

Brockman, S. W. and Eddie J. Eubank, Nov. 29th

Belew, Robt. T. and Martha A. Belew, Dec. 5th

Batton, Edw. H. and Emma Marshall, Dec. 21st

Brubeck, Wm. D. and Ida V. Hawkins, Mar. 16th

1888

Ballard, Jno. E. and Lucillia Austin, Jan 2nd

Batis, W. K. and W. A. Lewis, Jan. 3rd

Birckhead, Jo. E. and Pinkey Munday, Jan. 11th

Ballard, Ira L. and Dora Brown, Feb. 6th

Bryant, D. P. and Mattie Hudson, Mar. 13th

Bauce, Thos. C. and Lula B. Carter, Mar. 20th

Bulter, Phillip and Mercie B. Lordaree, Apr. 2nd

Bruffy, J. F. and B. L. Martin, Apr. 26th

Blackwell, R. B. and Ada M. Gardner, July 23rd

Belew, J. W. and Nellie J. Layne, Apr. 11th

Bailey, William W. and Sally J. Clements, June 23rd

Ballew, John W. and Sally L. Gardner, Oct. 8th

1889

Brown, Thos. A. and Mollie Melton, May 29th

Barksdale, Claid J. and Ida J. Parr, Sept. 2nd

Burnett, R. M. and Nena B. Dobbins, Dec. 26th

Beck, J. T. and A. L. Birckhead, Mar. 11th

Bruffey, T. R. and N. S. Davis, May 20th

Ballew, C. H. and C. J. Shanks, Nov. 23rd

Birckhead, Richd. and Anna Dowling, Nov. 25th

Buck, W. R. and Annie L. Wallace, Dec. 2nd

1890

Baber, Chas. and Jimmie Hunt, Jan. 20th

Bryan, Ed. and Peachy Munday, Feb. 18th

Branham, A. L. and Ellen M. Cambell, May 30th

Beddow, J. T. and Jdella Mallory, Dec. 24th

Birckhead, William J. and Mary L. Brock, Apr. 22nd

Burruss, R. D. and N. S. Marshall, June 2nd

1891

Blake, G. S. and Lizzie Maupin, Jan. 21st

Brookman, J. C. and N. M. Hall, Feb. 16th

Bishop, C. W. and N. J. Ricks, June 20th

Bruce, R. D. and M. J. Lamb, June 30th

Bishop, Geo. W. and M. L. Burgess, Sept. 14th

Ballew, J. A. and Selina Maupin, Oct. 7th

Bruce, Chas. E. and Ida Shiflett, Nov. 11th

Bibb, H. G. and Maggie Timberlake, Nov. 25th

Bruffy, H. E. and A. F. Lewis, Dec. 29th

Beck, J. M. and W. L. Owens, Jan. 26th

Bryan, E. F. and Hattie B. James, May 11th

Baber, Lee and Dolly A. Parr, Nov. 23rd
Butler, Y. P. and M. A. Blackwell, Dec. 28th
Balew, Charles E. and Addie C. Wood, Dec. 29th

1892

Bragg, G. M. and Emma J. Spincer, Feb. 22nd
Bird, G. B. and M. B. Page, Feb. 29th
Birstin, R. S. and A. G. Carver, Mar. 7th
Bispham, N. C. and M. S. Richard, Apr. 19th
Bell, E. J. and Lula B. Thurston, July 7th
Bruffy, S. L. and Rosa Lee Gay, July 19th
Bowen, Geo. W. and J. H. Griffin, Oct. 19th
Bing, Henry H. and Sally Burrus, Oct. 29th
Bowen, Geo. W. and J. H. Griffin, Oct. 19th
Breeden, J. W. and M. E. Johnson, Nov. 26th
Broocks, A. H. and M. A. Monday, Dec. 5th
Birckhead, F. and Julia Burr, Dec. 21st
Bugg, L. W. and D. A. Wingfield, May 2nd
Birckhead, T. E. and A. B. Wilkerson, July 11th
Beck, Geo. S. and Ida G. West, Sept. 29th
Bryant, Jack and Hen. Davis, Nov. 29th

1893

Beasly, A. F. and F. A. Durdin, Feb. 4th
Bishop, J. C. and C. L. Dudley, Mar. 28th
Barksdale, E. A. and L. H. Barksdale, Apr. 25th
Blackwell, Jerome and Martha A. Bolton, May 1st
Batton, J. N. and Lucy A. Goff, Aug. 10th
Bell, Jas. F. and Lina B. Christian, Dec. 12th
Blencome, F. and A. M. Geiding. Feb. 7th
Ballard, Jno. M. and Nora B. Day, Feb. 25th
Baber, Marvin P. and Nellie W. Eubank, Apr. 4th
Bruce, A. C. and M. A. Dinwiddie, July 18th

1894

Bowman, Louis M. and Clara L. Childs, Feb. 13th
Bass, Ro. and M. J. Wash, Apr. 21st
Butler, J. W. and E. C. Phillips, May 8th
Banks, Robt. and Eliza E. Harris, May 10th
Birckhead, L. and Lula Taylor, May 21st
Blair, Edw. and Susan A. Wood, June 19th
Bibb, G. R. and Clay Minza Lang, Dec. 17th
Barnett, P. L. and L. G. Houchens, Dec. 18th
Bickers, W. and A. P. Thurman, Dec. 22nd
Butler, Wm. H. and Nancie N. Butler, Aug. 1st
Bussenger, G. M. and Fanny Walker, Dec. 1st

1895

Burgess, R. L. and Mettie J. Taylor, Jan. 16th
Blackwell, Eugene and M. Shiflett, Feb. 5th
Bondurant, S. R. and Sally Bocock, Feb. 11th
Bridgewater, M. and F. Creasy, Mar. 13th
Blair, Joseph P. and Susie M. Powers, Apr. 1st
Britton, J. I. and R. T. Bush, Sept. 24th
Brown, Geo. W. and Ida J. Watts, June 19th
Bellamy, Lewis W. and Annie M. Robinson, July 6th

Butler, Wesley H. and Bettie B. Melton, July 30th
Ballard, Jno. and Lutie Herndon, Aug. 30th
Ballard, E. M. and Sally B. Wood, Sept. 6th
Baird, B. H. and L. P. M. Davis, Oct. 2nd
Barksdale, H. S. and A. C. Thacker, Oct. 12th
Butler, Jas. W. and Bettie Thurmond, Nov. 5th
Branzell, Geo. W. and Onie T. Hicks, Dec. 4th
Brockenbrough, J. N. and M. A. Martin, Dec. 12th
Britton, J. L. and R. T. Bush, Sept. 24th

1896

Beddow, W. E. and Bettie E. Morris, Jan. 1st
Byrd, O. W. and A. M. W. Butts, Feb. 25th
Burnett, L. H. and M. E. Dobbin, June 4th
Burgess, G. A. and L. B. Snell, July 14th
Briggs, Leslie Edw. and Va. Kate Cole, July 22nd
Baugher, Chas. W. and Lavina F. Johnson, Aug. 27th
Boone, H. B. and Francesca Brown, Apr. 24th
Baker, W. E. and E. D. Garland, Oct. 13th
Brown, J. Thompson, Jr. and Belle C. Bolton, Nov. 20th
Bell, A. G. and Aunie S. Powers, Nov. 24th
Brown, Tilden and Rosa Bell Scruggs, Nov. 24th
Buck, Wm. W. and Josephine Crawford, Dec. 30th

1897

Blair, A. and S. M. Thurston, Mar. 27th
Beazley, G. W. and Mattie Clements, Apr. 15th
Brenton, R. L. and M. S. Thurston, June 12th
Bales, W. J. and Grace E. Barksdale, June 29th
Burgess, Jno. A. and M. L. Spradling, Oct. 5th
Brooks, W. L. and Frances H. Mallory, Oct. 27th
Burton, Jno. D. and Mary S. Goods, Nov. 2nd
Bradshaw, H. D. and Laura B. Maupin, Nov. 11th
Butler, Claud and Mary L. Morris, Nov. 11th
Barnett, Reuben Jas. and Letitia E. Barnett, Nov. 17th
Barksdale, W. G. and Nannie P. Woods, Dec. 8th
Ballard, J. C. and Ella P. Austin, Dec. 13th
Bowcock, C. S. and Anna G. Early, Dec. 13th
Bellamy, Jas. D. and Carrie E. Gay, Dec. 27th
Benshaw, James O. and Mary Susan Hale, Jan. 9th
Burford, H. W. and Lucy Mallory, Nov. 16th

1898

Burton, H. C. and Mamie Thomas, Jan. 3rd
Barnett, S. D. and Fanny Gibson, Jan. 3rd
Bruce, Richard and Ella Walton, Jan. 4th
Butler, Jas. Cally and Irene Butler, Jan. 20th
Bailey, Newton D. and L. B. Sandridge, Mar. 21st

Burgess, Jno. E. and Mary L. Mayo, Apr. 2nd

Bowles, A. P. and V. C. Lewis, Apr. 19th

Bellew, S. W. and G. H. Humphreys, May 30th

Butler, Henry and Clara Price, June 11th

Brubeck, Jas. A. and Annie M. Yowell, June 14th

Browning, E. C. and Emma E. Rhodes, June 20th

Berryman, W. M. and Dora H. Craddock, July 9th

Butts, C. S. and Fanny N. Moon, July 13th

Brooks, Jas. H. and L. B. Pace, Sept. 6th

Browning, P. C. and Willie M. Warren, Sept. 19th

Bybee, H. W. and Eller A. Scruggs, Oct. 24th

Bowen, James H. and L. L. Thacker, Nov. 9th

Bashaw, E. P. and Anne E. Ward, Nov. 28th

Betters, W. S. and Mamie Loving, Dec. 20th

Burks, W. H. and A. A. Burks, Dec. 27th

1899

Bramham, E. Carter and Rosalie B. Temple, Oct. 31st

Black, Wm. W. and Florence E. Harris, Nov. 6th

Brown, Jas. W. and Wesley Wood, Nov. 21st

Bolton, L. C. and Eliza J. Kirby, Nov. 25th

Bruce, Pierce and B. E. Bales, Nov. 27th

Beck, Jas. J. and Ida M. Dowell, Dec. 22nd

Bing, H. L. and Clara E. Via, Dec. 25th

Bramham, J. O. and Mary H. Dillard, Dec. 26th

Bailey, S. G. and R. V. Mooney, Dec. 27th

Butler, W. P. and C. F. Black, Jan. 5th

Ballard, Vinceint D. and Mattie R. Long, Jan. 30th

Brubeck, Harry A. and Lorena Mayo, Feb. 16th

Ballew, M. J. and L. B. McAuby, Mar. 20th

Birckhead, Littleton and B. A. Harlow, Apr. 27th

Bishop, W. M. and Jas. M. Brown, July 24th

Burnley, Chas. W. and M. A. Worthington, Sept. 14th

Bragg, W. B. and Lizzie Wilkey, Sept. 27th

1900

Bingler, J. E. and A. E. Houston, Jan. 5th

Beddows, Henry B. and Lillie B. Bruce, Feb. 5th

Baily, C. W. and L. M. Sandridge, Feb. 13th

Butter, Jas. W. and Lillie B. Cash, Feb. 28th

Batton, W. T. and M. B. Haney, Mar. 5th

Byer, J. A. and M. E. Norris, Apr. 27th

Brown, M. and M. Gibson, May 12th

Bishop, J. W. and Cora J. Tillman, June 6th

Blackwell, P. A. and V. Shiflett, June 13th

Ball, O. M. and B. Moon, June 15th

Bush, E. J. and Addie L. Smith, June 26th

Baber, E. R. and Mattie S. Smoot, Aug. 16th

Browning, Harry G. and L. H. Sneed, Aug. 27th

Bryant, Jno. and Martha Scott, Sept. 25th

Bishop, Jno. W. and Fannie L. Kirby, Sept. 26th

Balton, L. L. and L. S. Gentry, Sept. 26th

Beddows, L. N. and Fannie E. Marshall, Oct. 16th

Birckhead, Frank and Leah B. McCauley, Oct. 29th

Bragg, Jos. B. and Mary E. Bowen, Nov. 5th

Burford, Tinsley and Lilly C. Mallory, Dec. 11th

Burgess, A. C. and Mittie Maddox, Dec. 11th

Burnett, J. A. and S. F. Dudley, Dec. 24th

Brown, Chas. O. and Lelia G. Harlow, Dec. 26th

Barnett, W. and M. Gibson, Dec. 30th

1901

L. H. Burgess, and N. A. Smith, Jan. 22nd

Birch, C. E. and Lillian D. Clark, Feb. 4th

Balew, E. E. and M. B. Bredsie, Mar 6th

Bingler, L. H. and Tilly Ray, Mar. 19th

Ballard, J. T. and C. B. Brown, April 18th

Bell, Edw. J. and Minnie J. Hall, Apr. 29th

Blair, Jno. and Julia F. Bowles, May 25th

Burgess, Eugene and Perry Eades, Aug. 8th

Batton, Chas. D. and Cora L. Powell, Aug. 31st

Bramham, W. W. and J. E. Goin, Oct. 2nd

Brooks, R. and P. Langhorne, Nov. 7th

Bishop, D. W. and Ada A. Gay, Nov. 12th

Brown, Chas. P. and Mrs. Maud Via, Nov. 23rd

Bargamin, Rus. and H. M. Wayland, Dec. 17th

Beard, Wm. A. and Maggie B. Wood, Dec. 18th

Bowen, M. Jarman and Mary E. Maupin, Dec. 18th

Birckhead, Charlie and Rena Herndon, Dec. 20th

Buston, Richard L. and E. E. Mawyer, Dec. 23rd

1902

Barnett, C. L. and E. Doswell, Jan. 23rd

Bishop, Rives and Mollie Tate, Feb. 6th

Burnley, C. D. and M. B. Wood, Mar. 3rd

Bowen, Chas. and B. M. Crickenberger, Mar. 5th

Buzly, Henry L. and Bessie B. Brown, Apr. 14th

Baptist, H. L. and M. E. Boyle, Apr. 19th

Burton, Thos. E. and Sally T. Ellinger, May 15th

Brent, W. M. and M. E. Rogers, June 18th

Bruce, Geo. W. and Blanch'Raynor, June 19th

Bugg, Samuel L. and Willie A. Maxwell, July 31st

Birckhead, Frank and Nannie Pritchett, Aug. 14th

Barks, Robt. P. and Eliz. L. Moore, Aug. 18th

Birckhead, W. J. and Nancy Clatterbuck, Aug. 26th

Brown, D. H. and L. R. Shackleford, Sept. 23rd

Bailey, J. H. and V. T. Milton, Sept.   27th
Bramham, Wm. W. and Emma J. Carroll, Oct. 29th
Bragg, Jas. A. and Hethe M. Bowen, Oct. 30th
Bishop, Edw. H. and Lillie D. Davis, Dec. 26th
Baunney, J. L. V. and M. L. Masters, Dec. 19th
Blake, C. E. and E. E. Cobbins, Dec. 22nd
Bevill, H. W. and A. G. Shepherd, Dec. 20th

1903

Bunton, Geo. F. and P. H. Ellinger, Jan. 13th
Barnett, Jno. and Lottie Sprouse, Jan. 17th
Baxter, C. R. and A. Hutchinson, Feb. 2nd
Baber, J. F. and L. M. Pugh, Feb. 14th
Birckhead, Wm. Edw. and Annie Marsh, Feb. 14th
Boyne, Geo. and Estiech, Via, Mar. 13th
Brown, Samuel and F. L. McDowell, Mar. 20th
Beach, Ray and Bessie King, Mar. 31st
Barlow, Wm. Henry and Helen Kate Worthington, April 14th
Brown, G. D. and E. M. Smith, Apr. 22nd
Bishop, J. H. and S. A. Morris, July 24th
Bibb, G. R. and F. P. Wingfield, Oct. 12th
Bering, F. C. and K. C. Landram, Oct. 20th
Burch, L. H. and A. M. Sutherland, Oct. 21st
Bruce, Horace and Lillie Baber, Dec. 12th
Butler, Perry H. and Martha J. Nuckles, Dec. 21st
Barr, Worth and Mrs. Iza Gosnell, Nov. 28th
Barr, Worth and Mrs. Iza Gosnell, Nov. 24th

1904

Birkhead, Wm. Everton and Hattie Pearl Crenshaw, Jan. 2nd
Barnett, Henry Thos. and Ruth Ann Gibson, Jan 5th
Black, Ernest Linwood, and Annie L. Howard, Jan. 20th
Brice, Otis Henry and Ethel Birckhead, Jan. 20th
Beckhan, Paul W. and Maude Hamner, June 7th
Brasie, Newton E. and Jane Lewis Perkins, Aug. 15th
Biggs, Henry W. and Lucy C. Baber, Oct. 19th
Beal, J. T. and A. D. Graves, Oct. 19th
Bryant, Wm. T. and Daisey Tisdale, Nov. 16th
Bugg, Ross Linwood, and Lucy Isabell Turner, Dec. 7th
Brown, T. A. and Winnie Amiss, Dec. 16th
Bailey, C. B. and Mary E. Taylor, Dec. 24th
Burks, Samuel M. and M. S. Craig, Dec. 24th

1905

Broun, M. Howard and Lelia C. Phillips, Feb. 2nd
Birckhead, Luther Allen and Fanny Mays, Feb. 16th
Brooks, Andrew Harris and Minnie Jane Durham, Feb. 16th
Barksdale, Jas. W. and Rosa M. Black, Mar. 2nd

Black, Robt. L. and Lottie Lee Robertson, Mar. 18th
Bibb, Chas. Massey and Martha Va. Baltimore, Apr. 26th
Bishop, Lee and Victoria Robinson, June 5th
Best, Maulesly R. and Fannie L. Morris, July 24th
Barnett, Lauman L. and Sarah Eliz. Bruffey, July 26th
Bunch, Jesse Lee and Mary Alice Hurt, Jan. 9th
Bruce, Jno. L. and Fannie S. Maupin, Sept. 23rd
Balew, Wm. E. and Lizzie Bragg, Oct. 5th
Branzell, Geo. Wm. Wash. and Mamie Gooch, Nov. 17th
Batton, Lewis and Lelia Wood, Dec. 23rd
Barnett, James Oscar and Carrie Lee Bruffey, Dec. 30th
Bowen, Harry Moore and Charlotte Stevens Goodloe, Dec. 30th
Burton, Mathew Farice and Emily Jane Drumheller, Dec. 26th
Bunch, Jesse Lee and Mary Alice Hurt, Jan. 11th
Balew, William E. and Lizzie Bragg, Oct. 5th
Brice, John L. and Fannie S. Maupin, Sept. 23rd
Burton, Mathew Fariee and Emily Jane Drumheller, Dec. 26th

1906

Brokenborough, T. W. and Alberta Farrar, Feb. 7th
Bethel, James T. and Essie M. Chisholm, Jan. 26th
Bishop, Andrew and Nellie Barnett, Jan. 9th
Batton, Jesse Davis and Martha Garver, June 15th
Barrett, Bernard and Clara B. Sprouse, Aug. 29th
Blackwell, Wilmer C. and Pauline C. Blackwell, Aug. 29th
Brown, James W. and Emma Brown, Aug. 25th
Boyne, Thomas L. and Mildred Via, Sept. 19th
Baltimore, G. J. and Luetta McDaniel, Oct. 31st
Breen, Andrew C. and Selina J. Clements, Oct. 31st
Balew, K. F. and Pearl A. Thomas, Dec. 19th
Breeden, W. M. and S. S. Evans, Dec. 12th
Birckhead, Thomas E. and Lena E. Marsh, Dec. 26th

1907

Beach, James P. and Gracie Hughes, Jan. 14th
Bishop, James R. and Mrs. Henrietta Rhodes, Jan. 8th
Brown, Russel L. and Julia N. Elsom, Feb. 15th
Burton, John H. and Mary V. Burton, June 26th
Bolton, L. L. and F. E. Harlan, May 22nd

Breeden, J. W. and Emma Shiflett, Aug. 20th

Bowden, E. B. and Ella N. Faris, Oct. 16th

Blake, H. H. and Sallie Ramsey, Oct. 16th

Birdisell, John D. and Blanche E. Radford, Oct. 7th

Begg, Robert B. H. and Addah Mann, Sept. 5th

Briant, S. F. and Mary Moore, Oct. 31st

Batten, Willie T. and Minnie R. Garver, Dec. 25th

Batton, Emmett H. and Ida Haney, Dec. 22nd

Bass, C. P. and A. I. Gutuonith, Dec. 31st

Bowen, James W. and Adelia B. Spes, Dec. 29th

Bunch, L. W. and Mirtie Chandler, Dec. 25th

1908

Bruce, Robt. and Mollie Bedows, Jan. 15th

Bragg, Charlie W. and Lillie F. Carver, Jan. 15th

Branham, Joseph Meade and Mary E. Gragg, Jan. 1st

Brooks, Andrew H. and Martha E. Clements, March 10th

Browning, T. M. and F. M. Goolsby, Feb. 24th

Barnett, Samuel D. and Emily L. Hicks, Feb. 5th

Bowman, John R. and Cornelia Winstar Clark, May 14th

Bruce, Robert L. and Fanny E. Young, May 13th

Bibb, Lewis A. and Mattie A. Via, July 1st

Bishop, George and Kansas Munday, June 17th

Brown, Henry B. and Nannie A. Rea, June 17th

Blair, Archibald E. and Estelle W. Dawson, June 3rd

Brown, James R. and Lillie M. Smith, Aug. 12th

Branham, Alexander L. and Margaret A. Fisher, July 24th

Bryan, William Minor and Henrietta K. White, Nov. 4th

Barnett, Oscar and Bettie Ruth Rhodes, Nov. 12th

Becker, Fred and Sallie M. Sinclair, Sept. 10th

Baughan, Maxcy and Eleanor P. Yowell, Dec. 31st

Barrett, Ernest C. and Willie B. Ship, Dec. 24th

Bass, John W. and Beulah E. Burgess, Jan. 1st

1909

Barnett, Thomas and Lizzie Street, March 24th

Bailey, Alvin and Gussie E. Proffit, March 9th

Black, Charles E. and Maud M. Sutherland, March 3rd

Brodt, Calvin and Lena Carson, April 24th

Balew, Woodridge and Georgia Gibson, July 22nd

Breedon, Harry and Myrtie Walton, Oct. 6th

Birch, Chas. W. and Mazie Bunch, Dec. 8th

Bayley, Warfield B. and Sallie J. Michie, Dec. 28th

Baltimore, Jesse R. and Nora Taylor, Dec. 27th

Baltimore, J. W. and M. M. Starks, Dec. 23rd

1910

Bunch, John E. and Gealie E. Birch, Feb. 15th

Bell, Edgar M. and Minnie A. Clarke, Feb. 10th

Brooks, Harrison and Josephine Minter, Feb. 10th

Brown, Thomas H. and Mary Jane Horde, Jan. 15th

Barnett, Warwick and Maude Gibson, March 30th

Branham, Lee A. and Mattie Cox, July 4th

Barnett, William H. and Agatha E. Martin, July 7th

Bumpass, Henry C. and Sadie B. Mahanes, Oct. 24th

Blundon, Robert J. and Eunice S. Campbell, Sept. 21st

Burke, Charles A. and Mary L. Durrett, Dec. 14th

Bussinger, Thomas J. and Mary R. Tinsley, Dec. 27th

1911

Broodhead, Harry J. and Ellen E. Kinber, Jan. 18th

Branham, Selden and Hattie Marrs, June 20th

Backers, Chas. Bedford and Marion Patricia Hensledwood, Aug. 21st

Blackwell, Ellis L. and Reecy Proffitt, Aug. 9th

Batten, Henry F. and Fannie Lee Coleman, July 27th

Beale, Bryon S. and Roxa Landes, Oct. 2nd

Black, Jr., Samuel and Lola Cox, Sept. 13th

Birckhead, Dabney O. and Uppie M. Morris, Nov. 8th

Bibb, James Henry W. and Mary E. Eades, Nov. 7th

Bliss, Joel Z. and Cora L. Batton, Nov. 6th

Bacon, Leland S. and Claudie A. Thacker, Oct. 21st

Bryan, Thomas Lee and Eva Bramham, Oct. 18th

Baber, Hitdra and Effie Kennedy, Dec. 29th

Brown, Arthur and May Atkins, Dec. 25th

Bennett, Charlie W. and Mattie J. Sullivan, Dec. 21st

1912

Bing, Charles E. and Sallie V. Ferneyhaugh, Feb. 14th

Banks, Robert and Addie Cornett, Jan. 27th

Baber, Frank and Edna O. Martin, April 24th

Birckhead, Samuel and Callie A. Woodson, April 3rd

Banks, Robet H. and Hallie B. Rothwell, June 26th

Bagby, John W. and A. Gladys Drumheller, Sept. 11th

Butler, Jack and Mrs. Sophia Edwards, Aug. 13th

Butler, J. C. and Bettie Patterson, July 29th

Beddows, Frank and Cora Huff, July 7th

Birckhead, Noah T. and Annie W. Estes, Oct. 7th

Bunch, Ellis and Annie B. Martin, Sept. 22nd

Balsley, May and Edna Parr, Sept. 7th

Barksdale, William I. and Gertrude Kennedy, Dec. 4th

Baird, John W. and Hattie Kirby, Oct. 22nd

Bishop, Willie and Bessie Pritchett, Dec. 24th

Brookman, Richard and Bettie Colvin, Dec. 25th

1913

Biggers, Hunter T. and Elsie Walker, March 13th

Brown, Victor H. and Nellie Boltwood, April 20th

Buntly, J. B. and Elsie A. Nicholas, June 7th

Bickers, George E. and Eva L. Bethel, May 24th

Bishop, John T. and Rosa Melton, Sept. 3rd

Banton, William and Martha May, Aug. 13th

Buck, James E. and Ruth S. Pace, July 3rd

Burton, George G. and Iva Eads, Sept. 3rd

Blackwell, Artenus and Rosa L. Birckhead, Dec. 1st

Blake, Walter L. and Hattie M. Bishop, Nov. 27th

Burton, H. B. and W. B. Gallaher, Oct. 31st

Baber, Andy and Rosie Deane Toms, Oct. 29th

Brooks, John G. and Lula P. Howard, Dec. 23rd

1914

Baber, Hunter C. and Annie Barnett, Jan. 19th

Black, D. N. and Sadie Dollins, Feb. 9th

Black, Will and Hettie Robinson, May 11th

Beagle, Walter J. and Mrs. Cora Garrison, May 5th

Bowcock, John O. and Alice D. Kline, April 21st

Bagby, T. J. and Margaret Kelley, July 2nd

Bibb, Ernest L. and Ethel Gay, June 23rd

Busenger, John W. and Hettie M. Bowen, Sept 1st

Beard, B. O. and Montie Wood, Aug. 31st

Barksdale, Jessie and Nina Bolling, Aug. 19th

Bruce, Harry C. and Virginia Walton, July 18th

Bishop, Sidney Thomas and Mary Eliza Moon, Oct. 27th

Bass, Reuben B. and Marie P. Brown, Oct. 15th

Bradley, Emmett C. and Mary C. Woodson, Oct. 7th

Ballowe, Sidney and Mrs. Lillian Davis, Sept. 23rd

Batton, John E. and Florence J. Walton, Sept. 19th

Bailey, Josh and Anita Hancock, Nov. 25th

Baber, Harry Wilson and Lucy Viola Craig, Dec. 7th

Beck, A. B. and Norma Turel, Dec. 30th

Butler, Guy V. and Mabel Boatwright, Dec. 24th

1915

Blair, Edward G. and Mary Golden, Feb. 1st

Bishop, Litt and Maggie Lee Sprouse, Feb. 8th

Balew, Lacy H. and Cora B. Henry, Feb. 17th

Bishop, Joseph and Iola Bellomy, Feb. 24th

Berthe, Frank R. and Mabel G. Morris, May 10th

Bass, Obediah and Alva M. Harris, May 12th

Beck, Robt. S. and Florence Beggers, July 14th

Burton, John I. and Grace Woodson, Aug. 14th

Bryant, Joseph N. and Eunice C. Coffney, Aug. 27th

Branham, Everett, and Nellie Biard, Oct. 19th

Butler, Charlie S. and Lena B. Phillips, Oct. 28th

Bryant, William and Lillian Clement, Nov. 6th

Ballard, John and Davis Gentry, Nov. 25th

Batten, Allen and Sadie Via, Nov. 26th

Baker, Chas. and M. Dillard, Dec. 9th

Bryant, William and Sally Harris, Dec. 12th

1916

Brown, Robert and Mary Jones, Jan. 1st

Burnett, Aome and Elsie Ferris, Jan. 12th

Bellomy, Eainley and Leola Ruth Adams, Jan. 31st

Blickwell, Ernest A. and Annie Sandridge, Feb. 3rd

Brown, Thomas and Rosa Kesterson, Mar. 22nd

Bragg, Herbert and Edna Pearl Davis, May 1st

Bolick, Geo. A. and Olivia K. Bledsoe, Apr. 19th

Bledsoe, William G. and Pearl Stubbs, Apr. 26th

Ballard, Brady P. and Elsie F. Jones, June 6th

Balew, H. L. and L. M. Critzer, June 14th

Bibb, Branch and Mary Chisholm, June 28th

Bailey, Woodruff and Carrie Lee Parnell, July 3rd

Byer, Bower Baxton and Vertie Viola Ponton, Aug. 23rd

Breeden, Zebb and Ethel B. Gibson, Oct. 14th

Bishop, Diggs Edward and Dora Belle Allen, Dec. 6th

Baiten, Otis D. and Ethel G. Coleman, Dec. 27th

1917

Bateman, John S. and Mrs. Lelia Gentry, Jan. 7th

Birckhead, Andrew J. and Willie E. Shepherd, Jan. 6th

Bibb, George R. and Rosa Lee Phillips, Feb. 3rd

Blew, Clarence and Mary E. McDonnell, Feb. 7th

Beasley, Mason Lee and Mary Lois Burton, Mar. 30th

Boyd, John M. and Sidney F. Vaugh, Mar. 19th

Baber, Ernest and Annio B. Mawyer, June 3rd

Bobst, Joseph and Nina Wood, July 3rd

Bishop, John R. and Riva E. Hawkins, July 28th

Bouz, William H. and Velna C. Merrifield, Aug. 21st

Boissian, Ray S. and Alma M. Hamner, Sept. 12th

Branham, Battle and Maude Pritchett, Sept. 24th

Battle, Henry and Florence Ragland, Nov. 6th

Burnley, Dewey W. and Sarah E. Parrish, Nov. 22nd

Batton, Jas. Henry and Maude E. Batton, Nov. 28th

Burrus, Willie W. and Virginia A. Wood, Dec. 13th

Bibb, Elmo B. and Bettie G. Butler, Dec. 22nd

Bowen, Walter and Evy Dodd, Dec. 25th

1918

Butler, Calvin S. and Mamie L. Cranwell, Feb. 9th

Boatwright, James W. and Alma P. Thomas, Feb. 26th

Branham, Robert and Eva Estell Baird, Mar. 22nd

Branford, Lawrence C. and Minnie L. Tapscott, May 4th

Bragg, Thos. H. and Lillian Robinson, May 25th

Baker, Benj. Chas. and Louisa N. Higginson, June 4th

Boland, Jas. W. and Lucy Fernyhough, Aug. 12th

Barnett, Richard and Ethel Garrison, Sept. 28th

Blackwell, Amherst L. and Vertie Doughty, Nov. 9th

1919

Berry, Willis F. and Gracie S. Craddock, Feb. 12th

Brown, James F. and Katie Kesterson, May 4th

Batton, Geo. W. and Delia Emory Batton, May 15th

Beddow, Frank and Fannie Cox, Mar. 29th

Bean, Edgar W. and Mary S. Bernwanger, Jan. 16th

Brown, Daniel R. and Mary Hall McCue, June 16th

Blackwell, Elmer F. and Susie E. Fisher, June 17th

Branzell, Geo. W. and Viola Sepe, July 10th

Briggs, Loyd A. and Doris H. Easton, Aug. 27th

Brown, Eugene P. and Margaret B. Nottingham, Sept. 11th

Britton, Stuart L. and Margaret Thurck Morton, Sept. 12th

Busby, Robert and Emma Harlow, Sept. 30th

Brown, John and Isabel Minter, Dec. 25th

1920

Butler, Elias A. and Mary K. Payne, Jan. 21st

Breeden, Ernest R. and Virginia E. Eades, Mar. 27th

Bailey, Eugene F. and Annie A. Morris, Mar. 30th

Bennett, James A. and Grace B. Vaden, Apr. 27th

Bunch, Horace N. and Alma N. Norris, May 18th

Burnett, Aubrey H. and Mary G. Durrer, June 2nd

Blake, Gilliam D. and Antonetta L. Johnson, June 26th

Baylor, Winsore C. and Sallie Morris, July 5th

Burgess, Willie and Rosebud Moyer, Aug. 1st

Bond, Edward R. and Estelle May Mitchell, Aug. 28th

Bruce, Creed F. and Mrs. Reva Dotson, Sept. 1st

Bugg, Samuel Leroy and Mrs. Georgia Hackett, Sept. 11th

Brooks, James H. and Lydia Morris, Sept. 14th

Birkhead, Lyn A. and Eva L. Leake, Sept. 27th

Barnes, Paul Alfred and Mary Hazel Dovel, Oct. 5th

Brown, Willie E. and Edna M. Giannie, Oct. 9th

Bing, Robert J. R. and Mary Helen Famer, Oct. 20th

Branzell, Branch H. and Florence E. Berry, Nov. 7th

Brochu, Urbian J. and Mattie M. Butler, Dec. 25th

Batten, Robt. F. and Carrie Garrison, Dec. 28th

1921

Bradshaw, Herbert G. and Lola R. Goolsby, Jan. 2nd

Ballard, John Weslie and Alice Pearl Gentry, Mar. 12th

Bishop, Willard and Ella I. Rhodes, June 19th

Bolick, Andrew Henkle and Ethel Pearl Detamore, June 21st

Bedden, James E. and Carrie L. Breedon, July 5th

Bingler, Richard H. and Emma G. Durham, July 30th

Benton, Roland and Hattie Dudley, Aug. 22nd

Breeden, Lewis and Addie Harlow, Nov. 8th

Buttner, Ernest F. and Mary Elizabeth Johnson, Nov. 16th

Brown, Edward and Lena Wood, Dec. 21st

Bovchure, Lewis and Katherine S. Snow, Dec. 27th

Beck, W. J. and Mary Goodman, Dec. 31st

1922

Bibb, Chas. A. and Dapleru Allen, Apr. 18th
Berry, Ernest T. and Virgie E. Driges, Apr. 15th
Baber, Fred T. and Agnes M. Jones, Aug. 2nd
Branham, James and Lula Green, Aug. 22nd
Barnett, Isaac L. and Lottie M. Wyant, Aug. 30th
Boatwright, Jr., Sam and Dorothy Harris, Oct. 31st
Borchin, Louis and Eva Martin, Nov. 13th
Bryant, George M. and Susan M. Moon, Nov. 22nd
Bagby, John W. and Sallie Ann Payne, Dec. 7th
Breeden, Elmer and Mattie Clements, Dec. 25th

1923

Batten, Jimmie and Elsie Garrison, Jan. 17th
Blincoe, Harold and Rena Marrs, Feb. 3rd
Brown, Geo. W. and Almer Adcock, Feb. 25th
Belew, William F. and Helen Parr, Apr. 7th
Bishop, Donald O. and Nora Scantling, May 5th
Barnette, Jessie and Myrtle Barnette, May 7th
Bruce, Julian and Lillie Mahoney, May 31st
Black, John W. and Pearl Brockenbrough, June 6th
Beasley, John L. and Francis W. Jarman, June 27th
Barnett, Robert and Mary E. Barnett, July 2nd
Burn, Joseph and Mary E. Davis, July 9th
Beck, Frank B. and Annie G. Thomas, Aug. 27th
Batten, Irving M. and Lessie G. Garrison, Oct. 2nd
Barksdale, Lewis O. and Alma V. Martin, Oct. 8th
Biggers, Arthur H. and Ruth Wood, Oct. 10th
Brown, Clarence and Winnie Farish, Oct. 10th
Burton, Hebson E. and Lillian Marsh, Nov. 8th
Beal, Willie S. and Ethel R. Faulconer, Dec. 20th
Bruce, Enoch and Mamie E. Keyton, Dec. 30th

1924

Bingham, Samuel and Iowa Sarah Smith, Jan. 2nd
Bruce, Lester W. and Annie Shiflett, Jan. 10th
Baber, Deane W. and Clara Toms, May 20th
Barnhart, Nat. G. and Katie E. Rea, Sept. 3rd
Black, Benjamin L. and Florence V. Dawson, Sept. 11th
Belew, Manis J. and Margaret L. McNeill, Oct. 4th
Brooking, Chas. T. and Vertina E. Bledsoe, Oct. 25th
Baltimore, Harry B. and Rosa L. Armstead, Dec. 24th
Bethel, Samuel P. and Susie F. Carter, Dec. 27th

1925

Burnley, George H. and Elsie Kelley, Feb. 16th
Baber, Charles M. and Sarah Harris, Apr. 3rd
Breeden, Joe and Mary Shaver, Apr. 9th
Brown, Obed O. and Maude B. Wheeler, June 12th
Barnett, Emmett and Jessie M. Goddin, June 24th
Blackwell, Allie and Joosie V. Turner, July 6th
Black, John W. and Mollie E. Tilman, Aug. 13th
Bailey, Claude J. and Catherine E. Duff, Oct. 23rd
Bishop, Stanley and Emma Johnson, Nov. 16th
Brightberry, Shepherd M. and Lucy E. Walsh, Dec. 23rd
Butler, Basil P. and Gladys C. Barden, Dec. 24th
Burton, Henry B. and Mary R. Craig, Dec. 26th

1926

Balser, Robt. L. and Nicie D. Thurston, Jan. 9th
Brown, Chas. Roy and Salone A. Deane, Feb. 3rd
Bussinger, Curtice L. and Maggie Birckhead, May 10th
Burton, Walker and Sadie Pylls, May 29th
Bing, Herbert R. and Gladys L. Dickerson, May 23rd
Branham, Percy C. and Virginia L. Boatwright, July 7th
Bell, George C. and Elizabeth M. Hayman, July 9th
Burgess, Clarence and Josie Lang, July 23rd
Birckhead, Edward R. and Rena Alice Parr, Aug. 18th
Boocock, Laurence and Lila May Blandey, Sept. 20th
Bingler, Eugene C. and Lilly May Durham, Sept. 30th
Bolling, Jr., Bartlett, and Eudora Sampson, Nov. 17th
Brooks, Alvin N. and Hallie L. Jones, Dec. 21st
Butler, John L. P. and Mazie D. Dudley, Dec. 28th
Britts, Jesse J. and May Mahanes, Dec. 28th

1927

Bramen, John W. and Cora Lee Martin, Jan. 8th
Bruce, Walter S. and Clara B. Trainham, Jan. 22nd
Banten, Theodore R. and Myrtle Dudley, Jan. 22nd
Bruce, Horace B. D. and Catherine McAllister, Mar. 7th
Batten, Floyd H. and Pear Shiflett, Mar. 14th
Birckhead, Albert and Mary Birckhead, Apr. 5th

Bradford, Jas. R. and Mary A. Wells, May 13th

Bailey, Jas. O. and Annie F. Via, June 4th

Burgess, Lawrence E. and Belle L. Meredith, June 21st

Barnett, Drury and Rena Sprouse, Sept. 24th

Brown, Hoyt G. and Grace F. Omohundro, Dec. 9th

Branham, Jamie W. and Ashlie G. Mundy, Dec. 24th

1928

Bellomy, Oscar R. and Annie E. Meeks, May 3rd

Bishop, Frank W. and Elsie M. Lanery, May 26th

Bailes, James F. and Ruth V. Rea, July 10th

Birckhead, Thos. E. and Pearl L. Shiflett, Aug. 3rd

Brown, John Edwin and Myrtle M. Valentine, Aug. 25th

Best, Harry Lee and Pearl V. Weitzel, Sept. 3rd

Brown, Douglas and Susie J. McCauley, Oct. 8th

Bush, Henry M. and Katie L. Minor, Oct. 9th

Bruns, Thos. Nelson C. and Bernard P. L. Early, Oct. 25th

Brookman, Harry and Mary S. Harris, Nov. 15th

Barnes, James E. and Mary J. Winn, Nov. 30th

Bledsoe, Wm. A. and Hester V. Shiflett, Dec. 1st

Birckhead, Edward F. and Rosa L. Sprouse, Dec. 18th

1929

Bonavita, Fred W. and Mary E. Pierce, Jan. 19th

Brennen, Edward E. and Willie J. Thomas, Jan. 29th

Bickley, James R. and Cornelia Laing, Feb. 8th

Boswell, Wm. W. and Willie G. Michie, Feb. 28th

Bailey, Floyd W. and Bessie E. Snead, Mar. 5th

Bolden, John D. and Muriel C. Jones, Mar. 9th

Brown, George and Beatrice Morris, Mar. 18th

Ballard, Walter L. and Edna M. Critzer, Mar. 30th

Brown, Rubin and Edna Wood, Apr. 5th

Boatwright, Russell and Ruth Adcock, May 2nd

Brown, Edgar P. and Elizabeth D. Sprouse, May 11th

Blackwell, Roy B. and Virgie M. Morris, June 4th

Brooks, Geo. Edward and Bessie H. Critzer, June 12th

Bryant, Wm. Percy and Ruth H. Martin, July 20th

Bruce, Lacy and Carrie M. Shiflett, July 30th

Birckhead, Jack and Luanna Geer, Sept. 7th

Bragg, Henry B. and Jessie C. Marion, Sept. 14th

Beverley, Robt. L. and Ruby M. White, Sept. 21st

Beverly, Rennie and Lucy Hall, Oct. 17th

Baugher, Gilbert L. and Martha Ann Via, Oct. 21st

Brockenborough, Thos. W. and Daisy A. Kent, Nov. 5th

Berry, Dewey L. and Annie B. Gray, Nov. 11th

Birckhead, Wm. H. and Ruby E. Baber, Nov. 14th

Black, Jas. Henry and Mamie Shiflett, Nov. 20th

C

1781

Clarkson, William and Molly Smith, June 12th

Cross, Thomas and Mary Goolsky, Nov. 20th

1782

Calloson, Elnathan and Margaret Duffy, April 16th

Carter, Richard and Susannah Nivans, June 15th

1783

Campbell, William and Sally Geke, June 19th

Carr, John Fendall and Elizabeth Dalton, Jan. 1st

Cobbs, Thomas and Betsy Martin, Aug. 13th

Cooper, Robert and Margaret Blaine, Feb. 4th

Crockett, Joseph and Elizabeth Woodson, Feb. 13th

1784

Cobbs, James and Patsy Martin, June 12th

Connor, John and Mary Hanie, May 17th

1785

Cammel, Archibal and Mary Grogg, Dec. 1st

Carrell, John and Sarah Jopling, Dec. 1st

Carter, George and Sully Carter, Jan. 16th

Carter, Henry and Sarah White, Dec. 13th

Collins, Hezekiah and Ann Wheeler, June 1st

1786

Carsey, John and Jane Bailey, Aug. 3rd

Clarkson, Alphine and Letty ?, June 8th

Cluseman, Frederick and Hannah Bryan, May 4th

Coleman, Harves and Ann Harris, March 16th

1787

Carr, John and Jane Lewis, July 12th

Crosthwait, Thomas and Mary Stone, Dec. 8th

1788

Cosby, William and Hannah Smith, March 7th

1789

Catterton, William and Elizabeth Foster, Oct. 20th

Clark, Micajah and Sarah Henderson, Jan. 15th

Clemmons, John and Sarah Britt, Nov. 12th

1790

Carter, Charles and Agness Horner, Dec. 29th

Carter, Edward and Mary Randolph Lewis, Oct. 14th

Cobbs, John and Susannah Hamner, June 21st

1791

Chapman, William and Sally Alphin, March 30th

Chinn, John and Nancy Fitch, Dec. 24th

Clark, John and Susannah Henderson, Nov. 12th

Coleman, William and Franky Garrison, Aug. 11th

Cox, George and Mary Shiflett, March, 15th

1792

Catterton, William and Aggy Sims, Dec. 26th

Chandler, John and Ally Sneed, Feb. 9th

Clark, Moses and Ann Deadman, Oct. 16th

Cleveland, Oliver and Jane Buckner, Dec. 19th

Cofer, Thomas and Elizabeth Taylor, March 15th

Crosthwait, John and Nancy Dickerson, Oct. 11th

1793

Carr, Meckins and Nancy Wood, Jan. 19th

Coopwood, Benjamin and Milly Thomason, Feb. 11th

1794

Clayton, John and Sarah Rickson, Sept. 11th

Collins, Elisha and Hannah Upstigrove, June 17th

Craig, David and Milley Watson, June 18th

1795

Carrell, Lewis and Elizabeth Naylor, Jan. 5th

Carter, Thomas and Susannah Dudley, Sept. 5th

Carver, Jurald and Nancy Beck, Oct. 16th

Collins, Elijah and Elizabeth Spears, Dec. 28th

Cosby, Joel and Lucy Garland, Aug. 26th

Crawford, Charles and Sarah Wood, July 18th

Cummings, Robert and Delphy Bowling, Jan. 19th

Cunningham, William and Nancy Carr, Dec. 24th

1796

Carrel, Jesse and Elizabeth Fitz, July 6th

Clark, John and Elizabeth Wood, March 17th

1797

Carver, Noel and Excey Becks, Dec. 4th

Clarkson, Julius and Elizabeth Price, Dec. 22nd

1798

Carter, Robert and Mary Elizie Coles, June 26th

Crews, John and Cristenna Clemens, April 5th

1799

Carver, William and Selah Carver, Oct. 7th

Cloar, Jacob and Annoh Gilmore, March 28th

Crosthwait, Thomas and Elizabeth Rogers, Nov. 14th

1801

Clemens, John and Elizabeth Phillips, Dec. 22nd

Coltranter, John and Milly McGehe, June 8th

1802

Cheatham, Robert and Milly Moore, June 28th

Collins, Hezekiah and Elizabeth Surface, Nov. 20th

1803

Carr, William and Sally Douglass, Nov. 14th

Clark, Jacob C. and Catharine Allen, Dec. 5th

Clarkson, John and Ann Harrison, Oct. 18th

Clemons, Drury and Sally Joseph Durham, Dec. 26th

Copeland, William and Charity Kirby, Dec. 28th

Craig, Robert and Polly Murry, Dec. 19th

1804

Carrel, William and Nancy Perry, Sept. 18th

Carver, Enoch and Sally Carver, Dec. 5th

Clark, Nathaniel and Nancy Hall, Feb. 7th

Clark, Thomas and Polly Jones, Feb. 24th

Clarkson, Reuben and Sally Wingfield, Nov. 16th

Clemens, Thomas and Nancy M. Burton, Oct. 11th

Coleman, John and Jane Norris, Jan. 7th

Colyer, Preston and Eliza Hayna, Nov. 7th

1805

Carr, Thomas and Peggy Solman, Dec. 20th

Cary, Wilson and Virginia Randolph, Aug. 27th

Craddock, Thomas and Patsy Becks, Oct. 7th

1806

Carr, James W. and Polly Carr, Feb. 3rd

Cook, William and Betsy Gouldin, Oct. 6th

Crenshaw, Thomas and Mary Goodman, Sept. 10th

1807

Carr, Elijah and Margaret Butler, Feb. 18th

Carr, John and Elizabeth Horsby, Sept. 26th

Carr, William and Henretta Brown, Aug. 27th

Carter, James and Judy Wade, Dec. 5th

Cobbs, David and Elizabeth Lewis, Aug. 5th
Cowell, John and Elizabeth Mayo, Jan. 22nd

1808

Carr, Anderson B. and Julia A. Brockman, May 6th
Carter, Goodloe and Mary Crenshaw, Feb. 19th
Carter, William F. and Jane Howard, Nov. 23rd
Clark, James and Margaret Lewis, June 7th
Cord, John M. and Nancy Jameson, Jan. 19th
Cosby, Minor and Ann J. Moore, Dec. 15th
Crank, George and Margaret Gains, Dec. 14th

1809

Campbell, John and Patsy Ballard, Aug. 7th
Carr, Jonathan B. and Ann B. Carr, May 31st
Carver, Josiah and Polly Craddock, April 18th
Clarke, Thomas R. and Elizabeth Garth, Aug. 3rd
Clarkson, James and Marie Wood, May 17th
Colvin, Sam and Elizabeth Britt, Dec. 25th
Cooke, Thomas and Elizabeth Clayton, April 20th

1810

Clements, Charles and Martha Durhum, Dec. 24th
Cowardin, John and Polly White, Oct. 8th

1811

Carroll, James and Patsy Harlow, May 15th
Carver, John and Nancy Carver, Dec. 8th
Childress, Samuel and Nancy Hamner, March 21st
Coffman, Joseph and Mary Yancey, Jan. 14th
Colyer, Horton and Philisha Rodes, Dec. 19th

1812

Cocke, Warner and Sally Stone, Sept. 22nd

1813

Cox, Edward and Martha Oglesby, June 27th

1814

Cleveland, Jeremiah and Elizabeth Moon, Dec. 27th
Craddock, John and Mary Gardner, May 28th

1815

Carr, Frank and Virginia Terrell, May 29th
Carr, John H. and Malinda Clarkson, Dec. 21st
Carr, Micajah W. and Ann Thurmond, Dec. 19th
Catterton, Francis and Nancy Clarkson, Oct. 2nd
Childress, John C. and Matilda Branham, Oct. 14th
Clarke, Parsons and Mary A. Maxwell, May 16th
Coleman, James and Elizabeth Coleman, June 5th

Crenshaw, William and Mary W. Troyman, Sept. 7th

1816

Carey, Soloman and Aggy Grass, Jan. 1st
Carr, Charles Lewis and Ann M. Watson, March 27th
Carter, Charles W. and Mary Hughes, April 27th
Chiles, John G. and Elizabeth L. Wells, Aug. 22nd
Chiles, Washington and Mary Hughes, April 27th
Clarkson, James M. and Sarah Clarkson, Feb. 8th
Coleman, Thomas and Laterda Snow, Oct. 19th
Colvin, William and Frances F. Burton, Jan. 17th

1817

Carr, Dabney and Mary Appleberry, March 11th
Carr, James O. and Mary A. Allen, Nov. 22nd
Clam, Wiliam and Patsey Graves, Dec. 23rd
Cleveland, William and Sarah Moon Jan. 18th
Coleir, Martin and Fanny Marshall, Jan. 30th
Coram, Stephen and Keliah Battles, March 19th

1818

Carr, Bernard and Nancy Rothwell, Dec. 23rd
Carr, Samuel and Maria Dabney, Dec. 1st
Carrell, Henry W. and Martha Carrell, Nov. 14th
Carthron, Charles and Elizabeth Brown, Oct. 5th
Carver, Lawrence and Frissry Sullivan, Sept. 29th
Carver, William T. and Jane Houseright, Feb. 19th
Chisholm, John R. and Nancy Gaines, Dec. 23rd
Cleveland, Oliver and Susan Gay, Dec. 22nd
Coatler, William B. and Lucinda Rodes, June 25th
Coleman, William and Nancy Dowell, June 9th
Crawford, Ezekiel and Judith Shifflett, Dec. 22nd

1819

Coles, Reubin and Sucy Bowles, Jan. 7th
Coley, William and Milly McClary, June 3rd
Cox, Charles and Maria Mooney, Dec. 2nd
Craig, Elijah and Sarah Maupin, Nov. 1st

1820

Carr, Willis and Mary Ann Gains, Dec. 14th
Chilel, Henry and Sophia Davis, June 14th
Coleman, John H. and Sarah Nicholas, May 1st
Craven, J. and Mary Clarkson, Oct. 17th

1821

Carden, William F. and C. Thomason, June 4th

Carr, John B. and Susannah Hamner, Nov. 7th

Carter, James and Nancy Thompson, Nov. 15th

Carver, Reubin and Elizabeth Eubank, June 3rd

Cobbs, Samuel and Mary Campbell, Feb. 5th

Craven, John D. and Jane C. Wills, Dec. 20th

1822

Carver, Nimrod and Caroline Craddock, Dec. 12th

Chilores, Samuel and Polly Smith, Dec. 11th

Cullock, James M. and Mary Smith, Nov. 6th

1823

Campbell, Joseph and Amanda Rogers, Jan. 15th

Carr, Mekins and Mary S. Hamner, Oct. 22nd

Collins, James and Mary Clarkson, Sept. 1st

Craig, Samuel and Margaret McCord, March 19th

Crosthwait, Isaac D. and Mary T. Rippeto, Sept. 23rd

1824

Cave, James and Elizabeth Beald, May 28th

Chapman, James E. and Polly Thompson, Nov. 24th

1825

Carver, Elliott and Nancy Davis, Feb. 10th

Carver, Reuben and Lucy C. Beck, Dec. 22nd

Chamberlain, Nathaniel and Margaret Marsheller, March 2nd

Cheatham, William and Sarah Wolfe, Oct. 1st

Clarkson, Julius W. and Margaret M. Thomas, Aug. 19th

Coleman, William N. and Elizabeth Bailey, Jan. 3rd

Colvin, Alexander and Ann Hall, Jan. 3rd

Coolidge, Jes and Ellen W. Randolph, May 29th

Crawford, Malcolm F. and Amanda Craven, July 14th

1826

Carr, Dabney L. and Sidney L. Nicholas, April 21st

Catterton, Michael and Lucy Mills, May 2nd

Clayton, Alex M. and Mary W. Thomas, Jan. 25th

Compton, James and Catherine H. Roberson, Nov. 31st

Crosthwait, William and Sarah Rogers, April 12th

1827

Carr, Samuel and Martha Fretwell, Jan. 3rd

Carter, Thomas and Ann Black, April 25th

Catterton, Benjamin W. and Ann Austin, Feb. ?

Catterton, William and Matilda S. Durrett, Oct. 13th

Chandler, Abram and Mary Ann Bonds, Oct. 13th

Crosthwait, Isaac D. and Nancy Herring, Jan. 4th

1828

Caruthers, John and Ann N. Martin, Nov. 17th

1829

Carpenter, Ira and Charlotte Littlefield, Dec. 18th

Chandler, David and Mary Rippeto, Oct. 5th

Clarke, Jefferson and C. M. Spencer, July 11th

Cooper, David and Ellen Essek, Dec. 19th

Craig, William W. and Emily L. Brown, Dec. 14th

Crenshaw, Edmund B. and Eliza L. Brand, Oct. 14th

1830

Carter, James and Sarah A. Cromwell, April 28th

Chick, Melton W. and Ann D. Wingfield, Nov. 27th

Chinchinun, George and Jemima H. Beckett, Dec. 25th

Clarke, David H. and A. D. Maupin, March 30th

1831

Captain, Isaac and Ellen Salmons, Dec. 5th

Carver, Elliott and Peachy Beaver, March 16th

Crosthwait, John and Nancy Taylor, Nov. 2nd

1832

Campbell, Abner and Elizabeth Bradley, Sept. 3rd

Carr, Thomas O. and Mary S. Patrick, April 28th

Chapman, William F. and Lucy D. Thompson, Dec. 19th

Childress, Benjamin W. and Susan T. Brown, Dec. 18th

Childs, Richard and Margaret Snell, Feb. 2nd

Clark, Thomas and Sydna Estes, Feb. 8th

Coiner, George and Mrs. Mary Wren, May 17th

Collins, Hezekiah and Sarah Wood, May 17th

Cox, William H. and Mary E. Lacey, Aug. 8th

1833

Clarke, John and Mary S. Maupin, Nov. 28th

Collins, Zachariah and Mary Ann Lowry, Jan. 28th

1834

Colbert, Burwell and Elizabeth Battles, Dec. 5th

Collier, John and Susan A. Kersey, Dec. 24th

Crewoson, James L. and R. V. Hoult, Dec. 11th

Critzer, Andrew and Maria Toms, Sept. 15th

Crobarger, George and Mrs. Elizabeth Blain, June 30th

1835

Calhoun, Andrew and Lavina Harris, Sept. 16th

Campbell, Lewis S. and Eliza D. Brown, Nov. 18th

Coleman, Anderson B. and Emily Pace, July 6th

1836

Carr, William G. and C. M. Duke, April 26th

Carter, Henry and M. Emmerson, Feb. 10th

Clements, Charles M. and F. E. Johnson, Dec. 21st

Cox, James M. and M. Draffin, Aug. 23rd

Craddock, James and Frances G. Craddock, Sept. 25th

1837

Clarke, Micajah M. and Margaret A. Sampaon, Nov. 7th

Clarke, William G. and Martha U. Huckstep, Nov. 28th

Clive, George and Patsy W. Carr, June 20th

Collier, Caswell and Elizabeth Haney, April 27th

Cox, John W. and Emma M. Stockton, Nov. 12th

Craven, George W. and Susan Ann Henkell, Nov. 14th

Crawford, James and Sarah Ann Simms, Aug. 9th

1838

Cashman, Robert and Margaret M. Clarkson, Sept. 20th

Clarke, John and Sarah Kidd, Dec. 22nd

Clements, John B. and Martha A. Houchens, Sept. 18th

Currier, Washington and Cary Ann Sprouce, Nov. 2nd

1839

Cabell, James L. and Margaret Gibbons, Feb. 5th

Calhoun, John and Marietta Harris, March 25th

Caruthers, Edward G. and Elizabeth A. Rogers, Nov. 7th

Chandler, Howell and Martha Pace, Feb. 7th

Clements, Lewis H. and M. J. Walker, Oct. 7th

Cocke, Horace and Elizabeth A. Wood, Jan. 10th

Corley, John N. and Elizabeth Mundy, Dec. 16th

Cox, Tazewell and Sarah Wood, Jan. 11th

Criddle, William and Mary Ann Kinnadey, Jan. 23rd

1840

Carter, Barnett and D. C. A. Shiflett, Nov. 26th

Childress, James and Mary Ann Gay, Aug. 10th

Coleman, Roderick S. and M. A. Fitch, Oct. 29th

Collins, William and Sarah Ann Taylor, Jan. 3rd

Connoly, John and Elizabeth Lowell, Dec. 1st

Cooper, William M. and Emma Littleford, Sept. 30th

1841

Childress, William M. and Martha J. Terrell, Jan. 16th

Clarke, James H. and Elizabeth F. Estes, Oct. 6th

Clormoach, David M. and Sarah F. Wood, March 25th

Coleman, John S. and Mary M. Jones, Dec. 4th

1842

Campbell, James M. and Sarah J. Pettet, Nov. 26th

Carver, Seimon W. and Julia A. Holbert, July 11th

Chisholm, Hugh D. and Catherine Georning, Sept. 22nd

Cleveland, Oliver E. and Sarah Ann Carr, Nov. 17th

Cobbs, Thomas H. and Ann Eliza Wood, Oct. 17th

Collins, Dillard and Mary Luck, Dec. 4th

Collins, Tandy and Lawrencia M. Dowell, April 17th

Coward, J. Mitchell and Sarah C. Sneed, Nov. 30th

1843

Carr, John M. and Mary J. Thurmond, Dec. 21st

Carr, John M. and Sarah Ann Brown, Jan. 30th

Cleaveland, Porter and Frances E. Ballard, July 28th

Craddock, Hugh and Elizabeth Hughes, March 3rd

Cullen, Hugh M. and Mary Ann Boothe, June 22nd

1844

Carpenter, Alfred and Frances A. White, Feb. 19th

Cave, Hiram A. and ? Shiflett, June 1st

Clarke, James F. and Lucy F. Boyd, Jan. 31st

Cobbs, John and Ann E. Wheeler, Dec. 23rd

Connoly, Charles and Mildred Blackley Jan. 5th

Cook, William and M. J. Simmons, Jan. 4th

Cooke, Thomas J. and Emily Stockton, Sept. 7th

Critzer, Spottswood and Dicy Ann Toms, Oct. 17th

1845

Carr, Peter and S. S. Lewis, Oct. 23rd

Carroll, John and Sophia Woody, Jan. 21st

Carter, James C. and Virginia F. Beazley, Oct. 27th

Childress, George W. and W. Shiflett, Nov. 24th

Childress, Thomas and M. F. Johnson, May 12th

Cleaveland, F. H. and William B. Winn, July 21st

Cox, Thomas and Judy F. Garrison, Aug. 27th

Craddock, W. R. and E. J. Rodes, July 16th

Cross, John G. and Sarah H. Davis, Feb. 1st

Carr, Samuel D. and Jane Mornas, Dec. 2nd

1846

Carson, Edward Jr. and Elizabeth Marshall, Jan. 29th

Chisholm, John B. and Hardenia Marr, March 17th

Clarke, Thomas J. B. and Velina A. Kingsolving, Nov. 10th

Clements, William D. and Susan F. Kirby, Feb. 3rd

Clopton, John C. and Marietta B. Thompson, Jan. 28th

Coatney, Edward H. and Virginia P. Howard, July 6th

Cole, Reuben and Sally Cottrell, Nov. 26th

Coleman, Reuben S. and Elizabeth E. Hart, Aug. 17th

Collins, Burrell and Lucy Becks, March 7th

Critzer, George W. and Catherine Hipport, Aug. 4th

1847

Carr, Francis E. G. and Sallie A. Carr, Feb. 4th

Carter, Richard H. and Rebecca Thurmond, Dec. 28th

Carter, Thomas P. and Caroline Hudson, Jan. 18th

Cleaveland, Albert H. and M. E. Lowell, Sept. 29th

Colquett, Caleb A. and M. C. Shackelford, Aug. 31st

Crawford, Samuel D. and P. C. Sims, Jan. 11th

Crickenbarger, Lewis and Ann Batton, June 8th

Cross, Patrick A. and Mary J. Kenney, April 26th

1848

Carr, Overton and M. A. Eastham, Feb. 24th

Crenshaw, David G. C. and Mary E. Harris, Nov. 23rd

Cropper, Jese and Jane Kelly, May 30th

1849

Carroll, Mayor A. and Martha C. Payne, Jan. 8th

Carver, William A. White and C. M. Broadus, Jan. 19th

Cox, Abner and Frances C. Estes, Aug. 5th

Craig, William A. and Elizabeth C. Via, Nov. 30th

1850

Carr, James B. and Sarah A. Woodson, Dec. 20th

Chapman, Samuel T. and Elizabeth D. Rodes, June 27th

Childress, Charles and Mary S. Hays, Sept. 19th

Cole, Jacob and Sarah E. Battles, Jan. 31st

Coleman, John S. and Elizabeth Traman, May 16th

Coles, Edward and Sally Ann Wheat, March 6th

1851

Carr, John D. and Agness Simms, Dec. 16th

Carver, C. F. and Elizabeth Sprouce, Nov. 2nd

Carver, Dabney C. and Sarah A. Payne, Dec. 20th

Chisholm, William D. and Lavinnia Pace, July 1st

Clarke, William S. and Ann E. Garth, Dec. 19th

Cleaveland, Albert H. and Elizabeth J. Barksdale, April 19th

Coleman, James T. and Sarah E. Lain, Oct. 9th

Craddock, A. J. and Ann E. Thompson, March 25th

Craig, George B. and Laura Bryant, June 10th

Crutchfield, Thomas J. and Martha I. Backinsto, March 17th

Currier, William and Nancy Gardner, March 5th

1852

Campbell, John M. and M. I. E. Lupton, Nov. 23rd

Carroll, James M. and Margaret A. Pippin, Feb. 5th

Cheatham, William and M. A. Bishop, April 22nd

Cobbs, Peyton S. and Julia I. Coles, March 15th

Comann, Robert S. and Tracy Dunken, Jan. 4th

Cornelle, William F. and Sarah E. Bowyer, Nov. 18th

Courtney, Thomas S. and Sarah I. Walton, Nov. 23rd

Crebs, John C. and Mary A. Bacon, Feb. 26th

Crouch, Bernard S. and M. E. Woodson, June 16th

1853

Coleman, John L. and Eliza J. Tompkins, Aug. 30th

1854

Carter, John A. and Louisa I. Hudson, March 14th

Carter, James T. and Martha J. Perry, Feb. 13th

Cavedo, Peter F. and Marietta M. Merritt, Feb. 27th

Cleaveland, N. A. and M. A. Marshall, Dec. 15th

Cox, Horace and Catherine Wood, Aug. 8th

Crawford, John L. and M. A. H. Gillum, April 11th

Crenshaw, J. P. M. and L. E. Wood, Dec. 7th

Crenshaw, J. M. and Lucinda E. Wood, Dec. 7th

1855

Carr, George and Linda C. Poore, Feb. 28th

Cochran, E. L. and E. A. Caruthers, Jan. 18th

Cornell, William O. and Mary Ford, Dec. 13th

Caven, Jas. S. and Mary Dunkun, Dec. 19th

Cockran, E. L. and E. A. Cauthur, Jan. 18th

Carr, George and Malinda Poore, Feb. 20th

1856

Clarke, George M. and Frances R. Watson, Jan. 5th

Cleaveland, William F. and Mary W. Moon, May 7th

Coleman, Dabney C. and Sarah H. Gardner, March 9th

Coleman, Thomas G. and Isabella Rives, Nov. 25th

Collins, Andrew J. and Martha A. Modena, Dec. 23rd

Cook, George W. and Cynthia A. Foster, April 28th

Cox, Charles B. Jr. and Lucy W. Bailey, Nov. 11th

Cox, Charles B. and Lucy W. Bailey, Nov. 11th

Coleman, Dabney J. and Sarah F. Gardner, Mar. 9th

Cook, Geo. W. and Cynthia A. Foster, Apr. 28th

Carter, James H. and Mary E. Good, Oct. 8th

Childress, R. M. and Ann E. Wiant, Mar. 7th

Cleveland, Wm. F. and Mary W. Moore, May 14th

1857

Carter, James H. and Mary E. Good, Oct. 5th

Childress, Robert M. and Ann E. Wyant, Mar. 7th

Craig, Samuel J. and Sarah E. C. McCord, Dec. 7th

Cullen, Addison M. and Elizabeth A. Staton, July 1st

Cullen, John C. and Sarah F. Farrish, April 16th

Cullen, Addison S. and Eliz. A. Staton, Oct. 21st

1858

Cocke, Albert and Henrietta Farrar, Jan. 14th

Crop, Patrick A. and Angelina Kenney, Feb. 5th

Cross, Patrick A. and Angelina Kenney, Feb. 7th

Cox, Albert and Henrietta Farrar, Jan. 20th

1859

Cole, James and Elizabeth M. Poindexter, Dec. 24th

Coleman, William G. and Pirena F. Sandridge, Oct. 17th

Collins, John O. and Catherine F. Scruggs, April 4th

Crow, Abraham and Sarah F. Boothe, Nov. 3rd

Cullen, James H. and Rosella H. Shelton, Jan. 3rd

Cullen, James H. and Rosello H. Shelton, Jan. 18th

Collins, Jno. A. and Martha A. Scruggs, July 24th

Cade, Bowyer, Jr., and Mary Jane Matthews, Nov. 29th

Cole, James and Elize M. Poindexter, Dec. 25th

Criddle, R. J. and Eliz. Gillispie, Nov. 24th

Coleman, Wm. G. and Travis F. Sandridge, Nov. 1st

1860

Cochran, Howe E. and Nannie L. Carrington, Dec. 18th

Cole, John G. and Ann M. Duke, Jan. 2nd

Collins, W. H. and Martha A. Scruggs, Jan. 17th

Criddle, Robert J. and Elizabeth Gillespie, Nov. 22nd

Critzer, James F. M. and Lucinda Toms, Oct. 15th

Cole, J. G. and Annie M. Duke, Jan. 3rd

Collins, Wm. H. and Martha A. Scruggs, Jan. 18th

Cochran, Howe P. and Ann L. Carrington, Dec. 18th

Critzer, J. F. M. and Lucinda Toms, Oct. 18th

1861

Carson, William and Elizabeth West, Dec. 28th

Carver, James D. and Mary S. Baughn, Aug. 22nd

Cloar, John and Elizabeth Pollock, April 29th

Carter, Capins and Fannie S. Green, Sept. 27th

Crow, Abram and Sarah F. Boothe, Oct. 28th

Carson, Wm. and Eliz. Vest, Dec. 29th

Catterton, Geo. N. and Malinda Woodson, May 16th

Carver, Dabney and Eliz. Bellamy, Mar. 2nd

Cloar, Jno. and Eliz. Pollock, Apr. 29th

1862

Cogbell, Wm. R. and Rebecca E. Farrar, Oct. 22nd

Corse, Genl. M. D. and Eliz. Beverly, Nov. 22nd

Casy, James and Catherine Lasy, Sept. 4th

Clauss, Henry S. and Martha R. Watson, April 24th

Carver, James D. and Mary S. Vaughan, Feb. 13th

1863

Coleman, H. N. and Ann Eliza Watson, Jan. 28th

Clarkson, Geo. W. and Mildred A. Beck, June 25th

Cox, A. S. and Susan A. Snow, April 20th

Craig, David F. and Liza J. Humphreys, April 28th

Craven, Peter H. and Willie M. George, June 6th

Clemens, F. D. and Eliz. Harslip, Sept. 25th

Chanceller, Chas. W. and Mary A. Taliaferro, March 13th

Carver, Tandy J. and Susan J. Fitz, Feb. 12th

1864

Clements, Wm. and Mary Hicks, Jan. 28th

Crenshaw, Thos. A. and Gillie M. Bramham, July 13th

Cornett, Henry and Mary E. Herndon, July 14th

Crew, Peter J. and Maria S. Rodes, Nov. 1st

Clark, Thos. J. and Lucy Ann Herren, Dec. 15th

1865

Criddle, Ben. F. and Eliz. Campbell, Nov. 16th

Criddle, Benjamin F. and Elizabeth Campbell, Nov. 15th

Critzer, Chas. and Julia A. Haskins, Sept. 5th

Critzer, Christian and Julia A. Haskins, Sept. 4th

Critzer, Wm. and Nancy Kennedy, Sept. 7th

Critzer, William and Nancy Kennedy, Sept. 4th

Chiles, Jno. H. and Emma Omohendro, Aug. 16th

Chiles, John H. and Emma Omohundro, Aug. 16th

Clifton, N. G. and Marian O. T. Bowyer, May 7th

Clifton, N. G. and M. O. T. Bowyer, May 6th

Cobbs, Jno. M. and Frances D. Wheeler, April 13th

Cobbs, John W. and Frances D. Wheeler, April 7th

Chamblin, Chas. M. and Mary F. Anderson, June 11th

Chamblain, Charles W. and Mary F. Anderson, Jan. 4th

Carter, Cashian and Fannie S. Green, Sept. 28th

Coleman, Thos. C. and M. A. Pieman, Dec. 29th

Coleman, Thomas C. and Mohala Greman Dec. 27th

1866

Carr, Albert and Eliza Younger, Nov. 3rd

Catterton, George N. and Malinda Woodson, May 9th

Chapman, Thomas A. and Sally Jane Chapman, April 11th

Chidsey, Strong Minor and Virginia A. Branham, March 21st

Clark, George W. and Angelina Burch, Aug. 29th

Clayton, John and Lucy Ann Wood, Oct. 1st

Crenshaw, O. A. and Susan W. Anderson, June 5th

Critzer, William H. and Louisa Critzer, Sept. 5th

Crenshaw, Oct. A. and Susan W. Anderson, June 6th

Chapman, Thos. A. and Sally J. Chapman, April 15th

Clark, Geo. W. and Angelina Bunch, Aug. 29th

Critzer, Wm. H. and Louisia Critzer, Sept. 5th

Clayton, Jno. and Lucy A. Wood, Oct. 11th

Chidsey, S. M. and Virginia A. Bramham, March 26th

Clark, Chas. D. and Emma M. Childress, Dec. 10th

Childress, Tho. H. and Molly A. Clarke, Dec. 10th

Chapman, Bernard T. and Virginia M. Chapman, Dec. 12th

Chapman, B. T. and V. M. Chapman, Dec. 13th

1867

Clark, Wm. N. and Barbara E. Houchens, Jan. 1st

Caum, Ro. A. and Annie B. Calston, Oct. 21st

Clayton, Gale and Lucy Dabney, Oct. 6th

Cannady, Wm. and Ang. Garton, March 3rd

Clarke, Chas. D. and Emma M. Childress, Jan. 8th

Childress, Thos. H. and Molly A. Clarke, Jan. 8th

Clark, Wm. N. and B. E. Houchens, Jan. 15th

Clarke, Geo. P. and Eliza M. Goode, May 30th

Crittenden, Wm. A. and Ann E. Taylor, June 28th

Casey, Ed. L. and Sophie Loving, April 27th

Clark, Wm. E. and Anna Macon, Nov. 21st

Chancellor, J. E. and Gabriella Mays, Nov. 14th

Clements, Step. E. and Mary F. Bishop, Nov. 28th

Cavindy, Wm. and Angelina Gaston, March 2nd

Carter, Walker and Margaret Grant, April 20th

Clarke, Geo. P. and Eliza M. Goode, May 29th

Cabell, Winston, and Susan Washington, July 1st

Clayton, Gale and Lucy Dabney, Oct. 5th

Clements, Thos. M. and Mary Frances Maupin, Aug. 15th

Cavin, Ro. A. and Annie B. Colston, Sept. 11th

Cockran, Jno. Henry and Charlotte Carr, Sept. 26th

Crockitt, David, and Lauisanua Dillard, Oct. 7th

Clements, Miles E. and Eloe A. Gibson, Oct. 12th

Clarke, Wm. Edw. and Anna Maron, Nov. 19th

1868

Cleaveland, R. L. and Alice T. Trowers, Jan. 20th

Clay, Thos. and Dosser Washington, Jan. 31st

Collins, J. P. and Fannie O'Neil, Feb. 18th

Clarkson, Thos. M. and Mary E. Ferguson, March 16th

Coleman, Henry F. and Mary Jane Patrick, April 6th

Carroll, U. Joshua and Emma M. Mayo, May 12th

Cosby, Robt. O. and Marry Farrar, May 30th

Cave, Wm. and Susan H. Cave, Aug. 22nd

Cochran, Jno. S. and Mary Massie, Aug. 26th

Criddle, Jas. and Sarah Ann Hogg, Sept. 12th

Carr, Wm. and Susan H. Carr, Aug. 24th

Collins, J. P. and Fannie O'Neil, Feb. 26th

Clark, T. C. and Nannie F. Clark, Oct. 17th

Cotwell, Granville and Georgia Williams, Oct. 17th

Catterton, Wm. and Sarah A. Elliott, Oct. 25th

1869

Coleman, Jos. S. and Emma V. Thompkins, Feb. 17th

Carr, Jack and Emma Terrell, May 29th

Coffman, Samuel H. and Lucy Page Anderson, Aug. 5th

Carter, John and Nellie Somel, Aug. 21st

Craddock, Thos. J. and A. E. Dramheller, Sept. 26th

Caldwell, H. C. and Rosa D. Pools, Oct. 5th

Clements, Wm. D. and Isabella Thompson, Dec. 19th

Cleveland, R. M. and Mary E. Lindsey, Dec. 15th

1870

Camp, Thos. H. and Bettie M. Warwick, July 12th

Coleman, Geo. W. and Sallie A. Day, Sept. 22nd

Critzer, Alex and M. L. Wade, Nov. 17th

Carey, Fred and Mary Watson, Dec. 8th

Carr, D. F. and R. E. Dicke, Dec. 11th

Carmichael, W. and Martha Jordan, Dec. 31st

Cleaveland, Luther J. and Lucy M. Shelton, Feb. 15th

1871

Clements, James W. and Ann L. Jones, Jan. 12th

Cox, L. W. and Eliza A. Foster, June 27th

Clayton, Jos. and Callie Renah Baber, Nov. 3rd

Catterton, B. N. and Sarah A. Smith, Nov. 16th

Carroll, Ed. Eugene and Lucy Jane Goin, Dec. 28th

1872

Carver, Meredith and Milly Ferguson, Jan. 5th

Callahan, Patrick B. and Kate Reynolds, Jan. 15th

Cox, Elijah D. and Sarah M. Dunn, Feb. 15th

Clemits, John M. and Josephine Rix, Aug. 15th

Critzer, Albert S. and Mary F. Carter, Nov. 7th

1873

Crawford, W. H. and M. F. Bellomy, Feb. 13th

Catterton, Finks and S. E. Parrott, May 5th

Carpenter, Chas. F. and S. S. Marshall, May 13

Claytor, Geo. W. and Lucy W. Dudley, Nov. 10th

Craig, Samuel A. and Lucella Mayo, Dec. 22nd

1874

Currier, Wm. and Sarah Gordan, Jan. 28th

Chisholm, Jno. N. and Victoria Rhodes, Jan. 19th

Crow, Jno. W. Jr., and Bettie W. Catterton, May 27th

Cooke, Jno. S. and Sallie A. Drumheller, May 23rd

Clements, Benj. M. and Mollie F. Bashaw, Aug. 18th

Clay, Geo. W. and Sally H. Crank, Oct. 5th

Carroll, Geo. H. and Amanda B. Shaw, Oct. 29th

Crenshaw, Geo. W. and America A. Wood, Nov. 30

Crenshaw, Benj. E. and Mattie S. Jones, Dec. 14th

Carr, Bernard O. and Sallie E. Ballard, Dec. 18th

Carroll, Jno. A. and Mary T. Goodman, Dec. 26th

1875

Coleman, Matthew R. and Annie N. Page, Jan. 8th

Carter, Walter H. and Ella A. Keller, Jan. 12th

Clarke, Geo. E. and Marcella Clarke, Feb. 1st

Craddock, Calvin B. and Caroline Clifton, March 23rd

Carter, Wm. T. and Sally M. Ferguson, April 19th

1876

Carter, Jno. P. and Mary E. Schackeford, Feb. 2nd

Cleveland, Albert B. and Sallie P. Carr, Feb. 2nd

Carpenter, Jno. A. and Martha F. Brown, March 4th

Clarke, Robt. W. and Martha G. Ferguson, June 20th

Cox, Chas. B. and Fannie A. Brown, Sept. 18th

Cason, Jas. C. and Nannie Clemens, Sept. 23rd

Carver, Dabney C. and Lucy A. Johns, Oct. 2nd

Clements, Robt. R. and Mary V. Tomlin, Dec. 11th

Clarke, George E. and Ida E. Walters, Dec. 18th

Coleman, Jas. D. and Tina A. Brown, Dec. 19th

1877

Critzer, Andrew and Virginia B. Toms, Jan. 19th

Campbell, Jas. F. and Mary L. Tyler, Feb. 6th

Clements, Geo. F. and Susan E. Farish, April 4th

Culen, Geo. W. and Seaba Scruggs, Sept. 4th

Crews, Jno. W. and Berdie Williams, Oct. 15th

Calfee, Albert P. and Ida M. Hughson, Nov. 20th

Casby, Thos. M. and Patty A. Thompson, Dec. 8th

Clarke, Kimrod T. and Martha T. Kidd, Dec. 10th

1878

Croberger, John C. and Annie Johnson, Jan. 5th

Carr, James B. and Georgia Rippoito, Jan. 26th

Clarke, Mann G. and Dora E. Furneyhough, Feb. 4th

Cunningham, Thos. A. and Maria W. Gilmer, Oct. 22nd

Crickenberger, Albert S. and Lucy M. Munday, Oct. 28th

Criddle, Wm. and Louisa J. Strange, Dec. 19th

1879

Cox, Horace J. and Mary E. J. Coleman, May 23rd

Carroll, Phillip A. and Mildred W. Goodman, May 15th

Clemons, John R. and Elizabeth Kirby, Sept. 12th

Chewning, John E. and Dollie H. Bailey, Nov. 3rd

Critzer, James P. and Alice A. Meeks, Dec. 9th

Coleman, Wm. J. and Lady Rugg Bishop, Dec. 24th

Cannady, H. and Eoeline Wade, Nov. 24th

Cooke, Calvin, E. and Emma C. Bacon, May 28th

Connor, Al Thomas and Frances A. Martin, Dec. 31st

Clark, Edgar J. and Emma G. Bishop, March 21st

Coleman, Charles L. and Bettie T. McAllister, Nov. 10th

1880

Coleman, C. H. and S. E. Kirby, Nov. 24th

Cornell, Geo. E. and Sallie A. Robinson, July 26th

Crawford, Charles W. and Eugene O. Edwards, Oct. 29th

Currier, William J. and Kate E. Tomlin, Oct. 21st

Cummings, Richard and Emily Gooch, Nov. 13th

Carter, John J. and Mary J. Rise, Dec. 1st

1881

Critzer, Bernard and Cora Burton, Feb. 17th

Chisholm, John Isham and Amanda Sneed, Feb. 9th

Clemmons, Stephen E. and Louisa E. Thacker, Nov. 7th

Cason, Franklin P. and Mary C. Garner, Dec. 22nd

Craig, Logan and Mary E. Bryant, Oct. 20th

1882

Clarke, David A. and Josephine W. Keyton, April 6th

Coles, James T. and Senora Slaughter, May 18th

Chaplin, Henry C. and Annle Brockman, Nov. 15th

Chapman, Thos. R. and Emma E. Woods, Dec. 21st

1883

Clements, Jno. Rhodes and Emma James Harris, Sept. 3rd

Cleaveland, Emmet H. and Ella Florence Jennings, Jan 17th

Cos, Eugene Augustus and Bertha Heuning Wood, Feb. 7th

Carver, George F. and Pamelia L. Colman, April 31st

Clark, Joseph Louis and Fanny E. Day, May 10th

Crickenberger, Jno. Wm. and Sarah Frances Wood, May 20th

Crow, Abraham and Susan F. Stokes, July 4th

Carr, Joseph and Lucy Kinney, ??

Clarke, W. S. and N. P. Wyant, Sept. 27th

Chambers, Jno. Willis and Martha Jane Butler, Oct. 7th

Craig, Alex M. C. and Alice R. Jameson, Nov. 8th

Carr, Edgar H. and Lizzie L. Douglass, Dec 31st

1884

Canden, Jesse Buford and Lula Bell Bacon, Oct. 7th

Carpenter, Wm. C. and Nannie Alberta Gay, Dec. 17th

Cobbs, Isaac and Milly Worley, Dec. 18th

Craig, John W. and Bettie E. Howard, Jan. 17th

Colman, Wm. Lewis and Mary Jane Via, April 7th

Craig, Sam'l Jameson and Josie Warren, June 11th

1885

Caldwell, Jm. F. and Alice Gerom Rice, Oct. 12th

Carpenter, Stephen A. and May Teel, Jan. 22nd

Carver, Peter and Lucilla W. McCauley, March 26th

Castick, Chas. and Annie A. Harris, June 3rd

Caunady, Horace and Annie E. Kirby, Nov. 10th

Chisholm, Napoleon B. and Laura B. Mullins, Dec. 27th

Cocke, Lucian H. and Lelia M. Smith, Sept. 17th

Cooke, Chas. C. and Nannie K. Eubank, Nov. 15th

Cornell, Casey A. and Theresa V. Quick, July 29th

Cox, Edward A. and Mauetta Cox, Dec. 27th

Creasy, Jas. A. and Anna E. Rodes, Nov. 25th

Critzer, Wm. T. and Gabriella D. Hilderbrand, Dec. 30th

1886

Carpenter, Geo. S. and Lena A. Hughes, Feb. 1st

Chisholm, Alex, and Amanda E. Gianniny, April 22nd

Cornell, Joseph J. and Kate C. Davis, June 20th

Coleman, Gilbert M. and Ellen Sullivan, Oct. 5th

Criddle, Henry F. and Mineua W. Goode, Nov. 11th

Castleman, Robt. A. and Fannie L. Funsten, Dec. 6th

Cockran, Campbell C. and Sallie O. Rosser, Dec. 22nd

1887

Clarke, Wm. Marcus and Have Ella Smith, March 3rd

Chisholm, Charlie and Laura Dudley, June 7th

Carver, Chas. and Ida Lee Chistmas, June 15th

Copps, Washington T. and Agnes E. Smith, July 5th

Carter, Edw. D. and Daphine Allen, July 12th

Carter, Robt. E. and Annie D. Gleason, Nov. 10th

Clements, Wm. H. and Georgulla Mooney, Dec. 8th

Critzer, Wm. H. and Sarah Wolford, Dec. 27th

1888

Clements, T. M. and M. A. Reynolds, April 2nd

Charles, J. A. and Amelie Rives, June 11th

Crenshaw, A. J. and Annie E. Sykes, Jan. 19th

Currier, H. L. and Mary A. Criddle, Feb. 1st

Carver, Thos. P. and Litia M. Herndon, May 7th

Cornell, Geo. E. and Kate V. Bruffy, June 5th

Cox, G. W. M. and W. A. Birckhead, Dec. 13th

1889

Cosby, C. W. and Fanetta Martin, Jan. 19th

Carter, F. D. and N. L. Coles, Jan. 25th

Critzer, L. L. and Maggie Critzer, March 25th

Cresey, R. N. and Helan F. Chambers, May 9th

Childress, Wm. T. and Lucy E. Branham, May 25th

Coleman, Ro. J. and Fannie R. Via, Sept. 30th

Carlton, Jno. T. and Lucy M. Gay, Oct. 1st

Carlton, C. F. and L. G. Bugg, Oct. 9th

Childress, J. and Willie Scott, Dec. 18th

Crump, E. D. and M. F. Farish, Dec. 24th

1890

Critzer, J. L. and Delie Graves, Feb. 18th

Connors, Jno. O. and M. L. Munday, Feb. 24th

Chewning, R. F. and Eunice D. Jones, March 3rd

Creasy, Jesse W. and Virginia V. Seay, March 31st

Craddock, Wm. B. and A. L. Hicks, April 16th

Coleman, Sam and Mary Lewis, May 7th

Caldleck, S. W. and K. M. Knapp, June 4th

Collum, Strange and Laura A. Marshall, June 23rd

Crickenboyer, W. and Artie Davenport, Sept. 1st

1891

Currier, W. S. and Cath. Browning, Jan. 12th

Cooke, T. G. and E. S. Ellenger, March 16th

Carrer, D. C. and C. L. Nimmo, June 10th

Craver, Wm. and L. B. Downer, June 16th

Currier, Geo. and C. L. Martin, June 22nd

Carter, R. W. and A. H. Lewis, Sept. 7th

Currier, Wm. F. and S. E. Suddarth, Sept. 29th

Craig, Buster, and Salley Johnson, Oct. 23rd

Cox, Chas. B. and Susan C. Munday, Nov. 10th

Carter, W. H. and M. L. Melton, Dec. 15th

1892

Crams, Willard T. and Susie F. Libbey, April 2nd

Critzer, A. and W. B. Hall, April 6th

Carver, W. O. Whites and Maria Field, June 18th

Carr, Wm. J. and Mary H. Turner, Aug. 2nd

Clements, R. A. and S. M. Thomas, Aug. 20th

Chandler, Dab. and J. C. Proffits, Sept. 22nd

Carter, H. J. and M. F. Maupin, Oct. 29th

Carter, Chas. and Elivira Allen, Nov. 18th

Clark, H. W. and C. F. Clark, Dec. 19th

1893

Chambers, J. W. and S. A. L. Keister, Oct. 7th

Crenshaw, W. R. and L. C. Walton, Oct. 19th

Craig, Jas. S. and Emma J. Harlow, April 12th

Colvin, Jno. G. and L. A. Mitchell, Oct. 21st

Critzer, Edw. W. and Georgie A. Maupin, Nov. 9th

Campbell, B. T. and V. B. Campbell, Nov. 10th

Cook, E. S. and S. B. Wingfield, Dec. 15th

Chisholm, W. D. and L. B. Burgess, Dec. 18th

1894

Cranwell, J. E. and Katy E. Baily, June 27th

Campbell, Jno. R. and R. B. Stevens, Nov. 28th

Coleman, J. D. and F. E. Via, Nov. 5th

Cummings, J. H. and Mary F. Via, Nov. 5th

Clark, Wm. N. and Rebecca A. Houchens, June 5th

Cerak, R. S. and Susie M. Edge, Sept. 8th

Creasy, L. R. and H. Bridgewater, Nov. 28th

Criddle, Chas. A. and Ollie V. Bolton, Dec. 19th

Cason, W. R. and A. T. Lang, Dec. 20th

Craig, J. M. Jr. and Ella Ballard, Dec. 24th

1895

Coleman, Thos. H. and Charlotte Mehring, Feb. 25th

Cabell, Aylett J. and Adelaide W. Wash, April 6th

Collins, Jno. Z. and Mirtie A. Harlow, June 17th

Carter, H. T. and Elizabeth Bussenger, June 3rd

Chisholm, L. A. and V. F. Scruggs, July 9th

Cox, Wm. J. T. and Irene Marshall, Sept. 12th

Cook, Geo. F. and Susie C. Howard, Sept. 23rd

Critzer, D. and O. L. Mawyer, Sept. 9th

Chamberlain, Wm. C. and Mary C. Peyton, Oct. 7th

Catlett, J. B. and E. G. Michie, Oct. 23rd

Carter, R. Z. and A. L. Lafferty, Oct. 30th

Carroll, J. Payne and F. B. Clarke, Nov. 20th

Craig, L. E. and O. L. Sneed, Nov. 23rd

Colthurst, Wm. B. and Eveline Michie, Nov. 25th

Clements, T. M. and Maggie Ellis, Dec. 12th

Cook, J. L. and Julia Sprouse, Dec. 26th

1896

Critzer, R. and E. L. Martin, Dec. 21st

Chapman, Edmund T. and Eliz. B. Beckwith, Jan. 7th

Collins, A. J. and Edna B. Smith, May 23rd

Chisholm, J. A. and Grace Clark, June 1st

Clements, J. W. and Drucilla Sulvan, June 3rd

Crawford, J. B. and M. L. Burgess, June 5th

Currier, T. G. and C. C. Barnett, June 19th

Claud, Mansen and Mollie J. Goodlow, Oct. 19th

Cox, John B. and Maggie L. Munday, Oct. 26th

Chambers, Lillian and Minnie Logan, Nov. 14th

Critzer, Samuel H. and Rosa E. Pugh, Dec. 7th

Coleman, S. W. and E. W. Bailey, Dec. 21st

1897

Cook, John B. and Fannie Morris, Oct. 18th

Carpenter, W. L. and Ira M. Worthington, Feb. 22nd

Cheape, J. A. and M. T. Minor, Feb. 27th

Clarke, Wm. and M. E. Suddarth, March 9th

Carter, Geo. E. and Katie Keener, April 17th

Critzer, Ches. and M. H. Shulty, April 26th

Cheape, H. W. and K. M. McMurdo, June 9th

Cormock, Gilbert R. and Anna B. Mahanes, June 19th

Crawford, C. E. and J. W. Houchens, July 7th

Clements, D. J. and Rosa B. Harris, July 24th

Carpenter, Ordway and Annie E. Smith, Aug. 10th

Campbell, Chas. and Mary O. Hart, Aug. 31st

Chandler, Geo. F. and Rosa B. Eaton, Nov. 15th

Critzer, Arthur and A. J. Thomas, Dec. 16th

Clark, Wm. and L. L. Wash, Dec 29th

1898

Critzer, J. W. and C. E. Parr, Feb. 14th

Clemons, J. H. and Fanetta Suddarth, March 5th

Craft, J. N. and Cora L. Maupin, March 12th

Clements, James M. and Mary E. Pace, March 21st

Collins, J. P. and S. H. Wood, June 20th

Carver, D. C. and Aurelia Woodson, July 25th

Clark, W. J. and Emma K. Smith, Sept. 13th

Colvin, Dr. J. A. and Annie E. Rea, Oct. 15th

Cribbs, M. M. and A. F. Bragg, Oct. 31st

Critzer, Geo T. and Sarah J. Toms, Nov. 7th

Craig, Wm. A. and E. E. Johnson, Nov. 7th

Catterton, W. Z. and I. B. Davis, Dec. 19th

1899

Coleman, James D. and Virgie Morris, Oct. 3rd

Coleman, Emmett L. and Bettie W. Powell, Dec. 13th

Chapman, J. Thomas and Gertrude D. Plunkett, Dec. 18th

Coiner, S. F. and Lelia E. Gardner, Dec. 23rd

Clark, J. T. and S. B. Clark, Jan. 17th

Crawford, Wm. A. and Junita Crawford, Jan. 30th

Collins, J. R. and S. E. Alexander, March 27th

Clements, L. J. and H. H. Kidd, May 17th

Carter, James and Sarah Palmer, Aug. 7th

Carroll, Joshua M. and Nannie V. Carroll, Sept. 1st

Cleveland, W. P. and Mary W. Collins, Sept. 13th

1900

Catterton, Herbert and Bertie Garland, Feb. 5th

Coles, E. P. and Zac. Hammond, Sept. 25th

Claiborne, J. W. and E. L. Vest, Oct. 13th

Critzer, Robt. and Daisy Baber, Nov. 5th

Crenshaw, J. T. and R. O. Pace, Dec. 15th

Cobbs, E. L. and Maggie N. Edwards, June 13th

Coleman, S. W. and A. S. Woodson, June 13th

1901

Carr, Ed. H. and Katie Douglass, Feb. 18th

Clatterbuck, Thos. and Sadie B. Mitchell, May 13th

Crawford, L. W. and F. E. Crawford, Aug. 9th

Clements, L. E. and E. C. Jones, Aug. 17th

Cleveland, E. C. and V. F. Gorden, Aug. 20th

Cobb, Ebenzerh and Georgia L. Chiles, Sept. 4th

Clements, R. W. and B. L. Fretwell, Sept. 17th

Carr, W. B. and J. J. Ballard, Sept. 27th

Clemmer, J. A. and Daily Landes, Oct. 9th

Critzer, Frank and Esther Hall, Oct. 21st

Cannady, S. and P. A. Toms, Nov. 11th

Coles, T. T. and M. M. Rhodes, Dec. 16th

Craft, G. A. and Catherine V. Kinney, Dec. 17th

1902

Critzer, Robt. Louis and Minnie McClue, May 28th

Craven, Samuel and Isabella Sandridge, April 29th

Clarke, J. E. and B. B. Bishop, May 31st

Cleveland, Wm. E. and J. Gertrude Morris, July 9th

Clayton, Willis T. and A. Fannie Hackett, July 22nd

Carver, Hammie T. and Carrie B. Shipp, Aug. 4th

Crenshaw, Wilbur and Mary Smith, Sept. 2nd

Craig, O. H. and Eliz Mann, Sept. 22nd

Conway, Jas. R. and Ella Spears, Oct. 21st

Chisholm, Vernie and Sally Baltimore, Nov. 8th

Crenshaw, S. W. and Annie J. Smith, Dec. 15th

Crisp, Jno. A. and Louisa Mason, Dec. 15th

1903

Clark, Wm. H. and C. E. Moon, Jan. 21st

Coleman, Jas. W. and Mollie Morris, April 11th

Campbell, A. J. and C. T. Johnson, July 24th

Cook, H. E. and P. M. Bragg, Aug. 25th

Crews, V. M. and C. Moon, Aug. 29th

Criddle, Jas. and Caroline Gibson, Oct. 19th

Casey, H. N. and A. M. Greaves, Nov. 12th

Cogghell, E. L. and M. W. E. Wood, Nov. 16th

Clarity, Jos. C. and Alice V. Failes, Dec. 22nd

Craddock, Geo. Henry and Annie Jane Amos, Dec. 23rd

1904

Carroll, Jno. W. and Polly Ann Ragland, April 13th

Colvin, Geo. and Annie Crawford, April 23rd

Crawford, Wm. H. and Maggie V. Walker, April 25th

Clements, Samuel T. and Louisa J. Hall, June 28th

Creasy, Sandy S. and Annie E. Cunningham, Aug. 26th

Currier, John Henry and Mary Eliz. Ferish, Nov. 8th

Clements, Henry Jackson and Mary Ellen Edwards, Nov. 12th

Cason, Mann Hasting and Lena Harlow, Dec. 22nd

Craddock, A. J. and Jane E. Craddock, Dec. 28th

1905

Chapman, Eugene and Nellie Jarman, Oct. 27th

Crawford, Columbus Lee and Elizabeth C. Maupin, Dec. 14th

Cooke, William Henry and Annie Virginia Snell, Dec. 18th

Critzer, W. S. and Agnes W. Stargell, Sept. 20th

Crist, J. H. and Fannie M. Phillips, Sept. 26th

Cox, Robt. L. and Carrie Norvell, Feb. 4th

Coleman, Edw. A. and Ida L. Thumers, March 28th

Clements, Jas. W. and Daisy Bell Hicks, April 11th

Clark, Clyde L. and Nettie A. Marshall, July 29th

Crest, J. H. and Fannie M. Phillips, Sept. 26th

Chapman, Eugene and Nellie Jarman Key, Oct. 27th

Cook, William Henry and Annie Virginia Snell, Dec. 18th

1906

Cannady, William T. and Fannie Cannady, July 21st

Crawford, John Sell and Zodie Lee Crawford, Aug. 6th

Crawford, Luther V. and Mary Alice Staton, Sept. 30th

Cooper, James H. and Grace Edge, Nov. 21st

Carver, John E. and Virginia A. Vaughan, Nov. 21st

Craig, Luther H. and Lelia L. Moyer, Dec. 23rd

Cobbs, Joseph M. and Eula B. Kirby, Dec. 23rd

Carr, Thomas O. and Edna E. McAllister, Dec. 27th

Carnell, Moses L. and Bettie J. Clements, Dec. 26th

1907

Critzer, Thos. S. and Loula A. Drumheller, April 3rd

Cushing, William A. and Elsie L. Hall, April 15th

Cleveland, Harry B. and Bettie C. Ballard, June 12th

Child, Lathom and May L. Rogers, June 12th

Clements, Floyd S. and Ada P. Southard, July 15th

Clements, S. E. and Emma Mooney, Aug. 18th

Clarke, Linwood and Annie E. Davis, Oct. 14th

Clarke, Charles H. and Carrie L. Thurston, Nov. 27th

Coleman, Grant L. and Atlee Spencer, Dec. 11th

Calhoun, D. Speck and Emily A. Simms, Dec. 17th

Cook, Charles H. and Willie Pugh, Dec. 26th

Colman, Charles H. and Lillie J. Sandridge, Dec. 22nd

Carver, Jim and Cora Hunt, Dec. 25th

Crickenberger, William E. and M. F. Norford, Dec. 30th

1908

Coles, Roberts and Mary W. Minor, Jan. 7th

Clements, Robert and Sadie L. Via, Jan. 16th

Clements, James Martin and Catherine Burnett, March 18th

Cox, Floyd E. and Ludie E. Crawford, April 20th

Cox, Aubrey G. and Mattie L. Marshall, April 20th

Coleman, James D. and Roney Batton, June 11th

Campbell, Willie E. and Pearl Walton, June 26th

Cook, Charles A. and Lucile Richards, June 30th

Carr, Samuel G. and Minnie S. Woods, July 22nd

Cole, William C. and Lillie B. Booker, Sept. 4th

Clements, William H. and Iness Brown, Nov. 15th

Critzer, Ernest T. and Nava Ashia Hackett, Dec. 16th

Critzer, James P. and Josephine Drumheller, Dec. 23rd

Chapman, George and Lula Wood, Dec. 22nd

1909

Craun, Samuel and Fannie L. Naylor, Jan. 21st

Craig, Jacob S. and Julia H. Kidd, March 2nd

Clements, James W. and Ada M. Meeks, July 11th

Collins, Joseph L. and Nora A. Wood, Aug. 22nd

Clarke, John and Annie Butler, Sept. 7th

Carver, Lywood J. and Florence J. Easton, Nov. 3rd

Cobbs, Carl and Electra Tooly, Nov. 10th

1910

Campbell, John and Esther Maddox, Jan. 19th

Childs, John William and Grace Herndon, March 17th

Call, Irvine and Minnie Kidd, May 11th

Campbell, Edward D. and Mildred Lankford, June 29th

Colvin, Robert L. and Eaerline Hinny, July 8th

Clarke, James W. and Carrie W. Owens, July 26th

Critzer, Raron A. and Maggie Bacon, July 27th

Craig, Bernard and Myrtle Fox, Aug. 22nd

Cunningham, John C. and Eveline Sneed, Sept. 10th

Clarke, Marvin S. and Mildred Woodson, Oct. 27th

Compton, Robert French and Mary Barbam Rixey, Nov. 8th

Criskenberger, Elma S. and Daisy H. Beck, Dec. 8th

Clarke, Hugh and Rosa Petitt, Dec. 27th

Craig, Harry N. and Lizzie Martin, Dec. 27th

Clements, William J. and Bertha Newton, Dec. 31st

1911

Clarke, Jacob N. and Josephine E. Garrison, Jan. 3rd

Carpenter, Early and Mattie Lee Munday, Jan. 7th

Cox, Willie and Annie Thomas, Feb. 6th

Canady, Leonard and Ida Barksdale, March 1st

Clements, William H. and Sarah Eubank, March 7th

Campbell, John and Ester Hall, May 11th

Cunningham, William Edwd. and Wilma N. Luck, June 22nd

Collin, Howard M. and Lula M. Elliott, Sept. 5th

Call, Jesse M. and Ruth Critzer, Sept. 6th

Cox, James and Ollie Thomas, Oct. 15th

Cleveland, Emmett H. and Julia Ann Powell, Oct. 18th

Craig, Luther and Chalkey Baber, Nov. 15th

Carroll, Harry and Gracie Critzer, Nov. 22nd

Critzer, Claude and Edna Lee Estes, Nov. 30th

1912

Clarke, Edwin and Myrtie Proffitt, May 29th

Clark, Stuart and Rosa E. Cason, June 2nd

Cash, Leonard and Annie Woodson, Sept. 11th

Carter, William L. and Annie B. Morris, Sept. 25th

Carter, William and Susan Maupin, Oct. 26th

Clark, Robert W. and Carrie L. Gentry, Oct. 30th

Cox, Hunter H. and Fleda E. Wood, Nov. 24th

Carrier, Robert H. and Ada M. Blackwell, Dec. 5th

Craig, John and Fannie Fisher, Dec. 11th

Crickenberger, George D. and Eva G. Durrett, Dec. 24th

1913

Craig, Howard E. and Rosa V. Leake, Feb. 24th

Coupela, Joseph M. and Minnie Carroll, June 1st

Critzer, William A. and Susie H. Harris, June 15th

Carver, Samuel D. and Nannie E. Lynch, July 23rd

Cook, Linwood W. and Lena Elliton, Oct. 22nd

Clayton, A. Y. and Gracie Mawyer, Oct. 29th

Coffman, Hiram D. and Mamis Bickers, Nov. 8th

Campbell, John W. and Fannie Durham, Dec. 4th

Critzer, Richard W. and Freda C. Wood, Dec. 24th

Callis, William S. and Virginia Edwards, Dec. 27th

Crenshaw, Charles E. and Ada M. McCauley, Dec. 31st

1914

Clark, William D. and Lillie B. Jones, Jan. 28th

Crickenberger, William D. and Lewallis B. Sandridge, Jan. 29th

Clark, Malcolm D. and Esther P. Moon, Feb. 2nd

Childs, Charles J. and Julia Kesterson, March 15th

Clements, Ned and Madie L. Critzer, March 26th

Coiner, Samuel H. and Sarah B. Alexander, April 14th

Coleman, L. A. and Ruth C. White, April 29th

Currier, Harry E. and Mabel L. Collins, May 20th

Carver, Willie C. and Laura Hunter, May 28th

Clark, Andrew J. and Mary E. Taylor, Aug. 8th

Cox, Downey and Eunice Marshall, Aug. 20th

Critzer, Sidney and Erie Dudley, Sept. 9th

Calhoun, Frank H. and Hannah M. Morris, Sept. 14th

Cougdon, Cary S. and Mary K. Wingfield, Sept. 22nd

Cobb, Thomas L. and Zoe Kirby, Nov. 3rd

Carver, Bessie A. and Elwood D. Shisler, Nov. 17th

1915

Caskie, Jasqulin Ambler and Margaret Lee Miner, Feb. 9th

Crawford, M. C. and M. M. Davis, April 5th

Chisholm, B. Lesley and Margaret E. Vasselor, April 12th

Cummings, George H. and Emma Ruth Collins, April 20th

Chummings, Geo. E. and Mary E. Dudley, May 5th

Collin, John C. and Nell Chisholm, May 17th

Carven, Robert and Kama Carven, May 24th

Crowe, Roy and Rachel Robey, Aug. 11th

Craig, Luther and Blanche Carter, Oct. 20th

Clarke, Nathan and Fannie Durham, Dec. 3rd

Cromer, C. L. and Ruby Chandler, Dec. 16th

Clarke, George and Minnie Buck, Dec. 29th

1916

Crawford, William and Julia Shiflett, Feb. 21st

Carner, Ollie W. and Daisy Carner, Feb. 24th

Carr, Coldwell A. and Bertha Pugh, April 1st

Clements, Willie and Martha Stone, May 5th

Chisholm, Lindsoy, and Alice Bishop, June 28th

Clements, Charlie and Nellie Sipe, July 4th

Cook, Charles T. and Mrs. Lulie W. Nolting, July 17th

Craft, C. C. and G. R. Taggart, Nov. 1st

Crenshaw, Hunter J. and Marian Ida Smith, Nov. 9th

Carver, William and Minnie S. Larter, Dec. 1st

Carroll, Herbert A. and Margaret S. Catterton, Dec. 11th

Critzer, Harry and Blanche Annie Mawyer, Dec. 27th

Cross, Jr., Chas. Felix and Mary V. White, Dec. 25th

1917

Craig, Julius H. and Feora Opal Bunch, April 10th

Clements, Luciaw S. and Minnie Jane Henry, April 13th

Cartie, Briscoe and Lizzie Fisher, April 22nd

Camden, Harry T. and Ester N. Spencer, May 5th

Cone, John W. and Juliet Graves, June 18th

Cason, Leonard E. and Mary L. Pitman, Aug. 1st

Conway, Clarence J. and Sally D. Garland, Sept. 4th

Coleman, Jas. M. and Mrs. Susie M. Mundy, Nov. 7th

Coffey, Wm. T. and Page M. Kirby, Nov. 24th

Clark, George L. and Julia E. Critzer, Dec. 2nd

Coffey, Raymond H. and Mary E. Kirby, Dec. 24th

1918

Callier, Quinton H. and Florence Easton, Jan. 7th

Chamberlain, Chas. Addison and Elizabeth M. Kidd, Jan. 10th

Clements, Jasper L. and Nellie K. Hunt, May 16th

Chambers, Wesley S. and Ella Morris, June 1st

Callahan, Claude S. and Lora E. McDaniel, Nov. 6th

Chisholm, Lewis and Viola Moubry Dec. 3rd

Cash, Robt. G. and Mary L. Geer, Dec. 22nd

1919

Craig, Thos. H. and Lula Fisher, Jan. 30th

Cason, Mann B. and Dora Wood, Feb. 17th

Clements, Willie H. and Minnie Hogue, Feb. 20th

Colliver, J. H. and Lillie F. Morris, April 26th

Carver, Dabney C. and Ada E. Harris, June 18th

Coffey, Willie Lee and Dolly A. Oliver, July 19th

Clements, Laurence O. and Mary E. Dudley, Aug. 14th

Chiles, Charles J. and Helen G. Shepherd, Oct. 8th

Currier, Henry L. and Anyelina E. Weaver, Nov. 5th

Cheape, Charles W. and Florence L. Nuttycombe, Nov. 26th

Clements, Samuel F. and Amanda I. Harlow, Nov. 26th

Collins, Ernest M. and Sallie P. Cutler, Nov. 27th

Clements, Ernest A. and Bertha Marrs, Dec. 31st

1920

Colvin, Jas. R. and Elizabeth F. Blackwell, Feb. 25th

Crickenberger, John O. and Emma Fisher, April 11th

Carter, Emmett G. and Carrie T. Carter, May 17th

Cook, George A. and Julia C. Rea, June 19th

Collins, Herbert W. and Cary Jane Corbett, July 3rd

Croft, Bedoe F. and Margaret S. Hines, July 23rd

Craig, George D. and Mammie B. Martin, Sept. 15th

Collins, Lonna Earl and Mary Agnes Kirby, Sept. 18th

Coffman, Benjamin F. and Jane M. Watts, Oct. 6th

Critzer, James William and Virginia Leona Tomlin, Oct. 1st

Clements, Robert and Susie Spradlin, Oct. 28th

Coleman, Moses J. and Lilly J. Batton, Oct. 29th

Crawford, Thomas Walter and Elsie Ray, Nov. 29th

Clarke, Roy S. and Eunice Smith, Dec. 22nd

Crickenberger, Eugene G. and Eunice L. Gentry, Dec. 23rd

Cox, James William and Effie May Beddow, Dec. 24th

1921

Cox, Frank Edward and Laura M. Harris, Jan. 5th

Colvin, Robert and Estelle Hamm, Jan. 24th

Carter, Stanley George and Thelma Black Wood, Feb. 14th

Crawford, Cornilus B. and Mary L. Gibson, Feb. 17th

Crickenberger, Dallas S. and Lena Belle Morris, Feb. 19th

Crickenberger, John S. and Mrs. Nora M. Bobst, March 2nd

Cardwell, Edward B. and Edna M. Bruce, June 6th

Critzer, George W. and Lilia Josephene Thurston, June 22nd

Christan, Mortimer H. and Amelia M. Money, July 5th

Clements, John and Lena Irving, July 19th

Colvin, Aelic and Patsie J. Estes, July 26th

Cash, Thurman S. and Carrie Lee Sneed, Aug. 12th

Clary, Wiley G. and Pearl Humphrey, Dec. 21st

Carter, Roy O. and Rachel Wolfe, Dec. 26th

1922

Cunningham, Joe S. and Nannie M. Kidd, June 9th

Collins, Edgar M. and Anna Elizabeth Newman, June 19th

Clinch, Douglas W. and Frances H. Bogert, June 29th

Chisholm, Chas. E. and Lula Krickbourne, July 4th

Clements, James F. and Bessie Moses, July 9th

Cross, Richard S. and Mary E. Woodruff, Aug. 5th

Clarke, Randolph B. and Nellie DeMasters, Aug. 19th

Cassell, Clair F. and Mary C. Hildreth, Aug. 28th

Campbell, Harrison and Mattie Napier, Dec. 26th

1923

Cook, John F. and Julia Sprouse, Jan. 11th

Critzer, Gilbert B. and Clara Mawyer, April 5th

Cook, Luther and Helen Quick, April 27th

Critzer, Massie W. and Claudie R. Carter, July 14th

Critzer, Murry and Sally Farish, July 16th

Critzer, Slaughter and Tinet Critzer, Aug 10th

Carter James Lewis and Martha Jane Donald, Aug. 31st

Clements, Edward L. and Mary G. Carver, Oct. 20th

Clements, William E. and Vertie W. Hunt, Dec. 18th

1924

Clements, Dalton M. and Annie M. Sprouse, Jan. 21st

Campbell, John C. and Cora K. Diggs, May 17th

Cobbs, James W. and Mary L. Proffitt, May 31st

Crowder, John J. and Lora M. Garrison, June 16th

Collins, Russell M. and Annie Kirby, June 16th

Cleveland, Rolor and Lillian Sprouse, July 3rd

Chisholm, Melvin and Velessa Iris Pugh, July 10th

Cash, Harvey S. and Lora M. Johnson, July 19th

Cash, Floyd D. and Crystal O. Gilford, Aug. 7th

Cook, Jacob S. and Lilly E. Durham, Aug. 14th

Cash, Robt. and Clave Dorman, Aug. 25th

Clarke, Jacob N. and Josephine Garrison, Sept. 19th

Cleveland, John W. and Mary M. Thacker, Sept. 24th

Critzer, James P. and Myrtle Lee Tilman, Oct. 25th

1925

Critzer, Dabney and Bessie Melton, Jan. 21st

Cooper, Charles R. and Ada L. Thacker, Feb. 24th

Critzer, Overton A. and Mannye P. Woodson, April 9th

Clarke, Lacy and Bethe Staley, April 14th

Carter, C. W. and Evelyn Galloway, April 18th

Cooke, Walter G. and Florence B. Pace, Aug. 1st

Collins, Lloyd and Pearl Sprouse, Aug. 13th

Creasey, Walker and Pearl Flynt, Sept. 19th

Carver, Reuben D. and Sadie F. Young, Oct. 9th

Cook, Minor E. and Zeta E. Lewis, Nov. 9th

Carpenter, Charles and Elsie Morris, Dec. 21st

1926

Cook, Harry D. and Ruth S. Douglas, Jan. 23rd

Carruth, Emmett L. and Ruby Poyn Maupin, Feb. 17th

Critzer, Jr., Chesterfield C. and Katheryne Sebrell, June 14th

Crawford, Warren H. and Lilia Haney, June 23rd

Carter, James M. and Katie V. Ragland, July 17th

Carver, Roy and Mae Beal, July 19th

Carpenter, Johnson L. and Virginia E. Turner, Nov. 17th

Clatterbuck, Jas. E. and Lillian H. Owen, Dec. 10th

Conner, Archie and Mildred Marshall, Dec. 27th

1927

Callier, Bogge and Mamie Morris, March 13th

Chisholm, Roy M. and Gladys S. Stephens, May 28th

Cash, Aubrey L. and Lucy Garrison, May 28th

Childs, William C. and Hattie M. Sandridge, June 13th

Cooley, Gery R. and Constance Martin, June 22nd

Carver, George and Maude Middleton, July 1st

Crawford, Bruce D. and Bertha M. Bailes, July 9th

Clark, Earl A. and Reva H. Hackett, Aug. 6th

Critzer, Lucian and Lula A. Mitchell, Oct. 26th

Carter, Albert H. and Ruth V. Hudson, Nov. 19th

Cake, David V. and Lelia W. Haden, Dec. 23rd

Cook, Walter S. and Mary E. Pugh, Dec. 14th

1928

Collier, Irving and Hattie Lee Collier, Feb. 16th

Chisholm, Bernie E. and Thelma H. Taylor, March 1st

Calvin, Joe and Ella Amos Brookman, March 12th

Craddock, Chas. E. and Dorothy M. Craddock, June 23rd

Carr, Alvin B. and Ruby E. Pritchett, July 16th

Clements, Roy M. and Willie V. Hudson, July 27th

Cash, Jessie Wm. and Daisy B. Pugh, Oct. 15th

Craddock, Harry J. and Lelia W. Gianning, Dec. 24th

Childress, Lloyd and Maggie Lawson, Dec. 29th

1929

Critzer, Walter E. and Mary J. Seay, March 30th

Cash, Homer and Goldie Dorman, March 30th

Clark, Gilbert D. and Alice L. Townes, May 10th

Crawford, John H. and Louise C. Shiflett, June 17th

Calvin, Lewis Chas. and Eleanor Dorothy Petitt, July 15th

Capelle, Joseph A. and Mary Eva Ballard, Aug. 14th

Cash, Reuben L. and Myrtle M. B. Dudley, Oct. 5th

Chapman, Geo. Wm. and Virginia D. Walters, Oct. 29th

D

???

Darnold, Moses and Frances Clarkson, July 4th

1782

Davis, Thomas and Elizabeth Fritz, April 15th

Denton, John and Sally Baber, Nov. 18th

1785

Davenport, Martin and Milley Murrell, Aug. 29th

Dedman, Dixon and Sarah Buster, Feb. 10th

Dowell, John and Martha Hall, Jan. 30th

1786

Davis, William and Betsy Chaney, Dec. 19th

Dawson, Benjamin and Mary Martin, ? 10th

Dedman, Nathan and Elizabeth Gooch, March 30th

1787

Dolton, Isaac and Susanna Garth ??

Douglass, James and Mary Wells, Jan. 24th

1788

Davis, Lenord and Mary Marshall, Dec. 23rd

Delaney, William and Nancy Rodes, Sept. 10th

Dunn, Reubin and Nancy Lane, Feb. 11th

1789

Drumheller, George and Betsy Helander, Dec. 10th

1790

Dickerson, Wiley and Polly Carr, May 20th
Dickinson, John and Elizabeth Dolton, Dec. 19th
Dudley, James and Sarah Hurt, March 12th

1791

Dickerson, William and Elizabeth Foster, April 15th

1792

Davis, Lewis and Patsy Walton, Nov. 8th
Dickerson, John and Judith Douglass, May 28th
Dollins, James and Elizabeth Dollins, March 9th
Donovan, Daniel and Nancy Rae, March 20th
Dowell, Richard and Frankey Bullock, Dec. 19th

1794

Dalton, Isham and Elizabeth Walton, Jan. 20th
Davis, Jacob and Mary Hurmond, Sept. 27th
Davis, Jeconias and Baby Lowry, Dec. 13th
Dotson, James and Delinay Jackson, Dec. 26th
Dowell, Reuben and Nancy Taylor, Sept. 25th
Dunn, Zacharias and Mary Davis, March 28th
Durham, Melton and Jane Coleman, March 10th

1795

Dowell, Elijah and Sally Dowell, Feb. 17th

1797

Davis, Nathaniel and Susannah Goolsby, Dec. 13th
Dollins, David and Nelly Collins, Dec. 18th
Dollins, William and Plebe Dollins, Dec. 23rd

1798

Dawson, William and Sally Jobling, Nov. 5th
Dovel, Bolser and Nancy Greening, March 12th
Dove, David and Abbagin Moore, Feb. 5th
Dudley, John and Polly Hurt, Dec. 29th

1799

Davenport, William and Sally Harris Rodes, Aug. 24th
Davis, Bartlot and Dalley Lowry, Feb. 2nd
Dawson, John and Nancy Martin, Nov. 5th
Day, Ambrose and Nancy Bowcock, Feb. 6th
Dowell, John and Elizabeth Bradley, Dec. 23rd
Drumheller, Jacob and Salley Davis, Feb. 4th

1801

Day, Hundley and Mary Garland, Dec. 27th

Deane, Finch and Jamima Harper, Oct. 27th
Dickenson, James and Milly Watts, Nov. 24th
Dickenson, James and Nancy Brown, Dec. 7th
Dougherty, Daniel and Rebecca Stone, Dec. 31st

1802

Davenport, Charles and Nancy Davenport, Aug. 1th
Davenport, Jesse and Susannah Thompson, June 22nd
Davis, Joh and Caty Downs, Sept. 18th
Davis, William and Ably Douglass, Nov. 1st
Dedman, Elijah and Salley Everitt, Jan. 19th
Dollins, John and Sarah Davis, Oct. 6th
Douglass, Achillis and Nancy Bowcock, Nov. 2nd
Douglass, William and Rebecca Bussey, June 9th
Durrett, Robert and Susanna Massie, Dec. 17th

1803

Dawson, Thomas and Nancy Fortune, Nov. 7th
Dollins, Richard and Margaret Alexander, Oct. 20th
Durrett, Larkin and Anne Maupin, Jan. 19th

1804

Davis, Edmond and Polly Riddle, Dec. 21st
Davis, Edmund and Susannah S. Mills, Aug. 7th
Dickenson, John and Sarah Blackwell, Oct. 24th
Dollins, John and Henry Wood, March 10th
Douglass, John and Nancy Edwards, Oct. 29th
Dowell, Major and Frances Jones, Oct. 1st

1805

Davis, Benjamin and Jane Jones, Dec. 21st

1806

Davis, Elijah and Elizabeth Jones, Dec. 18th
Dawson, Allen and Lucy Wingfield, Jan. 27th
Dawson, Elijah and Patsy Gentry, Oct. 13th
Dickerson, Wiley and Nancy Walls, Jan. 7th
Duke, Richard and Maria Walker, Aug. 8th
Durrett, Achillis and Hanah Shaver, Feb. 22nd
Durett, Achillis and Hanah Shaver, Dec. 4th

1807

Davis, John K. and Sally Davis, Jan. 4th
Dowell, James and Fanny Dalton, Dec. 27th
Dowell, John and Susan Roberson, Sept. 17th
Dowell, Major and Elizabeth Martin, April 20th

1808

Davis, Richard and Patsy Michie, Dec. 22nd
Davis, Thompson H. and Nancy McClary, May 12th

1810

Douglass, George and Rhody Bingham, April 5th

Douglass, William and Polly Barksdale, Dec. 10th

Dowell, William and Sally Pickett, Jan. 17th

1811

Davis,   and Cordelia Dowell, April 10th

Davis,   and Sarah Harvy, March 21st

Draffin, Thomas and Nancy Douglass, Feb. 11th

Durham,   and Mourning Burrus, Jan. 28th

1812

Dowell, Harrison and Nancy D. Hall, Dec. 26th

Dowell, Richard and Mildred A. Hall, Dec. 26th

Dowell, William and Lucy Hill, Jan. 13th

Dunn, Reubin and Maria Musin, Dec. 7th

Dunson, Benjamin and Dolly Watherehildrep, May 11th

Durrett, Richard and Peggy Richardson, Jan. 6th

1813

Dickerson, Robert and Sarah Crostwaite, Nov. 1st

Dickerson, William and Margaret Head, Feb. 12th

Dowell, Thomas and Fanny Collins, May 6th

Drumheller, Adam and Nancy Hicks, April 24th

Dudley, John and Patsy Lively, Aug. 2nd

Dunn, John and Susannah Maupin, Feb. 1st

1814

Davis, Lewis and Susanna Dandridge, Feb. 15th

Devinielle, John and Sarah W. Johnson, Jan. 4th

Dowell, John and Emily Walton, Dec. 9th

1815

Davis, Robert and Lucy Shiflett, March 16th

Dickerson, John and Ann Brown, Jan. 17th

Dickinson, Douglas and Frances Fourney hough, Nov. 13th

Diggs, George P. and   Richards, Nov. 9th

Dowell, Barnett and Nancy Munday, Sept. 28th

1816

Davis, Zachariah and Delphy Quick, Dec. 12th

Dossey, John and Nancy Marshall, Dec. 12th

Douglass, John and Mildred Bowcock, Oct. 23rd

Draffin, William and Nancy Marr, Oct. 7th

Duke, Archibald B. and Sarah P. Dickinson, Dec. 19th

Dunn, John and Mildred Watts, March 21st

1817

Davis, Isaac and Harriot Garth, April 29th

Durham, David and Polley Burrus, March 19th

1818

Davis, Edmund and Keronhopouch Walton, Jan. 17th

Davis, John and Mary Hall, Jan. 5th

Dollins, John and Nancy Wood, March 2nd

Drumheller, Adam and Sally Thomas, Dec. 30th

Drumheller, George and Jane Suddarth, Jan. 3rd

Dunn, James and Betsy Collins, Nov. 11th

Dannell, Ellis M. and Nancy Shiflett, June 3rd

Detter, John and Aliza Faris Harris, Aug. 21st

1819

Dowell, John and Elizabeth Garrison, Jan. 14th

Dowell, Pleasant and Nancy Hill, Nov. 11th

Drumheller, Jacob and Johanna F. Pleasants, Oct. 16th

Dunn, Fontaine D. and Nancy C. Via, Dec. 24th

Durrett, Robert D. and Elizabeth Price, Feb. 1st

Durrett, Robert D. and Mary D. Wood, Oct. 4th

1820

Dobbs, Martin and Elizabeth Bowen, Sept. 27th

Drumheller, William and Elizabeth Thomas, Jan. 11th

1821

Dallon, James and Martha Wood, Sept. 26th

Dettor, Mathwes and Elizabeth Suddarth, Oct. 9th

Dowell, John and Joanna T. Moon, Sept. 19th

Drumheller, Leonard and Sally Finder, Oct. 22nd

Douglass, Merry and N. McAllister, Dec. 19th

1822

Dollins Jeremiah and Ribba Merrett, July 16th

Dove, Henry and Rachel Wood, Dec. 18th

Downing, Charles and Rebecca Gray, Jan. 16th

Dunn, John and Elizabeth Johnson, Nov. 7th

1823

Dedman, Dixon and Sarah Drumheller, March 5th

Depraw, William and Patty Smith, Dec. 1st

Dequisee, Thomas and Ellen Thomas, Sept. 11th

Doling, William and Nancy Stone, May 15th

Dudley, William and June Thacker, June 10th

Dunkum, William and Frances Gentry, Dec. 18th

1824

Dopsey, Richard and Mildred Howard, Jan. 15th

Dudley, William and Jane Hurt, June 23rd
Durrett, Thomas and Emily Wood, Dec. 23rd

1825

Dowell, Atwell and Elizabeth Starkes, Aug. 4th
Drumheller, Samuel and Mary Ballard, Sept. 1st
Dudley, Isham and Agnes Bailey, March 7th
Dunn, James and Elizabeth Via, Dec. 20th

1826

Day, William and Sally Hicks, March 10th
Defoe, John and Matilda Rothwell, Sept. 17th
Dickerson, John and Rebecca Dopey, Nov. 2nd
Dickinson, Barnett and Nancy Crosthwait, Feb. 26th
Douglass, James Jr. and Mary McCullock, Dec. 11th
Drumheller, John A. and Susannah Hestand, Dec. 19th

1827

Douglass, Tanoy and Martha A. McCullock, Sept. 20th
Dowell, Marshall and Anne Starke, May 5th
Davis, Matthews P. and Matilda Dowell, April 7th

1828

Drumheller, Thomas and Harriot Eastham, Jan. 31st
Durham, David W. and Alvia Jane Borden, Aug. 22nd
Durrett, Marcus and Sarah Ann Moore, Sept. 4th
Durrett, Paul H. and Ann C. Gates, Dec. 12th
Durrett, William and Frances Calling, Feb. 4th

1829

Dolson, David and Sarah Bailey, March 7th
Davenport, Edward and Emily Case, Feb. 27th
Davis, Isaac and Martha Langford, Nov. 26th

1830

Dawson, Martin and Louisa Gore, Jan. 5th
Day, Musco G. and Julia A. Ballard, July 20th
Dickerson, Nimrod and Elizabeth Robinson, Dec. 16th
Dudley, George and Anna Anderson, Oct. 6th
Dudley, Hudson and Jane Dudley, Oct. 9th
Dudley, Nathan and Susan Thacker, Sept. 6th
Dunkum, John and Elizabeth M. Durrett, Oct. 30th
Durrett, Thomas G. and Frances Simms, Sept. 30th

1831

Davis, John W. and Alice Meriwether, June 23rd
Davis, Richard and Martha Harris, Oct. 25th
Dickerson, William and Ellen Lane, Jan. 25th
Dollins, Hugh A. and Isabella McCord, April 9th

Drumright, William and Christeance Carver, Aug. 18th
Durrett, James and Susan Goodman, April 14th
Durrett, Richard M. and Elizabeth Piper, Feb. 24th
Durrett, Richard W. and Lucy C. Twyman, March 1st
Durrett, William W. and Mary Martin, Feb. 7th

1832

Davis, James and Catherine Walton, Dec. 20th
Drake, Simmons G. and Elizabeth Noel, March 7th
Drumheller, Albert and Mary W. Hall, Nov. 5th
Durrett, Roy S. and S. J. Pomberton, April 19th
Durrett, William H. and Mary J. Dunkum, May 15th

1833

Diggs, John and Lucy B. Carr, Oct. 8th
Dowell, John H. and Mary Eubank, Nov. 1st
Duggins, Thomas C. and Elizabeth W. Jackson, Oct. 30th
Dunn, Thomas R. and Jane B. Salmon, Nov. 5th
Doak, John S. and Mary A. Porter, April 22nd
Dodd, John B. and Ann Polkenhorn, Jan. 12th

1834

Dudley, John and Nancy Hurt, May 15th
Dunn, James M. and Elizabeth Gentry, July 7th
Dyer, Robert and Sarah Ann W. Morris, Aug. 5th

1835

Day, Willis and June Barksdale, May 11th
Duke, Alexander and E. K. Garrett, Oct. 12th

1836

Dobins, David and Elizabeth Booth, May 19th
Dowell, Samuel and S. A. Binghum, Dec. 27th
Dudley, George and Nancy Bowen, Nov. 3rd
Dudley, Nelson and Jane E. Gibson, Jan. 9th

1837

Daniel, George M. and Elizabeth Hall, Oct. 11th
Daniel, James H. and Mary E. Jones, Oct. 31st
Davis, George W. and Eliza T. Winn, Oct. 12th
Davis, John B. and Jiney McCord, Dec. 19th
Dickerson, Moorman and Elizabeth Johnson, July 3rd
Druin, John and Jane A. Brown, June 20th
Dudley, William and Mary Dove, Sept. 7th

1838

Drumheller, Neb. and Elizabeth Drumheller, Dec. 3rd

Dunkum, Elijah and Elizabeth Ficklin, Dec. 17th

Dunn, Lewis and Elizabeth Bruce, Dec. 21st

1839

Dawson, Stephen and Dicy Wade, May 4th

Desper, Shelton and Rhodo Ann Desper, April 13th

Drumheller, William S. and Elizabeth F. Thomas, Jan. 4th

Dunn, James L. and Caroline M. Salmon, Sept. 19th

1840

Doak, Alexander S. and Ann H. Porter, March 3rd

Dudley, William and Malinda Britt, Feb. 10th

Dunlop, John W. C. and Margaret Kinney, Feb. 6th

1841

Davis, John and Caroline Wood, Oct. 27th

Drinkard, William and Frances Pace, Oct. 7th

Drumheller, Jacob and Martha Sudderth, Sept. 23rd

Dudley, William and Sarah Goodwin, Dec. 29th

1842

Dudley, Ralph S. and F. Hughes, Feb. 21st

1843

Darnelle, James M. and Mary M. Clarke, Nov. 18th

Dickerson, Edward and Julia M. Wood, Dec. 24th

Dudley, Robert and Elizabeth Dudley, March 6th

Dunn, John J. and Susan Dunn, Nov. 10th

Dunn, Miletus S. and Eliza P. Thurmond, Nov. 2nd

1844

Davis, Mathew and Edna T. Davis, Nov. 8th

Dove, David and Patsey Dudley, Aug. 6th

Durrett, Branton B. and Ann E. William, May 30th

1845

Darrow, Henry A. and S. M. Sudderth, June 23rd

Davis, James H. and Sarah E. Harris, Nov. 3rd

Devicks, Thomas W. and Martha Garner, March 20th

Dowell, Joseph and Martha Dowell, May 20th

Duke, John T. and Jane Bailey, Aug. 5th

Duncan, Andrew B. and S. E. Moon, April 24th

1846

Dodd, Francis W. and Virginia Wayman, Jan. 28th

Douglass, Edwin T. and Elizabeth D. Gillum, Sept. 26th

Douglass, Francis E. and Selvina M. Head, Feb. 27th

Dowell, Richard and Sarah F. Dowell, Dec. 17th

Dowell, Roberson and Amandy Mallory, Oct. 5th

Drumheller, Nicholas and Mary J. Harlow, Sept. 22nd

Dudley, William M. and Mary Ann Dudley, Oct. 5th

1847

Douglass, Archibald N. and E. F. Ross, Jan. 25th

Douglass, Magill O. and D. H. Hamm, Dec. 23rd

Douglass, Newton J. and Nancy Jarroll, Dec. 26th

Douglass, Rice G. and Ardena M. Head, Nov. 4th

Dudley, Lindsay and Mary A. Turner, Dec. 12th

1848

Dabney, Madison and Nancy Gillaspie, Nov. 27th

Davis, George and Rebecca A. Singleton, Dec. 20th

Davis, John T. and E. F. Cogbill, Oct. 4th

Davis, R. C. and S. M. Wyant, April 20th

Dawson, James M. and S. J. Carr, Sept. 11th

Deviney, William A. and M. A. Campbell, Sept. 21st

Dollins, Tyree and S. J. Alexander, May 1st

Due, Reuben B. and Lucy A. Diggs, Oct. 26th

Dulaney, A. G. and F. M. Shackelford, Sept. 20th

Dunavint, S. A. and M. R. Gilmore, March ?

1849

Douglass, Thomas M. and Susan E. Thompson, Sept. 13th

Dowell, John and Malinda Pritchett, Dec. 24th

Dunkum, John and Elizabeth Burgess, Feb. 8th

1850

Davis, Braxton and Agness M. Craig, March 6th

Douglass, John B. and Mary F. Old, Dec. 23rd

Drumheller, John B. and M. L. Drumheller, Dec. 12th

Drumheller, S. A. and Emily N. Thomas, Feb. 11th

Drumheller, William and Francis A. Powell, March 18th

Dudley, Fleming and Levine Chisholm, Feb. 5th

Dudley, John H. and Mary Frances Dudley, Dec. 26th

Duncan, John H. and Mary A. Travellian, June 11th

1851

Dabney, James and Lucy J. Pace, Oct. 5th

Dettor, James W. and Elizabeth A. Bowen, Feb. 19th

1852

Davis, Elizah and Sarah F. Walton, Jan. 3rd

Davis, Ira L. and Charity H. Davis, March 8th

Davis, James H. and M. A. Graham, May 13th

Davis, M. P. and N. B. Gibson, Aug. 2nd

Davis, William D. and Phannel Staples, Aug. 20th

Dawson, Wiliam L. and Maru A. Lama, April 6th

Dollins, John B. and M. Tilman, Nov. 3rd

Drumright, James E. and M. A. Bellomy, Dec. 20th

Dudley, William and Sarah E. Priddy, Sept. 23rd

Duke, Thomas and Judenia Garner, Feb. 26th

Dunn, F. D. and Mary F. McAllister, Oct. 1st

Dunn, M. L. and Mary A. Walton, Feb. 17th

1853

Davenport, William E. and Sarah A. Eubank, Nov. 16th

Davis, Benjamin F. and Ann Carden, March 17th

Davison, George W. and Sarah S. May, Oct. 26th

Dawson, Benjamin H. and Q. A. E. Harris, May 26th

Dillard, Robert F. and Lucy J. Shepherd, Dec. 28th

Doll, John A. and Sallie A. Hoye, Oct. 22nd

Dowell, Charles P. and Nancy Hall, Sept. 6th

Drumheller, William M. and Mary J. Thomas, Nov. 7th

Dudley, James H. and Eliza A. Britt, Oct. 18th

1854

Dobbs, Ira and Susan F. Dudley, Dec. 4th

Dobbs, William and Adeline Bowen, July 16th

Dodd, John B. and Ann E. Scott, Feb. 22nd

Dowell, Ezekiel and S. J. Vaughan, March 28th

Drumheller, I. L. W. and Susan D. Bailey, April 13th

DeYamport, A. H. and C. H. Turpin, Oct. 26th

Dowell, Ezeckiel and S. J. Vaughan, March 28th

Drumheller, Jas. W. and Susan D. Bailey, April 13th

1855

Deskins, Harry and Sarah F. Duke, Nov. 27th

Drane, Joseph K. and Mattie W. Poindexter, Oct. 23rd

Dudley, John and M. T. Hughes, March 27th

Durrett, Robert D. and Eliza M. Terrell, July 24th

Durrett, William T. and Sarah A. Howard, Nov. 27th

Deskins, Henry and Sarah F. Duke, Nov. 27th

Durrett, Wm. T. and Sarah A. Howard, Nov. 29th

Durrett, Rob't. D. and Eliz. M. Terrell, July 24th

Drane, J. K. and M. M. Poindexter, Oct. 23rd

1856

Davis, Patrick M. and Mary Ann Norris, May 8th

Dedman, Samuel L. and Annie C. Paull, Jan. 17th

Drumheller, John W. and Elizabeth C. Drumheller, June 17th

Dedman, Samuel L. and Ann C. Panll, Jan. 17th

Detter, John M. and C. R. McAlexander, Dec. 11th

Dickinson, Thos. M. and Mary E. Dillard, March 25th

Deis, Thos. R. and Bettie B. C. Hart, Sept. 22nd

1857

Dallum, Edward and Virginia S. Macon, Nov. 24th

Detter, John W. and Constance K. McAlexander, Dec. 10th

Dew, Thomas R. and Bettie B. C. Hart, Sept. 21st

Dickerson, Thomas M. and Mary E. Dillard, March 9th

Dunkum, Christopher L. and Ann M. Burgess, Jan. 5th

Dalbum, Edward and Virgilia S. Maran, Nov. 26th

1858

Daniel, John and Lucy A. Mayo, April 5th

Dawson, Thomas J. and Joanna Thomas, July 28th

Dickerson, James B. and Eliza A. Durrow, Jan. 7th

Duke, Edwin P. and Ellen B. Craddock, April 27th

Durham, Walter and Sarah A. Clements, Nov. 19th

Daniel, Jno. and Lucy Ann Mayo, April 6th

Durham, Walter and Sarah R. Clements, Nov. 23rd

Duke, Edwin P. and Ellen Craddock, May 4th

1859

Dabney, W. S. and M. L. Dickinson, Dec. 7th

Davis, Franklin B. and Mildred A. Fulcher, Feb. 11th

Davis, Livingston N. and Frances E. Craig, April 12th

Dollin, Thomas R. and Ann E. Thomas, July 11th

Dowell, Samuel and Mary Etta Beck, July 18th

Dowell, Samuel and Mary E. Beck, July 24th

Drumheller, Leonard T. and Mary E. Crank, Jan. 24th

Dulaney, Sextus and Susan Harriet Estes, Oct. 24th

Dunn, Addison and Jane M. Via, Dec. 5th

Dunn, Thomas M. and Sally S. Thompson, Nov. 12th

Davis, S. M. and Frances E. Craig, April 13th

Davis, F. B. and Mildred A. S. Fulcher, Feb. 13th

Dunn, Tho. M. and Sallie S. Thompson, Nov. 15th

Dunn, Addesole and Jane M. Via, Dec. 13th

Dabney, Walter S. and Susan H. Estes, Oct. 27th

1860

Davis, Dabney C. T. and Mary B. Anderson, July 23rd

Dawson, A. J. and Mildred B. Childress, May 23rd

Dollins, Daniel M. and Elizabeth Lane, Dec. 17th

Dudley, James and Mary S. Quick, June 4th

Dudley, William and Martha Sprouse, Oct. 15th

Duff, Robert F. and Mary F. Hall, Aug. 6th

Duff, Sanford B. and America B. Hall, Oct. 22nd

Dunn, Henry T. and Clementine W. Garrison, Feb. 10th

Dunn, James L. and Sarah F. Dosey, Feb. 16th

Dudley, Wm. and Martha Sprouse, Oct. 16th

Duff, S. B. and America B. Hall, Oct. 25th

Dunn, James S. and Sarah F. Dossey, Feb. 23rd

Dunn, Henry T. and Clem. W. Garrison, Feb. 16th

Duff, Robt. F. and Mary F. Hall, Aug. 7th

Dudley, James and Mary S. Quick, June 28th

Dawson, A. J. and Millie B. Childress, May 31st

Dollint, Samuel M. and Eliz. Lane, Dec. 20th

1861

Davis, Franklin B. and Charlotte C. Wood, July 19th

Dunn, Elijah J. and Susan A. Sandridge, July 7th

Durham, Wilkey S. and Mary Geonia, Nov. 4th

Dunn, Elijah J. and Susan A. Sandridge, July 30th

Durham, Wilky S. and Mary Geomnia, Nov. 7th

1862

Davis, Geo. D. and Malinda A. Hays, Dec. 24th

Druen, James A. and Margaret A. Lindsay, July 7th

Dudley, Nathan J. and Lucy Jane Dudley, July 10th

Davis, Albert F. and Susan C. Brown, March 20th

1863

Donohot, Alexis M. and Cornelia E. M. Lee, Jan. 15th

Davis, Peter S. and Maria F. Lang, Oct. 1st

Dunn, Edw. W. and Bettie E. Thompson, April 5th

1864

Dejarnette, E. H. and E. M. Magruder, July 18th

Duffell, N. J. and Sydia Sprouse, March 3rd

Dinwiddie, Wm. and Emily A. Bledso, June 28th

Downing, Jno. and Mary Murphy, Oct. 17th

1865

Dudley, Charles W. and Mary Brubby, Jan. 19th

Dudley, Chas. W. and Mary Bruffey, Jan. 19th

1866

Davis, William F. and Ella V. Sampson, Aug. 30th

Dillard, Joseph H. and Sally M. Barksdale, May 1st

Dillard, Nicholas and Samantha Brown, June 9th

Donella, Schuyler A. and Mary V. Dunnington, Feb. 5th

Driskell, Augustine and Mildred Morris, Nov. 1st

Drumheller, Hiram C. and Sally H. Fatwell, Sept. 24th

Dudley, George W. and Elenora Critzer, Aug. 4th

Durrett, James T. and Susanna Gaines, March 14th

Durrett, William and Sallie W. Johnson, Feb. 26th

Dobbins, Jas. A. and Lucy J. Johnson, Dec. 30th

Durrett, Wm. and Sallie W. Johnson, Feb. 27th

Durrett, Jas T. and Sue A. Gains, March 27th

Dillard, Joe. H. and S. M. Barksdale, May 10th

Dudley, Geo. W. and Elmora Critzer, Aug. 9th

Damon, H. C. and Sally H. Fretwell, Sept. 27th

Diskell, A. and Mil. A. Morris, Nov. 6th

Douglass, Lewis and Esther Ann McField, Dec. 22nd

1867

Durrett, Thos. D. and Mary A. Hall, Jan. 21st

Davis, Martin V. and Eliza M. Sandridge, Jan. 25th

Day, Wm. and Sarah Ann Eliz. Mayo, March 12th

Davis, Robt. S. and Susan C. Draper, May 18th

Dabney, Geo. and Louisia Reesby, Dec. 25th

Davis, Benj. F. and Milton G. Wood, Dec. 17th

Detter, R. J. and Columbia A. Jones, Oct. 22nd

Durrett, Thos. D. and Mary A. Hall, Jan. 29th

Dobbins, R. L. and Mary S. Richards, Dec. 5th
Davis, Henry T. and Sarah E. Maupin, Dec. 19th
Detter, R. J. and Columbia Jones, Oct. 25th
Dobbins, R. L. and Mary S. Richards, Dec. 2nd

1868

Dunn, Albert S. and Mary T. Catterton, Feb. 11th
Durrett, Jas. F. and Morea S. Moon, April 6th
Durrett, Frank S. and Maria S. Moon, April 8th
Douglass, Chas. and Mary Louisa Taylor, May 4th
Dickerson, Wm. and Lucy J. Harris, Oct. 29th
Davis, Albert F. and Henrietta Parr, Dec. 31st
Durrett, John D. and Susan H. Vandergift, Jan. 19th
Douglass, Richard and Nancy Jackson, Dec. 31st

1869

Davis, J. W. and Nannie I. Critzer, Jan. 21st
Dabney, W. C. and Jane Bell Minor, March 12th
Davis, Henry and Rhody Lewis, July 10th
Dudley, John W. and Mary S. Dudley, Sept. 29th
Douglass, A. P. and Sallie E. Jones, Oct. 19th
Daughty, John C. and M. F. Ballard, Nov. 30th
Douglass, Jas. T. and Eliza A. Woods, Nov. 28th

1870

Dudley, Chas. and Mary Critzer, Feb. 3rd
Deorick, A. J. and Ida L. Keller, Feb. 16th
Dinwiddie, M. and Lucy A. Leake, Feb. 24th
Dillard, Jesse P. and Minnie Hall, May 22nd
Dorsett, John L. and M. B. More, June 10th
Davis, R. A. and F. S. Tate, Nov. 11th
Darnella, C. N. and Mary J. Smith, Dec. 21st
Dyer, Philip and Betsey Bird, Dec. 24th

1871

Dudley, Jas. H. and Mary Ann Dudley, Feb. 9th
Dorset, Orarr and Alexina P. Jeffires, April 11th
Duren, Wm. D. and M. C. Loving, May 11th
Durett, Robert and Eva W. Gault, Dec. 19th
Dudley, William Jr. and Va. Ellen Rhodes, Dec. 28th

1872

Drumheller, David H. and Catharine F. Spears, Jan. 11th
Duncan, Archer G. and Eliz. G. Hamner, March 27th
Durrett, Wm. and Delicia K. Betts, April 17th
Daniel, Zachary L. and Fannie G. Anderson, July 18th

Day, Charles D. and Mary E. Vaughan, Nov. 7th
Dudley, Jeremiah M. and Martha E. Melton, Nov. 27th
Dinwiddie, Walter and Lillie S. Shepherd, Dec. 4th

1873

Durham, Wm. S. and G. E. Bishop, March 17th
Davis, Almond W. and Columbia E. Durrett, Aug. 6th

1874

Douglass, Alex. H. and Judy Morris, Jan. 9th
Davis, Z. Leonard and Annie E. Bellomy, Jan. 5th
Dunn, A. L. and Bettie S. Catterton, May 19th
Durrett, Jas. W. and Rosalie Wood, Oct. 23rd
Durrett, Francis and Clara Teel, Oct. 26th

1875

Drumheller, Leonard and Mary A. Brooks, Feb. 18th
Dunn, Jas. T. and Sarah A. E. Gibson, May 19th
Dunn, George F. and Bettie Luck, Aug. 26th
Dameron, Jno. H. and Emma R. Dameron, Sept. 15th
Dulaney, Jas. F. and Louisa D. Wilhoit, Oct. 25th
Du Bose, Wm. R. and Katie W. Bibb, Oct. 25th
Dandridge, Wm. B. and Mary S. Carver, Nov. 1st
Durrett, Richard W. and Susan Early, Nov. 8th
Drumwright, Jas. E. and Fanny O. Shepherd, Nov. 14th
Dunn, Newell A. and Julia E. Bailey, Nov. 29th
Dorman, Jno. H. and Ann M. Painter, Dec. 11th
Duren, Jno. F. and Fanny A. Geanini, Dec. 22nd

1876

Dowell, Benj. F. and Mary L. Ellis, Feb. 12th
Dowel, Overton V. and Parmelia A. Shotwell, May 1st
Dudley, Henry W. and Mary A. Harris, Nov. 27th
Dunn, Henry D. and Sally E. Timberlake, Dec. 4th

1877

Davis, Jno. W. and Ella M. Madison, April 30th
Drumheller, Henry A. and Bettie A. Groves, Sept. 7th

1878

Dudley, Reuben A. and Willie A. Hurt, Jan. 7th

Davis, Wm. H. and Alice F. Davis, April 18th
Dollins, J. A. and W. A. Woodson, May 25th
Dove, William E. and Bettie Via, May 31st
Dabney, Walter D. and Mary B. Douglass, Sept. 23rd
Durrer, Chas. E. and Adeline A. Gibson, Nov. 18th
Dudley, F. F. and Ida E. Quick, Oct. 7th

1879

Dunn, William M. and Martha A. Newcomb, April 19th
Davis, Peter L. and Octavia M. Wood, Aug. 26th
Davis, Henry F. and Susan J. Patterson, Dec. 29th
Drumheller, Garrett E. and Barbara A. Pleasants, Dec. 29th
Drumheller, Miles W. and Ella J. Drumheller, Dec. 30th

1881

Davis, Fountain B. and Reubenia V. Goss, Jan. 26th

1882

Duncan, Andrew L. and Sarah E. Clevland, May 18th
Drumheller, William and Julia P. Wade, Nov. 23rd
Dickenson, William S. and Mary E. Thompson, Nov. 30th
Douglass, Henry B. and Mildred E. Edwards, Dec. 5th
Davis, Wm. L. and Mannie T. Blake, Dec. 25th

1883

Davis, Benjamin Ira and Mittie Margaret Wood, Feb. 8th
Drumheller, Lewis F. and Josephine Jones, Nov. 8th

1884

Davis, Jno. T. and Lelia C. Walton, Dec. 18th
Dowell, Zach and Lilly E. Wilkinson, Dec. 18th
Durrer, Frank D. and Sallie J. Gibson, Dec. 6th
Dawson, James L. and Georgia A. Via, Dec. 12th
Davis, Andrew J. and Sadie E. Rea, April 30th
Dickenson, Thos. Winston and Rosa Lewis Brown, April 7th
Douglas Wm. Henry and Martha Spears, July 8th
Drumheller, Leonard Smith and Margaret C. E. Spears, Nov. 13th

1885

Dabney, Jno. Fleming and Josie V. Clarke, Oct. 26th
Davis, Geo. W. and Sarah Ann Davis, Dec. 10th

Duke, Jno. Thomas and Mary Proffit, June 21st
Dunn, Wm. M. and Adella M. Wood, Dec. 23rd

1886

Dowell, Jesse H. and Sarah A. C. Wilkinson, March 23rd
Duncan, Jno. E. and Clarie V. Comer, June 22nd
Durham, Jno. W. and Fannie A. Bishop, June 9th
Davis, Benj. M. and Mary L. Garnett, July 22nd
Davis, Samuel L. and Sarah M. Layman, Sept. 21st
Dabney, Jno. F. and Jane M. Lunasden, Aug. 23rd
DuBose, Dudley, and Emma C. Robertson, Oct. 7th
Davis, Com. Jas. and Sally F. Mahanes, Nov. 24th
Durrer, Dennis, and Ira E. Brown, Jan. 5th

1887

Dold, Wm. E. and Willy T. Brown, April 7th
Duke, Richard W. and Kate H. Hedges, July 18th
Dunn, Percival L. and Rosa Scott Thompson, Nov. 17th
Durrer, Henry J. and Rosa Wood, Dec. 20th

1888

Deane, Sianly and Josaphine Donell, Oct. 17th
Dowell, B. F. and L. L. Wingfield, Oct. 22nd
Durrett, Isaac G. and M. F. Ballard, Oct. 20th
Day, J. B. and Clara Smith, Nov. 6th
Drumheller, L. T. and B. L. Davis, Nov. 26th
Dollins, A. and A. A. Ellinger, Nov. 26th
Dobbs, Jno. T. and Alice Dudley, Dec. 26th
Dickerson, Jno. H. and Juliet O. Garnett, Dec. 30th

1889

Dowell, Jas. R. and Mildred Carter, Feb. 4th
Dudley, S. J. and F. M. Pace, March 7th
Drumheller, Wm. H. and Fanny Powell, April 3rd
Durrer, Geo. B. and E. P. Garnett, Aug. 6th
Dulton, Geo. E. and Carrie E. Morris, Sept. 10th
Dickerson, Joseph and Linda Wood, Oct. 7th
Davis, Geo. D. and Mary J. Pugh, Dec. 18th
Dudley, Austin and Alice Willis, Oct. 7th
Davis, Wm. W. and Alice Norford, Oct. 31st
Davis, Wesley and Bettie Minor, Nov. 12th

1890

Dudley, Arthur H. and Maggie E. Spradlin, June 12th
Davis, J. B. and M. E. Cox, Dec. 19th
Davis, Wm. H. and Emmie Burton, Oct. 28th
Dudley, W. W. and Mary M. Dudley, Dec. 24th

1891

Dobbins, Chas. D. and Susia V. Bennett, April 2nd

Dudley, Wm. and Nellie Bishop, Dec. 31st

1892

Davis, M. P. and Maud Mathews, May 30th

Dulaney, E. L. and M. G. Lupton, June 13th

Duncan, W. J. and L. J. Harris, July 27th

Detamore, J. W. and F. V. Moran, Nov. 7th

Dusenbury, J. J. and R. J. Patterson, Feb. 4th

Dickerson, Chas. E. and Annie E. Pritchett, June 6th

Dunn, Wm. M. and S. R. Newman, Aug. 27th

1893

Dallon, C. and C. McVenable, June 1st

Day, Wm. E. and Ada L. Carter, Aug. 29th

Dowell, Jeremiah and Lilly Alice Vaughn, Aug. 31st

Davis, A. B. and May McAlister, Oct. 2nd

Detemore, David D. and Mattie McAuley, Dec. 23rd

Donald, James and Maria L. Dowling, Dec. 23rd

1894

Dunkum, C. H. and F. H. Foland, Dec. 11th

Dickerson, J. R. and L. M. Wood, March 19th

Dickerson, C. E. and Anna Pritchett, April 9th

Davis, R. F. and Ida Powell, April 25th

Duke, Wm. R. and Edith M. Coleman, June 4th

Dunn, Robt. E. and Mettie J. Larn, Oct. 3rd

Duncan, R. W. and L. E. Johns, Dec. 20th

1895

Dudley, Dennis H. and Mardia J. Thacker, June 12th

Dudley, J. T. and Helen Farish, Feb. 9th

Draper, Wm. K. and Lula E. Marsh, March 7th

Dunn, Old. and M. B. Powell, Aug. 5th

Durrett, J. R. and Lulu Yancy, Sept. 16th

Douglass, G. W. and Estelle Thomas, Oct. 29th

Davis, Geo. W. and Permilia Norford, Dec. 5th

Diggs, Irvine and Martha Coles, Dec. 23rd

1896

Davis, H. E. and Nettie M. Wood, Jan. 6th

Durham, J. R. and Lillie Brooks, Jan. 28th

Donald, Geo. and Lucy M. Harlow, July 23rd

Dudley, W. L. and B. B. Critzer, Sept. 4th

Dunn, J. M. and Susie Hild, Sept. 28th

Dawson, F. G. and D. E. Brockenbraugh, Dec. 1st

Deulls, Robt. A. and Margaret M. Long, Dec. 31st

1897

Dean, Eddie B. and M. M. Giannini, Feb. 11th

Davis, M. B. and C. L. Lamb, March 20th

Dickerson, R. G. and Orie L. Moon, June 24th

1898

Dowell, Jno. H. and Lucy B. Woodson, May 14th

Dodd, Jno. T. and D. L. Spradlin, July 3rd

Drumheller, Jno. and L. N. Powell, Nov. 23rd

Dudley, Louis P. and Florence E. Wells, Dec. 13th

Daly, F. G. and Lucy Quick, Dec. 20th

1899

Davis, S. L. and E. McAllister, Feb. 9th

Dickerson, Tinsley and Ollie Herring, June 1st

Draper, R. L. and E. B. Birckhead, June 28th

Davis, S. O. and Lucy J. Thacker, July 3rd

Donald, J. A. and Bulah T. Bailey, Sept. 4th

Druen, John A. and Nellie S. Thomas, Oct. 5th

Dudley, Dennis H. and Mardia J. Thacker, June 12th

Dinwiddie, M. and M. S. Durrette, June 19th

Dabney, R. H. and L. H. Davis, Nov. 27th

Damron, W. T. and A. M. Robinson, Nov. 28th

Davis, O. M. and R. A. Walton, Dec. 23rd

Davis, H. H. and Flossie Mawyer, Dec. 22nd

1900

Davis, J. H. and Mary E. Tomlin, April 11th

Day, E. H. and S. P. Ward, Oct. 1st

Dean, Chas. and Lottie E. Gibson, July 14th

Davis, Jno. S. and Eliz. D. Staples, Sept. 19th

DuPre, M. M. and A. C. Jones, Sept. 22nd

Davis, Daniel F. and Lizzie Hensley, Dec. 19th

Dudley, Wm. H. and Susie B. Sprouse, Dec. 24th

Durrett, Thos. T. and Lillie Bramham, Dec. 28th

1901

Douglass, W. C. and L. C. Edwards, Jan. 29th

Dunn, Jas. A. and M. M. Lee James, April 6th

Durrett, Jos. D. and Sarah J. Durrett, May 16th

Dinwiddie, H. B. and Maude Hasbrauck, June 11th

Davis, G. and I. B. Powell, Aug. 12th

Dorman, J. and S. N. Munday, Aug. 20th

Dudley, Edw. and Viva Critzer, Oct. 21st

Davis, J. E. and V. B. Bishop, Dec. 17th

Dove, Thos. E. and Jennaby Gianniny, Dec. 17th

1902

Davis, Alex and Nora Norris, March 11th

Davis, Robt. H. and Lonnie F. Wood, April 1st

Deane, Andrew J. and Pearl A. Martin, Aug. 19th

Duffey, Edw. F. and Daisy G. Carroll, Dec. 2nd

Dudley, C. P. and M. R. Kinzer, Dec. 9th
Davis, H. J. and N. R. Bruce, Dec. 17th
Davis, Harry B. and Bertha Pace, Dec. 27th

1903

Dunlop, Chas. W. and Dallie A. Turner, Jan. 8th
Duke, W. D. and A. Hotopp, Jan. 22nd
Deans, Gray S. and Ellie T. Williams, April 17th
Durham, B. D. and Maud Brooks, April 30th
Dandridge, J. P. and J. H. Vaughan, Oct. 31st
Dudley, Eugene and Fannie Farish, Dec. 16th
Davis, Jess and A. M. Johnson, Dec. 21st
Dowling, Chas. Thos. and Eddie Jane Wash, Dec. 31st

1904

Dudley, Elmer and Minnie Brooks, May 17th
Davis, Ira S. and Ida B. Davis, June 6th
Daniel Thos. H. and Sarah B. Dunnington, July 18th
Dunn, Richard O. and Ella C. Shiflett, Aug. 4th
Durham, Chas. Edw. and Minnie C. Barnett, Sept. 7th
Davis, Zephamiah and Mary Frances Crawford, Sept. 14th
Drumheller, Wm. and Nannie Powell, Nov. 16th

1905

Davis, Willie and Masey Walton, March 24th
Davis, Samuel L. and Ellen Anderson, April 17th
Dorman, John and Ella Gibson, May 31st
Dameron, Jas. Elmo and Mary Ida Kirby, June 5th
Davis, Royal and Lucy Mary Walker, Oct. 4th
Disney, Fred W. and H. D. Dudley, Oct. 16th
Dull, Lewis Henry and Janie Sarah Ballard, Dec. 9th
Dudley, Alonza and Bessie Ann Gibson, Dec. 20th
Dunn, D. J. and I. L. Martin, Nov. 20th
Davis, Oscar and Flossie Pearl Gunter, Nov. 29th
Darnell, George and Mary S. Hawley, Nov. 27th
Davis, Oscar and Flossie Pearl Guester, Nov. 29th
Dull, Lewis Henry and Janie Sarah Ballard, Dec. 11th

1906

Davis, George W. and Laura Clements, Jan. 8th
Dunn, Percy Thomas and Florecne Linden Goss, Feb. 12th
Davis, Robert A. and Virginia Graham, May 17th
Deane, Thomas S. and Anne E. Gibson, June 20th
Darriel, Walter M. and Leah Ann Cox, Aug. 1st

Davis, James R. and Lillian J. Via, Sept. 11th
Dodd, James M. and Ina L. Sprouse, Sept. 19th
Driscoll, William W. and Lucy May Wyant, Oct. 24th
Dillian, F. Lee and Rosa P. Gooch, Nov. 21st
Davis, Bryon and Caldonia Lee Holloway, Dec. 12th
Drumheller, Freddie W. and Ella Thacker, Nov. 22nd

1907

Dowell, Cyrus B. and Mary B. Beck, Feb. 21st
Douglass, Henry and Sarah B. C. Ward, March 27th
Day, S. W. and Ludie B. Wayland,   ??
Dovel, J. J. and Eula L. Hiddle, July 26th
Dabney, W. O. and Mabell L. Williams, Aug. 28th
Durham, S. A. and Sallie S. Craig, Nov. 20th
Dawson, W. A. and Gertrude E. Hamner, Dec. 18th
Draper, Edgar M. and Annie M. B. West, Dec. 25th

1908

Davis, William E. and Lilian Cunningham, Jan. 1st
Dunn, Auburry M. and Cora E. Wood, Feb. 19th
Deane, Robert E. F. and Tidy E. Herndon, March 24th
Dalton, Bennie F. and Bertha Mooney, June 12th
Davis, C. A. and L. S. Glass, June 29th
Digh, Chas. S. and Annie L. Clark, July 4th.
Douglass, Carroll R. and Nora Hamner, Nov. 4th
Davis, Bruce R. and Olivet E. Marshall, Nov. 18th
Dodd, Egbert E. and Annie Quick, Nov. 30th
Dunn, George and Annie Wood, Dec. 17th

1909

Davis, Charles P. and Laura F. Shiflett, Jan. 14th
Dodd, Enoch and May Stribling, Jan. 20th
Dean, William C. and Millie A. Harris, March 24th
Damron, John and Nettie Edwards, April 10th
Dollins, Richard M. and Julia A. Burton, April 28th
Dunn, Alva and Minnie Dunn, Aug. 12th
Dickerson, Charles E. and Eliza A. Ragland, Sept. 1st
Dabney, Joseph S. and Minnie E. Payne, Nov. 26th

1910

Dudley, Aldrich and Louisa G. Littig, Jan. 12th
Davis, Letcher B. and Mary C. Gibson, Feb. 23rd
Deane, Whitler and Maggie Martin, March 28th

Downer, J. W. and Jessie B. Goodloe, April 3rd

Davis, Samuel M. and Mary E. Pace, April 20th

Davis, Jr., Dabney C. T. and Mrs. Mary Rhett Elliott, April 26th

Dotson, Bernard E. and Reva A. Payne, May 11th

Douglas, John C. and Lydia L. White, June 16th

Davis, Henry E. and Mary S. James, Sept. 15th

Davis, Bernard and Sallie Jones, Dec. 28th

Dean, Willie R. and Adua J. Collins, Dec. 24th

1911

Day, Henry W. and Lottie V. Morris, April 14th

Dunn, George C. and P. Ella Patterson, July 20th

Davis, Albert D. and Isabel M. Lewis, Oct. 14th

Dickson, Karl and Marchie Ballard, Oct. 11th

Dorrier, Charles R. and Clara Lee Pitts, Oct. 25th

Drumheller, Herbert L. and Mary Trusler, Nov. 18th

1912

Drumheller, John and Mattie V. Fitzgerald, Feb. 22nd

Drumheller, Miles and Norene V. Graves, March 5th

Dawson, John S. and Maude O. Shackelford, April 10th

Dukes, Harold and May Baber, April 16th

Dowell, Edgar L. and Lula A. Walker, April 21st

Dowell, Walter F. and Bertha L. Davis, June 5th

Dowell, Clarence and Lorena Fox, July 31st

Davis, Meredith and Annie Lee Maupin, Aug. 6th

Dowell, Henry C. and Mary Tomlin, Oct. 2nd

Dowell, Granutle A. and Beulah H. Dowell, Oct. 30th

Dameron, Houston and Pearl Kirby, Nov. 20th

Dean, Frank and Nellie Martin, Nov. 27th

Dudley, H. B. and Martha M. Dudley, Dec. 16th

1913

Davis, John W. and Nettie Maude Bruce, Jan. 16th

Dowdy, Cleveland M. and Clara Bell Davis, March 24th

Davis, William P. and Bessie Pugh, Sept. 9th

DeForest, Henry A. and Mrs. Annie E. Huff, Sept. 25th

Dudley, William N. and Lucy Maupin, Oct. 29th

Deane, Robert and Lillie Deane, Nov. 6th

Davis, Dr. Carroll A. and Lucinda Rothwell, Dec. 24th

1914

Dinwiddie, Harry E. and Margaret S. Maupin, April 22nd

Daughtry, Henry T. and Minnie O. McAlester, May 27th

Dudley, Claudie F. and Lillian E. Maxey, Nov. 11th

Dunham, George and Georgia Thomas, Nov. 15th

Davis, W. L. and Sallie B. Powell, Dec. 29th

Daughtery, J. R. and Sarah K. Wood, Dec. 23rd

Dodd, Woody and Bettie Bowen, Dec. 24th

Davis, Andrew J. and Lola N. Creasy, Dec. 30th

1915

Drumheller, Cary W. and Florence O. Hamner, March 4th

Dodd, Albert Gilmore, and Daisy Lee Drumheller, April 19th

Diggs, Emmett R. and Frances M. Flowers, June 2nd

Davis, Virgil E. S. and Mattie Sprouse, June 2nd

Drumheller, Hammie and Laura Morris, July 29th

Drumheller, Luther and Hattie Tussler, Aug. 18th

Drumheller, Jno. H. and Carrie Dameron, Oct. 9th

Dulaney, Robert L. and Mamie E. Cox, Oct. 27th

Dowdy, Henry and Amanda Thorp, Dec. 18th

1916

Dunn, Wm. L. and Catherine Davenport, Feb. 23rd

Douglas, Charlie and Bessie E. Critzer, March 4th

Dudley, Henry Ellis and Maud E. Tomlin, April 19th

Dudley, Eusie and Evie Woodson, May 16th

Dean, Gilbert Lee and Mary Rodgers, July 21st

Duling, Astin E. and Mildred N. P. Lewis, Sept. 21st

Dowell, Joseph and Callie Lang, Oct. 7th

Dillard, Dr. B. L. and Mildred Horsley, Oct. 7th

Druin, Jr., Wm. P. and Annie P. Page, Oct. 21st

Dickerson, Willie R. and Willie V. Seamonds, Nov. 8th

Dobbin, Chaobs W. and Esther E. Keller, Nov. 16th

1917

Drumheller, Clay and Ethel Dudley, Feb. 8th

Dowell, James R. and Josephine Clarke, April 26th

Dudley, John G. and Ethel V. Thompson, July 4th

Duler, Phillip A. and Lillie V. Morris, Sept. 29th

Davis, Lawrence G. and Lottie Watson, Oct. 31st

Douglas, Maury D. and Ada Garland, Dec. 23rd

1918

Davis, General C. and Maggie Gibson, April 5th

Dunivan, Jake C. and Victoria Shiflett, June 3rd

DeMasters, Eber C. and Winnie L. Moyer, June 23rd

Dunn, Thos. McK. and Olive M. James, Aug. 21st

Duke, Nelson P. and Mabel P. Wood, Sept. 19th

Deacon, Elmer H. and Rachael Beale, Oct. 24th

Douglas, Aro Tinsdale, and Ann Eliz. Harris, Nov. 16th

Drumheller, Jno. and Lillian Hall, Nov. 18th

1919

Detamore, Daniel and Grace Powell, Feb. 12th

Dickerson, Robt. and Hattie Elliott, June 18th

Dougherty, James A. and Maude Mason Dillard, Aug. 28th

Dudley, Richard H. and Mary Cornelia Gibson, Sept. 1st

Davidson, Troy M. and Margaret B. Nottingham, Sept. 11th

Dudley, Linwood and Annie R. Woodson, Sept. 21st

Doughtry, W. C. and Cornelia A. Wood, Nov. 19th

Dudley, Ernest P. and Bertie E. Bolton, Dec. 22nd

1920

Dudley, Henry H. and Cora Sprouse, April 7th

Davis, John Henry and Lillian F. Marshall, April 21st

Drumheller, Roy W. and Bertie Beverly, July 17th

Dollins, John M. and Alma L. Sutherland, July 19th

Dollings, Philip H. and Bettie Cook, Aug. 18th

Dickerson, Edwin J. and Amy L. Douglas, Sept. 15th

Dowell, Henry C. and Lottie Sprouse, Oct. 22nd

Durrer, Willie M. C. and Deare Louise Durrer, Dec. 22nd

1921

Dudley, James F. and Carrie Vanderhoff, April 3rd

Davis, Claurence C. and Hattie L. Wells, May 3rd

Dowell, Homer S. and Mary Mawyer, June 9th

Davis, Allen T. and Helen Hayman, Nov. 24th

Dollins, Jenning P. and Lena G. Maupin, Nov. 30th

1922

Davis, Roy C. and Mattie H. Gentry, Jan. 14th

Dudley, Hubert L. and Sallie R. Hutchinson, Feb. 26th

Davis, Floyd D. and Pearl T. Dunn, March 15th

Dowell, Eppie H. and Grace D. M. Daniel, March 28th

Davis, Wm. W. and Bessie Lee Davis, May 31st

Desmond, John M. and Isabel H. Blair, Sept. 6th

Dedder, Fedenck and Roby Comack, Sept. 12th

Dudley, Jr., Austin and Hazel Dudley, Sept. 19th

Downs, Luther L. and Frances F. Coopper, Oct. 11th

Drumheller, Roy and Ethel Sprouse, Nov. 4th

Davis, Wm. F. and Lucy G. Powell, Dec. 19th

1923

Dabbs, Henry and Willie V. Loving, April 18th

Dawson, James L. and Nooen Bugg, May 16th

DeHaven, Louis G. and Grace A. Hamilton, June 6th

Davis, Lyle M. and Lena Morris, June 28th

Dollons, Robt. A. and Burnice Lee Tanner, Nov. 7th

1924

Desper, Jas. J. and Lotie A. Tyler, Jan. 9th

Dunn, G. F. and Susie Estes, Jan. 9th

Deane, Willie C. and Ada E. Caldwell, Feb. 16th

Dudley, Roy and Elizabeth Moore, April 28th

Douglas, Archie and Violett Snow, May 17th

Drumwright, Allen W. and Elsie H. Smith, June 7th

Detamore, Robt. M. and Maggie V. Dulaney, June 13th

Denny, Jr., Victor Lyle and Margaret A. Hibbert, June 17th

Dorman, Charlie and Sallie Ramsey, June 28th

Dunn, Wm. D. and Theodosia E. Branham, July 25th

Dovel, Chester and Blanche C. McCauley, Aug. 15th

Douglas, Tommie L. and Vester A. Crenshaw, Sept. 3rd

Dobbins, Tennyson and Mary E. Snead, Dec. 23rd

1925

Dulaney, Homer L. and Stella M. Powell, Feb. 18th

Dodson, Garfield E. and Northie W. Baber, March 21st

Drumheller, Geo. W. and Annie Brunner, April 18th

Denson, Wm. R. and Elizabeth C. Craig, May 28th

Dudley, Ollie and Pearl Lee Moore, Aug. 29th

Dedder, Lewis G. and Alice Mae Allen, Dec. 23rd

1926

Dennis, Otis and Carrie Dorrier, May 29th

DuBose, L. Vaughan and Martha L. Burnley, June 1st

Downer, Bailey and Selma Beasley, July 3rd

Dickerson, Russell and Lila Davis, Aug 10th

Davis, Lewis D. and Sadie A. Haney, Sept. 10th

Duffy, Jr., Wm. J. and Mary E. Sandy, Sept. 11th

Davis, Russell T. and Carrie E. Maupin, Sept. 22nd

Durham, Geo W. and Virginia E. Lamb, Oct. 16th

Drumheller, John A. and Estelle L. Moneymaker, Dec. 18th

Davis, Thomas J. and Josie G. Lane, Dec. 28th

1927

Drumwright, Jas. Donald and Anna E. Woodson, March 7th

Davis, Wm. H. and Frances S. Amiss, March 25th

Davis, Lewis E. and Nannie E. Burruss, May 26th

Dudley, Wm. H. and Dolly Wood, Aug. 6th

Denny, George H. and Elizabeth B. Herold, Aug. 30th

Drumheller, Alfred and Coral Gertrude Thacker, Sept. 14th

Davis, Thomas G. and Ann N. Meredith, Oct. 24th

Durham, Arthur E. and Ethel M. Thomas, Nov. 12th

1928

Draper, Robert L. and Agnes Winn, April 7th

Desper, Thos. H. and Susie P. Jarman, April 30th

Durrett, Roy B. and Virginia L. Maupin, June 26th

Duff, George W. and Susie M. McTutie, July 2nd

Day, David A. and Mable G. Dudley, July 3rd

Durrer, Henry and Meta Wood, Aug. 4th

Delaney, Wm. and Bettie Sprouse, Nov. 10th

Dressler, Luther C. and Nora Lee Bowen, Nov. 23rd

Davis, Thomas O. and Zenobia McCarey, Nov. 28th

Drumheller, Curtis H. and Grace M. Thacker, Dec. 15th

Dudley, Albert L. and Mazie Armistead, Dec. 24th

Deane, Geo. L. and Olive S. Deane, Dec. 27th

1929

Davis, Mervin W. and Blanche M. Hall, Jan. 9th

Day, Robt. M. and Mary D. Winebarger, May 6th

Davis, Randolph T. and Lillian M. Hall, May 7th

Dunn, George F. and Agnes J. Teel, Aug. 16th

Deane, Richard G. and Eunice D. Michie, Sept. 3rd

Davis, Donovan H. and Pearl F. Hall, Sept. 11th

Durham, Lewis and Myrtie Armistead, Sept. 19th

Drumheller, Henry T. and Rosa Lee Wray, Sept. 24th

Davis, Lee E. and Mabelle B. Fultz, Nov. 30th

Davis, Robert E. and Nellie F. Davis, Dec. 10th

Diggs, Caskie L. and Lillian M. King, Dec. 31st

E

1781

Evans, Thomas and Mary Armistead, Aug. 12th

Eyre, John and Mary Carter, Oct. 25th

1787

Eubank, John Jr. and Winny Cheatham, Dec. 7th

1788

Epperson, John and Elizabeth Bowen, Dec. 22nd

Epperson, William and Nancy Hicks, June 21st

Eves, Abraham and Elizabeth Sharp, Jan. 1st

1790

Elliot, Abraham and Elizabeth Wansley, Aug. 28th

Eubank, George and Nancy Wingfield, July 8th

1791

Epperson, Charles and Sarah Lamb, Dec. 16th

1793

Eubank, William and Betsy Nally, April 11th

1794

Ealum, John and Avey Cocks, Oct. 28th

1795

Eastham, James and Sally Mitchell, Dec. 10th

Emberson, Zacharias and Deanna Southerland, Dec. 7th

Emra, Michael and Sisley Johnson, Oct. 5th

1798

Emmerson, Pleasant and Elizabeth Turlang, May 29th

1799

Eastham, John and Polley Rothwell, Aug. 1st

England, Dabney and Nancy Kindred, Dec. 2nd

1802

Ellis, Dudley and Elizabeth Watts, June 9th

Emmerson, William and Elizabeth Cosby, May 18th

Eves, Bennett and Milly Burrus, Aug. 2nd

1803

Eades, Peter and Sallie Henderson Sandridge, May 28th

Early, John and Sarah Durrett, Jan. 10th

Estes, Coleman and Clary Gaines, Jan. 25th

1805

Ellis, John B. and Malinda Maupin, May 22nd

1806

Eastin, James and Polly Munday, July 23rd

Enin, Shadaick and Betsy Martin, Feb. 6th

Eubanks, Daniel and Polly Martin, Nov. 3rd

1808

Ellenow, Richard and Elizabeth Graves, Jan. 4th

Eller, Dabney and Fanny Watson, March 7th

Elsom, Reubin and Elizabeth Dawson, Nov. 2nd

Emmerson, Jepe and Judith Grayson, Oct. 3rd

Everitt, John and Sally Woodson, Oct. 6th

1809

Engor, Henry and Jane Miller, June 21st

Eubank, Charles and Sally Childress, Sept. 11th

Eubank, Reubin and Elizabeth Old, Oct. 2nd

1810

Edwards, John and Ann Sandridge, Dec. 12th

1812

Early, James Jr. and Sarah Carr, July 6th

Embre, William W. and Elizabeth Brockman, Nov. 2nd

Estes, Merry and Elizabeth Wood, Feb. 20th

1813

Early, Joab and Elizabeth Thompson, Dec. 6th

Estes, Coleman and Mary C. Oglesby, May 3rd

Eubank, Thomas and Nancy W. Old, Sept. 6th

1814

Edwards, Samuel and Lucy Rhoades, Dec. 27th

Eubanks, James and Mary Hunt, Feb. 8th

1816

Ellarton, Micajah and Mary A. Strange, Jan. 1st

Elliott, George and Judah Martin, Jan. 26th

1817

Eades, John and Jincy Lively, July 26th

Edwards, Brice and Anney Dickman, March 6th

Edwards, Thomas and Aggy Brockman, Dec. 23rd

Eubank, John and Sarah Flinnt, Sept. 25th

1819

Elliott, Shephen and Sally Holmes, Jan. 16th

1820

Eades, George and Elizabeth Casney, Aug. 9th

1821

Eddins, Robinson and Sarah Collins, Dec. 5th

Elliot, William and Mary R. Hall, Nov. 11th

Ellis, Thomas and Mary Ballard, April 5th

Epese, J. B. and Isabella Williams, Dec. 18th

Eskridge, James W. and Lucy I. I. Peyton, June 27th

1822

Epps, Franks and Elizabeth Randolph, Nov. 28th

1823

Early, John and Margaret Timberlake, March 5th

1824

Eastham, James and Rachel Carr, Nov. 25th

1825

Eades, James and Rhoda Copeland, Dec. 14th

Eagan, John and Mildred Yancey, Nov. 14th

Eastin, Stephen and Sarah Rothwell, Dec. 22nd

Epen, Benjamin and Elizabeth Bunch, Nov. 7th

Eubank, Charles and Mildred Currier, Dec. 6th

1827

Emmet, John P. and Mary B. Tucker, July 19th

Early, James T. Jr. and Milly Thompson, Dec. 11th

1828

Eubank, John W. and Catherine Norvell, Nov. 3rd

1829

Eatherton, Anderson and Melisent Hall, June 18th

Epex, John B. and Elizabeth Grass, Nov. 24th

1830

Eastin, Ewell and Martha Shackelford, Oct. 7th

Edwards, Hiram G. and Elizabeth M. Douglass, Dec. 14th

1831

Elliott, T. G. and S. Childress, April 21st

Ellis, Ira H. and Mary Overstreet, April 11th

1834

Estes, Marshall and Cynthia Ann Estes, April 1st

1835

Ellis, William and Ann W. Johnson, Sept. 14th

1836

Eddins, William and G. M. Branham, May 13th

Eubank, Garland and Jane Eubank, Dec. 29th

Evens, Jerman and A. Isaacs, Oct. 20th

1837

Eades, Shepherd and Sarah Napper, Jan. 2nd

Elsom, Nelson W. and Evelina T. Herndon, Nov. 6th

Epex, Joseph and Elizabeth C. Bishop, Sept. 4th

1838

Elsom, Martin D. and Amanda M. Herndon, May 31st

1839

Eddins, Thomas J. D. and C. C. Barksdale, Dec. 12th

Estes, Lively T. and Frances Wood, Nov. 11th

1840

Early, John T. and Lucy Ann Watson, Jan. 17th

Earley, Thomas J. and Caroline Wood, Feb. 18th

England, David and A. Gillum, Dec. 25th

Estes, James W. and Martha Woodson, May 11th

1841

Emmerson, Luther and Catharine J. Minor, June 14th

1843

Early, William T. and Mary E. G. Michie, May 31st

Elliott, Parrott and Amanda A. Catterton, Oct. 2nd

Etterton, James B. and Susannah Shultz, Feb. 4th

1844

Ellis, Bentley B. and Cynthia A. Gardner, Nov. 5th

1845

Early, James B. and Sarah F. Catterton, Oct. 13th

Etterton, Fleming and Adeline Tomblin, Aug. 19th

Eubank, Thomas and Elizabeth J. Kelly, Jan. 25th

1846

Early, Isaac D. and Dorotha Thompson, Dec. 23rd

Early, Jacob W. and Sarah E. Martin, Nov. 19th

Early, Jeremiah A. and Mildred S. Wood, Sept. 24th

Elliott, Marshall D. and Malinda Shiflett, April 6th

Ellis, William and Eliza A. Durkam, March 9th

Eubank, Benjamin and Jane E. Turner, Sept. 16th

1847

Edge, Phillips and Sarah A. Dunkum, Aug. 30th

Edwards, James and J. W. Wells, March 13th

Elsom, William H. and M. J. Rittenhouse, April 22nd

1848

Ellis, Tyree J. and Lucy Jane Sneed, Dec. 18th

1850

Eubank, Matthew and Eloysa N. Wingfield, Sept. 22nd

1851

Eddins, Bluford R. and Susan R. Smith, Jan. 18th

1852

Edwards, Tazewell and Julia E. Munday, March 18th

Estes, Robert G. and Elizabeth Wood, Dec. 6th

1853

Ellis, Charles and Jane G. Burwill, Dec. 19th

1854

Eades, James and Wilhelmina Wells, April 11th

Elliott, William E. and Sarah Cary, Oct. 3rd

Elliott, Wm. E. and Sarah H. Carr, Oct. 3rd

Engleman John B. and Mildred Cox, April 2nd

Evans, David, and Ann E. Bailey, July 30th

1855

Eades, William F. and Matilda Gardner, Aug. 1st

Early, John R. and Sarah T. Brown, Feb. 22nd

Edge, Philip and Elizabeth B. Dunkum, Sept. 29th

Eubank, Overton G. and Lucy E. Burmin, Oct. 2nd

Engleman, Jno. B. and Millie M. Cox, April 2nd

Edge, Phillip and Eliz. Dunkunn, Sept. 30th

Early, Jno. R. and Sarah F. Brown, Feb. 22nd

Eubank, O. G. and L. E. Hamner, Oct. 2nd

1856

Eheart, Adam G. and Frances Sheela, Oct. 27th

Etherton, Dabney O. and Nancy F. Catterton, Oct. 27th

Eubank, Thomas P. and Mary S. Herron, Dec. 14th

Eubank, Thos. R. and Mary S. Herron, Dec. 14th

Estes, Littleton and Cor. F. Keister, Sept. 10th

Easten, Jas. D. and Eliz. Doswell, Aug. 27th

Easten, Jas. R. and E. M. Faris, April 16th

Edwards, Taswell S. and Mary E. Norvell, Dec. 22nd

Ewing, Dan'l P. and Mollie J. Woods, May 21st

1857

Eastin, James D. and Elizabeth Dowell, Aug. 26th

Edwards, Tazwell J. and Mary E. Norvell, Dec. 7th

Estes, Littleton E. and Cornelia F. Keister, Sept. 7th

Eweing, Price and Mary Wrods, May 18th

1858

Elliot, Marshall and Mary F. Jennings, Dec. 6th

Estes, William J. and Sarah M. Cox, Nov. 22nd

Elliott, Marshall and Mary F. Jennings, Nov. 15th

Estes, Wm. I. and Sarah M. Cox, Nov. 25th

1859

English, William O. and Elizabeth D. Gooch, Aug. 2nd

1860

Elsom, R. M. and Mary F. Simpco, Oct. 1st

Elson, Reuben W. and Mary F. Simpco, Oct. 2nd

1861

Ellis, James B. and Maria Singler, Aug. 13th

Eves, Nimrod and Lucy Ann Graves, March 4th

Ellis, James B. and Mary M. Singor, Aug. 14th

Eves, Nimrod and Lucy Ann Goens, March 15th

1862

Elson, Martin D. and Clorrenlina R. Luck, Dec. 16th

Ekheart, Chas. and Margaret Powell, July 3rd

1863

Edmonson, Wm. B. and Fannie C. Dolin, Aug. 25th

Elliott, Edmund and Jane S. Perkins, March 18th

1864

Early, Wm. D. and Parmelia M. A. E. Wilhoit, Aug. 23rd

Ergenbright, Rich. B. and Ann Eliz. Gibson, Aug. 30th

Ellis, Alfred and Margaret Sneed, Sept. 21st

1865

Earle, William E. and Bettie Price, Dec. 19th

Estes, Francis M. and Sarah M. Estes, Aug. 27th

1866

Ellis, James W. and Agnes E. Teel, Jan. 16th

Ellis, Jas. H. and Mary E. Teel, Jan. 25th

1867

England, Wm. T. and M. Sally Ann Nally. March 5th

England, Wm. T. and Sally A. Wally, March 5th

Ellis, Wm. T. and Lizzie B. Teel, Nov. 27th

Evans, Edward and Margarett T. Morris, Sept. 11th

1868

Estes, Francis M. and Catherine C. Austin, Jan. 14th

Elliton, Jas. and Cynthia A. Craig, May 25th

Elliott, J. Woods and Bettie D. George, June 17th

Escue, L. H. and Lutie Brown, Dec. 15th

1869

Estes, Albert M. and Mary W. Watson, March 25th

Ellyson, Jim and L. E. Catchikis, Dec. 2nd

Edward, Phil. and Charlotte Key, Dec. 29th

1870

Eiseman, Louis and Betty Obderoffer, May 4th

Eastham, J. B. and M. A. Richard, May 18th

Engleman, F. M. and M. F. Cox, June 2nd

1871

Easham, Jas. M. and Mrs. Sarah E. Harris, Sept. 26th

Early, E. W. and Celine C. deKock, Oct. 19th

Eaton, Wm. Henry H. W. and Mary Eliz. Robinson, Dec. 24th

1872

Evans, Wm. F. and Molly A. Bailey, Jan. 16th

1873

Early, O. W. and M. S. Brown, Jan. 2nd

Eddins, Q. G. and C. M. Marshall, April 7th

1874

Eddins, Henry M. and Saretha M. Smith, Sept. 7th

Ellis, Wm. H. and Sarah A. Durham, Nov. 18th

1875

Ellison, James M. and Willie B. Woods, Oct. 29th

1876

Early, Jas. T. and Sally Mary Brown, April 3rd
Edwards, Jas. W. and Frances A. Wood, June 21st
Elliott, Henry J. and Virginia M. Madison, Dec. 4th
Estes, Golden J. and Susie A. Wilkinson, Feb. 14th

1877

Early, Eugene and Patty W. McIntire, Jan. 2nd
Eubank, Wm. E. and Margaret F. Rice, Jan. 5th
Elson, Wm. H. and Susan A. Fretwell, Oct. 17th

1878

Edwards, John C. and Nancy Pritchett, Nov. 4th
Edward, Brice W. and Mary Etta Marshall, Nov. 25th
Eddins, Oscar and Sally E. Marshall, Nov. 26th
Easton, Wm. and Mahala W. Melton, Dec. 9th
Edwards, Valentine G. and Fanny A. Herndon, Dec. 11th

1879

Estes, John H. and Laura C. Creel, March 10th
Edward, John W. and Ermine W. Jones, May 15th
Eastham, Phillip and Mary W. Mills, Sept. 11th

1880

Elliott, Jas. F. and M. F. Powell, June 29th
Ellis, Wm. and M. Williams, Sept. 13th
Edwards, H. P. and Mattie L. Head, Oct. 9th
Eubank, Alexander N. and Sarah R. Jones, Sept. 22nd

1881

Eheart, Chastine and Willie Ann Durrett, Jan. 30th
Echols, Edward B. and Mary Jane Newell, March 28th
Eads, Wm. J. and Sally Dodd, Aug. 10th

1882

Esten, Nathanel R. and Georgianna Bishop, Dec. 26th
Early, Thos. L. and Nannie H. Brown, Jan. 24th

1883

Elliton, Samuel Martin and Bettie Davis, Jan. 17th
Elliott, James A. and Hester C. Fifer, April 19th
Estes, Christopher I. and Mattie W. Elsom, Sept. 12th

1884

Ehart, Adam G. and Sarah E. Tate, Dec. 11th

Eads, Jas. Washington and Emma P. Thomas, Jan. 10th
Eades, Thomas A. and Millie V. Brubeck, May 6th
Earley, Peachy H. and Annie Lewis Burnley, Aug. 6th

1885

Elsom, Wm. Marshall, Nettie L. Charles, July 15th
Echols, Wm. H. and Mary E. Blakey, Sept. 7th
Elliott, Henry I. and Fannie J. Madison, Sept. 20th

1886

Early, Jno. D. and Eliza J. Catterton, April 6th
Eltin, M. Ree and Evie M. Walters, June 2nd

1887

Etherton, Jos. E. and Mary Susan Ward, May 5th

1888

Estes, Robert E. and Nancy F. Wood, Jan. 6th
Everett, Aylett L. and Sadie S. Fry, Jan. 21st
Early, Thos. J. and Ida V. Wood, Feb. 11th
Elliott J. R. and L. B. Davis, Dec. 4th
Ellis, W. E. and Maggie M. Tyler, May 21st

1889

Estes, Geo. T. and Lucy B. Seamonds, Feb. 19th

1890

Edwards, Taswell A. and Mamie Davis, June 3rd
Edwards, W. C. and Virg. H. Johns, Dec. 23rd

1891

Eheart, C. A. and M. J. Drumwright, Aug. 4th
Eiserman, Hy. and Emma Hatopp, Oct. 15th

1892

Eastem, J. R. and L. H. Dolen, Aug. 1st

1893

Estes, Wilson J. and Tulie F. Sumands, Jan. 17th
Easton, G. R. and V. C. Harris, Oct. 9th

1894

Estes, W. M. and E. F. Wood, Nov. 6th

1895

Eubank, Geo. and Nellie Toms, July 10th
Estes, W. A. and E. E. Powell, Sept. 23rd

1896

Ellinger, G. E. and G. W. Rea, Jan. 24th

1897

Estes, L. L. and Carrie Lawson, May 1st

1898

Eades, Willie and Annie Durham, Jan. 11th
Emerson, Ruel and M. S. Wayland, March
10th
Ergenbright G. R. and S. C. Gibson, May 2nd
Earehart, J. W. and Birdie Bingham, Nov.
21st

1899

Eppard, Jasper L. and Callie May Ford, April
5th
Edwards, W. and S. E. Bracket, April 22nd

1900

Edwards, Elias and Sophie Butler, Aug. 16th
Ehart, C. E. and Blanch May, Dec. 27th
Edwards, R. A. and L. B. Mundy, May 26th

1901

Edwards, D. W. and M. E. Bibb, June 22nd
Elsom, R. M. and E. F. Nelson, Oct. 22nd

1902

Easton, G. W. and T. A. Mitchell, May 21st
Elliott, E. S. and M. C. Mallet, Oct. 7th

1903

Ellis, Roy H. and Agness E. Durrett, June 3rd
Estes, R. M. and Rena Wilkerson, Aug. 5th
Edwards, M. and C. L. Durham, Aug. 15th
Ellis, W. W. and E. N. Shackleford, Sept. 3rd
Early, Jno. D. and Mrs. Mary Compton, Dec.
3rd

1904

Enochs, Edw. L. and Sarah P. Gibson, July
27th
Ennis, Carroll C. and Overton W. Hicks, Oct.
22nd
Eubank, Jesse E. and Berdie G. Farish, Oct.
29th

1905

Edgar, Morton Bledsoe and Bertie Bell Bram-
ham, Dec. 16th
Easton, Henry Franklin and Georgia Melton,
Dec. 30th
Easton, Willie Wallace and Ella Clements,
Nov. 7th

1906

Ellis, N. G. and F. I. Moon, May 17th
Elliott, Andrew M. and Emma I. Deane, Oct.
3rd
Elliott A. B. and Margurete Rosser, Oct. 9th
Ellenton, Edward and Gabriella Dudley, Nov.
1st
Estes, Hugh F. and Nettie May Davis, Nov.
21st
Eddins, F. O. and S. A. Munday, Nov. 29th
Early, Fred Roy and Annie E. Fansler Dec.
25th
Elliott, Melton C. and Lucy H. Cocke, Dec.
29th

1907

Eubank, Halla L. and Bessie L. Eades, April
22nd
Easton, James M. and Lillian L. Davis, July
7th

1908

Edwards, James W. and Mrs. Lucy F. Glass,
Jan. 30th

1909

Eheart, Willis A. and Carrie A. Hall, March
25th
Eubank, Horace and Laura Kidd, Oct. 27th
Edwards, William M. and Ella Durham, Nov.
26th

1910

Elvery, Dudley J. and Emma B. Leake, July
14th
Easton, Harry and Evie Mitchel, Sept. 25th
Euiss, William F. and Idill M. Clark, Dec.
31st

1911

Estes, Hugh and Emma Clements, April 16th
Edwards, Tazwell S. and Sallie B. Ballard, Oct.
30th
Edwards, Jesse J. and Annie E. Marshall, Nov.
29th

1912

Elliott, William A. and Agnes F. Kemper,
Oct. 5th
Edwards, Thomas and Susie M. Giannini,
Nov. 26th
Emmons, Vernon and Minnie L. Bernwauger,
Dec. 18th

1913

Essig, George and Vinnie B. Glass, Aug. 4th
Elam, John R. and Grace J. Thurston, Aug.
17th
Elliott James F. and Eliza M. Wood, Oct. 15th

1914

Eades, John G. and May P. Maupin, July 3rd
Eliton, John E. and Lizzie Bailey, July 13th
Eubank, Elik and Edith Carter, Sept. 24th
Edwards, Jenny W. and Edna Sprouse, Oct.
23rd

1915

Edwards, Gordon G. and Lottie A. Nonull,
June 23rd

1916

Eliton, Walter Ellis and Blanche Siple, April
22nd

1917

Estes, William E. and Evelin E. Sandridge,
April 15th
Evans, Peyton R. and Janitta Fitz Hugh, Oct.
9th

Eggleston, Thos. L. and Arnette J. Siler, Dec. 1st

Elliott, Wm. H. and Della F. Shiflett, Dec. 26th

1918

Evans, Lloyd E. and Lena Mooney, Dec. 22nd

Estes, Woodie O. and Bertha Dickerson, Dec. 24th

1919

Evans, John W. and Lucy F. Reynolds, Jan. 8th

Easton, Wm. M. and Beulah V. Clemens, July 5th

1920

Elliott, Joseph H. and Cornelia M. Marshall, Jan. 19th

1921

Edwards, Dewey and Goldie C. Belew, May 5th

Edwards, Roy Alibest and Bessie Lee Farish, Aug. 17th

Estes, Willie Lee and Lutie May Fray, Nov. 24th

1922

Eppard, Arthur C. and Cordelia L. Allen, Dec. 22nd

1923

Eppard, Reece M. and Elsie M. Payne, May 15th

Eddins, George T. and Julia C. Hildebrand, July 12th

1924

Elswick, Robt. H. and Alma L. Watson, Aug. 6th

1925

Estes, Floyd and Virgie Marsh, April 7th

Estes, James W. and Rachel A. Harris, Sept. 1st

Eppard, Russell and Lillie V. Wood, Aug. 29th

Eubank, Cady B. and Grace Pace, Nov. 8th

1926

Eubank, Horace and Mury Moon, Dec. 28th

1927

Eppard, Andrew H. and Emma C. Lang, June 2nd

Ellis, Thomas S. and Annie K. Gibbon, Aug. 31st

1928

Estes, Eugene E. and Nannie K. Woodie, Nov. 17th

Elliott, Marshall B. and Ruby Lee Bing, Dec. 31st

1929

Edwards, Charlie Lee and Evelyn Lee Wood, Feb. 25th

Evans, Luther and Mannie R. Thomas, March 30th

Edwards, Raleigh M. and Janey E. Thurston, April 13th

Evans, Jr., Judson and Rosalie Meredith, Sept. 7th

Estes, Irone L. and Anne E. West, Oct. 1st

F

1781

Federa, John and Rachel Woods, Aug. 24th

1783

Feler, George and Sally Robertson, Nov. 20th

Flint, Thomas and Sally Flint, Feb. 20th

Fry, Joshur and Peachy Walker, Sept. 1st

1785

Faris, John and Anne Bunnel, July 22nd

Fitzgerald, Bartlot and Maske Coleman, Feb. 3rd

Fortune, John and Nancy Henderson, Nov. 11th

1786

Farell, James and Mary Wells, Sept. 22nd

Fortune, Nicholas and Frances Henderson, Dec. 12th

Foster, James and Patsy Humphrey, Dec. 15th

1787

Ferguson, James and Mary Robertson, Sept. 27th

Fitzpatrick, Thomas and Frances Gentry, Dec. 31st

1788

Foster, Anthony and Rachel Foster, Dec. 11th

1789

Fitzpatrick, John and Jean Blain, Oct. 8th

Fitzpatrick, Joseph and Elizabeth Jones, April 9th

Flint, Richard and Franky Sims, April 28th

Fowler, Samuel and Marget Cofer, Dec. 24th

1790

Fitzpatrick, Benjamin and Peggy Cocks, Nov. 30th

1791

Ferguson, Daniel and Nancy Eastin, Dec. 28th

1793

Faulkner, Daniel and Mary Hogan, June 5th

Ferguson, William and Caty Gilmore, Oct. 28th

Fitchpatrick, Hamner and Hannah Davis, Jan. 22nd

Foster, Edmund and Betsy Powers, Dec. 13th

Franklin, Bernard and Patsy Cleaveland, March 14th

1794

Franklin, Joel and Susannah Lewis, Jan. 7th

1795

Field, John and Sally Wood, Sept. 11th

Fletcher, Thomas C. and Susannah M. Janett, Nov. 19th

Foster, William and Peggy Buster, Dec. 24th

1796

Fitzgerald, Lawrence and Susannah Hill, April 4th

Fortune, John and Nancy Milton, Jan. 26th

Fox, William and Elizabeth Durham, Jan. 16th

1797

Faris, George and Susannah Sneed, Dec. 24th

Fitzpatrick, Joseph and Polly Perry, Nov. 21st

1798

Fenwick, James and Milly Sprouls, Sept. 24th

Frailey, William and Polly Burrus, Feb. 15th

1799

Fatham, William and Liddy Campbell, Jan. 26th

Ferguson, Daniel and Elizabeth Thomas, Oct. 29th

Field, Robert and Sally Durrett, Oct. 19th

Ford, Reuben and Jane Monroe, Dec. 20th

Foster, Joel and Betsy Golman, Dec. 16th

Fretwell, John and Mildred Garth, March 18th

Fretwell William and Nancy Hailey, Jan. 7th

1801

Fitzpatrick, Edward and Ruth Blain, Sept. 8th

Fortune, Pleasant and Polly Fortune, Aug. 1st

1802

Farrar, Joseph and Elizabeth Tindall, Dec. 20th

Fox, Samuel, and Betsy McAmory, Jan. 18th

Furgason, Lawrence and Ann Terry, Sept. 25th

1803

Fitzpatrick, William and Fanny Turner, Nov. 25th

Fortune, Richard and Martha Thacker, Aug. 13th

1804

Fogg, William and Nancy Alphin, Nov. 6th

Fortune, John and Delpha Dawson, March 28th

Fretwell, Alexander and Jane Hughes, Sept. 26th

Furgason, Hawkey and Elizabeth Norris, April 10th

1805

Fagg, Daniel and Polly Johnson, Sept. 4th

Fulcher, Thomas and Jane Gentry, Nov. 23rd

1806

Fagg, John and Betsy Oglesby, Dec. 27th

Farrar, John and W. Bailey, May 31st

Fields, Ralph and Milly Wood, Oct. 13th

Fitz, William and Mary Leake, Jan. 18th

Franklin, Richard and Mary Thompson, April 7th

1807

Fox, Josephin and Elizabeth Sneed, Sept. 7th

1809

Fields, Joseph and Mary Wood, Oct. 2nd

Fisher, George and Fanny Ray, April 1st

Foster, John D. and Ann Crenshaw, Dec. 18th

1810

Farish, John and Catherine Rogers, Feb. 17th

Flynt, James and Elizabeth Dowell, Feb. 15th

1813

Furk, Archibal and Lena Maupin, Oct. 11th

Fall, Sampson M. and Susannah Wood, Jan. 28th

1814

Foster, Thomas and Elizabeth Foster, Jan. 18th

Fowler, David and Susannah Butler, July 28th

Fretwell, William and Mary Askne, Nov. 7th

Furguson, David and Elizabeth Buck, Sept. 3rd

1815

Furke, Hiram and Martha W. Harris, May 15th

1816

Ferguson, Charles and Patsey Carver, Jan. 15th

Figgon, Willis and Nancy L. Suddarth, March 19th

Fitzpatrick, Thomas and Elizabeth Thomas, July 15th

Fretwell, Hudson and Elizabeth Burnley, Jan. 1st

1817

Finley, Samuel and Sally Golaing, April 7th

Fry, Wesley and Sophia M.   Jan. 15th

1819

Faris, John and Susan Rogers, March 1st

Fretwell, John and Peggy E. Marr, Sept. 6th

1820

Farrar, John and Nancy Carroll, Oct. 17th

Foster, James E. and Lucy T. Rogers, Dec. 22nd

1821

Fulcher, Jo and S. W. Durrett, Dec. 23rd

1822

Ferguson, David and Cynthia Jopling, Nov. 16th
Fretwell, Richard and S. Barksdale, Sept. 2nd
Fry, James F. and Mary Barksdale, Jan. 24th

1823

Foster, Grief and Eliza Battles, Oct. 20th

1824

Farneyhough, Edward and Elizabeth Earley, Feb. 19th
Farrar, John L. and Martha P. Walton, June 20th
Foster, William W. and Elizabeth Hamner, Nov. 1st
Frasier, John and Nelly Gowing, Nov. 4th
Frish, Nicholas P. and Virginia I. Randolph, Dec. 16th

1825

Farrer, Elijah and Maria Barnett, June 16th
Farrer, James and Critty Hawkins, Aug. 8th
Ferguson, David and Prudence Thomas, Nov. 3rd
Ferguson, Elias and Nancy Burford, Jan. 18th
Fitch, Henry H. and Elizabeth Watson, Dec. 25th
Fitch, Wilson and Mary Ann Carver, July 14th

1826

Faris, Reuben and Ann Watson, Dec. 7th
Fender, Ephraim and Nancy Morris, Dec. 15th
Fleming, Tarlton and Rebecca E. Coles, Nov. 30th
Foster, Norborne and Jane Hamner, Aug. 7th

1827

Ferrell, James L. and Mary Napier, Feb. 7th
Fishbourne, Daniel and Ann B. Rodes, March 19th
Fletcher, Daniel and Hannah A. Wimer, Oct. 11th

1828

Ferguson, Wiley and Lucy Robinson, Oct. 9th
Foster, Hugh and Jane Browning, Aug. 20th
Foster, Thomas and Elizabeth Rothwell, July 12th

1829

Field, Robert and Nancy Piper, Oct. 8th
Fisher, George D. and Elizabeth Higginbotham, June 29th

1830

Fretwell, John M. and Mary Ann Foster, Sept. 12th
Fretwell, Samuel and Mary Askne, May 3rd

1831

Ferguson, Stephen and Elizabeth Beck, Jan. 13th
Fisher, George R. and Lucy C. Johnson, Dec. 29th

Fisher, Robert and Nancy Walton, Jan. 6th
Foster, Allen and Martha Carrol, Oct. 13th

1832

Field, Robert and Virginia Toms, June 7th

1833

Finks, William M. and Demaris Hamner, Dec. 25th

1834

Flippen, Alfred W. and Minerva T. G. Staples, July 3rd
Frazier, Livingston and Delitha Rosanber, Aug. 18th

1835

Farrer, Thomas and Sarah Battles, May 7th
Fitz, John C. and Angelina Huckstep, Dec. 1st
Flint, William and Catherine Priddy, Dec. 7th
Foland, Valentine and Fran Smith, June 22nd
Foster James and C. M. Kirby, Nov. 28th

1836

Farneyhough, Edward and Mary B. Thrift, Oct. 24th
Fortune, McKinsey and S. Gazaway, March 24th
Frazier, John H. and Mary J. Morris, April 5th

1837

Ferguson, Samuel A. and Eliza J. Barksdale, Aug. 10th
Fisher, George and S. A. Balew, July 3rd
Fray, James and S. S. Barksdale, June 26th

1838

Foster, William W. and Mary A. Spears, Oct. 9th
Fray, John Jr. and Elizabeth Gooch, March 7th

1839

Fisher, William and Elizabeth S. Walton, April 3rd
Foster, Nelson and Eliza Ann Oaks, April 1st
Fox, Alexander and Verindy Huse, March 13th
Fray, Robert B. and Sarah Wilhoite, Aug. 28th

1840

Ferguson, Fendal and S. M. Clarke, Dec. 12th
Fisher, John and Jane T. Coles, Nov. 10th
Fretwell, William G. and E. E. Brum, Dec. 16th

1841

Fenwick, John and Rebecca Gilmore, Dec. 28th
Ferguson, David and Leannah Emmerson, Oct. 18th
Fisher, Robert and Elizabeth Mooney, June 7th

Flannagan, Benjamin C. and Ann V. Timberlake, March 8th

Foster, James and Elizabeth Cook, Nov. 1st

1842

Fox, John and M. W. Herrin, Jan. 31st

1843

Fletcher, Erron and Sarah C. Jury, April 18th

1844

Farish, Andracio J. and M. G. Crank, April 28th

Farneyhough, John and Eliza Thrift, Sept. 3rd

Fretwell, Burlington and Elizabeth F. Jarman, Dec. 11th

Fry, William H. and J. M. Watson, April 4th

1845

Faulconer, W. H. and Eliza Maury, Dec. 11th

1846

Faber, John G. and Ann M. Wingfield, June 1st

Flannagan, William A. and Martha Bishop, Sept. 15th

Fretwell, William C. and Verina S. Kinsolving, Dec. 8th

1847

Flynn, Owen R. and M. E. Perkins, Nov. 1st

Forbes, J. F. and Jane Dawson, Sept. 30th

Frazier, Shedrick and Naomi Shiflett, Sept. 13th

1848

Feilder, M. J. and M. F. Mathews, Oct. 5th

Foster, Miles S. and Sarah Baber, Nov. 23rd

Fox, William and Harriet Baber, April 24th

Fretwell, John R. and C. B. Saltmarsh, Oct. 4th

Fretwell, W. E. and Amanda Moon, April 24th

1849

Finder, Ephraim A. and Mary J. Abell, April 19th

1850

Farrar, John M. and Elizabeth Eubank, May 29th

Fleisher, Henry H. and Elizabeth C. Detter, Feb. 12th

Fox, Alexander P. and Mary P. Hart, Aug. 1st

Fry, John J. and Mary C. Lewis, Feb. 3rd

1851

Fisher, James M. and Margaret Moses, Oct. 4th

Fretwell, Franklin and Ann C. Jarman, Dec. 11th

1852

Farrar, Thomas M. and S. E. A. Durrett, May 11th

1853

Fortune, William B. and Ann R. Anise, Dec. 22nd

Fry, Matthew H. and Sallie F. Heiskell, Nov. 1st

1854

Farrar, Micanus C. and E. J. Mathews, Feb. 13th

Field, James G. and Frances E. Cowherd, June 20th

Ford, George L. and Ann E. Bowyer, March 20th

Fortune, Joel and Lucy I. Farrar, Oct. 5th

Foster, John C. and Sarah E. Fricks, March 16th

Frazier, James A. and Nancy K. Snow, Aug. 10th

Funsten, O. R. and Mary Bowen, July 10th

Foster, Jno. C. and Sarah E. Finks, March 16th

Funsten, D. O. R. and Mary Bowen, Jan. 10th

1855

Frazier, Jas. A. and Nancy K. Snow, Aug. 10th

Farrow, Wm. F. (F. N.) and Jounna Battles, Dec. 9th

Farrow, William F. and Joanna Battles, Dec. 8th

Ford, Geo. L. and Ann E. Bowyer, March 20th

1856

Frazier, James and Hannah Sprouce, Oct. 27th

Fry, Jesse L. and Frances E. Dunkum, Nov. 17th

Fry, Jesse S. and F. E. Dunkum, Nov. 18th

1857

Fretwell, Bright and Susan A. E. Herndon, Oct. 22nd

1858

Farrar, Micanus and Elizabeth B. Powell, Feb. 18th

Fennesel, Dennis and Jane Sprouce, Nov. 8th

Fishback, M. M. and Sallie A. Steff, Jan. 26th

Fishback, Wm. H. and Sallie A. Stiff, Jan. 26th

Farneyhough, Milton and Victoria B. A. Byers, March 16th

Feunesll, Denniss and Jane Sprouce, Dec. 11th

Farrar, Meanus, C. and Eliz. B. Powell, Feb. 21st

1859

Farmer, Nelson H. and Mary E. McAlister, Nov. 7th

Ford, John P. and Lizzie Hamner, June 23rd

Fortune, A. G. and Mary C. Fall, June 6th

Foster, John O. and F. I. Drumheller, May 30th

Funcott, Thomas R. and Mary A. Smith, June 13th

Faneette, Tho. M. and Mary A. Smith, June 14th

Farrar, Nelson H. and Mary E. McAllister, Nov. 27th

1860

Fulcher, James and Sarah Owens, Jan. 10th
Fulcher, Jas. and Sarah Owens, Jan. 12th

1861

Farrar, James S. and Eliza Ann Pace, Oct. 3rd
Fauck, George N. and Sarah F. Bunch, March 6th
Ferguson, Charles M. and Julia Ann Herring, Feb. 18th
Ferguson, George N. and Teresa N. Branch, Feb. 25th
Finks, William S. and Catharine Gardner, July 20th
Finton, Jeremiah S. and Catharine Coleman, Dec. 20th
Finks, Wm. S. and Catherine Gardner, July 10th
Farrar, James S. and Eliza Ann Pace, Oct. 6th
Finton, Jeremiah and Catherine Calleman, Dec. 28th
Ferguson, Chas. M. and Julia Ann Herring, Feb. 21st
Farish, George W. and Sarah F. Bunch, March 7th

1862

Furguson, James H. and Sarah Jane Farrar, Nov. 26th

1863

Faust, Anthony and S. E. Thompson, June 10th
Franks, Wm. and M. A. V. Dobbins, May 11th
Fatwell, Wm. W. and Mary E. Currier, Sept. 10th
Fray, John, Jr. and Fanny L. Terrell, Oct. 22nd

1864

Farish, Andrew J. and C. W. M. Laughlin, Nov. 1st

1865

Ferneyhough, G. N. and Fannie W. Goss, Nov. 18th
Figgins, Mauthebert and Elizabeth Hudson, Dec. 25th
Fray, Albert G. and M. A. Wilhoit, Aug. 7th
Farrar, Jas. T. and Ann J. Sullivan, Nov. 2nd
Fagins, Manslobert and Eliz. Hudson, Dec. 26th
Fray, Albert G. and Martha A. Wilhoit, Aug. 8th

1866

Failes, John S. and Eliza J. Priddy, Aug. 13th
Ferrell, Abraham D. and Lucy V. Hunt, Jan. 16th
Flint, M. and Ann Eliza Thomas, March 13th
Foster, William and Mildred Lewis, July 21st

Fretwell, John O. and Mary Jane Day, Jan. 17th
Fitzpatrick, Jno. M. G. and Endora Snead, Nov. 21st
Fretwell, Jno. A. and Mary J. Day, Jan. 18th
Flint, Wm. and Ann E. Thomas, Nov. 14th

1867

Fishburne, Clement D. and Lizzie Wood, June 10th
Flannagan, Andrew and Jane McCrae, Dec. 24th
Foster, Jno. W. and Serona F. Foster, Nov. 28th
Fulcher, James and Cornenilia J. Etherton, Oct. 1st
Fulcher, James and Cornelia J. Etherton, Oct. 3rd
Foster, Jno. W. and Lerona Foster, Nov. 21st

1868

Fagins, Henry and Martha Fagins, June 19th
Fisher, Wm. J. and Louisa Madison, Dec. 27th
Ferguson, J. H. and Mary J. Clark, Oct. 11th
Fulcher, Thos. J. and Harriet R. Goodwin, Oct. 1st

1869

Farrer, John K. and Fanny E. Edgs, May 19th
Farloins, John W. and Virginia C. Bailey, Oct. 28th
Faulkner, Chas. J. and Sally Winn, Nov. 25th
Fleming, Wilson and Mary Smith, Dec. 28th

1870

Fielding, Jas. and Mary McAllister, Jan. 5th

1871

Funkhauser, Filden S. and Emma Harman, Aug. 9th
Fry, Melvin and Rhody Gohanna, Sept. 23rd

1872

Fink, Rudolph and Care Nicholas, Nov. 7th
Fortune, James A. and Amanda A. Luntzofrd, Nov. 28th

1873

Floppo, S. W. and M. V. Martin, Jan. 22nd
Fox, John G. and C. A. Jones, Jan. 30th
Farrar, C. S. and E. G. Gilmer, Feb. 4th

1874

Fretwell, Dabney H. and Bettie M. Woodson, May 25th
Fretwell, John T. and Nannie A. Payne, Dec. 2nd

1875

Fallwelle, Jas. M. and Eliza J. Carrier, Dec. 11th

1876

Farrow, Thos. J. and Annie M. Jones, July 10th

1877

Flynt, Richard O. and Berta E. Leake, Jan 3rd
Faldwell, Edw. and Emma L. Martin, July 16th
Farrish, Frank P. and Emma S. Farish, Sept. 25th
Foster, Robt. A. H. and Sallie D. Sutherland, Oct. 18th

1878

Ford, Wm. V. and Lydia H. Price, Aug. 30th
Faris, John N. and Mattie A. Edge, Dec. 12th
Fugirary, Thos. B. and Sally M. Elson, Aug. 10th

1879

Fielding, Chas. H. and Martha T. Munday, Sept. 16th
Feinsley, James A. and Fanny B. Smith, Oct. 14th
Farish, Richard J. and Lizzie G. Sutherland, Oct. 20th

1880

Farish, Jno. A. and Lucy J. Kirby, April 12th
Fisher, James H. and Sarah A. McCauley, Sept. 24th

1881

Fansler, Jacob and Sallie Bacon, Feb. 23rd
Fry, James M. and Jennie Ann Dudley, March 1st
Farish, Benj. F. and Georganna Gooch, March 28th
Folks, Wm. R. and Cora Lee Hartnagle, Aug. 10th
Farish, Geo. W. and Mary E. Collins, Aug. 10th
Fox, Robert and Sally Ashly Glass, Sept. 29th
Field, Wm. W. and Lizzie White Martin, Dec. 21st

1882

Fray, Abram D. and Nettie M. Wood, Jan. 18th
Fry, Thomas H. and Mildred A. Via, Feb. 21st
Fuchterrberger, C. A. and Sophia Hartman, May 30th
Fenn, Francis M. O. and Lottie Benson, Nov. 23rd

1883

Fonville, Wm. Drakeford and Nannie Winn Yancey, Sept. 18th

1884

Frazier, Thomas and Elizabeth Garrison, Jan. 1st
Farish, Wm. P. and Lilly L. Harris, Nov. 5th

1885

Faulkner, Erasmus G. and Mattie J. Lupton, Oct. 25th

Fleming, Jno. Henry and Susan M. Catterton, Apr. 26th
Fox, Andrew Jackson and Mineroa F. Napier, Nov. 26th

1886

Fistier, Wm. A. and Martha A. Bayne, Jan. 13th

1887

Flannagan, Broadus and Lotty G. Green, Jan. 26th
Fielding, Robt. Lee and Lucy E. Crickenberger, Feb. 26th

1888

Farish, T. M. and J. S. Randolph, Nov. 27th
Farish, W. L. and Emma J. Bishop, Dec. 25th
Foster, Wm. F. and Molly F. Batten, March 13th
Follit, J. Lucus and Bettie Lewis Mix, May 31st

1889

Farby, Robt. A. and Marritta Anderson, June 14th
Faris, O. L. and V. G. Quick, July 27th
Fuller, Geo. W. and Ora M. Marshall, Sept. 9th

1890

Flowers, Wm. and Mary P. Leis, Oct. 25th
Fenwick, Wm. W. and Mary S. Thomas, Dec. 3rd
Fry, Jno. W. and Julia A. Gibson, Nov. 10th

1891

Fisher, Peter F. and Annie J. Crickenberger, May 18th
Flint, Wm. R. and Mollie Modena, Oct. 19th
Fielding, Wm. J. and Sally J. Bailey, Dec. 7th
Farrar, Wm. E. and M. E. Mallory, Jan. 30th

1892

Fisher, J. L. and Va. Eubank, Mar. 14th
Fielding, L. E. and L. A. Bolton, Apr. 2nd
Ferneyhough, G. F. and J. A. Ferneyhough, Oct. 17th

1893

Fleming, Thos. and Lucinda Minor, Aug. 15th
Fallit, R. F. and B. G. Durrett, Oct. 11th
Farrar, M. and J. H. Baber, Dec. 13th
Foster, C. E. and E. D. Rea, Dec. 16th
Fallet, Wm. and Flosine Alexander, June 3rd

1894

Frincke, M. C. and Pauline Hotopp, Sept. 18th
Faulconer, J. C. and S. E. Smith, Oct. 30th

1895

Fenneyhaugh, Ch. ? and Em. Fenneyhaugh?, Apr. 20th
Fields, R. L. and Carrie Edwards, May 27th

1896

Flannagan, R. K. and Lucy Jones, Oct. 19th
Furr, David and Mollie Crickenboger, May 4th
Ferneyhough, H. C. and Mary S. Douglass, Oct. 5th
Fray, A. D. and Sally E. Douglass, Oct. 22nd
Farrar, C. C. and L. B. Maupin, Dec. 21st
Freeman, Jas. E. and Annie G. Lyone, Dec. 30th

1897

Farish, Wm. and Dora Smith, June 30th
Fawcus, Thos. and Lucile Clark, Oct. 25th

1898

Fitzgerald, Dd. and Lula Harris, Nov. 4th
Fowler, David W. and Alice J. Fry, Oct. 8th
Fleming, Thos. and Maggie Quarles, Dec. 21st

1899

Fasler, Robt. and A. E. Banks, March 24th
Fisher, Louis and Ella J. Felter, July 21st
Farrar, I. J. and M. L. Harris, Dec. 22nd
Fishburne, C. D. Jr. and Annie W. Price, Dec. 23rd

1900

Farrish, Jas. S. and Bessie A. Newton, Jan. 16th
Foot, Alvin K. and Ada S. Page, March 2nd
Faluner, W. H. and L. E. Eubank, Sept. 3rd
Farrar, Thos. L. and Jennie C. Shackleford, Nov. 13th
Farrar, W. J. and Julia Barrton, Dec. 19th
Faulconer, J. C. and S. N. Houchens, Dec. 21st

1901

Fuller, W. C. and C. T. Woods, Jan. 30th
Fogg, J. U. and Annie T. Marshall, June 5th
Fisher, C. R. and Mattie Evans, Sept. 16th
Fitch, G. S. and M. L. Elsom, Oct. 2nd
Fitzgerald, G. W. and M. F. Newton, Oct. 7th
Fulcher, Lewis and Matilda E. Clark, Dec. 2nd
Farmer, Hizerl and Mattie Bailey, Dec. 17th
Foster, Virgil H. and Minnie L. Baber, Dec. 19th
Forloines, D. B. and F. C. Summers, Apr. 29th
Fitzgerald, W. D. and Mary E. Powell, Aug. 21st

1902

Fuller, Chas. and Fairfax Loving, June 4th
Farish, Henry L. and Sarah E. Gibson, Aug. 20th
Faris, Wm. L. and Fannie L. Dowell, Dec. 13th
Farrell, Jno. M. and A. F. Clements, March 31st

1903

Faulconer, W. B. and C. L. Harris, Aug. 11th
Flesham, R. T. and Cora Harris, Sept. 23rd
Farish, Jake and Cornelia Falwell, Nov. 3rd
Farish, Jno. D. and M. J. Fisher, Dec. 31st

1904

Faulkner, R. E. and Emma C. Austin, Aug. 15th
Fitch, Geo. A. and Bernard L. Green, Oct. 20th
Frames, Samuel J. and Julia C. Priddy, Dec. 22nd

1905

Faulkner, Wm. H. and Eugenie Moore, May 29th
Fisher, Eddy M. and Bessie L. Wilkerson, June 27th

1906

Fitch, Peter M. and Frances Clark, March 2nd

1907

Fretwell, Harry B. and Bessie M. Gibson, April 3rd
Farrish, William F. and Mollie Marshall, Feb. 5th
Fisher, Albert T. and Liggie O. Doss, June 27th
Flannogan, James F. and Jannett Wharam, Sept. 25th
Frazier, Frank and Sarah Breeden, Oct. 22nd
Flint, Austin and Annie Vannosdoll, Dec. 18th

1908

Ford, Andrew J. and Flora E. Durrett, Aug. 19th
Fisher, Joe and Eliza Ann Sprouse, Sept. 14th
Feuchtenberger, Otto C. and Florence Va. Jones, Sept. 29th
Fore, James R. and Carrie Lee Payne, Dec. 23rd

1909

Fitch, James F. and Mary D. Eddins, Feb. 27th
Faris, John F. and Maria C. Cavfints, June 16th
Fox, Jim and Elizabeth Harlow, Dec. 29th

1910

Fox, Filmore J. and Ruth Clarke, Feb. 16th
Ford, Thomas E. and Sarah E. Hilderbrand, March 30th
French, Claude L. M. and Annie L. Wade, April 10th
Frazier, Cleveland and Janie Garrison, Dec. 29th

1911

Frazier, Nathaniel and Mary L. McAllister, Jan. 18th
Fox, David and Lutie Herring, Feb. 12th
Flint, Olie and Evie Crickenberger, Aug. 2nd
Fitzgerald, Lloyd W. and Annie Lee Sprouse, Dec. 21st

1912

Fergusen, Roy Herman and Fannie D. Munday, May 10th

Forloines, Wallace G. and Susie Mitchell, June 26th

Fox, Richard W. and Luetta E. Head, Sept. 3rd

Foster, Henry N. and Fannie O. Ballard, Sept. 26th

Fry, George W. and Margery Harris, Oct. 4th

Figgins, William and Dora C. Garrison, Oct. 9th

1913

Fisher, Claybourne and Nora E. Sandridge, Sept. 21st

Foltz, Tecumch S. and Maude Watts, Nov. 25th

1914

French, Cabele L. and Ella S. Wade, Feb. 17th

Forsyth, George L. and Elsie F. Miles, May 5th

Fisher, George W. and Lydia T. Fatwell, June 14th

Faber, Jerry M. and Mary S. Judy, June 15th

Foster, Willie F. nad Ruth C. Ballard, Oct. 2nd

Fisher, Clinton and Lena Edwards, Nov. 24th

1915

Fry, Charles W. and Bertha E. Bolick, Apr. 21st

Ford, Jesse R. and Juanita Patterson, June 11th

Flannagan, Eric G. and Beryle Morris, June 26th

Farley, Thos. K. and Lottie A. Farley, July 2nd

Foster, Grover C. and Myrtle P. Sutherland, Aug. 13th

Funkhouser, Hunter and Gracie O. Rush, Sept. 1st

Fishburne, George P. and Esther C. Moon, Sept. 16th

Farish, Robert and Evelyn Critzer, Oct. 20th

Fitzgerald, Clinton M. and Florence J. Vess, Oct. 23rd

Farish, Walker and Lillie Quick, Oct. 30th

1916

Flannagan, Andrew S. and Mrs. Lizzie Blake, July 12th

1917

Fray, Ira C. and Mildred G. Maupin, June 2nd

Freeman, Philip E. and Pearl M. Justice, June 7th

Faris, Clarence A. and Annie P. Dudley, Aug. 1st

Fox, Clarence H. and Alma V. Smith, Sept. 4th

1918

Fields, Carman E. and May T. Birckhead, Feb. 2nd

Faris, Jas. F. and Dora Robinson, Sept. 31st

1919

Frazier, Billy and Gracie Shiflett, Jan. 7th

Foster, Jno. Wm. and Janie E. Mawyer, June 10th

Fry, John W. and Alice H. Everett, June 14th

Frazier, Thomas W. and Betty F. McAllister, June 12th

Farish, Wm. M. and Otey B. Thomas, Aug. 3rd

Fuller, Hugh H. and Rosa L. Maupin, Aug. 20th

Flint, Herbert C. and Thelma E. Cornett, Dec. 15th

Fisher, James and Katie S. Crickenbarger, Dec. 25th

1920

Fray, Charles M. and Sallie B. Parrott, Apr. 20th

Frazier, Lew and Ollie Shiflett, May 3rd

Fox, Ashby D. and Martha G. Layman, Aug. 17th

Flynt, Percy Lee, and Mary Motie Maupin, Oct. 1st

Fulcher, Edward L. and Rosa Bell Carter, Dec. 23rd

Fisher, Jacob F. and Viola Wolf, Dec. 31st

1921

Fitzgerald, Haywood and Ruth Wheeler, Nov. 23rd

1922

Fox, Gilbert F. and Mary Lou Tomlin, March 8th

Fraser, Donald and Josephine Cook, June 29th

Fox, Roy and Fleta Powers, Nov. 12th

Fox, Joseph P. and Eunice E. Garrison, Dec. 26th

1923

Franckle, George L. and Viola M. Marshall, Feb. 10th

Frazier, Dave and Virgia Via, Apr. 10th

Faurnile, Paul and Minnie Long, June 23rd

Funk, Roscoe L. and Ruby L. Durrer, Aug. 28th

Flowers, Edward and Bolling Lowry, Nov. 9th

1924

Fitzgerald, Claude E. and Hallie Turner, Feb. 4th

Fitzgerald, P. H. and Martha McDaniel, April 19th

Fox, Russell R. and Jessie R. Haven, Aug. 17th

Ford, Leslie W. and Mary V. Hamner, Sept. 4th

Frazier, Philip and Twittie Garrison, Dec. 31st

1925

Foster, Edward B. and Edna P. Belew, May 25th

Fuell, Shirley and Virgie Bishop, Aug. 23rd

Frazier, Luther and Gertrude Shiflett, Sept. 3rd

Fore, James O. and Eva Bragg, Dec. 26th

1926

Fossen, Lloyd L. Van and Bertha Bledsoe, Jan. 2nd

Farish, Walter and Lutie Farish, Feb. 4th

Fielder, Chas. H. and Annie E. Banton, Oct. 19th

Fain, Jas. Rhea and Lucy E. Bouldin, Nov. 20th

1927

Ferneyhough, Jesse C. and Sidneye E. Alexander, Feb. 3rd

Frazier, Sidney and Susie Lee Morris May 3rd

Farish, Daniel W. and Mary Melton, June 15th

Fitzgerald, Frank and Roberta B. Lamb, Sept. 5th

Flagg, Paul M. and Alma L. Humphreys, Sept. 23rd

Fletcher, Marshall and Sarah B. Hildreth, Oct. 15th

Flynt, Guy B. and Ketwah A. Pritchett, Nov. 15th

Ferrier, David and Nannie F. Zerkel, Dec. 24th

1928

Ferneyhough, Charlie R. and Fontaine T. Morris, April 6th

Fechtig, Frederick H. and Eula B. Wright, May 21st

Ferguson, William H. and Elma Fore, June 9th

Froxell, Wm. H. and Sallie A. T. Maupin, July 3rd

Feets, Asa F. and Virginia M. Critzer, Dec. 24th

1929

Faulconer, Chas. B. and Lois E. Davis, Feb. 23rd

Frezzell, Charles R. and Daisy S. Garth, May 18th

Finchons, Wm. Elwood and Ruby Lee Gibson, June 24th

Faulconer, Louis H. and Lola E. Thomas, July 5th

Fitzhugh, Oscar G. and Mary C. Boaz, Oct. 5th

Freeman, Robbie W. and Virginia F. Cobb, Oct. 26th

Farish, Samuel E. and Ella Parr Smith, Dec. 4th

G

Grayson, Thomas and Rhodes Merrett —

1781

Gilliam, Archer and Judith Tuley, Dec. 15th

Gilliam, John and Mary Tooley, Nov. 22nd

1783

Garth, John and Ann Rodes, June 17th

1784

Gentry, Richard and Jane Harris, March 12th

Grady, John and Scota Bocock, Sept. 17th

1785

Garland, Edward and Sarah Old, Aug. 6th

Garland, Rice and Elizabeth Humner, Feb. 22nd

Gillum, John and Elizabeth Baley, Dec. 22nd

Grogg, Berriah and Jane Early Kyle, Feb. 14th

1786

Garrison, Samuel and Mary Johnson, Aug. 13th

Goodman, Joseph and Nancy Michie, Dec. 2nd

Greening, James and Sarah Crosthwait, Nov. 19th

Greening, Robert Jr. and Patty Crosthwait, April 12th

1788

Gillum, William and Sarah Watson, July 10th

Grayson, Thomas and Jenny Field, July 11th

1789

Garth, Thomas and Susanna Durrett, Dec. 10th

Gentry, Josiah and Nancy Thompson, Dec. 10th

1790

Goodman, John and Frances Dickerson, Dec. 13th

Goodman, William and Elizabeth Gentry, Jan. 20th

Goulding, Zackey and Nancy Davis, Dec. 7th

Griffen, Burgess and Jenny Page, Dec. 27th

1791

Gowing, Sherwood and Susannah Simmons, June 5th

1792

Gardner, William and Elizabeth Epperson, Feb. 29th

1793

Garrison, Jeremiah and Saluda Davis, Jan. 27th

Gillum, Bennett and Betsy Cleaveland, Jan. 29th

Gunter, Reuben and Patience Dowel, Oct. 5th

1794

Gibson, Henry and Dicy Harvey, Feb. 6th

Gillum, Elisha and Lucy Wood, Sept. 1st

Gooling, Harding and Caty Bruce, Aug. 30th

1795

Garth, Elijah and Susannah Fretwell, Nov. 6th

Goodman, Nathan and Mildred Clarkson, Dec. 1st

1897

Garner, William and Mary Carden, Dec. 25th
Garrison, Zachariah and Sally Bruce, Dec. 26th
Garth, Jesse and Elizabeth Brown, Dec. 18th
Goolsby, Fulton and Mildred Walker, Dec. 4th

1798

Gibson, John and Elizabeth Harvie, Aug. 3rd
Gillaspy, Alexander and Jenny Hill, Jan. 6th
Goodman, Rowland and Elizabeth Rothwell, Feb. 5th
Goodridge, John and Lucy Currell, Dec. 3rd
Goulding, Peter and Betsey Moles, Dec. 22nd
Goulding, Richard and Ann Walton, April 27th

1799

Gambill, Richard and Elizabeth Tunstall, Oct. 15th
Gentry, Claborn and Jannis Maxwell, Nov. 19th
Gilbert, Nathaniel and Lucy Leak, Sept. 2nd
Goings, James and Becky Ailstock, Dec. 2nd
Goings, Jesse and Jenny Ailstock, Dec. 2nd
Grofton, Phillip and Ann L. Slaughter, Jan 9th

1801

Gaines, Henry and Elizabeth Kirby, Dec. 8th
Gentry, Aaron and Polly Ogg, Nov. 14th
Gentry, Christopher and Juriah Woods, July 13th
Gillum, John and Tempy Travillion, June 17th
Grant, Robert and Susannah Melton, Oct. 12th
Griffin, Sherrod and Polly Page, Dec. 16th

1802

Gaer, Ransom and Polly Lamb, Feb. 23rd
Gentry, John and Caty Gentry, Oct. 16th
Gillaspy, John and Milly White, Nov. 22nd
Gillaspy, Lewis and Nancy Ellis, April 13th
Gillaspy, William and Judith Herrin, Nov. 22nd
Gillum, John and Rebecca Wingfield, May 20th
Goodman, Charles and Sarah Tallcock, Jan. 30th
Greer, Jonathan and Sarah Trackwell, Jan. 26th

1803

Garland, Anderson and Nancy Buster, Aug. 8th
Garth, Elijah and Caty Wayt, June 18th
Gay, Thomas and Peggy Gay, July 8th
Gentry, Aaron and Peggy Ogg, Jan. 10th
Gilmer, E. R. and Mary House, Sept. 14th

1804

Gentry, John and Polly Thurman, Nov. 20th
Gentry, John and Patsy Hicks, March 5th
Gentry, Thomas and Ann Carr, Dec. 12th
Gibson, Randolph and Dicey Sprouse, July 4th

Gillaspy, Lewis and Sally Rogers, June 2nd
Goodman, Augustine G. and Polly Clarkson, Jan. 10th
Grant, John and Polley Denis Bruce, Aug. 4th

1805

Garrison, James and Nancy Garrison, July 25th
Garrison, William and Sally Garrison, Jan. 23rd
Gentry, William and Lucy Carr, Jan. 14th
Gillaspy, William and Elizabeth Colvin, Feb. 4th
Gooch, Nicholas and Judah Nash, Nov. 16th
Gooch, Thomas and Nancy Irvin, July 22nd
Grass, Jacob and Jenney Moore, March 4th

1806

Gillaspy, William and Mary Owens, Dec. 25th
Gillock, Robert and Nancy Burrus, June 2nd
Goodall, Charles and Patsy Wood, June 23rd

1807

Garrison, Elijah and Jinny Owens, Jan. 9th
Gianinny, Nicholar and Polly Pace, March 13th
Gillum, James and Sally Shelton, Nov. 28th
Grady, Jepe and Polly Hoy, Oct. 6th

1808

Garrett, Alexander and Evelina Bolling
Gentry, George and Elizabeth Dunn, Nov. 1st
Gentry, James and Elizabeth Tuly, Aug. 1st
Gianinny, Thomas and Judith Butler, Oct. 20th
Gillock, Thomas M. and Ann Burrus, Sept. 29th
Grady, Reubin and Nancy Read, Dec. 29th

1809

Gentry, Nicholas and Polly Maxwell, Jan. 21st
German, Pleasant and Elizabeth Ballard, Jan. 7th
Goulding, Thomas and Nancy Harlin, March 22nd
Griffin, Harrison and Amediah Cosby, Nov. 11th

1810

Garland, Clifton Jr. and Deara Kinsolving, Nov. 6th
Garrison, Early and Susan Gillaspie, Sept. 3rd
Gentry, Christopher and Sally Dunn, Aug. 2nd
Gentry, David and Sarah Harrison, Nov. 6th
Gillum, Frederick and Kelly Huckstep, May 15th
Goodall, Davis and Lucy Wood, Jan. 1st
Gowen, John and Ann Gowen, Jan. 11th

1811

Gibson, ? and Juda Dudley, May 21st
Gowen, and Louisa Eviers, Jan. 17th

1812

Garner, Richard and Patsy Ashly, March 25th

Gillum, John B. and Rebecca B. Porter, Nov. 26th

Grayson, John and Susannah Britt, July 16th

Grimstead, William and Elizabeth McCoy, Dec. 3rd

Grymes, William and Polly Wood, Dec. 7th

1813

Garland, William and Nancy Hamner, Oct. 19th

Gilloch, Benjamin and Sarah Thomason, June 7th

Gordon, William F. and Elizabeth L. Lindsey, June 19th

1814

Gillum, John and Elizabeth Moore, May 2nd

1815

Gains, Nathan T. and Harriet Suttles, Dec. 21st

Garth, William and Elizabeth S. W. Martin, Feb. 27th

Garton, Thomas and Elizabeth Priddy, Sept. 20th

Gladden, Edward and Nancy Howard, Feb. 6th

Gladden, John T. and Sally Pleasants, Feb. 19th

1816

Gardner, ? and Lucinda Martin, Dec. 12th

Garrison, Valley and Sarah Dowell, Aug. 29th

Garton, Thomas and Palsey Gillaspie, Sept. 1st

Gentry, James and Nelly Gibson, Aug. 5th

Goodall, Parks and Elizabeth Austin, Nov. 4th

Goodman, Charles and Polly Barksdale, Jan. 9th

Goodman, William and Sarah S. Durrett, Aug. 20th

1817

Garland, Peter and Betsey Martin, Feb. 18th

Garrett, Ira and Elizabeth I. Watson, March 14th

Gay, Samuel L. and Elizabeth Hamner, Jan. 6th

Gibson, William and Jemimor Gentry, Dec. 23rd

Gillaspy, Lewis and Elizabeth Owens, Jan. 9th

Gilmore, John and Mary Ann Harlan, Sept. 11th

Gilmore, William and Elizabeth Eubank, April 10th

Gooch, Thompson and Elizabeth Jarman, Dec. 11th

Grayson, Joseph and Roody White, Dec. 1st

1818

Gillaspy, Jonathan and Matilda Breedlove, Dec. 29th

Givins, Thompson and Susannah Brown, Aug. 24th

1819

Garrison, Achillis and Sidne M. Harris, Dec. 18th

Garton, Zachariah and Lucy Baber, Feb. 2nd

Gillum, Henry and Nancy Lobbin, Oct. 4th

Glascock, William H. and Mary Harper, Aug. 2nd

Gordon, James and Eliza S. Gordon, Oct. 30th

1820

Gardner, Wilson N. and Milly Ballard, Nov. 8th

Gay, Thomas and Minney Wood, Dec. 21st

Gibson, Samuel and Elizabeth Langford, Nov. 6th

Gowing, Henderson and Malinda I. Giving, Jan. 4th

Graves, James and Susan Moran, Aug. 7th

1821

Gentry, Robert and Mary H. Wingfield, Jan. 23rd

Gibson, Jon and Elizabeth Stone, Dec. 17th

Gilbert, Edward and Susan S. Sandridge, Jan. 5th

Groves, Benjamin and Susan Browning, June 28th

1822

Gaines, Mortimore and Emily Fretwell, Jan. 10th

Gardner, Garland and Mary Ann Garrison, Oct. 17th

Garland, Thomas and Mildred Moon, Nov. 13th

Gay, John and Susan Spradling, Feb. 6th

Gentry, William and Ann Moore, July 15th

Gibson, James and Mary Mays, Dec. 19th

Gibson, John and Eliza Collins, Jan. 28th

Gillaspy, William and Patsy Hundley, Aug. 15th

Gillum, Charles P. and Elizabeth Gillum, Aug. 20th

Goodwin, William Jr. and Ann Simpson, Jan. 17th

Gray, John and Nancy Sudderth Dec. 26th

1823

Gentry, Fountaine and Ann Kingtel, Feb. 9th

Gentry, James and Peachy Langford, Oct. 1st

Goodman, Thomas D. and Lucy H. Moon, April 15th

Graves, Jacob and Ann Williams, May 5th

Gregory, William L. and Jeannetta Robinson, April 24th

Groves, Hezekiah and June Moore, May 2nd

1824

Garth, James and Mary C. Wood, Sept. 27th

Garton, Spencer and Maria Davis, May 2nd

Garton, Stephen and Lucy Spradling, Dec. 23rd

Gates, John and Ann F. Bailey, Dec. 30th

Gilbert, Weston and Melinda Pritchett, Feb. 26th

Gillaspy, George and Peggy Dotson, June 18th

Gitchell, Godfrey and Sally Wood, Dec. 21st

Gooch, William F. and Mary J. Gooch, Feb. ?
Goodman, Horsley and Mildred L. Bumgardner, Oct. 15th
Goodman, Nathan C. and Sarah W. Terrill, Nov. 17th
Graham, David and Elizabeth Baily Nov. 14th
Greening, Isaac and Polly Stone, Dec. 23rd

1825

Gardner, William and Martha Woody, Dec. 29th
Garth, Benjamin B. and Susanna W. Gillum. Sept. 14th
Gentry, Thomas T. and Elizabeth M. Mullins, Feb. 14th
Gibson, Henry and Polly Maupin, Sept. 5th
Gilmore, William and Martha Roberts, Dec. 24th
Graves, Thomas W. and Mildred P. Thrift, March 7th
Groomes, Madison and Mary Bailey, Feb. 2nd
Guy, Robert and Gilly D. Rodes. May 25th

1826

Gibson, John and Polly Sprouce, Nov. 23rd
Gibson, John and Elizabeth Smith, Dec. 4th

1827

Gamey, William and Nancy C. Gentry, Dec. 15th
Garland, Nathaniel and Eliza Armond, May 16th
Gaulding, John and Mary Brill, Feb. 17th
Gibson, Thomas and Fanny Gentry, Nov. 5th
Glenn, Hugh and Susan Taylor, Feb. 14th
Goodman, Charles C. and Ann G. Crank, March 7th

1828

Gardner, John A. and Elizabeth Hale, March 10th
Garrison, Gelly and Nancy Pearce, Dec. 31st
Gaston, James A. and Nelly Sullivan, Dec. 18th
Gentry, Dabney and Elizabeth Drumheller, Jan. 16th
Gregg, Daniel H. and Maria R. Day, Feb. 6th

1829

Garrison, Richard Q. and E. A. Marr, March 19th
Gibson, Randall and Mary Sprouce, June 11th
Gilbert, Thomas and Dolly Farneyhough, Feb. 8th
Goodall, Charles and Elizabeth Goodall, Jan. 19th
Goodman, Austin and Lucinda Mayo, Jan. 29th
Goodwin, Elijah and Easter McCline, Dec. 21st
Gray, John G. and Susan R. Lindsay, May 1st

1830

Gabbermo, Washington and Peggy Gillaspy, Jan. 27th

Gillum, Granville and M. A. Huckstep, Dec. 23rd
Grimstead, Joseph H. and Sarah Yancey, Nov. 27th

1831

Garrison, Ralph and F. Marshall, Dec. 22nd
Garth, Parchal S. and Lucy E. Garth, March 1st
Gibson, Tandy and Elizabeth Sprouce, March 30th
Gillispie, Alexander and Ann R. Stout, May 19th
Gilmore, George C. and Seeana Lewis, Aug. 22nd
Goddard, James and Amelia C. Wood, July 14th
Grettor, John A. and Mary J. Winn, Aug. 3rd

1832

Garrison, Clifton and Susan A. Mallory, Feb. 15th
Garrison, Robert F. and Sarah S. Dunn, Aug. 6th
Garton, William and Elizabeth Thomas, May 17th
Gillum, Charles and Mary J. E. Estes, Oct. 16th
Gowens, Henderson and Agness Gowens, Jan. 16th
Gowen, Staples and Margaret Burrows, Aug. 6th
Gratton, Robert and Martha D. Minor, Aug. 10th

1833

Gardner, Brightberry B. and Lucinda, Wood, Nov. 7th
Garland, Fleming and Elizabeth Wade, Dec. 24th
Garland, William V. and Lucy Martin, Feb. 4th
Garrison, William and Nancy Sullivan, Jan. 17th
Gentry, Austin and June Frances Nailor, Jan. 3rd
Gobban, John and Barbara Martin, May 23rd
Goodin, James and Elizabeth D. Uyelate, Dec. 31st
Gowing, Levy and Frances Gowing, Sept. 19th
Graves, Leonard and Susan Day, April 18th

1834

Gardner, George W. and Rebecca Thurmond, Dec. 15th
Gardner, James D. and Mary Wood, Oct. 6th
Gentry, Benjamin and Amanda Browning, Dec. 8th
Grimes, Jacob and Etta Mallory Dec. 9th

1835

Garland, James and Matilda Wheeler, Dec. 30th
Goings, Charles and Matilda Middlebrook, July 22nd

Gooch, Edwin O. and Mary E. Huckstep, Nov. 16th

Goodman, Willis C. and Sarah A. J. Garth, Feb. 2nd

Grayson, William and Dulcinia Hays, Feb. 2nd

Grimes, Morris and Patsey Sprouse, May 13th

1836

Garrison, Ryland and Rhoda Kester, Dec. 16th

Gibson, William and D. Sprouce, Feb. 4th

Gillock, Reuben and Rebecca Boyd, May 12th

Gilmer, F. H. and M. J. W. Walker, Feb. 7th

Goodman, William A. and G. M. Hamner, June 11th

Graves, John and Martha Haskins, March 5th

1837

Garner, William G. and Jane Garner, Feb. 18th

Garrett, Allen Jr. and Martha Simpkin, June 8th

Gentry, Paseal B. D. and Susan M. Dunn, Nov. 6th

Gillaspy, Porterfield and Mary Shiflett, March 19th

1838

Gibson, Tandy and Elizabeth Dudley, March 12th

Godwin, John M. C. and Sarah Jane Jones, Feb. 20th

Gooch, William B. and Sarah M. Amiss, Dec. 24th

Grettor, David B. and Martha J. Winn, Oct. 24th

Grimes, Jacob and Elizabeth Finch, July 2nd

1839

Garrison, George K. and M. A. S. Garrison, Dec. 2nd

Garth, Garland A. and Mary J. Burnley, May 16th

Gillum, James A. and Mary Wilhoite, Aug. 28th

1840

Garland, Goodrich and Mary A. Wheeler, Jan. 6th

Garrison, Charles and Nancy Collins, Dec. 16th

Garrison, Elijah and Polly Melton, March 17th

Garth, B. G. and Emily A. Burnley, May 5th

Gay, A. G. and E. R. Pettett, Dec. 3rd

Goings, Durrett and Goshia Jackson, May 11th

Goings, Robert and Patsy Cole, April 5th

Graves, Thomas and Phebe Ames, April 2nd

1841

Gameson, John and D. A. Mundy, Dec. 16th

Gates, Joseph and Frances Garland, June 21st

Gray, Soloman and Jemima Gibson, Dec. 28th

1842

Garrison, Austin and Sarah Jane Taylor, Dec. 12th

Garrison, James and Caroline E. Hart, Dec. 20th

Gianniny, Francis and Amanda Burgess, Feb. 7th

Gordon, William and Charlotte Cooke, Nov. 7th

Graves, Haws and Elizabeth Haskins, Jan. 3rd

Griffin, John and Martha Ammonet, Dec. 21st

1843

Garrison, Foster and Eliza A. J. Dunn, Jan. 28th

Gooch, Edwin H. and Louisianna Johnson, Dec. 6th

Goodloe, Paul H. and Maria S. Gooch, July 24th

Gray, James W. and Mary A. Hickok, April 20th

Grayson, Thomas H. and Mary A. Jones, March 6th

Grow, George and Frances Ann Wood, Dec. 25th

1844

Garland, Allen and Martha Smith, April 5th

Gay, James H. and Lucy Burch, May 16th

Gianniny, Anderson and Maria Rodes, April 24th

Gillum, John N. and Susan A. Buck, July 20th

Gilmore, John and Mary E. Seay, Sept. 2nd

1845

Garth, James W. and Frances W. Branham, Feb. 1st

Gentry, Addison and Marguerite Walters, Jan. 2nd

Gentry, James A. and Suthonia A. Sandridge, Oct. 21st

Gianinny, James S. and A. M. Price, June 12th

Gilbert, Joseph and M. Higginbotham, Nov. 11th

Gins, Charles W. and Nancy Hamner, Oct. 9th

1846

Garrison, Clifton and Mildred M. Eubank, Sept. 4th

Gentry, James C. and Mary C. White, Jan. 15th

Gentry, John W. and Martha Dawson, Feb. 19th

Gillum, James A. and Henrietta M. C. Shiflett, Nov. 25th

1847

Gentry, Henry and Susan Gibson, Nov. 16th

Gibson, Andrew W. and Elizabeth McDaniel, Aug. 4th

Gillaspy, Andrew and Susan Bragg, Dec. 23rd

Gray, Hartwell H. and S. M. Timberlake, Feb. 28th

1848

Gault, A. W. and M. E. Jefferson, Jan. 3rd

Goings, Walker and M. J. Goings, Aug. 23rd

Goodman, William A. and M. W. Johnson, March 30th

Goodwin, James D. and M. A. Martin, Jan. 27th

1849

Gardner, James D. and S. N. Thompson, Sept. 3rd

Gay, William A. and Martha A. Seay, Aug. 22nd

Gentry, Albert H. and Mary E. Sowell, April 11th

Gentry, John and Jane Coleman, Aug. 31st

Gibson, Richard O. and Mary A. Harvey, Oct. 1st

Graham, Samuel and Louisa Kelly, Jan. 3rd

Graves, Hezekiah and Susan Moyer, July 15th

Graves, John and Kesuh S. Rogers, Feb. 22nd

Graves, Rue and Elizabeth Mawyer, Sept. 13th

1850

Garland, James and S. M. Wingfield, Dec. 11th

Gentry, James A. and Nancy F. Johnson, Feb. 6th

Goodin, James and Martha Dudley, Feb. 4th

Goodman, Charles G. and Keziah Laughlon, Aug. 20th

Goodman, Mariellus S. and Sarah E. Harris, Dec. 20th

Gordon, William F. Jr., and Nancy W. Morris, Nov. 12th

Gray, Isaac and F. M. Mathews, Feb. 1st

Grimes, James H. and Lucy J. Batchler, March 19th

1851

Gardner, Ira T. and Julia Ann Marshall, March 2nd

Garland, Anderson and Jane Dudley, Oct. 15th

Garman, William D. and Catherine G. Lindsay, Sept. 17th

Gibson, Jesse and Elizabeth Sandridge, Nov. 18th

Gibson, Merriman and Mary I. Thomas, Aug. 30th

Gilbert, William and F. E. Payne, Dec. 11th

Gilmer, George C. and Mildred W. Duke, Aug. 7th

Goodman, Charles, N. and Mary Moon, Oct. 15th

Gregory, Joseph F. and Malinda M. Bowen, July 8th

1852

Garland, William H. and A. M. Shepherd Dec. 21st

Gatewood, Asy B. and Jessie A. White, Nov. 2nd

Gates, James A. and Sarah A. Smith, Sept. 19th

Gianinny, Horace and Lucy J. Starks, Dec. 22nd

Goodman, Samuel W. and M. W. Moon, Dec. 31st

1853

Gibson, Peter Jr. and Nancy E. Gibson, May 5th

Gilbert, Edward and Susan Hamm, Nov. 13th

Gillaspie, D. H. and Sarah A. Roberts, Feb. 3rd

Goodman, John P. and Susan Ashlin, Sept. 29th

Gray, William E. and Eliza H. P. Moon, Aug. 3rd

Grayson, William D. and Mary L. Wood, March 25th

Greiner, Patterson and Martha Spears, Dec. 28th

1854

Goff, Charles W. and Mary A. West, Nov. 24th

Goodman, Horace A. and Mary C. Wingfield, April 4th

Goodman, James D. and Ann E. Fry, Nov. 21st

Graves, William and Susan A. Mawyer, April 29th

Goff, Chas. A. and M. A. West, Nov. 24th

Grayson, John and Mary E. Woods, Jan 25th

Goodman, J. D. and Ann E. Fry, Nov. 21st

Goodman, Horace A. and M. C. Wingfield, April 4th

1855

Gibson, James A. and Mildred C. Via, Dec. 9th

Grayson, John and Mary E. Woods, Jan. 25th

Green, Andrew and Elizabeth M. Davis, May 23rd

Gibson, Jas. A. and Mildred C. Via, Dec. 9th

Green, Andrew and Bettie A. Davis, May 23rd

1856

Gardner, John F. and Isabella C. Nelson, Oct. 22nd

Gennant, William and Hetty J. Brown, April 8th

Glover, Chapman and Emma Garett Sept. 8th

Glover, Chapman and Emma Gault, Sept. 7th

Goodwin, William and Ann E. Mayo, March 11th

Geurrant, Wm. and Hetty I. Brown, April 8th

Gardner, Wm. G. and Cath. E. Wood, April 16th

Goodman, W. H. and Mary C. Gentry, Oct. 21st

Gleeson, Michael S. and Martha D. Jury, July 2nd

Gardner, Ira I. and Julia A. Marshall, March 8th

1857

Gardner, William G. and Catherine E. Wood, April 6th

Glesson, Michael S. and Martha S. Jury, July 2nd

Goodman, William Henry and Mary C. Gentry, Oct. 20th

Graham, William and Ellen F. Atkins, Dec. 16th

1858

Gardner, Bright B. and Amanda Dowell, May 19th

Garrison, George C. and Mary J. Roberts, Sept. 23rd

Garton, Horace S. and Mary J. Mallory, Oct. 21st

Gay, Jno. H. and Cath. W. Harlan, Feb. 24th

Giles, Joseph R. and Frances E. Bowen, May 25th

Gillaspie, Jona H. and Susan M. Hughes, Feb. 11th

Gardner, Horace G. and Mary J. Mallory, Oct. 28th

1859

Gibson, Isaac and Elizabeth Marshall, Nov. 2nd

Gilbert, Edward T. and Lucy E. Creel, Jan. 28th

Giles, Joseph S. and Frances Ellen Bowen, May 26th

Gibson, Isaac and Eliz. Marshall, Nov. 10th

1860

Garrison, James T. and Frances H. Toombs, Nov. 12th

Gentry, William F. and Maria L. Lucas, Feb. 27th

Gibson, Abraham and Pauline N. Griems, Oct. 11th

Gibson, Randolph Jr. and Elizabeth J. Gibson, Sept. 5th

Gilchrist, P. P. and Alice Garth, Aug 22nd

Gooch, Horace C. and Sally A. Jarman, Feb. 6th

Goodloe, John and Elizabeth G. Garland, May 16th

Gentry, Wm. F. and Maria L. Lucas, Feb. 28th

Gooch, Horace and Sallie A. Jarman, Feb. 8th

Gibson, Rand Jr., and Eliz. J. Gibson, Sept. 6th

Goodloe, Jno. and Eliz. G. Garland, June 14th

Garrison, Jas. T. and Frances A. Toombs, Nov. 15th

1861

Garth, James D. and Lucy V. Michie, Nov. 4th

Gibson, William F. and Sarah F. Rodes, Aug. 5th

Glass, Jesse M. and Martha F. Garrison, Dec. 19th

Glover, P. J. and Kate R. Stockton, July 30th

Gordon, John O. and Mary C. Pegram, June 3rd

Gordon, Jno. C. and Mary B. Pegram, June 4th

Gibson, Wm. T. and Sarah F. Rhodes, Aug. 6th

Glass, Jesse M. and Martha F. Harrison, Dec. 19th

Garth, Jas. D. and Lucy V. Michie, Nov. 6th

1862

Gibson, Alex and Jane Dobbs, June 19th

Geomnia, Jno. and Mary Parish, Oct. 16th

1863

Gibson, Garrett M. and Mildred Fisks, Sept. 28th

Goodwin, Fleming C. and Lucy A. Daniel, Dec. 29th

Gibson, Mann B. and Eliz. F. Rix, Dec. 24th

Garrison, Geo. W. and Sarah E. Hill, Oct. 20th

Glenn, Alphias C. and Emma M. Matthews, Oct. 15th

Green, Jno. T. and Milly A. McQuarry, Sept. 15th

Guy, Wm. H. and Susan E. Madison, Aug. 11th

Gillaspy, Geo. W., and Hester E. McClain, Apr. 9th

Garrison, Francis and Eliza E. Filmore, Jan. 1st

Grantham, Jno. J., and Mary E. Bowen, March 18th

Gillum, Jas. S. and Mary J. Tayler, Dec. 17th

1864

Gliddon, Jno. Thos. and Susan Johnson, March 21st

Gaugh, Elem and Rebecca F. Sandridge, May 8th

Garrison, Clif. and Ellen Wolfe, March 29th

Gardner, Walker R. and Cornelia T. Wood, Feb. 16th

1865

Garrigas, H. H. and Kate V. Powell, April 19th

Garrison, Edward C. and Cora F. Collins, April 3rd

Gianniny, William J. and Teletha C. Drumheller, Dec. 26th

Gibson, Joel H. and Virginia C. Snow, June 21st

Gibson, William C. and Louisa E. Gibson, Oct. 10th

Gillispie, John and M. A. Loving, Sept. 4th

Goings, Hezekiah and Mary Eliza Wood, Sept. 18th

Goodman, John T. and Mildred P. Bishop, Nov. 29th

Green, Henry A. and Georgia A. Baber, Feb. 13th

Gregory, Benjamin F. and Bettie M. Keith, Jan. 2nd

Gardner, Jno. B. and Amanda M. Thurston, Dec. 14th

Goodman, Jno P. and Mildred P. Bishop, Nov. 30th

Gibson, Wm. C. and Louisa E. Gibson, Oct. 26th

Gibson, James W. and Martha A. Sprouce, Sept. 11th

Garrison, Ed. C. and Cornelia F. Collins, April 5th

Gillaspie, Jno. and Martha A. Loving, Sept. 7th

Garngins, H. H. and Kate V. Powell, Apr. 20th

Green, Henry A. and Georgia A. F. Baber, Feb. 14th

Gregory, Ben F. and Bettie M. Keith, Jan. 5th

1866

Garrison, Henry E. and Mary F. Marsh, Feb. 14th

Gibson, Abram and Emily Jane Sprouce, March 13th

Gilbert, Edward T. and Annie E. Creel, Oct. 3rd

Gildersleeve, B. S. and Bettie F. Colston, Sept. 15th

Green, Albert and Creasy Watson, March 31st

Grimstead, Richard J. and Sophia L. Leake, Jan. 3rd

Gully, George A. and Lucy F. Keblinger, July 19th

Garrison, Zack and Lavina M. E. Gentry, Dec. 12th

Garrison, Tyret P. and Lucy J. Smith, Dec. 20th

Grinstead, Rich. J. and Sophia L. Leake, Jan. 4th

Gulley, Geo. A. and Lucy F. Keblinger, June 19th

Garrison, Henry E. and Mary F. Marsh, Feb. 15th

Gibson, Abraham and Emily S. Sprouce, March 13th

Gilbert Edw. T. and Ann E. Creel, Oct. 15th

Gildersleeve, B. L. and Bettie Colston, Sept. 18th

1867

Goolsby, Lewis, and Nancy Ellis, Jan. 17th

Glenmore, Henry and Nannie S. Keitle, Feb. 4th

Gentry, Richard and Lucy Desper, March 12th

Gibson, Henry D. and Mary E. Wheeler, May 6th

Gillum, John and Willie J. Drumheller, May 22nd

Grymes, Wm. W. and Frances C. Martin, Dec 17th

Gibson, J. W. and Ellen P. Gibson, Aug. 6th

Glenham, Henry and Nannie S. Keith, Feb. 7th

Gantt, Price P. and Tempsett Eppes, Aug. 15th

Gaines, Samuel M. and Ada S. Leake, Dec. 18th

Garner Samuel M. and Ada Leake, Dec. 18th

Gilehrest, Jno. A. and Ada S. Michie, Oct. 1st

Goens, Henry and M. J. Carey, Dec. 12th

Garett, P. P. and Tumps W. Epps, Aug. 14th

1868

Garrison, H. W. and Susan P. Brown, Jan. 11th

Griffin, Wm. H. and Mary Ellen Camden, Feb. 3rd

Garland, Albin and Moria C. Kirby, April 17th

Gibson, Benj. and Mary Ann Gibson, June 10th

Gully, J. W. and Narapa Perry, July 6th

Gilbert, Beverly and Milly Solmon, July 7th

Goodwin, Wm. and Mary Hays, Oct. 6th

Geurant Wm. J. and Sarah J. Ellis, Dec. 24th

George, H. H. and Nannie E. Alexander, Jan. 26th

Goodwin, Jno. A. and Louisa C. Mayo, July 19th

Gibson, James E. and Ann E. Leathers, June 9th

Gardner, Hugh R. and Lucy G. Robertson, May 19th

Gilmer, Tho. W. and Petty L. Mince, Aug. 25th

Gibson, Jas. E. and Anna E. Leathers, June 10th

Garden, Hugh R. and Lucy G. Robertson, May 20th

Gordon, Reubin and Belle Robinson, July 5th

Going, Rob. S. and Saman E. Kidd, Oct. 8th

Gilmer, Thos. W. and Pattie L. Minor, Aug. 25th

Goodwin, Jno. A. and Louisa C. May, Jan. 22nd

Gibson, Abra, and Frances Sprouce, Nov. 10th

Greaver, Jas. J. and Lucy Johnson, May 27th

1869

Graves, Alfred and E. A. Graves, Feb. 25th

Gay, David G. and Annie E. Goodwin, Apr. 15th

Gibson Wm. L. and Milly A. Gibson, Dec. 30th

1870

Grady, F. F. and Helen M. Lautham, Jan 11th

Gibson, Robt. and Eliza Wolfe, Jan. 26th

Griffin, Jno. H. and M. A. Hardin, Feb. 24th

Gray, John and A. F. Eubank, March 7th

Goings, Henderson and S. E. Tyre, April 20th

Gohannon M. and M. Wood, April 16th

Garland, Jas. R. and M. J. Matthews, May 5th

Gilmer, Reuben and Charlotte Smith, Dec. 27th

Gentry Albert H. and Sally S. Wingfield, Feb. 19th

Garland, Anderson and Maria C. Kirby, Dec. 23rd

1871

Gillespie, W. W. and M. P. McAlister, June 25th

Gray, Wm. H. and Ida Eubank, Sept. 28th

Gibson, Tucker, F. and Eliz. Kirby, Oct. 12th

1872

Garth, John W. and Matilda E. Welsh, March 20th
Graves, John G. and Susan E. Shackleford, Feb. 8th
Garrison, Jonath W. and Mary F. Via, Aug. 25th
Gentry, James A. and Eliz. Woodson, Oct. 2nd
Gentry, Thos. A. and Mary E. Bailey, Nov. 16th
Gibson, John and S. J. Sprouce, Dec. 5th
Garrison, Wm. E. and Nannie M. Ball, Dec. 4th

1873

Good, Jas. M. and Sarepta Creel, Sept. 9th
Garrison, Geo. C. and Catherine E. Gardner, Nov. 27th
Grady, Jno. J. and Mary E. Carson, Jan. 16th
Gardner, Edgar M. and Joanna Craddock, July 15th

1874

Garrison, T. B. and M. V. Dunn, April 18th
Geannini, Sidney, R. and Frances A. Wingfield, May 25th
Gay, Geo. W. and Martha Goodman, Oct. 26th
Goode, Jas. L. and Sarah E. Bailey, Oct. 12th
Garland, Thos. P. and Lucy R. Scott, Nov. 5th
Gibson, Jefferson R. and Mary A. A. Faris, Dec. 24th
Gibson, Shepherd and Alice Sprouce, Aug. 13th

1875

Gibson, Samuel L. and Angeline Hicks, Feb. 15th
Graves, John and Josephine Norvell, Feb. 18th
Gillespie, Wm. F. and Julia P. Dillard, Feb. 23rd
Grady, Patrick and Anne Rooney, Sept. 6th
Gillispee, Wm. J. and Sarah E. Martin, Oct. 21st
Gay, Wm. J. and Sallie E. Carter, Oct. 25th
Gasther, Wm. H. and Adeline A. Walton, Nov. 1st
Gilbert, Jas. R. and Rodolin P. Furlones, Dec. 6th
Graves, Marshall R. and Anne E. Norvell, Dec. 22nd

1876

Graves, Francis M. and Mary E. Fatwell, Jan. 10th
Gleason, H. M. and Maggie Bibb, June 1st
Gibson, Henry D. and Margaret A. Morris, July 10th
Graves, Francis S. and Lena N. Edmonds, Sept. 13th
Gilbert, Geo. P. and Agness Lynes, Oct. 5th
Garrison, Geo. W. and Lucy D. Collins, Oct. 7th

Garver, Reuben and Louisa A. Proffitt, Nov. 24th
Garver, Peter and Frances E. Walton, Jan. 15th

1877

Graves, Weston K. and Betsy A. Hunt, Jan. 16th
Gentry, Wm. L. and Alice C. Taylor, March 5th
Goebing, Chas. and Annie M. Bishop, May 28th
Gibson, Isaac and Eliz Currier, Aug. 17th
Garnett, James W. and Mary M. Goodman, Oct. 30th
Garrett, Isaac R. and Bettie Spencer, Dec. 15th
Garrison, Henry W. and Nannie J. Walton, Dec. 8th

1878

Geove, Noah and Ella L. Wood, March 25th
Gish, John G. and A. B. Whitehurst, May 7th
Garrison, Jonathan and Lula Dunn, June 15th
Gillespie, W. W. and M. J. Blake, Sept. 5th
Geiger, Sylvester, E. and Lilly B. Bowcock, Oct. 21st
Garrison, Jesse F. and Martha W. Gilliam, Oct. 30th
Gay, Thomas A. and Texana Gay, Nov. 4th
Grooms, Jas. G. and Mary A. Thacker, Dec. 25th
Garrison, F. M. and T. A. Z. Bruce, Apr. 8th

1879

Gibson, George Ira and Sarah M. Sandridge, Jan. 11th
Garland, Robert and Katie Hall, Feb. 13th
Graves, Brenon and Willie A. Graves, March 1st
Gleason, James E. and Annie E. Perley, Apr. 24th
Gardner, James A. and Martha E. Rogers, Sept. 27th
Garrison, William and Sarah M. C. Herndon, Dec. 1st
Garnett, James M. and Cornelia M. Wingfield, Dec. 10th
Garland, James and Mary Langford, Nov. 6th
Golding, Thomas J. and Mary C. Wood, Jan. 28th
Goodwin, Julias S. and Rebecca H. Lassiter, Oct. 22nd
Garrison, Charles E. and Cornelia A. Mitchell, Nov. 26th
Gibson, William L. and Martha E. Sprouse, Nov. 20th
Goode, George W. and Susan M. Loving, July 15th
Garland, Eugene S. and Maggie E. Sneed, July 15th

1880

Gillock, Wm. C. and Adeline V. Kent, March 6th

Goolsby, A. J. and V. C. Bails, Oct. 16th

Garner, Chas. R. and Ella F. Marshall, Nov. 25th

Goodman, George W. and Mollie W. Mehring, Feb. 6th

Gillum, James A. and Ellen F. Lindsay, Feb. 9th

1881

Gordon, Wilson and Dilly Trip, Jan. 5th

Goss, John Preston and Eliza Ashley Goss, Jan. 26th

Gibson, Peter T. and Milly Ann Davis, Nov. 7th

Garth, Burwell, G. and Mrs. Sallie M. Early, Nov. 8th

Garrison, Thomas and Milly Sprouce, Dec. 5th

1882

Gates, Thomas J. and Ada F. Gallus, June 15th

Gibson, Randolph and Caroline M. Drumheller, Aug. 31st

Grumbo, Louis C. and Sarah Grooms, Oct. 7th

Garner, Samuel R. and Annie B. Brown, Nov. 1st

Gibson, James Wm. and Nancy Ellen Gibson, Nov. 15th

Garrison, Henry White and Sally Agnes Walton, Dec. 21st

Garrison, Henry H. and Semantha J. Gardner, Jan. 1st

Garrison, George S. and Emma T. Collins, March 22nd

1883

Graves, Preston and Sallie Marrs, June 12th

Gaines, Absalom and Fanny Jones, June 21st

Garth, Wm. Anderson and Emma C. Barksdale, Sept. 6th

Gibson, James I. and Sarah F. Madison, Nov. 8th

Garnett, Thos. E. and Mollie B. Garth, Nov. 14th

1884

Glass, James Hoy and Alice L. Brockman, July 27th

Garland, Thomas and Mary Ella Powell, Aug. 9th

Gentry, Edgar H. and Gertrude Taylor, Sept. 9th

Garnett, Walter and Idella H. Gilbert, Oct. 1st

Gilbert, Geo. Percy and Mamie H. Edge, Oct. 8th

Gianniny, Louis Overton & Ida Florence Gleason, Oct. 8th

1885

Gardner, Jno. Wesley and Alice Jane Tater, Jan. 13th

Griffith, David H. and Lucy A. Locke, June 3rd

Graves, Thomas and Stella Florence Moore, March 31st

Gardner, Elizy A. and Penkie W. Coleman, May 6th

Gentry, Edwin and Jennie Y. Rea, July 15th

Graves, Warren S. and Rebecca C. Fansler, Dec. 24th

1886

Going, N. B. and M. J. Branham, Jan. 10th

Goering, Charles and Francisca Meekel, Jan. 20th

Goodwin, Weir R. and Mildred W. Murray, Sept. 15th

Greaver, Jas. Thos. and Nannie C. Ganeson, Oct. 18th

Goolsby, Geo. W. and Annie L. Barger, Oct. 21st

Gillum, Felix M. K. and Frances M. M. Nair, Nov. 11th

Garrison, Wm. Edgar and Anna W. Dolen, Dec. 15th

1887

Gentry, Wm. R. and Ida B. Wood, Jan 6th

Gianniny, Wm. Jas. and Susan A. Leiler, March 2nd

Garland, James and Minervia E. Gibson, March 3rd

Giles, Wm. A. and Mary M. Gianniny, April 7th

Gibson, Jeremiah M. and Pinky L. Sprouse, June 8th

Garvier, Walker L. and Mary A. Smith, July 23rd

Garth, Wm. and Josie Blackwise, Aug. 13th

Gibson, B. and S. J. Sacree, Aug. 30th

Garrison, Geo. C. and Lucy E. Donnell, Sept. 3rd

Gay, Samuel G. and Ada F. Garland, Nov. 8th

Grasty, Isaac B. and Helen C. Coleman, Nov. 25th

Glass, Nath'l. and Va. Watson, Dec. 27th

1888

Gleason, A. S .and M. Ida Burgess, Feb. 29th

Greaves, Jno. and Geo. Harridge, Apr. 18th

Guemany, Ele and Sadiet Mix, May 30th

Garth, H. L. and Lucy Speck, Oct. 23rd

Gipson, J. P. and M. E. Sprouse, Nov. 21st

Gibson, Wm. M. and Flo. Barnett, Nov. 27th

Gibson, Loyd M. and F. A. Clemens, Dec. 28th

1889

Gibson, Wm. L. and Plin. Gibson, April 18th

Gibbs, Henry and Rosa Bocock, Sept. 17th

Garrison, J. F. and M. C. Pritchett, Oct. 12th

Goss, Peter and Sarah Chamber, Dec. 19th

Gibson, R. E. and M. R. Sprouse, Dec. 20th

1890

Graves, John and Lulia Critzer, Feb. 3rd

Garrison, S. A. and Geo. Via, March 3rd

Givin, P. H. and M. W. Minor, Sept. 5th

1891

Goodson, J. W. and Cora L. Lane, March 10th

Goodyear, G. B. and A. W. Payne, May 5th
Giles, J. A. and A. F. Hall, June 19th
Giddings, C. G. and J. L. Garland, July 20th
Gough, C. E. and L. E. Bishop, Dec. 13th

1892

Gentry, E. E. and L. E. Douglas, Jan. 11th
Garrison, Samuel and Geo. Via, Feb. 12th
Goss, L. H. and T. H. Tell, Feb. 29th
Garrison, Wm. K. and Mattie J. Madison,
   April 15th
Gianniny, G. W. and L. C. Gianniny, June 6th
Granger, Gordon, and Lucy C. Maury, July
   13th
Gardner Wm. and Eliz. Dudley, Aug. 3rd
Garner, E. W. and C. S. Sandridge, Sept. 18th
Grasty, Isaac and Lucy May, Oct. 4th
Greerway, J. R. and M. T. Smith, Nov. 30th
Garrison, C. G. and N. B. Davis, Dec. 26th

1893

Gibson, Benj. and L. F. Strange, Jan. 4th
Gault, Jas. F. and Marg. B. Collins, Jan 16th
Graves, M. R. and P. A. Thurston, April 1st
Garrison, M. P. and L. J. Wilkerson, April
   4th
Goolsby, S. T. and M. F. Wheeler, June 17th
Gardner, B. E. and Emma Gibson, July 27th
Graves, Louis and Louisa Thacker, Sept. 29th
Garth, Chas. P. and A. L. Birckhead, Oct. 23rd
Garrison, A. J. and Bettie E. Lively, Nov. 11th
Garrison, J. F. and A. E. Marsh, Nov. 13th
Garland, Jas. N. and Emma J. Marshall; Dec.
   4th
Garrison, Oliver and J. A. McAlister, Dec.
   11th

1894

Grigsby, Hughes S. and Maud Lewis Harris,
   Jan. 3rd
Gibson, Ed and C. L. Garland, Jan. 11th
Garnett, W. J. and Cornelia J. Hayms, Sept.
   17th
Graves, T. A. and E. S. Wood, Sept. 20th
Gibson, A. P. and W. B. Ergenbright, Nov.
   27th
Glover, R. L. and L. G. Harler, Nov. 21st
Gibson, Lorinzo A. and Mollie B. Gentry, Dec.
   24th
Goodwin, Bernard N. and Georgie Dunn, Feb.
   13th

1895

Glass, J. D. and Lucy Brown, Jan. 31st
Garirson, Wm. G. and Sarah J. Bruce, March
   4th
Gibson, Ben and Sally A. Young, June 26th
Garrison, Alex and Lucy E. Dowell, Aug. 23rd
Green, W. A. and F. M. West, Sept. 11th
Graves, A. N. and Callie R. Parr, Nov. 12th
Gentry, John S. and Ann. J. Dowell, Dec. 16th
Garland, Geo. and Ella Lunsden, Dec. 24th

1896

Graves, Lincoln, and M. M. Houchens, Jan.
   11th
Gibson, Tandy and Nellie Tate, April 6th
Giles, John H. and D. E. Hawkins, April 15th
Gebson, Jno. P. and Lena Sprouse, June 2nd
Gibson, Abram and Josephine Rea, June 13th
Gardner Lewis C. and A. W. Leake, July 3rd
Gibson, Jas. H. and Elenora Reynolds, Aug.
   18th
Gibson, Jno. A. and Mary L. Sprouse, Sept. 5th
Gibson, Chas. E. and Rachail Sprouse, Sept.
   7th
Garrison R. F. and S. A. Beddows, Sept. 5th
Gough, R. J. and Laura F. Bussenger, Sept.
   4th
Garth, J. Winston and Mattie Lewis, Sept. 8th
Garrison, Samuel and Mary J. Garrison, Sept.
   28th
Guthrie J. R. and Theodore Blair, Dec. 7th

1897

Garrison, J. C. and Bettie L. Martin, March
   31st
Giannini, R. N. and Willie A. Hudson, May
   5th

1898

Geaves, Frank M. and Sophia Irvin, June 2nd
Gay, Willia A. and Susie E. Dudley, Aug.
   22nd
Garrison John W. and G. L. Payne, Oct. 10th
Garrison, J. W. and Georgie F. Payne, Oct.
   11th
Gore, C. H. and Annie F. Comptin, Nov. 7th
Gardner, Wm. L. and M. M. Jones, Nov. 8th
Garth, J. Woods and Anna E. Maupin, Nov.
   23rd
Gentry, Allen and Lena Edwards, Dec. 16th
Gibson, Walter B. and Carrie M. Jones, Dec.
   27th
Gibson S. D. and K. A. Sprouse, Dec. 27th

1899

Gibson, W. T. and Georgietta Norris, Feb.
   11th
Gibson, Jean A. and Minnie Sprouse, Feb.
   20th
Gibson, James W. and Clara Gibson, March
   1st
Gockenver, L. B. and B. C. Via, April 26th
Gibson, W. M. and Minnie Gibson, May 1st
Gentry W. A. and H. L. Lucas, Sept. 7th
Gentry, Walter B. and Mary E. Gianniny,
   Nov. 14th
Gentry, C. L. and H. T. Clements, Dec. 25th
Gooch, W. E. and E. V. Perkins, June 5th
Graves, G. T. and M. E. Edwards, Aug. 1st

1900

Gibson, Chas. L. and Ellen M. Sprouse, July
   2nd
Gentry, James A. and Minnie W. Gentry, July
   2nd

Gibson, Samuel and L. L. Shiflett, Aug. 22nd
Goodloe, W. T. and C. B. Hill, Sept. 4th
Gentry, Albert B. and Susan L. Abell, Sept. 24th
Gilmore, J. A. and M. M. Lyman, Oct. 9th
Graves, Wm. R. and Minnie D. Sneed, Nov. 5th
Griffiths, Robt. T. and Dora H. Sinclair, Jan. 15th
Grimstead, James H. and Estelle Foster, June 18th
Gibson, J. W. and Pearly Gibson, June 25th

1901

Garrison, Wm. E. and Jenny May, Jan. 14th
Gentry, Jas. R. and Blanche Mays, March 4th
Gilbert, Jno. E. and T. E. Dudley, March 18th
Gay, Jno. H. and B. E. Dudley, April 22nd
Goodman Wm. and Lizzie Payne, May 15th
Goodall, Chisney and Julia G. Ellison, May 27th
Gardner, A. N. and Lucy E. Bruce, July 8th
Gibson, Bernard and Alice Sprouse, Aug. 5th
Gibson, S. D. and Dora J. Barnett, Aug. 21st
Garrod, Chas. Holmes S. and Mildred J. Goodman, Sept. 9th
Goolsby, Jno. R. and Laura Proffit, Oct. 28th
Garrison, S. K. and Georg Belew, Oct. 29th
Gibson, Alphonso and Cornelia C. Sprouse, Nov. 13th
Gibson, Stonewall J. and Mary E. Sprouse, Nov. 13th
Gibson, B. W. and H. V. Gibson, Dec. 26th
Gentry, F. H. and L. B. Batton, Dec. 26th

1902

Glass, Benj. A. and Susan J. Clark, March 15th
Gibson, R. V. and Iola P. Lane, April 1st
Gibson, John I. and Virgie Wood, June 13th
Ganter Samuel L. and Annie Harlow, July 10th
Gibson, Jesse and Burthe Hurb, Oct.6th
Glass, Mitchell H. and Hewana L. Campbell, Oct. 17th
Gibson, Robt. W. and Annie Lee Hicks, Nov. 10th
Gibson, Geo. T. and P. J. Thacker, Dec. 22nd
Garrison, J. R. and I. B. James, Dec. 24th

1903

Garrison Moletus E. and Sarah Frazier, Feb. 14th
Gibson, C. E. and M. S. Kirby, March 9th
Gibson, U. and P. C. Kirby, Aug. 15th
Gibson, Z. and Bettie Sprouse, Aug. 21st
Gibson, Randolph and Lina Sprouse, Sept. 17th
Gibson, W. F. and M. J. Shiflett, Oct. 14th
Gooch, Arthur and Julia Moon, Oct 15th
Graves, H. and P. A. Clements, Oct. 28th

1904

Gilbert, Andrew Jackson and Susan Frances Hall, Jan. 28th

Glass, Edw. and Jessie Bill White, Feb. 16th
Garth, L. C. and Fannie M. Plunkett, April 12th
Garland, Eugene and Bessie B. Craig, April 13th
Glass, C. H. and Bessie Campbell, May 18th
Garrison, Jas. W. and Lizzie C. Wood, June 6th
Gentry, Edw. and Amy A. Busby, June 9th
Gianniny, Robt. N. and Georgia E. Marshall, June 28th
Gibson, Ernest and Clara Robertson, July 4th
Gibson, Flint and Willie Barbur Thumers, Dec. 30th

1905

Garland, Chas. Emmett and Mary Wilkins Critzer, Jan. 2nd
Garrison, Geo. and Syddie Ann Shiflett, April 13th
Garrison, Willie and Mollie Davis, May 6th
Godsey, H. F. and Bessie M. Johnson, May 20th
Goodwin, Earnest Wm. and Virgie Baret Smith, June 2nd
Granger, Chas. E. and Alice E. Glass, July 3rd
Garner, W. D. and Etta P. Crenshaw, July 27th
Glass, Wm. G. and Texie Anna Sprouse, July 31st
Gibson, Benj. W. and Mary A. Minter, Aug. 4th
Gibson, J. F. and A. L. Walton, Aug. 29th
Goode, G. E. and E. A. Stumbock, Nov. 20th
Gibson, Johnson and Rachel Sprouse, Nov. 29th
Gibson, J. F. and A. L. Walton, Aug. 29th.
Gooch, William J. and Annie B. Dowell, Sept. 14th
Gough, F. L. and Sallie C. Mooney, Sept. 25th
Gibson, John W. and Bessie M. Jones, Sept. 27th
Gentry, Granville and Sarah Sprouse, Oct. 21st
Garrison, Richard and Lillie May, Nov. 14th
Goode, G. E. and E. A. Stumbocker, Nov. 20th
Gibson, Johnson and Rachel Sprouse, Nov. 29th
Gibson, George and Pinkey Gibson, Dec. 1st
Garrison, Charlie Wm. and Annie Rebecca Walton, Dec. 13th

1906

Gibson, Walker and Ella Harrison Stokes, Feb. 12th
Griman, St. George Tucker and Susan Fitzhugh Dabney, April 17th
Garton, John Z. and Lottie B. Ship, June 2nd
Gunter, Robert Castle and Lena May Snead, June 21st
Gibson, Harry L. and Annie C. White, Sept. 12th
Graves, Oscar and Carrie Jones, Sept. 13th
Gay, J. S. and A. F. Carroll, Dec. 23rd

Garrison, George R. and Mary A. Via, Dec. 26th

Glass, Arthur D. and Maggie Morris, Dec. 31st

1907

Gibson, James L. and Laura D. Jones, Jan. 1st

Gay, William and Maggie L. Clements, Feb. 13th

Garrison, Henry and Lola Shiflett, June 26th

Gruber, J. Harlin and Martha V. Painter, June 18th

Gibson, J. H. and Annie Ralston, Sept. 4th

Garnett, James T. and Irene Garnett, Nov. 16th

Garth, Edwin B. and Margaret G. Kemper, Nov. 19th

Goursette, Edward and Ethel Moses, Dec. 10th

Grissenger, Walter K. and Carrie R. Shepherd, Dec. 22nd

1908

Givins, J. E. and May K. Gressenger, Jan. 16th

Gibson, John and Mary E. McClamour, Feb. 18th

Glass, William D. and Mattie P. Johnson, Feb. 17th

Gibson, Oscar and Mollie McCauly, Feb. 19th

Gentry, Oscar and Minnie Powell, July 25th

Gibson, R. A. and M. L. Mallory, July 29th

Graves, Stonewall and Dokey K. Fitzgerald, Sept. 2nd

Garrison, Bousey and Bessie Garrison, Sept. 4th

Glozebrook, Haslett M. and Emily H. Robinson, Sept. 8th

Goodson, James M. and Sallie A. Bragg, Nov. 24th

Gray, Walter Gose and Leonora Lake, Dec. 16th

1909

Gardner, Arthur and Grace Goolsby, March 17th

Giannine, Robert L. and Clara A. Ragland, April 21st

Gilbert, Kemper J. and Maggie Wright, April 20th

Gill, Orman G. and Mamie E. Woodson, June 2nd

Garrison, E. S. and Cora M. Dickerson, July 4th

Galding, John F. and Annie E. Brown, Aug. 22nd

Glass, John L. and Bessie M. Wilkerson, Aug. 21st

Gibson, John P. and Rosa Shiflett, Aug. 25th

Glenn, Garrard and Rosa A. Wood, Sept. 9th

Garrison, Charles T. and Cora Garrison, Oct. 10th

Groves, James G. and Ethel H. Yowell, Oct. 11th

Goolsby, William L. and Mittie J. Fitzgerald, Oct. 24th

Gibson, George A. and Edna P. Garrison, Nov. 16th

Garrison, Morgan and Lena Rubush, Dec. 27th

Green, Chambers R. and Myrtle E. Weeks, Dec. 22nd

Geer, Otis and Salln Walker, Dec. 23rd

Gibson, Elsie and Minnie Vest, Dec. 25th

1910

Gay, William J. and Sallie J. Maddex, Jan. 3rd

Guerrant, William S. and Lula M. Childress, March 23rd

Gregory, Emanuel S. and Eva M. Smith, Sept. 7th

Gibson, Charlie S. and Mollie S. Smith, Sept. 14th

Graham, Othor R. and Mabel R. Bayliss, Dec. 26th

Gibson, Walter D. and Rosa F. Patterson, Dec. 26th

1911

Glass, Edward and Lizzie Via, Jan. 8th

Garrison, Edgar F. and Nina Peckerring, Jan. 18th

Gurnell, Tom and Gracie Sprouse, Jan. 24th

Gibson, Aubrey and Gracie Canady, Jan. 30th

Garner, John W. and Ethel Davis, March 1st

Gibson, Charlie E. and Willie May Hicks, April 5th

Gills Edgar C. and Sallie Morris, June 12th

Garrison, Joseph C. and Angie N. Morris, June 20th

Graves, Robert and Nannie Moore, July 5th

Graves, Carter E. and Myrtie L. Wilhoit, Sept. 6th

Garth, Charles Thomas and Lula Mae Brown, Oct. 4th

Garwood, Harry W. and Cora L. Livich, Nov. 6th

Gianniny, Frank N. and Helen F. Bibb, Nov. 22nd

Gilmer, George K. and Rosalie G. Wheeler, Dec. 18th

Garrison, Robert W. and Annie Sandridge, Dec. 25th

1912

Gibson, Edward and Lucie M. Hicks, Feb. 10th

Garrison, Dosh and Reva Shiflett, April 17th

Glass, Dan G. and Ella Via, July 28th

Gibson, Archie and Gabie Sprouse, July 31st

Graves, Pat F. and Amanda J. Hunt, Aug. 11th

Gentry, Raymond A. and Annie M. O'Neill, Aug. 21st

Gibson, Philip O. and Edna Sprouse, Oct. 9th

Garth, Jr., William A. and Beatrice V. Gentry, Nov. 6th

Gay, William Harry and Marie J. Dudley, Nov. 12th

Graves, Robert and Gracie Beal, Nov. 16th

Gentry, Robert E. L. and Gracie F. Saunders, Dec. 4th

Garton John Z. and Lora L. Lang, Dec. 25th
Garrison, Price and Loney Walton, Dec. 26th

1913

Goodman, Jesse and Bettie Parr, May 14th
Graham, W. C. and Elizabeth P. Harlor, June 3rd
Gordon, George L. and Sarah T. Anderson, June 11th
Gibson, Bernard and Idora Sprouse, June 15th
Gilliland, Patrick H. and Sarah M. Howard, Aug. 28th
Garrison, John H. and Gusie Thompson, Oct. 8th
Gulley, Edward F. and Lina E. Ballard, Oct. 15th
Goodloe, Aboyn J. and Mamie L. Estes, Dec. 24th
Glass, R. R. and Lillie E. Morris, Dec. 25th

1914

Glass, John and Rose Lee Sprouse, Jan. 14th
Gibson, Elisha and Flora Sprouse, March 25th
Gibson, Robert B. and Mittie B. McCauley, April 22nd
Garrison, Edward C. and Elsie C. Bishop, May 7th
Garland, Percy C. and Ethel Woodson, June 23rd
Gay, H. Frank and Isabella Boltwood, Aug. 31st
Giles, Harry M. and Nannie C. Vasseur, Sept. 17th
Graves, Robert L. and Katherine B. Bishop, Nov. 9th
Gentry, Tucker W. and Estelle Gentry, Nov. 11th

1915

Geer, Howard and Mary L. Carnell, Jan. 20th
Grady, W. B. and Minnie McFadden, Feb. 17th
Gibson, William L. and Nora E. Maddox, April 3rd
Gentry, Overton and Mae Thomas, June 16th
Gentry, Ollie and Sallie Larrie, July 1st
Goode, Raymond M. and Edith P. Branzell, July 5th
Gore, Willington L. O. and Annie Walker Mawyer, Sept. 29th
Garth, Lewis W. and Martha E. Wingfield, Oct. 20th
Garrison, Eugene and Ida Bishop, Dec. 22nd
Godsey, J. E. and Ethel V. Gentry, Dec. 27th
Graves, Forest and Lozethe Chisholm, Dec. 29th

1916

Gibson, Thomas and Mary Barnett, Jan. 6th
Garrison, Robert and Flossie Madison, Jan. 4th
Gentry, Bryan and Carrie Mooney, Jan. 29th
Gibson, George E. and Maggie E. Norris, May 28th

Gentry, George T. and Gladys Mahanes, June 21st
Garth, James W. and Jane C. Hancock, June 28th
Garrison, Lacy Jefferson and Mannie Ellen Ray, Aug. 1st
Gibson, Raleigh and Virgie Hicks, Aug. 15th
Gibson, Elizie and Laura Goode, Aug. 26th
Grasty, Clarence W. and Myrtle Ellinger, Oct. 2nd

1917

Gianning, William G. and Maggie M. Harris, April 17
Gibson, Lawrence M. and Bessie A. Henry, April 18th
Glass, Levie and Rosa Via, June 24th
Gibson, Lewis T. and Ida Shifflett, Sept. 3rd
Garrison, Reuben and Susan Morris, Oct. 6th
Gibson Lacy and Victoria Gibson, Oct. 8th
Gibson, Sidney and Anna Edwards, Nov. 9th
Goodwin, Willie Lee and Pearl Lee Garland, Dec. 26th
Goolsby Thos. C. and Myrtle Lee Byer, Dec. 31st

1918

Gibson, Albert and Maud Anderson, Aug. 17th
Greene, Christopher A. and Honor Price, Oct. 28th
Glassgo, John F. and Annie E. Baltimore, Nov. 6th
Garrison, Dewey and Pearle Shiflett, Dec. 21st

1919

Gibson, Franklin Mathew and Cary E. Woodson, March 3rd
Garrett, Harry and Lena Fitzgerald, March 18th
Gianniny, Irby Lawerence and Hester Irene Durham, April 21st
Good, Donald E. and Rena E. Hackett, June 2nd
Garth, Jas. Fendal and Edith C. White, Sept. 10th
Gibson, Claude W. and Josephine I. Perry, Nov. 18th

1920

Glass, Henry H. and Maggie L. Dollins, March 6th
Garrison, Henry Clay and Marjorie Arbogast, April 24th
Garrison, James W. and Martha E. Cox, May 27th
Greenwood, Robert Lee and Eleanor D. Pinkerton, Sept. 15th
Goodloe, Jr., Judson Cary and Sally Francis Ladd, Oct. 20th
Gamble, Jr., Edward W. and Eleanor D. Kent, Nov. 24th

1921

Gibson, Douglas H. and Sarah E. Rea, Jan. 5th

Gibson, Eugene Earnest, and Willie Minor Morris, Jan. 5th

Gleason, J. Emmett and Helen B. Simmons, Jan. 25th

Garrison, Thomas E. and Margaret G. Klise, Feb. 1st

Gibson, Thos. J. and Lucile V. Snead, Feb. 24th

Gibson, Arthur and Nellie Gibson, May 30th

Gowe, Luther E. and Lellia Garrison, June 9th

Glass, Wiley W. and Annie Ruth Harlow, June 17th

Gibson, Austin and Ella Marshall Woodson, Aug. 2nd

Glover, Ellis and Gracie L. Shiflett, Aug. 18th

Gentry, Granville and Mattie Mayo, Aug. 20th

Gibson, James E. and Julia Ann Kirby, Aug. 22nd

Graves, Gordon G. and Lucy Poe, Nov. 18th

Grunbine, John D. and Emily C. Madigare, Nov. 30th

1922

Gibson, Lawrence A. and Virgie Mary Kirby, March 8th

Graves, Julian M. and Addie L. L. Brown, June 21st

Gentry, Raymond and Blanche Sprouse, June 20th

Gentry, Everett N. and Thelma Brockenbrough, June 29th

Gardner, Charles B. and Audrey V. Wood, June 27th

Garwood, Samuel F. and Bessie E. Perry, July 12th

Gooden, Jessie C. and Bettie Rossan, July, 15th

Glass, John S. and Henretta Pendleton, Sept. 24th

Glass, J. Carlton and Myrtle E. Walters, Oct. 18th

Goolsby, John D. and Hattie E. Craig, Dec. 4th

Gaskins, Horace L. and Grace B. Rolley, Dec. 25th

1923

Garrison, Davis and Lillie V. Batten, Feb. 5th

Glass, Olices G. and Eva D. Stump, Feb. 7th

Goolsby, Rufus P. and Katherine Wilkinson, Feb. 12th

Garrison, Eley and Cornelia B. Hilderbrand, Feb. 16th

Gentry, Litt and Gladys Marsh, March 1st

Gibson, Henry and Florence Via, March 12th

Garth, Robert B. and Edith B. Thurman, June 11th

Garrison, Carl and Carrie Lee Garrison, July 11th

Gianniny, Horace M. and Sarah J. Durham, Aug. 2nd

Garver, John Wm. and Ruth McAlister, July 21st

Garrison, Jack and Lula Garrison, Nov. 22nd

Gill, Arthur B. and Gladys A. Yancey, Nov. 29th

Garrison, John B. and Meta S. Gardner, Dec. 20th

Gibson, Clarence I. and Mary Woodson, Dec. 24th

1924

Garrison, George M. and Edna J. Via, Jan. 2nd

Gianniny, Wilbur and Margaret Smith, Jan. 23rd

Gray, Larcey E. and Virginia Faris, March 12th

Garrison, Anda and Celia Keyton, April 11th

Goolsby, Robt. L. and Mary A. Riffles, April 15th

Gentry, Kenneth B. and Eugenia Ramsey, May 20th

Gianniny, Curtis and Evelyn Fennick, Jan. 23rd

Guffin, John and Mamie Kent, Sept. 1st

Grubbs, Herbert L. and Bessie E. Brown, Sept. 27th

Glass, Liovey and Hattie Beasley, Oct. 2nd

Gibson, Alfred B. and Willemner Woodson, Oct. 14th

Gibson, John L. and Netie Woodson, Oct. 20th

Gibson, Floyd and Nannie Woodson, Nov. 2nd

Gay, Chas. E., III and Ouida A. Wattler, Nov. 22nd

Goodwin, Harry N. and Blanche W. White, Dec. 9th

Gibson, Arthur and Christine Gibson, Dec. 29th

1925

Good, Charles F. and Ada M. McCary, Jan. 19th

Gibson, Fletcher and Mattie E. Lynch, March 7th

Gregory, Herman F. and Sallie M. Gills, March 9th

Garver, Peter L. and Julia Bell Hicks, March 9th

Gibson, Robt. P. and Leola Shiflett, May 9th

Graves, Theodore and Mary Thomas, May 20th

Gardner, Phillip H. and Annie L. Dowling, June 14th

Green, Garfield and Honssell Abell, July 9th

Garth, Frank and Wyatt Catterton, Aug. 6th

Gianniny, Robt. N. and Daisy Beery, Aug. 1st

Gentry, William H. and Ora Carn Short, Sept. 8th

Gibson, Ophery and Lorine Eubank, Sept. 17th

Gibson, Eugene and Rebecca Woodson, Oct. 15th

Gibson, Lyn and Maggie Barnett, Dec. 16th

Garrison, Dash and Myrtie Garrison, Dec. 24th

1926

Gibson, Henry and Lelia M. Shiflett, Jan. 4th

Gentry, Jas. A. and Emily Mahanes, March 2nd

Goodman, Joseph M. and Elizabeth Johnson, May 29th

Graham, Dr., Andrew S. and Nancy Hart Gordon, June 26th

Gough, Bernard L. and Daisy L. Bragg, July 3rd

Gentry, Thomas P. and Alice W. Goode, Oct. 9th

Gibson, Morton and Stella M. Fisher, Nov. 6th

Garrison, William E. and Louise F. Via, Nov. 10th

Garrison, John and Ethel McAllister, Dec. 28th

1927

Goodwin, Herbert T. and Effie Vasseur, Jan. 26th

Garrison, Irving and Fannie Morris, April 19th

Gibson, Claude and Dora Currier, May 7th

Garrison, Whilton R. and Ethel May Sprouse, May 16th

Graves, Harry Lee and Bessie Va. Critzer, June 11th

Gillispie, Augusta R. and Mary Q. Bird, Aug. 20th

Gibson, Leonard and Fannie Morris, Dec. 22nd

1928

Gibson, Lovil and Emma Hutchinson, Mar. 19th

Garrison, Lee R. and Dora K. McCauley, Apr. 4th

Gibson, James A. and Pearl Morris, April 11th

Garnett, Wm. E. and Bettie Wingfield, April 20th

Goodwin, Charlie and Sallie H. Morris, May 1st

Gianniny, Horace N. and Bessie L. Albert, June 1st

Gill, Wm. C. and Addie Whittlesey, July 1st

Gibson, Charles Otis and Edna L. Sanders, July 13th

Grater, Allen and Isabel Eustsler, July 14th

Goodman, Wm. R. and Thelma A. Morris, Aug. 1st

Grenger, John A. Claudine M. Cunningham, Aug. 2nd

Gray, Lawrence R. and Mary E. Page, Aug. 7th

Gitchell, John D. and Allie F. Omohundro, Aug. 30th

1929

Gilbert, James F. and Daisey M. Gentry, Feb. 4th

Gardner, Horace S. and Dorothy Ellen Wood, March 30th

Gianniny, Albert Lee and Susie H. Harris, April 27th

Gilmer, Estes E. and Della M. Link, May 6th

Gibson, Jas. L. and Lula W. Wood, May 29th

Garrison, Richard F. and Laura McAllister, June 1st

Garnett, Robt. F. and Fannie C. Durrette, June 13th

Graves, John L. and Nellie Lula Spencer, June 15th

Gentry, Jno. Wm. and Sara E. Rogers, Sept. 6th

H

1781

Higgins, William and Margaret Mooney, Sept. 17th

1783

Horsley, Goodman and Betsey Rodes, May 8th

Huckstep, Charles and Moze White, Sept. 20th

1784

Hammer, John and Ann Wingfield, June 23rd

1785

Haggard, Bartelott and Martha Dawson, Nov. 10th

Hall, James and Mildred Humphrey, Oct. 14th

Harris, Benjamin and Mary Woods, Oct. 3rd

Harris, John and Margaret Maupin, April 14th

Hicks, John and Nancy Davis, Feb. 5th

1786

Harrison, Hiram and Sally Richardson, Sept. 12th

Hart, Andrew and Elizabeth Leake, Dec. 14th

Hines, John and Frances Henderson, Dec. 21st

1787

Haden, Anthony and Anna Darbney, Nov. 30th

Harris, John and Nancy Claybrook, March 7th

Horn, John and — Chandler, April 7th

1788

Harrison, James and Sarah Harris, Dec 13th

1789

Harlow, Nathaniel and Elizabeth Gilbert, Sept. 10th

Hopkins, William and Elizabeth Moon, Oct. 8th

Houseright, Joseph and Elizabeth Lenders, June 22nd

Howard, William and Elizabeth Marshall, Dec. 14th

Huckstep, John and Aggey Watts, July 15th

1790

Haggard, David and Nancy Dawson, Nov. 6th

Hancock, Benjamin and Priscilla Frankling, April 5th

Harris, James and Mary McCullock, Jan. 11th

Hughes, Edward and Elizabeth Chisholm, Dec. 19th

1791

Hancock, John and Fanny Farrar, Dec. 13th
Harris, William and Hannah Hanson, Oct. 13th
Herring, David and Jenny Ramsey, March 23rd
Hogg, ? and Molly Eads, —
Howard, James and Dizy Ballard, June 9th
Howell, Matthew and Salia Johnson, July 28th
Hughes, John and Mary Johnson, March 5th

1792

Harris, Henry and Mary Ferguson, Nov. 13th
Harris, John and Nancy Mays, Dec. 13th
Harris, Samuel and Sally Burk, Dec. 13th
Hazlering, Richard and Polly Eubank, Feb. 23rd
Hurt, William and Rittoi Page, June 5th

1793

Haden, John and Nancy Gianniny, Dec. 24th
Hamner, Hendley and Elizabeth Wingfield, Dec. 23rd
Harden, George and Sally Gentry, May 13th
Harlan, Samuel and Jane Goolsby, Dec. 25th
Hart, Andrew and Elizabeth Beckler, Oct. 10th
Henderson, Ambrose and Susannah Fargason, Nov. 14th
Hopping, Jeremiah and Phely Hughes, Nov. 25th
Horner, Joseph and Martha Carter, April 17th
Houchings, William and Franky Britt, Dec. 16th

1794

Hall, William and Martha Edwards, July 10th
Harkins, John and Nancy Bent, April 29th
Henderson, John and Ann Barber, Nov. 25th
Henderson, Joseph and Jinny Murrell, Dec. 22nd
Herring, Christopher and Elizabeth Lucus, March 6th
Horseburgh, Alexander and Jane Jopling, Nov. 22nd

1795

Herndon, Richard and Sarah Tool, Dec. 21st
Hill, Charles and Molly Hill, Dec. 30th

1796

Harding, Daniel and Ann Bussey, Jan. 13th
Higdon, John and Mary Ross, June 21st
Hogg, William and Polly Gianniny, Jan. 19th
Hughes, Henry and Elizabeth Parish, July 19th
Hains, John and Elizabeth Langford, Nov. 22nd
Herrin, Benjamin and Nancy Hill, Dec. 27th

1798

Haden, Isaah and Polly Spears, Jan. 24th
Hall, Joseph and Liddy Scott, April 22nd
Harlow, Edmond and Hannah Barnett, Oct. 17th

Harlow, Nathaniel and Salley Thacker, Jan. 30th
Harlowe, Hezekiah and Mildred Ford, July 22nd
Hill, Richard and Elizabeth Hill, Sept. 3rd
Horner, John and Sally Proctor, March 12th
Hurt, George and Polly Mabrey, April 15th

1799

Haden, Richard D. and Sally Lewis Tompkins, March 7th
Hall, William and Susannah Davis, Dec. 30th
Harlan, Thomas and Salley Eubank, March 3rd
Harris, Reuben and Nancy Burke, Dec. 21st
Harris, Wiley and Betsey Jamerson, Dec. 20th
Henderson, Joseph and Mary Durham, Jan. 2nd
Herndon, John and Mary Cosby, Jan. 19th
Hicks, David and Jemima Tennal, Dec. 3rd
Huckstep, Josiah and Nancy Watts, April 15th

1801

Harlow, Bartlett and Lucy Thacker, July 13th

1802

Hamaker, John and Elizabeth Spears, Aug. 27th
Hensley, Benjamin and Polley Melton, Dec. 6th
Hill, John and Jane Munday, Dec. 18th
Homan, Reuben and Lucy Wills, Sept. 29th
Hope, Michael and Patsy Snead, Feb. 2nd

1803

Hamner, William and Theodophy Ricks, Nov. 27th
Henderson, John and Susannah Kirby, Jan. 17th
Henderson, Joseph and Jane Whitesides, Oct. 14th
Henderson, Thomas and Nancy M. Terril, April 27th
Henderson, William T. and Rebecca L. Hudson, Oct. 7th

1804

Hall, Nathan and Jemima Scott, Nov. 17th
Hamner, Nicholas and Mary Garland, June 18th
Harris, William and Mildred Sebrel, June 21st
Harvey, Richard and Dolly Gentry, Dec. 31st
Huckstep, David and Fanny Brand, June 4th

1805

Hailey, Benjamin and Ann Sisk, April 26th
Hall, Dabney and Milly Leake, Sept. 2nd
Hall, Nathan and Jeeley Ham, May 3rd
Heizer, Samuel and Polly Ware, Nov. 10th
Horsley, William and Lillie Nailor, March 26th
Hughes, John and Polly Jean, April 29th
Hunt, Benjamin and Sarah Strange, Oct. 7th

1806

Hanson, ? and Ann Cook, May 2nd
Harris, Morton and Elizabeth Brockman, Dec. 19th
Harvie, ? and Molly Mayal
Henderson, John and Sally Harris, Sept. 6th
Herndon, Thomas and Molly Mayal, Nov. 6th
Hill, Henry and Thomas Modena, Dec. 22nd
Horsley, ? and Polly Carr, May 24th
Hoy, William and Peachy Ballard, Dec. 24th
Huckstep, Charles and Martha Gillum, Feb. 22nd
Hurt, ? and Mary Patterson, Sept. 1st

1807

Hackly, Richard and Peggy Draffin, July 7th
Hall, Ambrose and Elizabeth Marr, Dec. 24th
Hamler, Joseph and Cynthia Sneed, Sept. 7th
Harlow, Sherod and Nancy Bowdin, Feb. 7th
Hore, Wiliam and Jurrel Moorman, Jan. 14th

1808

Hall, Cornelius and Rhody Wood, Dec. 27th
Hamner, Francis and Sally Eubanks, Oct. 29th
Harvey, Martin and Elizabeth Gentry, Jan. 16th
Hoy, George and Eliza Monroe, Sept. 28th

1809

Ham, Elijah and Susan Farney. Feb. 5th
Herring, Jonathan and Susan Hill, Dec. 30th
Hicks, Charles and Judy Walton, Jan. 7th
Holston, Thomas and Susan Wheeler, Feb. 14th
Houchens, Obediah and Polly McQuarry, Jan. 7th
Hudson, George and Polly Ropson, Oct. 11th

1810

Harris, Jarrot and Jane Ramsey, Nov. 19th
Harris, William and Elizabeth Harris, Sept 1st
Hill, John and Aggy Brockman, Aug. 23rd
Hinyon, Willis and Polly Pierce, Nov. 28th
Holston, William and Marcarina Baily, Oct. 25th

1811

Hamner, ? and Elizabeth Hamner, Dec. 2nd
Hamner, John and Susan Fretwell, March 11th
Harris, Henry T. and Mary W. Harris, April 9th
Henderson, William and Sarah Dollins, July 25th
Herndon, William and Sarah McAllister, March 13th
Holston, ? and Nancy Bailv. Nov. 24th
Houck, John and Elizabeth Hoy, May 27th
Huckstep, James and Betty Bacon, Feb. 25th
Hudson, Larkin and Polly Wingfield, Nov. 4th

1812

Hays, James, Jr. and Margaret Yancey, March 21st
Herron, Alexander and Jane Clovin, Oct. 21st

Hundley, Thomas and Elizabeth Hensley, Oct. 10th

1813

Herren, Spencer and Lucy Breedlove, Dec. 28th
Harris, William B. and Eliza Hart, March 27th

1814

Haden, John Jr. and Polly Maupin, Dec. 19th
Hamner, Ed and Charlotte Clarkson, Feb. 15th
Harris, William and Patsey Maupin, March 1st
Harrison, John C. and Fanny Rhodes, July 25th
Henderson, Charles and Frances Lane, Aug. 19th

1815

Hall, James and Polly Herring, June 17th
Hamner, James and Isabella Maxwell, Dec. 11th
Harris, William and Mary Con, March 4th

1816

Harris, Clifton and Mary H. Lewis, Jan. 8th
Hays, David and Elizabeth Yancey, March 4th
Herren, John and Larat Hill, Jan. 29th
Hicks, Charles and Rebecca Thomas, Jan. 4th
Hoy, Isaac and Nancey Taylor, Aug. 13th
Hughes, William R. and Elizabeth Goodwin, Jan. 8th

1817

Hancock, Benjamin and Malinda Hogg, Dec. 25th
Hunter, Joseph and Parthiney C. Snead, July 14th

1818

Hall, John and Anny Wilkinson, Dec. 29th
Hall, Richard and Nancy Morris, Oct. 12th
Harris, John and Sarah C. Barclay, Dec. 30th
Harris, Samuel and Catherine Garrison, Oct. 24th
Harris, Thomas and Mary Depoor, Dec. 16th
Heiskill, Alexander and Sarah T. Lewis, June 4th
Herring, George and Polly Carver, Dec. 17th
Herring, John and Lucy Carver, Dec. 3rd
Holston, Thomas and Elizabeth Wheeler, Nov. 9th
Houchens, Reubin and Elizabeth Black, Dec. 24th
Howard, John and Virginia Pettitt, Dec. 9th

1819

Hall, Thomas and Elizabeth Pickett, Feb. 23rd
Harris, Robert M. C. and Lucinda Maupin, Oct. 28th
Hart, James and Sophia Harris, Nov. 4th
Harvey, Francis and Malinda Dawson, Nov. 25th
Herring, John and Maria Hill, Nov. 11th
Humphreys, John and Elizabeth W. Woods, May 20th

1820

Hall, James and Judah Herring, Dec. 20th
Harris, David and Elizabeth Newcomb, June 6th
Holiday, Edward and Sarah Moore, Jan. 5th
Hopkins, William and Maryaziance P. Haden, April 7th
Houchens, James and Elizabeth Harden, Dec. 21st
Hughes, Anderson and Ann B. Mullins, Dec. 19th

1821

Harris, Lansy and Dosha A. Baily, Aug. 9th
Herndon, George T. and Patsy Price, May 11th
Hicks, William and Mildred Sprouce, Sept. 6th
Hildlebough, John and S. G. Williams, Dec. 18th

1822

Hamner, William and Elizabeth Blain, Dec. 4th
Hany, John and Elizabeth Watson, Dec. 10th
Harlow, Reuben and Sophia Martin, Aug. 5th
Harlow, William and Elizabeth Taylor, Dec. 19th
Hulls, David and Mary Sunco, Aug. 29th

1823

Hare, Frederick and Nancy Fogers, Sept. 7th
Hawes, Daniel M. and Maria Chewning, Sept. 13th
Head, Walker and Harderia P. Garth, Sept. 9th
Hendree, John and Herriot Brown, May 20th

1824

Harlow, Henry M. and Elizabeth Hawley, Jan. 6th
Harper, Gabrill L. and Sarah L. Anderson, Dec. 8th
Hart, John E. and Ann Rodes, Jan. 14th
Hogg, John and Jane Lively, April 15th
Howard, Richard and Eliza Pettett, Nov. 2nd
Huffman, Milton and Feliccia Peyton, Jan. 22nd

1825

Haden, William P. and Sarah A. Durrett, May 19th
Hall, James and Martha Morris, Sept. 14th
Hall, Willis and Barbara Banzzem, Dec. 19th
Hameasby, William and Malinda Hays, June 1st
Harslip, Samuel C. and Mary Morris, Dec. 1st
Hawkins, Joseph and Harriet Butler, April 13th
Herndon, Joseph and Surany Cave, Dec. 12th
Hopkins, William and Rebecca Estes, Jan. 4th
Humphrey, David and Mary Smith, Aug. 15th
Humphrey, Meriwether T. and Susan Thurston, Feb. 23rd

1826

Harvey, James and Nancy Gibson, Sept. 12th
Hays, Nathaniel and Mary Wood, Sept. 26th
Heiskell, Colvin and Nancy Durrett, Nov. 8th
Hicks, Thomas and Ann Thomas, Jan. 5th
Houchens, Joshua and Nancy Wood, Nov. 20th

1827

Hamner, John T. and Mary Blain, Jan. 4th
Harris, Benjamin and Susanna Carter, Jan. 18th
Harris, Thomas W. and Elizabeth Maupin, Dec. 19th
Herring, Nathan and Susan Hill, Jan. 11th
Hicks, David and Mary Sudderth, Dec. 1st

1828

Hamner, Jesse B. and Sarah W. Herndon, Oct. 16th
Harlow, Wm. H. and Lucy A. Davis, June 13th
Harris, Benjamin and Rebecca Harris, Jan. 17th
Herndon, Bartley and Mary Boyd, June 6th
Hudson, Charles and Agness Lewis, March 5th

1829

Haden, John and Nancy Modeana, May 14th
Haskin, William and Mary Carter, May 19th
Hawley, William and Mary Ann Gillum, Aug. 18th
Herndon, Manson and Frances Rodes, Feb. 19th
Humphrey, George W. and Elena Robinson, Dec. 5th

1830

Hall, Martin H. and Lucy Beck, Sept. 6th
Harlow, George and Elizabeth Carmon, June 29th
Harris, Randal and Martha Ferguson, Jan. 6th
Harrison, Gesno and Elizabeth G. Tucker, Dec. 15th
Herron, George and Lucy Simes, Dec. 28th
Hicks, James and Susan Wilhoit, Feb. 8th
Hoskins, Fraw and Ann E. Higgenbotham, July 6th
Humphrey, David and Nancy Nabers, Dec. 9th

1831

Hare, Richard Jr. and Martha Martin, Aug. 1st
Hareslip, Robert M. and Susan Merritt, Aug. 1st
Harris, Julius A. and Caroline C. Pettet, Nov. 28th
Hemmings, Madison and Mary Hughes, Nov. 21st
Henderson, John H. and M. C. Hopkins, Sept. 1st
Hoy, Isaac and Mildred Hamilton, March 15th

1832

Hall, Lewis and Elizabeth Seamons, May 9th

Harrison, Julius C. and Elizabeth Strange, Jan. 5th

Hawkins, William W. and Ellen T. Rogers, June 6th

Henly, Thompson and Sarah E. Hall, Nov. 5th

Highlander, Jacob and Sally Haskins, July 5th

Hill, Richard and Nancy T. Tatrum, Dec. 26th

Hogg, William and Nancy Bishop, Sept. 12th

Hull, Edward and Ellen J. Clark, June 7th

Hummings, Ester and Julian Ann Isaacs, June 14th

Humphrey, Lewis D. and Sarah A. Thurston, April 3rd

1833

Harlow, Nathaniel and Susan West, Jan. 23rd

Harlow, Pleasants and Martha Ferguson, Sept. 11th

Harris, Alanson and Sophia Ann Harris, Feb. 12th

Harris, William and Nancy Jordan, Jan. 31st

Herndon, John M. and Lucy Ann Wingfield, Oct. 31st

Herring, James B. and Margaret J. Butler, Feb. 7th

Hoskins, Thomas and Jane Harris, July 9th

Hudson, John J. and Ann R. Hudson, Sept. 17th

Hunter, James A. and Martha C. Watson, March 7th

1834

Halback, John P. and Ellen W. Gates, March 4th

Hall, John B. and Adela A. Head, May 12th

Hall, Samuel and Betsy Dowell, Sept. 30th

Hamner, Thomas and Maria B. Garland, Sept. 13th

Harden, William and Mary Stults, Nov. 11th

Harvey, James and Frances Keister, Jan. 20th

Haskins, Robert and Harriett Toms, Dec. 15th

Henly, Wilson and Elizabeth Thompson, Dec. 15th

Holbert, Alexander and Martha Ann Moseley, April 7th

Howard, Eli and Ann Marshall, May 12th

Huffman, John and Ann Hilldrup, June 5th

1835

Harris, William O. and Sarah Pritchett, Jan. 17th

Hicks, Joseph and Jane Price, Dec. 17th

Hicks, William R. and Ann R. Deltor, Dec. 10th

Hill, Willis and Elizabeth Simpco, Jan. 19th

Huckstep, John F. and Mildred M. Estes, Nov. 17th

Huffman, Robert and Harriot Garner, Dec. 8th

Harris, William and Martha White, Nov. 29th

Hawkins, Allen W. and Martha Pinkard, Dec. 17th

Holladay, Albert and Ann G. Minor, Oct. 27th

1836

Houchens, Miner and Mary F. Batcheller, Sept. 20th

1837

Hackett, William R. and Mary P. Johnson, Dec. 4th

Hall, John A. and Elizabeth Gillock, Feb. 8th

Hall, William D. and Sarah A. Gillock, March 16th

Hamner, Warwick W. and Ann Eliza Moore, Aug. 22nd

Harris, John M. and L. F. Marshall, Jan. 19th

Harris, William A. and Mary Ann Milliway, Nov. 9th

Harton, Benjamin F. W. and Elizabeth D. Hays, Feb. 15th

Herring, Nimrod and Amanda Price, Nov. 22nd

Hoy, Joseph and Elizabeth Snow, Sept. 18th

Hughes, Reuben and Susan M. Smith, Aug. 29th

Humphreys, John P. and Margaret J. Fouster, Oct. 24th

1838

Hall, Woodson K. and Sarah Wilkinson, Oct. 30th

Harris, Henry and Mary Martin, Dec. 20th

Head, Valentine and Lucy J. Barksdale, Nov. 27th

Houchens, George W. and Martha C. Johnson, April 5th

Huffman, John F. and Sarah S. Norris, Jan. 1st

Hughes, John F. and Eliza A. Thomerson, June 5th

1839

Harris, Andrew F. and Sarah F. Antrim, Aug. 21st

Haskins, John M. and Aireene Toms, Jan. 8th

Hawkins, Allen W. and Elizabeth Burch, May 7th

Haxall, R. W. and Jane R. McMurdo, Nov. 13th

Hopkins, Stephen D. and Mrs. Elizabeth McClun, March 20th

Houchins, John R. and Charlotte Kidd, Dec. 2nd

1840

Hamner, Robert and V. E. Childress, Oct. 27th

Hamner, W. W. and J. M. Branham, Nov. 11th

Harden, James O. and D. A. Farrish, Dec. 7th

Harris, Lively and F. S. Norford, Dec. 29th

Hays, Murphy and Mary A. Smith, Feb. 7th

Hill, Thomas T. and Ariadne L. Jones, Oct. 27th

Hutcherson, Jere and Amanda Sims, Oct. 8th

1841

Hall, John and Angelina A. Fretwell Jan. 7th

Harris, Andrew J. and Frances Ann Woodson, Jan. 18th

Harris, Robert M. and Jaama Woodson, Jan. 22nd

Harris, Tandy and Emily Marshall, Aug. 12th

Heiskill, Jese S. and Eleanora Martin, Oct. 18th

Hernsly, Chris and Rebecca Price, Sept. 8th

Holloway, Joseph S. and Ann C. Burgess, Oct. 7th

Humphrey, Elijah and Mary Graham, Nov. 10th

1842

Hamner, Walter S. and Sarah A. Morris, Dec. 20th

Harlow, James M. and Jerusha M. McCord, July 25th

Harris, Ribert and Frances Owens, Dec. 26th

Hawley, James O. and Mary M. Jones, Dec. 6th

Henderson, John A. and Almeida Brown, March 15th

Herndon, George T. and Matilda B. Mayo, Dec. 22nd

Hicks, Samuel and Elizabeth Reynolds, Jan. 25th

Houchens, Nathan G. and F. E. Houchens, Feb. 7th

Hoy, William and Susan Cox, Aug. 15th

Hudson, Edward N. and Susan Johnson, Nov. 30th

Hughes, Silbrun J. and Mildred Kirby, Feb. 9th

1843

Hall, Richard and Mary J. Harding, Aug. 19th

Harris, G. W. and Susan A. Carr, Nov. 10th

Head, James E. and Ann E. Kinsolving, Oct. 30th

Hickok, William and Lucinda S. Noel, Feb. 6th

Holbert, Robert and Sarah Pritchett, Sept. 22nd

Hopkins, John and Sarah Wingfield, Feb. 8th

Houchens, William and Mary E. Broadhead, Sept. 3rd

Hudson, Joseph S. and Elizabeth M. Wingfield, April 22nd

Humphrey, George N. and Eliza Via, March 20th

1844

Hall, Mace P. and Tipton P. Walton, Nov. 16th

Harlen, William R. and M. M. Harlen, Nov. 26th

Harlow, Henry S. W. and Elizabeth Harlow, Sept. 13th

Harlow, James S. and Drusilla Luck, June 2nd

Harper, Louis A. and Sarah M. T. Harris, Aug. 27th

Harris, Wyatt and Ellen Battles, Jan., 18th

Herron, John C. and Elizabeth A. Sheffler, Dec. 27th

Hicks, Soloman R. and Elizabeth Jackson, Feb. 10th

Hunter, William C. and Rosalee Pollard, Sept. 6th

1845

Hamlett, Elias and R. Eubank, May 8th

Harlow, William and Sarah Herring, Dec. 7th

Harper, Joseph and Mary Ann Wood, Aug. 4th

Hays, D. T. and Sally Hays, Dec. 12th

Heppard, George and Sarah A. Critzer, Oct. 21st

Houchens, William and S. A. Garland, Feb. 3rd

1846

Hager, Eldridge H. and Sarah Thomas, Oct. 31st

Hall, Richard P. and Sarah Given, July 16th

Hallbrook, John H. and Severna Brown, Sept. 7th

Hamm, Joab C. and Martha D. Douglass, Dec. 24th

Harlow, James M. and Jenetta M. Robertson, Jan. 20th

Herndon, George J. and Martha M. Elsom, Oct. 5th

1847

Hamner, James and Lucy Ann Gay, May 12th

Harlow, Hudson M. and Jane Moore, Jan. 16th

Harris, Benjamin G. and Ann C. Lewellyn, Oct. 4th

Harris, George W. and Jane Shackelford, Nov. 30th

Harris, Henry F. and Eliza Gibson, Sept. 4th

Harris, William H. and M. J. Wayland, Jan. 18th

Herndon, Samuel and Emily A. Cloar, Aug. 18th

Hodges, William S. and Elizabeth Nimno, Dec. 7th

Houchens, Thomas B. and C. C. Powell, Nov. 15th

Hurt, Morris and Mary Bruffy, Sept. 22nd

1848

Haden, William D. and P. M. Brown, Feb. 29th

Harris, Denton H. and J. E. Harris, Dec. 21st

Harris, William B. and E. T. Harris, Sept. 14th

Harrison, P. R. and M. F. Rodes, May 5th

Henshaw, James W. and R. A. Batcheller, April 27th

Herndon Joseph and Mary Nunineo, Jan. 4th

Hughes, J. C. and Anne E. Timberlake, June 3rd

1849

Hall, Daniel and M. E. Harris Jan. 1st

Hall, Henry F. and F. Crickenberger, May 15th

Hancock, Francis W. and Virginia Hancock, Oct. 11th

Harlow, Nicholas and Anna Sprouce, Jan. 3rd

Herndon, Elisha M. and Martha G. Clour, Nov. 15th

Houchens, George L. and Jane E. Goodman, July 26th

Humphrey, Daniel and Mary J. Thacker, Oct. 16th

Humphrey, James G. and E. J. McAlexander, July 12th

Humphreys, Joab O. and V. E. Humphreys, May 11th

1850

Hall, Mace P. and Frances W. Seamond, Dec. 29th

Hall, William and Matilda Hall, May 16th

Harlan, Thomas S. and Mary E. Harlan, May 15th

Harlow, Reuben M. and Susan E. Hare, April 22nd

Harris, Lafayette and Martha J. Minor, June 3rd

Harris, William T. and Nancy F. Maupin, Nov. 4th

Hawley, James A. and Catharien S. M. Baily, Nov. 24th

Heck, Tilford B. and Estelline M. Boyd, Feb. 26th

Herron, Charles A. and Mary Jane Martin, July 7th

Hicks, John and Frances Pritchett, Dec. 12th

Hudson, Richard N. and Ann Cary, May 20th

Humphreys, John M. and Sarah Jane Garland, May 14th

1851

Hamner, James F. and Cornelia P. Lewellyn, Sept. 2nd

Harlan, Joseph and Levinna Bowen, April 23rd

Harris, Albert W. and Margaret E. Scott, Oct. 8th

Harris, Henry and Martha Davis, Aug. 20th

Harris, James and Z. E. Goodman, Dec. 28th

Haversham, S. E. and Lucy E. Pollard, July 13th

Houchins, Thompson G. and E. V. Campbell, Dec. 24th

1852

Harris, Lively and M. S. Smith, Aug. 1st

Hawkins, Thomas S. and M. E. Wheeler, March 24th

Hogg, Mulenburg, and Mary Marion, Sept. 13th

Hourton, J. C. and M. W. Wolfe, Oct. 27th

Howard, Thomas D. and Lucy A. Bibb, Dec. 22nd

Hughes, Elijah and Sarah Ashlier, Nov. 18th

Hurst, Scyum and Ann Craddock, May 21st

1853

Harris, Charles W. and Augustine M. Brown, March 16th

Harris, John H. and Betsy Anne Wade, July 21st

Harris, William M. and Mary W. Watson, Nov. 9th

Haskins, Marcus W. and M. F. Baber, Oct. 16th

Herndon, James H. and S. A. Haislip, Feb. 3rd

Humphrey, John O. and Willey A. Hamner, Jan. 1st

Hurley, Daniel and Catharine Murphy, Jan. 5th

Hurt, James and Sarah E. Bunch, Jan. 6th

1854

Harmon, Edward D. and Frances E. Stone, Aug. 31st

Harris, R. F. and Elizabeth W. Wayland, Oct. 31st

Harris, Reuben and Elizabeth Ann Harris, Dec. 14th

Hartman, St. Clair and Jennie Tompkins, Feb. 8th

Hartnagle, Frederick and Martha J. Johnson, Aug. 10th

Herndon, Elisha M. and Virginia A. Perry, Nov. 27th

Hicks, Edwin L. and Martha A. Rothwell, March 14th

Houchens, John R. and Sallie Houchens, Jan. 12th

Hughson, Frederick and Lucy A. Detter, Jan. 9th

Harris, Geo. D. and Sarah E. Foster, Jan. 10th

Houchens, Jno. B. and Sally Houchens, Jan. 12th

Harris, B. F. and Eliz. W. Wayland, April 31st

1855

Haden, William H. and Susan M. Brown, Dec. 11th

Hall, Richard M. and Sarah J. Wilkerson, Sept. 9th

Harlow, Franklin J. and Mary Tisdal, Oct. 23rd

Harris, George D. and Sarah E. Foster, Jan. 10th

Harris, James E. and Hettie M. Harris, Dec. 17th

Harris, James E. and Hettie Morris, Dec. 20th

Higgins, Roger and Mildred Kerby, Nov. 11th

Holbert, Alex and Sarah E. Bragg, Sept. 3rd

Hoye, John L. and Mary S. Calhoun, July 16th

Hoye, Thomas P. and Isadora Tompkins, July 3rd

Hudson, Larkin and Lucy C. Wingfield, Jan. 9th

Hughson, Fred and Lucy A. Dettor, Jan 9th

Higgins, Roger and Mildred Kirby, Nov. 1st

Hoye, Jno. J. and Mary S. Calhoun, July 17th

Hartnagle, F. and Mania J. Johnson, Aug. 10th

Hamner, Edw. D. and Frances A. Stone, Aug. 31st

1856

Hardesty, J. R. L. and Susan M. Ficklin, June 18th

Harlow, Lewis J. and Catharine Smith, Jan. 3rd

Hartnagle, Frederick and Mary E. Goodwin, Sept. 1st

Hawkins, Joseph and Sarah E. Carver, April 23rd

Hawkins, Robert A. and Emeline Hawkins, Nov. 27th

Head, Willis M. and Ann E. Woodward, July 1st

Hippert, Jacob M. and Louisa Hays, Oct. 8th

Hudson, Andrew J. and R. Ellen Bachelor, April 8th

Huff, Samuel P. and Bettie Jurey, Aug. 7th

Humphrey, John and Sarah F. Page, Jan. 15th

Hardest, Jo. R. L., and Susan M. Ficklin, June 18th

Hudson, Andrew J. and Rebecca E. Bachellor, April 8th

Huff, Samuel P. and Bettie A. Jurey, Aug. 7th

Hennesey, Jno. and Sarah F. Page, Jan. 15th

Hawkin, Robert A. and Emiline R. Haskins, Nov. 27th

Hancock, Chas. and Kate Thurmond, July 8th

Hartnagel, Fred and Mary E. Goodwin, Sept. 14th

Haislip, Henry and Mary Harlow, Dec. 3rd

Hepburn, And. D. and Henrietta McGuffey, July 10th

Humphreys, P. H. and Ann E. Harlow, May 28th

Harris, B. F. and Nancy F. Wood, Sept. 16th

Harris, C. W. and Angelina E. Via, Oct. 1st

Hinkle, John and Maria L. Keaton, Sept. 24th

Hapkins, Joseph J. and Mary E. Stratton, Dec. 9th

Hurt, Wm. and Mary Dudley, May 31st

Hix, William, Jr., and S. A. Sprouce, Feb 5th

1858

Hamner, Robert and Agnes C. Hamner, Jan. 25th

Harris, J. S. and Mary S. Maupin, Dec. 16th

Harris, Julius A. and Elizabeth E. Lipscomb, Jan. 15th

Harris, William M. and Cynthia J. Maupin, Dec. 16th

Hedrick, George and Nancy F. Catterton, Oct. 20th

Henderson, Frank W. and Mary S. Crawford, Jan. 1st

Horton, John S. and Rachel M. Hernson, Feb. 25th

Huckstep, Benjamin J. and Mildred A. Wood, Feb. 20th

Hughes, Lilburn and Elizabeth Ashlin, May 1st

Humphrey, James T. and Susan M. Clark, Nov. 22nd

Harris, Julius A. and Eliz. E. Lipscomb, June 17th

Hughes, Lilbun and Eliz. Asklin, May 2nd

Humphrey, Jas. T. and Susan M. Clarke, Nov. 24th

Hedrick, Geo. and Nancy F. Catterton, Oct. 28th

Harris, Oswin S. and Mary S. Maupin, Dec. 21st

Harris, Wm. M. and Cynthia J. Maupin, Dec. 21st

Hamner, Robert and Agnes E. Hamner, Jan. 28th

Harlon, John S. and Rebecca M. Herndon, March 3rd

Henderson, Frank M. and Mary S. C. Crawford, Jan. 7th

1859

Haislip, Henry and Mary Harlow, Dec. 29th

Harlow, James S. and Margaret Birkhead, Dec. 27th

Harrison, William B. and Ellen W. Randolph, May 9th

Head, William S. and E. E. Head, Dec. 19th

Herring, Tandy and Mary Jane Carver, Dec. 20th

Houchens, Robert M. and Emily F. Beach, Nov. 7th

Howard, Thompson P. and Emily E. Eastham, Oct. 22nd

Howard, Thompson P. and Emily E. Eastham, Oct. 25th

Herring, Tandy and Mary Jane Carver, Dec. 22nd

Head, Wm. S. and Eliza E. Head, Dec. 22nd

1860

Harlow, G. W. and M. G. Beach, Dec. 24th

Harris, Jacoby F. and Columbia A. Norris, Oct. 16th

Harris, James O. and Maria L. Sparrow, Oct. 16th

Herndon, Edward J. and Margaret A. Burch, March 12th

Herrick, James B. and Sophia M. Bledsoe, June 18th

Hubard, James L. and Isetta C. Randolph, Nov. 13th

Harris, Jas. O. and Maria L. McSparron, Oct. 23rd

Harris, Hawkey, F. and Columbia A. Morris, Oct. 22nd

Hubbard, Jas. L. and Isretta C. Randolph, Nov. 13th

Herndon, Edw. L. and Margaret A. Burch, March 13th

Harlow, Geo. W. and Mary F. Beach, Dec. 27th

1861

Hancock, Gustaver A. and Lillie J. Wunbest, June 15th

Harden, James and Eliza Goodman, May 8th

Harris, S. A., and V. L. Harris, Oct. 17th

Harris, William H. and Susan A. Garrison, Dec. 18th

Harts, David and S. Highlander, Dec. 3rd

Head, Henry E. and Lucy F. Jeffries, Jan. 7th

Haskell, Alex C. and Rebecca Singleton, Sept. 10th

Hudson, B. G. and Sarah A. Wingfield, Oct. 30th

Hutchinson, George W. and Lucy Jane Johnson, Oct. 28th

Harden, James and Eliz. A. Goodman, May 9th

Hartz, David and Stima Highlander, Dec. 4th

Harris, Wm. A. and Susan A. Garrison, Dec. 19th

Hall, Reuben W. and Lucy F. Flint, Dec. 26th

Houchens, Geo. W. and Lucy A. Johnson, Oct. 29th

Head, Henry E. and Lucy F. Jefferies, Jan. 16th

Hancock, G. A. and Lilly J. Wimbish, June 8th

Harris, S. A. and V. S. Harris, Oct. 17th

Hudson, B. G. and Sarah A. Wingfield, Oct. 31st

1862

Hanison, Chas. A. and Martha F. Garrison, Nov. 13th

Herbert, Benj. and Lutelia M. Bailey, Oct. 29th

Hancock, David E. and Nettie H. Thurmond, April 21st

Heiskell, Felix and Louisia S. Halback, Aug. 5th

Hansbrough, David and Viena S. Fretwell, Feb. 18th

Huff, James W. and Molly A. McSparren, Dec. 24th

1863

Henson, Wm. H. and Maria A. Hoage, Jan. 1st

Harris, Bernard and Aug. S. Powell, Nov. 17th

Harris, Henry and Emma J. Bibb, Nov. 25th

Head, Agretus W. and Lavina Updike, Dec. 22nd

Harlow, Allen M. and Eliza Ashland, Sept. 3rd

Hidgen, Wm. I. and Mildred E. Moon, July 31st

1864

Hodges, David and Elizabeth Via, March 10th

Head, T. V. and Mary F. Feaganes, Jan. 14th

Hancock, Rich'd. J. and Thomasia O. Harris, Nov. 19th

1865

Hall, John E. and Isabella H. Turner, Feb. 22nd

Hall, Reuben W. and Lucy C. Bishop, Oct. 16th

Harden, John N. and Susan C. Eubank, Jan. 6th

Harlow, Thomas J. and Margaret S. Gibson, Feb. 27th

Harrison, Charles C. and Cornelia E. C. Rives, Dec. 23rd

Hays, Thomas C. and Emilia J. Johnston, Jan. 30th

Herron, John H. and Lucy A. Priddy, July 20th

Hobgood, John H. and Jannie Twole, Dec. 12th

Houchins, Charles S. and M. S. Kent, June 18th

Hobgood, Jno. H. and Jimmie Toole, Dec. 14th

Hall, Reuben W. and Lucy C. Bishop, Oct. 19th

Herron, Jno. H. and Lucy A. Priddy, July 27th

Houchens, Chas. L. and Martha L. Kent, June 22nd

Harlow, Tho. J. and Margaret L. Gibson, March 6th

Hall, Jno. E. and Isabella H. Turner, Feb. 22nd

Hays, Tho. C. and Emily J. Johnson, Jan. 31st

Harrison, Chas. C. and C. E. C. Rives, Dec. 25th

1866

Haislip, William H. and Frances Haislip, Feb. 26th

Hall, John W. and Anne E. Dillard, May 18th

Hall, Reuben W. and Lucy F. Flint, Dec. 23rd

Hame, Lewis D. and Lucy E. Young, Oct. 3rd

Harman, Daniel and Susan Wood, March 13th

Harris, Lewis and Sarah Rives, Oct. 25th

Hedgiman, Obediah and Mary Scott, May 18th

Hester, Forester and Martha Smith, May 18th

Hughes, Madison and Lucy Jones, May 5th

Humphreys, George S. and Samantha S. Wood, Oct. 15th

Hutchins, George D. and Sarah Ann Gibson, March 1st

Herndon, Theo. and Isabella F. Wood, Dec. 12th

Hawkins, Robt. A. and Mary E. Smith, Dec. 18th

Harman, Daniel and Susan Wood, March 14th

Harden, Jno. W. and Susan C. Eubank, Jan. 11th

Hutchenson, Geo. D. and Susan A. Gibson, March 1st

Haislip, Wm. H. and Frances A. Haislip, March 1st

Hall, Jno. W. and Ann E. Dillard, May 16th

Humphreys, Geo. A. and Samantha S. Wood, Oct. 18th

Haine, Lewis D. and Lucy E. Young, Oct. 9th

Herns, Lewis and Sarah Rives, Oct. 27th

Hawkins, Robt. A. and Mary E. Smith, Dec. 18th

Harris, Hardy and Polly Taylor, Dec. 24th

Hall, Wm. S. and Sarah F. Wilkerson, Dec. 17th

Hoodward, Theodore H. and Molly A. Wyatt, Dec. 22nd

1867

Hashingle, Andrew and Ellen Taylor, Jan. 15th

Harrison, Geo. F. and Susan Matthews, Jan. 21st

Hawkins, Samuel A. and Emaline R. Hawkins, March 28th

Harris, Daniel and Malinda Morris, April 22nd

Harris, Geo. and Betty Miller, Dec. 25th

Humphreys, I. S. and Susan M. Wood, Nov. 7th

Harris, Wm. and Eliz. Houchens, Nov. 12th

Herndon, Samuel S. and Rose Key, Oct. 8th

Harrison, Geo. F. and Susan Matthews, Jan. 22nd

Hill, Demas L. and Louisia I. Wolfe, July 8th

Harlow, Wm. S. and S. C. Beckhead, Dec. 20th

Harris, Winston and Ellen Coleman, Sept. 14th

Hughes, Burwell and Ella Jackson, Oct. 15th

Harris, James M. and Mollie F. Maupin, Dec. 12th

Herndon, Sam'l S. and Maria E. Trint, Feb. 18th

Humphrey, Wesley J. and Lucy A. Wood, May 6th

Hall, Rich'd. and Emma E. Rives, May 22nd

Hall, Johnson A. and Harriet Wilkerson, Dec. 31st

Hartnagle, Andrew and Ellen Taylor, Jan. 15th

Hall, Rich'd. and Emma E. Rives, May 25th

1868

Houchens, Jesse and Bettie H. Johnson, Feb. 3rd

Himmiman, Chas. F. and Jane Sprouce, March 28th

Humphreys, John B. and Laura J. Munday, June 3rd

Holman, Edmund and Maria Banks, July 6th

Henwes, W. A. and Virg. L. Sinclair, Nov. 18th

Hamner, Wm. J. and Martha E. Tompkins, Dec. 22nd

Harris, Bernard L. and Isabella Gay, Feb. 26th

Humphreys, James F .and Amanda Humphreys, May 9th

Henderson, Henry and Helen Leay, May 26th

Hall, Julian A. and H. E. Wilkerson, Jan. 2nd

1869

Hooper, Napoleon and Ella Mitchell, March 7th

Hopkins, Jno. A. and Sally M. Parrot, April 15th

Hite, R. M. and Susan R. Rose, June 3rd

Huffman, Henry M. and Sarah Lupton, June 10th

Hull, George R. and Columbia Mallory, June 24th

Heath, Thos. S. and Mary S. Cocke, July 11th

Hicks, Ira and E. R. W. Stake, June 29th

Huffman, James H. and Sarah M. Mitchell, July 13th

Harris, Joseph and Mary Maupin, July 4th

Hicks, Waller and M. F. Cangean, Aug. 19th

Hudson R. F. and Elizabeth Gay, Sept. 9th

Hughes, C. May and Mary M. Buck, Sept. 1st

1870

Henderson, Wm. and Sally Brown, Jan. 29th

Hawkins, Addison and M. A. Shelton, Jan. 20th

Hamner, R. M. and S. M. Wingfield, Jan. 20th

Hally, Skiler and Permillia Lane, Feb. 12th

Heller, A. B. and F. A. Litterman, March 13th

Harris, Beverley and Julia Gohannah, April 16th

Hays, Thomas H. and Mildred J. Robertson, Feb. 17th

Harris, W. and Mary White, April 24th

Hart, J. A. and M. A. Spears, May 23rd

Howard, James and Julia Maupin, Dec. 17th

Howard, Jacob and Nancy Michie, Dec. 29th

Hicks, Geo. W. and Millie Scott, Dec. 23rd

1871

Harris, Geo. and Lydia Wiatt, Jan. 15th

Harlan, Isaac H. and Oct. S. Elliott, Feb. 23rd

Hudson, James R. and E. C. Minor, June 21st

Henderson, Thos and Ella Reisley, Sept. 10th

Howard, Conway R. and Jane Colston, Sept. 12th

Hempstead, Fay and Gertrude O'Neal, Sept. 13th

Harlow John and Martha Dove, Sept. 26th

Hemphill, David and Lucy Everett Singleton, Nov. 1st

Hudson, James Walter and Laura Abney Jefferies, Nov. 29th

Hanckel, Louis Frapman and Ida Macon, Dec. 19th

1872

Hall, Richard W. and Maria O. Turner, Jan. 9th

Harlowe, Richard L. and Adeline Dudley, Jan. 25th

Harris, James A. and Margaret A. Gionanni, March, 21st

Hill, Olengo and Sallie B. Robertson, Sept. 17th

Harrison, John and Anne C. Pegram, Nov. 19th

Hall, Richard and Louisa F. Norvell, Nov. 6th

Hall, Lucien and Henrietta Jarman, Nov. 7th

Herndon, Theophilus and Lucy M. Clements, Nov. 7th

Hurley, Patrick and Mattie Mann, Nov. 23rd

Hall, Wm. Frank and M. A. Bramham, Nov. 27th

Houchens, W. T. and B. E. Bailey, Feb. 18th

Harrison, John and Anne C. Pegram, Nov. 19th

1873

Howard, N. B. and Susan E. Hall, April 7th

Herring, H. C. and Mary E. Edwards, April 15th

Holladay Waller and Kate M. Emerson, June 21st

Houchens, Jas. R. and Rebecca Prico, Sept. 9th

Hamner, Zach. T. and Laura J. Brown, Nov. 3rd

Hill, Wm. C. and Fannie A. Crewdson, Nov. 13th

Herron, Walker Alex and Bettie D. Baber, Dec. 13th

Henderson, Alexander and Suky Mickie, Dec. 27th

1874

Hamner, S. N. and Willie P. Childress, Jan. 9th

Hoard, Dr. R. L. and Fanny M. Stack, Oct. 5th

Herring, John H. and Nancy M. Smith, Oct. 13th

1875

Houchens, Chas. W. and Emma J. Davis, Feb. 16th

Harlowe, Jas. M. and Sally F. Johnson, Jan. 13th

Hill, J. F. and Sarah E. Estes, Feb. 25th

Herring, Alfred C. and Betty A. Smith, March 29th

Hogg, Francis and Georgianna Heath, March 29th

Hurt, John and Emma J. Dudley, April 26th

Hanf, Angush and Mary Bachrack, May 11th

Hall, Jno. R. and Mary S. Walton, June 23rd

Hurt, Jno. A. and Martha A. Bunch, Sept. 22nd

Herring, Bland and Mary Shiflett, Nov. 19th

1876

Huff, Jas. Wm. and Sallie Twyman, April 10th

Hudson, Chas. B. and Anna P. Giles, Sept. 23rd

Hamner, Robt. M. and Ellen M. Wingfield, Oct. 14th

Holloway, Jas. N. and Emma W. Foloines, Nov. 6th

Hicks, James Carter and Willy Ann Sprouse, Jan. 25th

Huck, Henry J. and Margaret D. Brown, Feb. 28th

Holliday, Albert S. and Nannie W. Eastham, May 14th

1877

Hanger, Jacob A. and Marietta W. Dawson, Feb. 3rd

Harlowe, Jno. L. and Eliza A. Madison, July 7th

Hamner, Edw. C. and Bettie White, Sept. 26th

Hale, Benj. F. and Florale Maupin, Nov. 26th

Hoffman, Jas. F. and Mary E. Lane, Nov. 28th

Hill, Jas. H. and Marcy C. Estis, Jan. 23rd

Houchens, Sam'l. D. and Elizabeth E. Strange, May 12th

1878

Houchens, Franklin C. and Betty K. Clarke, Jan. 17th

Henry, William and Fanny C. Brown, Feb. 20th

Harding, Lewis A. and Bettie J. Hawkins, Sept. 21st

Herring, James A. and Mollie E. Raynor, July 1st

Hawthorne, Jno. T. and Jeannie B. Harris, Dec. 2nd

Harmon, Chas. W. and Annie M. Warwick, Dec. 18th

Haggard, Henry F. and Willie P. Thomas, Dec. 25th

Harlow, Thos. J. and Margaret S. Shackleford, Jan. 15th

Herndon, George P. and Druisilla L. Seamond, Nov. 28th

Haney, John M. and Maria Garland, July 25th

1879

Howard, Charles M. and Virginia McCamant, Feb. 10th

Harris, Ellis F. and Ida E. Woodson, Feb. 14th

Harris, Samuel W. and Mary E. Meeks, Feb. 25th

Herring, William W. and Mary F. Herring, Sept. 23rd

Hamner, Zachariah F. and Eva Boag, Dec. 10th

Hicks, Peyton and Mildred Sprouse, Dec. 9th

Harrison, James P. and Mary J. Davis, Feb. 13th

Harlow, Rubin N. and Elizabeth M. Phillips, Aug. 21st

1880

Hughes, Wm. F. and Rosa Dudley, Nov. 15th

Harlowe, O. S. and M. J. Raynor, Aug. 26th

Hamner, Samuel H. and Virginia A. Dillard, March 2nd

Herndon, Rascal R. and Doriah M. Creel, Oct. 28th

Hall, William J. and Mahala T. Harlowe, Dec. 6th

Hardin, Winfield S. and Mollie S. Beale, Dec. 22nd

Harris, John C. and Fannie B. Salmon, Dec. 20th

1881

Henderson, Micajah and Angelina Mosby, Jan. 29th

Hanfs, Chas. and Callie Talbertha Bachanah, March 23rd

Hull, James P. and Nannie B. Modena, Sept. 2nd

Harlow, John and Tabida Mitchell, Dec. 29th

Herndon, Mat and Ann Lindsay, Jan. 22nd

Hunter, Clarence J. and Eliza M. Bailey, Feb. 16th

1882

Holliday, James P. and Mary E. Dillard, Feb. 8th

Hackett, Chapman J. and Mary E. Murray, Feb. 10th

Harris, James F. and Catharine L. Hall, May 25th

Harris, Chas. E. and Josephine G. Rogers, Sept. 6th

Hughes, George S. and Nellie Johnson, Oct. 25th

Herring, William E. and Sarah P. Johnson, Dec. 7th

Hicks, William W. and M. J. Sprouse, Dec. 28th

Harris, Edgar T. and Parmelia O. Hilderbrand, 'May 23rd

1883

Hamner, James E. and Ella Nora Elsom, Jan. 25th

Houchens, Joseph B. and Mary L. Thornton, May 6th

Humphrey, Peter Anderson and Ida Chapman Wood, May 23rd

Hilbers, William and Alice Maria Stephens, June 5th

Hayden, James Luther and Ellen McGregor Maury, June 12th

Herndon, Zachary B. and Julia K. DeVeaux, July 26th

Harris, Wm. Samuel and Sarah Eliz Shackleford, Oct. 21st

Holmes, James Henry and Nanny Spicer, April 30th

Hopkins, Alfred and Mary Turner, Oct. 15th

1884

Herring, Henry A. and Eliza Marshall, Dec. 6th

Hurt, Wm. and Mary Annie Wingfield, Dec. 21st

Hogan, Wm. Allen and Sarah Jane Wood, Dec. 15th

Hancock, John C. and Sally E. Dodd, Dec. 20th

Hall, John Rice and Mary F. Hilderbrand, Jan. 21st

Harrison, Robt. Lucius and Lillian Elsom, Jan. 30th

Houchens, R. B. and Molly R. Walsh, March 16th

Hopkins, Floyd and Ann Williams, April 1st

Hart, Morris, Jr. and Mary E. Leonard, May 15th

Hissch, Sam'l. Edgar and Gussie Lazams, Oct. 8th

Harris, James C. and Mattie P. Atkins, Oct. 22nd

Harris, Frank W. and Alice F. Bishop, Oct. 22nd

Hawkins, Young and Willie Ann Powell, Oct. 30th

Hawkins, Edward P. and Emma Jane Hughson, Nov. 6th

1885

Holley, Wm. L. and Alice L. Snow, Jan. 22nd

Hadin, Wm. E. and Sarah A. Turner, Feb. 3rd

Hagawin, James and Sophia H. Leterman, March 3rd

Hunt, Jas. M. and Laura C. Baber, April 26th

Hawley, Jno. Thos. and Fanny Eilburt, June 25th

Harlis, Jas. Henry and Florena Aimes, Sept. 12th

Hartman, Jacob N. and Mary S. Boothe, Oct. 21st

Hayslett, Wm. G. and Lucy F. Hughson, Dec. 22nd

Herman, John and Margaret Munday, Dec. 24th

Hughes, John and Molly Jarman, Dec. 24th

1886

Hudson, Clarence H. and Annie P. Terrell, Jan. 26th

Hinkle, Sam. W. and ·Matla W. Marshall, Feb. 24th

Henry, John F. and Mary F. Lamb, March 6th

Harman, Dan'l. Jr., and Fannie Murphy, March 9th

Haden, Camillus B. and Sallie B. Hawthorne, July 17th

Houidges, Richard J. and Margaret L. Cuer, Aug. 26th

Hattesley, John and Mary S. Garland, Oct. 19th

Haislip, Walter B. and Anne Lee Elsom, Oct. 26th

Hall, John R. and Millie W. Mayo, Dec. 1st

Hawley, Chas. E. and Mattie J. Gillum, Dec. 6th

Haecker, J. F. and Susannah Leis, Dec. 26th

1887

Harlowe, Walter L. and Maggie Paverill, Jan. 6th

Herring, Alfred and Alfretta M. Shiflett, May 19th

Harris, J. Leigh and Adeline Dudley, June 8th

Hawkins, B. F. and L. J. Powell, Dec. 14th

1888

Harris, Jas. W. and Dora L. Estes, Jan. 3rd

Heron, Jno. A. and Emma J. Moran, Feb. 23rd

Hinley, Robt. L. and Emma F. Hall, March 5th

Hinshelwood, G. G. and Annie M. Dawson, March 29th

Howell, Chas. E. and Jennie Womack, April 13th

Harris, Fred and Malvin Huff, Feb. 24th

Harlow, J. H. and E. M. Bunton, June 6th

Harlow, Richard and Peggy Harlow, Aug. 15th

Hoeberle, J. and L. M. Hacker, Dec. 21st

Hall, Dock and Josh A. Blackwell, June 19th

1889

Hall, Asa R. and Laura M. Bruce, Feb. 18th
Hurt, M. Jr., and M. S. Laumo, Feb. 25th
Henry, Thos. and Mary S. Marshall, March 28th
Holly, Eugene and Lucy F. Durrett, June 20th
Herring, T. B. and A. F. Marshall, Aug. 9th
Hendon, Geo. I. and Nannie F. Walton, Sept. 4th
Harris, G. S. and Annie I. Gilliam, Oct. 15th
Hackett, C. F., and N. M. Shanks, Dec. 23rd

1890

Hall, Edgar and Eliza Powell, Feb. 5th
Hunt, H. S. and D. L. Wood, Feb. 26th
Harlow, Clifton and Mary S. Harlow, April 7th
Haynes, W. H. and M. F. Baber, May 19th
Hite, Benj. and Ida A. Harris, June 4th
Humphrey, Jno. D. and D. M. Johnson, July 5th
Herron, L. H. and J. B. Baber, July 22nd
Harris, T. A. and M. V. Childress, Sept. 29th
Horsby, A. C. and W. C. Gilmer, Oct. 21st
Harlow, Jno. L. and Lucy Jane Sprouse, Oct. 28th
Hasnold, W. and A. M. Kellerer, Oct. 28th
Hooper, N. B. and Cora L. Melton, Nov. 18th
Harlow, E. J. and Olive B. Hall, Nov. 26th

1891

Harlow, Jno. W. and Mary Amos, Jan 28th
Hilderbrand, J. W. and W. C. Hilderbrand, April 30th
Hite, J. W. and C. J. Thornton, June 3rd
Hughes, E. L. and Jennie L. James, June 1st
Harris, Lewis H. and J. L. Wood, Sept. 28th
Harley, Clement and Mary L. Bragg, Nov. 7th
Hass, O. B. and N. J. Baber, Dec. 24th
Harvie, Wm. and Lilly Clements, Dec. 26th
Hicks, Henry and Lucy Brown, Dec. 31st

1892

Harris, Wm. H. and A. C. Stargell, Feb. 15th
Hughes, J. H. and A. M. Collins, April 11th
Houchens, E. J. and A. B. Pace, May 23rd
Hilman, L. G. and C. M. Wingfield, July 11th
Huckstep, J. D. and S. L. Via, Oct. 17th
Harbuer, Jo. and M. E. Leathers, Oct. 24th
Harlow, Chas. E. and Anetta Mallory, Nov. 21st
Hunt, Jas. B. and Dora L. Parr, Dec. 27th

1893

Helfrick, D. A. and Rusha Goodloe, Jan. 24th
Harlow, W. B. and M. C. Price, June 15th
Herndon, Jno. W. and Sarah N. Brown, June 26th
Harris, R. N. and Fanny Rodes, Sept. 22nd
Hopkins, R. D. and G. L. Porter, Oct. 4th
Hudson, Willis H. and Annie C. Mowyer, Dec. 26th
Hudson, Geo. and Laura Price, Sept. 6th
Hall, Lewis and M. C. Thacker, Dec. 4th

1894

Hughes, E. B. and W. T. Dudley, March 10th
Hall, R. M. and E. E. Wilkerson, April 20th
Huckstep, P. J. and M. S. Lupton, June 4th
Harlow, Geo. M. and Mollie A. Hall, Sept. 18th
Herring, Geo. I. and Lyda L. Yowell, Nov. 27th
Haynes, R. B. and K. D. Gentry, Oct. 27th
Hoy, L. J. and Leanna Holly, Nov. 5th
Hunt, H. W. and M. D. Kirby, Nov. 12th
Herring, Lorin Zo. M. and Alice Creasey, Dec. 24th
Hines, J. L. and A. A. Winn, Dec. 25th

1895

Harlow, Miles B. and Ida B. Birckhead, Jan. 28th
Harris, G. T. and C. A. Perkins, Feb. 19th
Harlow, Robt. O. and Alice Gianny, Feb. 27th
Harris, E. G. and B. E. Morris, Feb. 27th
Harlow, Jno. and L. M. Mitchell, Mar. 24th
Hughes, H. C. and Nora Leake, April 21st
Hart, Jno. M. and C. O. Harris, May 1st
Head, C. A. and L. B. Sinclair, June 19th
Haislipe, Wm. J. and C. E. Thomas, Sept. 16th
Humbert, G. L. and N. C. Wood, Oct. 3rd
Hamilton, Jno. B. and N. C. Bragg, Nov. 9th
Harlow, J. H. and Christian Maddox, Nov. 27th
Hamm, G. S. and L. R. Taylor, Dec. 18th
Hicks, M. and Lucy A. Wood, Dec. 21st
Head, Charlie W. and Lucy A. Smith, June 14th

1896

Hoffman, Chas. and Farie Phillips, June 23rd
Hoffman, Jas. R. an Nora O. Harlow, June 23rd
Harris, Jacob Dexter and Bertha Drene Newcombe, July 22nd
Henson, H. E. and Sally Shelton, Nov. 2nd
Harris, E. L. and F. M. Bowen, Aug. 8th
Hewett, F. R. and F. M. Meade, Sept. 2nd
Hicks, J. W. and L. B. McAllister, Sept. 11th
Harris, H. A. and Mrs. Bessie James, Nov. 3rd
Houchens, J. F. and Birdie Amoes, Nov. 15th
Harlow, E. E. and F. K. Marsh, Nov. 18th
Hapkinson, Jno. and Florence R. Barlow, Dec. 8th
Hunt, Wm. and Lula F. Drumheller, Dec. 10th
Harris, R. A. and Sallie J. Harlow, Dec. 23rd

1897

Hase, Geo. A. and Augie L. Sullivan, Jan. 19th
Hunt, Harry H. and Edna E. Sutherland, Jan. 22nd
Hudson, T. P. and Julia Thacker, Jan. 26th
Harlow, W. M. and M. G. Leake, March 3rd
Harlow, Dudley F. and Emma I. Harlow, April 17th
Holt, Fred G. and Mamie A. Payne, June 1st

Herndon, W. H. and A. J. Bishop, June 21st
Hudson, Wm. L. and L. C. Bennett, Aug. 3rd
Halvis, G. and K. V. Barnes, Aug 27th
Harlow, E. F. and S. B. Sandridge, Sept. 13th
Humphreys, J. D. and Mattie Carter, Oct. 23rd
Haislip, Napolean and Mary C. Meeks, Nov. 24th
Hulvey, E. G. and M. M. Davis, Dec. 16th
Humphreys, E. E. and M. E. Keener, Dec. 25th
Harris, Lewis H. and Gertrude Brown, Dec. 27th

1898

Hitchcock, J. S. and Mary W. Bryan, April 1st
Houchens, C. N. and Kate Gianniny, April 9th
Hill, T. M. and E. E. Gentry, Sept. 6th
Howlin, Dr. J. B. and Roberta E. Hall, Sept. 20th
Hamner, Jno. L. and L. B. Wingfield, Oct. 10th
Houchens, Felix and Daisy A. Lane, Oct. 19th
Harlow, E. W. and Elsie Blake, Nov. 16th

1899

Harris, L. V. and S. C. Ballard, Jan. 2nd
Hutchins, G. S. and K. B. Hill, Jan. 17th
Harrison, J. C. and Rosalie Smith, Jan. 24th
Hall, Jerry M. and Lois E. Norford, April 15th
Huffman, S. H. and Julia Green, April 21st
Howell, G. S. and Mary S. Canaday, June 12th
Harding M. L. and M. E. Pace, June 14th
Harlow, E. L. and Lucy Morris, July 5th
Harris, H. S. and M. B. Bishop, July 24th
Herron, Dowell W. and Maud M. Baber, Oct. 14th
Henson, H. E. and Sally Shelton, Nov. 2nd
Haynes, Thomas and Eliz. F. Maury, Nov. 2nd
Harris, Henry H. and Sally Thomas, Nov. 2nd
Houchens, S. L. and R. E. Mawyer, Nov 11th
Haynes, J. E. and F. L. Eades, Nov. 25th
Hegro, Antonio and Emma J. Morris, Dec. 21st
Harlow, Newton and Susie Kennan, Dec. 26th

1900

Haden, Victor B. and Octavis A. Gibson, July 14th
Howell, G. W. and E. Amiss, Sept. 4th
Head, P. and A. S. Norris, Sept. 12th
Harris, Joseph and Rosa Shiflett, Sept. 18th
Head, J. W. and C. E. Rhodes, Oct. 2nd
Hamner, J. E. and Sallie Dudley, Oct. 10th
Herring, G. Wm. and Carrie P. Norvell, Nov. 5th
Harlow, Nath. and Ellener Clements, Nov. 5th
Hanckel, Louis L. and Amy C. Nelson Nov. 15th
Haynes, M. L. and S. M. Wingfield, Nov. 28th
Hartley, G. W. and Stella Lyons, Dec. 8th
Houchens, J. W. and M. R. Barnett, March 6th
Harding, A. J. and Mary L. Martin, April 6th
Harlow, Horton and Mary Wingfield, May 8th
Harris, J. O. and M. E. Harris, Dec. 15th

Harrington, Addison S. and Laura Baxter, Dec. 18th
Humphrey, W. T. and Lizzie C. Thurston, Dec. 19th
Horton, Geo. K. and Sarah A. Jones, Dec. 26th
Humphrey, Jas. L. and Mary A. Garrison, Dec. 29th

1901

Harlow, M. C. and B. F. Baltimore, Jan. 2nd
Hall, Jake and Mollie Jones, Feb. 26th
Harmon, C. L. and S. T. Moss, April 23rd
Harris, E. B. and L. E. Omohundro, April 23rd
Herron, Eddie P. and Cora V. Dickerson, April 30th
Harlow, Rosser and Lizzie Hill, July 11th
Herring, Chas. R. and M. V. Madison, Sept. 10th
Hanley, E. and S. Owen, Nov. 8th
Hawley, T. J. and L. M. Starks, Dec. 10th
Harris, Clinton V. and Annie L. Crawford, Dec. 24th
Harler, R. E. and M. A. Spencer, Dec. 26th

1902

Heiman, Geo. E. and Bertie B. Howard, Feb. 8th
Hisle, C. R. and K. V. Gentry, Feb. 18th
Harris, W. H. and Lottie B. Haney, Feb. 22nd
Humbert, J. L. and M. L. Durrett, March 22nd
Hudson, L. R. and L. L. Giddings, May 15th
Hall, J. M. and S. B. Ballard, June 3rd
Harlow, W. B. and H. A. McDonald, June 5th
Hendricks, Frank S. and Mary A. Garrette, July 1st
Harlow, Teed A. and Fannie W. Payne, Oct. 4th
Harlow, Sam and Laura Etta Kirby, Oct. 15th
Herring, Lucian C. and Ada B. Thurman, Oct. 30th
Hartman, B. C. and Carrie Cox, Oct. 8th

1903

Harris, Ed. A. and Emma G. Sipe, Jan. 29th
Hudson, W. W. and P. Brokinbraugh, Feb. 25th
Head, Weller H. and Mary E. Propes, March 6th
Herring, Jack and Lula Maude Madison, May 25th
Hensler, J. E. and M. F. Marshall, Sept. 21st
Harbottle, Geo. and S. Alice Sinclair, Oct. 27th
Huckstep, J. H. and N. A. Marshall, Nov. 2nd
Herndon, M. P. and Lula W. Garrison, Nov. 17th
Hurt, Wm. H. and Mary Eliz Wills, Dec. 21st
Hany, Normand M. and Sally Mary Sandridge, Dec. 26th

1904

Harris, John Calvin and Mrs. Fannie M. Spicer, Jan. 21st
Hall, Manice B. and Hester A. Shiflett, Feb. 18th

Hogshead, Geo. H. and Millie Lee Page, March 8th

Haggard, J. M. and S. E. Hall, April 4th

Henrichs, Jacob H. and Laura M. Shepherd, May 4th

Hilderbrand, J. W. Jr. and Susan A. Fielding, May 30th

Hurt, Jas. E. and Mattie V. Newton, June 29th

Harris, Jno. L. and Mattie L. Stargall, July 27th

Herring, J. A. and Laura E. Purvis, Aug. 6th

Herndon, S. N. and I. J. Tilman, Sept. 27th

Harlow, Walter and Alice Rhodes, Dec. 15th

1905

Hawkins, Robt. S. and Bessie Perkins, Feb. 15th

Hutcherson, Arthur and Myrtle Ann Harlow, May 13th

Harris, Kelley Y. and Alice P. Dickerson, May 31st

Hackett, Thos. I. and Laura E. Heflin, June 20th

Hamm, Jno. Edmund and Eula Shelton, July 1st

Hickes, Jessie and Maggie Lee Sprouse, Oct. 5th

Hiserman, Russell L. and Edith Bessie Smith, Oct. 10th

Huckstep, Chas. E. and Nora O'Neill Lupton, Nov. 6th

Harris, Charles Henry and Sallie Willis Stargell, Nov. 15th

Hall, B. F. and Emma McDaniel, Oct. 13th

Hoord, Groves C. and Eva V. Brown, Dec. 9th

Houchens, Lucien G. and Nora C. Mawyer, Dec. 22nd

Herring, Bernard and Fanny Shiflett, Dec. 30th

Hall, B. F. and Emma McDaniel, Nov. 13th

Harris, Charles Henry and Sallie Willie Stoigall, Nov. 15th

Hoard, Grover C. and Eva V. Brown, Dec. 11th

Houchens, Lucian G. and Nora C. Mawyer, Dec. 20th

1906

Huff, Walter George and Eva Baber, Feb. 27th

Hunt, John Calvin and Florie Belle Via, April 4th

Harlow, Lee and Cora Reynor, April 17th

Hopkins, John William and Birdie Williams, June 1st

Holloway, Chas. Burgess and Nannie Virginia Bellamy, June 19th

Hosberle, Jacob L. and Martha J. Sutler, July 18th

Hughes, John J. and Mary L. Johnson, July 25th

Hunt, William H. and Dora L. Harris, July 25th

Hall, Lewis and Mrs. Louisa Jane Campbell, July 27th

Houchens, Thomas E. and Annie Ray, Oct. 21st

Harris, William R. and Dora Jennie Oliver, Nov. 3rd

Hopkins, Edward P. and Mabel Y. Williams, Nov. 6th

Hawkins, Archie W. and Edith V. Warren, Nov. 21st

Hardisere, Patrick T. and Mary A. Lane, Nov. 24th

Hutchinson, Lacy E. and Katie Vest, Dec. 25th

1907

Hodger, C. S. and S. Amelia Sweaney, Feb. 2nd

Houchens, Reuben J. and Maggie Birkhead, March 1st

Hall, W. I. and D. V. McClary, June 23rd

Humphrey, Melvin A. and Sallie M. Eheart, July 17th

Herndon, W. L. and Bettie C. Burton, Sept. 19th

Hall, Eddie and Nettie Bruce, Nov. 27th

Holt, Fred G. and Mrs. Lillie M. Kirig, Nov. 17th

Hobbs, Chas. K. and Mattie Y. Page, Nov. 19th

Haggard, Maury E. and Helen G. Carter, Nov. 21st

Hudson, James E. and Lucy R. Amos, Nov. 27th

1908

Harlan, G. T. and Fannie V. Payne, Jan. 8th

Harper, George Russell and Fannie Mary Burgess, Jan. 20th

Hamner, Robert A. and Laura B. Robinson, June 3rd

Hawkins, James L. and Mrs. Willie R. Rinehart, June 10th

Harlow John and Lizzie Tomlin, July 27th

Hurtt, James W. and Mary Estelle Kirby, Sept. 23rd

Hatfield, William H. and Lida H. Rankine, Oct. 1st

Hall Benjamin F. and Clara N. Maddex, Nov. 4th

Holladay, William D. and Laura Smith, Nov. 12th

Houchens, William R. and Edna E. Mawyer, Dec. 6th

Hanger, Stuart and Minnie Ross, Dec. 9th

Henry, Thomas and Virginia Bettor, Dec. 22nd

Hughes, Sam C. and Bessie Harris, Dec. 23rd

1909

Herron, William and Ida Mawyer, Jan. 23rd

Huff, William and Berta Sacre, May 5th

Hardin, Samuel L. H. and Mrs. Irene Herndon, May 6th

Humphrey, Wesley J. and Dora Jones, Sept. 26th

Humphreys, Melvin and Sadie Morris, Sept. 28th

Harris, R. Frank and Carrie Munday, Oct. 16th

1910

Hall, Charlie and Lucy M. Shiflett, Jan. 26th

Harris, Allen C. and Mary E. Hicks, May 4th

Hackett, Alfred and Lila Sneed, May 25th

Holberton, Richard R. and Mary A. Whately, June 29th

Hill, Henry and Mannie Atkins, Aug. 1st

Haden, Abner E. and Clara B. Shepherd, Sept. 7th

Hunt, Arthur and Rosa Baber, Sept. 15th

Harler, Herbert E. and Anna C. Easton, Oct. 25th

Harris, Willie J. and Aeba J. Thomas, Oct. 27th

Hibbet, Robert W. and Adonna J. Hamner, Nov. 10th

Herndon, Ben Louis and Pearl Mayo, Dec. 18th

Hughes, John J. and Sallie M. Cleveland, Dec. 22nd

Hubbard, James B. and Edmonia G. Douglass, Dec. 26th

Houchens, C. B. and Annie L. McGhee, Dec. 27th

1911

Hilderbrand, Edward P. and Lucy Peregoy, Jan. 19th

Herron, Leonard L. and Annie L. Miller, Feb. 15th

Henderlite, John and Bessie Raynor, April 9th

Holly, Cary and Alice Shiflett, April 25th

Hill, Henry D. and Lydia Bowen, July 29th

Humphreys, John D. and Lula Jackson, Aug. 17th

Henry, N. L. and S. F. Anderson, Aug. 19th

Heck, William Harry and Anna S. Tuttle, Sept. 9th

Hale, Willie Greene and Bettie Lee Hurtt, Sept. 21st

Hackett, Japas and Olive Minter, Nov. 12th

Hitchinson, Arthur and Bertie Gibson, Nov. 19th

Herron, Elwood D. and Sarah L. Hackett, Nov. 22nd

Hackett, Otis and Alma Farley, Dec. 2nd

Hansberger, Wilbur T. and Ruth E. Hamner, Dec. 23rd

Hensley, Hearst and Annie Henning, Dec. 30th

1912

Henderson, Howard and Violer Perry, Jan. 1st

Hicks, James E. and Mary S. Kirby, Jan. 21st

Hopkins, Edward and Bessie B. Marshall, April 21st

Hensley, Joe and Lou Marshall, May 15th

Herring, Alvah and Marier Leibeck, June 26th

Holly, Fleming and Pearl Mitchell, July 16th

Hawkins, William B. and Grace A. Kirby, July 20th

Haden, W. D. and Sallie C. Pugh, July 25th

Houchens, H. S. and Ruth Clark, Aug. 7th

Harris, Jr., Charles B. and Alexina L. Harrison, Oct. 2nd

Hurt, William and Mary Nicholas, Oct. 6th

Hall, John Marvin and Emma I. Railey, Oct. 16th

Hunt, James William and Lucy Wood, Oct. 27th

Hick, Walter C. and Fannie V. Goolsby, Dec. 22nd

1913

Huckstep, Josiah P. and Mrs. Ethel Bruce, April 8th

Harbottle, Arthur and Lotta V. Falwell, April 15th

Harlow, Samuel E. and Mary Stone, May 18th

Hoy, John G. and Sally Kesterson, May 15th

Hicks, Edgar and Minera Gibson, June 11th

Harlow, George C. and Emma E. Adlington, June 18th

Harrell, Theodore C. and Ruth Jones, June 25th

Holler, Cleaveland and Pear Dillard, July 14th

Hensley, Herbert and Lillie Mitchell, Sept. 1st

Herndon, William L. and Amanda B. Carroll, Oct. 30th

Herring, Wilmer and Alice Herring, Dec. 24th

1914

Houchens, William A. and Nellie V. Bailey, Feb. 18th

Herring, Henry L. and Virginia Morris, April 8th

Hackett, Halimore and Lillian Critzer, April 13th

Henckel, John R. and Mattie L. Drumheller, April 14th

Hilton, R. S. and Ethel F. McLeod, May 30th

Hoy, Silvester and Maggie Parr, July 10th

Herron, J. A. and Mattie Mawyer, Aug. 24th

Harris, Frank S. and Mrs. Bettie M. Lewis, Sept. 23rd

Harlow, Richard and Lucy R. Bibb, Oct. 22nd

Hughson, Robert B. and Emily L. Williams, Nov. 24th

Hall, Charlie E. and Edith C. Dolen, Dec. 17th

Haly, Samuel and Gertie Shiflett. Dec. 23rd

Houchens, Ernest L. and Margaret I. Loving, Dec. 26th

Hutcherson, James and Viola Crickenbarger, Dec. 28th

1915

Hunt, Richard C. and Susie Ward, April 11th

Hargrase, Boyd W. and Myrtle R. Rea, April 24th

Hamner, Walter G. and Lettie B. Stargel, June 5th

Harris, James S. and Ada M. Butler, July 5th

Harlow, Henry C. and Alice E. Mars, Aug 16th

Howdyshall, S. H. and Susie M. Viar, Aug. 17th

Herring, Russell E. and Willie G. Sandridge, Sept. 16th

Houchens, Harry and Rosa Powell, Sept. 26th

Herdt, Louis J. and Alice L. Bolick, Oct. 10th

Harding, George S. and Clara Pace, Oct. 27th

Hart, Henry and Nobb Winn, Oct. 28th

Herdon, R. B. and Lelia King, Nov. 25th

Houchens, Aubrey and Ethel B. Quick, Dec. 23rd

Hudson, Wm. J. and Joanna Via, Dec. 24th

1916

Haislip, James and Beula Moyer, Jan. 31st

Hensley, Emmett E. and Florence Watson, March 2nd

Haney, C. Franklin and Rosa May Morris, May 30th

Hicks, Leslie and Virgie Sprouse, Sept. 27th

Harris, William D. and Mary V. Campbell, Oct. 18th

Holmes, Alan L. and Lucy M. Whakely, Oct. 18th

Hensley, Sim and Eva Birckhead, Nov. 1st

1917

Hall, Price L. and Sarah E. Powell, Jan. 6th

Hensley, Charles Edward and Clemima Conley, Feb. 7th

Hutchinson, Clinton and Nannie Gibson, March 17th

Hall, Wardie and Pearle Wood, May 31st

Hippert, Maxwell A. and Cora Lee Thomas, June 15th

Harlan, William B. and Mary E. Pirkey, July 18th

Harlow, Nat. P. and Sidney Clark, July 25th

Harrower, Harry N. and Annie L. Kidd, July 31st

Howell, Geo. A. and Nora Snow, Aug. 8th

Hamner, Charlie E. and Iris Isabell Newcomb, Oct. 13th

Hall, Archie J. and Gertie M. Allen, Nov. 4th

Harris, Douglass and Edna Burton, Nov. 8th

1918

Harlow, Jefferson C. and Pearl E. Kirby, Jan. 2nd

Harding, Clarence B. and Myrtle V. Layman, Jan. 16th

Hensley, Garfield and Nancy Birckhead, Feb. 5th

Hall, Thomas and Madi Shiflett, April, 5th

Hurtt, Morris, Jr., and Lellie Farish, April 23rd

Huff, Oswin T. and Julia Marshall, Dec. 5th

1919

Harman, John and Vertie McDaniel, Jan. 25th

Hall, Massie and Gladys Maupin, March 7th

Hunt, Judson W. and Florence H. Kirby, April 20th

Harris, Thos. C. and Irene Hughes, April 19th

Hancock, Philip G. and Jessie McW. Sinsel, May, 12th

Hibbert, Robt. Wm. and Mollie Maddox, June 3rd

Higginson, John M. and Helen Carpenter, Aug. 5th

Hunt, Jas. B. and Maggie Wills, Aug. 28th

Hensley, Silas W. and Cora M. Breedin, Sept. 23rd

Haggard, Henry M. and Annie L. Marshall, Nov. 8th

Hall, Robt. M. and Josephine Wood, Dec. 27th

1920

Herron, Hawthorne H. and Margaret E. Freed, Feb. 18th

Howe, Ralph W. and Anna D. Van Wayenen, April 24th

Hall, Robt. Brent and Zada Atlee Walsh, May 29th

Harler, Robt. W. and Susan Ann Smott, Aug. 20th

Huffman, Chauicey O. and Daisy L. Dandridge, Aug. 24th

Haigh, Edward N. and Katie C. Colthust, Sept. 4th

Haisles, J. R. and Sallie Graves, Oct. 1st

Hall, John R. and Elsie M. Bell, Nov. 15th

Harris, Walter Everett and Mable Adline Dudley, Nov. 18th

Herron, Mitchell D. and Frances A. Marshall, Dec. 11th

Haven, Bennie P. and Annie C. Jones, Dec. 27th

1921

Herring, Archie C. and Mrs. Bulah Garizert, Feb. 22nd

Hayslip, Henry E. and Annie E. Clements, March 29th

Hawthorne, Dr. Allen T. and Dorothy Turner, June 1st

Humphrey, William E. and Fannie Va. Wood, June 6th

Hudson Thos. P. and Estelle E. Houchens, July 18th

Hall, Jack and Mary E. Thomas, Sept. 7th

Hunt, William D. and Georgie E. Drumheller, Dec. 21st

Herring Benj. F. and Lolie Bruce, Dec. 29th

1922

Harlow, Bernice E. and Lula R. Johnson, Jan. 13th

Humphrey, Willie and Lottie Sipe, Feb. 25th

Hurtt, Edgar G. and Ruth Houchens, April 14th

Haskins, John W. and Cora E. Warubl, April 19th

Harris, Graham H. and Genevieve P. Langhorne, April 29th

Henwood, James M. and Lydie Sandridge, June 13th

Haynes, Francis A. and Aline C. Smith, July 5th

Hall, John P. and Lula M. Wood, July 9th
Hunter, Albert C. and Eva Ray, Aug. 21st
Hutcherson, Harry L. and Ethel Mae Marrs, Dec. 9th
Harlow, James H. and Carrie E. Johnson, Dec. 26th

1923

Hill, Fred David and Bessie May Blackwell, Jan. 2nd
Hunt, Walker C. and Maggie W. Wood, Jan. 14th
Haney, Lurty and Anna Thomas, March 13th
Haskin, Dyle and Virginia M. Pace, Apr. 11th
Harris, James W. and Edith M. Gentry, April 11th
Hunt, Robert Lee and Rusha B. Smith, April 17th
Herring, James and Olie Kirby, May 7th
Harris, Willie R. and Gladys Bourne, June 16th
Hensley, Roland H. and Ruby M. Robertson, June 16th
Herndon, Geo. W. and Nellie Jones, July 2nd
Horton, George E. and Virginai M. Graham, Sept. 6th
Huffman, Patrick H. and Katie Minter, Sept. 24th
Hall, Athol Asa and Maiden Sanford, Sept. 30th
Harlow, Channing B. and Arline Lucas, Nov. 21st
Hicks, Lewis E. and Mary V. Hilderbrand, Nov. 29th
Harris, Chas. H. and Perrelye Mundie, Dec. 6th
Hall, Elwood and Nellie Jennings, Dec. 26th
Hoover, Marion H. and Hazel A. Gienger, Dec. 30th

1924

Houchens, Jas. H. and Mary G. Woodward, Jan. 14th
Hoddinott, Harry A. and Lucy A. McCauley, Jan. 15th
Holt, Rufus K. and Rosa L. Mason, Feb. 23rd
Haney, Whitelow R. and Christine Thomas, April 16th
Hughes, Cecil W. and Fannie L. Goolsby, June 2nd
HHarris, Edgar L. and Daisy M. Harlow, June 7th
Hairley, Homer and Maggie Goode, July 7th
Head, Wm. A. and Eva B. Wood, July 19th
Harlow, Monroe and Violet Pumphrey, Sept. 23rd
Huffman, James L. and Eunice M. Morgan, Oct. 17th
Herring, Ashton and Rachael Bishop, Dec. 4th
Harris, Dewey and Bessie W. Hustt, Dec. 24th
Heddings, Robert E. and Addie L. Wood, Dec. 24th
Hutchinson, Winfrey and Mattie Beasley, Dec. 29th

1925

Harmon, John and Susie Sprouse, Feb. 24th
Herndon Schuyler and Eula Dunn, March 9th
Halderman, Aey H. and Inez R. Deane, March 13th
Hughes, John F. and Virginia Jones, May 18th
Hoke, Harvey and Sallie L. Hossaphe, June 13th
Hudson, Thomas and Agnes Claments, June 24th
Harris, Hugh and Nellie Hunt, Aug. 16th
Hooper, Curtis F. and Dorothy F. Thurston, Sept. 2nd
Hughes, Wm. E. and Thelmer E. Grasty, Nov. 24th
Hall, Jr., Oscar B. and E. Pamplin Jones, Dec. 23rd
Hanna, John and Clarissa I. Sparks, Feb. 10th

1926

Hunt, Clinton C. and Louise E. Carroll, Feb. 11th
Henton, Arthur W. and Ruth R. Proffit, June 2nd
Harper, Ward E. and Margaret J. Wolfe, June 24th
Harlow, Walter and Bertha Clements, June 28th
Hunt, John H. and Jennie Wells, July 1st
Hitchinson, Thomas and Maggie Fitzgerald, Aug. 31st
Hunt, Raymond and Gertie Gray, Nov. 23rd
Harlow, Claude B. and Margaret L. Clark, Nov. 24th
Harding, Eldred and Evelyn Blake, Nov. 30th
Harmon, Lewis and Virginia Frazier, Dec. 27th
Hurtt, Benjamin L. and Vivian I. Brown, Dec. 28th

1927

Hackett, John and Emma Taylor, April 12th
Hall, Dennis and Marjorie Bruce, April 23rd
Hamm, Geo. L. and Edna Sprouse, July 19th
Hunter, Carl D. and Ruby L. Austin, Aug. 8th
Hunt, Joseph D. and Mary L. Key, Sept. 2nd
Haggard, Otis L. and Mabel E. Crawford, Oct. 22nd
Harlow, Bernard T. and Mamie E. Melton, Oct. 22nd
Hicks, Bledso and Virginia B. Sandridge, Nov. 3rd
Harris, Henry H. and Mary L. Burgess, Dec. 3rd
Hunt, Jas. A. and Lucille M. Carver, Dec. 3rd
Hughes, Samuel H. and Mrs. Carrie G. Manley, Dec. 14th
Houchens Rat H. and Mabel L. Barnett, Dec. 16th

1928

Harlow, Edward and Elsie Marshall, Jan. 7th

Holloway, Wm. J. and Clara M. Caldwell, Jan. 8th

Hibbard, Ford and Elizabeth A. Kearny, May 5th

Harmon, Dan and Mattie Shaver, May 14th

Hensley, Whitelow E. and Mary E. Haney, Aug. 29th

Head, O'Neill B. and Lucille Thomas, Sept. 1st

Herring, Clarence W. and Alice M. Powell, Nov. 30th

Haislip, Walter and Alice D. Shiflett, Dec. 22nd

1929

Humphreys, Marvin W. and Mary G. Carter, Jan. 15th

Hunt, Ollie H. and Ruby A. Key, Jan. 28th

Harris, Aubrey D. and Lena A. Beach, Feb. 16th

Hunt Roy F. and Janie G. Wood, Feb. 16th

Harlow, Nathaniel P. and Mary M. Jones, June 4th

Houchens, Ethelburt and Mary Houchens, July 3rd

Hall, Geo. Wilmer and Helen Va. Walton, July 13th

Humphreys, Boyd J. and Josephine L. Thurston, Aug. 17th

Hughes, Rubin N. and Lillian H. Byrd, Sept. 3rd

Herndon, Harmon J. and Mildred E. Marshall, Sept. 19th

Tall, Lenuel P. and Dorothy L. Maury, Oct. 21st

Harris, Melvin C. and Theresa V. Napier, Nov. 23rd

Hammock, Liffie and Evelyn Norvell, Dec. 23rd

I

1783

Irving, Charles and Milly Jordan, May 20th

1784

Ivyman, Samuel and Frances Rogers, Nov. 20th

1791

Irvin, Samuel and Sally Hughes, March 28th

1796

Irvin, Joseph H. and Elizabeth Cole, July 4th

1805

Irvin, Matthew and Peggy Irvin, July 22nd

1824

Isbell, Livingston and Mary Edmondson, Feb. 26th

1848

Isaacs, Tucker and Elizabeth Foster, Jan. 10th

1849

Isaacs, Fred and Susan Gasoway, April 17th

1850

Irving, Robert J. and Susan Jackson, Jan. 30th

1858

Iseman, William and Cynthia C. Brown, Oct. 11th

Isman, Wm. and Cynthia C. Brown, Oct. 21st

1871

Iseman, Isaih P. and Mary V. Proffit, March 30th

1874

Irving, Robt. W. and Jsetta Rass, Dec. 7th

1885

Inge, Z. Taylor and Sarah J. McDeamon, Oct. 7th

1893

Irving, W. A. and M. E. Snead, Feb. 20th

1896

Iseman, J. B. and M. L. Goodwin, April 20th

1904

Irvine, C. M. and A. M. Garland, May 24th

1914

Irving, Willie C. and Sadie I. Early, July 8th

Isgett, J. W. and Bertie Lankford, Aug. 13th

1924

Inman, Acie O. and Lucille M. Bugg, Dec. 4th

1926

Irvine, Dewey G. and Myrtle Lee Meeks, Feb. 20th

Irving, Charles K. and Susie B. Kent, Oct. 26th

J

1781

Jefferson, Randolph and Anne Lewis, July 30th

1782

Johnson, John and Milley Randolph, Jan. 1st

Jordan, Reuben and Janett Harvie, Aug. 17th

1784

Jones, Erasmus and Judith Francis, Oct. 8th

1785

Johnson, Benjamin and Elizabeth White, Feb. 16th

Johnson, Richard and Peggy Sneed, Oct. 21st

Johnson, Thomas and Mildred More, Nov. 10th

1786

Jameson, Nathan and Martha Page, Aug. 23rd

1787

Johnson, William and Susanna Coleman, Sept. 28th

1788

Jameson, Thomas and Rachel McCollock, April 10th

1792

Johnson, Thomas and Lucy Watson, Nov. 12th
Jones, Landy and Lucy Farrar, Dec. 1st

1793

Johnson, Benjamin and Betsy Moorman, June 3rd
Johnson, Benjamin and Sarah Fitch, Nov. 23rd

1794

Johnson, Benjamin and Sally Clarkson, June 1st

1795

Jennis, William and Frances Martin, Jan. 27th
Jones, James and Matlaid Watson, Dec. 22nd

1799

Jackson, John and Susannah Graves, Nov. 11th
Jacobs, Hickerson C. and Susannah Martin, Nov. 4th
Jennings, William and Acbriah Young, Oct. 2nd

1801

Jones, William R. and Sally Kay, Dec. 14th
Jopling, Ralph and Jane Thomas, July 22nd

1802

Jeffries, James and Writter Wood, Jan. 23rd
Johnson, Absalom and Sally Brown, Feb. 1st
Johnson, Richard and Elizabeth Thorpe, Feb. 2nd
Jones, Russel and Dicey Walton, Aug. 30th
Jones, Walter and Salley Freeman, March 23rd

1804

Johnson, Absalom and Polly Mitchell, Sept. 24th
Johnson, Nathaniel and Elizabeth Burch, Dec. 21st
Jopling, Thomas and Mary Poor, April 10th

1805

Johnson, Martin and Polly McClary, Dec. 6th
Johnson, William and Jane Ford, May 25th
Jones, Thomas and Mary Maupin, Dec. 16th

1806

Jackson, Thomas and Peggy White, April 22nd
Jameson, Thomas and Evelina Alcocke, April 7th
Johnston, ? and Susanna Leake, Nov. 5th

Jones, ? and Nancy Carr, Oct. 29th
Jones, ? and Elizabeth White, July 21st
Jordan, Samuel and Polly Murrell, March 13th

1808

Jefferson, Thomas and Polly Lewis, Oct. 3rd

1810

Jarman, William Jr. and Peggy Wallace, April 2nd
Jones, George and Rhody Matthew, March 5th

1811

Jameson, John and Rebecca Maupin, Jan. 28th
Jarrell, John and Elizabeth Harrin, April 24th
Johnson, Andrew and Sally Jean, Nov. 14th
Jones, Powhatan and Lyndia Rodes, Dec. 20th
Jopling, Joseph and Margaret Grayham, Jan. 2nd

1812

Johnson, Thomas and Nancy Downs, Dec. 1st

1813

Johnson, James and Mehulaah Crank, Nov. 6th

1814

Jameson, William and Rebecca Maupin, Sept. 15th

1815

Johnson, ? and Dorothy Moormern, April 3rd
Johnson, Benjamin and Ann B. Robertson, Dec. 26th
Jones, Sosomon and Elizabeth Kirby, Dec. 11th

1816

Johnson, Michael and Sophia Lewis, Nov. 12th

1817

Jones, Masias and Frances Claytor, Sept. 23rd

1818

Jarman, Dabney M. and Fanny D. Maupin, Nov. 12th

1819

Johnson, Samuel and Ann M. Barksdale, Sept. 6th

1820

Jones, Turner and Sarah Garner, Feb. 16th

1821

Jones, John and Susan Martin, Dec. 4th

1822

Jefferson, Isham R. and Margaret Peyton, July 3rd
Johnson, Carmon and Mary Johnson, April 2nd

1823

Johnson, George and Elizabeth Owens, Jan. 9th

1824

Johnson, James and Franky Gentry, April 17th
Jones, Lain B. and Mary J. Hopkins, May 20th

1825

Jackson, John and Nancy Toms, Nov. 16th
Jones, Armstead and Patsey Wood, June 17th
Jones, Tandy and Isabella Maupin, March 30th

1826

Johnson, David and Susan Rittenhouse, Sept. 21st
Jones, Abram M. and Mildred Crenshaw, Jan. 19th

1827

Jameson, Alec and Frances Ann Overstreet, Oct. 15th
Jets, John T. and Ann S. Noel, July 12th
Johnson, James C. and Elizabeth A. Shickles, April 19th
Johnson, Richard H. and Elizabeth D. Twyman, April 4th

1828

Jefferson, Robert L. and Ann E. Moreman, Oct. 16th
Johnson, Nicholas and J. Garrison, Dec. 22nd

1829

Jarrall, Willis and Malinda Hamm, June 4th
Johnson, Thomas and Susan J. Garrett, Oct. 20th
Jones, Isaac W. and R. C. Via, Dec. 24th

1830

Jameson, A. H. and C. R. Logan, March 18th
Johnson, Belfield C. and Eliza A. Dickerson, Jan. 12th
Johnson, Edward F. and Mary Gillaspy, Aug. 18th
Johnson, James and Eliza Borden, Nov. 10th
Johnson, Reuben and C. D. Apperson, Aug. 10th
Johnson, Thomas L. and Nancy Hooker, Jan. 18th
Jones, James and Lucy A. Maury, Jan. 5th

1831

Jackson, Stephen and D. Gowen, Feb. 3rd
Jones, A. G. and Martha A. Goodman, March 23rd
Jones, Schyler and Margaret Bailey, Nov. 30th

1832

Johnson, Clifton O. and Polly Moon, Jan. 26th
Johnson, William D. and Martha Payne, Nov. 3rd
Jones, Jesse W. and Ann E. Proctor, Nov. 7th
Jones, John T. and Sarah Ann Campbell, Dec. 20th

1833

Johnson, John M. and Margaret Alexander, Nov. 28th
Johnston, Jeremiah M. and Eliza A. Moon, Aug. 19th
Johnston, William H. and Angelina Moon, Feb. 20th
Jones, William H. and Mary Ann Lane, May 20th

1834

Jennings, Samuel B. and Martha E. Watson, Oct. 7th
Jones, James and Catharine S. Page, Feb. 27th

1835

Jackson, Joshua and Amandott Early, Nov. 23rd
Jeffries, David and Mary Shelton, Feb. 2nd
Johnson, John and Mary F. Kersey, Sept. 29th
Jones, James M. and Mary M. Baily, Jan. 16th
Jones, Thomas S. and Christianna Huckstep, Nov. 17th

1836

Johnson, John W. and Matilda Craddock, Sept. 22nd
Johnston, Thomas and Marry Burkhead, Oct. 17th

1837

Jarman, Edward B. and I. W. Maupin, Feb. 8th
Jarman, William P. and Mary Ann Rothwell, Dec. 21st
Johnson, Joshua H. and Frances A. Via, Feb. 6th
Jones, Thomas W. and Doreas B. Ramsey, Nov. 7th

1838

Jarrall, James and Kiziah Huffman, April 16th
Johnson, Thomas J. and Mary F. Hudson, Oct. 22nd

1839

Johnson, James A. and Nancy Sims, July 16th
Johnston, Fountain and Winnifred H. Moon, Jan. 22nd
Jones, William H. and Mary Ann Key, Feb. 26th

1840

Jackson, Joel and Eliza Graves, March 24th
Johnson, James R. and Martha E. Yancey, Sept. 8th
Jones, Jese W. and Elizabeth Zigler, Dec. 16th

1841

Jeffries, William and Harriet C. Rothwell, Oct. 27th
Johnston, Edward S. and Sarah Jane Griffin, May 10th
Jones, Henry W. and Mary Stout, Dec. 21st

Jones, Raphael and Martha A. Beddo, Sept. 3rd

1842

Jackson, Andrew and Lucy S. Goolsby, Nov. 18th

Jackson, Robert S. and Ann C. Watson, March 17th

Johnson, Reuben and M. A. Davis, Feb. 5th

1843

Johnson, Thomas A. and Matilda T. Nelson, Feb. 20th

Jopling, Holman and Rebecca Norvell, April 25th

1844

Johnson, Reuben and M. A. Davis, Jan. 5th

1845

Jewell, Albert and Catherine Ramsey, Jan. 20th

Johnson, Robert and Frances Keaton, June 21st

Jones, Benjamin H. and M. W. Tilman, Dec. 22nd

Jones, Charles E. and M. A. Smith, April 5th

Jones, William H. and D. M. Brown, Feb. 3rd

1846

Jones, James D. and Sallie R. Faris, Dec. 29th

1847

Johnson, David and Eliza Etta Baber, Jan. 6th

Johnson, Thomas J. and Susan G. Gasten, April 22nd

1848 .

Jones, D. N. and S. M. Farrar, May 16th

1850

Jones, Isaac F. and Amanda T. Keaton, Oct. 15th

1851

Jennings, Benjamin T. and Mary F. Durrett, Oct. 20th

Jones, George T. and Marianna Monlandor, Feb. 27th

Johnson, Robert F. and M. E. Leay, July 20th

1852

Jones, B. H. and Elizabeth Shepherd, May 6th

Jones, William H. and Mary M. Johnson, Nov. 29th

1853

Jarman, James H. and Jerema Fretwell, Dec. 15th

Jones, James L. and Ann E. Shiflett, Aug. 11th

1854

Jarman, M. B. and Sarah C. Ballard, Nov. 23rd

Jarman, M. B. and S. C. Ballard, April 23rd

1855

Jameson, Samuel and Lucy H. Martin, Dec. 14th

Johnson, Richard A. and W. J. Woodson, Nov. 20th

Jones, Jefferson S. and Lucy J. Strange, Nov. 13th

Jamison, Samuel and Lucy H. Martin, Dec. 20th

1856

Jackson, Ira and Martha M. McKinney, Dec. 4th

Jackson, James W. and Sallie A. Goodloe, Jan. 3rd

Jarrall, William G. and Rachel Herndon, Dec. 9th

Jones, John and Etty Garrison, Jan. 1st

Jones, Jesse W. and Mary F. Wiant, Sept. 29th

Jefferson, Thomas and W. E. Barker, Jan. 4th

Jones, John and Etty M. Garrison, Jan. 1st

Jackson, Ira and Martha W. McKinny, Dec. 4th

Jones, Jesse W. and Mary F. Wiant, Oct. 1st

Johnson, Fred J. and Mary A. M. Nornora, Dec. 7th

1858

Johnston, Fred J. and Mary A. McNamara, Dec. 7th

Jones, Horace W. and Susan J. Duke, Sept. 1st

Jury, John S. and Sarah F. Wolfe, Sept. 20th

Jury, Jno. S. and Sarah F. Wolfe, Sept. 21st

1859

Jallet, James T. and Lucy Ann Shiflett, Nov. 17th

1860

Jarman, John L. and Mary C. Fry, Dec. 10th

Jarman, Thomas T. and Henrietta Woods, May 12th

Johnston, T. H. and Sallie W. Holladay, March 19th

Jones, Thomas A. and Caroline A. Walton, Dec. 3rd

Jarman, Thos. T. and Henrietta Woods, March 15th

Jones, Thos. A. and Caroline A. Walton, Dec. 18th

Jarman, Jno. L. and Mary C. Fry, Dec. 12th

1861

Jones, Moses H. and Susan M. Fielding, April 22nd

Jones, Horace M. and Susan M. Fielding, April 25th

1862

Jenkins, Boswell and Lucy Ann Kenney, Sept. 14th

1863

Jones, Richd. D. and Virginia A. Pace, Jan. 15th

Jones, Philip B. and Bettie G. Morris, March 12th

Johnson, Jno. J. and Emily C. Gooch, March 11th

Javins, Jno. W. and Mary E. Marr, Dec. 1st

Jenkins, Henry and Anne C. Halback, April 7th

Jones, Ben F. and Mary F. Wood, April 7th

1864

Judson, T. A. and Anna E. Evans, Feb. 11th

Jennings, Henry R. and Julia Ann Walton, Jan. 5th

Jones, Jno. S. and Mary E. Omohundro, Feb. 11th

Jurey, John A. and Susan C. McCauley, Sept. 25th

1865

Jackson, Andrew and Sally Crenshaw, Dec. 27th

James, John M. and Frances A. Via, Jan. 27th

Johnson, Nicholas W. and H. A. Mallory, Sept. 28th

Johnson, Richard and Mary G. Simmons, Aug. 14th

Johnson, Isaac and Margaret Barbour, Oct. 21st

Johnson, Richard T. and Mary G. Saunders, Aug. 22nd

James, Jno. M. and Frances A. Via, Jan. 31st

1866

Jackson, Matt and Frances Nicholas, May 30th

Jones, Calvin H. and Mary E. C. Coleman, Aug. 20th

Jones, William S. and Elizabeth McDaniel, April 10th

Jordan, Sam and Betty Muse, Nov. 7th

Jones, H. Scyler and Martha M. Davis, Dec. 18th

Jones, Nathl. and Mary E. Houchens, Nov. 29th

1867

Johnson, Geo. T. and Mary E. Dennis, April 17th

Jefferson, Thos. and Eliza Nelson, Oct. 4th

Jameson, Harvey A. and Mary E. Mathews, March 5th

Jones, John and Sally Wiginn, Jan. 5th

Jasper, David N. R. and Ellenora F. Pettet, June 20th

Johnson, Geo. T. and Mary E. Dennis, Oct. 17th

Jefferson, Anderson and Fannie Beck, Dec. 10th

Jones, Bernard and Cynthie Williams, Oct. 12th

1868

Johnson, Deck and Fannie Simms, Jan. 6th

Jones, Barclay S. and Sallie E. Houchens, Feb. 5th

Johnson, Burwell and Milly Jones, May 25th

Jones, Martin and Mary Carter, May 28th

Johnson, Beverley and Martha Modena, Feb. 9th

Johnson, Burwell and Adeline Chambers, Aug. 16th

Janner, Edw. D. Haes and Juliet G. Minor, Nov. 10th

Jackson, John and Mary S. Massie, July 4th

1869

Jordan, Robin and Michie Famer, June 5th

Jordan, James and Julia Randolph, Dec. 28th

Johnson, Frank and Virginia Smith, Dec. 30th

1870

Johnson, Chas. L. and Sally F. Hunter, Jan. 18th

Jefferies, Jas. W. and S. A. Wood, Jan. 27th

Jackson, Andrew and L. June Robertson, June 5th

Johnson, Chapman and Sally Reives, July 24th

Johnson, W. W. and Willie C. Anderson, Dec. 22nd

Jnborden, J. A. and Eliz. S. Smith, Dec. 17th

1871

Jones, Calvin T. and Susan E. Thacker, April 12th

1872

Johnson, Thomas J. and Mary L. Bingham, Oct. 8th

Jones, J. J. and M. F. Garrison, Dec. 19th

1873

Johnson, J. J. and M. A. Johnson, Jan. 16th

Jones, Robert R. and A. M. Pace, April 5th

Jones Osgood K. and Molly E. Herndon, April 21st

Jenkins, C. A. and Lillie S. Cocke, June 30th

1874

Jefferies, V. B. and Anne W. Lewis, Jan. 21st

Johnson, Geo. T. and Mattie Hawkins, Nov. 5th

1875

Jacoby, Simon and Lena Lazerous, June 15th

Jarman, Jno. B. and Annie B. White, Nov. 6th

Johnson, Harvey and Clara Broun, Nov. 22nd

Johnson, Jas. and Sallie M. Garland, May 17th

1876

Jones, Andrew J. and Eliza A. Thacker, Jan. 10th

1877

Jefferies, Geo. W. and Martha H. Tilman, Feb. 17th

Jarman, Jas. E. and Mary E. Jones, April 10th

Jones, Bernard O. and Bettie A. Carr, Oct. 17th

1879

Jones, Charles B. and Sallie O. Gillum, April 24th

Jones, Isaac F. and Louisa M. Wood, Sept. 22nd

Johnson, Moses M. and Augusta V. Croburger, Dec. 1st

Johnson, Benj. R. and Sallie A. Tilman, Dec. 16th

Jones, Llewellyn and Susan F. Carr, Dec. 22nd

Jones, Thos. C. and Virgilia A. Pettit, Dec. 22nd

1880

Jones, George M. and Annie L. Crobauger, Nov. 30th

1881

Johnson, John F. and Charlotte E. Vapem, Sept. 14th

1882

Jones, Andrew J. and Sarah L. Morris, June 28th

Jones, James Frank and Lucie Belle Hill, Dec. 24th

1883

Johnson, John Walter and Bettie Alice Rogers, June 7th

Johnson, Montillian S. and Drusilla F. Harris, Oct. 24th

Jones, David W. and Dora Ellen Carr, Nov. 8th

1884

Jones, Jeter Chapman and Kate Nelson Gilliam, Jan. 17th

Johnson, Wm. Henry and Martha R. Melton, Dec. 31st

Joseph, Chas. Stuart and Mattie M. Walker, Jan. 21st

Johnson, Jas. H. and Mary C. Burke, April 30th

1885

Johnson, Geo. T. and Mary A. Hawkins, May 27th

Johnson, Richard R. and Emma F. Armstrong, Sept. 30th

Jones, Rich. Buckner and Lucy Lee Smith, Sept. 17th

1886

Johnson, James Edgar and Flora Anne Dabney, March 31st

1887

James, Wm. E. and Sallie B. Sandridge, Jan. 6th

Johnson, Jas. F. and Ella Watson, Dec. 21st

Jarman, Jno. J. and Ada M. Nicholas, Dec. 22nd

James, John T. and Bessie Harlow, Dec. 27th

1888

James, Lem H. and Maggie C. Beck, July 5th

Jarman, J. H. and M. A. Broodhead, Oct. 20th

1889

Johnson, H. J. and Helen Russell, March 7th

Johnson, G. W. and E. J. Taylor, Oct. 26th

Jones, T. A. and F. R. Ladd, Nov. 28th

James, Isaac F. and Orie L. Gentry, Dec. 23rd

Johnson, Jno. W. and B. F. Dabney, Dec. 24th

1890

Johnson, Reuben E. and Hister A. Tilman, March 22nd

Jones, M. H. and M. L. Herndon, Sept. 1st

Jett, Robt. C. and Annie A. Funster, Oct. 28th

Johnson, Crosbin and F. N. Ashlin, Dec. 6th

1891

Johnson, Ed. S. and Cora E. Marshall, April 27th

James, Jas. T. and S. S. McNair, June 30th

Jones, A. L. and A. R. Brown, Aug. 22nd

Johnson, T. B. and N. J. Payne, Aug. 31st

Jones, Mannis and S. M. Martin, Dec. 23rd

Johns, W. N. and Cora A. Edwards, Dec. 1st

Jenkins, D. C. and Sally E. Rea, Dec. 10th

1892

Jameson, James S. and Fannie M. Kent, Sept. 28th

1893

Johnson, R. G. and Ada B. Meeks, Aug. 8th

Jarman, T. W. and Mamie Rea, Sept. 29th

1894

Jarman, E. L. and M. N. Webb, Dec. 10th

1895

Johnson, Wm. M. and R. L. W. Rea, Feb. 28th

Johnson, Joseph F. and Va. A. Burgess, July 16th

Johnson, P. N. and Myrtle Mansfield, Oct. 12th

1896

Jarman, R. M. and I. E. Smith, Aug. 8th

Johnson, Jas. E. and Mary C. McDonald, Sept. 28th

Janvier, Meredith and Sarah E. Minor, Oct. 27th

Jones, Horace E. and Jeddie F. Gentry, Nov. 24th

Johnson, J. W. and V. B. Davis, Nov. 28th

Johnson, C. F. and Laura R. Gianniny, Dec. 3rd

1897

Jones, B. M. and E. R. Lang, April 15th

Johnson, Lloyd C. and Willie E. Bryant, May 20th

Johnson, L. S. and L. M. Mahanes, Dec. 29th

1899

Johnson, R. H. and Stella Dameron, March 6th

Johnson, G. M. and Mary L. Perkins, April 30th

Jones, T. Thompson and E. H. K. Nelson, May 16th

Jones, W. T. and L. W. Walker, June 5th

Johnson, Oscar F. and Blanche M. Dudley, Aug. 25th

Jones, Chas. W. and Cora A. Sheppard, Oct. 7th

Jones, S. H. and Annie L. Davis, Nov. 27th

Jones, John H. and S. Lillian Petitt, Dec. 20th

Johnson, J. E. and K. M. Gillispie, Dec. 25th

1900

Johnson, John B. and G. Lenna S. Blake, Nov. 9th

James, Lemuell and S. A. McAlister, Jan. 26th

1901

Jennings, G. C. and O. L. Hall, Jan. 12th

Jones, B. F. and L. P. Jones, Jan. 22nd

Jenks, B. H. and Vora Hall, June 10th

Johnsten, M. G. and K. Aubrey, Sept. 4th

Johnson, Thos. and Mary L. Hicks, Sept. 14th

Jones, N. and L. E. Mayo, Oct. 7th

1902

Jones, O. F. and C. E. Martin, March 3rd

Johnson, J. W. and C. R. Payne, March 25th

Jackson, Geo. and Lula Kirbey, May 29th

1903

James, George and Katie Ergenbright, March 28th

Jones, C. R. and J. B. Dabney, June 22nd

Jennings, H. E. and Nettie Jones, Sept. 8th

Jones, B. M. and A. E. Workham, Sept. 15th

Jones, G. W. and Ella N. Ladd, Nov. 20th

Jones, F. J. and L. F. Davis, Dec. 22nd

1904

Jones, Samuel and Mollie C. Jones, Feb. 8th

Johnson, Ryland and Essie Estes, Aug. 6th

Johnson, W. W. and Edna Gamble, Dec. 19th

Jarman, W. B. and N. C. Young, Dec. 27th

Johnson, William Thomas and Annie E. Desper, Oct. 19th

1905

Jackson, C. A. and Lena B. Ward, Feb. 29th

Jones, Percy Gordon and Ony Profitt, April 11th

Jellett, Chester C. and Cora E. Morris, June 1st

Jones, Harry L. and Lottie Baber, Oct. 16th

1906

Jones, N. L. and I. P. Sandridge, June 30th

Joslin, Edward H. and Carrie R. Randolph, Aug. 1st

Johnson, Andrew J. and Lola J. Morris, Oct. 6th

1907

Jones, Willis B. and Rosa Lee Hill, April 28th

Johnson, Joseph L. and Carrie E. Kidd, April 12th

Jordan, Joseph and Mary Mitchell, July 20th

Jackson, James H. and Bessie Brown, Aug. 29th

James, Jessie and Neonie F. Blackwell, Oct. 27th

1908

Johnson, A. S. and A. L. Richards, Jan. 1st

Jones, Rives R. and Rosa A. Feuchtenberger, April 22nd

Jones, Benjamin J. S. and Stella Alleyree, May 27th

Johnson, Wilelma V. and Mary E. Hiserman, July 1st

Johnson, Obed W. and Sallie Mildred Dgerle, Aug. 12th

Jarman, Thomas W. and Martha Grimstead, Nov. 11th

Jones, Charles B. and Rosa R. Fry, Dec. 1st

1910

James, Alfred R. and Julia W. Renshaw, Sept. 10th

Jones, William C. and Mamie V. Martin, Oct. 4th

Johnson, Willie W. and Mary F. Long, July 4th

Jones, James Henry and Lucy M. Wyant, Dec. 21st

1911

James, John L. and Ida Coleman, Aug. 10th

1912

Jones, Frank J. and Lucy Jones, Jan. 16th

Johns, Albert J. and Grace L. Williams, Aug. 13th

1913

James, John R. and Martha A. Blackwell, May 10th

Jones, Grover and Lula Sullivan, May 20th

Johnson, Willie and Rosa E. Robertson, June 9th

Josselyn, Rollen O. and Sallie F. Maupin, June 29th

Jones, Thomas and Lizzie Lamb, July 3rd

Jones, Coles C. and Susie Dunn, Aug. 27th

1914

Johnson, Henry E. and Kate R. Wayland, Jan. 7th

James, Hiram and Bertha F. Via, Dec. 23rd

1915

Johnson, James I. and Anna J. Branham, March 20th

James, Franklin and Ida L. Via, April 1st

Jones, John Porter and Ann Roberta Garth, April 21st

Jones, Osevin H. and Maude E. Showalter, June 26th
Jones, Willian and Lena Coleman, June 26th
Johnson, John G. and Nina Smith, Dec. 15th
Jones, Geo. N. and Va. B. Lamb, Dec. 22nd

1916

Jacobs, David and Florence V. Rhodes, Jan. 26th
Jefferies, Jno. D. and Oris Anna Poats, March 11th
Jarman, Geo. Ballard and Mattie May Massey, Feb. 23rd
Johnson, Charlie M. and Sadie Ann Chambers, May 16th
Jones, Abraham I. J. and Laura Herndon, Aug. 17th
Jones, William A. and Elizabeth G. Hart, Sept. 12th
Johnson, Clarence Edward and Lizzie Jane Perry, Nov. 20th

1917

Jones, Thomas K. and Virginia L. Yowell, June 27th
Johnson, Early P. and Sadie Saunders, July 31st
Jones, Robert M. and Mrs. Rose E. Mayo, Sept. 22nd
Jones, Kelly and Nettie M. Frye, Nov. 7th
Jenkins, Jno. E. and Lucy Payne, Nov. 10th
Jones, Frank G. and Ann Louise White, Dec. 24th

1918

Johnson, Wm. O. and Katie E. Moyer, Sept. 29th
Johnson, Wm. W. and Elizabeth N. Amos, Feb. 15th
Joseph, Charley R. and Mary F. Brown, May 15th
Johnson, Geo. W. and Grace C. Thuma, June 16th
Jones, Robt. D. and Mary A. Paulett, Aug. 21st
Johnson, Bryan K. and Helen Payne, Aug. 27th
Jenks, Wm. H. and Grace Morris, Sept. 15th

1920

Jones, Hardy and Mary Dudley, March 17th
Johnson, Luther Frank and Minnie Lowery, Nov. 27th
Jones, Wylis P. and Elevyn B. S. King, Dec. 13th

1921

Jones, Jesse N. and Janet V. Crawford, March 28th
Johnson, Kaufman H. and Pearl J. Currier, July 5th
Jones, Edward F. and Bernice T. Breeden, July 26th
James, Dewey and Susan Bowen, Aug. 9th
Jamerson, J. H. and Lois I. Amiss, Sept. 12th

Jackson, Clarence H. and Rosetta J. U. Flowers, Nov. 21st
Johnson, Hobard W. and Viola H. Buttner, Nov. 22nd

1922

Jarrell, Nathaniel and Elma Otis, March 29th
Johns, Edward Wm. and Jennie E. Wood, April 12th
Johnson, Geo. Arthur and Lola Estelle Jones, July 22nd
James, Charlie W. and May L. Via, Sept. 7th
Journey, Elwood H. and Bettie Alma Bragg, Oct. 23rd
Jones, John P. and Cora L. Ward, Nov. 11th
John, Jordan and F. Ineza Gentry, Dec. 23rd
Jones, Henry W. and Ellen Layne, Dec. 26th

1923

Johnson, Thos. H. and Mooelle Scantilier, April 18th
Jones, Elizah H. and Nellie M. Hughes, May 5th
Johnson, Jimmie A. and Alma Halloway, June 16th
Jones, James C. and Lillie L. Snall, July 27th
Jennings, Ernest and Eva Bragg, Oct. 11th

1924

Jenkins, Wallace F. and Cardyn Lovejoy, Feb. 16th
Johnson, John H. and Emma J. Willis, Dec. 27th

1925

Jones, Harvey and Lucy Harris, Feb. 19th
Jones, Thomas R. and Thelma Huffman, June 24th
Jones, Morgan B. and Nell K. Bragg, Oct. 6th
Jimbro, Herbert and Hattie Wyant, Oct. 27th

1926

Jones, Lewis and Vernie Moore, Jan. 25th

1927

Johnson, Chas. Lee and Nannie E. Leake, April 16th
Jones, Geo. W. and Emma C. Johnson, June 1st
Johnson, Benj. and Bessie Monger, Nov. 3rd
Jarrell, Wm. and Sadie L. Hunt, Dec. 24th

1928

Jennings, Russell H. and Pansy D. Wood, Feb. 9th
Johnson, Charlie B. and Edith L. Bingler, June 13th
James, Lorenza D. and Mae J. McAllister, July 12th
Jafferson, Prince Albert and Dorotha Childress, Oct. 13th
Johnson, Carey A. and Belva L. Dodd, Oct. 20th

1929

Jennings, Geo. C. and Daisey L. Thomasson, Feb. 7th

Johnson, Christhoper and Lucie B. Garrison, June 6th

K

1781

Kindred, Bartholomew and Milly Lively, Dec. 29th

1782

Key, William Bibb and Mourning Clark, Dec. 23rd

Kirkpatrick, Roger and Elizabeth Blaine, April 4th

1784

Kerr, David and Dobes Robes, Nov. 25th

Kileon, William and Susanna Spencer, April 11th

1787

Kindred, Edward and Elizabeth Haggard, Oct. 23rd

1788

Kinney, Jacob and Ann Morris, Dec. 6th

1792

Kidd, John and Lucy Melton, May 2nd

1794

Kerr, John R. and Sarah Henderson, Nov. 24th

Kirbey, Noel and Sally Bishop, Jan. 14th

1795

Kidd, Joseph and Ann Johnson, Sept. 13th

1796

Kerr, Henry and Elizabeth Eucle, March 8th

Kesterton, William and Polly Bailey, May 13th

1798

Knight, Ephraim and Mary Carrel, Jan. 22nd

1799

Knight, William and Elizabeth Rogers, Jan. 26th

1802

Keaton, Nelson and Edna Davies, Jan. 5th

Kelly, John and Mary Alcock, Sept. 11th

Kidd, Pleasant and Sarah Farrell, Dec. 20th

1805

Keaton, Larkin and Ann Davis, March 4th

Kindred, Edward and Polly Izar, Jan. 25th

Kinsolving, George W. and Anny Barksdale, Sept. 30th

Kirby, Larkin and Elizabeth   , March 4th

1806

Kennedy, Joseph and Sally Johnson, March 17th

Kerby, Joel and Nancy Henderson, July 29th

Kindred, Thomas and Lurorn Hawly, Sept. 4th

1807

Kembrough, James and Peggy Foster, June, 10th

1809

Kennerly, Reubin and Tabetha Wayh, June 15th

Kerby, John and Mary Roberson, Nov. 18th

1811

Kinkoad, John and Sarah Speers, Nov. 11th

1812

Kirby, Henry and Frances F. Bailey, Feb. 27th

1814

Kirby, William and Nancy Smith, Feb. 11th

1815

Kinsolving, James and Margaret Brown, Nov. 6th

1816

Keblinger, David and Lucy M. Maupin, Feb. 6th

Kinney, William W. and Judith Mahanes, July 31st

1817

Key, Daniel Price and Elizabeth Durrett, Nov. 18th

Kimbrough, Merideth and Sally Gaines, Nov. 11th

Kimbrough, Thomas and Susan Gaines, Jan. 6th

1818

Key, Jepe P. and Sarah J. Woods, Jan. 20th

1819

Key, Nelson and Nancy Hall, May 10th

Knight, William and Matilda S. Burns, Dec. 23rd

Kricer, William and Aisana Tomes, Nov. 13th

1820

Keith, Daniel and Elizabeth McCarnelle, April 22nd

1821

Kerby, John and Judah Kerby, Feb. 13th

1822

Kenney, C. P. M. and Hetty Rodes, Dec. 5th

1823

Keadle, James G. and Lucinda Eades, Dec. ?

1825

Kerby, Anderson and Mary Ann Moyer, Nov. 7th

1826

Keister, Phillip and Celina Marshall, Oct. 12th
Kelly, Abraham and Mildred Watson, Oct. 7th
Kinsolbing, Madison B. G. and America Watts, Sept. 12th
Knight, William and Caly Shiflett, June 7th

1827

Kelly, Garrett and Mary R. Garner, Jan. 2nd
Kidd, William and Mahala Damron, Sept. 3rd

1828

Keaton, Nathan and Jane Keaton, May 29th
Kennedy, James and Sophia Harlow, April 22nd

1829

Keaton, James and Sarah McCauley, Oct. 27th
Koach, Hiram and C. A. Mayo, Jan. 8th

1831

Keister, Peter and Frances E. Wood, Dec. 20th
Kenney, John and Lucy Ann Cole, April 21st

1832

Kerby, Coleman and Lucinda Morris, Oct. 29th
Kerby, Fayette F. and Martha D. Roberts, March 6th
King, George R. and Ann Elizabeth Winn, May 13th

1833

Keaton, John W. and Catharine Garrison, April 11th
Kizer, Lewis and Patsy C. Hill, Oct. 10th

1834

Keenan, John C. and Doratha A. Faris, May 3rd
Kidd, William H. and Mary A. Kidd, Feb. 26th

1835

Kennedy, William and Mary A. Widderfield, Nov. 2nd
Kermerly, Samuel and S. A. Fretwell, June 9th
Kidd, Joseph and Lucy J. McKerney, June 1st
King, Sabrit and Jarneia Herring, Oct. 12th
Kirby, Frank and Sarah Rodes, Dec. 4th
Knight, Washington and A. Sullivan, Oct. 13th

1836

Kent, Spots F. and Mary A. Fagg, Jan. 12th

1838

Keaton, Lively and Sophia Shiflett, Jan. 5th
Kemper, George W. and Mary A. Brown, Aug. 2nd

Kirby, Coleman H. and Elizabeth H. Johnston, Dec. 1st
Kirkpatrick, John L. and Mary E. Turner, May 7th

1839

Kidd, Lessy and Mrs. Eliza Slater, April 4th
Kirk, Rollin H. and Georgianna Garth, May 13th
Koiner, John B. and S. D. Maupin, Oct. 28th

1840

Keaton, John B. and S. E. Harris, Nov. 23rd
Keblinger, David and Mrs. Elizabeth McCord, March 19th
Kirby, Calvin M. and Mary A. Martin, Jan. 26th

1841

Keaton, James and Betsy Powell, Jan. 18th
Keblinger, William M. and Mary C. Jarman, Nov. 6th

1843

Kent, Joseph H. and Elizabeth J. White, May 4th
Kirby, William J. and Elizabeth Bailey, April 4th

1844

Keaton, Elijah and Hardena J. Wood, Dec. 14th

1845

Keith, James D. and Sucretia Byers, Jan. 14th
Kims, Dellimer and Sarah A. Ray, April 3rd
Kidd, Elias and Martha Garland, Aug. 19th
Kidd, J. B. and Ann Johnson, March 6th
Kirby, Albin and M. J. Harlow, April 23rd

1846

Kidd, George W. and Susan G. McKinney, Oct. 14th
Kinney, William and Nancy Cole, July 31st
Kirby, Allen and Mary Thacker, June 1st

1847

Kinney, John and Susan Battles, Oct. 28th

1848

Keller, Thomas C. and S. E. Garner, Aug. 24th
Kent, Walter J. and Mary J. Fitz, Nov. 29th
Kerby, Jefferson N. and C. M. Amiss, April 26th
Kerby, John and Eliza Kerby, Feb. 14th
Kirby, William and Nancy Bailey, Oct. 2nd

1849

Keller, Spotswood M. and G. Balthis, Jan. 4th
Kidd, George M. and Minnie Ann Wash, Nov. 13th
King, James M. and Susan F. Hodges, Nov. 22nd
Kirby, William O. and Mary A. Mayfield, June 13th

1850

Kennedy, Morris and Harriett Bunch, Feb. 17th

Kirby, Benjamin and Elizabeth Eades, May 3rd

1851

Kerby, John Jr. and Catharine Kirby, March 10th

Kirk, James and Gabricia Garth, Nov. 3rd

1852

Knight, John I. and Susan C. Tilman, Sept. 5th

1853

Kirby, Francis M. and Sarah V. Smith, March 2nd

Kirby, John R. and Sarah Sprouce, Jan. 5th

1854

Kean, Robert H. and Jane N. Randolph, April 20th

Kennedy, James and Maria O. Carroll, Aug. 24th

1855

Kirby, William R. and Martha E. Harlow, July 31st

1856

Kirby, James and Elizabeth Cawthorn, June 19th

Kerby, Francis M. and Lucy Jane Bailey, March 24th

Kemper, Koseusko and Iratta C. Garrett, Feb. 10th

1858

Kirby, Francis M. and Lucy J. Bailey, March 24th

Kemper, Koseusko and Irattea C. Garrett, Feb. 10th

1859

Kemper, Koscrinsko and Iraetta C. Garrett, Feb. 9th

Kerby, Jefferson N. and Sarah E. Humphreys, Nov. 4th

Kerby, Jeff M. and Sarah E. Humphreys, Nov. 1st

1860

Keith, Nathaniel C. and Maria L. Hamner, March 27th

Kidd, Fields A. and Martha A. Mays, Nov. 20th

Keith, Nath. C. and Maria S. Hamner, March 28th

Kidd, James S. and Mary Jane Via, April 10th

Kidd, Fields A. and Martha Ann Mayo, Nov. 24th

Keaton, Jno. W. and Lillie T. Brown, July 1st

1861

Keaton, John W. and Sallie T. Brown, June 27th

Kerby, David and Elizabeth Calmon, Feb. 9th

Kerby, Frank and Margaret Ward, Dec. 31st

Kidd, James S. and Mary Jane Via, March 28th

1862

Kerby, Ro. E. and Sarah W. Hutchenson, March 2nd

Kerby, Frank and Margaret Ward, Jan. 1st

1863

Kilby, Thompson A. and Rebecca Wheeler, Jan. 3rd

Kennerly, Alfred and Eliza J. Herron, Feb. 17th

1864

Keener, Lewis and Catharine B. Jackson, Dec. 8th

Kenney, Horace and Mary F. Cole, Jan. 10th

1865

Kidd, Ben. W. and Alice B. Goodwin, Sept. 3rd

1866

Kennon, Henry and Willie A. Hall, Feb. 26th

Kenslin, Samuel B. and Susanna Elizabeth Wood, Jan. 30th

Kent, William S. and Mary E. Winston, Feb. 26th

Keysooar, Hugh P. and Susie M. Branham, Sept. 18th

Kemper, Chas. M. and Sarah E. Parrott, Nov. 29th

Kent, Thos. J. and Mary J. Toms, Dec. 6th

Keaton, Wm. L. and Mary E. F. Via, March 6th

Keister, Levi B. and Susanna E. Wood, Feb. 6th

Kennon, Henry and Willie A. Hall, Feb. 28th

Kent, Wm. S. and Mary E. Winston, March 7th

Keysear, Hugh P. and Lucie M. Bramham, Sept. 20th

Kent, Thos. J. and Mary Jane Toms, Dec. 3rd

1867

Kappes, Wm. H. and Frances Jane Winn, May 7th

1868

Keister, Peter and Eliz. Pritchett, Jan. 31st

1869

Kenny, Lian, O. S. and Sallie Bunn, July 18th

Kembral, Moses and Cela Gillet, Aug. 26th

Kaufman, Moses and K. Lutterman, Oct. 5th

Kase, Alva and Sarah M. Fray, Nov. 11th

1870

Kirtley, F. W. and M. M. Lofland, April 29th

Kirby, L. F. and S. E. Gardner, May 24th
Kelly, Jas. and Emmal Ball, Dec. 22nd

1871
Kirby, Lewis and Sally Kennedy, Oct. 12th

1872
Kirby, James W. and Angeline B. Baker, Feb. 29th
Kubyen, William and Mary Kennedy, April 18th
Key, James W. and Lucy H. Jameson, Sept. 16th

1873
Kidd, James S. and Lucy F. Dunn, July 19th
Kirby, Jas. H. and Sallie S. Clemons, Nov. 21st
Kidd, Mathew Le B. and Mary E. Morris, Dec. 23rd
King, John W. and Helta E. Wilcher, Aug. 30th

1874
Keyton, Jno. and Lucy McAllister, July 20th
Kirby, Jas. J. F. and Sarah F. Bass, Oct. 5th

1875
Kirby, Wm. Nall and Mary June Dudly, Sept. 2nd

1876
Kemper, Fontain L. and Sally B. Brown, Oct. 4th
Kirby, G. W. and Ida J. Pace, Nov. 21st
Kennedy, Thos. and Mary C. Fox, Nov. 22nd
Kirby, Thos. C. and Martha Price, Dec. 26th

1877
Kertz, Adam H. and Rebecca Tomlin, Nov. 5th

1878
Kennedy, David and Cornelia Wade, Jan. 19th
Kirby, Geo. W. and Eliza Snead, April 22nd
Key, John and Polly Kirby, Sept. 10th

1879
Kidd, Wm. J. and Sallie D. Johnson, March 17th

1880
Kirby, John H. and Martha E. Morris, March 1st
King, Miles B. and Clara M. Kents, Oct. 6th
Kanney, Chas. and Catharine Kirby, Oct. 19th
Kice, George A. and Mary L. Jackson, Nov. 3rd

1881
Kirby, John Wm. and Elizabeth Farish, Sept. 6th

1882
Kirby, Hamilton and Josephine Carter, Dec. 21st
Kirby, James W. and Elizabeth Dudley, Nov. 15th
King, Abram L. and Sally K. Moore, Dec. 25th

1884
Kidd, Jas. Wm. and Eliza Pritchett, Dec. 31st
King, David Wm. and Sallie Smith, Feb. 26th
Kincaid, Archie and Juliana Gardner, June 2nd
Kidd, Joseph M. and Ada Ellis Bruffy, July 24th
Kent, N. B. and M. J. Carr, Sept. 17th
Keyton, Jno. W. and Mary Jane Brown, Nov. 9th

1886
Kirby, Jeff. R. and Nannie A. Sprouse, Jan. 6th
Keon, Jas. Wm. and Mary Nelson Davis, Aug. 24th
Kirby, Jno. Wm. and Margaret E. Harlon, Sept. 16th
Ketcham, Benj. P. and Lilian Lee Brand, Oct. 14th
King, Willard and Luttie K. Burgess, Jan. 19th

1887
Ketala, Edw. M. and Margaret L. Chewning, July 11th
Kline, John F. and Alice Dobbins, Nov. 23rd

1889
Keaton, Ro. J. and Cora Bruce, Oct. 3rd
Knight, Chas. and Hesterline Sprouse, Dec. 28th

1890
Kelly, Geo. O. and N. C. Marsh, Feb. 26th
Kruckbaum, J. G. and Willie A. Burgess, June 2nd
Kirby, C. O. and Annie Criddle, June 2nd

1891
Kidd, J. F. and Lizzie Byers, June 20th
Kidd, J. L. and N. F. Johnson, July 6th

1892
Kirby, S. R. and Ella N. Taylor, Jan. 7th
Kidd, Charles W. and N. S. Farrer, Jan. 12th
King, W. W. and Emma J. Currier, March 7th
Knig, W. W. and L. E. Morris, June 6th
Kirckpatrick, S. P. and N. I. Morris, June 20th
Keaster, W. B. and Margaret Pritchett, July 27th

1893
Keller, J. W. and A. C. Bush, April 25th

Kirby, Willie W. and Lula E. Watts, July 18th
Kirby, L. C. and Eliza Martin, Nov. 11th

1894

Kirby, E. H. and J. E. Pleasants, Sept. 4th

1895

Kidd, J. L. and D. E. Jones, Feb. 11th
Kent, C. W. and Mrs. E. Miles, June 3rd
Kirby, Robt. and Sallie Eades, Sept. 2nd
Kirby, Wm. O. and Mary A. Graves, Nov. 7th
Kent, Thos. L. and Sally M. Harris, Dec. 14th

1896

Kent, Jas. W. and V. L. Newman, Oct. 29th

1897

Kell, A. D. and A. V. Houchens, Feb. 19th
Koiner, Kemper and Willie A. Bolton, June 5th
King, Jo A. and L. M. Herndon, Aug. 30th
Knighton, Percy W. and Fannie M. Johnson, Aug. 31st
Kirby, E. J. and Lilly Cash, Dec. 6th
Kirby, Broadus E. and Mollie L. Moon, Dec. 9th

1898

Kearny, J. W. and E. M. Harrison, March 12th
Kirby, Wm. E. and Mary McCrasy, April 4th
Kirby, Robt. L. and Hattie Barnette, May 11th

1899

Kent, J. O. and Viola Young, June 1st
Kidd, Chas. L. and Alice J. Payne, Nov. 27th

1900

Kidd, Oscar and Minnie Carroll, Sept. 18th
Key, Jas. W. and Eva H. Dudley, April 18th
Kirby, Jas. H. and S. F. Bower, June 13th
Kennedy, W. S. and M. L. Scruggs, June 18th

1901

Killimayer, J. M. and Lenora Houchens, May 3rd

1902

Kirby, Frank and Julia F. Norford, Jan. 22nd
Kirby, J. R. and Susie Bishop, March 3rd
Key, J. B. and M. Alice Schultz, April 21st
Keyton, L. S. and L. Garrison, July 2nd
Kirby, J. L. and Daisy Faris, Oct. 21st
Keen, Thoc. J. and M. M. Garrison, Dec. 24th
Keaster, Geo. and Virgilia Dowell, Dec. 30th

1903

Kidd, John W. and Minnie Phillips, Feb. 17th
Kidd, S. R. and M. E. Morris, March 18th
Kirby, E. N. and M. E. Ricks, Oct. 1st
Keyton, R. J. and Aeph Pedoon, Oct. 19th
Kanny, G. C. and M. S. Tomlin, Oct. 20th
Kirby, Wm. Allen, and Lula B. Irving, Dec. 17th

1904

Kirby, Jas. F. and Willie Scott McCary, Aug. 16th
Kirby, Wm. Lloyd and Margaret Delaney Craig, Aug. 30th

1905

Kennedy, David Currie and Mary Eliz. Leake, June 27th
Kirby, Jno. Thos. and Lottie Kirby, June 28th
Kellam, J. H. and Ada H. Martin, Aug. 21st
Kennady, Hy E. and Florence Kennady, Sept. 23rd
Klugh, Henry W. and Mamie Birckhead, Dec. 19th
Kidwell, Jas. W. and Lillie S. Hancock, Oct. 16th
Key, Thos. J. and Mary B. Goude, Nov. 7th
Key, Charles J. and Mary B. Youde, Nov. 7th

1906

Kirby, Lewis and Irene Henry, Jan. 6th
Kelly, William and Susie Norvell, May 17th
Kidd, J. O. and E. B. Disher, Oct. 18th

1907

Kennedy, Robert and Annie Toms, March 27th
Keaton, William and Jennie A. Shiflett, Aug. 28th
Kysie, J. B. and Mary A. Young, Oct. 20th

1908

Kurtz, James F. and Alice Thompson, March 17th
Kirby, Ellis and Annie Shiflett, March 4th
Kelly, Joseph and Fannie Gay, July 8th
King, Ashby and Ludie E. Carver, Sept. 16th
Killingworth, Julian and Irene Marsh, Dec. 24th
Kirby, Laurence and Pearl Walker, Dec. 29th

1909

Kemper, Boyd P. and Elizabeth E. Garth, Jan. 6th
Kirby, Edward and Mittie Davis, Jan. 25th
Keyton, Ozro and Daisy Hill, June 9th
Kennedy, Chastine and Dora Toms, Dec. 24th

1910

Kinney, Andrew and Lillie James, Jan. 10th
Keener, Charles R. and Lizzie Mitchell, June 30th
Keener, Andrew J. and Anna P. Carter, Dec. 21st
Kidd, Robert and Elsie Morris, Dec. 28th

1911

Kennedy, Charlie and Lillian Henry, Jan. 12th
Kidd, Molie L. and Lora Moon, Sept. 27th
Kirby, Charlie H. and Agnes Morris, Oct. 16th

1912

Kirby, Ross and Clara Johnson, Aug. 24th
Keenan, Jim A. and Estelle M. Campbell, Oct. 24th

1913

Kirby, Percy and Alberta Woodson, April 16th

Kirk, Edwin and Page Taylor, June 26th

Kenney, McCray A. and Bertha M. Merritt, Sept. 10th

1914

Keyton, Zra and Oriella Madison, Jan. 23rd

Koiner, G. R. and F. M. Wood, June 2nd

Kirby, John H. and Reba L. Critzer, June 9th

Kirby, James Lucy and Annie V. Kirby, July 3rd

Kirby, Charles H. and Inez Ragland, Oct. 7th

Kingsbury, Henry G. and Bertie E. Drumheller, Nov. 30th

1915

Keister, Carlos S. and Louise D. Balthis, Oct. 20th

Kirby, Frank and Estelle Massie, Dec. 27th

1916

Kelly, James D. and Isabel D. Money, April 25th

1917

Kirby, Carroll and Myrtie E. Jones, April 11th

Kent, Thomas W. and Ora Grace Toms, May 5th

Kibler, Joseph W. and Ula V. Leake, Dec. 22nd

1918

Keerny, Frank P. and Roxy M. Brooks, Feb. 13th

Keyton, Lee and Florence Garrison, May 20th

Kirby, Richard F. and Alma G. Moore, Aug. 21st

1919

Keais, Michael and Clarkie Haynes, April 28th

Kent, Robt. S. and Narcissa Florence Gray, July 3rd

Kent, Thomas Harris and Lelia Faith Brigg, Aug. 16th

Kirtley, Jas. H. and Mary Lou Dudly, Aug. 27th

Key, Jas. W. and Mary M. Hogue, Dec. 24th

Kirby, Kenneth and Edna Sandridge, Dec. 31st

1920

Kennedy, Leslie and Margaret P. Powers, Jan. 25th

Kidd, Robert B. and Mary H. Ellinger, April 19th

Kapp, Herbert and Elsie I. Schree, July 6th

Kirts, Wallace B. and Clara G. Keller, Aug. 2nd

Kinzer, Josh Francis and Luttie Margaret Reynolds, Oct. 4th

Kennedy, Graham H. and Sadie E. Meeks, Nov. 18th

Kyger, Earl Whitfield and Maude Fray, Nov. 19th

1921

Knave, Edward Daniel and Reiver Kidd, April 13th

1922

Kessler, Harry W. and Lillian C. Gentry, July 8th

Kirby, Clarence R. and Edith P. Smith, July 21st

1923

Kidder, Delas B. and Mary E. Cheape, June 25th

Kirby, Early F. and Jennie L. Mawyer, July 1st

Kirby, Robert and Janie Jones, Sept. 8th

1924

Kidd, Allen W. and Jennie P. Pollard, April 12th

Kennedy, Tom R. and Mary E. Smith, Sept. 8th

1925

Kelley, Thos. L. and Mary K. Heflin, May 27th

Kephatt, Wm. D. and Ruth J. Plemmons, Aug. 16th

Knight, James F. and Hettie Frazier, Dec. 1st

1926

Key, Henry and Thelma Truslow, Feb. 23rd

Kent, Albert and Dorothy Goodman, Aug. 25th

King, Thos. M. and Mary Moses, Sept. 22nd

Kirby, Alfred and Elizabeth Critzer, Nov. 13th

Kennedy, Claude Henry and Lillie May Norvell, Nov. 23rd

King, Charlie and Mary Critzer, Dec. 24th

1927

Kyle, Bernard J. and Julia B. Shirley, May 3rd

Krattz, Clarence and Virginia Wash, July 28th

Kessler, John M. and Lucille Ann Carver, Sept 5th

Knight, Edd. Cole and Eva M. Shiflett, Sept. 7th

Kirby, John B. and Susie Kister, Dec. 24th

1928

Knight, Isaac F. and Etha Morris, May 4th

Keyton, Gilbert and Lena Shiflett, May 30th

Kirby, Gaines J. and Mazie M. Critzer, July 28th

Kennedy, John L. and Lena M. Davis, Sept. 10th

Kidd, John W. and Nettie Loudree, Sept. 29th

Kennedy, Allie Fulton and Mary E. Tidsdale, Oct. 15th

Kent, Aubrey L. and Effie M. Tomlin, Oct. 31st

1929

Kennedy, George T. and Alece M. Tomlin, March 5th

Kanney, William M. and Ruby M. Kirby, March 23rd

Kindrick, A. B. and Ethel M. Via, July 3rd

Kirby, Charlie and Ola M. Wheller, Oct. 7th

Kidd, Newton S. and Sedorah E. Ginter, Dec. 24th

Keyton, John H. and Sallie Garrison, Dec. 28th

L

1781

Lewis, Hopkins and Molley Henderson, Nov. 11th

1783

Lewis, James and Elizabeth Maury, June 19th

1785

Lane, John and Nancey Langford, Nov. 25th

Langford, John and Kerenhabuck Perry, Jan. 26th

Lewis, Francis and Polly Hudson, Nov. 26th

Livingstone, James and Elizabeth Jopling, Oct. 22nd

1786

Lewis, Jesse and Nancy Clarkson, April 14th

1788

Lane, John and Patients Beaber, Aug. 2nd

1789

Lavender, George and Nancy Fortune, Feb. 10th

Lobbin, John and Elizabeth Copland, July 21st

1790

Lane, Isham and Nancy Lamb, March 6th

1791

Laughn, James and ? Burns, March 21st

Lively, Charles and Elizabeth Bishop, Dec. 23rd

1792

Lanford, John and Sally Shepherd, June 18th

Low, Benjamin and Ann Clark, Dec. 20th

Luse, Zephariah and Elizabeth Douglass, July 12th

1793

Landers, Meredith and Elizabeth Kidd, April 11th

Lane, Joseph and Lucy Herring, Jan. 12th

Lane, William and Mary Mills, July 13th

1794

Laine, John and Ann Defore, Oct. 24th

Lively, John and Mary Jameson, Dec. 8th

Lively, Shederick and Sally Burrus, March 4th

1795

Lane, Richard Norman and Rachel Herron, June 1st

1796

Lewis, Edward and Elizabeth Gillaspy, June 29th

1798

Landcraft, Nathaniel and Sarah Harden, Sept. 26th

Landon, Benajmin and Mary Syron, May 8th

Lane, John and Felithy Crew, Dec. 21st

Leffler, David and Nartty Page, Dec. 24th

Lilly, John and Elizabeth Lackly, June 18th

Lloyd, William and Polly Hill, Aug. 3rd

1799

Lacy, Stephen and Bersey Davenport, June 3rd

Lanham, William and Molly Bailey, Dec. 19th

Lucudo, James and Hannah Mabry, April 24th

1801

Leake, Samuel and Sophia Farrar, Nov. 2nd

1802

Linton, Benjamin and Peggy T. Parriott, Feb. 11th

Lively, Mack and Bersy Bailey, Oct. 26th

1803

Lowry, Albon and Nancy Lowry, June 13th

1804

Lamb, William and Elizabeth Herring, March 25th

Langford, John and Mildred Thurmond, Oct. 3rd

Langford, Pleasant and Ellenton Thacker Sprouse, Jan. 21st

1806

Lively, Mark and Rachel Mansfield, March 6th

Lowry, Overton and Mary Wheeler, Dec. 24th

1808

Lowell, Elisha and Elizabeth Gillum, Jan. 9th

1809

Lanford, Augustine and Nancy Breedlove, Aug. 10th

Landers, Benjamin and Nancy Shiflett, Oct. 11th

Langford, Parks and Patsy Dudley, March 11th

Lewis, John W. and Nancy Sneed, March 6th

Lively, Carmon and Lucy Dunkerm, March 6th

1810

Leake, James and Emmily Mahanes, May 9th

Lindsay, Reubin and Nancy Rogers, Aug. 6th

1811

Leake, Kob S. and Nancy Hestaned, Dec. 10th

Leitch, James and Polly Lewis, Feb. 5th

Lobbin, John and Hannah Wallace, June 11th

1814

Lizer, Daniel and Jane E. Watts, July 20th

1815

Lane, Edward and Susannah Mooney, Oct. 25th

Langford, James H. and Jane Morton, Sept. 7th

Lightfoot, William F. and Catharine Maury, May 5th

Lively, John H. and Sally H. Taliafond, April 13th

1816

Lane, William and Susan Hoge, March 25th

Lupton, Jacob C. and Susan Colvin, Nov. 4th

1817

Leigh, James W. and Mary Kinsolving, June 23rd

1818

Langster, Robert and Sally Irvin, Jan. 10th

Lively, John and Ametra Shackelford, Jan. 9th

1819

Lindsay, Reubin and Mary M. Goodman, Aug. 19th

Locker, Andrew and Sarah Turner, Oct. 14th

Long, John and Susanna Anderson, April 10th

1820

Lindsay, Henry and Fanny D. Maupin, Nov. 1st

1821

Lane, Frederick W. and Darkin McCord, Aug. 8th

1823

Leon, John and Susan Bolling, May 15th

Lewis, Gilly M. and Phaniel Campbell, Nov. 13th

1824

Lane, John W. and Sarah McCord, Nov. 1st

Lowell, Pleasant and Sarah Garland, Dec. 15th

1825

Lane, Elkin H. and Ann I. Timberlake, July 15th

Lee, John and Evelina R. Perry, July 14th

1826

Lane, Thomas W. and Jennet Tullock, Jan. 9th

Langford, James and Elizabeth Morris, Dec. 15th

Lewis, James and Polly Marks, Oct. 17th

Lewis, James H. and Sarah A. Stanford, Dec. 15th

Lockhart, Reubin and Jane E. Hudson, July 4th

Long, George and Harriet Selden, Dec. 18th

1827

Lane, Thomas and Mildred Thurston, Jan. 22nd

1828

Lacy, Edmund T. and Eliza Burruss, May 6th

Lane, Robert and Mahala Thurston, Dec. 15th

Locker, David and Maria Modena, Dec. 16th

Long, Abraham and Ann Watson, Nov. ?

Lowell, Lewis and P. A. Dunkin, Feb. 7th

1829

Lobbin, Samuel and Sarah S. Hamersly, Jan. 3rd

1830

Langford, Anderson and Martha Dove, Nov. 2nd

1831

Lane, Aaron W. and Frances Dickerson, Jan. 26th

Lane, Benjamin and Elizabeth Watson, Dec. 29th

Lane, James and Ann Coleman, Feb.   ?

Lewis, Robert and Sarah A. Craven, March 14th

Littleford, Richard W. and Patsy S. Sudderth, Nov. 18th

1832

Langford, Garrett and Jane Sandridge, Dec. 4th

Lines, Benjamin M. and Jane Ballard, Nov. 15th

1833

Lewis, John and Mrs. Catharine Spicer, Sept. 2nd

Loyd, Richard and Martha J. Ellis, Nov. 7th

1834

Lane, Edward W. and Elizabeth Birkhead, Jan. 1st

Latterson, Charles and M. F. Wingfield, Nov. 24th

Lewis, Charles H. and Ann J. Bowles, Oct. 8th

Lobbin, John G. and Jane B. Ramsey, Aug. 23rd

1835

Leitch, James A. and Ann Pool, Aug. 24th

Lucas, William W. and Dianna Marshall, Dec. 7th

1836

Leake, Samuel A. and M. A. Boyd, Oct. 10th

Leake, William F. and Mary Ann Snow, Dec. 27th

Lively, John and Priscilla Hogg, Nov. 26th

Lobbin, James and Diannah Martin, Dec. 8th

1837

Lamb, Johnson and Nancy Vermal, April 25th
Lane, Gideon and Rebecca Ballew, July 13th
Levy, Charles and Belvidena Garner, Jan. 18th

1839

Longinatto, John and Mary A. Thurmond, April 9th
Lupton, Benjamin and Catharine H. Jury, Feb. 19th

1840

Langford, Warner and Frances F. Walton, July 14th

1841

Lane, David and F. A. C. Via, Nov. 27th
Langford, Robert and Jenetta Hays, Dec. 14th
Leobrick, George and Nancy Kidd, Nov. 18th
Lewis, John and Sarah Lewis, Jan. 3rd

1842

Langford, West and Martha Woodson, July 4th
Lobbin, James and Mary H. McGehee, Jan. 13th
Luck, Richard and Sarah Collins, Dec. 14th

1843

Lee, John and Susan Ann Burns, June 27th
Lupton, William A. and Martha Dollins, Dec. 21st

1844

Lively, John W. and Ann M. Thomas, Dec. 26th
Lobbin, John G. and M. C. Wingfield, Aug. 19th

1845

Lane, Presley C. and S. E. Fearneyhough, Sept. 25th
Leake, Walter and Elizabeth Stephens, March 18th
Linton, John C. and E. S. Watson, Nov. 2nd

1846

Leitch, James A. and S. Y. L. Poore, Nov. 11th
Loving, William H. and Eliza M. Travellian, Nov. 5th

1847

Lane, Edwin W. and Emily Bornce, Oct. 28th
Leake, Austin and Ora Mechams, May 3rd
Lewis, James and Lucy Brock, Dec. 11th
Lobbin, James and Catharine Saunders, Feb. 3rd
Lofland, George M. and Elizabeth Cox, Sept. 2nd
Lovell, Lewis and E. J. Gentry, Nov. 27th

1848

Laurine, J. J. E. M. and M. E. Maddox, May 29th

Leitch, Andrew and Mary Watson, Jan. 20th
Lewis, James M. and Catharine A. Jury, Dec. 21st
Lewis, Z. R. and Mary E. Gault, July 14th

1849

Lewis, William F. and Matilda F. Creel, Nov. 20th
Lupton, David H. and S. W. Cockerill, Aug. 9th

1850

Lamb, William J. and Mary J. Sandridge, Oct. 17th
Leake, Francis M. and Cornelia Mehanes, May 25th

1851

Lamb, John R. and Jane E. Keinnon, June 28th
Lewis, John M. and M. E. R. Tapp, Dec. 24th
Luck, John K. and Clem R. Terrill, June 16th

1852

Leathers, Jonathan and Polly Sowell, Feb. 17th
Lightbaker, J. M. and Sarah N. Garner, Dec. 5th

1853

Lilly, Joshua and Sarah Mosby, Jan. 11th
Lowery, Albert T. and Elizabeth Wheat, May 4th

1854

Lewis, William I. and Fanny Campbell, June 7th
Lewis, Wm. S. and Fannie Campbell, June 7th

1855

Lamden, Henry and Dolly Bailey, March 8th
Latane, James A. and Mary M. Holladay, Nov. 7th
Layne, William P. and V. A. Suddarth, Nov. 20th
Lenehan, Thomas and Sallie A. Rodes, Sept. 12th
Lewis, Samuel H. and Louisanna Dabney, Aug. 30th
Lewis, Sam'l. H. and S. S. Dabney, Dec. 15th

1856

Lacy, Robert and Ann M. Proffett, Jan. 16th
Layne, Wiliam S. and Dianna J. Hoey, Feb. 14th
Lacy, Robert and Anna M. Proffit, Oct. 19th
Lane, John R. and Irena Kennon, March 1st
Lipscomb, C. B. and Sallie P. Turner, Feb. 5th
Leack, James H. and Sarah E. Harlan, Feb. 24th
Lane, Nehemia and Agnes Madison, April 15th

1857

Lane, John R. and Irena Kennon, Feb. 28th

Lipscomb, Chris B. and Sally P. Turner, Feb. 3rd

1858

Ladd, John M. and Mary E. Hawley, Feb. 24th

Lane, Jeremiah and Angelina Madison, March 1st

Leech, James H. and Sarah E. Harlan, Feb. 23rd

1859

Lane, George W. and Eliza Thurston, Dec. 15th

Lang, Garie and Virginia A. Crawford, Sept. 21st

Layne, John H. and Elizabeth P. Jackson, Oct. 17th

Loving, Leaton H. and Martha J. E. Tompkins, Aug. 30th

Lane, Jno. H. and Eliz. T. Jackson, Oct. 20th

Loving, Seaton H. and Martha J. E. Tompkins, Aug. 31st

Lang, Garie and Virginia A. Crawford, Sept. 22nd

Lane, Geo. W. and Eliza Thurston, Oct. 20th

1860

Lafferty, John J. and Martha A. Brown, April 24th

Langford, Warner and Sarah E. Hicks, Jan. 31st

Leake, William J. and Mary E. Wood, April 2nd

Lipscomb, William H. and Texie Wolfe, July 16th

Louthan, William P. and Helen M. Bibb, July 5th

Loving, Ewell A. and Henrietta Hudson, Oct. 16th

Lowery, George T. and Mildred A. Morris, Sept. 5th

Laffuty, Jno. J. and Mattie A. Brown, April 20th

Langford, Warren and Sarah E. Hicks, Feb. 6th

Leak, Wm. J. and Mary A. E. Wood, April 5th

Lowery, Geo. T. and Mildred A. Morris, Sept. 6th

Lipscomb, Wm. H. and Texie M. Wolfe, July 17th

1861

Lang, N. G. and Lucy N. Mahanes, Dec. 21st

Lewis, Henry D. and Elizabeth Meeks, Oct. 15th

Lightbecker, Charles and Sallie E. Huffman, Jan. 9th

Lowery, John T. and Martha A. Stone, Dec. 24th

Luther, Ada and Eliza J. Houchens, April 24th

Lang, Nath. G. and Lucy N. Mahanes, Dec. 26th

Lewis, James T. and Alice S. Lewis, Jan. 11th

1863

Lane, Jno. J. and Kate M. Genutham, Dec 20th

1864

Lewis, Ro. W. and Lizzie Minor, Sept. 21st

1865

Lewis, Geo. and Sarah A. Speers, March 16th

Lane, Andrew J. and Margaret F. Nicholas, Jan. 12th

London, Lewis and Grbraella Wood, Jan. 5th

Lane, Andrew J. and Mars F. Nicholas, Jan. 11th

London, Lewis and Gabrella Wood, Jan. 3rd

1866

Lewis, George W. and Amediah Jackson, Sept. 1st

Lewis, John W. and Susan F. Dobbs, March 21st

Lupton, James W. and Lucy C. Marshall, Feb. 17th

Lang, Mandeth B. and Eliza A. Beck, Dec. 3rd

Long, Meredith B. and Eliza. A. Beck, Dec. 5th

Lane, Jas. A. and Lucy A. Sandridge, Dec. 4th

Luckett, Wm. L. and Macy E. Wheeler, March 22nd

Lupton, Jas. W. and Lucy C. Marshall, Feb. 22nd

Lewis, John W. and Susan F. Dobbs, March 6th

1867

Leake, Samuel A. and Lucy H. Boyd, Jan. 21st

Lewis, Cary and Lucy Cobbs, Jan. 26th

Logans, Stephen and Ruth Ann Williams, Dec. 24th

Lipscomb, Oscar C. and June M. Jefferies, Dec. 17th

Long, Jno. W. and Cormora H. Shiflett, July 26th

Lupton, Jno. H. and Susan M. Foster, Oct. 16th

1868

Lott, Samuel and Nellie Cole, June 1st

Luck, John R. and Ann Frazier, July 7th

Lawson, Jas. R. and Mary A. Wash, Nov. 4th

Laffland, George and Sallie E. Farish, March 24th

1869

Loftland, Geo. and Sallie Farish, March 4th

Lewis, James and M. Jane Stewartz, May 2nd

Lipscomb, Wm. C. and Maria E. Rae, March 10th

Lanve, Alphinse and C. C. M. Samuels, June 1st

Loeb, J. and Patty Minor, Oct. 1st

Longs, Lewis S. and Cornelia F. Bamley, Oct. 13th

Lane, Moses and Jane Williams, Dec. 14th

Lane, Thos. W. and Mary L. Bragg, Dec. 29th

Leay, Oracha F. and Virginia Vaughn, Dec. 23rd

1870

Lamb, M. and Oartilia C. Wood, Jan. 30th

Lee, Warfield and Anna J. Walton, March 15th

Lightfoot, Jas. A. and M. E. Mays, June 1st

Lott, James and P. Jones, June 11th

Leake, F. C. and Helena Snead, Sept. 8th

Lane, Jas. T. and S. J. Tyler, Feb. 16th

1871

Landstreet, Chas. and Laura M. Early, Jan. 17th

Lewis, Jno. W. and Isabella V. Bruffy, April 13th

Linsey, Jacob and Alice Watson, May 29th

1872

Lane, Henry W. and Eliza D. Easton, July 11th

Leake, Wm. and Mary E. Abell, Aug. 20th

Lancaster, Samuel C. and Cornelia A. Crank, Aug. 29th

Little, Lewis and Eliza Key, Sept. 23rd

1873

Lyons, John W. and M. P. Burton, Jan. 9th

Leake, N. P. and C. B. Winn, Feb. 5th

Leake, E. M. and A. M. Sandrum, Feb. 10th

Lewis, Jno. C. and Lucy W. Austin, July 7th

1874

Lanum, Jas. L. and Dollier A. Critzer, Jan. 26th

Lane, Jno. R. and Anne E. Biggers, June 2nd

Lobban, Wm. F. and Maggie L. Wood, Oct. 13th

Langford, Shepherd and Annie Barnett, June 4th

1875

Lewis, Thos. W. and Jane W. Page, Jan. 8th

Leitch, James S. and Nannie D. Carver, Sept. 28th

Leake, Nathan F. and Fanny S. Goolsby, Oct. 9th

Lindsay, Asberry and Cynthia J. Harris, Nov. 3rd

1876

Lemmon, B. H. and Eliz. L. Maury, July 28th

Leake, Luther G. and Susan F. Etherton, Sept. 26th

Lucado, Wm. J. and Mary C. Brigg, Dec. 22nd

1877

Leathers, Jno. P. and Louisia H. Stevens, Dec. 29th

1878

Lewis, James T. and Annie M. Wood, May 10th

Leake, Samuel J. and Kitty A. Elliton, Sept. 24th

Lankford, Jno. B. and Martha A. Wren, Sept. 25th

1879

Layman, Samuel R. and Kate E. Tomblin, Sept. 22nd

Loving, Andrew and Marian L. Kirby, Nov. 4th

1880

Lucus, Wm. Elverton and Alice Metta Gibson, Dec. 29th

1881

Lockwood, George R. and Annie P. Davis, Nov. 23rd

1882

Lamb, Ezekiel and Perlersa Thacker, Nov. 11th

Lewis, Henry C. and Ella J. Maupin, April 20th

Lewis, D. John and Rosa S. Parrott, May 16th

1883

Leake, John C. and Bettie Glenn Hilderbrand, March 15th

Lazand, Louis and Fannie A. Helles, Sept. 13th

1884

Layman, John T. and Mildred J. Robertson, ?

Lang, Jno. L. and Theodosia Gianiny, Feb. 10th

Londree, Thos. H. and Bettie L. Harrison, May 6th

Lea, John W. and Kate H. W. Wilson, May 5th

Letellier, Wm. W. and Ida B. David, Nov. 7th

1885

Lankford, Wm. A. and Bettie E. Walter, Aug. 11th

Lewis, Zack R. and Nannie L. Scott, Sept. 2nd

Lester, Jm. Brown and Kate Alkins, Oct. 13th

Liebrug, R. C. A. and Ida J. Hotoff, Oct. 21st

1886

Langford, Jno. D. and Julia A. Smith, June 27th

Leamon, Wm. Henry and Punie L. Coleman, Oct. 27th

Longfellow, Jno. D. and Julia M. Harris, Nov. 11th

Lipscomb, Wm. P. and Anna A. Goodloe, Nov. 25th

1887

Lewis, Geo. Wash. and Kitty Wood, Jan. 1st

Lewis, Robert D. and Caroline R. Thompson, Feb. 8th

Liebeck, Frederick and Salle M. Faulkner, Feb. 22nd

Lemmis, Thomas and Margaret B. Funsten, June 1st

1888

Lambert, Kemp L. and Kate H. Carter, March 20th

Lane, Henry L. and Laura L. Morton, March 21st

Londeree, Jno. and Ela Aromstrong, May 3rd

Lang, L. L. and L. G. Norford, May 17th

Lee, W. S. and E. J. Minor, July 23rd

Lang, L. J. C. and T. Gianniny, Oct. 9th

1889

Ladd, Chas. E. and Lucy A. Flint, Jan. 17th

Leckie, Geo. W. and Ella M. Cleveland, April 8th

Lacey, Walter H. and Sarah A. Craddock, Sept. 23rd

Loving, C. G. and S. C. Hamner, Oct. 21st

1890

Lamsden, Geo. W. and M. S. Smith, Feb. 22nd

Leonard, Chas. and Caroline Drumheller, June 11th

Loving, D. C. and Mamie W. Johnson, Aug. 4th

Lewis, W. H. and A. E. Strayer, Sept. 22nd

Lang, Mongomery L. and Vistie Dabney, Oct. 27th

Loving, C. H. and L. V. Hamm, Dec. 18th

Lang, A. P. and M. E. Jones, Dec. 24th

1891

Lirch, Mc. and Ellen V. Goobly, Oct. 13th

Louny, M. C. and E. M. Bacon, Dec. 2nd

Lamb, Jno. L. and Pirlissie Shiflett, Dec. 15th

1892

Lenham, W. D. and N. A. Kirby, April 14th

1893

Lawson, Robt. G. and Sallie Lawson, Feb. 6th

Lupton, Chas. S. and Jenny C. Eddins, March 6th

Leake, James and Auslia Leake, May 23rd

Lively, W. M. and B. C. Coleman, Sept. 25th

Limerick, Chas. H. and Berdie B. Omohundro, Nov. 7th

Laivson, Jessie and Amanda Herring, Nov. 14th

Lucas, Jas. W. and Sally Gilliam, Dec. 16th

Lee, H. C. and Annie Dudley, Dec. 21st

1894

Lane, Wm. H. and H. J. Graves, Jan. 15th

Lawson, Robt. and Minnie Sepe, Dec. 4th

Lauman, Robt. F. and Catherine Stickma, Dec. 19th

Lipscomb, K. M. and M. M. Woods, Dec. 25th

1895

Lupton, H. J. and M. J. Via, March 21st

Lamb, Emmet and Minnie B. Herring, July 29th

Lang, W. L. and S. E. Gainniny, Sept. 9th

1896

Landerer, Geo. W. and Cathering L. Bishop, Feb. 12th

Littell, J. F. and F. C. Burnley, June 17th

Leake, G. S. and L. M. Young, Sept. 22nd

Lang, M. L. and N. F. Giannini, Sept. 30th

Lang, C. V. and L. E. Terry, Dec. 24th

1897

Lamb, Chas. F. and Anna F. Gentry, Feb. 18th

Long, W. S. nd M. L. Sullivan, Feb. 27th

Leake, N. F. and Emma Lange, April 24th

Leitch, Wm. A. and Mary C. Ballard, Dec. 18th

1898

Layman, Loyd and Lelie Mose, March 9th

Long, M. H. and B. L. Harris, May 23rd

Lupton, W. N. and C. E. Lupton, June 14th

Lewis, M. B. and J. B. Hancock, June 28th

Loudere, T. H. and Helen Bishop, July 24th

Lawson, Geo. Ro. and Mollie Herring, Sept. 13th

Lankford, Wm. and Mary A. Thomas, Sept. 13th

1899

Landes, D. and Ora E. Page, April 24th

Leake, R. Henry and Nellie F. Preddy, Sept. 18th

Lang, Maynard B. Jr. and Lucy L. Smith, Sept. 26th

Lipscomb, R. A. and Maude Williams, Nov. 28th

Landrum, V. W. and E. V. Bowen, Dec. 25th

Lane, C. W. and Annie Graves, Dec. 25th

1900

Lowery, R. L. and Geo. Powell, Jan. 23rd

Lamb, Chas. F. and Mattie F. Gentry, July 17th

Lyons, Geo. W. and Maggie B. Taylor, Dec. 17th

1901

Lafferty, Wm. C. and S. E. Owens, Feb. 5th

Leake, J. S. and M. L. Durrett, Dec. 31st

1902

Lamb, J. L. and M. F. Shiflett, Feb. 12th

1903

Lawson, Eugene and Edna Bailey, April 13th

Lurnesten E. R. and Ida J. Sprouse, May 26th

Layhs, Wm. R. Jr. and Elmer S. Huntington, June 10th

Lewis, Walker G. and B. F. Norris, Aug. 20th

Lamb, Newton and Bettie Miller, Nov. 16th

1904

Lang, A. B. and Lillie C. Lang, April 4th

Landram, Lewis E. and Eliz. L. Hall, July 16th

Laitenen, H. and H. Sunderland, Dec. 27th

1905

Landram, G. C. and Mary I. Critzer, Aug. 12th

Lonzey, George Christopher and Florence Wilson Hughes, Aug. 21st

Lewis, Minor B. and Jeanette E. Hancock, Oct. 10th

Loyd, Ezekial and Cora Lee Colvin, Dec. 30th

Lankford, Burnley and H. E. F. Grant, Nov. 7th

Lloyd, George W. and Minnie Rea, Dec. 16th

Lee, Claude Marshall and Mary Willingby Duke Slaughter, Dec. 19th

Langley, George Christopher and Florence Wilson Hughes, Aug. 21st

1906

Lamb, William N. and Lincinda Shiflett, Jan. 9th

Lamb, William Newton and Maggie Sprouse, March 5th

Lanum, James Loving and Mrs. Willie Ann Stanton, April 2nd

Leist, Charles F. and Ethel J. Simmons, May 2nd

Lambert, James Burdette and Sallie Davis Morris, June 4th

Larunw, James E. and Bestie M. Startctore, Sept. 20th

Lang, William P. and Lula May Lang, Dec. 26th

1907

Lilly, James W. and Florence R. Graves, Jan. 10th

Lanum, Howard W. and Lottie L. Kirby, April 17th

Loeser, J. W. and Maggie A. Mitchell, June 8th

Lourey, Sidney L. and Carrie L. Powell, Oct. 17th

Langhound, Thomas Henry and Edith A. Forsyth, Oct. 26th

Lipscomb, L. D. and Maud R. Winn, Nov. 27th

1908

Ladd, Hugh S. and Elizabeth F. Walker, Jan. 29th

Leake, Fulton B. and Dollie A. Wood, June 24th

Leays, Joseph and Georgia Gardner, Dec. 23rd

Lane, Thomas H. and Fannie L. Bragg, Dec. 30th

1909

Landow, Dr. Frank P. and Nora Mary Austin, April 14th

Lewis, Darriel H. and Annie Lilly Farrar, June 16th

Lamm, Hoy E. and Lizzie M. Davis, Aug. 4th

Londree, Garfield and Minnie Moore, Aug. 12th

Looney, John J. W. and Eveline C. Mackreth, Nov. 23rd

1910

Lawson, Oscar and Bessie Sipe, March 14th

Lamb, Walter and Alice Thomas, April 26th

Littlejohn, James C. and Mary E. Poates, June 22nd

Lewis, Austin and Texan Garrison, Aug. 4th

Lemhan, John I. and Eliza W. Fox, Aug. 22nd

Lynch, Ashby and Pearl E. Wells, Jan. 5th

Leake, Claude M. and Mary E. Oliver, Jan. 18th

Leake, Charles F. and Gracie A. Toms, Jan. 19th

Ladd, Charlie E. and Cornelia Loyd, March 7th

Leake, William Reginald and Vivla Agnes Ladd, April 25th

Lewis, Maryan B. and Maude L. Parr, June 1st

Lilly, Chas. M. and Grace F. Jones, Oct. 22nd

Loyd, Andrew and Cora Crawford, Nov. 13th.

1912

Lightfoot, John B. Jr. and Nan Maury Lemmon, April 20th

Lamb, Charles W. and Lela Sprouse, May 27th

Leake, Wilmer S. and Blanche J. Tyler, Aug. 22nd

Landes, Robert C. and Mollie Carver, Nov. 26th

1913

Lee, Alonzo J. and Mrs. May G. McMillan, March 5th

Lewis, Ed and Lelia Chamber, Jan. 15th

Lang, L. M. and Ethel J. Giannini, June 8th

Lang, John J. and Bessie L. Durham, June 30th

Lunn, Charles J. and Ellen Griffith, July 17th

Lucy, Herbert D. and Grace B. Smith, July 22nd

Lewis, Enoch J. and Florence I. Parr, Sept. 10th

Layne, George L. and Cora E. Layne, Oct. 21st

1914

Lamb, Robert E. and Alice Garrison, April 15th

Lane, Robert W. and Bell D. Smiley, June 10th

Littleton, Samuel C. and Sarah E. Perkins, Nov. 8th

Lefeere, George and Julia Faris, Dec. 20th

1915

Lockridge, Clifton H. and Obedience D. Loving, Aug. 16th

Lewis, Charles and Beatrice Cobbs, June 23rd

Long, John F. and Josie A. Critzer, Aug. 2nd

Lane, Lonnie Lee and Nora Annie Davis, Aug. 6th

Leuke, J. N. and Olie McCauley, Oct. 14th

Leake, Robert and Myrtle Munday, Nov. 22nd

Lockman, Russell and Amanda Sprouse, Dec. 20th

Ladd, Joseph and Magnolia Chander, Dec. 21st

Ladd, Elzia and Maude Carven, Dec. 23rd

1916

Lamb, Champe and Fannie E. Gibson, Feb. 24th

Lapsley, James W. and Mildred Jameson, June 15th

Lacy, John Peyton and Ethel M. Brown, July 8th

Leake, Perry H. and Lydia V. Cox, Sept. 20th

Louhoff, William H. and Mabel Critzer, Oct. 25th

Leake, Herbert F. and Kathleen Woodfolk, Dec. 27th

1917

Lawhorne, Lucian N. and Hattie V. Garrison, May 16th

Larner, Matthews W. and Caroline L. Bishop, July 16th

Lamb, Moody N. and Mary Glenna Beddows, Aug. 5th

Lively, Jacob and Maggie Collins, Sept. 10th

Leathers, Johnson F. and Birdie L. Clements, Oct. 9th

Londered, Albert and Rosa Lee Harris, Nov. 11th

Lanum, Chas. C. and Blanche L. Smith, Nov. 9th

Layne, Charles Wesley and Lillie Dudley, Dec. 21st

1918

Lang, James E. and Jessie L. Gianniny, Jan. 27th

Ladd, Liah C. and Lelia M. Chandler, March 23rd

Lively, Laurence and Nellie Bishop, Sept. 23rd

1919

Lang, Waddell and Edna Alice Misenheimer, June 11th

Lacy, Medford W. and Mattie A. Bolsie, Aug. 6th

Lloyd, James and Hattie Wayland, Oct. 7th

1920

Lamb, John Henry and Mary Ethel Abell, Nov. 18th

Lamb, Chas. F. Jr. and Annie L. Bolton, Nov. 27th

Lane, Arthur Lee and Carrie Belle Butler, Dec. 31st

1921

Leake, Herring W. and Mary Cleveland, Feb. 5th

Ladd, Maurice Robert and Melva G. Kirby, April 8th

Lang, Charlie L. and Maggie A. Humphrey, Aug. 9th

Layman, George D. and Lottie L. Baber, Aug. 14th

Lamb, Arthur and Nettie Morris, Dec. 23rd

1922

Luce, Geo. D. and Lovena D. Watson, Jan. 21st

Lapsley, Samuel N. and Virginia E. Howsoin, Feb. 21st

Lummins, Irvine L. and Evelina N. Magruder, June 6th

Lanier, Willie E. and Nola E. Long, Dec. 28th

1923

Lamb, W. Newton and Rachael Sprouse, Jan. 23rd

Layne, John Robert and Mary Lee Smiley, May 17th

Lewis, Linwood and Lizzie Shiflett, June 27th

Layne, Walter A. and Cora E. Young, Aug. 22nd

Loving, Benton and Mary Anderson, Oct. 18th

1924

Lewis, Clarence B. and Elizabeth L. Brown, Feb. 6th

Layne, Marvin T. and Mary Lucy Young, Aug. 3rd

Lilly, Miles and Catherine A. Gable, Aug. 20th

Lewis, Peyton S. and Marie A. Shepherd, Oct. 14th

1925

Lewis, Oscar and Lessie Garrison, Feb. 21st

Lucas, Kenneth and Ruby Dowell, Feb. 18th

Long, Teddy E. and Marie M. Buttner, April 16th

Layman, Clarence V. and Rachel Foster, April 26th

Layne, Robert and Stella Stuart, June 27th

Layman, Haller W. and Nora M. Currier, July 1st

Lane, Charles E. and Sally Kesterson, Aug. 6th

1926

Lamb, Mathew D. and Susie A. M. Dickerson, March 3rd

Lamb, Lester and Maggie Ola Geer, June 7th

Late, Burleigh and Carrie Ryan, July 5th

Larrimore, Frederick G. and Margaret G. Price, July 30th

Lang, Harvey and Florine Barnett, Sept. 18th

Lang, Percy L. and Bessie Lloyd, Oct. 20th

Lewis, Maupin and Maupin Martin, Nov. 16th

Lawry, Aubrey and Edith Henry, Nov. 23rd

1927

Lotts, Harry Lee and Va. Wade, Jan. 19th

Lowry, Neal J. and Mary E. Henry, June 21st

Lewis, Thos. J. and Bertha Reid, June 21st

Lam, Carl E. and Ruby A. Cox, June 30th

Lawson, Theodore R. and Betty L. Lamb, July 19th

Lawrence, Ollie and Melva Winebarger, Aug. 2nd

Lee, Willie A. and Carrie L. Parr, Aug. 20th

Londeree, Larkin and Eula V. Carter, Dec. 24th

1928

Laster, Angrus G. and Ruth T. Campbell, July 11th

Leonard, James J. and Annie B. Cleveland, Dec. 7th

Lamb, Geo. W. and Edith Viola Shiflett, Dec. 27th

1929

Lamb, John A. and Nellie Lynch, April 6th

Landes, Forest Lee and Emily M. Barnett, Aug. 9th

Lamb, Edward N. and Emma J. Amiss, Aug. 12th

Lowry, Julian and Cora Currier, Aug. 24th

Leadom, Benjiman and Lunidia Shiflett, Aug. 31st

M

1781

Mackie, Alexander and Milly Smith, Aug. 28th

Murrel, George and Sally Blain, Oct. 8th

1782

Maupin, Daniel and ? Jarman, Jan. 14th

1783

Mills, John and Elizabeth Fields, Jan. 6th

Moore, Edward and Mildred Lewis, March 3rd

Moore, James and Elizabeth Hamner, Jan. 13th

1784

Maupin, Thomas and Anny Spencer, June 10th

Mullins, Anthony and Polly Clark, Nov. 2nd

1785

Mageke, Charles and Cate Bishop, Dec. 21st

Mansfield, Robert and Mourning Clark, May 4th

Martin, Peter and Elizabeth Henderson, Dec. 24th

Maupin, David and Sarah Spencer, Oct. 13th

Mills, Nathan and Betty Harris, Aug. 20th

1786

McCord, William and Darkis Rosel, July 29th

McKinsey, Alexander and Tabitha Hill, March 29th

McNally, Elijah and Jane Hulcey, Oct. 16th

Moore, Richard and Kilturea Austin, March 9th

1787

Melton, Benjamin and Susanna Updegrave, Dec. 21st

Modred, Adam and Jean McCord, Nov. 27th

1788

Mansfield, Samuel and Martha Shelton, Jan. 8th

Maupin, John and Elizabeth Mills, Dec. 7th

Mooney, Richard and Milly Carroll, Dec. 24th

Moore, Plat and Milley Langford, Sept. 29th

Murray, James and Milley Cook, Feb. 27th

1789

Marshall, Benjamin and Mary Coffer, Jan. 7th

Martin, John and Sarah Wingfield, Nov. 7th

McCauley, David and Susannah Goulding, Nov. 2nd

McCue, Charles and Anne Maxwell, May 23rd

Monroe, Andrew and Ann Bell, Oct. 24th

Muse, Samuel and Elizabeth Smith, Nov. 14th

1790

Mansfield, John and Mary Smith, Dec. 22nd

Mansfield, Reuben and Nancy Massie, Dec. 22nd

McNalley, David and Ann Kyle, March 12th

Michie, William and Mary Ann Nancy, Dec. 23rd

Miller, Isaac and Polly Lewis, May 9th

Monroe, Joseph J. and Elizabeth Kerr, ?

1791

Maum, Dennis and Patsey Lewis, Jan. 15th

Maupin, Daniel and Betsy Gentry, April 21st

Maupin, Gabriel and Polly Mullins, Aug. 26th

Maupin, Thomas and Elizabeth Michie, Nov. 21st

Micks, Richard and Peggy Gianniny, March 9th

Mills, Minan and Frances Janett, April 28th

Munday, Reuben and Anne Dowell, Dec. 27th

1792

Marshall, Thomas and Susannah Rodes, Dec. 12th

Marshall, William and Mary Connerly, Jan. 2nd

Maupin, Daniel and Susannah Sandridge, Feb. 27th

Maupin, Gabriel and Susannah Holman Bailey, Feb. 16th

Maxwell, John and Katy Squaire, April 12th

McCauley, Ezekiel and Margarett Ray, Dec. 27th

McKnight, Archibald and Rachel Bishop, March 21st

Mooney, Martin and Patsy Gray, July 14th

Moore, William and Mary Mighers, Oct. 13th

Moore, William and Milly Littrell, Dec. 7th

Munday, Sam and Anna Hall, Dec. 31st

1793

Marshall, Richard and Taba Cofer, Dec. 28th

Martin, Abraham and Jany Trible, Dec. 2nd

Maxwell, James and Jane Gentry, Feb. 14th

Meaks, William and Catherine Gianniny, July 17th

Middlebrook, Jesse and Winny Tyree, Oct. 9th

Miller, Daniel and Susanna Wood, Nov. 25th

Myers, Christian and Susannah Southerland, Dec. 24th

1794

Martin, George and Sally Henderson, Feb. 24th

Maupin, Bland and Sarah Brown, Dec. 23rd

Morrison, John and Mary Buckner, Nov. 24th

1795

Mallory, Henry and Ann Jones, Jan. 9th

Marshall, James and Milly Hensley, July 2nd

Martin, Benjamin and Caty Bailey, June 17th
Martin, Elisha and Barbara Henderson, Oct. 7th
Mullins, John, Jr. and Mury Mickie, Jan. 25th
Mullins, John and Milly Mullins, Dec. 12th

1796

Mars, John and Sally Jones, June 22nd
Moore, Moses and Nancy Hurt, Jan. 4th

1797

Meador, Thomas and Frances Gilmore, Nov. 14th
Morgan, Gideon and Betsy Hardin, Dec. 15th
Morris, Thomas and Ann Davis, Dec. 12th

1798

Maupin, John and Polly Michie, Feb. 6th
Mayo, John W. and Mourning Mayo, Dec. 3rd
McCauley, Daniel and Patsey Slater, June 8th
Mills, Zachariah and Mary Catting, Dec. 6th
Moran, William and Lucretia Pemberton, Dec. 22nd

1799

Mansfield, John and Nancey Carr, Feb. 16th
Martin, Thomas and Mary Ann White, March 21st
Matthews, William and June Dunbar Hall, Oct. 7th
McClure, Alex and Nancy Foster, July 12th
McDaniel, Stacey and Sally Lamb, April 6th
McDonnall, Sam and Nanny Kirby, Dec. 9th
Merewether, John and Mary Bowles, Aug. 24th
Merrett, Nicholas and Elizabeth Smith, Jan. 1st
Moore, Charles and Polley Cleveland, Nov. 4th
Moore, George and Elizabeth Buster, Feb. 4th
Moore, Stephen and Mary Royster, May 5th
Moul, George and Polly Thacker, Oct. 25th

1801

Mansfield, Isaac and Nancy Copeland, July 7th
Moore, Joseph and Rhoda Harper, Nov. 19th

1802

Martin, Reuben and Susannah Eads, Dec. 9th
Massie, James and Catherine Chrisholm, March 20th
Maupin, Cornelius and Polly Paul, May 18th
Maupin, William and Jane Jameson, Nov. 27th
Mayo, James and Nancy Scott, Dec. 6th
McFall, Cornelius and Mary Musick, Sept. 15th
Moss, Thomas and Polly Farrar, Oct. 26th
Morris, Elijah and Elizabeth Gaer, Jan. 18th
Morton, Nathaniel and Elizabeth Thompson, Sept. 8th
Mullins, John and Elizabeth B. Elllis, April 20th

1803

Martin, Nelson and Rebecca Austin, July 25th
Maupin, John and Nancy Cobbs, Oct. 3rd
Mayo, Claudius and Nancy Bailey, Jan. 3rd

1804

Marshall, Henry and Eleanor Wood, Dec. 26th

Martin, William and Sarah Michie, April 5th
Matchett, Richard and Caty Davis, Oct. 1st
McCloud, John and Mary Elliott, Dec. 14th
Montgomery, Thomas and Jane Lewis Witt, Jan. 2nd

1805

Martin, Cary and Nancy Pemberton, Nov. 18th
Matthewson, James and Polly Hering, Sept. 9th
Maupin, Chapman W. and Polly Spencer, Dec. 26th
Maupin, Thomas and Margarett Maupin, July 27th
Maxwell, Bezaleel and Polly A. Rice, Dec. 5th
McClary, Robin and Mary Spears, Jan. 12th
Minor, Dabney and Eliza Johnson, March 30th
Moran, William and Ruth Fitzpatrick, Dec. 24th
Moss, Drury and Lucy Howel, April 2nd

1806

Maupin, Bernard and Betsy Harris, Dec. 13th
McClure, John and Ann Mapie, Oct. 18th
McCullock, Rob, Jr. and Patsy Mills, Sept. 18th
Mills, Nathan and Kelly Jameson, Feb. 18th
Minor, Peter and Lucy Gilmer, May 31st
Moses, Samuel and Patsy Quick, March 30th

1807

Marshall, Reubin and Sally Elliott, Jan. 6th
Maupin, Pleasant and Lucinda Wood, Dec. 1st
McCauley, Peter and Agnes Garrison, Jan. 8th
McGehee, Benjamin and Betsy Reynolds, Nov. 2nd
Moore, Platt and Polly Grymes, May 17th

1808

Mahanes, Lewis and Ducilla Brockman, Jan. 1st
Mason, William and Polly Carden, ?
Matthew, Ben and Nelly Scott, Dec. 30th
Maury, Reubin and Elizabeth Lewis, Nov. 10th
Miller, Zach and Mary Calling, Dec. 6th
Moon, Martin and Polly Burch, Oct. 3rd
Moore, William and Mary G. Marks, May 2nd
Munday, John and Sally Harper, June 29th
Marshall, Richard and Elizabeth Rodes, Dec. 19th
Maupin, Thomas and Polly Clarkson, Jan. 21st
McGehee, Joseph and Lucy Mullens, June 25th
Michie, William and Susan Michie, Jan. 18th
Minor, James and Christian Tompkins, Dec. 12th
Moore, John and Susan Barnett, May 28th
Mullens, Anthony and Sally Reynolds, Jan. 20th

1810

Marshall, Henry and Elizabeth Walton, Jan. 22nd
Marshall, James and Sally Moore, Dec. 19th
Marshall, Joseph and Mary Boswell, Jan. 16th
Martin, John and Lucinda Starling, Nov. 18th
Martin, Merideth and Peggy Ramsey, June 5th
Maury, Garland and Jinny Rea, May 7th
Maxwell, Thomas and Caty Norvell, Nov. 5th

McAllister, Nathaniel and Elizabeth Dowell, Dec. 29th

Merry, John and Priscilla Rollings, July 7th

Moore, Pleasant and Orpha Harlin, Dec. 14th

1811

Maupin, Charles W. and Polly Harrison, Sept. 19th

Maupin, William and Polly Perry, May 6th

Moon, Nathaniel and Rozey Moon, Oct. 5th

Moore, John and Nancy Thacker, March 4th

Morris, Samuel F. and Elizabeth Johnston, Nov. 13th

1812

Maupin, Daniel and Hannah Harris, Dec. 24th

Maupin, David, Jr. and Jerusha Snow, Feb. 3rd

Maupin, John and Rosanna Maupin, Nov. 9th

Maury, Hudson and Peggy Ray, Nov. 9th

Maury, James W. F. and Elizabeth S. Thomas, Jan. 28th

Minor, Samuel O. and Lydia Lewis, Jan. 11th

Moore, Noble and Martha R. Rogers, Dec. 7th

1813

Marr, Janes and Jane M. Paine, Feb. 1st

Maupin, Carr and Nancy Burch, Aug. 2nd

Maxwell, Robert B. and Sally C. Norvell, Jan. 4th

McCauley, Samuel and Sarah Grimstead, Feb. 27th

Melone, James and Fanny Watts, Oct. 21st

Melton, Benjamin and Sarah Burford, Dec. 21st

Moore, Thomas and Mary Ann Spradling, June 2nd

1814

Mason, Matthew and Fanny Marshall, Jan. 3rd

McFall, Thomas and Nancy Hall, Aug. 23rd

Moore, Tope and Susanna Moore, March 28th

Moyer, John and Mildred Moore, Sept. 5th

1815

Markwood, David and Rebecca Williams, April 29th

Marshall, James and Fanny Robinson, Oct. 10th

Martin, John and Macy Wood, April 1st

Massie, John and Mary Smith, Aug. 24th

Maupin, Thomas and Nancy Harris, April 15th

McCloud, Joseph and Elizabeth Pritchett, Oct. 10th

McDaniel, Armistead and Julia McCauley

McMulhin, Charles and Tabetha McQuincy, May 6th

Moore, John W. and Mary Downs, Dec. 4th

Morrison, John and Mary Hays, Jan. 27th

1816

Mahanes, Samuel and Nancy Humphreys, June 5th

Maiden, William and Sally W. Gardner, March 12th

Martin, James and Robena Wingfield, Dec. 25th

Martin, Pleasant and Maria Turner, Dec. 28th

Marye, John S. and Anne Maria Burton, Oct. 10th

Mayo, James and Nancy Mayo, April 23rd

Michie, James and Francis Durrett Garth, June 16th

Milliway, John and Judith H. Mahanes, Sept. 26th

Milton, Samuel and Matilda Watts, Aug. 24th

1817

Mason, Armistead T. and Charlotte E. Taylor, April 3rd

Maupin, Joel and Polly M. Maupin, Dec. 9th

Meyers, John and Elizabeth Grayson, Dec. 9th

Miller, Jepe and Lucy Baber, Dec. 1st

Mitchell, Johnson and Falatha Herring, Dec. 1st

Moore, William and Martha Wheeler, Oct. 6th

Munday, Thomas and Fanny Ferguson, Nov. 6th

1818

Mahanes, Samuel and Elizabeth Harris, Dec. 22nd

Martin, David and Patsy Baber, Nov. 9th

Maupin, Galride and Polly Marr, Nov. 9th

McCord, William and Sally M. Field, Dec. 22nd

McKinney, William and Elizabeth M. Mastin, Jan. 4th

Meriweather, Peter M. and Mary W. Meriweather, June 9th

Mills, Martin S. and Elizabeth Boyd, Aug. 13th

Minor, Dabney and Martha I. Terrell, Dec. 24th

Morris, Simpson and Judy Shiflett, Aug. 23rd

1819

Marshall, Thomas and Patsey Marshall, March 2nd

Martin, Reubin H. and Sarah H. Foster, Aug. 3rd

Matthews, Francis and Elizabeth Smith, Sept. 23rd

Maupin, Richard C. and Lucy Harris, Sept. 14th

McKinney, John and Mildred Wood, Oct. 4th

Meeks, Edmund and Mary Branham, Feb. 18th

Munday, Achillis and Polly Wilkinson, Dec. 20th

1820

Maupin, Rice and Mary A. Carr, Dec. 2nd

Maxwell, Foster and Polly Ann Mason, Feb. 3rd

McWilliams, Alex C. and Jane Breedlove, April 10th

Miller, Thomas, Jr. and Matilda Johnson, Dec. 11th

Monday, Jonathan and Mary Edwards, Nov. 6th

Moon, John D. and Mary E. Barclay, March 18th

Moore, Henry O. and Eliza Moore, Oct. 19th

1821

Mallory, Nathan and Elizabeth Thompson, Oct. 22nd

Marshall, Eppa and Nancy Dunn, Jan. 11th

Martin, Lindsay and Polly Abell, Jan. 9th

Maupin, Overton and Polly Marrs, Nov. 18th

Maury, Thomas W. and E. A. Clarkson, Jan. 11th

McAllister, James and ? Brock, June 6th

McKenny, John H. and Mary S. Garth, Dec. 17th

Montague, Dudley T. and Elizabeth R. Brooks, Feb. 24th

1822

Maxwell, Fountaine and Sally Mason, Nov. 14th

McQuary, John and Martha Noel, March 10th

Meriwether, W. G. and Jane Lewis, Nov. 27th

Murphy, John and Eliza Munday, Aug. 20th

1823

Madison, Winston and Elizabeth Mooney, Feb. 25th

Martin, John and Elizabeth Wheeler, Dec. ?

Martin, Land W. and Sally White, March 22nd

McClary, John and Jane Davis, March 23rd

Meriwether, George D. and Alice Lewis, Feb. 5th

Minor, John and Jane Bell, Jan. 15th

Morris, Jacob and Eliza Eubank, Feb. 6th

Munday, Roling and Matilda Munday, June 19th

1824

Madison, Tom and Sarah Elliott, Sept. 23rd

Mandose, John H. and Sarah Carr, March 4th

Marshall, Wiley and Sarah Dopsey, Jan. 11th

Marvy, John and Susan White, Aug. 4th

Matthews, Joseph and Peggy Ballard, Dec. 2nd

McCord, James and Sidna Brown, Oct. 11th

Meriwether, John W. and Anne C. Nelson, Dec. 7th

Moon, Thomas and Rebecca Harper, Sept. 11th

Morris, Jeremiah and Peachy Shiflett, Sept. 24th

Morris, William and Nancy Digges Durrett, Aug. 5th

1825

Marrs, James J. and Maria Maupin, Feb. 21st

Marshall, D. W. and Emily Marshall, November 22nd

Marshall, Eppe and F. Gibson, Aug. 3rd

Marshall, Henry and Dilly Shiflett, Oct. 5th

Mason, Nathan and Nancey Collins, Nov. 7th

Matthews, John A. and F. Daniel, Aug. 18th

Maupin, Thomas and Susan Gibson, Dec. 13th

Milliway, Isaac and Judith Milliway, Jan. 12th

Munday, Charles and Elizabeth Solman, Jan. 15th

1826

Madison, Dabney and Sarah Barksdale, Sept. 11th

Madison, Thomas S. and Rebecca Elliott, Dec. 27th

Mahanes, William and Martha Mullievery, Aug. 14th

Marshall, Early and Claripa Collins, Nov. 6th

Meriwether, Francis and Margaret D. Meriwether, June 5th

Middlebrook, Hasten and Maria Gowing, Nov. 14th

Moon, Samuel O. and M. A. P. Moon, March 14th

Morris, Peter and Pina Shiflett, Oct. 2nd

Morris, Panhell and Susan Morris, Oct. 7th

1827

Marshall, Louden and Jincey Langford, Jan. 1st

Maupin, Joel R. and Martha Gentry, Dec. 17th

Mawyer, John and Nancy Harris, Feb. 24th

McCue, William B. and Frances Wineborger, Dec. 31st

Meriwether, Charles A. and F. E. Thomas, Feb. 14th

Michie, Robert and Elizabeth F. Walker, Oct. 25th

Mooney, John and Frances Blackley, April 17th

Moore, William and Sarah Wheat, Feb. 21st

Morris, Starling and Elizabeth Jones, Dec. 26th

Mullins, Walter and Margaret Rhoades, Jan. 31st

1828

Marshall, Greensville and Frances Marrs, Jan. 1st

Marshall, Wilson and Sophia Beddors, Jan. 6th

Maupin, Clifton and Elizabeth Maupin, Sept. 17th

Martin, David and Elizabeth Garland, Aug. 18th

Maupin, Tilman J. and Purena D. Brown, Jan. 17th

Mayo, Allen and Mary Farish, Dec. ?

Morris, Henariah and Frankey Haney, Dec. 9th

1829

Marshall, Brice and Elizabeth Martin, Dec. 31st

Marshall, William and Malinda Price, Dec. ?

Martin, Benjamin and Sarah Yancey, Nov. 23rd

Maupin, Cornelius and Polly Ellis, June 28th

McAlexander, Joseph and S. S. Foster, Aug. 25th

McClary, Isaac and Amanda Davis, Dec. 10th

McCord, James and Betsy Rupell, Jan. 10th

McFull, Ephraim and Sarah E. Johnson, Oct. 1st

Merchant, John A. and Malinda W. Marrs, March 19th

Morris, Sterling and Eliza K. Norvell, Aug. 3rd

Myers, John and June Gillum, Dec. 4th

1830

Martin, N. T. and S. A. Harper, March 9th

Matthews, Joel E. and Elizabeth W. Poage, Oct. 5th

Maupin, Walter C. and E. M. M. J. Scott, Oct. 20th

McCauley, Thomas and Polly Keaton, June 15th

McCrea, William and Jeretta Borden, Oct. 4th

Montgomery, Samuel and Susan Baber, May 27th

Moon, E. H. and Anna M. Barclay, Oct. 11th

Moore, Benjamin and Mary Bowen, Feb. 6th

1831

Massie, Nathaniel and Elizabeth F. Rodes, March 24th

McAleer, Robert and Malinda H. Beal, June 25th

McClary, George and Betsy Walton, Feb. 16th

McClure, William W. and E. H. Durrett, Feb. 22nd

McCord, Alexander and E. Maupin, Jan. 31st

Moon, Simleberry and Martha P. Moon, Aug. 4th

1832

Madison, James F. and Mary M. Collins, Dec. 3rd

Mahanes, William and Polly B. Harris, Dec. 30th

Mallory, Nathan and Cally Harris, Oct. 1st

Martin, David and Caroline McLain, Sept. 13th

Maupin, David W. and Virginia Ann Mills, March, 27th

Maupin, Lilbourn and Eliza A. Kent, Dec. 20th

Maupin, Nimrod and Susan E. Maupin, Dec. 19th

McAllister, Turner and Jane Hall, Oct. 18th

McMurdo, Thomas B. and Jane R. Higginbotham, Dec. 24th

Mooney, John and Vienna Sullivan, Aug. 6th

Mooney, Thornton and Elizabeth Sullivan, Feb. 22nd

Moore, Thomas and Susan Barnett, Sept. 25th

Morris, Absolum and Nancy Knight, Jan. 13th

1833

Marshall W. and Mildred Martin, Nov. 13th

Martin, Azanah and Susan D. Eubank, Sept. 11th

Mayo, Samuel S. and Savina R. Shiflett, Dec. 10th

Michie, John J. and Martha A. Michie, April 18th

Michie, William J. and Susan Anne Hartman, Sept. 11th

Milliway, William S. and Mary Garrison, May 30th

Mooney, David and Patsy Beaver, July 1st

Moore, John and Elizabeth Bragg, March 13th

Morris, Johnson and Frances Tailor, Jan. 2nd

1834

Marshall, Thornton and Polly Shiflett, Feb. 25th

Martin, Patrick and Susan Wertenbaker, Dec. 29th

McCoy, Daniel E. and Frances Burton, March 25th

Minor, Franklin and Lucy Ann Gilmer, Dec. 15th

Minor, John B. and Martha M. Davis, Dec. 23rd

1835

Mahon, James and Mrs. Margaret Woods, Jan. 8th

Martin, Barnett W. and Mary Golding, Nov. 7th

Maupin, Giles B. and Mary J. Norris, Dec. 5th

Maupin, Nicholas and Lucinda Ballard, March 30th

Maupin, Paschal and Frances Maupin, Dec. 10th

McGehee, Joseph and Polly Kirby, April 18th

Merchant, John A. and D. Shackelford, Dec. 23rd

Minor, Charles and L. W. Minor, May 19th

Morris, William F. and Frances E. Via, Dec. 19th

Morrison, John N. and Mary F. Anderson, Feb. 11th

1836

Mann, John T. and M. A. Suddarth, June 18th

Marshall, Fountaine and Judith Gardner, Dec. 19th

Marshall, Tavernor and Airy Gibson, Sept. 5th

Martin, Richmond and Maria Cole, March 28th

Martin, Samuel and Martha Cole, March 28th

Mason, Thompson D. and Harriett Cave, Jan. 20th

Maupin, Arthur T. and Mary B. Harris, Dec. 17th

Maupin, John D. and Marciscia Davis, Feb. 27th

May, John and Clarisa Jorden, March 25th

McCord, Samuel J. and Eliza J. Wolfe, Nov. 17th

McDaniel, Reubin E. and Sally Dunn, Dec. 19th

Melton, James C. and Martha Pritchett, Nov. 30th

Meriwether, Peter M. and F. W. Tapp, Oct. 6th

Minor, Hugh and Mary Ann Carr, Dec. 27th

Mitchell, Robert and Susan Boothe, Dec. 24th

Mosely, John A. and Mary J. Wingfield, July 4th

Mosely, Reubin and S. Burkhead, Aug. 5th

1837

Magginson, Benjamin C. and Frances A. Blain, May, 19th

Marshall, Blufoot and S. A. S. Crenshaw, June 8th

Marshall, William and Mary A. Shackelford, May 4th

Martin, Hudson and Mildred W. Minor, Oct. 30th

Maupin, Pleasant W. and Sarah Catterton, Aug. 31st

Mawyer, Shelton and Matilda J. Critzer, Oct. 17th

McClure, James and Eliza Brooks, May 24th

Morris, Aniel and Eliza Lane, Jan. 12th

Morris, Fountaine and Patsy Morris, Jan. 12th

Morris, Gorden and Margaret Douglass, March 23rd

1838

Madison, George H. and Frances Gibson, May 28th

Mallory, John B. and Elizabeth Roberts, March 4th

Marshall, Winston and Jane Norford, July 26th

Maupin, Chapman C. and Sarah M. Jarman, Jan. 8th

Maupin, C. D. and V. D. Harris, Oct. 3rd

Maupin, Sil G. and Martha Tilman, Dec. 17th

Maury, James M. and Sarah Goodwin, May 26th

Mawyer, Wilson F. and Mary A. Pugh, Aug. 20th

Mecklehan, David S. and Septima Randolph, Aug. 31st

Moore, John W. Jr. and Eliza Pace, Dec. 27th

Morris, Reuben and Polly McCauley, Dec. 26th

Murrell, John T. and Candice E. Warwick, Nov. 8th

1839

Marshall, James M. and Eliza Ann Barton, March 4th

Maupin, Albert A. and M. A. Jarman, Dec. 14th

Maupin, David S. and Frances A. Cobbs. May 16th

Maupin, Merritt R. and M. J. Maupin, Dec. 17th

McAllister, Benjamin and Frances Wilderson, Feb. 5th

McIntyre, George and C. A. Clarke, Nov. 19th

Michie, John and Mildred A. Palmer, June 10th

Moore, Samuel R. and Mary E. Minor, Feb. 26th

Morris, Lachareak and Sarah Highlander, Aug. 5th

1840

Marshall, Parks and Judah S. Batton, Feb. 14th

Martin, John S. and M. A. Staples, Nov. 3rd

Mayo, George L. and Eliza E. Houchens, Feb. 3rd

Minor, Peter C. and Lucy S. Carter, Oct. 16th

Monroe, Levi N. and Hannah P. Antrim, Jan. 31st

Moore, Richard A. and M. F. Pugh, Oct. 21st

Moorman, S. A. and Merry C. Maupin, Sept. 1st

Morris, William F. and Lucinda Turner, July 15th

Murray, Powhatan and Lethe Ann Bules Jan. 17th

1841

Marrs, John and Martha Hall, Jan. 7th

Martin, Patrick and Martha Mann, Oct. 19th

Martin, Willis and Virginia Cooper, Dec. 20th

Maupin, Logan J. and Eliza Sims, Dec. 6th

Mayo, James and Sally Ann Wilson, Jan. 14th

McClung, James H. and Elizabeth Wingfield, Jan. 24th

McKee, Charles R. J. and Theresa J. Hilton, Aug. 18th

McPhail, Benjamin G. and A. C. White, Dec. 25th

Moore, George W. and Elizabeth M. Mahanes, May 26th

Mosely, John O. and H. T. Page, Dec. 30th

Moss, John O. and Catharine Brown, July 9th

Mundy, John D. and Cynthia, A. Birkhead, June 29th

1842

Marr, Gaswell and Maria S. Burns, March 15th

Marshall, James S. and Emily J. Gorton, Oct. 14th

Maupin, John M. and Mary F. Thompson, March 8th

Mayo, John and Martha J. Wilson, Dec. 21st

Miller, Warwick N. and Maria J. Carr, March 22nd

Minor, Benjamin and Sarah Burch, April 14th

1843

Maupin, William C. and Jane A. Smith, Oct. 28th

Mawyer, Childress S. and Margaret A. McLain, Sept. 25th

Maxwell, Augusta E. and Sarah Brockenbrough, May, 22nd

McCauley, Jackson and Amanda Turner, Nov. 4th

Melton, William W. and Elizabeth Garrison, Feb. 15th

Minor, Francis and Virginia L. Minor, Aug. 31st

Moore, Pleasant and Nancy Ricks, July 4th

1844

Manning, M. Jacob and Frances E. Sprouce, Nov. 7th

Marshall, James T. and Jane F. Gibson, Nov. 26th

Marshall, Tazewell and Sophia R. Williams, Dec. 31st

Maury, Fleming and Lucy J. Price, July 8th

Maury, T. H. and Sarah J. Bails, April 23rd

McCauley, Alfred F. and Lurama F. Coleman, July 29th

Morris, John and Sarah E. Wingfield, May 7th

Munday, James and Judy Pratt, Oct. 7th

1845

Madison, George and Elizabeth Becks, Feb. 10th

Madison, John R. and E. A. Norford, Dec. 9th

Mann, William H. and Arabella Keith, Feb. 1st

Martin, Garrett W. and S. M. Wood, Nov. 3rd

Mawyer, James and S. E. Harlow, April 17th

Mayo, Claudius B. and M. E. Crenshaw, May 17th

McAllister, James and Susan Harvey, May 25th

McCauley, Miletus and Mildred Turner, Dec. 29th

McQuerry, Thomas H. and Sarah J, Garland. Feb. 13th

Michie, Reuben T. and S. E. Crank, Nov. 26th

Mills, David W. and Sarah E. Richard, Feb. 18th

Misgrove, Robert A. and M. J. Wolfe, Nov. 19th

Monday, Merideth and M. Hall, April 17th

Moon, Richard A. and F. C. Moon, Nov. 4th
Morris, Benjamin and W. A. Madison, Dec. 25th
Morrison, John N. and Eliza T. Davis, June 3rd
Mosby, Benjamin and M. A. Peake, Oct. 14th

1846

Marshall, Parks and Elizabeth Wood, Oct. 5th
Maupin, Thompson and Mildred C. Kiblinger, May 22nd
Mayo, Harden M. and Elizabeth Pugh, Dec. 29th
Mayo, Joseph R. and Isabella C. McKinney, Dec. 19th
McGrath, John and Nancy H. Singleton, Sept. 13th
Michie, Thiodore A. and Margaret M. Michie, Nov. 12th
Miller, George E. and Sarah A. Digges, Oct. 20th
Moon, Jacob and Pamelia A. Mawyer, Jan. 10th
Moore, Charles C. and Leonora Hicks, May 26th
Mosby, Robert H. and M. J. Anderson, July 29th

1847

Madison, Dabney and Nancy Gillaspy, Nov. 27th
McAlister, T. A. and Caroline M. Byers, April 9th
McAllister, T. A. and P. A. Beddor, July 25th
McLane, Smithson and Hardenia Pace, March 12th
Moon, John S. and Elizabeth Tompkins, Feb. 1st
Moore, James A. and Henrietta Hall, Aug. 12th
Morris, Samuel S. and Ella Garrison, Jan. 31st
Munday, Jefferson B. and Sally Flint, Dec. 23rd

1848

Mallory, William H. and M. E. Chapman, Jan. 14th
Marshall, George and Jane T. Murian, Dec. 23rd
Marshall, Zermesville and Virginia E. Fray, Dec. 5th
Martin, Benjamin and S. M. Meeks, Sept. 4th
Martin, Richard D. and M. S. Critzer, July 27th
McCurdy, John and E. R. Beal, April 3rd
McDaniel, John S. and M. E. Brooks, Feb. 21st
McLain, Christopher and S. A. Rice, March 27th
Michie, Octervus G. and Martha A. S. Michie, Oct. 21st
Mitchell, William and Morhula Jarrell, Nov. 23rd
Mosley, Robert B. and M. A. Gooch, June 25th

1849

Madison, John R. and Frances A. Smith, Nov. 1st
Mason, Charles and Maria C. Randolph, Sept. 20th
Maupin, John and Virginia Latham, Aug. 8th
McCauley, William T. and R. M. Royall, July 30th

Minter, Jacob and Catherine Mayo, June 18th
Munday, Wiley C. and Polly Ann Oaks, Sept. 3rd

1850

Marshall, James S. and Margaret Thomas, Aug. 13th
Marshall, Schuyler W. and Ann E. Woody, Feb. 21st
Mawyer, Jacob and Sarah Jane Kirby, May 19th
McAlexander, Jack L. and Susan C. Roberts, Oct. 24th
Moore, John and Nancy Hays, Oct. 29th
Mosby, Henry B. and Adeline Wright, March 21st
Mundy, Castleton H. and C. W. Drumheller, Aug. 5th
Mundy, Horace and Lucy Jane Thomas, March 4th

1851

Marr, Thomas and Nancy Parish, April 9th
Martin, James and Frances Akers, Oct. 13th
McGuffy, William H. and Laura P. Howard, Sept. ?
McMullen, William H. and Margaret S. Rice, Dec. 16th
Moon, Richard and Martha Bowen, Jan. 5th
Moon, Samuel N. and Ellen E. Dameron, Sept. 24th
Mooney, John and Nancy Becks, July 31st
Moore, Anderson D. and Susan Harris, June 3rd

1852

Maker, James and M. A. Martin, May 26th
Mallory, Daniel and Mary Ralchire, Dec. 15th
Maloney, Daniel and Mary Ralehan, December 15th
Maupin, Pleasant W. and M. J. Batton, Feb. 26th
Morris, Benjamin F. and S. G. Morris, Dec. 29th
Muloin, Jeremiah and M. Brown, May 20th

1853

Marshall, N. K. and M. A. Gardner, Jan. 20th
Massie, N. H. and Eliza S. Meriwether, Jan. 17th
Maupin, John and Eliza Jarman, March 16th
Maupin, Wayland W. and Lucy A. Dunn, April 7th
McCarty, John and Elizabeth Page, April 3rd
Michie, John W. and Georgianna C. Powers, Dec. 20th
Miller, John and Sarah Shiflett, Aug. 27th
Monterio, Aristides and Mary F. Cocke, Oct. 4th
Moon, William F. and Marietta Appling, Dec. 21st
Munday, Roland and Pelisa Hall, Jan. 18th
Murray, George W. and M. J. Bellomy, Feb. 24th

1854

Maloney, Patrick and Horiang Flynn, July 17th

Martin, George and Sarah E. Durrett, March 28th

Martin, William S. and Eliza A. Powell, Dec. 21st

Maupin, George W. and Martha K. Jarman, Sept. 26th

Mawyer, John A. and Colyann Toms, Nov. 13th

Mays, Uriah B. and Mary Ann Garrison, Dec. 4th

McKenny, James L. and M. J. Jackson, April 13th

Meeks, Henry and Mary O. Mahanes, Dec. 1st

Michie, Alex H. and Lucy V. Brown, April 11th

Michie, A. H. and Lucy V. Brown, July 16th

Mitchell, John R. and Fannie P. Gantt, Oct. 11th

Mitchell, Jno. R. and Fannie P. Gault, October 11th

Mitchell, Thomas P. and Mildred A. Maupin, Nov. 12th

Moore, Benjamin S. and Mary Bowen, Feb. 14th

Morris, William M. and L. H. Alexander, Aug. 15th

Muse, Thomas R. and Mary M. Hartman, Nov. 23rd

Muse, Thos R. and Mary M. Hartman, November 23rd

1855

Madison, D. R. and Sarah Smith, July 26

Madison, Dabney R. and Sarah Smith, July 26th

Madison, James and Mary Harris, Sept. 15th

Madison, Jas. and Mary Harris, September 6th

Martin Wm. H. and Cath. Price, July 15

Marshall, Daniel W. and Emily Marshall, Nov. 22nd

Marshall, John W. and Amy Marshall, Nov. 22nd

Marshall, Jno. W. and Angelina Marshall, November, 22

Martin, Andrew J. and Susan N. Price, Feb. 24th

Martin, William H. and Catharine Price, July 15th

Mason, James W. and Sarah B. Glover, Oct. 4th

Mason, Jas. W. and S. B. Glova, September 12th

Maupin, Geo. W. and Martha K. Jarman, September 26th

McKinney, Jas. L. and Mildred J. Jackson, April 13th

McVeigh, Benjamin F. and Sarah E. Lane, Feb. 15th

Michie, I. A. and Susan R. Jackson, March 22nd

Miechie, J. Augustin and Susan R. Jackson, March 22nd

Mills, Western and Martha A. Hays, April 29th

Mills, Western and Martha A. Hays, April 14th

Moore, Benj. L. and Mary Bowen, February 14th

Morris, Thomas F. and Mary E. Bruffy, Jan. 3rd

Morris, Thos. F. and Mary E. Bruffey, January 3rd

Morris, Wm. W. and L. H. Alexander, August 15th

Moseley, M. A. and M. J. Bailey, Jan .9th

Moseley, Malcom A. and Martha J. Railey, January 10th

1856

Macon, George W. and Mildred N. Meriwether, Sept. 3rd

Macon, Geo. W. and Mildred N. Meriwether, September 3rd

Madison, Wm. B. and Sarah J. Sandridge, May 28th

Mallory, Andrew J. J. and Mary J. Gardner, July 23rd

Marchant, Edw. W. and Mary M. Madason, June 21st

Marshall, Thos. and Julia Pritchett, August 13th

Martin, Garrett, W. and Sallie F. Early, December 9th

Martin, John A. and E. Moore, October 23rd

Martin, J. W. and Frances J. Thompson, Dec. 9th

Martin, Jere W. and Frances J. Thompson, December 4

Martin, John A. and Ann E. Moore, Oct. 23rd

Martin, Jno. T. and Cor. F. Powell, January 8th

Martin, William J. and Susan A. McCoy, Jan. 3rd

Martin, Wm. J. and Susan A. McCoy, January 3rd

Matthews, Robt. H. and Susan M. Royal, February 2nd

Maupin, Benjamin F. and Drucilla D. Brown, Nov. 12th

Maupin, Benj. F. and Drissilla D. Brown, November 12th

Mayo, Joseph R. and Elizabeth Garland, Dec. 25th

Mayo, Jo. R. and Eliz. Garland, October 28th

McCauley, Miles A. and Eliza Harvey, Aug. 7th

McCherney, Adam and Julia A. Dolin, July 29th

McCauley, Miles A. and Eliza Harvey, August 7th

McDaniel, Wm. H. and Eliz. Dudley, May 26th

McManary, Patrick and Ellen Rotchood, Nov. 13th

Meeks, Hiram and Martha Wood, February 26th

Metheuy, Fielding and J. A. McCauley, July 16th

Montario, J. M. and Maria E. Cocke, January 15th

Morris, Ambrose and Sarah Ann Dudley, Aug. 6th

Morris, Ambrose and Sarah A. Dudley, August 6th

Munday, James A. and Sarah F. Martin, Nov. 25th

Munday, Jas. A. and Sarah F. Martin, November 25th

Murphy, John and Nancy Bailey, Oct. 18th

1857

Madison, William B. and Mary J. Sandridge, June 22nd

Mallory, Andrew J. J. and Mary J. Gardner, July 20th

Marchant, Edward W. and Mary M. Madison, June 22nd

Marshall, Thomas and Julia Pritchett, Aug. 11th

Martin, Garrett W. and ? Early, Dec. 8th

Martin, John T. and Caroline F. Powell, Jan. 7th

Matthews, R. H. and Susan M. Royall, Jan. 31st

Mays, Joel E. and Mary A. Trainer, Dec. 7th

McDaniel, William H. and Elizabeth Dudley, May 25th

McDonald, Lewis and Lewellyn, Aug. 6th

Meeks, Hiram and Martha Woods, Feb. 11th

Mitheney, Fielding and Frances A. McCauley, July 13th

Monterro, J. M. and Maria E. Cocke, Jan. 14th

Moore, Joseph N. and Nancy S. Scruggs, Nov. 24th

Munday, Samuel and Sarah A. Hall, Jan. 7th

1858

Madison, Thomas W. and Ann Lane, Sept. 6th

Magruder, B. H. and Ann E. Norris, Feb. 15th

Maloney, Patrick and Jane E. Wash, August 12th

Marshall, Richard and Margaret M. Harris, May 12th

Marshall, Richd. H. and Margaret M. Harris, May 19th

McCauley, Patrick W. and Margaret J. Jones, March 17th

McCauley, Robert W. and Margaret J. Jones, March 18th

Morgan, Geo. W. and Martha P. Criddle, May 3rd

Morris, Thomas F. and Mary F. Goodwin, Dec. 24th

Munday, Clifton S. and Lizzie Bruce, February 10th

Munday, L. and Lizzie Bruce, Jan. 8th

1859

Maupin, John M. and Ellen F. Goulding, April 12th

Mayo, Julius and Susan J. Mayo, December, 21st

Mayo, Julius and Susan Jane Mayo, Dec. 14th

McDermott, Thomas and Mary Jane Suddarth, April 16th

McDermott, Thos. and Mary J. Suddarth, April 20th

Migginson, Archer B. and Helen Brady, Oct. 18th

Miggison, Austin B. and Helen Brady, October 22nd

Mills, David and Sarah Dudley, Nov. 3rd

Minor, John B. and Nannie F. Colston, Feb. 28th

Minor, Jno. B. and Nannie F. Colston, March 1st

Moon, Fleming B. and Ann M. Seay, Oct. 7th

Moon, Richard A. and Sarah E. Goodman, Jan. 14th

Mooney, George W. and Elizabeth Mares, Feb. 28th

Moor, Fleming B. and Ann M. Leay, October 20th

Moran, Robert S. and Elizabeth Ann Graves, April 16th

1860

Maddox, James M. and Sally Hamner, Oct. 24th

Maton, Jas. N. and Sally Hamner, October, 25th

Matthews, James D. and Maria F. Simpson, June 16th

Maupin, Wayland W. and Virginia A. Maupin, Nov. 29th

McKnight, James W. and Elizabeth Garland, Sept. 17th

McMurdo, John R. and Susan M. Anderson, July 2nd

McKnight, Jas. W. and Eliz. Garland, September 20th

Michie, Lucian A. and Theresa E. Michie, Dec. 3rd

Mitchell, Andrew J. and Lucetta E. Brockman, November 29th

Mitchell, Andrew J. and Lucilla E. Brockman, Nov. 26th

Moon, Richard A. and Sarah E. Goodman, February 1st

Munday, Dabney and Mary J. Lee, Nov. 5th

Mundy, Dabney and Jane Lee, November 12th

1861

Mailey, Patrick and C. MacNamara, April 3rd

Major, James J. and Martha G. Devoucks, October 13th

Mallory, William T. and Mary E. Marshall, April 1st

Mallory, William I. and Mary E. Marshall, April 25th

Mape, James J. and M. G. Devericks, Oct. 12th

McPherson, Jno. H. and Mary Jane Hodge, June 12th

McPherson, John H. and Mary Jane Hoge, June 11th

Mead, Edward C. and Emily A. Burgoyne, Nov. 18th

Mead, Edward C. and Emily A. Burgoyne, November 21st

Munday, R. H. and Lucy E. Brand, Dec. 23rd

Mundy, R. H. and Lucy E. Brand, December 24th

1862

Maupin, Tho. R. and Mc. C. Maupin, April 14th

Maury, Richard and Susan E. Critchfield, July 17th

McPhail, C. C. and M. J. Powell, July 30th

Michie, Tho. G. and Sally D. Jackson, October 7th

Miles, Wm. T. and Maggie M. Darton, November 4th

Moody, Rob. B. and Sarah S. Davis, January 22nd

Moore, Michael and Sarah C. Herndon, June 20th

1863

Maddox, Jas. M. and Mary A. Maupin, May 20th

Madison, Elizah F. and Jane E. Gillaspie, March 19th

Marks, Wm. T. and Mildred A. Goodwin, February 3rd

Marshall, P. H. and Mary E. Gooch, November 19th

Martin, Wm. R. and Martha J. Shelton, February 7th

Martin, Rubin M. and Mary Jane Maupin, September 7th

Massey, Rodes and Betty G. Lewis, September 10th

Maupin, Jas. H. annd Sally E. Maupin, August 27th

Mayo, Wm. H. and Mary M. Jones, April 18th

McCauley, M. A. and Martha Walton, October 22nd

McDinold, N. T. and Sarah E. C. Page, April 19th

Mealey, Nep. B. and Louisa R. Batchler, Auguest 18th

Mitchell, W. B. F. and M. J. Munday, May 9th

Moffint, Jno. G. and Virginia E. Austin, July 23rd

Moore, Ro. S. and Mary F. Desper, April 13th

Moyer, Allison and Jane Holmes, February 6th

Moyer, Jas. E. and Mary S. Kent, May 7th

1864

Marshall, Rice D. and Sally M. T. Maupin, February 29th

Martin, Jno. T. and Nellie G. Lucas, February 17th

McCormick, Ro. and Martha Jackson, August 29th

Michie, James W. and Sarah Davis, June 22nd

Mullins, Walter and Mary Humphrey, October 27th

1865

Mallory, John T. and S. F. Marshall, Sept. 28th

Malloy, Jno. T. and Susan F. Marshall, October 12th

Martin, Samuel H. and Mildred F. Via, Jan. 2nd

Martin, Samuel H. and Mildred F. Via, January 5th

Mitchell, James N. and Sarah A. Munday, Sept. 4th

Mitchell, Jas. V. and Sarah A. Mundy, September 7th

Mitchell, W. B. F. and Lucy J. Pritchett, Oct. 13th

Mitchell, W. B. F. and Lucy J. Pritchett, October 15th

Mooney, J. M. and Mary L. Campbell, Dec. 18th

Mooney, J. M. and Nora L. Campbell, December 19th

Morris, M. R. and Willie J. Norris, Dec. 24th

Morris, Marshall R. and Willie J. Johnson, December 27th

Moyer, Hardin S. and Mary Ann Snead, Dec. 25th

Munday, James A. and Willie A. Bunch, Sept. 2nd

1866

Maddox, Ro. H. and Sallie C. Wingfield, December 6th

Madison, Ben T. and Eliza C. Marshall, October 4th

Madison, Benjamin T. and Eliza E. Early, Oct. 1st

Madison, E. F. and Lavinia Chisholm, November 15th

Madison, E. F. and Lavinna Chisholm, November 12th

Madison, Geo. A. and Judith Garden, July 5th

Madison, George A. and Judith Gardner, July 4th

Mahanes, Tavner O. and Emily V. Salmon, December 20th

Mann, Auburn annd Jennie N. Wheeler, Oct. 22nd

Mann, Auburn and Jennie L. Wheeler, October 22nd

Mann, Jno. P. and Ann E. Sutherlan, November, 13th

Mann, Jno. P. and Ann E. Sutterland, November 10th .

Marsh, W. F. and Susan E. Garrison, January 6th

Marshall, Gelrge T. and Jane Harris, Oct. 22nd

Martin, John A. and Martha C. Dudley, Sept. 24th

Martin, Jno. A. and Martha A. Dudley, September 24th

Martin, J. T. and Sarah N. Bourne, Nov. 7th

Martin, J. T. and Sarah M. Benson, November 7th

Martin, Thos. H. B. and Mattie V. Patrick, April 4th

Martin, Thomas H. B. and Mattie V. Patrick, April 2nd

Mason, Lewis and Malinda Givings, April 26th

Mason, Rob F. and Maggie Cooke, Sept. 11th

Mason, Robt. F. and Maggie Cooke, September 11th

Maupin, Bernard P. and Susan A. D. Maupin, November 3rd

Maupin, Bernard P. and Susan A. D. Maupin, Nov. 3rd

Maupin, J. Nathl. and Mary A. C. Maupin, December 10th

Maupin, J. Nathl. and A. C. Maupin, December 13th

Maupin, Pleasant W. and Eliza A. Wood, January 17th

Maupin, Pleasant W. and Eliza A. Wood, Jan. 13th

Maupin Tho. R. and Sallie E. J. Maupin, July 1st

Maupin, Thomas and Sallie E. J. Maupin, June 26th

Mawyer, William N. and Elenora Norvell, April 2nd

McCardle, Henry and Jane E. Smith, Oct. 29th

McClung, John H. and Bettie Lipscomb, Aug. 1st

McRea, Wm. and Martha Taylor, December 27th

McClung, Jno. H. and Bettie Lipscomb, August 2nd

McCaidle, H. A. and Jane E. Smith, November 1st

Melton, Henry W. and Eliz. Woodson, January 11th

Melton, Henry W. and Elizabeth Woodson, Jan. 10th

Miller, Alfred H. and Rebecca D. Fickeler, Nov. 6th

Miller, A. H. and Rebecca D. Ficklin, November 6th

Moon, James N. and Cary A. Coleman, Sept. 17th

Mooney, Thos. J. and Sarah A. Wood, November 27th

Mooney, Thomas J. and Sarah A. Wood, March 26th

Morgan, George W. and Martha P. Criddle, ?

Morris, Whitfield and Mary E. Galden, March 29th

Morris, Whitfield and Mary Elizabeth Galeton, March 26th

Moss, Samuel J. and Cynthia J. Ballard, November, 21st

Mowyer, Wm. N. and Elenora Nowell, April 5th

Moyer, Hundson S. and Mary A. Snead, December 28th

1867

Mackley, F. A. and Fannie M. Smith, February 18th

Madison, James and Mary Ann Belew, October 7th

Mahanes, Chas. E. and Louisa M. Salmon, December 21st

Mahanes, Merideth and Louisa M. Salmon, December 23rd

Mahanes, W. S. and Lucy J. Salmon, February 18th

Mahoney, Elias, Jr., and Mep Ellen Pace, April 22nd

Marrs, Wm. T. and Mary Sharp, November 19th

Marshall, B. J. and Susan E. Thomas, March 4th

Marshall, Henry and Murta Scott, February 2nd

Martin, Jas. and Sally Brooks, December 25th

Martin, Joseph and Sally Brooks, December 21st

Martin, Sylvetta G. and Mollie I. Thomas, December 13th

Maupin, Gabriel N. and Lizzie F. Harris, February 7th

Maupin, James R. and Lucy A. Maupin, March 25th

Maupin, Nelson Chapman and Fanny Key, January 26th

Maupin, Rice W. and Millie E. Martin, January 11th

Maupin, Richard H. and Mary A. Haislip, February 23rd

Maury, S. Talbott and Lucy Burley, September 20th

McAlister, John and Selina F. Marshall, January 10th

McCauley, Virgel D. and Lucy Ann Herndon, January 25th

McCauley, Wm. T. and Henrietta J. Tate, January 28th

McAlister, W. T. and Mrs. S. A. Goodwin, April 22nd

McGehee, Peter and Ann H. Gilmer, June 10th

McGehee, N. C. and Molly Lobban, November 13th

Meeks, W. S. annd Mary L. Vasieior, November 4th

Melton, Cornelius J. and Mary E. Marshall, March 19th

Michie, Wm. W. and Luwina Rea, December 27th

Mongomery, W. F. and Josephine Dobbins, July 21st

Mooney, Edward and Mary A. Norris, September 21st

Mooney, Edward and Mary A. Norris, September 21st

Moore, Frank and Aidelia Carey, December 28th

Morris, Thos. C. and Anna C. Payne, November 5th

Morris, Wm. T. and Mary Sharp, November 18th

Mosbey, Jordan and Mary A. Rall, October 20th

Moses, Samuel D. and Bettie O. Brown, August 1st

Munday, Jonathan and Mary J. Salmon, December, 14th

Murphy, Dennis and Augusta J. Herring, December 27th

1868

Martin, Abram D. and Mary A. Elson, January 6th

Martin, Jno. H. and Amanda F. Antrovelle, April 14th

Martin, Jno. H. and A. F. Ambroselli, April 22nd

Martin, Tho. and Marian Toombs, January 20th

Marshall, James and Laura Smith, December 22nd

Marshall, R. J. and Eliza Jane Norford, February 3rd

Maupin, Gab'l. W. and Matie A. Maddox, November 24th

Mayo, Dudley R. and Margaret J. Craig, October 5th

Mayo, James E. and Mildred F. Ballew, February 5th

Mayo Thaddens and Morea Hams, April 11th

Michie, Jno. T. and Sallie E. Case, January 15th

Moon, Moses J. and Emily Jackson, ?

Mooney, Joseph and Lucinda E. Tate, February 25th

Moses, Samuel D. and Bettie Overton Brown, July 31st

1869

Madison, Lee and Emily Jackson, September 25th

Magruder, H. M. and Sally G. Minor, April 7th

Martin, G. W. H. and Masy E. Dunn, December 13th

Martin, P. A. and M. J. Ward, May 27th

Martin, Reubin and Esther Johnson, August 26th

Mayo, G. S. and E. C. Johnson, September 8th

Mays, Alex and Mildred Wheeler, November 30th

McCue, Jno. W. and Masy A. Shepherd, November 2nd

McAlister, Wm. T. and Mary E. Walton, December 16th

Meeks, J. F. and M. L. Craddock, February, 25th

Milstead, Gideon and H. E. Madison, April 13th

Minor, Lancelot and Emma R. Minor, November 24th

Monroe, James and Louisa Johnson, ?

Monroe, Ned and Harriet Captain, December 27th

Morris, Reubin J. and Betty Hurt, August 9th

Munday, Jas. W. and Mary L. Gilbert, November 18th

1870

Marshall, Jno. R. and Harny S. Gibson, December 1st

McGhee, John W. and M. L. Anderson, May 24th

Meade, Francis A. and Mattie B. Mosley, July 28th

Moon, Jas. P. and M. J. Hughes, October 27th

Moore, Neil and Foky Brown, November 4th

Munday, Samuel and Sallie M. Talwell, December 6th

1871

Marchant, J. B. and Alice A. Tyler, July 24th

Mayo, James S. and Mattie E. Thomas, December 21st

McAllister, Jno. W. B. and Mildred W. Robinson, October 2nd

McClure, Jas. A. and Amanda S. Martin, October 9th

Moon, Jacob L. and Ann Martin, October 31st

Moon, Rich'd. C. and Emma S. Scantling, November 11th

Moose, George and Sally Wingfield, November 29th

Morgan, Robert S. and Maria R. Abell, June 12th

Moyer, Joseph Coleman, and Nannie Jane Kirby, December 21st

Murray, Wm. M. and Bettie Scruggs, July 10th

1872

Maddox, John C. and Sallie H. Cleaveland, September 10th

Marshall, D. W. and R. B. Towdsend, December 24th

Martin, Henry and Mildred J. McKenny, February 1st

Martin, John F. and Sally Baber, January 10th

Mason, James G. and Sue Jane Tyler, March 6th

Maupin, Thomas G. and Mary F. Robertson, January 8th

Maury, Matthew F. and Nannie Maury, January 1st

Mayo, William J. and Susas E. Bass, April 11th

Mays, G. W. and Texanna Wheeler, December 11th

McDaniel, John S. and Sarah E. Williams, January 17th

Miller, Silas P. and Georgianna Brown, March 28th

Minter, Thomas J. and Susan A. Kirby, June 2nd

Mitchell, B. F. and Rhody E. Douglass, December 30th

Moon, Ben F. and Frances P. Harris, October 1st

Munday, Alex C. and Frances A. Norwell, August 8th

Munday, Thomas Jr., and Mildred E. Preddy, October 17th

1873

Mann, M. L. and F. O. Morris, January 21st

Martin, J. N. and S. M. Garland, February 3rd

Marsh, J. W. and C. Garden, March 3rd

Marsh, R. J. and M. C. Marsh, June 20th

Martin, Benj. and Lucy McKennie, Feb. 19th

Mayo, Francis N. and Lucy Herndon, January 23rd

Mayo, Tandy R. and Mary J. Craig, September 15th

McGehee, M. W. and M. E. Munday, January 19th

McCary, Richard F. and Sally H. Goodman, September 15th

Moore, Rev. Frank D. and Lilly L. Brown, November 17th

Moore, William and Julia A. Drumheller, August 25th

Moyer, W. Lee and Louisa Beaver, November 3rd

Munday, J. W. and E. J. Marshall, March 31st

1874

Madison, Theodore A. and Columbia Sprinkle, December 12th

Marshall, Geo. B. and Mary E. Draper, September 14th

Mayo, Stephen L. and Henrietta Craig, October 21st

Miller Wm. H. and Lucy V. Ferguson, March 31st

Morris, Robt. L. and Bettie C. Biggers, May 4th

Moyer, Thos. W. and Betty A. L. Kirby, April 27th

1875

Madison, John A. and Martha J. Collins, December 16th

Madison, Jno. R. and Florance Hill, January 29th

Mallonee, Mathew and Jennie Carr, September 14th

Martin, Jas. H. and Clandias D'ONorthrop, March 9th

Martin, Wm. H. and Sally W. Powell, March 13th

Marshall, Jas. A. and Emma C. Lupton, October 18th

McDaniel, Taqwell C. and Sallie A. Harlow, September 7th

McPheters, Wm. A. and Mary C. Goodwin, August 12th

McAllister, Burrus N. and Susan A. Hicks, October 2nd

Metzinger, Jacob and Ginnie Morris, December 2nd

Moore, Harwell S. and Fannie A. W. Jefferson, November 23rd

Munday, Calvin P. and Cora A. Davis, August 11th

Munday, Jno. D. and Eliza B. Norris, August 21st

Munday, Jas. O. and Clara E. Wood, December 7th

1876

Mardaga, Wm. and Bertha C. Hase, May 18th

Marshall, Robt. T. and Lucy A. Via, December 29th

Martin, Jno. Wm. and Matilda J. Moyer, December 21st

Maupin, Henry C. and Mary L. Brown, February 16th

Maupin, Oscar D. and Mary Hall, December 16th

Maupin, Wayland W. and Appollonia Harris, April 3rd

McAllister, David A. and Bettie E. Blake, July 18th

McCutcheson, Frank and Florence Harris, November 21st

Mitchell, N. J. and Mollie A. Winston, June 5th

Morris, Jno. Wm. and Eliza J. Fox, May 29th

Muse, Jas. B. and Mary Liz Hartman, September 6th

1877

Mallory, Walter E. and Mary E. A. Tyler, February 22nd

Matthews, Wm. F. annd Bertie F. Parrott, March 14th

Mayo, Geo. L. and Francis A. Sneed, March 5th

Maverick, Albert and Jane Lewis Maury, March 19th

Martin, Jeramiah W. and Marietto B. Clapton, July 14th

Marshall, Geo. and Mary E. Pritchett, August 17th

Maupin, Jas. E. and Mary Gillispie, January 29th

Melton, Henry W. and Susan F. Etherton, September 12th

Mooney, D. G. and Mary A. Rodes, October 27th

Mallory, John and Harriet E. Milstread, December 26th

Mowyer, Andrew W. and Margaret Thoms, December 17th

Murray, Chas. K. and Texanna Garrison, December 19th

Morris, Jas. F. and Cornelia J. Shiflett, December 28th

1878

Mahanes, Sam'l G. and H. V. Taylor, June 3rd

Martin, Garland N. and Willie C. Harding, November 30th

McCauley, Henry D. and Sarah F. M. Thompson, March 13th

McIntosh, Roderick C. and Cora B. Lewis, November, 14th

Munday, David B. and Sarah J. Phillips, February 4th

Moon, John B. and Marian G. Dabney, March 18th

Massie, Benj. F. and P. E. Chewning, June 24th

Mayo, Wm. J. and Mary E. Bishop, December 20th

Meeks, Wm. N. and Cora S. Curren, November 2nd

Moffett, Robt. N. and Annie E. Harris, November 5th

Morris, Thos, J. and Esteline Dudley, November 6th

Moon Jacob, and Betty M. Harris, October 14th

Moyer, Jas. Wm. and Lucy Mary Leak, November 19th

Mahanes, Geo. R. and Frances C. Munday, December 2nd

Melton, Elisha J. and Cora J. Tilmon, December 25th

Maupin, Wm. L. and Eliza J. Garland, April 17th

Montcastle, Arthur L. and Mary A .Bruffy, July 2nd

Morgan, James W. and Mrs. Alice A. Marchant, October 30th

1879

Mann, John P. Jr. and Josephine Carter, December 13th

Massie, Wm. A. and Fannie L. Chewning, January 18th

Maupin, Clifton P. and Joanna A. Wood, September 2nd

Mays, Eugene R. and Fannie S. Lewis, February 4th

Marshall, George and Maggie Shiflett, February 25th

McAllister, Wm. N. and Addie C. Brown, October 14th

McPherson, Edgar P. and Mrs. Hinnie Watson, November 14th

McMullen, Richard L. and Martha M. Johnson, April 7th

McCue, Massie L. and Emma F. Purcell, November 8th

1880

Mawyer, Henry S. and Nellie Wade, February 9th

Mawyer, Preston F. and Mary Barber, November 8th

McNeale, Chas. A. and Nannie Goodyear, October 8th

Montague, Julius D. and G. P. Garth, June 9th

Mitchell, Thos. H. and Sarah F. Harlow, September 25th

Makely, Wm. F. and Rosa L. Adams, September, 28th

Mawyer, Charles and Anna Canada, November 15th

Muder, Charles H. and Mary E. Cullen, December 8th

Mars, Henry G. annd Eliz. B. Eades, December 25th

Martin, Thomas D. and Lilla Kirk, November 1st

1881

Moore, Alexander B. and Lucy Beverly Berkely, February 9th

Martin, John Lewis and Theodosia V. Carter, February 9th

Maury, William and Angelina Brown, February 16th

May, Joseph and Mary E. Crawford, March 15th

Morris, James B. and Lucie S. Wingfield, October, 25th

Maupin, William D. and Ella F. Childress, November 9th

Martin, Abram D. and Mrs. Harriet F. Crowbeyer, November 25th

Marsh, Wm. L. and Josephine McGreph, December 14th

McDaniel, James and Mary Sinclain Gibson, March 31st

McCue, Cyrus F. and Sallie Mann, December 21st

Mooney, Thornton T. and Sarah A. Whites Carver, September 15th

Moore, Thomas and Seline Birckhead, December 15th

Mowyer, George F. and Roas E. Robinson, December 29th

1882

Martin, John W. and Ellena L. Garland, March 8th

McLenore, Britain S. and Minnie F. Barksdale, November 8th

Moore, Samuel and Mary E. Birckhead, March 13th

Madison, Dabeney, M. and Rosalie A. Munday, March 23rd

Marshall, John H. and Willie S. Smith, April 28th

Marsh, William F. and Mollie C. Burgess, September 10th

Madison, Dabny M. and Dora A. Munday, October 22nd

Miller, Thomas W. and Ida M. Diggs, December 6th

Munday, George H. and Fanny A. Rhodes, December 13th

Maupin, James R. and Emma P. Sutphin, December 18th

Madison, Millard F. and Nancy F. Wilkerson, December 21st

Mayer, Laviree S. and Sally J. Barber, December 28th

Moyer, Ballard H. and Virginia E. Gibson, November 9th

1883

Marshall, Robert Angus and Lucy Matilda Dowell, February 28th

Madison, Henry Clay and Mary Alice Wilkinson, April 26th

Magonder, Dudley and Isabella Weass, ?

Maury, Walker and Hester H. Wheeler, July 12th

McCauley, Wm. T. and Ada V. Jurey, November 7th

Moore, Jno. R. and Sally Ann Sprouse, January 1st

Mundy, Lindsay Walker and Susan Vashtie Wood, October 11th

1884

Melton, Fielding J. and Edith O. Burgess, December 31st

Marshall, Wm. A. and Mary J. Douglass, April 16th

Mays, Thomas H. annd Clara Bell Harris, May 7th

Maze, Thomas G. and Fannie Bell Layne, May 18th

Massey, Walter and Nannie H. Edge, October 8th

Maxcoll, Chas. C. and Christina L. Haebule, October 7th

McAlister, Geo. J. and Mildred A. Brown, January 1st

McGee, Wm. Hugh and Lizzie St. Waddell, September 3rd

McCauley, Alfred F. and Mary Jane Martin, September 24th

Mitchell, Henry and Susie Rayner, October 30th

Minor, John B. and Ellen Temple Hill, November 12th

Mitchell, Lesley B. and Mary E. Dabney, December 4th

Munday, Leslie Y. and Annie E. A. Abell, December 18th

1885

Marshall, Geo. T. and Jeatta V. Jones, February 19th

Mudge, Edw. W. and Greta M. Beasley, June 22nd

Moses, John S. and Fannie M. Kirby, June 25th

Moore, Wm. H. and Eliza Jane Bryant, July 30th

Michier, Eugene O. and Julia Fox, December 10th

1886

Morris, Jas. Wm. and Mary Ellen Boyne, February 1st

Manly, Henry and Mary Tesdale, February 8th

Marsh, Geo. F. and Willie Irene Hall, February 24th

Milton, Jno. Henry and Mattie W. Wingfield, April 20th

Morris, I. A. and Mary Morris, May 13th

Mooney, Jno. M. and Willie M. Snead, August 14th

Morris, Wm. Lylasius and Roxy Anna Johnson, October, 7th

Meadows, Wm. Thos. and Saludee A. McCauley, October 21st

Marsh, Richard and Lucy F. Madison, December 23rd

1887

Moyer, Jacob Wm. and Mary Ellen Young, January 12th

Munday, Jas W. and Pyrena M. Criddle, March 27th

Marshall, Jackson and Annie Melton, April 6th

Maxey, Edw. F. and Mary T. Hanckel, June 22nd

Maupin, John H. and Bettie Harris, August 8th

Marshall, R. L. and Mary E. Wingfield, December 23rd

Moore, Jno. T. and Sarah A. Sneed, January 11th

Marsh, James E. and D. J. McAubey, February 27th

1888

Morris, Tho. R. and Clara S. Sutherland, April 2nd

Martin, W. H. and S. E. Herndo, April 24th

Mawyer, Jno. A. P. and Hester Parr, May 2nd

Mitchell, Mc. D. and Willie A. Smith, May 7th

Minchart, Theo. and Maria Russow, May 26th

Mooney, J. H. and A. E. Harlow, June 6th

Mackinzie, E. L. and Julia S. Coles, July 16th

Motley, T. H. and Fannie A. Loving, September 17th

Madison T. W. and M. S. Powell, October 24th

Martin, H. H. and B. L. Hamner, December 5th

Mallet, Jno. Wm. and Marie J. Burthe, December 14th

McCauley, Parris and Ada B. Marshall, January 3rd

McCauley, Doctor and Caroline Sprouce, May 26th

1889

Maupin, Ed. P. and S. C. James, February 14th

McMullan, R. L. and M. L. Garnett, March 6th

McCutchen, L. A. and Maggie V. Lane, June 18th

McDaniel, E. W. and Emma J. Carter, October 16th

Melton, Jerry and Nancy F. Bailey, April 22nd

Marsh, Alex and Lillian B. Madison, August 9th

Mooney, W. I. and Lily M. Sulliven, August 29th

Morris, Robt. Lee and Henrietta Bingler, September 12th

Maddox, Paul and Delia Mays, September 14th

Maupin, Jno. R. and Lillie M. Meeks, October 1st

Munday, H. L. and E. L. Munday, December 11th

1890

Martin, J. G. and Rosa Boaz, February 10th

Mayo, Wm. P. and M. A. Wood, March 17th

Moyer, M. L. and Isabella Norvell, May 26th

Mihanes, T. M. and A. B. Mihanes, June 28th

Mooman, J. H. and Bettie B. Pendleton, July 7th

Martin, Elizier and Laura F. Via, July 21st

Mace, G. W. and B. W. Humphrey, July 29th

Melton, Elisha and Cornelia Modena, August 9th

Meeks, Ed. and En. Shackleford, August 28th

Morsell, Dr. W. F. and J. M. Harris, October 18th

Mays, Henry and M. Critzer, October 30th

Milstead, Gil. and Josh. Pritchett, November 18th

Minor, C. L. and M. McVenable, December 9th

Morris, L. M. and L. A. Marshall, December 23rd

1891

Marks, B. A. and Kate E. Huff, January 21st
Madison, C. N. and M. F. Gibson, March 13th
Martin, Barney and Susan Curry, April 21st
McDaniel, G. W. and S. H. Dowell, February 12th
McCauley, Wm. and M. B. Hancock, June 26th
McAllister, Geo. and J. A. Garrison, November 30th
Minor, Jno. and L. L. E. Trice, May 23rd
Moore, J. W. and E. J. Martin, June 1st
Mitelun, G. G. and M. J. Childress, July 9th
Millorie, T. P. and E. B. Lyner, September 9th
Matheny, Robt. J. and L. B. McAuby, September 16th
Meadows, J. Tyler, and Minnie W. Earle, October 7th
Money, Ernie, G. and Susan S. Bacon, October 10th
Munday, David and Cor. Birckhead, October 16th
Melton, Chas. M. and S. M. Flannagan, November 11th
Marshall, G. E. and Willie Bailey, December 29th

1892

Moore, Sandins, S. and A. F. Profitt, March 24th
Marshall, Edgar and J. P. Gibson, April 23rd
McDaniel, Thos. and N. Townshend, September 27th
Munday, Evans Clarke and Emma Sledd Douglass, May 2nd
Munday, H. and S. A. Mooney, June 21st
Moore, J. F. and M. C. McCarey, July 13th
Mowyer, H. N. and Bettie Mathews, September 20th
Mullers, Andrew W. and Annie L. Rix, October 4th
Miller, J. O. and N. H. Hawkins, October 10th
Maupin, J. W. and Gab Wood, October 11th
Morgan, F. C. and M. S. Alexander, November 28th
Marshall, W. H. and L. S. Brown, December 13th
Madison, R. S. and L. E. Shiflett, December 15th
Miller, Isaac and Amanda Starks, December 22nd
Marshall, J. W. and Laura Toms, December 27th

1893

Mahanes, O. L. and Leva Rhodes, January 5th
McAvery, Columbus and S. Crittendens, June 16th
McCauley, A. F. and M. J. Meadows, September 14th
McDaniel, J. S. and M. J. Harlow, September 30th
McAau, A. G. and Mary R. Browne, October 6th

McAllister, H. F. and F. J. McAllister, December 18th
Munday, Wiley C. and Alice V. Via, January 23rd
Moss, W. W. and Lizzie Harmon, February 21st
Mowyer, Parker and Rify Mowyer, March 14th
Murion, L. H. and Lula B. Maupin, April 17th
Money, W. E. and M. M. Fiszeel, May 11th
Maupin, Jas. and Berrie Beagle, August 10th
Moon, Marshall and Susan Winston, October 11th
Melton, Wm. and Ann E. Walton, October 19th
Myers, Daniel J. and Eita C. Sandy, October 29th
Marshall, E. W. and L. E. Wood, November 20th
Morris, Allen, and Maggie Morris, November 27th
Maupin, T. C. and Hen Durham, December 7th
Maupin, G. A. and Nannie Garrison, December 11th
Melton, J. S. and E. J. Walton, December 14th
Munday, Th. and Anna Via, December 20th
Maupin, J. D. and S. M. Sandridge, December 20th
Mahanes, Luther G. and Katie R. Dabney, December 23rd

1894

Mooney, J. M. and S. E. Lee, April 28th
Mays, Chas. and Ada A. Barnett, May 2nd
Mitcham, Jas. and L. Barksdale, August 16th
Marshall, Wesley L. and Lula W. Garrison, December 4th
Morris, R. L. and A. J. Perkins, December 18th
Martin, O. J. and L. A. Herring, October 27th
Marshall, Thos. D. and M. D. Marsh, November 13th
Magruder, H. E. and J. M. Wallace, November 20th
Mayo, T. W. and E. F. Burgess, December 24th
Munday, W. and G. E. Garrison, December 26th

1895

Marshall, Geo. T. and Lucretia Dowell, January 7th
Mayo, Rossn. P. and Laura F. Black, March 4th
Maupin, Jno. W. and Emm N. Dunn, April 9th
Mawyer, Emmet and Mollie Mawyer, April 25th
Mann, John P. and Ida K. Rogers, July 8th
Maupin, Jole R. and L. J. Maupin, September 12th
Martin, M. and B. Douglass, November 2nd
Mansfield, E. E. and S. Johnson, November 12th
Mawyer, Alfred K. and Alice Critzer, December 9th
Manly, Richard C. and Ida E. Taylor, December 16th
McAllister, J. G. and Mary S. Via, February 25th

McCary, Edw. G. and Lixeama Sneed, June 3rd
McDonald, Jas. and Theo Wilkerson, Nov. 5th
McCue, C. M. and M. L. Hall, December 21st

1896

Marks, George and Bettie Powell, July 11th
Michie J. H. and L. L. Farish, September 12th
Marshall, O. F. and J. Y. Gentry, September 24th
Maupin, H. R. and Anna J. Maupin, October 5th
McGghy, W. W. and Lizzie O. Burnley, June 27th
McAllister, L. A. and Lorena Easton, September 24th
Munday, G. C. and Mary S. Maupin, January 6th
Milton, Jas. C. and Hester L. Carter, March 2nd
Michie, Jas. P. and Eliza D. Kase, March 11th
Morris, O. W. and Minnie Dudley, November 20th
Miller, Fielding P. and Eleanor A. Smith, December 23rd

1897

Morris, Wm. N. and Eugene Dabney, January 19th
Marshe, J. C. and Emma Via, May 4th
Martin, W. T. and L. O. Perkins, May 11th
McCarey, J. A. and N. W. Pace, April 13th
McAlister, Jno. W. and Sallie E. Eaton, December, 20th
McCauley, Geo. T. and Rosa E. Smith, December 27th
Minter, Thos. and Martha Riley, June 7th
Millan, Chas. H. and Maggie Watson, July 26th
Marsh, J. C. and Lenora H. Davis, August 25th
Michie, Edgar G. and Henleen C. Garth, August 30th
Morhart, Chas. C. and Augusta E. Hotass, September 7th
Morris, Monroe and Lillie L. Blackwell, September 14th
Moon, Littebery and Grabel Toms, September 28th
Mitchell, Geo. and W. Clatterbuck, October 2nd
Melton, Jno. S. and Ida R. Marshall, October 16th
Mallory, O. C. and Mattie L. Brooks, December 3rd
Mooney, Geo. S. and B. E. Shiflett, December 20th

1898

Morris, J. D. and Eliza Fatwell, February 7th
Mahone, R. T. and M. E. Worthington, February, 9th
McAuley, W. J. and Clara Madison, June 14th
McMahon, J. J. and S. Blanche Pace, June 24th
McCue, Leslie H. and Margaret T. Shirley, September 27th
McMudo, A. E. and H. L. Corbett, October 22nd

McAllister, W. B. and M. J. Dunn, December 21st
MacGregor, D. D. and Minnie A. Goodloe, October 11th
Murch, H. H. and Hettie S. Payne, March 19th
Michael, M. G. and Bertha Trumbo, March 19th
Marshall, James and Rosa Belle Melton, March 20th
Meeks, Edw. H. and Henreitta J. Dowell, June 13th
Maupin, Chas. and Sarah C. Breedin, August 1st
Marshall, Geo. F. and Sarah F. Keyton, November 4th
Mason, Jas. T. and Maggie V. Jones, December 1st
Maupin, Alphonsa and Fannie Drumheller, May 2nd
Minor, B. S. and M. V. Mason, December 19th

1899

Marshall, Thos. A. and M. Edna Norris, January 31st
Melton, Jos. S. and Mittie M. Beddow, February, 6th
Munday, Charles Hunter, and Emma W. Salmon, February 8th
Mahanes, Walker K. and S. Debora Madison, February 14th
Mallery, Evert R. and Gertie Smith, February 16th
Mayo, Geo. M. and Mattie N. Campbell, February, 20th
Mahanes, W. G. and Bessie Mahanes, February 20th
Maupin, E. J. and Rebecca S. Hughes, May 13th
Maupin, J. A. and Maggie J. Newton, December 14th
Michie, Edw. D. and Jessie Johnston, May 30th
Mitchell, C. F. and L. A. Fry, December 27th
Mahone, W. O. and Ada Wingfield, June 5th
Marshall, Wm. H. and Mary E. Smith, June 5th
Maupin, David R. and Lucy M. Wood, August 4th
Mawyer, Luther and Annie Norvell, December 16th
Munday, Jno. A. and Sallie E. Rush, September 18th
Marsh, C. R. and Callie C. Wingfield, September 28th
Moore, Arthur and Nancy Moore, December 19th

1900

Mallory, Robt. L. and Courtney E. Cobb, May 14th
Markham, Adrian and Oph. Rogers, March 3rd
Marsh, W. D. and M. E. Herndon, February 19th
Mathews, W. W. and F. A. Grove, February 13th

Mawyer, Harden and M. G. Pugh, May 19th

Maupin, Edw. P. and Sallie B. Doughtry, July 10th

Maupin, J. F. and Emma Mooney, June 11th

Maupin, E. J. T. and Willie M. Eddins, January 24th

Matthews, J. W. and Anne E. Powell, August 6th

Marshall, R. E. and Blanche B. Beddows, November 22nd

McCauley, E. L. and M. W. Thurston, September 5th

McIntire, R. W. and Kate W. Woods, December 24th

Moon, L. S. and L. E. Moore, December 11th

Moon, Roy C. and L. F. Zinnerman, May 1st

Mawyer, J. A. and Ann B. Fox, December 17th

Morris, Geo. S. and Vienna Shiflett, December 24th

Moris, L. L. and O. S. Morris, September 25th

Moseby, Wm. L. and Bessie R. Stackhor, June 21st

May, Oppie and Eula Edwards, December 24th

1901

Mawyer, H. S. and Minnie Sandridge, March 12th

Maupin, G. W. and Dora Maupin, May 21st

Maury, M. F. and F. E. Pagam, June 10th

Minor, A. W. and J. T. Holloday, June 25th

Mawyer, G. T. annd Ella Suddarth, July 10th

McDowell, Paul W. and Lottie L. Edwards, March 7th

McDaniel L. L. and Mary Hutcheston, May 6th

Murray, Jas. E. and Eva G. Hackett, August 3rd

Marks, R. I. and M. E. Houchens, August 21st

Mars, H. and M. Mars, September 5th

Mahanes, Jas. and Clara Lang, September 9th

Marshall, J. R. and F. B. Walton, October 18th

Munday, H. E. and M. E. Leake, November 11th

Maupin, J. H. and F. Staton, November 19th

Morris, Harvey andn Daisy Kirby, December 19th

Marks, Jno. H. and Ida S. Morris, December 21st

Morris, Wm. L. and N. M. Highlander, December 23rd

Maupin, W. D. and Minnie Dowell, December 24th

Morris, Chas. V. and L. Maude Shiflett, December 26th

Maupin, Stewart and Mary Slaughter, December 30

1902

Marshall, Jno. Y. and V. S. Shiflett, January 15th

Martin, Hudson, and M. A. Price, January 22nd

McDonald, Henry and Mary Smith, March 8th

McDaniel, Luther and Mary Hutchison, May 13th

Morris, B. O. and M. F. Lane, March 12th

Michie, S. J. and M. Grayback, April 28th

Miller, Harry C. and Annie S. Allen, April 28th

Moore, Jno. W. and Luda A Eddins, May 26th

Murfee, Walter Lee and Mary Turner Graves, June 5th

Marsh, Thos. J. and Cora R. Birckhead, June 24th

Mason, E. W. and M. B. Taylor, July 16th

Melton, Jos. and Lillie Martin, July 28th

Maddox, H. A. and L. D. Druen, October 8th

Miller, J. Barton and Mary L. Kemper, October 20th

Moon, A. B. and S. S. Wade, December 2nd

Mawyer, Cal and Bird Mawyer, December 3rd

Marsh, Ro. and Sallie Miller, December 17th

Mars, Dick and Laura Hogg, December 20th

Mawyer, Jno. W. and Carrie A. Mawyer, December 22nd

Man, Charles and Annie Breeden, December 26th

1903

McDaniel, W. A. and M. A. Bolding, April 6th

Munday, Lewellyn and Mattie Garrison, April 4th

Mays, J. R. and J. L. Irvins, May 15th

Morris, O. W. and Ora J. Payne, June 15th

Marshall, Lee and C. A. Phillips, June 18th

Mahanes, J. L. and Ada Quarles, August 8th

Morris, Sim and S. B. Bailey, August 13th

Madison, H. D. and M. A. Sandridge, August 29th

Marshall, W. A. and M. C. Beddows, October 15th

McComb, J. W. and L. M. Newman, July 13th

McCary, T. J. and Josephine Criddle, December 22nd

Morris, L. and S. Shelton, October 15th

Moses, Charles and Mamie Mawyer, September 13th

Marshall, Emmet E. and Eillie Malory, December 21st

Morris, C. R. and Lee Herron, December 21st

Mayho, Jno. Wm. and Rosa Ellen Bush, December 26th

1904

Mays, Aubrey M. and Lottie L. Oliver, August 19th

Melton, Jas. Oscar and Maggie E. Blake, February 19th

Melton, R. E. L. and Mary B. Davis, April 8th

Mahone, Geo. W. and Minnie B. Haggard, July 19th

Moyer, Jas. O. and Ethel M. Henry, August 11th

Mooney, Bernard T. and Josephine Davis, August 26th

Mahanes, W. L. and L. J. Salmon, September 13th

Mooney, Jas. E. and Emma N. Davis, October 7th

Morrison, Hackley and Elizabeth N. Boyden, October 10th

Marsh, Ivy and Jennie Scruggs, November 22nd

Mawyer, Ashby A. and Laura R. Dudley, November 23rd

Mawyer, Phillip Smith and Lucy Quick, December 17th

Mawyer, Howard and Frances Mawyer, December 23rd

Marsh, Edw. and Sadie D. Bishop, December 24th

McCary, Geo. L. and Senola Willis, January 25th

McAlister, Richard and Lillie Garrison, June 9th

1905

Miller Chas. Allen and Lelia Shepherd Dunn, January 9th

Mars, Jas. Robt. and Annie Mars, March 14th

McClue, Thos. E. and Lena Georgia Wood, February 14th

McMurdo, A. K. and S. G. Magruder, October 23rd

McComb, Wm. Jr. and Lelia Estelle O'Neill, November 7th

McCary, John L. and Jennie L. Mayo, December 19th

McCauley, Lucien and Eva Meeks, December 22nd

McCauley, Columbus D. and Eleanor B. Clements, June 20th

Moore, Wm. A. and Minnie B. Bacon, April 12th

Melton, Jerry and Mattie Bruce, May 4th

Marshall, Chas. E. and Matie B. Wood, May 6th

Moyer, Clarence L. and Cleaver Pearl Henry, May 20th

Melton, Thos. W. and Eva Rogers, June 13th

Mayo, J. Fred and Mable E. Burks, June 27th

Morris, Wm. and Virgie Judson, July 12th

Mann, R. C. and L. W. Harlow, July 17th

Maupin, O. M. and M. E. Faulconer, October 30th

May, William Walton and Nellie Warren White, November 15th

Mayo, Willie Marshall annd Emma Cornelia Houchens, December 4th

Maupin, J. G. and N. E. Maupin, December 5th

Mullins, Charlie Wren and Ada Rhodes, December 9th

Mooney, P. E. and L. M. Bailey, December 15th

Marsh, A. W. and A. E. Garrison, December 27th

Maupin, John William and Jurenia Estelle Humphries, December 28th

Moses, Charles and Mamie Mawyer, September 13th

McMurdo, A. K. and S. G. Magruder, October 23rd

Maupin, A. M. and M. E. Faulconer, October 30th

McComb, Jr., William and Lelia Estelle O'Neill, November 7th

Mayo, Willie Marshall and Emma Cornelia Houchens, December 4th

May, William Walton and Nellie Warren White, November 15th

Maupin, J. G. and N. E. Maupin, December 5th

Mullins, Charlie Wren and Ada Rhodes, December 9th

Mooney, P. E. and L. M. Bailey, December 15th

McCary, John L. and Jennie L. Mayo, December 19th

McCauley, Luther and Eva Meeks, December 20th

Marsh, A. W. and A. E. Garrison, December 27th

Maupin, John William and Jurenia Estella Humphries, December 28th.

1906

Mawyer, Archie Golden and Hattie Ann Mawyer, August 14th

Marshall, Edgar Thomas and Rosa B. Garland, September 22nd

Morrison, Hugh Stockdell and Frances Campbell Page, October 3rd

McDaniel, John R. and Mary Via, October 18th

Maupin, Gabriel E. and Carrie E. Jones, October 24th

Moyer, Richard D. and Annie Baber, November 11th

Marshall, James T. and Fannie Keatin, November 15th

Marshall, Charles H. and Lizzie Sprouse, November 15th

Marsh, William and Sadie Wilkerson, November 21st

Maupin, Orvander P. and Annie F. Dunn, November 28th

Maupin, George and Minnie Berry, December 12th

McCrarg, Craven P. and Amanda C. Hamner, December 20th

Maupin, Edward and Hester Blake, December 22nd

Maupin, John L. and O. A. Clements, December 26th

Morris, James B. and Rosa M. Miller, December, 27th

Marks, John Virgie and Beulah Rosa Munday, February 2nd

Martin, Walter Y. and Elizabeth Dudley, March 6th

Moore, John L. and Sally M. Ferguson, May 2nd

McLane, E. R. and Nettie E. Wilkerson, May 21st

Morris, Edgar and Mary Moore, May 31st

Marshall, Bennett Wyatt and Florence Ellen Norford, June 16th

McCormick, Charles and Elizabeth A. Smith, June 21st

1907

Moon, William F. and Julia L. Duho, April 25th

MacPherson, Thomas and Annie Hutcheson, April 19th

McCauley, Archie C. and Lelia B. Hall, April 24th

McClary, W. T. and M. C. Black, May 15th

Martin, J. L. and Josie Davis, May 15th

Martin, E. R. and Mada B. Abell, July 14th

Marshall, Aubrey F. and Susie P. Edwards, July 30th

Moore, Edward and Pauline Thomas, August 14th

Martin, R. L. and Amandy B. Gentry, August 19th

Madison, Piercy and Polly Munday, August 20th

Marsh, Newman L. and Susie Marsh, August 21st

McClummons, John R. and Annie F. May, August 28th

Mitchell, Seton L. and Mary L. Linahan, August 31st

Martin, James E. and Dora C. Kirby, September 1st

Morris, Sam. A. and Margaret Johnson, September 14th

McClammer, James A. and Mittie D. Cox, October 8th

Munder, Norman T. A. and Jerusha Goodloe, October 29th

Madison, A. M. and Emma Harlow, October 24th

Mays, T. W. and Victoria Eubank, November 6th

Morris, Robert A. and Edly F. Mayo, November 6th

Mars, John H. and Bessie L. Ferneyhough, November 14th

Moore, S. H. and Katherine Cobbs, November 27th

Mallory, Charles E. and Rosa L. Kirby, November 28th

Maupin, E. P. and Sallie W. Horton, December 17th

1908

Muse, C. C. and M. M. Smith, January 8th

Morris, Arthur and Lula A. Bruce, February 17th

Mawyer, Sidney and Edna Brag, March 11th

McCauley, David and Sarah Schaffer, March 29th

MacGregor, John M. and Gabrielle Winn, April 15th

McCary, Harvey P. and Armenia L. Ramsey, April 11th

McCauley, Samuel L. and Rena Crickenberger, April 14th

Melton, George H. and Annie Chewning April 22nd

Magness, William T. and Virginia W. Morris, September 2nd

Massie, Willie M. and Blanche Ross, September 6th

Martin, William H. and Sallie J. Thacker, September 30th

Maury, John Minor and Jane Bell Moon, October 7th

Meadows, Charles W. and Lucinda Shiflett, October 25th

Maddex, Willie W. and Alice L. Leathers, December 16th

Morris, William S. and Clara Smith, December 17th

Martin, Edward and Elie G. Black, December 23rd

Maupin, Clifton M. and Marg. S. E. Ward, December 29th

Morris, Louis E. and Lena Shiflett, December 29th

1909

Marsh, Edward and Martha Hunt, March 1st

Munday, Edward and Lizzie Mawyer, March 8th

Morris, Worth and Mary F. James, March 8th

Moubry, Ben and Gertrude N. Garrison, April 7th

Melton, Thomas H. and Nannie C. Barnett, May 1st

McClure, Edward C. and J. Elizabeth Bailey, May 19th

McDonald, William and Ida B. Shepherd, June 29th

Marshall, William H. and Virginia S. Bragg, August 5th

May, Erz Amus and Susie Davis, September 1st

Mawyer, Silas and Mignon E. Bunch, September 26th

McKinley, Michael L. and Mirian Anthony, October 9th

McKennie, Clarence and Bernard Phillips, October 6th

Mahanes, Samuel T. and Lelith Broadhead, October 15th

McAllister, William P. and Mary E. Carr, October 19th

Marshall, William H. and Myrtle Shiflett, October 28th

Moore, Joseph A. and Myrtle L. Spencer, October 27th

Meeks, Thomas E. and Lelia C. Londeree, November 9th

Marshall, Samuel W. and Lutie E. Davis, November 15th

Morris, Lunas and Althia Shiflett, December 9th

Moubry, Jim and Sallie B. Via, December 9th

Morris, Samuel and Lydia Sprouse, December 17th

Maupin, Willie B. and Sallie M. Dunn, December, 22nd

Moyer, George and Maud Williams, December 26th

Magann, Aubrey and Vertie Maupin, December 22nd

Mawyer, Otis and Susie R. Tomlin, December 22nd

Melton, Harry E. and Emma L. Craig, December 28th

1910

McGuire, Ignatus and Bessie Flynn, January 13th

McCauley, Henry H. and Mary S. Batten, January 26th

Martin, J. Gauley and Mannie E. Townley, February 2nd

Moon, Lindsay R. and Myrtle Robinson, February 1st

Moon, Schuyler J. and Martha Demars, February 12th

May, Otha T. and Grace E. Goodloe, March 22nd

Mallow, John A. and Sallie M. Humphrey, March 27th

Meeks, Luther and Lelia Bolton, March 26th

Morris, Charles F. and Mary L. Hilff, April 12th

Marshall, Zebbie E. and Bulah E. Price, June 1st

Morris, Robert and Elsie Wood, June 2nd

Mahaney, Thomas and Pt. Wayne Cox, July 4th

Matheny, Thomas L. and Rebeccah Maupin, July 20th

Moor, Howard C. and Ella C. Eubank, August 4th

Michie, Dr. Henry Clay and Clara Louise Robinson, September 28th

Moon, James L. and Margie L. Wade, October 17th

Martin, John and Ada Beasley, November 16th

Massie, William Russell and Susanne W. Buck, November 16th

Marshall, John W. and Mattie R. Meeks, December 26th

1911

Mitchell, Lloyd E. and Maud W. Ballard, March 15th

Mundy, Lemuel E. and Mary Inez Smith, April 12th

Marchant, Gouverneur W. and Elizabeth C. Mehring, April 26th

May, Robert L. and Louise Suddorth, May 17th

McAlister, Bernard and Bedy Wood, May 29th

Munday, Hunter and Melva Douglass, June 3rd

Marshall, Harry T. and Nancy Lea, June 17th

Marshall, Sidney M. and Zola Agnes Edwards, June 28th

Madison, Edgar and Minnie Mahoney, July 4th

Morris, Willie and Annie Thomas, August 15th

Maupin, John W. N. and Mamie Pritchett, August 28th

Mitchell, Sylvester and Mary E. Mitchell, September 7th

Morris, Harry and Mamie Shaver, September 6th

Meeks, Arthur and Ethel Hicks, September 7th

Marshall, Laurel F. and Luna M. Norford, October 18th

Martin, Stephen D. and Julia M. Clarke, October 21st

Morris, Charles Edlve. and Myra Porteh, November 1st

McClary, Ottie and Rose Johnson, November 2nd

Mays, George W. and Victona Eubank, November 10th

Martin, Marshall A. and Rosa M. Boatwright, December 28th

1912

Maddox, Frank and Virginia B. Campbell, February 4th

Marsh, Vernon H. and Hattie M. Davis, February 20th

McAllister, Emmett and Fannie Shiflett, March 9th

Moran, Charlie E. and Katherine M. Fontaine, April 2nd

Marsh, James C. and Marg B. King, April 7th

McDowell, Myron B. and Abbie M. Keyes, April 25th

Moon, William E. and Lillian E. Smith, April 29th

Morris, George M. and Eliza J. Shiflett, June 16th

Miller, Hiram M. and Mary F. Minor, June 26th

Martin, Amos and Elizabeth Mayo, July 13th

Marsh, Tom and Annie Hunt, August 30th

Martin, Robert and Leslie Bunch, September 4th

Montgomery, R. C. and M. R. Wheeler, September 7th

Melton, Dr. James M. and Emma F. Clark, September 25th

Mawyer, Cleveland and Lula Norvell, October 6th

Moon, John and Madaline Grasty, October 5th

Mann, Honny F. and Susie Alice Ponton, October 10th

Moim, Joe and Sadie Munday, November 5th

Mawyer, Jerry and Lillian Wood, November 21st

Martin, J. G. and L. J. Thoop, December 17th

Mawyer, Smith and Nora Pugh, December 25th

Mauers, E. L. and Alma Madison, December 25th

1913

McCauley, Oscar and Josie Shaffer, February 13th

McMillan, Prentis E. and Lena Via, March 22nd

Morris, William Louis and Audrey Reed, March 28th

Maupin, Stewart A. and Annie Lee Sprouse April 8th

Mitchell, Molieck E. and Mary E. Garnett, May 8th

Moore, H. W. and Elmer D. Bryant, June 4th

Moore, J. B. and Billie Garland, June 3rd

Mays, James and Addie Moore, June 8th

Moore, William E. and Ethel E. Vandevuder, June 18th

McDaniel, Richard and Minnie K. Lewis, June 29th

Morris, Charlie and Buchie Dudley, August 2nd

Marshall, Frank and Ada A. Gardner, August 11th

Morris, Joseph K. and Lucy A. Marshall, September 6th

McCray, Edward and Lucy Lie May, September 22nd

Mann, Jr., William J. and Louise S. Fontaine, September 27th

McCauley, Gaines C. and Eveline M. Payne, October, 1st

Mason, John Y. and Loulia W. Austin, October 1st

Morrow, Byron S. and Mannie T. Gentry, October 8th

Murphy, William B. and Hazel D. Hosterman, November 27th

Mayo, James S. and Nora A. Thomas, December 7th

Marshall, Willie and Bertie Clements, December 24th

1914

Maddex, Frank C. and Lila O. Hall, January 6th

Marrs, Richard and Effie Morris, January 18th

McGaugby, J. B. annd Frances Coleman, February 12th

McDaniel, Frank G. and Mary E. Kirby, February 23rd

McManus, Thomas L. J. and Emilie O'Connor, April 16th

McHenry, Edward R. and Mrs. Minnie, Vaughan, May 5th

McDaniel, Kelly and Edith Dunwaw, May 14th

Mawyer, Archie and Lizzie I. Mawyer, June 6th

Marshall, Charlie and Matilda Shiflett, June 26th

McWilliam, Howard C. and Julia W. Jones, August 10th

McCullers, V. L. and Bessie Williams, September 16th

Miller, Ashton C. and Maggie Tate, September 29th

Mathews, Henry A. and Emma H. Wood, October 7th

Morris, William H. and Coy E. Via, November 25th

McAllister, William and Addie Hall, November 30th

1915

Mawyer, Mac. M. and Cora M. Parr, January 17th

Martin, Steve and Bell Jerrell, March 22nd

Misenheimer, John and Mrs. Laura E. Vest, April 27th

McAllister, William B. and Amanda Weakley, July 1st

McCauley, John and Nannie Vest, July 15th

Mackreth, Hubert C. and Mary Iner Bonner, July 21st

Marshall, Hugh H. and Mabel Deane Radford, July 28th

Mawyer, Ernest and Viola E. Powell, August 15th

Mawyer, Walter and Maude D. Hudson, August 16th

Mills, Herbert J. and Gladys E. Chisholm, September 1st

Mayo, Charles H. and Cora Hall, September 16th

Middleton, George W. and Drucilla E. Wood, September 25th

Mawyer, Henry and Florence Mawyer, October 15th

Miller, Archie and Mattie Wood, November 8th

Marrs, Oscar E. and Ruth Short, December 28th

Maupin, Jarman and Mary Beasley, December 26th

Munger, William M. and Effie Lee Marshall, December 25th

Moyer, Clarence and Tina Brown, December 29th

1916

Mawyer, Clarence and Mary Ella Maupin, January 1st

Marshall, Jeter J. and Flona Austin, February 29th

Meeks, William Melvin and Addie Claments, March 23rd

Maddox, Graves C. and Nora Lee Gentry, April 26th

Mawyer, Whitfield and Florence Beasley, April 30th

Marshall, Andrew J. and Bettie Gardner, May 11th

Mayo, Artie V. and Grace E. King, July 15th

Moore, Milton and Nellie Snow, July 28th

Maupin, Henry C. and Eva C. Davis, August 2nd

Marsh, Jack and Grace Bussinger, August 31st

Massey, Joseph C. and Virginia D. Maupin, September 8th

McCury, Hunter M. and Mary Allen White, October 10th

Moffitt, Henry Harris and Virginia W. Page, October 21st

McCallister, Claudius B. and Clara L. Buckley, November 3rd

Mawyer, Montague and Bertha Houchens, November 19th

McCue, Charles P. and Mary Ellen Allen, November 22nd

Moore, James W. and Marian J. Moore, November 22nd

McCallister, Charles M. and Nettie F. Wyant, December 20th

McCormick, Emmett B. and Fannie E. Staples, December 25th

Mawyer, Harry and Thalia Mawyer, December 24th

1917

Miller, David Johnson and Meta Rodgers Rhoudes, January 17th

Mitchell, Eddie P. and Fannie Marsh, February 22nd

Mars, John and Nannie Butler, March 29th

Martin, Laurence J. and Josephine E. Marshall, April 11th

Moyer, Jacob A. and Florence W. Robinson, April 25th

Maulry, Herbert Lee and Annie Bell Poe, April 29th

Marrs, Joseph H. and Mary A. Walters, April 29th

Marshall, Thomas H. and Effie L. Lewis, May 23rd

Maupin, Tevi and Alberta Sandridge, June 2nd

Matthews, Albert C. and Mary A. Minor, June 1st

Marsh, Philmore and Mary E. Parr, June 2nd

Madison, John A. and Alice Irving, June 23rd

Miller, Eugene Davis and Tessie E. Dudley, June 23rd

Maupin, Ernest and Jennie L. Via, August 4th

Munday, John B. and Minnie E. Robertson, August 18th

Moon, Richard M. and Bertha A. Shackelford, September 4th

McCauley, Stephen O. and Anthoney Elizabeth Leake, September 5th

Meeks, Harry Frank and Carrie Gibson, September 9th

Morris, Newman and Lizzie Sprouse, September 15th

Moore, James R. and Glenna Smith, September 30th

Mann, Harry W. and France P. Morrison, November 3rd

Mawyer, Charles J. and Helen A. Toms, November 24th

Melton, William H. and Lillian E. Marks, November 28th

McClanner, Edward W. and Mary E. Walker, December 4th

Mawyer, Moncure L. and Nannie B. Critzer, December 24th

1918

Maupin, Bezell B. and Fannie B. Maupin, January 23rd

Morris, Robert and Reathy V. Reed, January 26th

Mawyer, Robert S. and Daisy P. Brooks, February 13th

Miller, Lonie H. and Agnes J. Belew, April 11th

Maupin, John W. and Evie, B. Norford, May 29th

Melton, Jas. C. and Lena M. Williamson, August 24th

Mundy, Basil and Ida Smith, August 29th

Maupin, Joseph W. and Ethel M. W. Belew, September 18th

Miller, Samuel C. and Sallie M. Maupin, October 28th

Maupin, James and Sally Jones, November 23rd

Moore, Davy M. and Blanche A. Bryant, December 5th

Maupin, Ernest H. and Bertha S. Calvin, December 24th

Moss, Chas. L. and Mary L. Morris, December 28th

Morris, Sherman annd Mattie Smith, December 28th

1919

Martin, Olie and Lula B. Carter, May 12th

Mays, Russell W. and Hilda K. Gallaher, April 28th

Moyer, Herbert O. and Cora Moore, April 30th

McFarlord, James E. and Helen Harris, May 21st

Maupin, Ernest H. and Ruth Wood, June 15th

Moore, Chas. Joe and Danna Zinnerman, June 13th

Moore, Henry W. and Eula E. Moyer, June 3rd

Marrs, Ernest R. and Margaret E. Dodd, June 27th

Moore, Lacy M. and Francis E. Ballard, July 5th

Mundy, Henry and Nannie Mundy, July 23rd

Mays, Frederick W. and Maggie R. Morris, September 17th

Miner, Peter Carr and Edith Emlie Gusie Frost, September 21st

Madison, Peerce W. and Evie Sprouse, September 27th

Marrs, Russell L. and Mary J. Gardner, October 24th

McCoy, Halliburton and Emma S. Garnett, October 25th

Miles, James F. and Jonnie Liniouiz, November 15th

Mussleman, Hansey and Mary Lively, November 18th

Mahanes, Julian A. and Etta P. McCauley, December 17th

Moses, Carroll annd Lottie M. Clements, December 24th

1920

Martin, Harry and Mamie J. Smith, January 15th

Mooney, Robert R. and Lizzie B. Morris, February 16th

Minter, Allen and Mary Humphrey, April 15th

Miller, Robert B. and Lois A. Young, May 15th

Miller, Allie and Florence Pace, May 15th

McCormick, Frederick A. and Nellie R. Campbell, June 9th

Mahone, Nelson A. and Lucille E. Wood, June 15th

Milton, John and Florence N. Kirby, July 12th

Morris, Daniel and Leithler Riley, July 24th

Morgan, William and Mary Dudley, August 10th

Melton, Thomas Wade and Herietta Walker, September 4th

Moon, Geo. F. and Grace H. Ellis, September 4th

McMillan, James P. and Marie R. O'Neill, September 8th

Maupin, Edward J. T. and Mattie Y. Wheeler, September 7th

Miller, French S. and Sarah J. Thacker, September, 14th

Maupin, Joseph Walker and Va. Margaret Thurston, November 10th

Moore, Phillip H. and Carrie M. Craig, November 20th

Mahone, Walter Wingfield and Thelma Ethel Tillman, December 22nd

Mowyer, Dewey S. and Nannie B. Loving, December 27th

1921

Madison, Odis A. and Eva K. Dunn, August 1st

Marshall, Homer W. and Alice J. Craddock, September 10th

Mayo, Robt. Lee and Clara C. Crank, November 26th

Mawyer, Aubrey M. and Fannie M. Drumheller, December 8th

Mahone, Robt. A. and Ida Belle Via, February 26th

Munday, Marcus M. and Virginia M. Shiflett, March 26th

Marsh, Percy H. and Clara M. Nofsinger, April 3rd

Morris, Fred and Julia Morton, May 10th

McCloud, John B. and Hilda Audrey Pace, May 11th

Morris, Elzie M. and Mertie A. Critzer, May 23rd

Mayo, Sylvester B. and Lillian E. Hurtt, June 20th

Martin, Wilbert and Mary Pace, June 25th

McCary, Mason W. and Ruby L. Swain, June 29th

Meeks, Douglas and Helen L. Locker, July 5th

Morris, James Thomas and Thelma E. Herring, July 9th

1922

Morris, Everett and Blanch E. Smith, March 10th

McAllister, Albert Guy and Mrs. Myrtie Shelton, June 12th

Mehring, Oscar Edwood and Minnie L. Marshall, June 23rd

Morris, Edgar B. annd Gurrie G. Shiflett, July 3rd

McDaniel, Lawrence C. and Gladys V. Beddow, July 21st

Martin, Ollie annd Luler Carter, August 24th

McClung, Oscar H. and Annie L. B. Wayland, October 4th

Moon, Samuel C. and Bessie L. Moon, October 18th

Maupin, Willie C. and Mary A. Leake, October 21st

1923

Moon, Roy O. and Lilly Kirby, February 3rd

Miller, Richard H. and Bessie Dunn, April 11th

Morris, Luther and Bertha Rogers, April 24th

Merritt, Wilmer B. and Mary Martha McCue, June 18th

Miller, Hughlet F. and Mary Sprouse, June 28th

Mills, William B. and Maude Durham, July 16th

Morris, Edward Lee and Mattie P. Wood, August 23rd

Moneymaker, Clarence E. and Mary E. Powell, September 4th

Mawyer, Sidney H. and Mary Taylor, September 10th

Moses, Victor and Mattie Zinnerman, September 15th

Munday, Daniel H. and Mable B. Glass, December 22nd

Mayo, William and Stella Smith, December 22nd

1924

McAllister, Richard and Ollie V. Wyant, February 11th

Micklem, Patt C. and Daisy Martin, March 19th

Morris, Layton and Maude A. Lloyd, March 21st

McDaniel, Jessie F. and Minnie O. Powell, April 19th

Mowbray, Walter C. and Lillian B. Shiflett, May 10th

Makielski, Stanislaw J. and Alice Lee Patton, May 20th

Martin, Merdith M. and Elva Stargall, May 24th

McEwen, Chas. E. and Lena B. Paulett, June 28th

Melton, George E. and Mary Lucy Kirby, July 30th

Mackey, Cary S. and Nancy V. Page, August 14th

Montgomery, Chas. M. and Alice H. Haynes, September 8th

Marshall, Robt. W. and Virginia F. Davis, September 13th

Martin, Sam D. and Ethel E. Garver, October 8th

Mahoney, Russell annd Ethel F. Walters, October 10th

McCauley, Malcolm A. and Edna A. Drumheller, October 11th

Mills, Abbot P. and Augustina D. Carr, October 21st

Maupin, W. L. and Eva M. White, November 26th

Moore, Bledsoe B. and Lelia O. Harris, December 7th

Morris, Claude and Rita Mayo, December 20th

Maupin, Jr. Wm. D. and Grace E. Clarke, December 20th

Moon, C. Blair and Agnes P. Pitts, December 24th

Morris, Robt. K. and Clara M. Morris, December 23rd

1925

Morris, Chas. W. and Mary D. Cobb, January 17th

Madison, Wm. M. and Ruth O. Munday, January 24th

Mink, Clifford J. and Bertie M. Munday, February 15th

Moore, Arthur L. and Bessie M. Harlow, March 7th

McDounel, Newton and Lizzie T. Harlow, March 30th

Marshall, Roy and Edna Critzer, April 7th

Morris, John C. and Marie M. Branham, April 12th

Mawyer, Dewey Lee and Maude D. Tomlin, April 26th

Mawyer, Granville and Gertrude Darnell, June 2nd

Moulton, Wm. T. and Hattie Foland, June 6th

Maupin, Arty and Madaline Moore, June 6th

Moore, William A. and Lula Dudley, June 19th

Mars, Leslie and Annie Mars, June 21st

Moon, Alonzo B. and Algie L. Baber, June 28th

Mayo, Ashby W. and Sallie P. Parr, July 22nd

Martin, Marvin M. and Helen E. Watts, September 1st

Miller, Joseph H. and Nellie M. Critzer, September 11th

Maupin, Benj. and Casey Jones, October 20th

McCauley, Jesse and Margaret R. Mahanes, November 4th

Maupin, Gaulay and Ethel H. Warick, December 24th

1926

Moore, Henry W. and Elsie D. Via, January 1st

Marsh, John C. and Alma Mayo, January 2nd

Marshall, James R. and Clara L. Kirby, February, 18th

McCary, Gei. L. and Zenobia McCary, February 26th

Moore, Wm. Robert and Va. Viola Bell, May 4th

Madison, Lester C. and Mary Shiflett, June 12th

Maupin, Nathaniel B. and Mabel Ann Douglas, June 18th

Melton, Hazzie and Grace Harris, June 29th

McCraw, Richard M. and Elizabeth, B. Watts, July 7th

Mayers, Lloyd C. and Ann G. Dawson, July 3rd

Marrs, Pendleton and Katherine Marrs, July 3rd

Marsh, Tommie and Virginia Walton, July 5th

Moon, Colie and Jannie Powell, July 6th

Martin, Henry E. and Beatrice Douglas, July 31st

Melton, John D. and Lelia P. Keister, August 7th

Mawyer, Theadore T. and Maude Martin, August 19th

McDonald, Therman N. and Mary A. Johnson, September 4th

Maupin, Gabriel N. and Eula E. Wood, October 31st

Moon, John S. and Katherine Clements, November 10th

Martin, Marion and Reba Shaw, November 10th

Morris, Amiss and Bertha McAllister, November 10th

Marshall, John W. and Dora Ann Wood, December 29th

Marrs, James J. and Flossie Marsh, December 29th

1927

Malory, Benj. F. and Mary C. Toombs, February 10th

Morris, Joseph C. and Gay Mills Frazer, February. 15th

Moore, Sam O. and Carrie Birchhead, March 5th

McCue, James G. and Frances M. de Truvillle, March 8th

Mundy, Martin M. and Mary L. DeMasters, March 14th

Morris, James F. and Carrie E. Gibson, March 21st

McReynolds, Stuart and Frances C. Melton, April 30th

Morris, Jessie J. and Nettie O. Shiflett, June 7th

Mitchell, Newton S. and Daisy C. Peton, June 8th

Moore, Romie L. and Lottie V. Smith, July 20th

Moore, Ernest C. and Nancy P. Tapscott, August 22nd

McAllister, Arthur R. and Evelyn Patterson, September 20th

Morris, Mathew M. and Alice L. Dowling, October 8th

Moses, Marion and Hazel Walters, October 22nd

Melton, Edward and Gertrude Houchens, October 25th

Meeks, Harry J. and Mary J. Critzer, November 18th

Mawyer, Dennis D. and Mary M. Mawyer, November 20th

Morris, Alvin D. Jr., and Mary A. Dowling, December 27th

1928

Morris, Edward and Lula Dowell, February 3rd

Mumsey, Thos. F. and Mary G. Moore, March 3rd

Marrs, Geo. M. and Bettie M. Ward, March 7th

Mawyer, Albert and Eva E. Drumheller, April 7th

Moore, Lacy M. and Evelyn B. Moyer, April 11th

Morris, Willie Wade and Bertie May Morris, April 21st

Maupin, Roy and Mary F. Maupin, May 1st

Minor, Eldred L. and Mary G. Humbert, June 14th

Miller, Otis L. and Effie L. Mundy, July 14th

Marrs, Howard L. and Nellie L. Davis, August 4th

May, Herman H. and Addie M. Ferneyhaugh, October 16th

McCauley, Wm. H. and Mary A. Ray, December 7th

McCarnell, Andrew D. and Martha D. Goodwin, December 15th

Melton, Edgar J. and Ethel B. Sprouse, December, 24th

1929

Morris, John L. and Myrtle Shiflett, January 4th

Malco, Henry J. and Nellie M. Mundy, March 31st

Mowbray, Gilbert and Beulah Marshall, April 3rd

Maupin, George W. and Hittie A. Wood, April 8th

Martin, Henry H. and Edith L. Butler, April 13th

Moses, Carroll and Annie Hayslip, May 23rd

McClary, Eugene L. and Dorothy M. McNeal, May 29th

Moneymaker, Henry and Barbra Herring, June 1st

Maupin, Grover C. and Pearl G. Kirby, June 19th

Mayo, Luther P. and Helen H. Harris, June 21st

McGhee Willie S. and Lora May Starks, July 5th

Morris, John C. and James Virginia Clements, July 8th

Marsh, Russell A. annd Essie L. Brookman, August 6th

Maupin, Carroll and Otie Via, September 4th

Morton, Powhatan M. and Virginia E. Cockran, September 2nd

Moon, Claude G. and Grace H. Ellis, September 13th

Mundie, Woodsie and Mary Birckhead, September 21st

Morris, Lloyd and Edna Roberts, October 16th

Marshall, C. H. and Gladys Gibson, November 15th

Morris, Jas. M. and Carnelia A. Ward, December 18th

Massie, Walter L. and Susie G. Wheeler, December 26th

N

1788

Norvell, Henry Holdscrost and Mary Norvell, February 13th

1789

Nicholas, Jeremiah and Ann Salmon, November 2nd

1791

Newcum, John and Nancy Carter, February 15th

Norris, Nathan and Sarah Craig, November 10th

1793

Nailer, George and Jane Nucomb, November 22nd

Nally, John and Mary Cheatham, October 4th

Newman, Richard and Agg Going, September 7th

179?

Napier, Janes and Sally Moarman, ?

1796

Nimms, Robert and Martha Austin, March 7th

1797

Norvell, Hugh and Matilda Sneed, December 23rd

1798

Nimmo, Hiram and Polly Harper, November 23rd

1799

Nailor, Thomas and Rosana Spencer, January 16th

Napier, Fortunatus and Prudence Ellerton, August 7th

Newcum, Lance and Fanny Harris Ballard, February 13

Nimms, James and Rhodes Hamner, September 15th

1801

Nailor, Edward B. and Fanny Ballard, Nov. ?

1804

Nailor, Benjamin and Mary Rodes, November 5th

1805

Nimms, David and Polly Sullivan, January 15th

Norvell, Thomas and Sally Eubank, March 2nd

1806

Nailor, John and Elizabeth Wells, December 4th

1811

Nally, William and Sarah Holston, December 26th

Norvell, John and Sally Maxwell, November 4th

1812

Norris, Cabel and Ollie Harris, June 16th

1813

Norris, Thomas and Mary Ann G. Barksdale, October 23rd

1814

Nailor, Thomas and Jane Walton, January 4th

Norford, Isaac and Elizabeth Madison, October 6th

1815

Newcum, William and Polly Wood, November 6th

Norris, Opie and Cynthia T. Kelly, October 28th

1818

Newcomb, John and Sally Holmes, December 24th

1819

Norris, John and Nancy Watson, October 25th

Norris, William and Margaret R. Watson, January 16th

1820

Nelson, Thomas and Mildred W. Nelson, November 18th

1822

Newcum, John and Sally Gray, July 29th

1823

Napier, David B. and Malinda Toms, April 7th

Newcomb, William P. and Elizabeth Mooney, February 3rd

1824

Newman, Jacob and Caroline Martin, September 20th

1825

Newcum, William P. and Dolly Garton, December 5th

1826

Newcum, Carter and Elizabeth Garton, November 23rd

Norvell, Elliott and Elizabeth Barksdale, July 31st

1827

Norvell, Leneca and Mary C. Parsons, February 13th

1828

Norvell, Lorenzo and M. Eubank, February 14th

1829

Noell, Charles W. and Sarah Dove, March 16th

Norris, Samuel and Lucy Bailey, December 21st

1831

Neville, James S. and D. S. Moorman, October 3rd

Norvell, George and Susan Snell, December 1st

1833

Newcum, Miletus and Matilda Smith, January 7th

Nicholson, George A. and Mary Jane Dyer, March 28th

1834

Nally, Joseph A. and Betsy H. Elsom, March 3rd

Norvell, George W. and Susan Findall, August 4th

1835

Napier Willian and M. W. Terrell,, December 21st

Nelson, Alexander F. and Mildred Rodes, February 27th

1836

Nicholas, George and Mary Eubank, December 26th

Nimmo, Henry and Mameroa Herndon, November 25th

Noel, Robert C. and S. Cooper, August 24th

Noland, George S. and Maria D. Lewis, July 28th

1837

Norris, Caleb and Hardena F. Harris, December 22nd

Nuckols, Richard and Jane Eubank, December 6th

1838

Napier, Richard A. and Nancy Ellington, September 10th

Norris, Thomas C. and Elizabeth Ware, June 25th

1839

Norris, William and Mary Gibson, January 29th

1840

Napier, James and L. A. B. Wood, November 24th

1841

Nailor, Hiram and Cynthia J. Via, December 22nd

Nelson, Keating and Julia Ann Rogers, October 19th

Nixon, Robert B. and Marth C. Shepherdson, July 12th

1842

Nelson, F. K. and Margaret D. Merewether, December 26th

Norford, William T. and Jane Gilbert, January 31st

Norris, Feudal and Nancy J. Harris, July 25th

1843

Nailor, Samuel C. and Eliza J. Gardner, September 7th

Nimmo, William and Susan Spencer, May 24th

Noel, Clarion J. and Mary Elizabeth Clune, November 28th

Noland, Richard W. N. and Mary S. Minor, November 1st

Norvell, Benjamin and Martha Walters, November 2nd

1844

Norford, James M. and F. A. Gilbert, March 21st

1845

Newcomb, Lawrence and N. Thompson, May 8th

1847

Noel, Richard A. and S. A. T. Brown, October 19th

Norris, Nathan B. and Mary E. Ward, March 1st

1851

Newcomb, L. W. and Ann E. Spradling, November 27th

1852

Norris, J. H. B. and Elizabeth Ward, May 20th

1854

Noonan, John and Mary Kelly, September 11th

1855

Nicholas W. D. and Sarah S. Farrar, March 22nd

Nicholas, Wilson C. and Sarah Farrar, April 10th

1856

Norris, Fendal and Cornelia F. Davis, March 26th

1857

Norris, Fendall and Cornelia Davis, March 16th

1858

Norvell, Nathan W. and Sarah A. Old, November 17th

Norris, Nathan B. and Ann E. Via, October 12th

1859

Nicholas, William H. and Isabella Beal, September 8th

Norris, James R. and Sarah E. Garland, January 19th

Norvell, Henry W. and Mary A. F. Mawyer, August 27th

Nuckols, Reuben J. and Arabella Dickerson, November 19th

Nicholas, W. C. and Hettie E. Goodall, May 15th

Norvell, Samuel W. and Sarah A. Old, November 18th

Norris, Jas. R. and Sarah E. Garland, February 3rd

1860

Newcomb, William H. and Julia A. Blake, December 24th

Nucum, Wm. H. and Julia A. Blake, December 27th

1864

Nay, James H. and Sarah F. Johnson, March 16th

Northent, Elisha and Margaret McCoy, January 12th

1865

Naylor, John T. and Louisa J. Powell, October 24th

Naylor, Jno. T. and Louisa J. Powell, November 16th

Nottingham, John B. and Caroline F. Moon, December 18th

1866

Nicholas, Albert and Emma Lee, October 5th

Norford, James M. and Susan H. Marshall, November 5th

Noel, Chas. W. and Sarah Dove, March 16th

1867

Norvelle, Richard W. and Mary E. Elliton, March 18th

Nimrod, James D. and Susan C. Via, June 10th

Nillerd, Chas. Fred L. and Henrietta Pearce, July 1st

Nicholas, Simon and Jane Rodes, August 17th

Norris, Eugene S. and Cecelia A. Powell, November, 19th

Nimmo, Jas. D. and Susan C. Via, ?

1868

Nicholas, Frank and Harriet Rives, February 26th

Norford, Wm. J. and Ella M. Taylor, October 18th

Nicholas, Hudson and Lucinda Minor, November 7th

1869

Neunfray, Wm. H. and Martha Frances Durham, September 1st

Nally, Wm. and Lucy M. Guard, February 17th

Norris, J. B. and Eliza E. Marshall, December 30th

Norris, Albert and Harriet Johnson, December 30th

1870

Newcombe, L. W. and V. E. Kerby, October 25th

1871

Nelson, Burwell and Eliza Brown, January 15th

1873

Norris, R. A. and E. M. Draper, February 18th

1874

Norvell, Daniel W. and Martha S. Mayer, September 28th

Norris, Wm. E. and Sallie T. Norris, November 4th

Nolley, R. E. and Lucie V. Cobbe, December 7th

1875

Norris, Jesse F. and Nellie J. Wood, February 27th

1877

Norford, James M., II, and Lucy A. Marshall, February 12th

Ninimo, Geo. T. and Susan V. Craig, March 5th

1879

Noel, Samuel M. and Willie E. Goodwin, November 17th

1880

Newell, Geo. W. and Margaret A. Drumheller, November 16th

Norford, Edward T. and Eliza E. Marshall, November 11th

1881

Norford, John B. and Magdeline Rebecca Thomas, December 18th

1883

Naylor, Herbert and Bettie Gentry, July 12th

1884

Northrop, Frank X. and Lydia V. Coles, May 26th

Nottingham, Jno. E. and Mary Catherine Wood, November 12th

1885

Nay, Robt. E. Lee and Mary E. Parr, May 6th

Null, Jos. F. and Mattie L. Dillard, October 22nd

1886

Norford, Geo. T. and Felicia F. Madison, May 15th

Norvell, Henry R. and Callie L. Critzer, December 15th

Norford, Millard Filmore and Susan Magnolia Wood, May 6th

1889

Napier, R. F. and B. E. Moran, February 25th

Newcomb, Wm. H. Jr., and Virginia A. Fatwell, May 27th

Norris, R. C. and M. B. Wood, March 18th

1890

Newcomb, J. D. and L. E. Amos, July 11th

Newton, J. E. and P. E. Wood, December 24th

1891

Newcomb, B. F. and E. R. Driver, April 14th

Norris, J. H. and M. A. Shiflett, December 31st

1892

Newman, W. R. and M. E. Booth, May 17th

Newcomb, Wm. H. and Va. E. Mays, August 7th

Norris, Claud and N. C. Mays, September 21st

1893

Newton, Geo. and M. E. Douner, January 2nd

Neve, L. W. F. and F. G. Taylor, June 7th

1894

Newcombe, S. T. and V. A. Clements, March 14th

Norvell, Emmet and Blanche Norvell, December 1st

1897

Norvell, Paul W. and Estelle P. Thomas, December, 18th

1898

Nuttycombe, H. Wm. and Laury Patton, June 27th

1899

Newton, James H. and Daisy D. Tomlin, November 6th

Nuttycombe, Thos. Robt. and M. L. Shepherd, November 20th

Norcross, J. E. and Natie W. Jones, December 12th

Norman, J. H. and S. E. Courtney, March 14th

Norvell, Chas. and Lacy Wood, March 22nd

Nuttycombe, W. R. and Sarah F. Hopkins, August 12th

1900

Norris, O. F. and Tommie Woodson, December 24th

1901

Norris, J. W. and L. B. Patterson, July 5th

Nicholas, Wm. M. and Mollie E. Page, October 29th

1902

Norford, Durell and C. L. B. Smith, July 30th

Neff, A. C. and M. A. Tucker, November 17th

1903

Nickell, Ralph and Mittie Pearl Gisener, April 13th

Norvell, Russell L. and Pearly G. Mawyer, June 22nd

Norvelle, Jas. and A. M. Kannedy, July 27th

Norvell, John N. and Josephine Norvell, January 13th

1905

Newman, William T. and Eliza C. Failes, December, 27th

Newman, William T. and Eliza C. Failes, December 27th

Norvell, Edward and Lottie Mawyer, February 13th

Noel, E. E. and A. J. Thurston, March 20th

Napier, W. B. and Mary J. Woodson, April 7th

1906

Norvell, Anvil Waller and Hattie Eliz. Mawyer, July 3rd

Norvell, John U. and Carrie Mawyer, December 26th

1907

Norris, Marvin E. and Lillian Feuchtenberger, June 18th

Noell, Richard A. and Eva Marshall, June 26th

Norford, William L. and Cora D. Smith, August 27th

North, G. W. and Hattie L. Barnett, September 16th

Norford, Tinsley and Bessie Madison, October 17th

Neill, J. A. O. and Mary E. Gentry, November 13th

Newell, J. G. and C. E. Businger, December 22nd

Norford, Mannis W. and Addie Maupin, December 25th

1908

Napier, Homer and Mattie E. Hunt, June 30th

Nairm, William and Julia A. Harris, August 24th

1909

Norvell, John H. and Annie E. Meeks, November 9th

1910

Napier, William W. and Nettie A. Mawyer, April 12th

Norvell, Robert and Curtis Norvell, August 15th

Nash, Joseph C. and Violet P. White, October 27th

Norflett, William J. and Mary E. Morris, November 9th

1911

Norris, Robert Clinton and Minnie Lee Walker, August 30th

Nolly, George M. and Margaret H. McCue, September 7th

Newbury, Guy H. and Sadie W. Clark, September 6th

Newton, Robert Acey and Virginia P. Carnell, December 4th

Noble, Edward W. and Browning E. Neff, December 23rd

1912

Newell, Jr., G. W. and Alline Scantlin, May 25th

1913

Newby, Theodore A. and Carolyn K. Payne, October 22nd

1914

Norford, John Q. and Alice W. Marsh, February 18th

Nunally, W. F. and Ida A. Woodson, April 4th

Norris, Wm. Thomas and Ollie C. Turyman, November 24th

Novell, Olie S. and Lelia Mawyer, April 7th

Norvell, Harry and Jonnie E. Mawyer, July 4th

1916

Norford, Willie and Maggie E. Davis, June 21st

1917

Norris, Randolph D. and Maria A. Shiflett, February 7th

Naite, Jr., Harrison and Mary C. Herring, July 23rd

Nelson, Francis P. and Ruth Lee Wayland, April 29th

Norford, Larrie M. and Carrie L. Powell, November 22nd

1918

Napier, Jackson and Ida G. Duncan, March 11th

Naylor, Charles B. and Bessie L. Sandridge, March 27th

1919

Newcomb, Cecil I. and Carrie E. Drumheller, September 1st

Newman, Chas. R. and Annie S. Pace, December 16th

1920

Nash, Charlie Y. and Annie C. Staton, September 10th

Naylor, Lyman H. and Nora Lee Haney, December 23rd

1921

Nunn, Arthur B. and Bessie Ellinger, June 25th

Napier, Harry T. and Donona Chisholm, December 6th

1922

Norvell, Henry R. and Esther F. Powell, October 12th

1923

Neill, George P. M. and Virginia L. Jackson, May 24th

1924

Northrope, Alfred B. and Mary F. Gibson, March 9th

Newcomb, Jno. L. and Grace L. Russell, October 21st

1925

Naylor, Kenneth and Eula M. Estes, February 19th

Napier, Forest and Annie Hunt, October 21st

1926

Newcomb, Roscoe B. and Catherine A. Johnson, January 17th

Newman, Geo. A. and Annie E. Payne, June 18th

1927

Napier, Wesley C. and Lillie B. Woodie, January 13th

Norvell, Percy and Lillie Dudley, January 26th

Nines, Charlie and Nora Shiflett, March 26th

Napier, Wm. B. and Julia E. Ward, April 4th

1928

Nuttycombe, Hopkins and Elizabeth T. Miller, July 20th

1929

Napier, Clinton and Gertrude M. Holsapple, March 30th

Norford, Colman S. annd Willie E. Clements, October 26th

O

1784

Orrd, William and Agatha Edwards, December 21st

1785

Old, John and Milley Wheeler, July 14th

1787

Offell, James and Elizabeth Holaday, March 15th

Oglesby, Pleasant and Elizabeth Gillum, December 20th

1792

Oaks, Henry and Susannah Randal, November 15th

1794

Old, William and Nancy Harper, December 23rd

1795

Owens, Stuart and Caty Harris, March 30th

1797

Old, John and Elizabeth Steele, December 16th

1799

Ogg, Daniel and Elizabeth Flynt, December 31st

1806

Omohundro, Thomas W. and Polly Cowell, May 24th

1807

Old, Abyah and Sally Fretwell, January 20th

1811

Oglesby, John and Elizabeth Thomas, September, 30th

Owen, ? and Polly Wood, November 26th

1818

Oneal, John S. and Frances Burnley, April 28th

1821

Oaks, Hudson and Lucy Wood, July 28th

Omohundro, George C. and Lucy B. Shelton, December 20th

1823

Oaks, Hudson and Sophia Ballard, January 21st

Oaks, Rice and Patience Sudderth, June 24th

Owens, William and Caroline Willis, August 3rd

1826

Oliver, William N. and Mary Bales, August 15th

1829

Overstreet, William and Sophia Harris, January 22nd

1830

Old, J. W. A. and Jemema Hudson, November 7th

1836

Oney, Isaac and Susan Burton, October 3rd

1847

Owens, G. T. and C. White, January 11th

1848

Oneal, John L. and C. B. Saunders, July 3rd

1850

Omohundro, Tipton T. and Frances M. Turner, January 15th

1851

Owens, James M. and Frances M. Points, September 18th

1854

Olden, William and Margaret Flynn, July 28th

1855

O'Brian, Daniel and Catherine Powers, October 1st

O'Connor, Michael and Martha Bowen, October 17th

Owen, Wm. M. and A. W. Lewellyn, November 2nd

Owens, William and A. W. Lewellyn, November 20th

1858

Omohundro, George C. and Caroline V. Thornley, October 4th

1860

Oberdofer, Benjamin and Malke Baum, October 15th

Omohundro, Thomas and Virginia Randolph, January, 2nd

Omohundro, Thos. and Virginia Randolph, February 2nd

1861

Omohundro, R. F. and Margaret Crank, May 29th

Omohundro, R. F. and Margaret G. Crank, May 30th

1862

Ogg, Rich'd H. and Marietta Via, June 10th

O'Connor, Owne and Eliza Morris, July 15th

1866

Owens, John W. and Albenia W. Owens, September 13th

1867

Omohundro, Wm. M. and Carolin Stone, July 10th

Oliver, Jno. H. and Mary E. Yates, November 28th

1868

Ogg, Wm. D. and Oliver Stevens, December 2nd

Otis, Joseph and Frances Suddarth, January 16th

1877

Obaugh, Jno. A. and Emma E. Naylor, March 14th

1878

Owens, Creed W. and Lucy E. Early, May 6th

1882

Orr, William A. and Lucy J. Gentry, December 27th

1883

O'Neill, John Thos. and Anna Isabella Robertson, April 25th

1890

Orange, J. P. and R. L. Farish, November 1st

1892

Ould, J. W. and M. W. Huckstep, December 12th

1893

Omohundro, T. T. and L. A. Shippard, December 20th

1894

Omohundro, Andrew D. and A. M. Breckenbrough, November 3rd

1897

O'Brien, David and Mary E. Moore, December 2nd

1902

Orrison, G. Devere and Myrtie G. Moore, March 20th

1903

Odell, Harlan B. and M. Josephine Bryant, April 11th

Omohundro, S. T. and P. A. Fowler, April 22nd

1904

Owens, Jas. Wm. and Lucy Catherine Marsh, November 19th

1905

Owen, Rupert Beartrice and Bessie Farrand Wood, June 16th

Ogg, Wesley Scott and Lucy Elmer Downer, December 12th

Ozy, Wesley Scott and Lucy Elma Douner, December 12th

1906

Owen, J. R. and M. H. Snell, February 12th

Otis, James and Emma Melton, March 7th

1907

Oslin, Arthur L. and Lucy Mann, March 20th

O'Neill, J. A. and Mary E. Gentry, November 13th

Ownsby, Charlie S. and Minnie B. Craig, December 22nd

1908

O'Brien, Charles and Fannie O. Lang, March 4th

1909

Oliver, Robert R. and Lucy M. Mann, April 28th

O'Neill, John K. and Ora Dickerson, September 28th

1911

O'Ferrell, James C. and Sallie Thacker, January 18th

1912

Osborne, Richard H. and Minnie G. Wood, May 18th

1914

Owsley, Albert P. and Mae E. Harris, October 24th

1916

O'Bannon, J. S. and L. M. Downer, December 1st

1917

Owns, Eustice C. and Martha G. Via, September 3rd

1918

Osborne, Percy and Josephine Houchins, March 28th

1919

Orange, Percy and Mary H. Woodson, September 21st

1922

Ogden, Cammie and Ruby Belle Smith, November 17th

1923

Owens, Henry S. and Emma J. Bragg, June 17th

1924

O'Quinn, Bernie Lee and Anna B. Napier, June 13th

1925

Olinger, Roland T. and Dorothy M. Humphrey, November 10th

1926

Omohundro, Jr., Geo. T. and Ruby L. Paulette, November 13th

1927

Offutt, Frank O. F. and Constance F. Disney, February 4th

1928

Overback, Clarence J. and Harriot Lee West, September 4th

1929

Oliver, John B. and Nannie M. Fenchans, April 3rd

P

1785

Payne, Benjamin and Anne Martin June 12th

Perry, Hildeburt and Sally Wade, October 22nd

Perry, William and Keziah P. Sowell March 28th

1786

Polson, Thomas and Nelly Ellis, August 24th

1787

Powers, Jacob and Ann Crosthwait, September 13th

1788

Perrow, Daniel and Anna Garland, February 12th

Price, Elisha and Nancy Hudson, March 19th

1789

Patterson, John Perry and Nancy Wansly, November 14th

1790

Page, William and Elizabeth Smith, November 2nd

Pettitt, Thomas and Patsy Ballard, February 5th

Phillips, Martin and Elizabeth Burton, February 9th

1791

Parsons, Richard and Sarah Moran, December 24th

Powers, Norman and Mildred Leake, December 26th

1792

Page, Leavell and Martha Dudley, September 6th

Peyton, Craven and Jean Lewis, September 4th

Pierce, John and Judah Hicks, October 25th

Polson, John and Patsy Bryan, December 24th

1793

Pritchett, James and Mary Solomon, December 5th

Pugh, Lewis and Polly Gooding, December 11th

1794

Poindexter, James and Polly Thomson, December 3rd

1795

Payne, Jesse and Jean Morgan, June 13th

Price, Thomas Johnson and Patsy Brown, March 7th

Pritt, James and Martha Hoy, August 26th

1796

Page, Edmundsen and Elizabeth Butler, April 15th

Petty, William and Elizabeth Sullivan, January, 9th

Poage, John and Elizabeth Davis, June 22nd

1797

Price, Abraham and Sucky Dawson, December 13th

1798

Page, Robert Jr. and Jeriah Morris Smithson, October 9th

Patrick, Charles and Dawkus Black, January 26th

Patrick, John and Susannah Snell, February 5th

Poindexter, Samuel and Sally Garth, February 10th

Poindexter, William and Judith Thompson, September 11th

Polson, Thomas and Judith Coleman, October 6th

Polson, Thomas and Susannah Dollius, November 28th

1799

Patten, Thomas and Sarah Lewis, June 13th

Phillips, John and Elizabeth Jones, April 3rd

1801

Padgett, John annd Elizabeth Watts, November 20th

Page, William and Mary Pearce, November 23rd

Pleasants, Robert and Sally Rogers, September 7th

1802

Pritchett, John and Peggy Russell, May 31st

1803

Patterson, David and Nancy Moore, April 4th

Payne, William and Mildred Copeland, July 4th

Pemberton, Thomas and Franky Blaine, March 28th

Pettus, Dabney and Elizabeth Turner, September 17th

Purkypile, John and Mary Boyer, November 5th

1804

Page, William and Sarah Melton, June 21st

1805

Porter, Peter and Nancy Hopkins, November 21st

Priddy, John and Elizabeth Gillaspy, December 6th

Putt, Soloman and Sally Horner, October 17th

1806

Page, Tucker W. and Milly Wheeler, December 3rd

Parrott, Charles and Sarah Brown, October 15th

Patterson, John and Mary B. Nicholas, May 28th

Pleasants, Richard and Zepporah Hicks, December 24th

Powell, Harvey and Polly Spencer, December 1st

Priddy, George and Polly Gartin, May 22nd

1807

Pace, John and Polly Groom, September 21st

Philips, Philip and Martha Gray, March 7th

Powell, John and Rainy Goulden, August 28th

Pritchett, Elijah and Nancy Carver, September 17th

1808

Pace, George and Peggy Mullins, April 22nd

Page, William and Christian McQuarry, August 1st

Pemberton, Charles and Susan Wood, February 25th

Pemberton, Henry and Milly Wood, August 2nd

Powell, Sam and Elizabeth Strange, March 12th

1809

Pace, Joseph and Ann Ricks, November 29th

1811

Proctor, James B. annd Hanah Matthews, December 2nd

1813

Parrott, George and Elizabeth Catterton, December 14th

1814

Perkins, John B. and Rachel B. Key, December 6th

Priddy, James and Fanny Carver, January 21st

1815

Page, Edmound and Rhoda Harper, January 20th

1816

Pleasants, John and Jane Spencer, November 23rd

Priddy, John and Polly Mooney, October 15th

1817

Parsons, James and Martha Lowell, September 27th

Philips, Matthew and Nancy Woodey, January 23rd

1818

Paul, Hugh and Elizabeth Fretwell, December 17th

Pettett, Fountaine and Nancy Wood, January 25th

Pettiss, Ira and Nancy Rhoades, September 16th

Philips, Philip and Eliza Walker, November 14th

Pitts, Johnson W. and Ann C. Bishop, December 10th

1819

Pence, John H. and Malinda Bennett, December 28th

1820

Powell, Jacob and Mildred Drumheller, February 24th

1821

Pace, Ben and Hardenia Thacker, December 3rd

Parsons, Adolphus and Patience M. Bishop, May 10th

Pickett, Charles and Jane Dowell, March 5th

1822

Panonser, Thomas and Mary Ann Martin, November 28th

Parsons, William M. and Mary Moran, December 19th

Payne, George M. and Eliza Dyer, May 4th

Poseton, John D. and Elizabeth Carr, July 19th

1824

Perry, William and Nancy Kerby, December 8th

1825

Peck, Limmonds and Mary A. West, March 3rd

Perry, Edmund and Mildred D. Barksdale, October 12th

Pleasants, Thomas W. and Susan H. Goodman, April 4th

Powell, Phillip and Mary Burton, October 14th

Pugh, Lewis and Susan McDaniel, July 25th

1826

Payne, David and Frances Norford, December 7th

Phillips, Matthew and Nancy Bailey, October 11th

Price, Stephen C. and Lydia Ann Harper, September 21st

1827

Peck, Lyman and Lucy B. Gaines, July 18th

Perkins, Schuyler and Rebecca Rittenhouse, November 5th

Perry, Calven S. and Mary A. Tutt, December 31st

Pitt, John and Frances Osbourne, January 2nd

1828

Perkins, Benjamin M. and Mary S. Dabney, December 11th

Pritchett, William and Nancy Salmon, December 18th

1829

Parsons, David and Sarah G. Anderson, July 7th

Payne, Richard and Darkey Taylor, December 21st

Pettet, Lyderer R. and Mary Proctor, December 16th

Powell, Robert and Nancy Shiflett, February 11th

Priddy, Willis and Maria Breedlove, November 19th

1830

Petitt, William J. and Lucy Jane Bernard, May 4th

1831

Page, William annd Mildred F. Sudderth, November 18th

Payne, James M. and Eleanor Robinson, May 2nd

Phillips, Charles and Sarah Drumheller, April ?

Piper, Jeremiah and M. C. Richardson, February 22nd

Polson, James and Mary Ann Watson, March 10th

1832

Pemberton, Thomas H. and Sarah A. Durrett, March 22nd

Pritchett, Walter and Julia Salmon, November 28th

1833

Page, R. F. and Sarah W. Jones, October 25th

Pickering, Thomas and Christianna Branham, February 20th

Pinkard, Richard N. and Mary J. Brand, December 19th

Piper, Willis W. and Bary S. Black, December 17th

Pollard, Henry and Courtney B. Burton, May 16th

Powell, Henry Jr. and Elizabeth Elliott, July 18th

Powell, Samuel M. and Jane Martin, December 3rd

Price, Abram H. and Sarah A. Drumheller, September 7th

Pritchett, Horace and Mary Beck, November 11th

1834

Poindexter, James W. and Mary E. Wayt, September 2nd

Price, Daniel and Eliza Breedlove, December 22nd

1835

Parrott, William T. and Nancy F. Thompson, February 23rd

Payne, Jesse and Mildred Rippito, November 28th

Perkins, Harden and J. Ann Harris, April 6th

Porter, Madison C. and Emily Staples, October 8th

1836

Peterson, Orange and Martha Watson, April 22nd

Poole, John and Mary Jane Suddarth, November 5th

Porterfield, Robert and L. L. Sudderth, April 16th

Powell, Nicholas and S. Drumheller, February 1st

1837

Payne, James A. and Lucy A. Rodes, April 19th

Porter, Rezen D. and Mary B. Watson, November 22nd

Price, John J. and Catharine C. Gillum, December 21st

1838

Pace, Edward H. and Sarah Payne, October 4th

Perkins, Daniel and Martha E. Wood, October 17th

Porter, Lewis L. and Mary Hays, August 20th

Powell, Michael and Elizabeth Spencer, August 6th

1839

Parnell, Samuel and Nancy Pugh, November 12th

Patterson, John and Harriet Shiflett, September 29th

Piper, William K. and Evelene Walters, July 2nd

Price, Henry G. and Malinda Sandridge, December 18th

Proffitt, William and Sarah E. Holbert, December 21st

1840

Pace, Jese and Nancy B. Moore, April 6th

Paris, George and Ann L. Liggon, August 13th

Pettit, Jese S. and Elizabeth O. Pollard, April 2nd

Powell, Benjamin S. and Mary Vandergrift, August 24th

1841

Page, Edward D. and M. J. Porter, December 7th

Powell, Caspier and Angelina Hundley, January 14th

Priddy, Anthony and Amanda Herring, December 16th

1842

Pace, James M. and Mary Marr, March 15th

Pace, Harner and Lucy Bailey, February 7th

Parrott, Charles H. and Martha W. Brown, November 18th

Patterson, James M. and W. A. Tompkins, January 20th

Payne, Elijah W. and Mary J. Bear, September 20th

Perkins, John F. and Eliza S. Perkins, August 23rd

Pettet, Jese S. and Sarah E. Pace, July 18th

Powell, Casper and Susan F. Abell, February 22nd

Pugh, Nicholas W. and Winifred S. Wood, November 24th

1843

Pace, Jese and Martha Norvell, November 30th

Pettett, Fountaine and Martha A. Roach, February 2nd

Piper, Garrett W. and Sophia J. Farrar, August 7th

1844

Parn, Alexander and Sarah C. Dettor, February 27th

Pugh, John B. and Adeline F. Critzer, September 16th

Pugh, William H. and Marian Thurmond, April 27th

Pullium, Thompson W. and Jane Moss, June 22nd

1845

Pace, Henderson W. and M. A. Dixon, April 2nd

Page, Edmond D. and M. Y. Hays, February 5th

Parrock, F. and S. S. Wertenbaker, October 8th

Peyton, William H. and M. C. Thurmond, December 23rd

Pollard, John F. and M. A. Barksdale, November 3rd

Poole, J. M. and Virginia Jones, December 17th

Powell, F. F. and M. F. Gentry, July 13th

Powell, Michael and S. Underwood, November 13th

1847

Pedler, William and Patience Bishop, December 23rd

Pendleton, George W. and Mary E. Gully, August 10th

Perkinlo, Stephen C. and C. A. Walker, July 21st

Perry, William D. and Rebecca Widderfield, December 21st

Phillips, Peter V. and V. H. Terrell, December 7th

1848

Pleasants, Joseph S. and Eliza A. Thacker, February 20th

Powell, S. Aleberry M. and Jane Norvell, October 9th

Powell, William H. and M. E. Norvell, February 21st

Pryor, Roger A. and Sarah A. Rice, November 8th

1849

Page, Nicholas M. and Mary E. White, October 9th

Patterson, Joab and P. J. Jones, September 17th

Pole, John G. and J. F. Clarke, June 11th

1850

Pace, James H. and Winifred C. Lyon, July 4th

Page, Frederick M. and Anna K. Meriwether, December 24th

Pettit, Joseph F. and Adeline R. Fielder, January 15th

Peyton, M. Green and Martha Champ Carter, November 6th

Poore, R. H. and Jeanette B. Magruder, August 8th

Pugh, Absolum C. and Marthana Critzer, December 10th

1851

Parr, Thomas and Elizabeth Dawson, March 19th

Payne, Samuel S. and Elizabeth N. Crawford, September 23rd

Pendleton, John O. and Ann L. Harris, September 13th

Peyton, George L. and Mary C. Omohundro, September 9th

Porter, Oswald and Frances Ann Gillaspy, June 9th

Powell, William and Mary Nicholas, April 3rd

1852

Powell, Robert W. and S. Norvell, September 9th

Powell, William R. and H. E. Roberts, August 2nd

Preston, Henry and Ann C. Carter, September 8th

Price, Charles H. and M. A. Wood, August 21st

Proffit, David A. and Sarah West, March 10th

Pryor, William H. and M. H. Walker, October 1st

1853

Pegram, R. H. and Jarnette L. Saunders, February 3rd

Powers, D. P. and Sarah Staples, June 13th

Pritchett, James and Parnelia Wood, October 30th

1854

Pace, Wm. J. and Mary J. West, April 26th

Pace, William J. and Mary J. West, April 28th

Page, William C. and Mary L. Purvis, December 20th

Pegram, Edward S. and Lucy W. Gilmer, February 1st

Pegram, Edw. S. and Lucy W. Gilmer, February 1st

Perkins, J. N. and Mary Jones, October 31st

Phillips, Richard S. and Ethelind Christian, February 2nd

Pleasants, John and Mary Pittman, October 12th

Powell, Gilbert W. and Anna Powell, December 7th

Powell, Geo. W. and Anna Powell, December 7th

Powers, Reuben S. and Mildred A. Ballard, May 4th

Powers, Reuben S. and Mildred A. Ballard, May 14th

Phillips, Richard L. and E. N. Christian, February 2nd

Powell, Benj. F. and Mary E. Bowen, February 7th

Powell, Andrew J. and Sallie W. Powell, February 7th

Pleasants, Marcus and Frances Price, January 24th

Pugh, Wm. C. and Sarah M. Tomblin, January 17th

Pugh, Nelson W. and Eliz. Gillock, April 3rd

1855

Pace, Benjamin H. and Sarah J. Campbell, September 18th

Page, Wm. C. and Mary L. Purvis, December 20th

Parrott, George W. and Susan M. Ward, June 7th

Parrott, Geo. W. and Susan M. Ward, June 7th

Perley, James and Mary J. Mooney, April 26th

Perkins, Jno. N. and Mary Jones, October 31st

Points, William J. and Cornelia V. Brown, December 4th

Powell, Thomas A. and R. C. Martin, March 1st

Powell, Thos. A. and R. C. Martin, March 1st

Pritchett, S. and Mary Pritchett, August 16th

1856

Patterson, Charles J. and Martha Goolesby, October 28th

Patteson, Charles J. and Martha S. Goolsby, October, 28th

Powell, Edward and Mary W. Wood, November 3rd

Powell, Edward and Mary W. Wood, November 6th

Powers, John and Joanna Flynn, June 17th

Price, William A. and Elizabeth H. Edwards, July 13th

Price, Wm. A. and Eliz. H. Edwards, July 13th

Pride, James E. and Sallie A. Price, September 10th

Pride, James E. and Sally A. Price, September 10th

Pugh, A. C. and Nancy J. Thacker, March 11th

Pugh, Absalom C. and Nancy J. Thacker, March 11th

Payne, Jno. E. and Nancy F. Draper, April 9th
Pleasants, John T. and Julia W. Thacker,
March 18th

1857

Page, John M. and Lucy E. Flanagan, September
14th
Page, R. A. and Alma M. Diggs, June 22nd
Patterson, David N. and Mollie S. Harris, October 29th
Payne, John E. and Nancy E. Draper, April 9th
Pugh, Edwin A. and Mary P. Johnson, November 9th

1858

Page, William E. and Lucy A. C. Oliver, February 1st
Page, Wm. E. and Lucy A. C. Oliver, February
14th
Payne, Barnett G. W, and Ann Humphrey,
September 30th
Payne, Benett G. W., and Martha A. Humphreys, September 30th
Peter, Jonathan and Lucy V. Wright, November
25th
Peyton, John B. and Ella J. Howard, September
27th
Peyton, Jno. B. and Ella J. Howard, September
28th
Peyton, Thomas Green and Carry Ann Carr,
November 8th
Porter, Jonathan T. and Lucy V. Wright, November 24th
Price, W. R. and Sammella Adams, January
18th
Price, Wm. R. and Sannella Adams, January
19th

1859

Pace, Bowyer and Mary Jane Matthews, November 27th
Pleasants, John T. and Julia W. Thacker,
March 17th

1860

Pace, John M. and Martha A. Jones, December
22nd
Pippin, Edward A. and Helen Hamner, March
Pace, Jno. M. and Martha M. Jones, December
25th
14th
Powell, Benjamin F. Jr. and Celina M. J.
Wood, June 28th
Powell, Franklin and Jane W. Thomas, January
6th
Purvis, O. W. and George E. Blankenberg,
December 3rd
Purvis, O. W. and Georgie E. Blankenburg,
December 4th

1861

Pace, John J. and Adie S. Rodes, February 4th
Pace, Jno. J. and Adeline S. Rodes, February
5th

Peyton, Hervey S. and Mary Eliza Pauli, November 25th
Peyton, Henry S. and Mary E. Pauli, November
26th
Powell, Walter M. and Sally W. Powell, September 3rd
Powell, Walter M. and Sally W. Powell, September 19th
Preston, Samuel D. and Texie G. Saunders,
December 5th
Preston, Sam'l D. and Texin Saunders, December 5th
Pritchett, Peter and Mildred Birkhead, August
30th
Pritchett, Peter and Susan M. Birkhead, September 4th

1862

Parsons, Tho. J. and Wilhel Moon, November
20th
Poole, Wm. M. and Emma J. Craven, September 24th
Poali, T. T. and S. C. Keller, January 29th

1863

Pace, Pleasant W. and Sarah C. Staton, May 7th
Pleasants, P. B. and Susan A. Martin, August
27th

1864

Preston, Jno. M. and Mary P. Cochran, Feb. 3rd
Parr, Ammanis and Harriet S. Baber, September 22nd
Powell, Lewis Wm. and Frances A. Naylor,
April 13th
Parr, Francis M. and Angelina Baber, August
2nd

1865

Page, Henry and Martha P. Turner, April 23rd
Parrott, William N. and S. Baker Cobb, December 4th
Perrot, Wm. N. and S. Bettie Cobbs, December
14th
Payne, T. W. and Sarah F. Herron, November
16th
Payne, F. W. and Sarah F. Herron, November
16th
Phillips, H. T. and Kate Dyson, July 11th
Phillips, H. T. and Kate Dyson, July 20th
Pleasants, James and Caroline Massie, November 7th
Pleasants, Jas. and Caroline L. Massie, November 8th
Poe, David and Susan D. P. Hays, November
21st
Pugh, Henry and Martha P. Turner, April 18th
Pugh, Silas C. and Jane A. Haskins, January
24th
Pugh, Silas C. and Jane A. Haskins January
31st

1866

Pace, Wm. A. F. and Mary A. Ricks, December
25th

Patterson, James H. and Susan M. Via, February 10th

Patterson, Joab and Susan E. Gary, July 5th

Patterson, Joab and Susan E. Guy, July 12th

Pettett, Thos. J. and Sarah A. Lupton, December 20th

Phillips, B. S. and Malvina H. Farish, January 13th

Phillips, B. S. and M. A. Farish, January 15th

Pittman, Jas. H. and Susan M. Via, February 15th

Pleasants, Chris. and Kosa V. Suddarth, February 19th

Pleasants, Chris and Kasandor V. Suddarth, February 17th

Powell, John D. and Rosanna E. Mawyer, February 6th

Powell, Jno. D. and Rivanna E. Maroy, February 6th

Preston, Charles H. C. and Mary E. Woodson, September 18th

Preston, Chas. H. C. and Mary E. Woodson, September 19th

Priddy, James F. and Mary E. Thomas, October 25th

Pugh, William H. and Mary P. Pugh, March 21st

Pugh, Wm. H. and Mary P. Pugh, March 6th

1867

Puringo, Geo. and Patsey Taylor, September 14th

Payne, Jno. E. and Cornelia E. Norvell, October 26th

Payne, F. A. and Susan F. Vaughn, October 29th

Peyton, Chas. S. and Sarah E. Bramham, November 19th

Pritchett, Bellfield and Nannie C. Wilkerson, November 26th

1868

Phillips, T. W. and Virginia W. Gardner, January 6th

Parter, Henry D. and Mary B. Teryll, January 13th

Perry, Jefferson and Maria Monroe, June 1st

Peteman, Robert C. and Fedora H. Via, June 18th

Patterson, Jno. V. and Sallie H. Carter, September 14th

Powell, A. J. and Milly A. Fretwell, September 26th

Powell, A. J. annd Milly A. Fatwell, October 1st

Price, Thomas and Mary P. Henderson, July 7th

Pugh, Absolum T. and L. E. Haskins, February 13th

Porter, Henry D. and Mary B. Payne, January 21st

Pitman, Robert C. and Federo H. Via, June 21st

Peyton, Chas. S. and S. E. Branham, November 21st

Phillips, T. W. and Virginia W. Gardner, January 7th

Purvis, Daniel J. and Mattie E. Dudley, January 12th

Perkins, Joseph and Sallie C. Maupin, December 3rd

Powell, Alfred N. and Henrietta Fincham, September 4th

Payne, Henry and Mary C. Taylor, January 6th

Pugh, Wm. H. and Ann L. Johnson, January 21st

1869

Page, Claiborne and Morning Monroe, August 8th

Parrish, Jno. T. and Ellen D. Tyler, November 16th

Poats, J. W. and Ella P. Grayson, November 25th

Porter, Warh and Phillis Page, December 23rd

1870

Payne, Robert W. and Nancy E. Ray, March 24th

Page, Chas. H. and June Leaton, May 19th

Phillips, Henry and Alice Madison, May 26th

Price, Chas N. and Sallie J. Woods, November 2nd

Price, Wm. A. and M. E. Woody, November 24th

Phillips, J. N. and Elize E. Gillispie, November 20th

Price, Richard and Mary E. Tilman, December 29th

Parrott, Wm. N. and Bettie J. Whitlock, December 1st

1871

Pearce, Jno. N. and Mary F. Garrison, January 19th

Percivall, Joseph J. and Amanda O. Beazeley, November 22nd

Payne, George Anderson and Rebecca Caldwell Vaughan, December 7th

Perkins, George and Eliza Norris Watson, December 13th

Pugh, John F. and Carrie C. Pugh, March 9th

1872

Pugh, Wm. A. and Mintie P. Catyre, September 26th

Pannell, Washington and M. S. Henderson, October 24th

Pleasants, John J. and M. S. Robertson, December 23rd

Pyle, Augusta J. and Loretta A. A. Jones, December 10th

1873

Paxton, H. E. and V. A. Wood, January 8th

Palmore, Newton R. and Sallie T. Tilman, July 14th

Price, Bowman F. and Mary Hancock, November 11th

Pritchett, Thos. W. and Julia H. Flynt, December 4th

Perkins, Randolph S. and Susan M. Wood, December 23rd

Payne, John and Willie Gillim, April 30th

1874

Plunkett, Algin W. and Susan B. Catterton, February 12th

Pugh, J. D. and Martha F. Graves, May 6th

Payne, John L. and Hetty S. Libbey, May 19th

Poallman, Wm. F. and Mary A. Enock, November 18th

Parrott, Bernard T. and Sallie A. Brown, December 7th

Price, Chas. A. and J. Josephine New, December 22nd

Perry, Eugene A. and Mattie J. Terrill, July 18th

Pettit, Jno. H. and Mollie C. Abell, March 4th

1875

Pace, Benj. R. and Kate L. Petitt, January 26th

Pugh, C. G. and Isabella F. Suthard, November 9th

Payne, Harry and Mary Barnett, December 29th

1876

Pinkerton, Brainard M. and Alice H. Harris, May 13th

Payne, Henry and Eliz. Fellinger, July 17th

Parr, Jas. M. and Mary J. Maxwell, November 11th

Page, Pleasant C. and Mollie P. Frazier, December 14th

1877

Powell, Walter A. and Willie C. Norvell, January 27th

Payne, Henry M. and Sarah M. Norford, April 2nd

Perkins, Wm. M. and Fanny Mason, June 7th

Powell, Geo. W. and Mary S. Shotwell, June 28th

Payne, Richard F. and Lucy E. Walker, August 1st

Payne, Jas. E. and Emma Pugh, August 11th

Payne, Chas. and Janes H. Dudley, October 11

Pearce, Napoleon B. and Willie H. Wheeler, December 3rd

1878

Patterson, Wm. and Mary B. Walton, January 4th

Pace, Geo. L. and Jsetta A. Bishop, May 1st

Pitts, David H. and Cora L. Staples, November 4th

Page, Frederick K. and Flora G. Lewis, November 11th

Powell, Sharod and Harriet C. F. Powell, December 9th

Payne, Alphonse D. and Anne S. Herndon, October 31st

1879

Powell, James C. and Martha F. Ballard, January 20th

Peunt, Wm. H. and Annie M. Johnson, February 27th

Pritchett, Benj. F. and Mary E. Marshall, April 24th

Petrie, Jacob H. and Mary H. Brown, May 5th

Powell, Eugene C. and Nellie M. Ferguson, September 29th

Pugh, Charles E. and Lucy J. Bailey, November 15th

Phillips, Jas. W. and Mary Richards, December 8th

1880

Phillips, Louis Otho and Duny C. Harris, January 21st

Pugh, Wm. L. and Bettie A. Herron, November 17th

Pugh, Walker W. and Mollie J. Herron, September 13th

Pugh, Charles T. and Eliz C. Phillips, December 20th

Paxton, Charles H. and Lizzie M. Smithson, December 21st

Pritchett, Wm. and Ella Watts, December 29th

Pryor, John and Caroline Dyer, December 30th

1881

Phillips John D. and Mary C. Elsom, August 12th

Poindixter, Royal Mc. C. and Effie Estel Johnson, January 25th

1882

Proffit, Edw. C. and Mary E. Chapman, February 2nd

Purvis, Albert A. and Ada J. Adams, February 22nd

Pritchett, Lemuel E. and Nellie G. Marshall, October 8th

Powell, William E. and Lucy E. Davis, October 26th

1883

Powell, Walter F. and Janie Lee Hudson, April 3rd

Pendleton, J. O. H. and Corine M. Digges, July 5th

Page, Frederick W. and Lucy C. Brent, November 15th

Powers, Thos. Edw. and Susan M. Early, November 14th

Pritchett, Samuel and Mary Cason, November 25th

1884

Pettus, Julian K. and Nannie P. Trevillian, March 5th

Page, Samuel Massie and Margaret W. Harris February 26th

Pace, Sidney W. and Va. A. Ancille, December 23rd

Powell, Chas. E. and Willie C. Via, December 24th

1885

Patterson, James and Sally A. Dures, January 22nd

Page, Walter Taylor and Marie Page, March 17th

Pleasants, Chriss and Jennie Pleasants, May 17th

Profitt, James R. and Willie E. Douglass, July 30th

Prince, Edwin G. and Mollie P. Maupin, September 9th

Pugin, Byom A. and Jennie L. Collins, November 3rd

1886

Page, Robt. S. and Nannie B. Cader, August 8th

Pearce, Lucian P. and Sarah E. Scruggs, September 28th

Price, Walter E. and Ellen Heath, October 5th

Phillips, Jno. C. and Ida M. Cattett, October 25th

1887

Pace, Broadus, C. and Willie L. Carter, February 15th

Pugh, Charles B. and Laura F. Baber, June 7th

Peyton, Henry S. and Nellie L. Gilbert, December 12th

Pritchett, Strother and Laura A. Watts, December 13th

1888

Parr, Littleton A. and Dollie W. Dawson, January 7th

Powers, Jno. B. and Eleanor Richards, February 20th

Perry, J. A. and R. T. Hase, April 3rd

Pace, John and Janie Kirby, October 24th

Payne, Alex and Mildred Melton, December 25th

1889

Powell, Wm. and Hosetta Hunt, January 5th

Phillips, W. L. and Clara G. Jones, January 15th

Powell, R. L. and Bettie Fretwell, March 14th

Powell, B. L. and S. M. Walton, March 29th

1890

Parry, Jas. R. and Viola M. Parry, January 9th

Perkinsons, W. H. and Jsabet Holms, April 29th

Perkins, Arch. and A. R. Jefferies, August 5th

Price, R. H. and Mary Morris, December 15th

1891

Pendleton, J. H. and M. L. White, June 25th

Payne, V. A. and Mary A. Worsham, November 18th

Pugh, J. W. and Algevline Baber, December 1st

Payne, W. B. and Lena J. Munday, December 15th

Pritchett, Simon and L. N. D. Keaster, December 29th

1892

Patterson, A. K. and M. A. Goolsby, May 16th

Pollard, C. J. and E. R. Eahart, May 24th

1893

Phillips, Jno. B. and A. M. Butler, April 3rd

Pleasants, McLain and H. R. Kyle, April 11th

Payne, Samuel E. and Sally P. Jones, April 18th

Payne, Winston and Virgie E. Garrison, August 21st

Pope, Danl. and Grace Goodson, September 6th

Pryor, B. A. and E. P. Wingfield, October 3rd

Parikey, C. L. and E. L. Wallace, November 14th

Pace, W. J. and C. M. Pace, December 25th

1894

Pritchett, Lee and Roberta Thomas, January 19th

Powell, Eugene and Cordellia Bruce, April 23rd

Parr, J. D. and Julia A. Hunt, May 14th

Payne, Thos. P. and Ada B. Hicks, June 11th

Ponten, Nelson and Alice V. Meeks, July 23rd

Powell, R. L. and Florence Drumheller, December 12th

Perkins, Frederick A. and L. H. Wills, October 10th

Parr, Samuel F. and M. E. Pugh, December 24th

1895

Parrott, N. B. and S. F. Douglas, February 19th

Pleasants, Thos. L. and L. O. Suddarth, April 1st

Pleasants, Chris and Nan Thacker, April 1st

Payne, W. P. and Rosella Thurston, May 20th

Parkins, Frank and J. L. Sykes, June 13th

Pace, J. C. and Mrs. S. A. Barnett, July 18th

Pace, B. H. and Lucy Ponten, September 2nd

Pitman, R. C. and W. A. Blackwell, September 26th

Pace, T. T. and Carrie Thousely, November 11th

Pierne, A. D. and F. M. Lipscomb, December 21st

1896

Purvis, Simon P. and Mattie Taylor, January 2nd

Priddy, Lawson, M. and Winnie J. Pace, May 9th

Porter, Horace and Susan Allen, July 1st

Prickett, Richard and Alice Sneed, August 19th

Patterson, David J. and Mollie M. Bruce, September 28th

Potts, Allen and Gerturde Rives, October 14th
Pugh, L. H. and M. E. Goolsby, December 17th
Page, Thos. E. and Eddie Moon, December 24th

1897

Powell, Chas. E. and Anna J. Powell, April 20th
Pierce, Chas. E. and Maud J. Harlow, June 23rd
Price, Julian and Ethel G. Clay, August 20th
Payne, Sidney A. and Carrie Smith, October 12th
Parish, Wm. J. and Ada E. Wood, December 20th
Pugh, Thos. J. and Mollie Critzer, December 25th

1898

Phillips, J. B. and R. L. Knight, February 10th
Parrott, C. C. and Saan N. Bruce, March 14th
Poindexter, J. G. and Lena Daniel, March 15th
Pritchett, Ephriam and Flora Thomas, August 16th
Pittman, Chas. R. and Lillie E. Harris, October 10th
Price, J. W. M. and Mrs. Jennie Biggers, October 29th
Pleasant, Thos. and Hattie Martin, November 12th
Plummer, T. C. and Alice A. Sprouse, December 14th
Payne, J. D. and Ida D. Mawyer, December 23rd

1899

Payne, Willis A. and Susie A. Goodson, March 4th
Ponton, Chas. E. and Minnie C. Via, March 16th
Pugh, N. H. and L. L. Brooks, April 8th
Proffit, W. J. and Olive T. Bybee, May 27th
Pyles, Geo. M. and Nannie J. Stargill, October 7th

1900

Page, Dr. J. M. and Elinore M. McGlore, July 21st
Purvis, O. M. and L. E. Marshall, September 11th
Pugh, Ed H. and Etta L. Rice, December 1st
Petitt, T. J. and S. E. Spencer, December 17th
Payne, Maurice and Nora Bibb, January 3rd
Philps, Jas. M. and Annie L. Elsom, April 20th
Phillips, Thos. V. and Rosa L. Wood, May 23rd
Payne, J. M. and Willie K. Fails, June 21st

1901

Price, Richard and L. C. Gardner, May 28th
Portch, J. W. and Josie M. Coleman, June 18th
Pritchett, J. F. and Rose Pritchett, September 19th

Phillips, Jerry and A. V. Poindexter, September 25th
Pirkins, J. T. and J. Johnson, October 8th
Pace, Herman annd A. S. Childress, October 29th

1902

Powell, Howard and Nannie Thacker, April 21st
Pugh, M. B. and Nannie Burnett, July 12th
Pugh, W. A. and Sally J. Parr, January 22nd
Page, F. W. and L. W. Bryan, September 10th
Powell, W. Y. and L. B. Ballard, October 2nd
Pitts, Wm. M. and Charity C. Sevarnger, November 17th
Pace, Joab K. and Maude E. Price, November 25th

1903

Pennybacker, Joseph F. and Lelie A. Flint, January 16th
Pace, Custis, C. and Clara Maybell Coleman, February 11th
Pamplin, Walter Marion and Blanch Gertrude Thomas, February 16th
Price, M. L. and H. M. Lewis, June 15th
Proctor, Wm. O. and Alice Harlow, June 24th
Pugh, V. F. and Rosa B. Baber, September 15th
Pinkerton, W. A. and E. M. Wayland, October 12th
Payne, Thos. and Ada Lee Bibb, October 21st
Phillips, R. and M. V. North, October 28th
Pace, Arthur and Gertie Carter, November 10th

1904

Pritchett, Zachariah and Sandy Frances Hamm, January 21st
Pugh, W. L. and J. E. Kent, May 24th
Payne, B. A. and C. R. Morris, May 30th
Pitman, Guy M. and Susie E. Garrison, June 6th
Pugh, C. M. and Susan R. Alexander, October 24th
Patterson, S. G. and Ella J. Dolins, December 7th
Powell, E. A. and S. W. McClammer, October 15th
Price, James and Carrie Jane Mayo, December 28th

1905

Phillips, Chas. Mason and Linda Bell Smith, February 27th
Pritchett, John and Mrs. Minnie Thomas, March 25th
Payne, J. E. and C. L. Garrison, June 8th
Pugh, William A. and Kattie J. Herron, September 2nd
Pugh, W. A. and Katie J. Herron, September 2nd
Pritchett, Robert and Minnie Mundy, November 15th
Parr, John William and Bessie E. Wells, December 20th

Parr, John William and Bessie E. Willis, December 20th

Payne, John D. and Ester Lively, December 27th

Pritchett, Charles and Florence Kidd, March 17th

Powell, R. L. and P. G. Baber, December 23rd

Payne, Robert Walker and Gertie Francis Payne, June 4th

Price, William Watkins and Leonora Eliz. Maloney, April 4th

Payne, O. C. and Ida B. Denton, September 12th

Pitman, George W. and Blanche McDaniel, September 19th

Parr, Dan and Julia Mawyer, September 19th

Payne, S. L. and May Ella Morris, November 12th

Pleasants, John W. and Lillie L. Mawyer, November 20th

Prichette, James and Lelia Kirby, December 11th

1907

Pugh, Elliott D. and Willie L. Grooms, January 30th

Payne, Thomas T. and Maud S. Taylor, January 26th

Preddy, W. M. and Carrie L. Norford, September 18th

Poitevent S. and Heomaal O. Hancock, September 19th

Poole John H. and Caroline M. Bolling, December 24th

Price, George and Lillie Johnson, December 17th

Pumphrey, William F. and Flora Busby, December 30th

1908

Pritchett, Ernest and Lucy Pritchett, February 17th

Palmer, Roy M. and Sue Duke Jones, January 8th

Pugh, Lacy and Nellie E. Wade, May 1st

Probasco, William R. and Clara M. Tuttle, June 30th

Purvis, Joseph E. and Alice M. Rohr, July 8th

Phillips, Robert L. and Minnie F. Willis, September 1st

Pugh, David T. and Mary L. Bowen, December 22nd

1909

Pace, Keller and Mabel Smith, February 24th

Pitman, Ellis J. and Mary E. Gibson, May 5th

Perkins, William Allan and L. Hazlehurst Bolton, June 1st

Payne, Henry and Sarah Soanes, August 1st

Payne, Willie A. and Willie A. Marshall, August 25th

Pugh, Elmer and Clara Spencer, October 20th

Phillips, James W. and Julia M. Wheeler, November 17th

1910

Payne, John D. and Maggie Marsh, January 8th

Purvis, Claude E. and Cassie W. Failes, March 24th

Pugh, Charlie S. and Maggie Clark, April 19th

Pritchett, Russel and Elittin Irvine, April 17th

Payne, Joseph A. and Ida E. Black, June 30th

Parker, Don E. and F. Eva Martin, July 12th

Poats, Louis J. and Mary S. Black, October 4th

Pitts, Marvin A. and Julia E. Holladay, October 12th

Phillips, Hubert F. and Hattie E. Woodson, November 9th

Pultz, Lloyd R. and Laura S. Ramsey, December 30th

1911

Parr, Lewis K. and Clara B. Tomlin, January 1st

Powell, John and Estelle Tooley, February 22nd

Perkins, Herbert W. and Mary Holloway, April 25th

Price, Edward Fiske and Mabel Moran, July 26th

Payne, Jr., Robert Lee and Mary E. Harmon, August 2nd

Pugh, Robert A. and Josie Mawyer, August 6th

Phillips, Ovanda W. and Lizzie V. Pritchett, August 24th

Payne, James L. and Sadie J. Walker, August 30th

Payne, John and Geo. Etta Nicholas, September 2nd

Powell, Pribble H. and Hazel M. Wood, September 6th

Parrott, Edward B. and Mary L. Brown, October 4th

1912

Pugh, Goldie S. and Katie E. Munday, March 27th

Pritchett, Mettie and Cassie Crenshaw, April 17th

Pack, Emmett H. E. and Mary F. Wells, April 26th

Pleasants, Robert and Annie F. Woody, September 28th

Patterson, William N. and Nora Martin, November 27th

1913

Peyton, William Herbert and Mary Elizabeth Garth, January 8th

Pritchett, Edward C. and Sarah Wayland, February 12th

Pritchett, Lionel W. and Annie Smith, February 12th

Pace, Theodore and Missie Lee Rhodes, April 9th

Phillips, Spiller V. and Eva L. Briggs, July 10th

Pumphrey, William H. and Mary S. Powell, December 8th

1914

Pugh, Roy and Eva Snow, February 27th
Pace, John P. and Carol D. Wood, January 28th
Price, Richard L. and Annie Kenzie, March 30th
Pugh, Nelson and Gertie Norvell, May 14th
Purvis, Jackson C. and Mary M. Martin, August 18th
Peregory, John D. and Florence Barger, September 12th
Patterson, Floyd and Cora Martin, September 21st
Parr, Gertie and Willie Woody, December 3rd
Perry, Robert and Cora Shiflett, December 22nd

1915

Pritchett, Obie and Esther Pritchett, March 20th
Pugh, Harris N. and Fannie Lou Henry, April 24th
Page, John W. and Gertrude Harris, May 4th
Parrish, George and Addie Morris, June 2nd
Payne, William T. and Mildred C. Watson, June 16th
Proffitt, Edward C. and Mary E. Clarke, June 30th
Putman, Albert and Ola E. Dudley, September 23rd
Payne, Henry S. and Lucy J. Tilman, October 24th
Powell, W. Alfred and Rosa Clements, December 5th
Portch, Wingfield and Minnie Clements, December 27th
Payne, Russell H. and Dorothy M. Creasy, December 26th

1916

Price, Tom and Grace Herring, January 3rd
Pote, Thomas J. and Lucy E. Dobbs, March 28th
Payne, Ollie C. and Luetta Knight, April 27th
Perkins, Joe P. and Mary Eva Allen, April 29th
Potz, John and Rosa Lee Warden, May 20th
Proffitt, Oscar L. and Rosa Lee Davis, June 21st
Peter, G. Freeland and Mrs. Lulie W. Nolting, July 17th
Parr, Norman and Emily E. Gardner, August 1st
Page, Frederick Byrd and Anne Radford, October 31st

1917

Phillips, Grover C. and Annie H. Phillips, June 20th
Payne, Bernard and Julia Harrison, July 31st
Peyton, Phillip B. and Ann D. Moon, October 20th

1918

Perry, John V. and Estelle Graves, January 30th

Pitts, Floyd L. and Martha G. Dillard, February 20th
Parr, Emmett B. and Eva M. Mawyer, February 20th
Parr, William L. and Sarah G. Hicks, December 28th

1919

Pugh, Phillip S. and Lucy E. Hicks, February 15th
Pipes, Hake Smith and Margaret B. Fralin, March 15th
Payne, Paul P. and Lou Baber, April 1st
Pirkey, Herbert and Mabel E. Wood, April 23rd
Powell, Benjamin C. and Flaxey Marshall, May 23rd
Pace, Samuel B. and Theresa Niedomier, July 3rd
Powell, Emmett R. and Ethel M. Norvell, August 23rd
Peyton, Robert and Margaret Branham, October 11th
Powell, Percy and Nora Norvell, October 16th
Parr, Vernon and Ruth L. Harris, October 18th
Poe, John J. and Edna Bryant, November 20th
Page, Cecil W. and Elizabeth A. R. Greaves, December 30th

1920

Pierce, Glenn A. and Ethel F. Ruthledge, March 8th
Payne, Thomas T. and Ruth Taylor, April 4th
Painter, John and Julia Kirby, May 3rd
Pace, Floyd P. and Katherine N. Huffman, October 20th
Patterson, Earl S. and Mary J. Woodson, November 2nd
Payne, James Frederick and Veora Clinton Colvin, November 3rd
Price, William Henry and Alberta Powell, December 17th
Pace, Harry H. and Linda G. Price, December 22nd
Payne, Richard F. and Sarah Herndon, December 30th

1921

Plumb, Walter W. and Lutie J. Wood, March 28th
Proffitt, James and Blanche Dabney, May 13th
Pitts, Lindsey and Hester McFarland, June 2nd
Powdin, Charles W. and Emma S. Hoove, September 6th
Pace, Roy C. and Grace M. Hunt, December 23rd

1922

Parry, James W. and Josephine Gibson, March 13th
Peyton, Henry S. C. and Sammie Lizzie Durrett, April 12th
Patterson, Roy and Cora L. Martin, May 5th

Payne, Samuel R. and Violet M. Bishop, July 7th

Payne, Tom Edward and Mary E. Payne, July 4th

Powell, Roosevelt and Nellie M. Morris, August 3rd

Patterson, Guy R. and Susan E. Via, August 8th

Pritchett, Jas. F. and Bessie Sprouse, October 4th

1923

Purvis, Oscar B. and Helen L. Martin, January 14th

Peters, Jr., William T. and Ruth E. Draper, February 12th

Payne, Wm. Thomas and Bertha May Farish, April 2nd

Patterson, Emmett W. and Carrie F. Woodson, May 16th

Pace, Aubrey W. and Edith L. Davis, June 20th

Price, Frank and Rose Taylor, September 11th

Platts, Harold and Hazel Harris, September 30th

Parley, Sherly B. and Helen V. Pitts, October 3rd

Payne, Richard M. and Margaret H. Fry, October 8th

Page, John W. and Annie B. Anderson, October 24th

Parr, Early L. and Susie M. Kent, November 30th

Pritchett, Virgil and Eva Pritchett, December 26th

1924

Patterson, Carmon H. and Elizabeth S. Jefferies, January 16th

Perkins, Daniel P. and Ruth M. Carter, March 27th

Price, Noah and Ruth H. Durrer, April 13th

Page, W. M. and Bertha Brockenbough, June 5th

Powell, Bud G. and Lena V. Powell, July 10th

Purvis, Clarence O. and Flossie M. Kirby, September 16th

Payne, Rogers B. and Sarah Lou Scruggs, October 15th

Powell, Edward M. and Nealie Herring, December 24th

1925

Pritchett, Ellis and Wilmer Birckhead, January 5th

Pfantz, John M. and Margaret P. Hogue. April 18th

Powell, Roy and Esther L. Graves, May 2nd

Prentice Max G. D. and Winnifred T. DeVoe, May 23rd

Pace, Harry H. and Ollie B. Sevain, June 10th

Proffitt, Thomas and Ethel Wood, July 6th

Phillips, John H. and Mallie V. Ramsey, July 20th

Powell, Walter C. and Daisy V. Bing, August 10th

Pugh, Nelson H. and Mary V. Burton, August 20th

Parrish, Robert R. and Elinore L. Page, November 21st

Price, James M. and Margaret C. Rea, November 25th

Pratt, Thomas R. and Lula E. J. Bailey. December 23rd

Pugh, Ellis and Lilly Critzer, December 27th

1926

Pyles, George N. and Florence Burton, February 19th

Pritchett, Thomas and Alice Fox, May 8th

Patterson Joseph I. and Caroline A. White, June 30th

Poindexter, Joseph B. and Helen E. Maupin, June 26th

Pritchett, Frank E. C. and Ruth C. Wilburn, September 15th

Pugh, Wm. H. and Ella F. Critzer, October 7th

Pace, Robert and Isabelle Ricks, November 22nd

1927

Patterson, Marion P. and Martha Showers, January 20th

Phillips, George C. and Mary C. Robertson, January 20th

Parham, Louis D. and Mairran Reeves, April 16th

Pugh, Joseph L. and Nellie J. Pugh, August 20th

Proff, Theadore G. and Lillian B. Toombs, August 22nd

Powell, Harry D. and Emmie Eubank, August 26th

Pate, Jamison L. and Nancy O. Sanders, September 30th

1928

Parrott, George H. and Georgia R. Johnson, January 3rd

Powell, William M. and Molly Carroll, September 17th

Pritchett, Richard D. and Lou W. Flynt, October 6th

Phillips, Henry and Lillie A. Batten, October 9th

Parr, Robert F. and Ola L. Coleman, December 1st

Pitman, Airs J. and Julia Ann Dale, December 19th

Pritchett, Aubrey B. and Rilla A. Hitt, December 24th

1929

Pugh, Aubrey C. and Katie M. Butler, February 5th

Powell, Robert J. and Nina S. Sandridge, May 8th

Powell, Grover L. and Ella K. Brown, July 25th

Phillips, David L. and Elizabeth Chamberlan, August 17th

Pleasants, Thomas R. and Mary Lee Sprouse, November 11th

Q

1787
Quinn, Thomas and Catharine Ford, April 12th

1818
Querry, Thomas M. and Frances Stout, December 12th

1820
Quick, Charles and Patsy Foster, July 14th

1822
Quarles, Albert G. and M. A. Minor, January 29th

1824
Quick, Joshua and Mildred Foster, January 5th

1827
Quick, James and Judah Carter, January 18th

1856
Quarles, Robt. E. and Virg. E. Dodd, September 29th

1857
Quarles, Robert E. and Virginia E. Dodd, September 28th

1860
Quick, James R. and Sally Thacker, December 18th
Quick, James R. and Sally E. Thacker, December 19th

1873
Quarles, J. R. and E. W. Wheeler, February 24th

1886
Quinn, Jno. A. and Martha A. Nimmo, May 2nd

1889
Quick, Wm. and Annie Farish, November 19th

1903
Quick, C. D. and D. R. Reynolds, April 20th

1906
Quick, John T. and Lucy E. Parnelle, December 20th

1908
Quarles, William E. and Ann Morgan, January 20th

1909
Quick, Arthur and Jennie F. Brown, October 6th

1912
Quick, William T. and Annie Mawyer, December 8th

1913
Quick, Jr., William H. and Martha Sacre, March 6th

1915
Quinn, James M. and Mary Ann Seiler, October 12th

1929
Quinn, Robert H. and Ora J. Waddell, May 31st
Quick, Clarence G. and Cora Lee Gray, October 25th

R

1785
Ramsey, William and Margaret Wallace, December 13th
Richardson, Richard and Mildred Butler, December 24th
Roberson, James and Amelia Clark, ?
Roberts, Morning and Elizabeth Harding, December 21st
Rush, John and Margaret Maupin, May 2nd

1786
Randolph, Isham and Mildred Lancas, October 12th
Richie, Daniel and Nancy Herrondon, November 9th
Roach, Samuel and Molly Medor, January 3rd
Robinson, James and Ann Embrey, April 8th
Rodes, David and Polly Yancy, December 14th
Rodes, John and Jane Stapleton Birch, May 23rd

1787
Ronalds, James and Nancy Berry, September 14th

1788
Ray, Robert and Elizabeth Maupin, January 10th
Roberts, Richard and Elizabeth Gillum, January 10th
Ryan, Patrick and Nancy Thomason, May 13th

1789
Ray, Thomas and Annis Ballard, August 13th
Robinson, Benjamin and Elizabeth Deckerson, December 21st
Rogers, John and Susanna Goodman, August 29th

1790
Richards, Benjamin and Lucy Michie, March 10th

1791

Rasor, Jacob and Elizabeth Sharp, October 8th
Reeds, Elijah and Sally Holt, April 10th
Reily, Peter and Ann Grady, September 19th
Richardson, Samuel and Mary Cross, May 24th
Roye, Leonard and Anna Parenett, October 13th

1792

Roper, William and Polly Moorman, April 27th

1793

Rodes, John and Fracina Brown, March 5th

1794

Rodes, Matthew and Ann Blackwell, May 28th

1795

Reynolds, Charles and Sarah Finley, April 4th
Rothwell, Thomas and Molly Fitch, December 4th

1797

Robertson, Charles and Nancy Ford, December 13th

1798

Robert, Peter and Rebecca Goodman, February 22nd
Robert, William and Salley Beaver, July 14th
Robinson, James and Salley Leake, May 2nd
Rogers, John and Milly Uyer, March 5th
Rogers, John and Elizabeth Night, December 8th
Roswell, John and Nally Ballew, August 9th
Rowe, Edward D. and Sally Trevillian, December 3rd

1799

Ready, Isham and Mary Garland, June 3rd
Rittenhouse, Samuel and Catherine Thurmond, October 29th
Robinson, Archilaus and Polly Carver, December 20th
Robinson, James and Polly Taylor, December 16th
Rothwell, John and Susannah Thurmond, January 7th

1802

Roderick, Frederick and Elizabeth Phillips, February 13th
Rodgers, Daniel and Catherine Austin, October 8th
Rippeto, James and Sarah Norfolk, January 1st

1803

Robertson, James and Kezia Garton, January 20th

1805

Robertson, John and Sarah Baber, November 7th

1806

Read, ? and Isabella Price, February 20th
Reynolds, ? and Jane Richs, January 1st
Rittenhouse, Samuel and Judy Thomas, June 15th

1807

Ramsey, John and Mary Black, November 17th
Reynolds, Fontaine and Nancy Foster, September 17th
Rop, Alex and Elizabeth Cooper, February 24th

1808

Read, Robert and Sally Thacker, September 10th
Reynolds, John and Gudieth Lively, February 19th
Reynolds, Walter and Nancy Burrus, November 7th
Richardson, David and Fanny Durrett, October 11th
Rogers, Benjamin and Mary Lewis, September 10th

1809

Rogers, Paul and Elizabeth Furgerson, December 19th

1810

Roberson, John and Elizabeth Lobbin, April 9th
Rossen, James and Eliza Wingfield, November 5th

1811

Robins, Wilson and Sally Morris, February 25th
Rowe, Jepe and Martha Sharp, September 11th

1812

Robertson, George and Ann Dyer, October 19th

1813

Rice, Charles E. and Julia Carr, June 18th
Rice, Holeman and Susan Hamner, May 21st
Rice, Jacob and Elizabeth Moore, December 1st
Rhodes, Thomas and Mary Brockman, April 5th
Robinson, John and Lucy Hamner, March 1st
Rothwell, William and Nancy B. Gillum, February 21st
Roller, Samuel and Mary Ann Colvin, December 8th

1814

Roach, James and Ann W. Doggett, February 5th
Robinson, Richard and Sally Gay, May 23rd

1815

Ragland, John C. and Sarah Eliza Kelly, September 7th
Randolph, Thomas J. and Jane Nicholas, March 6th

Rhoades, John and Mary Martin, November 2nd

Roathwell, Richard and Lucy Barksdale, January 17th

Robertson, John and Sally Brownel, July 31st

Rogers, Thornton and Peggy Hart, October 13th

Ross, Alexander and Elizabeth Armistead, December 4th

Ross, James and Easter Wallace, January 6th

1816

Reynolds, Tandy and Elizabeth Foster, April 1st

Robertson, Robert and Elizabeth Garton, March 23rd

Rutherford, John and Emily A. Coles, April 23rd

1817

Raner, James and Mildred Gillaspy, October 1st

Ray, Bland and Sarah Alexander, June 21st

Reynolds, Tinsley and Nancy Bustor, December 1st

Roberts, Jeremiah and Mary Ann Harris, April 7th

1818

Reynor, George and Lucy Herron, June 29th

Ricks, Gilbert and Nancy Mullins, November 18th

1819

Randol, George and Betsey Thacker, November 3rd

Reister, John and Lucinda Robinson, January 10th

Rives, William C. and Judith Walker, March 13th

Rogers, James B. and Margaret S. Wood, May 31st

1820

Rippeto, William and Judith H. Phillips, August 10th

Rogers, Thompson and Miney Browning, August 10th

1821

Rea, Daniel and Sarah Thomas, June 21st

Robinson, Tandy and Elizabeth Burrus, December 25th

1822

Ribemon, Cosby M. and S. Browning, May 26th

Roberson, Daniel and Frances McDaniel, November 19th

1823

Richards, Fountaine and Sophia Mills, April 10th

Rippeto, William and Rachel Stone, December 21st

Roberts, John H. and Margaret D. Hopkins, September 22nd

Robertson, John and Mira Field, November 6th

Roper, Daniel and Frances O'Neal, September 3rd

Rowen, ? and Sally Huckstep, December 11th

1824

Riner, Jacob and Matilda Estes, October 22nd

Roathwell, Anderson and Elizabeth Browning, February 20th

Rodes, Robert P. and Mildred Marshall, February 20th

1825

Railey, John M. and Mary R. Watson, March 29th

Railey, Silbourn R. and Lucy Jane Burks, January 27th

Rogers, John and Polly Harris, December 27th

Ryan, William W. and Sarah Hundley, January 20th

1826

Rea, Samuel and Matilda Farris, April 26th

Rives, George and Mary E. Carter, June 16th

Rodes, Jefferson and Sally Lively, January 25th

1827

Rhine, John and Eady Davis, April 16th

Rite, William and Martha Ann Dunkum, February 1st

1828

Reinhard, Elhaman and Catherine H. Minor, April 16th

Roberts, Jeremian and Lucy M. Fagg, October 21st

Robertson, Colby C. and Sarah A. Goodman, December 20th

Rodes, Skylor W. and L. Jane Walker, January 15th

Royal, Samuel H. and Martha Terrell, December 22nd

Rives, Alexander and Isabella B. Wydown, April 6th

Robinson, William and Amanda Blain, March 4th

1830

Roberts, John H. and Mary White, December 27th

Robertson, Peter and Frances McDaniel, November 16th

1831

Robinson, John C. and Lucinda Williams, April 27th

Rothwell, Joseph and Sarah Gillum, December 13th

1832

Reynolds, William and Polly Digges, November 22nd

Rodes, Thomas and Lavina Marshall, November 15th

1833

Roberts, Frederick and Caroline M. Huckstep, November 28th

Roberts, Robert and Mary Ann Baker, October 15th

1834

Randolph, Benjamin F. and Sarah Carter, November 10th

Ross, John and Frances A. E. Walton, March 10th

Rea, Bland and Elizabeth W. Jones, January 12th

Read, Robert and Frances A. Pendleton, November 3rd

1835

Ridd, Charles and Malinda Kidd, December 21st

Ring, Sabrit and Mary Mills, February 2nd

1836

Roberson, Buckner T. and Nancy Murray, January 4th

Ross, James W. and Ann P. Clarkson, December 19th

Ruffin, James F. and Eliza Wood, August 25th

1837

Rodes, John D. and Mrs. Ann D. Morris, January 9th

1838

Rennolds, Edward and Mary Roberts, February 1st

Rhodes, Horace G. and Jane Spicer, December 20th

Rhodes, Richard and Martha Pace, June 21st

1839

Randolph, William M. and Margaret S. Randolph, September 2nd

Rittenhouse, Henry G. and Ann M. Boyd, January 17th

Rittenhouse, John and Sally Emmerson, October 5th

Roberts, William R. and Mary E. Brown, September 21st

Robinson, Jeremiah J. and Mary E. Dawson, July 15th

Rodes, Robert and Elizabeth A. Rogers, November 7th

Rothwell, James C. and Mary S. Ramsey, February 5th

Rothwell, George W. and Ann S. Brown, January 1st

1840

Reynolds, William C. and Sarah Jones, November 23rd

Rice, Claiborne and Malinda F. Spencer, March 2nd

Rives, George and Maria R. F. Tucker, April 2nd

Roach, William and Sarah F. Watson, June 18th

Roberson, Benjamin W. and Lurietta J. Davis, March 26th

Ross, John B. and E. E. Young, September 12th

Ruffin, Frank G. and C. A. Randolph, December 23rd

1841

Rhodes, William B. and M. J. Mundy, January 5th

Rolls, John W. and Sarah Grimstead, January 24th

1842

Reynolds, Andrew J. and Julia Ann Woodson, March 5th

Ricks, Joseph and Lucinda Amiss, January 3rd

Riley, Littleberry and Frances E. Sadler, December 13th

Roberts, Henry H. and Nancy B. Harris, November 9th

Roberts, Weiddy W. and Francees A. Wingfield, July 18th

Robertson, William J. and Judith C. Farrar, April 4th

Robertson, William J. and Hannah E. Gordon, August 16th

Rothwell, Fielding E. and Sarah F. Tilman, December 6th

1843

Reid, Mark and Ann Hoy Dade, November 21st

Rucker, Larkin G. and Siverna A. Davis, November 21st

1845

Ray, Zachariah R. and M. A. Jackson, March 15th

Roberts, Joseph H. and J. A. Perkins, June 10th

1846

Reynolds, James R. and Judy A Hicks, March 9th

Rodes, James M. and Harriet S. Morris, August 4th

Rogers, Thompson and Lucy Wayland, April 15th

1847

Randolph, John T. and Ann M. Farrish, October 25th

Rayburn, John C. and Margaret J. Duncan, February 23rd

Robertson, Archilaus and Ann Woodson, December 6th

Robinson Jese W. and Ora S. Barksdale, December 22nd

Rodes, John Q. A. and M. E. Chisholm, March 6th

Rothwell, William J. and S. Yarborough, January 21st

1848

Richardson, C. G. and S. A. Thacker, August 25th

Robertson, James M. and F. J. Hunt, May 23rd

Robertson, Jeremiah and N. J. McLane, January 1st

Robertson, William J. and E. T. Farrar, February 23rd

Rodes, Thomas and A. E. Wood, September 5th

1849

Ramsey, William A. and S. F. Abelle, July 20th

Rice, Andrew J. and M. A. Drumheller, November 26th

Rogers, William G. and Marion Wood, September 17th

Rothwell, Thomas B. and Margaret F. Oaks, September 17th

1850

Rea, Absolum and Elizabeth Fisher, April 21st

Rice, William H. and Frances Wood, February 6th

Roberts, David W. and Mary Jane Rodes, June 26th

Robinson, Richard W. and Elizabeth F. Black, ?

Robinson, William H. and Martha E. G. Wingfield, May 1st

Rodes, James J. and Elizabeth A. Bishop, November 17th

Ross, Joseph and Martha Bowen, October 12th

1851

Richmond, Nick and Ammonett Sammonds, September 24th

Robertson, Thomas D. and M. H. Spradling, September 11th

Rogers, A. W. and Lavinnia M. Wallace, February 4th

1852

Ramsey, Joseph T. and S. E. Rothwell, December 15th

Rhodes, Schuyler T. and V. C. Wood, December 16th

Rittenour, Isaac and P. E. Brown, March 13th

Roberts, Pleasant and M. Roberts, April 16th

Robertson, John N. and N. L. Pleasants, June 8th

Rogers, B. F. and Mary A. Dollins, September 12th

1853

Rakes, William J. and Sarah A. Loyd, April 5th

Randolph, Thomas J. Jr. and Mary W. Merewether, July 18th

Rice, Andrew S. and Lucy Ann Acress, February 25th

Ricks, John A. and Paulina A. Humphrey, December 7th

Roberts, John P. and Julia Wingfield, November 10th

Rogers, Jonathan B. and Elizabeth Schultz, March 15th

1854

Rankin, James W. and Jestin E. Kenten, December 21st

Reynolds, James M. and Mary E. Morris, March 16th

Robertson, James S. and Sarah J. Pleasants, November 9th

Robertson, J. S. and Sarah J. Pleasants, November 9th

Rodes, John Q. A. and Mary J. Gillispie, January 5th

Rodes, John Q. A. and M. J. Gillespie, January 5th

Rogers, T. Oscar and Ammiville N. May, January 21st

1855

Rankin, Jas. W. and J. E. Keyton, December 27th

Reynolds, Jas. M. and Mary E. Morris, March 16th

Rhodes, Esaph and Julia A. Edwards, August 30th

Rhodes, Epaph and Julia A. Edwards, August 30th

Rhodes, Walker and Mary S. M. Lively, June 5th

Rogers, J. O. and S. N. May, January 4th

Robinson, John and Mary L. Peck, August 24th

Robertson, Spencer L. and Mary E. Martin, December 12th

Rothwell, John W. and Lucinda C. White, February 20th

Rothwell, Jo. W. and L. C. White, February 20th

Rothwell, William and Mary A. White, August 10th

Rothwell, Wm. I and Mary A. White, August 10th

1856

Rea, Andrew J. and Lavinia Claterbuck, November 18th

Rea, Andrew J. and Lavinice Claterbuck, November 18th

Riardon, Dennis and Martha Harlow, May 7th

Rice, William G. and Sarah F. Lyon, November 6th

Rice, Wm. G. and Sarah F. Lyon, November 6th

Roach, Thomas S. and Josephine Brady, December 28th

Robertson, Jacob W. and Sarah A. Mason, September 3rd

Rodes, Robert and Hardenia Williams, December 30th

Roson, Yancey P. and Martha E. Batten, February 26th

Roberts, Wm. D. and R. A. Shiflett, October 22nd

Robinson, A. S. annd H. H. Antrim, November 1st

Rosson, Joel F. and Malinda H. Batton, January 25th

Richards, Jno. T. and Mary E. Bramham, December 22nd

Robinson, Frank W. and Mary M. Perry, April 15th

1857

Reynolds, James R. and Susan Graves, May 26th

Roberts, William D. and Rhoda A. Shiflett, October 22nd

Robertson, John W. and Abigail H. Cocke, December 7th

Robinson, Arthur S. and Henrietta H. Antrims, October 31st

Rogers, William A. and Catherine Michie, November 2nd

1858

Randolph, W. C. N. and Ann E. Holladay, November 10th

Roberson, Frank W. and Mary M. Perry, April 15th

Ryner, John D. and Darah E. Marshall, December 6th

1859

Reynolds, J. M. and Harriet Kennedy, September 3rd

Richards, John T. and Mary E. Branham, December 21st

Risson, Joel F. and Malinda F. Batton, January 20th

Rittenhouse, David C. and Sallie E. Brown, April 23rd

Rittenhouse, David C. and Sallie E. Brown, April 28th

Rittenhouse, Hamilton and Sarah Jane Elsvin, October 31st

Rittenhouse, H. and Sallie J. Elson, November 3rd

1860

Robinson, James J. and Elizabeth E. Wilson, December 29th

Rodes, J. W. and C. A. Jarman, December 3rd

Rogers, James B. and F. A. Michie, August 30th

1861

Randolph, D. N. and Fannie A. Michie, October 31st

Randolph, R. W. and Fannie A. Michie, October 31st

Rea, John A. and Mary J. Grimstead, February 23rd

Rea, Jno. A. and Mary Jane Grinstead, March 1st

Remmely, Christian and Susan Balltins, December 12th

Reynolds, Nenjamin F. and Jane A. Wetcher, January 7th

Reynolds, Ben F. and Jane C. Wilcker, January 25th

Rhodes, William and Mary E. Brown, August 2nd

Rhodes, Wm. and Mary E. Brown, August 4th

Robertson, John T. and Julia N. Day, November 9th

Robertson, Jno. T. and Julia N. Day, November 10th

Robinson, J. I. and Eliz. E. Wilson, May 1st

Reinnaly, Christan and Susan Balthis, December 12th

1862

Randolph, Jno. and Millicest Payne, October 2nd

Reilison Oscar L. and Mary E. Flannagan, July 14th

Ross, Wm. H. and Pocakuntas Herndon, April 29th

Rodes, James E. and Judith A. Wallace, February 25th

Rogers, James R. and Margaret B. Rogers, Oct. 14

1863

Robinson, Wm. A. and Susan M. Perry, July 16th

Robert, Wm. A. and Eliz. A. Fretwell, December 9th

Railey, Wm. B. and Cornelia J. Maupin, July 6th

Rea, Overton C. and Va. A. Mallory, October 16th

Railey, James P. and Cornelia R. Burnley, December 6th

1864

Rodes, Andrew J. and Sarah Eliz. Lively, Sept. 27

Ryals, G. M. and Libbie Kennedy, February 24th

1865

Randolph, Thomas J. and C. N. Merewether, February 7th

Randolph, Tho. J., Jr., and C. N. Merewether, February 9th

Ray, Cancey B. and Bettie L. Johnson, December 15th

Ray, Chancy B. and Bettie L. Johnson, Dec. 17

Rensker, M. B. L. and V. V. Herring, March 2nd

Rodes, Hez'h. and Sarah C. Morris, Sept. 27

Roicker, N. B. F. and Victoria V. Herring, February 27th

1867

Rogers, Jno. H. and Mary D. Carr, January 7th

Roberts, Stephen and Sarah C. Layne, September 9th

Robinson, Jno. A. and Catherine V. Vaughn, October 29th

Robertson, Rexs O. and Mary H. Wallace, January 26th

Randolph, Jack annd Maria Mayo, March 14th

Robertson, Wm. J. and Ellen E. Moon, July 8th

Rhodes, Daniel H. and Catharine M. Poindexter, December 24th

1868

Rhodes, Thomas D. and Sarah Beck, January 28th

Rhodes, Thos. D. and Sarah Beck, January 30th

Robertson, Edw. and Eliza Wood, April 11th

Rawlings, Jas. M. and Helen C. Watson, July 6th

Reid, Edward and Manah Stewart, January 3rd

Rea, John R. and Ella J. Scantling, February 25th

Rawling, Jas. M. and Helen C. Watson, July 7th

Richardson, J. G. and Julia T. Whitehurst, November 4th

Rea, J. W. and Georgia A. Woods, February 3rd

Reed, Thos. W. and Sallie B. Hallbach, December 1st

1869

Rhodes, Geo. W. and Emma Hicks, February 7th

Richardson, Thos. and Phuney, A. Kinny, July 4th

Robinson, James H. and Olive Stephen, November 9th

Ramsay, Wm. S. and Lucy Goodloe, November 22nd

Roy Perkins, and Kitty Whipps, December 29th

1870

Ross, Jessie and Lucy Wingerton, January 1st

Randolph, James and Emily Tilman, July 12th

1871

Richards, Geo. W. and Lucy E. Carr, February 7th

Rhodes, Jos. Daniel and Joanna Chisholm, December 28th

1872

Reynolds, Wm. C. and Lucy J. Robinson, February 29th

Russow, Adolphus and Ida Lieback, November 18th

Rothwell, Wm. F. and Mary E. Woodson, December 9th

Riley, Frederick and Frances Clough, December 26th

1873

Rice, Wm. H. and Lucy A. Garrison, October 17th

Rogers, Benj. M. and Mollie J. Burgess, October 27th

1874

Ralls, Chas. E. and Susan C. Grove, July 14th

1875

Reynolds, Jos. J. and Bettie Thomas, May 7th

Rose, Ned and Susan Kinney, November 4th

1876

Rhodes, Jno. B. and Anzonetta T. Via, February 21st

Rogers, Jas. T. and Bettie A. Bruffy, February 18th

Rhodes, Hezekia and Catharine Wilkerson, April 8th

Reynolds, Jas. S. and Mary E. Tomlin, April 10th

Royster, Frank and Georgianna Via, May 26th

Rust, David N. and Mary N. Locke, October 9th

Riddle, Harrison and Susan Rice, November 14th

1877

Robinson, Geo. W. and Harriet M. Ruchcill, February 12th

Robinson, Jas. T. and Mollie P. Sutherland, March 5th

Rea, Chas. C. and Emma E. Robinson, April 2nd

1878

Riley, Wm. D. and Mary V. Phillips, January 26th

Reynolds, Jas. M. D. and Martha E. W. Tooley, March 4th

Rogers, Wm. N. and Bettie E. Pace, May 25th

Robertson, Elisha W. and A. B. Rothwell, September 2nd

Rayner, Richard and Harriet Herring, November 9th

Reynolds, Major H. and Mandana L. Wright, December 23rd

Rea, Wellington L. and Mary Cranwell, February 28th

1879

Robinson, Lafayette and Peachy E. Spencer, February 12th

Rodes, Dorse L. and Betty Lenohan, April 19th

Raymond, David E. and Mary S. Davidson, September 20th

Ricks, Thomas G. and Mollie J. Pace, Oct. 15

Robinson, Aleck G. and Willie A. Chiles, October 14th

Rea, James H. and Betty R. Black, December 1st

Rodes, Chas. L. F. and Emma Sneed, December 24th

1880

Riston, F. P. and Susan F. Gay, August 25th

Ranson, James M. Jr., and Mary C. Brown, November 17th

Rothwell, Paul E. and Josephine Wood, December 6th

Rice, Jacob Blaine and Sally Ann Pugh, December 23rd

1881

Robinson, Jas. H. and Julie M. Kirby, January 4th

Rossen, William and Ellen Via, November 13th

Riley, Emmit L. and Lizzie M. Fitch, November 17th

1882

Robinson, Richard A. and Nannie H. Deskins, September 5th

Robertson, Alexander and Eliz. Terrill, Apr. 4

Riley, Frederick and Esgotise Hicks, November 19th

1883

Randolph, Frank M. and Charlotte N. Macon, January 17th

Rodes, William S. and Nattie M. McCue, January 17th

Rossow, Geo. Franklin and Ada M. J. Batton, February 8th

Randolph, Robert Mann and Margurette C. Harris, June 21st

Rice, Jno. Henry and Maggie Lee Massey, September 20th

Robinson, Geo. Wash. and Victoria Bragg, September 26th

Rea, Wm. T. and Viate Warren, November 8th

1884

Rogers, Thos. Lewis and Virginia M. Burton, December 18th

Robertson, Jones N. and Sarah E. Moon, February 2nd

Rothwell, Wm. H. and Jennie N. Weed, May 14th

Robinson, R. J. and Lucy I. Bishop, September 4th

Runkle, Wm. H. and Irene I. Barksdale, September 1st

1885

Rea, Arthur J. and Lizzie Warren, September 27th

Rudisile, Wm. D. Jr. and Irene Lewis Jones, November 5th

1886

Reed, Allan and Marion H. Dickson, November 18th

Raynor, Thos. and Mary Munday, December 7th

1887

Rossiter, Jno. E. and Lucy Ann Wolford, December 31st

1888

Rinsland, L. and L. Hertman, June 19th

Roberts, Jno. P. and Edmonia P. Wingfield, September 28th

1889

Robinson, Albert and Charlotte Jefferson, February 2nd

Rife, J. M. and R. L. Bacon, November 16th

Reynolds, J. H. and M. J. Mooney, December 17th

1890

Robertson, A. L. and H. N. Clements, January 13th

Rodes, Jno. and Mollie Sprake, February 10th

Romtree, S. S. and M. C. Lewis, February 11th

Rhoades, Sam. and Mary Wells, February 25th

Reynolds, R. L. and Nannie Moony, May 24th

Rhodes, A. M. H. and Henrietta Kirby, July 2nd

Robertson, H. and M. L. Vawler, September 22nd

Rosser, T. L. and H. H. Gordan, October 13th

Rodes, Thos. L. and Junetta Creasey, December 2nd

1891

Rothwell, J. S. and L. K. Smith, February 9th

1892

Radford, C. E. and B. E. Herron, January 18th

Roger, Alfred and A. C. Clark, November 30th

Roark, J. A. and L. T. Munday, December 6th

1893

Rogers, H. P. and Annie E. Rea, February 13th

Rhinhart, C. W. and D. G. Fife, May 2nd

Raine, E. A. and C. L. Brown, June 2nd

Roudabush, W. O. and D. S. Cutshall, August 9th

Rowe, Wm. W. and Mattie S. Wayland, October 2nd

Rothwell, W. F. and W. M. Campbell, December 29th

1894

Ray, Dollie E. and Mollie E. Garrison, April 3rd

Rea, Robt. J. and Leonora Belton, December 3rd

Randolph, Dr. Wm. M. and Mary Walker Randolph, October 19th

Reynolds, W. C. and R. B. Holly, November 5th

1895

Rowles, R. S. and B. F. Crenshaw, October 16th

Railey, L. B. and Edna E. Lewis, October 29th

Roark, J. A. and Gabie Wheeler, November 26th

Ran, Wm. S. and Laura A. Bruce, November 27th

Robertson, Jno. W. and Lula W. Snow, December 24th

1896

Rea, Robt. and M. E. Thurston, Dec. 21st

1897

Roy, W. L. and L. E. Thacker, February 10th

Runkle, A. M. E. and C. L. Gibson, February 24th

Roberts, R. R. and M. C. Spotts, July 31st

Ryan, Wm. and Addie Cox, December 13th

1898

Ryals, Thos. H. and M. L. Marshall, February 2nd

Rhodes, E. L. and B. W. Thurston, April 21st

Rennels, J. H. and Lucy F. Shaver, October 14th

Rea, Dennis and Lena Gibson, December 29th

1899

Riley, Henry and Mollie C. Brown, January 2nd

Rogers, B. N. and Clara L. Wheeler, January 12th

Ramsay, W. D. and Daisy Wingfield, April 19th

Rhodes, H. P. and M. A. Jones, April 25th

Roberts, J. D. and Martha R. Farish, April 29th

Raymon, Jas. and L. A. B. Warren, July 6th

Rea, R. L. and V. L. Bailey, July 17th

Robinson, Alex and Emma Miller, October 5th

Randolph, H. N. and Caroline T. Walter, October 16th

1900

Reynolds, M. and A. B. Spradling, September 11th

Riorden, Frank L. and Julia A. Edward, October 24th

Reynolds, C. T. and Rosa L. Sprouse, November 29th

Rogers, W. H. and V. A. Jones, Jan. 23

Ricks, Robt. L. and Eliz. Loudere, Mch. 21

Rhodes, Chas. and Cornelia Irving, Apr. 18

1901

Rogers, J. W. and M. G. Mitchell, December 26th

Randolph, J. C. and Stella Mills, December 30th

1902

Robertson, John W. and Maude Pace, July 4th

Rhodes, Henry Lee and Grace D. Walters, July 10th

Revercomb, H. A. and Sallie Stephenson, August 6th

Rogers, E. R. and Mary Lile, October 15th

1903

Ray, A. C. and C. L. White, June 9th

Reed, Jas. A. and M. E. Martin, August 11th

Robinson, F. L. and Mabel Farish, October 13th

Ryals, John Hurley and Mather Susie Fansler, Dec. 24th

1904

Ragland, John W. and Maray Lee Ragland, Jan. 28

Ruggles, Liberty and Mollie H. Coleman, July 20

Robertson, P. T. and Lola M. Edwards, July 21

1905

Reed, Noah A. and Anna L. Wood, Feb. 15

Rea, Henry D. and Lelian Harlow, Aug. 2

Ray, John E. and Lizzie N. McCluer, Nov. 27

Rea, Virgil Rice and Essie Lena Hawkins, Dec. 26

1906

Robinson, J. T. and N. E. Pannell, May 8th

Rhodes, Aubrey Wash. and Lillian Chisholm, Oct. 4th

Rhea, Shaw A. and Fannie L. Baber, Nov. 25th

Rieves, Louis and Lottie Adams, Nov. 26th

1907

Rice, C. E. and Irene Hawley, June 17th

Rush, Henry U. and R. Elizabeth Weast, July 3rd

1908

Robinson, Richard W. and Edna Earle Maddox, March 25th

Rutledge, Robert and Eva Brown, March 29th

Rhodes, Eugene C. and Eva Smith, June 13th

Rogers, Jerry D. and Cynthia E. Wheeler, July 26th

Robinson, William C. and Katie V. Mitchell, Aug. 31st

Rothwell, James F. and Lena Colley, Nov. 19th

Rea, Harry B. and Julia D. Grasty, Nov. 24th

1909

Robinson, Emmett S. and Fannie L. Henry, June 12th

Rushton, Arthur T. and Annie L. Johnson, June 22nd

Roberts, John and Nora Shiflett, Sept. 9th

Reid, William H. and Mary T. Johnston, Oct. 28th

1910

Rea, Alfred E. and Bessie M. Thurston, Jan. 5th

Roberts, James A. and Eddie F. McAlister, Feb. 7th

Ragland, Grover C. and Gladys E. Newcomb, April 7th

Richard, Arthur W. and Daisy R. Wayland, June 27th

Rhodes, John N. and Susan N. Bass, July 20th

Railey, Mirritt M. and Ophelia C. Johnson, Sept. 14th

Ruffin, John F. W. and Sarah McE. Osborne, Oct. 17th

Ray, Charles E. and Addie Maupin, Oct. 24th

Ray, Ernest and Lena Maupin, Oct. 24th

Rhodes, Eugene H. and Josephine Harlow, Dec. 14th

Rhodes, Emmett and Leafy Stone, Dec. 24th

1911

Ragland, Paul and Katie Hackett, March 15th

Ragland, Wm. Balkman and Lillie Kate Linderee, Sept. 2nd

Robinson, John D. and M. G. Houchens, Oct. 18th

1912

Reid, George T. and Sarah Wood, June 8th

Rosser, Robert and Roberta W. Hunt, Nov. 12th

Robertson, George M. and Dora L. Martin, Dec. 18th

1913

Ray, M. R. and Minnie E. Boune, Jan. 30th

Ricks, Ernest and Masie May Rhodes, March 31st

Ralston, Eugene and Edna Thomas, May 5th

Rice, T. H. and Elizabeth M. Sherrod, May 28th

Ryan, John L. and Mary M. Mallory, June 25th

Reynolds, Bennie S. and Edna L. Tomlin, Sept. 17th

Romer, William A. and Lena Bragg, Oct. 14th

1914

Raynor, Arthur H. and Eleanor Harlow, Feb. 13th

Roston, John and Lessie B. Batten, March 24th

Reburn, John J. and Jennie E. Woodson, April 29th

Reynolds, Hall and Ethel Bishop, July 10th

Rhodes, Lloyd H. and Lutie M. Chisholm, July 20th

Redford, Edward L. and Sarah A. Lily, Sept. 1st

Robertson, James R. and Julia E. V. Burton, Sept. 6th

Russell, Sperry T. and Ada E. Barnett, Nov. 1st

Reed, Augusta S. and Florence Harlow, Nov. 25th

Ray, Everett and Virgie Gibson, Dec. 27th

1915

Robinson, J. Lesley and Fannie M. Mawyer, May 1st

Rae, Thurman and Mary Shaver, May 26th

Rae, Sidney R. and Susie M. Morris, May 31st

Ramsey, James A. and Viola P. Gay, June 8th

Richey, Homer and Eva Clarke, June 26th

Russell, Charles G. and Kathleen E. Earles, Sept. 8th

Rock, John F. and Agnes Lee Beck, Dec. 16th

Rutlege, George W. and Laura Jane Rice, Dec. 23rd

Raynor, Floyd and Kate Gardner, Dec. 27th

1916

Ryalls, Uylesses G. and Christine Ballard, Jan. 5th

Randolph, S. Welford and Deborah White, May 17th

Rogers, Willie O. and Levena Hubbard, July 21st

1917

Reynolds, Cecil C. and Flora Thacker, Mar. 17th

Rinchurtz, Herbert and Josephine C. Payne, June 3rd

Ray, Roy and Martha J. A. Sprouse, Aug. 15th

Remsbury, Norman B. and Warnitie Edwards, Nov. 29th

1918

Ray, Shaw C. and Virginia Sandridge, Jan. 18th

Rae, Thomas Edward and Annie Jones, May 20th

Railey, Linwood W. and Eleanor P. Birckhead, Aug. 25th

Riley, Sidney F. and Willie A. Kirby, Oct. 16th

Robertson, Sam and Fanny Lawson, Nov. 20th

Ross, Melvin and Lena McMillin, Dec. 21st

1919

Raines, Leonard and Nettie F. Shiflett, Jan. 7th

Rafferty, Jr., Gilbert Thos. and Charlotte Nelson Randolph, Jan. 25th

Roberts, Marcus Hunter and Ethel G. Clarke, July 10th

Rae, Frank H. and Mary F. Ross, Sept. 7th

Roberts, Ira C. and Elsie B. Collier, Dec. 11th

Ricks, Albert S. and Lillie M. Bishop, Dec. 24th

1920

Ryan, John D. and Carrie Lee Carver, Mar. 8th

Roche, Adolph and Annie E. Berry, Mar. 31st

Ray, Grover P. and Mabel A. Irving, Apr. 26th

Ridenson, Ira L. and Ruth M. Eades, June 1st

Roberts, Walker M. and Willie Lee Landford, Sept. 29th

Richardson, Clarence Warren and Maggie Elizabeth Bishop, Dec. 22nd

1921

Roberts, Earl D. and Margaret V. Gringer, May 1st

Ross, Jr., Hugh and Barbara J. Gable, June 15th

Ralston, Jerry W. and Evelyn Wood, July 10th

Ramsey, James S. and Richie B. Gibson, Sept. 9th

1922

Rowe, William M. and Carrie Humphrey, Jan. 17th

Rogers, Willie and Lula Watson, Oct. 5th

Riley, Lawrence and Myrtie Kirby, Nov. 11th

Rigsby, Lester and Pearl G. Eaton, Dec. 20th

Riley, Woods and Nellie Moore, Dec. 27th

1923

Roberts, Ira C. and Mary Goode, Aug. 19th

Roston, Jerry and Evy Lee Wood, Sept. 1st

Roberts, Allie E. and Elizabeth F. Story, Nov. 1st

Richardson, Regenale and Anna Lanforde, Dec. 18th

Ross, Givens and Pearl C. Dowell, Dec. 25th

1924

Rose, Esan and Ethel M. Leake, July 3rd

Ramsey, Gordon and Retter D. Alexandria, Nov. 10th

Roberts, Charlie O. and Earline E. Durrer, Dec. 17th

1925

Reid, George M. and Aida F. Hall, Feb. 11th

Rogers, George and Mary Lee Morris, Feb. 27th

Rea, Elmore and Nora Lee Kirby, July 1st

Ragland, Earl Lee and Viola Marie Pritchett, Sept. 7th

Reynolds, Robert H. and Rebecca Davis, Oct. 24th

Ray, Gentry and Alma Barnett, Dec. 16th

1926

Riggs, Frank W. and Mabel M. Walker, June 24th

Ruffin, Thomas E. and Ruth L. Boaz, Aug. 27th

Roudabush, Wm. S. and Marion Houchens, Sept. 25th

Ramsey, Homer L. and Lillie E. Kidd, Oct. 12th

Robertson, Russell E. and Ruby M. Fenwick, Oct. 27th

Robinson, Emmett S. and Ethel W. Payne, Nov. 6th

Ross, Arthur and Mabel Hutchinson, Dec. 6th

1927

Rush, Ellison and Fern Reeves, Apr. 16th

Rubush, Alvin S. and Ruby Lee Walton, June 5th

Ribble, Watkins L. and Constance Strobel, June 10th

Rittenhouse John B. and Margaret L. Deane, July 14th

Raynor, John W. and Mazie V. Cook, Aug. 31st

Rea, Thurman A. and Elsie M. Pugh, Sept. 2nd

Reynolds, Alvin R. and Elsie Mae Pickering, Sept. 7th

Ray, Charles and Edna F. Fisher, Nov. 13th

Rea, Earl and Elsie Barksdale, Dec. 24th

Rosten, Charlie C. and Virginia M. Belew, Dec. 3rd

1928

Rowan, William W. and Laura W. Earhart, Jan. 27th

Riley, James W. S. and Dora A. Sullivan, Apr. 30th

Ranlet, Jr., Robert and Suzanne Hanckel, June 13th

Rodgers, Hiram and Viola Watson, July 17th

Rhodes, William J. and Norvell C. Carver, Dec. 26th

S

1783

Sandidge, John and Molly Wood, Nov. 13th

Shelton, William and Fanny Maupin, Aug. 15th

Simms, John and Mary Dedman, Jan. 4th

1784

Sandridge, William and Susanna Dedman, ? 14th

Smith, Thomas and Susanna Shelton, Aug. 30th

Southerds, James and Jane Randolph, Dec. 9th

Sprouce, David and Lucy Sprouce, Oct. 1st

1785

Smith, James and Sally Gentry, ———

Smith, William and Polly Bailey, Dec. 12th

Spencer, John and Mary Humphrey, Nov. 4th

Stepp, James and Sally Burbridge, Jan. 4th

1786

Shiflett, Lewis and Sarah Haslerig, March 29th

Staples, William and Martha Tompkins, June 17th

Strange, David and Eliza Eubank, Nov. 14th

1787

Sharp, Robert and Susannah Razor, May 6th

Sherman, George and Elizabeth Parrott, Oct. 27th

Shiflet, Joel and Sally Grady, Nov. 1st

Smith, Samuel and Anne Davis, June 14th

Spencer, William and Jane Proctor, June 1st

1788

Shackelford, Mordeca and Sarah Jones, Oct. 12th

Shop, John and Sarah Gragg, Dec. 18th

Smith, George and Mary Harden, April 10th

Smith, Joel and Martha Patrick, Feb. 28th

Steel, John and Lucy Moon, Dec. 11th

1789

Sampson, Richard and Sarah Goff, Jan. 12th

Shackelford, Richard and Patsy Spears, June 4th

Shelton, Thomas and Mary Jameson, Nov. 2nd

Simpson, Samuel and Franky Burbage, Nov. 2nd

1790

Sanford, Richard and Sarah Twyman, Dec. 16th

Seebre, James and Millie Ferguson, Aug. 3rd

Shiflett, Thomas and Betty Lamb, May 15th

Skinner, Burdit and Nancy Austin, Jan. 25th

Skivers, Oan and Catharine Brown, Nov. 9th

1791

Shepherd, Peter and Elenor Smith, Sept. 9th

Shiflett, Bland and Elizabeth Shiflett, Sept. 9th

Shoap, Philip and Elizabeth Gregg, Feb. 21st

Smith, John and Molley Tomplin ———

Smith, —— and —— Humpey, Aug. 14th

Smith, John and Martha Wallace, Sept. 13th

Sneed, Claiborne and Mary Childress, March 9th

Sullivan, Thomas and Nancy Boswell, April 22nd

Sutton, Martin and Margaret Williams, July 5th

1792

Sneed, Elijah and Polly Barker, Feb. 9th

Spering, Henry and Elizabeth Frog, Sept. 19th

Spradling, Nathan and Mary Phillips, Nov. 21st

Stone, Henry and Elizabeth Crosthwait, Jan. 6th

Sutton, William and Sally Carr, Dec. 22nd

1793

Shirley, John and Susanna Gardner, Dec. 10th

Sneed, Berrell and Susannah Norwell, Dec. 9th

Snelson, Robert and Polly Thomas, Aug. 29th

Snow, Fielden and Sally Foster, Jan. 8th

Sullivan, Dennis and Caty Jones, Aug. 10th

1794

Smith, Peter and Elizabeth Wallace, Oct. 4th

Sullivan, Daniel and Nancy Reinolds, Feb. 25th

Swetnam, George and Polly Sutton, March 14th

1795

Seamonds, Barnett and Frances Estes, Jan. 13th

Shiflett, Stephen and Rachel Hicks, Jan. 16th

Simpson, John and Elizabeth Davis, Feb. 2nd

Smith, Austin and Sally Davis, Dec. 7th

Suddarth, Jarot and Sally Hensley, July 23rd

Sullivan, William and Suky Seamonds, Sept. 19th

1796

Shaver, Michael and Mary Davis, Aug. 8th

Sims, Nath and Susannah Johnson, Aug. 14th

Sowell, Benjamin and Annie Gentry, Feb. 20th

Stamer, Henry and Mary Biery, March 15th

1797

Stone, Kenzia and Sally Watts, Dec. 21st

1798

Salmon, John Downey and Nancy Dowell, Feb. 5th

Shiflett, John and Ann Hicks, Nov. 14th

Slape, Thomas and Elizabeth Archer, Jan. 30th

Smith, William and Nancy Hall, Sept. 3rd

Space, Benjamin and Secelia Melton, March 8th

Speace, Jacob and Sally Burges, Sept. 11th

Starks, James and Nancy Kindred, March 8th

Stephens, Abraham and Mary Via, Nov. 6th

1799

Sandridge, Austin and Sally Thurmond, Aug. 12th

Shepherd, William and Sally Craven, June 3rd

Shields, John and Mildred Reynolds, June 20th

Smith, Joseph D. and Ann Gillum, May 6th

Smith, William and Patsy Edwards, April 17th

Suddarth, Tandy and Betsey Hicks, Dec. 4th

1801

Shaver, John and Elizabeth Fisher, May 30th

Stark, James and Patsey Bowcock, Oct. 1st

1802

Scott, Jesse and Sally Jefferson Bell, Aug. 10th

Smith, William and Elizabeth Breedlove, Sept. 21st

Spears, Ephraim and Sally Walton, Nov. 23rd

Stone, Thomas and Charlotte Dalton, Jan. 1st

1803

Smith, Isaac and Betsy Mullins, April 5th

1804

Sneed, John and Anna Richardson, Dec. 26th

Spradlin, Richard and Elizabeth Beaver, Nov. 13th

Sprouse, Henry and Dicey Thacker, Mar. 5th

Sprouce, John and Rachel Wood, July 2nd

1805

Scott, Robert and Sally Henderson Price, Nov. 13th

Sharp, Isaac and Susannah Fitz, Nov. 2nd

Shelton, Weatherston and Elizabeth Harrison, Jan. 25th

Shepherd, Drury and Nancy Elsom, Nov. 4th

Smith, William T. and Polly Leake, March 1st

Spinner, John and Polly Battels, April 2nd

1806

Sandredge, —— and Elizabeth Proctor, Oct. 15th

Seamonds, Enock, and Nancy Gentry, Sept.
23rd
Singo, Archibald and Martha Cleveland ——
Smith, Burnett and Ann Wood, Oct. 27th
Smith, John and Kiza Patterson, July 28th
Smithson, —— and Catherine Triplet, Dec.
25th
Snow, —— and Jinny Harvie, Jan. 4th
Stewart, Robert and Jinny Bailey, Sept. ——

1807

Scott, James and Mildred Thompson, Dec. 9th
Shelton, Thomas and Susan Ballad, Dec. 10th
Shields, David and Elizabeth Smith, Feb. 2nd
Sprouce, Jack and Elizabeth Wood, March
2nd

1808

Salmon, Thomas and Elizabeth M. Carr, Dec.
17th
Scott, William and Lucy Hardin, Sept. 30th
Sharp, Richard and Nancy Rowe, Oct. 17th
Shepherd, Anthony and Mary Eads, Sept. 30th
Speer, John and Elizabeth Ricks, April 9th

1809

Sanford, Augustine and Nancy Breedlove,
Aug. 10th
Shackelford, Zack and Susan Gilmer, June
30th
Sharp, William and Fanny Sebre, Dec. 11th
Sims, Isaac and Nancy Catterton, Jan. 4th
Stykes, William F. Margaret Gibb, Nov. 21st
Smith, John and Nancy King, Jan. 26th

1810

Shelton, Austin and Elizabeth Ballard, Aug.
30th
Shiflett, John and Elizabeth Campbell, Oct. 5th
Sprouce, John and Betsy Carver, Dec. 6th
Stephens, William and Catherine Clark, Dec.
17th

1811

Shiflett, Anderson and Catharine, Nov. —?
Shiflett, Moddeque and Nancy Brock, Dec.
27th
Shultz, John and Elizabeth ? ——
Smith, John and Martha, ? ——
Snow, John and Jane Burrus, Dec. 25th
Sudderth, Thomas and Dicy Myers, Nov. 6th

1812

Savage, George P. and Elizabeth Miller, Dec.
25th
Shiflett, Nathaniel and Betsy Proctor, Jan. 7th
Simms, John and Nancy Millowry, Dec. 24th
Singleton, Richard and Rebecca Coles, Feb.
3rd
Speers, John and Ann Graves, March 3rd
Strange, Hudson and Sally Hamner, Aug. 4th
Sutherland, Joseph and Elizabeth Garland,
Nov. 19th

1813

Sandridge, Pleasant and Thomas Edwards,
June 22nd
Schniggs, Grove and Elizabeth Hamner, Sept.
6th
Shiflett, John and Frances Martin, Nov. 27th
Smith, John and Elizabeth B. Hirchus, April
5th
Stevens, James C. and Nancy G. Medearis,
April 3rd

1814

Shields, Samuel and Susannah Brock, Dec.
22nd
Sims, Richard D. and Elizabeth Clarkson,
Oct. 11th
Smith, John and Cary Ann Nicholas, Nov.
29th
Smith, Rice and Nancy Robertson, Oct. 3rd
Sprouce, Micajah and Polly Patterson, March
7th
Sprouce, Tandy and Nancy Sprouce, April 4th
Stone, Isaac and Elizabeth Keister, March 31st

1815

Shiflett, Bennett and Polly Shiflett, Dec. 28th
Smith, Richard N. and Mary Fry, Dec. 11th
Smith, Elisha and Susan Dowell, Sept. 4th
Sprouce, Benjamin and Elizabeth Dove, Oct.
24th
Stede, John and Eliza H. Moon, Oct. 25th
Stone, John and Elizabeth Wood, Dec. 22nd

1816

Sampson, John P. and Jannette Rogers, Oct.
31st
Sandridge, Austin and Ann Hall, Jan. 1st
Shackelford, James C. and Elizabeth Lively,
Feb. 22nd
Snetum, William R. and Mary Bolling, May
8th
Stevenson, Andrew and Sarah Coles, Oct. 17th
Suddarth, Randolph and Alley Norvell, July
1st

1817

Seamonds, Preston and Elizabeth P. Golding,
Dec. 11th
Shackelford, Daniel and Patsey Carr, Dec. 24th
Snead, Gregory and Nancy W. Heiman, Jan.
6th
Spencer, James and Riles Oaks, Sept. 7th
Spencer, William and Sally Hicks, Jan. 5th
Spicer, Dabney and Catharine Brockman, April
2nd
Staples, Thomas and Ann Tompkins, Oct. 6th

1818

Shackelford, William and Susan Bowen, Dec.
30th
Shiflett, Wily and Minerva Shiflett, Feb. 5th
Shope, John and Patsey Houchins, June 30th
Slater, John S. and Fanny Trevillian, July 29th
Slaughter, Robert H. and Mary R. Garland,
July 15th

Snow, Henry and Polly Dowell, May 25th

Stubbs, Bailey and Polly Dowell, Nov. 8th

1819

Shepherd, Anthoney and Lucy Thomas, Aug. 31st

Sims, Thomas F. and Ann E. Anderson Feb. 4th

Sobban, John and Harriot A. Patrick

Sobban, John and Harriot A. Patrick, ?

Spears, Henry and Nancy Smith, Dec. 27th

Staples, Beverly and Judith White, Aug. 14th

1820

Selden, Joseph and Harriot Gray, Oct. 8th

Sneed, Nicholas and Sally McDaniel, Jan. 10th

Southall, Valentine W. and Mary A. Garrett, Jan. 18th

Starke, Fielding and Elizabeth Gray, Sept. 12th

1821

Sandrekge, Stephen and Miry M. Gardner, March 22nd

Shiflett, Micajah and Sadia Pleasants, Nov. 7th

Simons, Thomas and Pinkerton T. Farrell, May 18th

Simpson, John and Ann Davis, May 8th

Slaughter, Waddy T. and Frances Ballard, Nov. 7th

Smith, Abraham and Spicey Humphrey, Aug. 30th

Smith, John and Mary Foster, Nov. 17th

Smith, William and Malinda Kirby, June 30th

Sneed, Richard and Lucinda Becks, Dec.. 30th

Sponer, George W. and Elizabeth W. Perry, Feb. 15th

Spradling, David and June Pleasants, Nov. 7th

Stewardson, William and Elizabeth Gibson, May 24th

Sutherland, Richard S. and Sarah A. Irvin, March 20th

1822

Shipten, Preston and Martha Anderson, Dec. 19th

Sneed, John and Mary Norvell, Feb. 20th

Snider, Jacob and Celia Hall, April 30th

1823

Scoutling, Edward and Mary Thurston, Oct. 16th

Shaver, Abraham and Mary Beaver, Nov. 4th

Smith, David B. and Nancy S. Crosthwait, Sept. 12th

Starkes, Allen and Matilda Carrier, July 5th

Starke, James T. and Mary Ann Estes, Feb. 25th

1824

Shackelford, James and Mous J. Garrison, May 11th

Shiflett, Joseph and Melissa Shiflett, Oct. 20th

Shiflett, Turner and Mildred Powell, Sept. 24th

Sprouce, Dabney M. and Eliza Gibson, Jan. 25th

Strange, George E. and Mary Watson, Nov. 11th

Sudderth, John and Mary Wills, Dec. 20th

Sullivan, Jeremiah and Frances Collins, Dec. 30th

1825

Scrigner, Samuel and Mary Wood, May 25th

Scruggs, George R. and Frances E. Noel, Dec. 24th

Sheckles, Thomas B. and Eleanor Johnson, Sept. 1st

Shiflett, Cowherd and Jinny Snow, Oct. 21st

Shumate, Bailey and Lucy Mills, Sept. 17th

Smith, William and Susanna Garrison, Nov. 14th

Southall, Valentine W. and Martha Cocke, Feb. 1st

1826

Shiflett, Clayton and Justin Davis, June 6th

Shorbes, John and Sally Shiflett, Oct. 24th

Sparraw, Erasmus M. and Louisa J. Harris, Dec. 11th

Sprouce, Randal and Rachel Thacker, Feb. 9th

Stockdal, John and Catharine Matthews, Aug. 7th

Strange, John and Frances Cloar, March 15th

1827

Shelton, Thomas D. and Susan L. Farrar, Dec. 17th

Shelton, Weathersnow and Sarah Thorpe, Jan. 15th

Shiflett, Bennett H. and Patience Shobe, Feb. 28th

Sivitzer, Lawrence and Nancy White, Aug. 14th

Savage, Moses and Sarah Lee, Sept. 4th

Smith, James W. and Mary Hall, Oct. 25th

Stevens, William and Lucy White, Aug. 22nd

Stewardson, William and Sally Wingfield, April 10th

1828

Sandridge, Lindsay and Lucy Smith, March 12th

Sandridge, Nicholas and Elizabeth Sandridge, May 1st

Shiflett, Benson and Tina Shiflett, November 8th

Simpson, John Jr., and Lucy Branham, May 14th

Smith, Wilson C. and Virginia S. Woods, November 1st

Smith, William and Joarma Finder February 5th

Spradling, David and J. A. Becks, January 23rd

Sullivan, Sinclair and Frances Luck August 7th

1829

Salmon, John and Mary D. Foster, December 23rd

Salmon, Thomas and Harriott Price, September 17th

Seargant, William L. and Elizabeth Watson, July 30th

Smith, John M. and Amanda Harris, August 4th

Spillon, Collier and Georgianna Gilmer, April 11th

Spinhed, John and Nancy Pritchette, February 17th

Sprouce George and Eliza Alfred, June 1st

Sprouce, John and Catharine L. Sprouce, March 21st

Suddarth, Joseph and Mary Fendrick, February 3rd

Sudderth, Benjamin and Mary Haskins, June 16th

1830

Shackelford, J. and Rebecca Bishop, November 13th

Shiflett, Washington and Sally Morris, March 2nd

Speers, William W. and Delidah Speers, May 6th

Sprouce, Washington and Caty Anderson, July 7th

Strange, David and Susan Wilson, December 16th

Sullivan, David and Polly Summons, December 23rd

Sullivan, William and Nancy Bishop, November 13th

1831

Sandridge, Joel M. and Frances Sandridge, November 24th

Sandridge, William and Elizabeth Garrison, January, 11th

Scott, Peyton H. and Frances Tyree, April 4th

Smith, John M. and Jacinta T. Rodes, February 17th

Sneed, Stapleton C. and Elizabeth N. Craven, July 12th

Sprouce, Henry and Sarah Sprouse, December 26th

Summons, William and Eliza Rosson, December 11th

1832

Sandridge, Nathan H. and Jane H. Gardner, January 3rd

Shackelford, Henry J. and Eliza A. Perkins, May 23rd

Shiflett, Brightberry and Tempy Shiflett, January, 17th

Shiflett, Valentine and Jane Shiflett, September 3rd

Simms, Bluford and Mildred Ann Austin, January, 30th

Sprouce, Zachariah and Sarah Munday, December 3rd

Sudderth Horace and Martha Clement, November 27th

Sudderth, James and Elvira Drumheller, January 2nd

Sutton, Wisdom and Sarah Hamilton, June 4th

Sweeney, John W. and Sarah J. Hickok, June 13th

1833

Sanders, Ephraim D. and Ann P. Gurion, November 13th

Seebrick, Frederick and Jane Fenwick, February 2nd

Shiflett, Leland and America W. Mallory, November 14th

Sprouce, Jefferson and Susan Thacker, April 27th

Stockton, John W. C. and Emily Bernard, November 5th

Suddarth, William and Nancy Scruggs, March 5th

1834

Salmon, Fendal and Sarah Foster, January 15th

Sandridge, Benjamin and Salliva Elliott, November 14th

Shelton, Stapleton C. and Eliza M. Terrell, January 1st

Shiflett, Burton and Nancy Frazier, December 1st

Shiflett, Fielding and Betsey Shiflett, October 27th

Shiflett, Lewis and Eliza Keaton, January 15th

Simpson, John and Elizabeth Boswell, May 27th

Sinclair, Samuel and E. H. Craven, October 24th

Smith, Christopher M. and Sarah Foster, January 8th

Smith, Pleasants and Lucinda Gasaway, December 11th

Smith, Wm. and Sarah E. Rolls, September 1st

Speers, John and Mary Stewardson, February 24th

Sprouce, Anderson and Mary Marion, April 9th

Sprouce, Pleasants and Anna Harlow, October 6th

Sprouce, William and Polly Dudley, January 8th

Stone, Michael and Mary Wayman, October 11th

1835

Sandridge, Michael and Nancy Taylor, November 17th

Settellier, John and Marrietter Wings, March 25th

Shan, Charles B. and Isabella P. Watson, December 7th

Shiflett, Archibald and Matilda Newcum, December 7th

Shiflett, Nelson and Carey Davis, November 18th

Simio, Reuben and S. C. Hill, May 19th

Slater, Christopher and Eliza Riley, October 23rd

Smith, Thomas and Elizabeth J. Harris, June, 4th

1836

Sandridge, Austin and S. Sandridge, August 1st

Sandridge, Joel M. and Susan Wood, September 26th

Scribner, W. W. and S. A. R. Twyman, January 21st

Seathers, Jonathan and R. A. Farish, September 5th

Shafer, Charles and Ellen Day, January 25th

Shiflett, Charles and Jinny Shiflett, April 19th

Shiflett, David and Judy Morris, March 19th

Shiflett, Isaac annd Susan Jorden, October 24th

Shiflett, Wiliam and Polly Shiflett, April 10th

Sims, Dabney Y. and Elizabeth Edwards, October 10th

Singleton, John C. and Mary S. Carter, September 22nd

Spitler, Samuel and M. B. Watts, September 20th

Snow, Obediah and Nancy Watson, April 16th

Subles, A. T. and Mary J. Leake, January 13th

1837

Sandridge, Natha W. and Parmelia Garrison, August 29th

Shiflett, Henderson and Milly Shiflett December 22nd

Shiflett, John and Elizabeth Shiflett, March 16th

Shope, Nicholas and Sophia Shiflett, February 4th

Smith, Hiram M. and Elizabeth G. Aimes, December 25th

Smith, Robert and Nancy Lamb, May 14th

Sneed, Benjamin and Mary J. Shiflett, December 18th

Snell, Albert G. and Mary Ann Page, October 5th

Sprouce, Tipton and Susannah Woody, May 22nd

Sprouce, Zachariah and Nancy Gaymer, July 5th

1738

Sandridge, Benpamin T. and Isabella E. Mundy, December 21st

Sandridge, Pleasant and Charlotte Wilkerson, December 6th

Shiflett, Asa and Jane Shiflett, December 10th

Shiflett, Wiley and Margaret Shiflett, January 22nd

Slattor, James and Mary Ann Via, October 16th

Smith, George W. and Gilly Dowell, September 13th

Smith, William M. and Catharine Mickleborough, October 2nd

Sprouce, William and Christine K. Sprouce, September 3rd

Strange, Reuben C. and Maria Zigler, September 27th

Stratton, Richard H. and Ann Eliza Brown, December 5th

Sutherland, Clifton G. and Mary M. Ammonett, September 17th

1839

Seay, Joseph and Martha E. Ryon, June 3rd

Shelton, Nelson S. and Sarah Jane Carr, April 11th

Shepperd, William R. and Martha Marr, May 28th

Sneed, John H. and Susan Roberson, November 12th

Stephens, Jese A. and Elizabeth A. McKinney, July 6th

1840

Shiflett, Golding S. and Sarah Shiflett, July 22nd

Shope, Nicholas and Ann Barnett, July 18th

Simpson, Robert and Frances Hall, February 27th

Smith, James D. and M. J. Herring, December 15th

Smith, Mathias and Nancy Riley, April 2nd

Snow, R. D. and S. A. Lane, December 22nd

1841

Sampson, Stephen F. and Ann C. Lindsay, September 7th

Shalter, John and Frances Estes, November 8th

Shepherd, Charles R. and Amanda M. Mahanes, October 26th

Sheller, Frederick and Barbara Pleasants, October 7th

Shields, Joseph D. and Elizabeth F. Conway, July 5th

Sims, Samuel and Lucy Jane Faris, March 3rd

Smith, Albert and Sophia Pleasants, October 7th

Smith, William T. and Mary J. C. Duke, July 26th

Snead, Robert and Nancy Thacker, June 7th

Sprouce, Weston and Nancy Payne, Jan. 20th

Stover, Simon W. and Mary A. Rittenhouse, Nov. 8th

Sudderth, Randolph and Abitha Sudderth, Aug. 24th

1842

Schaaff, John and Elizabeth Birkhead, Aug. 27th

Seal, Robert A. and Mary Jane McCullock, Dec. 26th

Smith, Henry T. and Angelina Coleman, July 11th

Smith, James and Nancy Thacker, Aug. 31st

Smyth, Thomas M. and Ann E. Garrett, Dec. 15th

Spears, Littleton and Lucy Mayo, May 3rd

1843

Shackelford, John A. and Elizabeth Moseley, Dec. 26th

Shiflett, Morton and Rosalonia Shiflett, June 5th

Shiflett, Nicholas and Nancy Lawson, Jan. 11th

Sibley, George H. and Frances Gillaspy, Jan. 2nd

Smith, Robert P. and Sarah E. Cocke, Jan. 2nd

Sprouce, Gustavus W. and D. A. Durrett, ——

1844

Sampson, Frances J. and Sarah M. Shiflett, Nov. 11th

Schneiff, Joyn and Martha M. Batcheler, Oct. 17th

Scott, Edward and Elizabeth R. Scott, Sept. 26th

Smith, William and Eliza Dudley, April 4th

Sprouce, Albert and Mary Cunin Sprouce, March 4th

Sprouce, Joseph and Celia Harlow, Oct. 10th

Stafford, John F. and E. J. Marr, Jan. 1st

Swan, Richard W. and Lucy W. Minor, May 16th

1845

Saunders, John S. and Elizabeth Jones, March 20th

Shiflett, Kertly F. and Mary E. Moore, Jan. 23rd

Smith, Colser and Malinda Rice, Feb. 18th

Sprouce, Benjamin and Elizabeth Wood, Jan. 23rd

Strange, John and Sarah Wingfield, Sept. 24th

1846

Sampson, Stephen F. and Sarah E. Campbell, Nov. 26th

Scruggs, William and Elizabeth Hughes, April 3rd

Scruggs, William G. and Paulina O. Norvell, May 4th

Seneal, Peter and Martha A. Wallace, April 18th

Shiflett, James and Frances Shiflett, Jan. 17th

Shiflett, John and Eliza Via, Dec. 10th

Sipes, Henry E. and Mary A. Dossy, March 11th

Smith, William and Mary P. Wallace, May 19th

Sneed, William and Sarah J. Clarke, July 1st

Strange, Callem H. and Sarah W. Wash, May 19th

Synars, William and Isabella Thompson, April 3rd

1847

Sandridge, Michael and M. C. Parsons, Aug. 29th

Sandridge, Nicholas and Polly Dunn, Oct. 4th

Scott, Charles and Eliza Brock, Nov. 17th

Smith, Childress and Mildred Thomas, Dec. 28th

Sormon, Rollins and Sarah B. Scott, Jan. 2nd

Sprouce, Shelton and Eliza Harlow, Aug. 23rd

Station, Harden F. and Elizabeth Station, Feb. 23rd

Sutherland, William and Lucy Bales, Sept. 2nd

Sutter, George W. and F. H. Underwood, Oct. 4th

1848

Shackelford, William and Sarah Moon, June 29th

Shelton, John and Sophia Battles, Nov. 26th

Shepherd, U. E. and F. E. Watson, Nov. 1st

Smith, John F. and Parmelia F. Wood, March 21st

1849

Schele, De Von Max and E. W. Rives, July 25th

Scott, George W. and Elizabeth Vermillion, Feb. 20th

Smith, William E. and H. A. Carver, Sept. 4th

Spotts, Michael H. and V. P. Dillard, April 12th

Sprouce, John and Sarah Pratt, June 22nd

Sprouce, Joseph and Margaret A. Hicks, Sept. 12th

Sutter, Thomas L. and Jane Hays, Oct. 14th

1850

Simms, James F. and Selena Jane Barksdale, March 5th

Smith, Charles D. and Elizabeth J. Hicks, Dec. 25th

Smith, Joseph and Eliza M. Harris, Oct. 31st

Snead, James M. and Ann E. Beach, Dec. 20th

Spencer, Robert and Parmelia A. May Feb. 14th

Spradling, William and Mary Ann Baber, June 22nd

Sprouce, Henry and Sarah Gibson, Dec. 6th

Summons, Hiram and Lucy P. F. Wood, Sept. 2nd

1851

Saunders, James G. and Ann A. Jones, March 18th

Saunders, R. C. and Caryetta Davis, May 28th

Scantling, William and Mary E. Claum, Sept. 18th

Scott, James and Kitty Pleasants, July 14th

Shelton, John and Elizabeth Farrow, March 12th

Shelton, James H. and Ann E. Grayson, May 22nd

Shiflett, U. Linton and Christine Powell, Feb. 4th

Shotwell, Jeremiah and C. Brockman, Dec. 23rd

Slack, Samuel R. and Sarah A. Key, May 14th

Smith, Joseph A. and Lucinda E. Smith, Dec. 1st

Spencer, Alex and Wilmer Bowen, April 3rd

Sprouce, Jacob and Lucy Barnett, Feb. 17th

1852

Scott, Charles A. and Polo R. Scott, Oct. 22nd

Shackelford, A. I. and Virginia Smith, Aug. 25th

Sheets, Andrew and M. Shaffer, Oct. 28th

Slater, Joseph and Margaret Clour, Oct. 14th

Snead, William H. and Susan Thacker, Feb. 5th

Sneed, William B. and Lavinia A. Hoid, Jan. 17th

Stephens, Paul and M. E. Goodloe, March 30th

Strange, John H. and Elizabeth A. Strange, March 6th

1853

Scruggs, Fred H. and Maria E. Staton, May 7th

Seal, Morgan and Sarah Booth, Dec. 2nd

Sheeler, David and Susan Heiper, Dec. 28th

Smith, Francis H. and Mary S. Harrison, July 21st

Spradling, John Z. and Martha Smith, July 23rd

Sneed, George C. and Lucy Eades, Aug. 23rd

1854

Sandridge, William and Frances Fisher, Sept. 10th

Shepherd, Richard W. and Mary J. Lindar, July 25th

Sims, Jno. C. and Mary J. Creel, Dec. 10th

Smith, B. William R. Elizabeth Tyler, Feb. 19th

Smith, Garland and Amanda L. Davis, April 6th

Smith, Horace W. and Mildred Ann Morris, Feb. 9th

Smith, John D. and Jane Dowell, Oct. 16th

Sprouce, Giden and Cornelia Thomas, Dec. 27th

Sprinkle, Wm. F. and H. C. Shiflett, Apr. 20th

Snead, John and Lucy Sandridge, Dec. 14

Smith, Wm. R. and Eliz. Tyler, Feb. 19th

Smith, Garland and A. L. Davis, Apr. 6th

Sandridge, Wm. and Frances Fisher, Sept. 10th

Stewart, Jno. W. and Mary H. McGuffey, June 15th

Semmonds, Joseph S. and Delia A. M. Ward, Jan. 14th

1855

Sellers, Theodore N. and June R. Dunkum, Aug. 22nd

Stephens, Joseph H. and Eliza P. Douglass, Dec. 13th

Suddarth, Charles and M. J. Littleford, Jan. 17th

Suddarth, Chas. and M. J. Littleford, Jan. 25th

Simour, M. P. and Mary L. Bruce, Oct. 9th

Sprouce, J. M. and Eliza A. Gibson, Oct. 3rd

Shiflett, L. R. and A. R. Gentry, Feb. 28th

Sumner Geo. I. and Lucy M. Jones, Nov. 29th

Stark, Wm. A. and Ann E. Herndon, July 22nd

Sellers, Theo. N. and Jane R. Dunkum, Aug. 22nd

Stephens, Jo. H. and Eliza P. Douglass, Dec. 20th

Sprouce Dyer M. and Dicey M. Gibson, July 17th

Sprouce, William and Julia A. Dudley, Feb. 15th

Smith, Horace W. and Mildred A. Morris, Feb. 9th

Sigourney, Henry and Amelia L. Rives, May 10th

Seamonds, Jo. G. and Delilah M. Wood, Jan. 19th

Shepherd, R. M. and Mary J. Tinder, June 25th

Strange, Tucker and Sarah J. Bramham, Dec. 24th

1856

Scott, John L. and Eliza M. Pendleton, Nov. 28th

Sharp, Charles and Lucy S. Sorthall, Nov. 27th

Sharp, Charles and Lucy S. Southall, Nov. 27th

Sutherland, Edward and Ann E. Shepherd, Nov. 20th

Sutherland, Edw. and Ann E. Shepherd, Nov. 20th

Sutherland, Joseph and Elizabeth Anderson, Feb. 26th

Sutherland, Joseph and Ann E. Anderson, Feb. 26th

Scott, Jno. L. and Eliza M. Pendleton, Nov. 28th

Smith, Edw. B. and Lucy W. Downing, July 15th

Smith, J. Henry and Mary K. Watson, Jan. 8th

Snead, John and Mary A. Tooly, Oct. 9th

Shultz, Jacob and Eliz. Suddarth, May 23

Shirey, G. H. and M. V. McAlexander, Nov. 12th

Scruggs, Fred H. and Mariah E. Slaton, May 7th

Shackelford, Jas. D. and Sarah J. Maddox, Aug. 20th

Strom, L. H. and Susan F. Clements, Aug. 9th

Suddarth, John and Frances Willis, Dec. 30th

Strayer, Jo. B. and Fannie C. Rodes, July 13th

Sprouce, John and Frances Bellamy, Mar. 28th

1857

Suddarth, John and Frances Willis, Dec. 29th

Suddarth, Nathaniel S. and Elizabeth H. Thacker, Nov. 30th

Sutherland, John and Sarah F. Suddarth, Jan. 13th

1858

Scott, Edward and Mary K. Scott, Oct. 21st

Staples, Silas and Sarah W. Dannielle, Nov. 16th

Spears, Andrew J. and Susan E. Bowles, Dec. 30th

Sodd, Jno. M. and Mary E. Hawley, Feb. 25th

Smith, Jno. M. and Manda A. Smith, Nov. 11th

Shaw, James and Tabellia M. Wash, Aug. 12th

Smith, Tho. H. and Sophia I. Sweeney, Sept. 9th

1859

Sandridge, Geo. W. and Eliz. Walton, Aug. 18th

Sandridge, George W. and Elizabeth Walton, Aug. 16th

Swiede, Jno. S. and Josephine A. Moon, May 18th

Smith, Joseph P. and Fannie E. Shiflett, Feb. 2nd

Sprouce, Edw. and Mary A. Hutchinson, June 1st

Sneed, Jno. S. and Josephine A. Moore, May 18th

Shackelford, Dabney F. and Mary E. Maddox, Jan. 25th

Strange, Tho. V. and Ann M. Spicer, Sept. 15th

Stocker, Alfred J. and Sallie E. Stone, Oct. 18th

Salmon, Wm. H. and Sarah J. Mundy, Oct. 13th

Stirling, Chas. H. and Sallie W. Jones, Oct. 27th

Starling, R. R. and C. A. Burch, Nov. 8th

Sellers, Jno. W. and Martha E. Wood, Sept. 1st

1860

Sandridge, Stephen G. and Susan Pritchett, June 26th

Shepherd, Richard W. and Martha L. M. Herndon, Feb. 4th

Shepherd, Richard W. and Martha M. Herndon, Feb. 19th

Sweet, Benjamin H. and Mary R. Wingfield, Jan. 16th

Sandridge, Stephen G. and Susan Pritchett, June 28th

Southan, Wm. P. and Helen M. Bibb, July 5th

Sweet, Benj. R. and Mary R. Wingfield, Jan. 16th

Snow, Pulaskers, and Va. C. Madison, Dec. 18th

1861

Sprinkle, Wm. B. and Frances J. McMullen, Apr. 18th

Spradling, D. H. and Margaret F. Lines, Oct. 2nd

Sutler, Asa and Eliza J. Houchens, Apr. 25th

Sprouce, Henry, Jr., and Sarah Thomas, Jan. 14th

Smith, Wm. G. and Malinda Wheeler, Jan. 30th

Sprouce, Tho. J. and Milly J. Harlow, Feb. 20th

1862

Stein, John and Sarah F. Herron, Nov. 28th

Sprouce, Jno. C. nad Mary Jane Sprouce, Aug. 20th

Summerson, Wm. and Eliza W. Estes, June 17th

Starks, Allen W. and Sarah F. McRea, Mar. 27th

1863

Snyder, Samuel K. and Mary F. Houchens, June 10th

Stafford, Henry S. and Sarah E. Dove, Dec 30th

Shackelford, Jno. A. and Clementina Marshall, July 30th

Sprouce, James A. and Mary J. Dudley, Aug. 18th

1864

Smith, Jno. E. and Lucy A. Marshall, Apr. 7th

Scruggs, Samuel M. and Susan W. Oaks, Apr. 21st

Sloan, Chas. N. and Sarah A. Whitley, Mar. 28th

Smith, Martin A. and Josephine Craddock, Jan. 6th

Shelby, Tho. H. and Emily F. Clements, Feb. 2nd

Samuels, Tho. S. and Henrietta C. Moore, Aug. 9th

Simms, Wm. J. and Sarah Ann Fray, Aug. 30th

Shackleford, Wm. C. and Sarah Jane Goss, Nov. 29th

Shumate, Jo. P. and Malinda S. Wilkerson, Dec. 27th

1865

Shepherd, A. A. and Sallie M. Shepherd, Oct. 14th

Shepherd, Albert G. and Bettie M. Elsom, Dec. 4th

Shepherd, Albert G. and Bettie M. Elson, Dec. 12th

Shackleford, Richard J. and Laura A. Vandergrift, Nov. 23rd

Suddarth, Charles L. and Elizabeth Fenwick, Oct. 2nd

Suddarth, Chas. L. and Eliz. Feswick, Oct. 5th

Sweeney, George W. and Ann C. Taylor, March 13th

Strange, Andrew and Emeline Wingfield, Oct. 12th

Sutherland, A. A. and Sallie M. Shepherd, Oct. 17th

Sprouce, Albert and Eliz. Gibson, Aug. 10th

Sprouce, Albert and Emily McRae, Nov. 15th

Sweeney, Geo. W. and Ann C. Tayler, Mar. 13th

Sandridge, Geo. M. and Wiedna I. Via, Oct. 5th

1866

Sandridge, William O. and Parmelia A. Sandridge, Sept. 22nd

Seiler, Samuel and Rebecca Johnson, Jan. 10th

Seiler, Samuel and Rebecca Johnson, Jan. 11th

Shepherd, Thomas H. and Bettie H. Elsom, Oct. 15th

Shepherd, Thos. H. and Bettie H. Elson, Oct. 23rd

Sprouce, Lilburn and Martha Wood, Jan. 18th

Sprouce, Richard and Frances Langford, Sept. 16th

Sprouse, Albert and Emily McRae, Nov. 10th

Sneed, Miles A. and Martha A. Hughes, May 2nd

Smith, Geo. W. and Mary A. Smith, May 1st

Smith, A. J. and Ellen O. Lewis, May 23rd

Strange, Stephen and Adeline Hoye, July 5th

Spears, Tucker and Dorothy A. Ellett, Sept. 2nd.

Smith, Edw. A. and Mary S. Burton, Nov. 1st

Smith, Minock and Jane Lewis, Dec. 24th

Sandridge, Zack and Mary S. Sandridge, Dec. 10th

1867

Sandridge, Ira G. and Mary S. Garrison, Jan. 17th

Suddarth, Wm. B. and Savinia Toms, Jan. 22nd

Spencer, Soloman S. and Sarah E. Drumheller, Mar. 11th

Shiflett, Lewis G. and Parthena Gardner, May 14th

Smith, J. Mafire and Nellie Timberlake, May 20th

Smith, Paul and Harriet Fredler, Nov. 3rd

Simms, George and Betsey Ann Pattern, Dec. 27th

Stephenson, Augustus T. and Georgie E. Shelton, Dec. 23rd

Stephenson, A. T. and Georgie E. Shelton, Dec. 24th

Shiflett, L. H. and Emily J. Bruce, Dec. 17th

Sampson, Charles and Martha Cave, Aug. 20th

Setellia, Jno. H. and Fannie C. Christian, Oct. 19th

Song, Jno. W. and Cornora H. Shiflett, July 25th

Simmons, Henry E. and Elza A. Harris, Nov. 30th

Stargall, Henry S. and Nannie J. Powell, Dec. 10th

Smith, Gilmore and Bettie Dodd, Dec. 12th

Spears, Andrew J. and Mary Drumheller, Jan. 10th

Smith, Nelson and Fanny Washington, Dec. 27th

Suddarth, Wm. R. and Lavinia Toms, Jan. 24th

1868

Smith, Theopkelin and Mary Bryant, Jan. 29th

Spencer, Garland and Martha Washington, Feb. 4th

Scott, Daniel and Sally Johnson, Mar. 9th

Sinclair, Geo. A. and Eglemna F. Dillard, Mar. 21st

Sargeant, Henry H. and Mary W. Burmham, May 28th

Smith, Harrison and Harriet Johnson, June 1st

Sprouce, Robert and Mildred Harlow, Aug. 26th

Sinclair, John C. and Sally M. Yager, Sept. 8th

Sinclair, Jno. C. and Sally M. Yager, Sept. 15th

Sprouce, D. M. and Maggy Wolfe, Sept. 26th

Stewart, Addison and Amanda Lewis, Jun. 7th

Southall, Randall and Bettie Moorman, Jan. 15th

Sargeart, Henry H. and Walker Burnham, June 2nd

Shiflett, Leake and Eliza J. Johnson, Dec. 24th

Sinclair, Geo. A. and E. F. Dillard, Mar. 24th

Smith, Theo. and Marg. Bryant, —— ——

Sprouse, Benj. and Cath. Sprouce, Sept. 10th

Scott, George and Judy Harris, Dec. 24th

Small, Albert A. and Milly Shaw, Dec. 17th

Sprouce, Kaskinsco and Eliza. J. Thacker, Sept. 7th

Snead, Luther R. and Emma R. Elliott, Nov. 10th

Shepherd, Thos. and Sarah F. Johnson, Dec. 27th

Smith, Geo. T. and Susan E. Lupton, Dec. 15th

Shay, A. K. and Julia B. Lewis, Feb. 8th

1869

Skenkler, Thos. K. and Bertha Rives, Dec. 8th

Salmon, Thos. B. and Maggie L. Smith, Dec. 18th

Slaughter, F. and Sallie Brown, Dec. 26th

Sprouse, Ezekial and Polly M. Gibson, Nov. 11th

Sandridge, C. T. and Ella E. Coleman, Dec. 2nd

Stewart, M. V. and Hermitta Gentry, Dec. 14th

Staley, Geo. A. and Susan F. Brown, May 25th

Shadrock, James M. and Emma Terry, June 8th

Scott, Davie and Titia A. Battles, April 7th

Sheets, William and Susan C. Sheffer, April 8th

Shelton, Fleming and Sophia Brown, Dec. 4th

1870

Slaughter, H. and Sally P. Miller, Feb. 23rd

Sinclair, C. G. and Willie G. Peyton, Mar. 16th

Shiflet, Ralph and Georgenna McAllister, Sept. 18th

Shiflet, J. A. and M. A. Shiflet, Dec. 15th

Sandridge, Henry A. and Sarah M. Jennings, Dec. 20th

Spears, Louis and Polly Rhodes, Jan. 13

1871

Southall, Caesar and Kate King, Jan. 15th

Sneed, Benj. N. and Caroline E. Moss, Feb. 23rd

Shope, Wm. S. and Virginia Batton, June 22nd

Suddarth, Jas. R. and Sophia Pleasants, Aug. 13th

Swink, John K. and Martha Garland, Oct. 30th

Sneed, Horace Alex and May Paulina Gentry, Dec. 5th

Sneider, Jacob Adrain and Mary Elmia Ross, Dec. 12th

Stargall, Richard D. and Zeppy Ann Pleasants, Dec. 21st

Ship, Wm. H. and Sally F. Raymond, Dec. 26th

Ship, R. G. and Willie B. Cobbs, Apr. 18th

Sutherlands, Jas. C. and Mary R. M. Robinson, March 30th

Shackleford, J. and L. A. Humphreys, June 27th

1872

Sprouse, Charles L. and Lucretia Harlow, Jan. 11th

Shipley, Francis H. and Va. L. Harman, Feb. 20th

Smith, William P. and Eliz. Gibson, Mar. 26th

Summerson, Jas. E. and Eliz. Nuckalls, Apr. 16th

Sprouce, Burwell and Ann E. Gibson, Nov. 29th

Shifflet, George H. and Matilda Via, Nov. 17th

Sneed, Charles F. and Nannie M. Heard, Dec. 23rd

Smith, John E. and E. B. Morris, Dec. 5th

1873

Sprouse Thomas J. and L. A. Gibson, Jan. 30th

Stovall, Dr. J. T. and M. E. Watts, Apr. 2nd

Sapiter, R. C. and Martha E. Spencer, Apr. 14th

Smith, Chas. R. and F. W. Herring, Sept. 1st

Shepperd, Nathl and Mrs. Mary E. Mitchell, Oct. 20th

Shackleford, Zachariap and Lucy E. Walker, Dec. 13th

Shirley, James W. and Julia T. Browen, Oct. 27th

Stone, Stephen R. and Lucie M. Keblinger, Aug. 18th

Sandam, D. F. and Drisilla Scruggs, Dec. 30th

1874

Sandridge, Benj. and Sarah C. Maupin, Dec. 7th

Sprouse, Dabney and Anne E. Rayland, Apr. 29th

Sharewood, Edward R. and Amelia Harrison, Sept. 17th

Shewalter, Jas. D. and Martha A. Hicks, Sept. 13th

Sneed, Jno. A. and Jeannie P. Railey, Dec. 14th

Smith, Downing L. and Willie M. Marshall, Dec. 16th

Seale, T. G. and Ida Thacker, Dec. 22nd

Sacred, Geo. and Sarah J. Clemons, Dec. 28th

1875

Sewis, Thos. W. and Jane W. Page, Jan. 8th

Shifflett, Benj. and Lucy E. Marshall, May 8th

Stuart, Henry L. and Lucy L. Carr, June 2nd

Sprouse, Zacheria and Eliz. Sprouse, June 21st

Sprouse, Wm. N. and Frances Sprouse, Sept. 2nd

Sutter, Richard and Josephine Graves, Oct. 16th

Smith, Wm. N. and Eliza E. Gibson, Dec. 21st

Sanum, Jno. and Mary S. Critzer, Dec. 14th

Smith, Nathan and Mary E. Chisholm, Dec. 28th

1876

Shiffer, Edward P. and Lelia A. Baker, Jan. 8th

Simms, Jas. Monroe and Mary Durrett, Jan. 10th

Sprouse, Albert J. W. and Catharine Clemens, Mar. 1st

Shiflett, Edw. and Cordelia C. Via, Mar. 10th

Sprouse, Pleasant and Jenny Thacker, Apr. 7th

Suddarth, Geo. W. and Louisa V. Reynolds, Apr. 12th

Sandridge, Alfred W. and Lucy J. Coleman, Oct. 30th

Smith, Jno. A. and Amanda V. Priddy, Nov. 26th

1877

Smith, Edgar B. and Eliza J. Coleman, Feb. 26th

Smith, Jno. Wm. and Eliz. Ricks, Feb. 5

Smith, Geo. W. and Margaret N. Herron, Dec. 3rd

Sneed, Alexander and Amanda C. Durham, Apr. 12th

Smales, Chas. B. and Lucella Powell, Sept. 15th

Sandridge, Jas. W. and Fannie M. Gibson, Sept. 17th

Scott, Bradford R. A. and Mary M. Anderson, Sept. 26th

Shackleford, D. Rbt. B. and Endora F. Sampson, Oct. 31st

Shiflett, Jas. and Matilda A. Morris, Dec. 28

Sprouse, Jno. W. and Lucinda Sprouse, Sept. 26th

Sandridge, Eugene E. and Fanny R. T. Walton, Oct. 22nd

Summerson, Jas. E. and Ella Dennis, Feb. 24th

Shipp, Ellis J. and Rosina C. F. Long, Apr. 3rd

Sprouse Albert J. R. H. and Mrs. Elize Sacre, June 4th

Slaughter, Wm. T. and Harriet E. Miller, July 31st

1878

Sacre, William and Lucy J. Gibson, Aug. 1st

Seamonds, Hiram J. and Susan A. Gibson, Jan. 21st

Shepherd, James F. and Alice S. Owens, Mar. 13th

Shepherd, Jas. B. and Sarah E. Haggard, July 3rd

Scruggs, Geo. W. and M. E. Chisholm, Sept. 19th

Smith, Pharish and Mary Smith, Oct. 7th

Sprouse, John W. and Sally Kirby, Oct. 15th

Shepherd, Garrett and Susan M. Haggard, Nov. 22nd

Stickleman, John L. and Mrs. Eddie J. Anderson, Oct. 22nd

Shepherd, Henry W. and Carmelia T. Norris, Dec. 5th

Smith, George T. and Mary E. Wood, Dec. 10th

Sandridge, Jas. F. and Sally H. Biggers, Feb. 20th

Shepherd, John H. and Sarah L. Collins, May 6th

Sandridge, Robt. W. and Jane E. Page, Dec. 24th

1879

Scantling, Chas. W. and Mildred A. Ladd, Feb. 10th

Smith, Chas. H. and Sarah C. Ricks, Feb. 10th

Smith, John D. and Mary E. Norford, May 1st

Smith, Wyatt, T. and Willie F. Chisholm, Dec. 24th

Sinclair, Cephus H. and Julis S. Farish, June 4th

Sprouse, Edward and Mary Lee Sprouse, July 21st

Smith, Benj. L. and Willie A. T. Dunn, Sept. 16th

Spears, Harrison and Margaret Thomas, Nov. 22nd

Sibley, Benj. D. and Laura A. Hartnigle, Jan. 1st

Sampson, John R. and Annie E. Woods, June 10th

Scott, Charles L. and Louise M. Everett, Aug. 26th

Sprouse, Wm. H. and Sarah A. Hale, Sept. 9th

Sampson, Eugene and Maggie D. Lewis, Dec. 16th

Sprouse, Shelton and Bettie Thacker, Dec. 16th

Shelton, Francis and Roberta S. Wilhoit, Dec. 22nd

Smith, Jerry and Alice Barnett, Dec. 4th

1880

Smith, F. M. and Emma S. White, July 2nd

Scott, John A. and Lucy P. Waddell, July 7th

Shackleford, Jno. A. and Mary J. Duke, Aug. 17th

Sneed, Geo. Wm. and Mrs. Sallie Ellis, Aug. 12th

Sandridge, Dabney L. and Nannie E. Coleman, Nov. 15th

Sander, Wm. F. and Jannie Marshall, Nov. 17th

Smith, Barton and Rosa Ricks, Dec. 1st

1881

Snead, William Henry and Lousetta Kirby, Feb. 24th

Smith, James E. and Florence E. Smith, Jan. 3rd

Sammons, Thomas N. and Fanny H. Bullock, Feb. 15th

Strange, Burton W. and Isabella F. Sneed, Oct. 21st

Shiflett, Wm. and Roberta Gardner, Nov. 7th

Starke, George W. and Lenna W. Teel, Nov. 22nd

Sandridge, Alexander A. and Willie A. Walton, Dec. 8th

Smith, John D. and Florence C. Williams, Dec. 15th

1882

Slaughter, Charles and Mary W. Duke, Apr. 26th

Saleman, Benj. and Hannah Hahn, May 7th

Sprouse, Henry and Willie McCral, June 29th

Sprouse, Reuben and Sally Marsh, Sept. 6th

Shiflett, Albert M. and Eliza J. Shiflett, Sept. 17th

Sprouse, John and Isabella Sprouse, Oct. 18th

Shields, John A. and Cynthia A. Black, Oct. 18th

Staples, Willie D. and Willie Omohundro, Nov. 29

Snead, James C. and Ada B. Dull, Dec. 13th

Simms, John F. E. and Daisy R. Garth, Dec. 21st

Sandridge, Emmett R. and Nancy Ann Gibson, Dec. 14th

1883

Smith, Henry Lewis and Lydia Laura Lewis, Jan. 10th

Sneed, Edw. W. and Ida L. Baltimore, Apr. 10th

Sprouce, Andrew Dyer and Mineova A. Gibson, May 3rd

Shiflett, Lindsay and Cinthia Morris, July 8th

Stern, Samuel Aarson and Hawnie Lazans, Sept. 5th

Sprouse, Jerry Prestin and Mattie Amiss, Nov. 29th

1884

Scantling, Fernando W. and Mary Blanche Shanker, Jan. 9th

Sprouse, Chas. D. and Mary A. Hutchinson, Mar. 19th

Stout, Wm. J. and Mary Lizzie Harris, Apr. 29th

Shiflett, Dick and Mary Breeden, Apr. 27th

Smith, Robt. P. and Ludie L. Gay, Apr. 29th

Standwick, Robt. C. and Sallie P. Lewis, May 15th

Shackleford, L. Geo. and Virginia M. Randolph, July 1st

Scruggs, Jno. T. and Georgia McEues, July 15th

Scott, Lyttleton E. and Kittie Hoys Waddell, Aug. 6th

Stindwant, H. L. and Mary L. Huff, July 25th

Smith, Phaneb and Mollie E. H. Johnson, Aug. 13th

Smith, George D. and Willie Lee Gleason, Oct. 1st

Smith, Edgar and Sallie J. Lenahan, Oct. 30th

Shields, Wm. H. and Nannie H. Childress, Nov. 26th

Sours, John S. and Alice L. Collins, Nov. 23rd

1885

Sneed, Chas. E. and Mary H. Herndon, Jan. 1st

Sibley, Benj. Daniel and Blanch A. Hackbager, July 19th

Scrugg, Wm. H. and Eliza V. O'Brien, ———

Spencer, Robt. Alex and Nannie L. Bugg, Sept. 17th

Smith, Lewis Wade and Emma Allen Lane, Nov. 11

Smith, Wm. Henry and Eliz. Susan Hall, Nov. 11th

1886

Shumate, Norman T. and Lizzie R. Parrott, Jan. 6th

Smith, H. W. and Sally F. Luchado, Jan. 14th

Smith, Jno. E. and Mary Fanny Gay, Feb. 24th

Sprouse, Wm. and Margaret L. Kirby, Mar. 18th

Small, Alex J. and Alice G. Beasley, Apr. 27th

Sprouse, Wm. W. and Mattie E. Sprouse, July 14th

Scruggs, Robt. E. and Ellen A. Vasseur, Sept. 28th

Saibner, Geo. B. and Carrie L. Rothwell, Nov. 11th

Smith, Thos. D. and Norella G. Johnson, Dec. 23rd

Scott, John and Maria F. Johnson, Dec. 23rd

Shiflett, Garland and Keziab C. Morris, Dec. 23rd

Shelton, John G. and Judia Robertson, Dec. 29th

1887

Sneed, Robt. and Nannie A. Madison, Jan. 6th

Small, Clarence M. and Fannie P. Chapman, Jan. 12th

Starkes, Henry Franklin and Eliz. Ellen Haislip, Mar. 24th

Sneed, Edgar M. and Stella V. Stark, June 2nd

Scruggs, Jno. Edward and Maria June Rhodes, June 8th

Staton, B. F. and Cora B. Shaw, Aug. 16th

Smith, Albert W. and Eveline Abell, Nov. 8th

Stubbs, J. A. and Emma Donald, Nov. 12th

Shelton, Jno. B. and Willie D. Early, Dec. 19th

Sacree, Geo. W. and Susan G. Farish, Dec. 27th

1888

Sandridge, Henry D. and Ann S. Robinson, Jan. 25th

Sesler, Samuel and Amanda Gianniny, May 7th

Sheffield, L. J. and A. J. Burgess, June 23rd

Shafer, Wm. H. and S. E. Sprouse, Sept. 10th

Stewart, Wm. H. and Sallie M. Magruder, Sept. 20th

Sutherland, J. B. and Lizzie P. Boyd, Sept. 26th

Sandridge, N. T. and M. M. Sandridge, Oct. 8th

Sergeant, G. A. and Lucy F. May, Oct. 26th

Shiflett, G. L. and Alice Madison, Dec. 4th

1889

Shiflett, A. S. and R. C. Lansu, Jan. 7th

Sprouse, S. E. and Alice Shope, Mar. 7th

Shepherd, B. M. and M. G. Hall, May 6th

Sandridge, L. W. and S. E. Coleman, Oct. 7th

Shackleford, J. S. and S. E. Harlow, Oct. 10th

Sprouse, Eb. and Rosa B. Harlow, Nov. 13th

Sneed, R. E. and C. A. Horton, Nov. 19th

Smith, A. J. and Eliza Dudley, Dec. 2nd

Sutherland, W. H. and M. E. Edge, Nov. 14th

1890

Sams, C. W. and M. M. Minor, Oct. 23rd

Stratton, T. H. and B. G. Catterton, May 17th

Semonsan, Clinton and M. A. W. McNair, June 3rd

Sandridge, J. A. and B. A. Sandridge, July 7th

Shisler, J. R. and Va. L. Worsham, Oct. 4th

Smith, Philip W. and Cora L. Alure, Oct. 28th

Sandridge, J. J. and M. S. Elliott, Nov. 6th

Sullivan, Jackson and Fannie Dowell, Dec. 15th

Sandridge, L. L. and C. T. Bailey, Dec. 15th
Sandridge, J. E. and F. D. Horton, Dec. 20th
Sneed, A. J. and M. L. Bishop, Dec. 23rd

1891

Shiflett, J. K. and M. M. Morris, Feb. 28th
Spicer, C. P. and Susan Kinnedy, Apr. 2nd
Smith, A. W. and M. O. Martin, May 20th
Stickleman, Jno. L. and Cashime Kirtey, Aug. 8th
Snead, Len and Lena Powell, Aug. 8th
Scruggs, Wm. H. and Bessie Birckhead, Sept. 9th
Sullivan, Ira H. and Mary A. Durrett, Sept. 19th
Smith, J. L. and L. G. Fulcher, Sept. 21st
Shaver, A. G. and Jos. Garrison, Sept. 30th
Sprouse, Jno. and Lydia A. Thomas, Nov. 3rd
Shaver, Jno. and M. L. Sprouse, Nov. 24th
Shiflett, Jas. and M. F. Shiflett, Nov. 30th
Smith, Thos. W. and Bettie C. Munday, Dec. 14th
Shiflett, Ro. L. S. and S. K. Shiflett, Dec. 31st

1892

Spencer, C. W. and L. W. Cleveland, Feb. 9th
Stargell, Andrew J. and Jannie E. Drumheller, Apr. 4th
Sands, C. R. and M. S. Bowcock, Apr. 4th
Scribner, Geo. B. and Addie E. Douglas, May 17th
Smith, Jno. F. and Nancy Lane, June 21st
Sibut, Harvie and Lavia Long, June 29th
Shotwell, E. F. and L. O. Herring, Dec. 22nd

1893

Sprouse, Jno. S. and Vic Hawley, Jan. 4th
Spears, S. A. and M. V. Hall, Feb. 5th
Shiflett, Wm. H. and Lucinda F. Breedin, Feb. 15th
Spradling, Wm. and L. L. Clements, Mar. 17th
Sneed, Jas. and M. G. Woodward, Mar. 20th
Staton, W. W. and N. E. Maupin, Apr. 22nd
Suddarth, G. W. and L. A. Campbell, May 20th
Smith, E. F. and Eula H. Smith, June 9th
Shiflett, Jno. T. and Annie Norris, Aug. 31st
Steel, Ch. and T. L. Garrison, Oct. 2nd
Suddarth, W. D. and Nettie Suddarth, Dec. 1st
Spears, Wm. W. and T. A. Drumheller, Dec. 8th
Smith, Jno. R. and S. E. Terrell, Dec. 16th

1894

Smith, Jas. M. and Hattie B. Norford, Jan. 15th
Stargall, Wm. H. and Irena Critzer, Feb. 5th
Shelton, J. T. and M. S. Sutherland, Mar. 19th
Son, Jas. Wm. and M. J. Drumheller, May 3rd
Sprouse, Lewis and D. A. Sacree, June 22nd

Shiflett, Noah and Lucie Bruce, July 14th
Shelby, J. M. and Elizabeth M. Estes, Aug. 6th
Scantling, C. W. and M. M. Graves, Aug. 12th
Spencer, Jas. A. and Eliza C. Broun, Apr. 15th
Scruggs, Richard E. and Jennie Scruggs, Aug. 20th
Shiflett, O. F. and C. Shiflett, Aug. 22nd
Smith, Thos. H. and Margaret L. Kirby, Dec. 5th
Spears, Thos. H. and M. C. Drumheller, Dec. 7th
Stokes, P. S. and Ida Shaw, Dec. 19th
Stephens, R. M. and Lula A. Wilhoit, Oct. 22nd
Stoneman, P. N. and M. B. Purvis, Nov. 15th
Swisher, J. M. and Jsobe Moon, Nov. 16th
Smith, G. W. and W. J. Houchens, Dec. 24th

1895

Stark, A. H. and M. Stone, Jan. 23rd
Sneed, Robt. and Va. E. Farish, Jan. 23rd
Shiflett, Jacob and Mary Lamb, Feb. 14th
Sprouse, J. R. Rosa Gibson, May 8th
Sprouse, R. S. and M. G. Marsh, June 25th
Sutherland, Marcellus and Lucy A. Sheppard, July 16th
Smith, R. R. and G. E. Falcner, Sept. 4th
Smith, Chas. H. and Lucy M. Milton, Oct. 20th
Spicer, A. N. and Annie Rhodes, Nov. 11th
Seamonds, J. A. and Bess Birckhead, Dec. 10th

1896

Sneed, Floyd and Ada Powell, Mar. 11th
Shiflett, Links and Sarah Davis, Apr. 16th
Smith, Geo. W. and Ella I. Sanford, Apr. 20th
Snead, W. B. and Mollie Houser, May 20th
Shaver, Benj. L. and A. L. Garrison, Aug. 13th
Sprouse, Jno. and Cora L. Thomas, Sept. 22nd
Smith, Walter A. and Jane V. Lewis, Oct. 7th
Sprouse, Albert and Bettie Houchens, Oct. 14th
Spradling, J. F. and Rosa Sprouse, Nov. 19th
Sampson, J. W. and M. R. Shackleford, Nov. 25th
Smith, Wm. D. and M. J. Parish, Oec. 8th
Simpson, Thos. R. and Josephine Pleasants, Dec. 21st

1897

Shiflett, Jos. L. and Martha L. Marshall, Jan. 18th
Shiflett, H. R. and M. C. Shiflett, Jan. 27th
Salmon, W. L. and G. M. Smith, Mar. 17th
Shiflett, Amos S. and Lutie Morris, Mar. 22nd
Sneed, Alex and Virginia Collins, Apr. 24th
Strange, Robt. M. and Birdie A. Wash, June 15th

Shanks, Jas. and Winnie Robinson, July 20th
Shisler, Louis and Katie C. Gay, Aug. 24th
Sanford, M. R. and L. B. Marshall, Oct. 6th
Strange, Julius and Norvilla Clements, Oct. 9th
Schultz, Chas. and Lettie Critzer, Oct. 18th
Shaw, R. G. 2nd and Nancy W. Langhorne, Oct. 26th
Simmons, L. J. and Annie Jones, Oct. 26th
Shepherd, Geo. A. and Mattie M. Hall, Nov. 3rd
Street, Geo. L. and Emma D. Clements, Nov. 11th
Suddarth, J. R. and Mary A. Bibb, Nov. 22nd
Staples, T. E. and C. L. Barnett, Dec. 2nd

1898

Shiflett, B. S. and F. M. Lewis, Jan. 17th
Sprouse, T. B. and E. Va. Barnett, Mar. 10th
Sullivan, J. S. and Mattie B. Rea, Mar. 14th
Stargall, Jos. H. and Ada J. Wade, Apr. 25th
Smith, Frank E. and Edna E. Gibson, May 14th
Stevens, A. L. and Bettie B. Railey, June 28th
Sullivan, E. S. and Mary L. Marshall, July 9th
Staber, Caleb and W. G. Laird, July 21st
Saulsbury, W. H. and T. M. Thomas, Aug. 3rd
Sullivan, Wesley B. and Alice Dimmon, Aug. 13th
Sprouse, Henry and Eunice Gibson, Oct. 11th
Salmon, W. H. and I. B. Beck, Nov. 9th
Shiflett, Edw. and Bessie Shiflett, Nov. 18th
Shepherd, Wm. P. and Mary A. Pendlitin, Dec. 6th
Sandreidge, E. W. and Annie W. Sandreidge, Dec. 20th
Smith, J. D. and A. C. Dowell, Dec. 20th

1899

Sadler, Wm. J. and Betty R. Riley, Nov. 6th
Shackelford, A. C. and L. W. Shackelford, Dec. 11th
Smith, Edward E. and Maggie L. Salmon, Nov. 17th
Smith, A. F. and V. T. Gillispie, Nov. 20th
Smith, E. D. and Emma M. Mehring, Dec. 23rd
Smith, Wm. M. and Jessie L. Rea, Dec. 27th
Sprouse, Robt. and Sallie Thomas, Jan. 2nd
Suddarth, B. N. and F. E. Clements, Jan. 20th
Sclater, E. R. and S. E. Rothwell, Jan. 27th
Suddarth, D. L. and N. V. Campbell, Mar. 20th
Scantling, R. M. and M. J. Vest, Apr. 22nd
Sipe, Jacob and Julia Via, May 29th
Snead, Alonza H. and Annie V. Burton, June 3rd
Sprouse, R. A. and Lena Gibson, July 29th
Sode, Andrew F. and Minnia E. Hotopp, Sept. 18th
Sprouse, Robt. L. and Lizzie Morris, Oct. 2nd

1900

Sacre, John and Virginia Fisher, June 11th

Simmons, Wm. and Georgie M. Clements, May 16th
Sprouse, Ben and Maggie Sprouse, Aug. 6th
Sprouse, Dawson S. and Laura L. Sprouse, July 2nd
Staton, Jas. and Susie Napier, July 19th
St. Clair, R. A. and H. V. Lanhone, Aug. 22nd
Smith, C. H. and O. Va. Elsom, Sept. 26th
Shanks, G. W. and Lillie B. Horton, Oct. 9th
Sclater, M. T. and E. M. Boyd, Oct. 15th
Stone, Lindsay and Lillie F. Pitts, Oct. 29th
Sprouse, K. H. and Emma Sprouse, Nov. 19th
Sprouse, Wm. H. and Fannie E. Morris, Dec. 22nd
Shackleford, W. C. and Leila Lewis, Dec. 24th
Shiflett, A. E. and M. Shiflett, Jan. 17th
Shiflett, James E. and Mary E. Jones, May 12th
Smoot, L. E. and Mary McNeale, Dec. 26th
Spencer, Howard and Lillie May Melton, Dec. 28th

1901

Stuart, F. Lee and A. M. Rives, Mar. 18th
Sprouse, A. J. and N. H. Sprouse, Apr. 3rd
Shepherd, R. T. and D. D. Deane, May 24th
Spears, A. J. and L. L. Clements, Aug. 14th
Southworth, W. B. and G. Elsie Brown, Aug. 27th
Sanford, Bertie and Grace Etherton, Oct. 1st
Sprouse, A. J. H. and Mary Langhorne, Oct. 8th
Shiflett, Conway and Alice E. Shiflett, Oct. 11th
Sadler, A. W. and E. P. Payne, Oct. 15th
Sprouse, W. H. and R. S. Sprouse, Oct. 15th
Sonner, W. B. and Maggie M. Baber, Oct. 21st
Sensbaugh, J. P. and E. M. Moses, Oct. 23rd
Shiflett, Newman R. and Attelia Via, Oct. 31st
Skinner, Samuel L. and Betty Graves, Nov. 13th
Smith, Jno. F. and Jennie S. Powell, Nov. 14th
Stephens, G. B. and Clara M. Coffman, Dec. 6th
Shepherd, J. B. D. and B. M. Timberlake, Dec. 31st

1902

Sandridge, S. and L. Shiflett, Jan. 13th
Sprouse, E. L. and M. L. Tate, Feb. 12th
Siple, A. K. and Ann Mallow, Mar. 10th
Spincer, G. W. and Carrie L. Gibson, Apr. 29th
Shiflett, Bernard and Flo Shiflett, Sept. 3rd
Smith, J. G. and Alice Warren, Sept. 9th
Sadler, I. H. and M. Williams, Nov. 7th
Sandridge, E. W. and V. Lee Evans, Dec. 15th
Sprouse, A. C. and M. Johnson, Dec. 24th
Dec. 31st

1903

Shiflett, A. L. and Rosa Breeden, Feb. 12th
Snyder, A. M. and J. D. Foster, Mar. 12th

Spencer, Alonza and Minnie B. Spencer, Mar-
16th

Sandridge, S. N. and Mabel Mayo, Mar. 23rd

Sprouse, H. L. and Emma Moon, May 15th

Smith, Jno. M. and L. Lu Johnson, July 1st

Sprouse, Mannis and Nannie Maddox, July
8th

Sandridge, Logan W. and H. Sandridge, July
27th

Street, A. L. and Dixey Clay, Aug. 24th

Sprouse, T. W. and Elenore Sprouse, Sept.
14th

Spenor, Clifford and Eliza Wood, Oct. 1st

Sprouse, J. B. and M. Minter, Oct. 3rd

Shiflett, E. and S. A. Dorman, Oct. 9th

Shiflett, N. A. and S. B. Gibson, Oct. 20th

Shipp, Doctor and Burrell Campbell, Sept.
7th

Shackleford, H. W. and W. J. Moore, Oct.
26th

Smith, G. B. and T. S. Jarrell, Nov. 10th

Sandridge, Earnest and M. E. Madison, Nov.
23rd

Sprouse, G. H. and Sarah Woodson, Dec. 7th

Smith, Robt. E. and Sally Lupton, Dec. 15th

Shanks, Geo. A. and Sidney B. Balew, Dec.
22nd

1904

Stacy, LeeRoy and Oliva Mahanes, Apr. 2nd

Shaver, Lindwood and Addie Ward, June 15th

Ship, Jno. R. and Bertha M. Leake, Sept. 26th

Shipp, Doctor and Burrell Campbell, Sept.
7th

Shiflett, Thos. and Mildred Ann Sprouse,
Sept. 26th

Shiflett, Chris and Georgie P. Marshall, Oct.
3rd

Staples, Jno. D. and Maggie Faulconer, Oct.
11th

Stout, John Henry and Lulah Davidson, Oct.
11th

Smith, Eugene D. and Mary Broadhead,
Nov. 21st

Shilton, B. L. and Ann A. Wingfield, Dec.
10th

Sandridge, Herbert Early and Susan Mary
Ward, Dec. 17th

Sullivan, Jas. and Lizzie Hoy, Dec. 17th

Soule, Wm. Jackson and Bessie Watson Mawyer, Dec. 23rd

Sprouse, Chas. Anderson and Bird Mary Bagby, Dec. 28th

Sprouse, J. R. and Carrie Clements, Oct. 19th

Shiflett, Geo. B. and M. B. Shiflett, Dec. 29th

1905

Sebrell, Wm. and Nora Wingfield, Oct. 4th

Sebrell, William and Nora Wingfield, Oct.
4th

Sprouse, Albert and Rebecca Gibson, Jan. 25th

Sprouse, Richard Aubry and Lucinda Glass,
June 17th

Sprouse, John and Bertha Durham, May 25th

Sprouse, John R. and Rosa Gibson, Sept. 2nd

Sprouse, J. J. and Fanny Ray, Sept. 20th

Sprouse, Wm. Sam'l and Rosa Lee Thomas,
Nov. 16th

Sprouse, William Samuel and Rosa Lee
Thomas, Nov. 16th

Sprouse, Richd. Aubrey and Lucinda Glass,
June 17th

Sprouse, John R. and Rosa Gibson, Sept. 2nd

Shiflett, Edw. and Addie Veliva, Feb. 8th

Shiflett, Edw. and Lottie F. Via, Feb. 29th

Shiflett, Scofield and Lillie Shiflett, Nov. 15th

Shipp, Edward Lewis and Alma Pearl Young,
Dec. 23rd

Suddarth, J. A. and Mary M. Clemments,
Mar. 6th

Smith, Oscar Lee and Ola Newman Norford,
May 6th

Snapp, E. E. and Cora Lucy Hughes, Aug. 22nd

Staton, Wm. Garland and Edan Willis, June
21st

Stinson, J. B. and L. T. Jones, June 26th

Stinson, Luther Randolph and Mannie Daniel Scruggs, July 24th

Stinson, Luther Randolph and Nannie Daniel Scruggs, July 24th

Shiflett, Dean and Judy America Shiflett, July
18th

1906

Sheffield, Thomas H. and Cora Lee Marsh,
Feb. 7th

Shepherd, William Edward and Fanny Mann,
March 13th

Shiflett, John and Nora Shiflett, April 4th

Seiler, Samuel Henry and Mary L. Houchens,
April 25th

Shiflett, Edward and Elizabeth Shiflett, May
10th

Sprouse, Robert J. and Bettie Hicks, June 6th

Sandridge, John A. and Julia A. Marshall,
Aug. 6th

Sandridge, Lewis J. and Lucie B. Via, Aug.
19th

Shiflett, Joseph and Cora L. Blackwell, Aug.
20th

Skinner, D. S. and E. J. Garrison, Sept. 14th

Swink, Elmer and Sammie Wood, Sept. 19th

Staton, James L. and Willie Margaret Bowen,
Sept. 25th

Smith, Freeman T. and Orer R. Hall, Nov.
29th

Shiflett, George C. and Amanda J. Hutcheston, Dec. 22nd

Shackelford, Grigsby and Evelyn M. Page,
Dec. 22nd

Sutter, Richard and Lillian Hoy, Dec. 23rd

Sprouse, Grover C. and Virginia W. Brown,
Dec. 26th

1907

Shiflett, William K. and Lucy J. Shiflett, Jan.
13th

Shiflett, William B. and Selina K. Jones, May 10th

Scruggs, Sam and Virginia A. Moon, May 15th

Snead, John and Annie McClure, June 12th

Steger, D. C. and Annie Hughes, June 18th

Shiflett, Hiram and Gracie Moore, June 18th

Sprouse, C. R. and Olie Fisher, June 29th

Selam, George and Etta Gardner, July 29th

Smith, J. W. and Josephine Moyer, Aug. 25th

Shiflett, William T. and Nettie V. Shiflett, Aug. 28th

Sutherland, M. Y. and Ethel M. White, Sept. 4th

Snoddy, Walter and Anna P. Branham, Sept. 25th

Shiflett, Benjamin and Altha Lewis, Dec. 25th

Shuffler, Ralph S. and Carrie D. Henderson, Dec. 28th

1908

Sandridge, G. G. and May F. Crickenberger, Jan. 1st

Shiflett, Thomas L. and Mannie Bggou, Jan. 7th

Sprouse, Jack and Mollie Marsh, Jan. 8th

Smith, Willie and Senada Butler, April 3rd

Shiflett, Willie and Mollie Shiflett, April 8th

Sprouse, Charles R. and Olie Lee Ross, April 8th

Sprouse, Rhodes and Laura Ann Gibson, April 15th

Snyder, Everett and Mary Ranier, April 14th

Sandridge, Newton H. and Mrs. Creve Wood, May 12th

Sprouse, Andrew D. and Melissa B. Clements, June 2nd

Smith, J. O. and A. E. Morris, July 1st

Shiflett, Linwood E. and Nettie F. Shiflett, July 9th

Stone, Leon N. and Nettie E. Gentry, July 29th

Smith, John W. A. and Bessie T. Omohundro, Sept. 9th

Sinclair, Eugene Y. and Lelia M. Hamner, Sept. 17th

Sulllivan, Jeremiah M. and Josephine Maupin, Sept. 29th

Sutherland, M. Clark and Rosa Timberlake Page, Oct. 19th

Salmon, William Price and Lillie May Beck, Oct. 28th

Smith, Charles and Henrietta Nimmo, Nov. 4th

Smith, Louis and Lennie Norford, Dec. 11th

Sandridge, Sandy and Blanchie V. Via, Dec. 30th

Simpson, Ben and Annie V. Sneed, Dec. 30th

1909

Stevens, Charles B. and Fanny H. Wingfield, Jan. 27th

Sims, Jerry and Rose Leigh Hamner, Jan. 28th

Sandridge, Dillard and Minnie Coleman, March 1st

Sprouse, Albert T. and Mary Sacre, March 15th

Staton, James L. and Annie L. Ward, May 16th

Soule, William J. and Octavia Carroll, May 15th

Sandridge, E. L. and N. F. Madison, July 7th

Showers, James and Sallie B. Scantling, Oct. 21st

Sandridge, Eugene and Amanda Marshall, Oct. 27th

Schwal, Henry C. and Namie Clark, Nov. 21st

Sandridge, Laura K. and Vertie M. Batton, Nov. 28th

Sprouse, Lester and Loula Gibson, Dec. 19th

Shiflett, Henry and Flerry Shiflett, Dec. 17th

Shiflett, Cornelius and Nellie R. Payne, Dec. 24th

Spicer, William A. and Bessie Johnson, Dec. 27th

Simms, Hugh F. and C. Janie Railey, Dec. 29th

Shotwell, Jacob B. and Bertha C. Birckhead, Dec. 28th

1910

Shoves, Emmett and Edna Moore, Jan. 20th

Slaughter, Thomas F. and Louise Carpenter, Jan. 12th

Saunders, Henry and Allie Reid, Jan. 26th

Shiflett, Merrieweather and Amanda J. Garton, Feb. 9th

Shackelford, Dr. R. B. and Mary Breld Bolling, Feb. 8th

Sprouse, John D. and Ethel M. Durham, Feb. 15th

Stevens, Bland and Nannie Steward, March 26th

Sandridge, Henry H. and Sallie F. Ward, April 4th

Stevens, Philip and Lula M. Sandridge, April 6th

Shaver, Martin and Ada Randolph, April 19th

Suddarth, Rosser and Arnlia Carter, May 11th

Smith, William D. and Annie P. Harris, June 3rd

Sandy, William H. and Flora V. Ladd, June 6th

Sneed, John L. and Mary Margaret Marshall, July 20th

Sandridge, Ernest and Lucy F. Walton, Sept. 15th

Sinclair, Ben P. and Julia S. Farish, Sept. 20th

Smith, John A. and Essie C. Critzer, Oct. 10th

Sandridge, Percy W. and Nannie T. Batten, Nov. 10th

Sprouse, Howell and Rebecca Childress, Dec. 12th

Schultz, Charles R. and Ruth C. Humphrey, Dec. 20th

Spencer, Oscar N. and Minnie H. Mawyer, Dec. 28th

1911

Spicer, Henry David and Martha Ann Holloway, April 4th

Stargell, Andrew and Stenna Bishop, April 9th

Sprouse, Lindsay and Nellie Trusler, June 16th

Smith, Jr., Albert J. and Johetta Oliver, June 28th

Smith, Nathaniel and Geneiuene Garland, July 2nd

Starke, William Frederick and Lura Lillian Hicks, July 2nd

Sadler, Morton P. and Jacqueline Burton, Aug. 22nd

Smith, Oliver T. and Olie B. Miller, Sept. 20th

Sprouse, John W. and Irene Humphreys, Nov. 6th

Sanders, Cecil and Mary E. Harris, Nov. 20th

Smith, William and Lizzie Kirby, Nov. 24th

Sandridge, Joseph R. and Pluma S. Sandridge, Dec. 21st

1912

Sprouse, Tom and Effie Lony, March 4th

Sims, Jr., Endaline A. and Ollie Shepherd, March 14th

Shiflett, William D. and Harriet E. Stevens, April 7th

Sprouse, Richard W. and Myrtle Harlow, May 8th

Shiflett, R. B. and E. E. Morris, May 26th

Sprouse, Luther W. and Martha E. Knight, July 1st

Smith, Harrison and Carrie Cash, Sept. 7th

Sprouse, Perley L. and Lucy Reynolds, Sept. 16th

Shiflett, Sel and Mildred Couley, Oct. 11th

Smith, John W. and Mary Crickenberger, Dec. 22nd

1913

Shaver, Austin and Lena McCauley, Feb. 19th

Smith, Arthur and Grace White, Feb. 28th

Surtzer, James J. and Annie Tomlin, March 15th

Sprouse, John W. and Ella Hicks, March 31st

Shiflett, Lemuel and Lola B. Shiflett, April 1st

Spencer, Orville F. and Mabel Powell, April 5th

Smart, Dr. Francis P. and Mary E. McLeod, June 25th

Smith, Lewis W. and Lillian G. Abell, Aug. 16th

Smith, Lawson R. and Hettie Bunch, Aug. 20th

Shiflett, James H. and Mary F. Robbins, Sept. 19th

Swann, Edward and Beatria Gardner, Sept. 24th

Scott, James R. and Annie R. Reynolds, Oct. 1st

Sealock, Willie M. and Elsie Crickenberger, Oct. 1st

Sprouse, Peyton and Lessie Gibson, Oct. 20th

Sandford, Fred T. and Willie L. Garrison, Nov. 1st

Shanks, George A. and Myrtle M. Thurston, Nov. 15th

Shiflett, John M. and Lucy M. Shiflett, Nov. 19th

Smith, Henry H. and Mrs. Sallie A. Long, Dec. 23rd

Sandridge, James W. and Dorothy B. Morris, Dec. 23rd

Stubbs, Arthur L. and Lottie L. Demasters, Dec. 26th

Smith, Rockwell E. and Jean M. Dunnington, Dec. 30th

1914

Small, John A. and Masie Ward, Jan. 14th

Stribling, Graham A. and Lottie A. Wood, Feb. 11th

St. John, Wille E. and Ollie M. Allen, March 9th

Sprouse, Henry and Lena Woodson, March 20th

Sprouse, Frederick and Bertha Gibson, March 25th

Shiflett, Thomas and Lula V. Frazier, June 9th

Staley, D. R. and Emma E. Wyant, June 19th

Soule, Edwin E. and Maggie B. Thurston, June 20th

Smith, J. A. and May E. Dudley, July 2nd

Smith, James A. and Mrs. Lelia G. Gianniny, July 9th

Souders, Leo Francis and Minnie Lee Gentry, Aug. 6th

Shafer, Samuel Sandridge and Sarah Maupin, Aug. 11th

Shiflett, John E. and Catherine Shiflett, Sept. 9th

Smith, James J. and Ella W. Bulk, Oct. 9th

Sprouse, R. A. and Elizabeth Flannagan, Oct. 18th

Saunder, Jr., Samuel and Annie T. Harding, Oct. 28th

Stargall, Richard and Lillie Thomas, Oct. 29th

Smith, Robert R. and Lucy Nell Nichols, Nov. 16th

1915

Shiflett, Elias and Mollie Via, Feb. 11th

Spradlin, S. S. and Susie Elton, Feb. 17th

Shiflett, Charlie and Minnie L. Morris, Mar. 23rd

Shiflett, Martin and Addie Lewis, Apr. 12th

Scott, Lewis and Dorothy Johnson, Apr. 18th

Speaks, Charles B. and Lillian E. Smith, May 8th

Stadden, Robert W. and Nora Apple, May 18th

Scruggs, William W. and Nellie F. Payne, June 23rd

Sprouse, Landy R. and Lula Gibson, June 27th

Stone, John W. and Lilly Thacker, July 1st

Spottswood, Harry and Virginia Neggro, July 22nd

Shiflett, Haley F. and Ethel Martin, Aug. 16th

Sprouse, Willie and Katie Morris, Sept. 1st

Simmons, Isaac S. and Mattie Walton, Sept. 9th

Snead, Floyd and Kate Durham, Sept. 14th

Swink, Gillispie B. and Myrtle A. Wright, Oct. 4th

Snead, Arthur and Clarice Critzer, Oct. 14th

Sinclair, Clement and Carry Dunn, Oct. 14th

Sullivan, Jack and Maggie E. Ward, Oct. 18th

Shiflett, Harry and Lizzie Warton, Oct. 23rd

Sawyer, Roscoe R. and Ethel Drain, Oct. 27th

Shiflett, Gallie and Lena P. Handyshall, Nov. 5th

Smith, Floyd I. and Beatrice Harding, Nov. 9th

Shores, John and Florence Bryant, Dec. 7th

Stanford, W. D. and Rena Kidd, Dec. 7th

Sprouse, R. and Estelle Gibson, Dec. 12th

Sandridge, Eugene and Lelia Baber, Dec. 18th

1916

Schultz, Peyton J. and Hallie Ruth Smith, Jan. 1st

Slachter, James and Grace Shipp, Jan. 19th

Shiflett, Woodfork and Louise Lewis, Mar. 6th

Shiflett, Andrew and Lela G. Shiflett, Mar. 27th

Sprouse, William J. and Rosa Breeden, May 3rd

Sprouse, William and Ellen Hamm, May 17th

Snead, Russell L. and Elizabeth P. Reives, June 10th

Shiflett, Morton and Sadie Bruce, July 6th

Scrogahar, Joseph F. and Nannie E. Shiflett, Sept. 10th

Sellers, Theadore E. and Sally H. Wingfield, Oct. 25th

Spangler, Charles L. and Mabel C. Williams, Nov. 5th

Sullivan, Walter and Lou Rosa Powell, Dec. 5th

Sprouse, R. and Lutie Tate, Dec. 7th

Snyder, Henry A. and M. May Walverton, Dec. 13th

1917

Sipe, Raymond and Maggie Shiflett, Jan. 22nd

Smith, Thomas J. and Elma G. Smith, Jan. 31st

Smith, George P. and Hallie H. Harlow, Feb. 17th

Shepherd, Jr., H. C. and A. E. Lang, Mar. 17th

Scruggs, George F. and Lydia M. Anderson, Apr. 15th

Street, Alvin and Maggie L. West, May 2nd

Saunders, Thomas R. and Mary Ballard, May 9th

Smith, John W. and Bessie E. Dudley, May 6th

Snead, Grover and Annie M. Dolen, July 15th

Seldominney, Charles L. and Annie K. Reed, July 18th

Shiflett, Samuel and Lizzie R. Cox, Aug. 10th

Shanklin, Aleneron W. and Aurelia M. Zirkle, Aug. 15th

Sullivan, Golden and Mannie Batten, Apr. 22nd

Shiflett, Phillip and Elizabeth Branham, Sept. 10th

Shiflett, Jessie and Virginia R. Roberts, Sept. 19th

Smith, James A. and Viola Dudley, Sept. 20th

Shiflett, McKinley and Laura B. Shiflett, Sept. 28th

Strange, Julius M. and Cora Spears, Oct. 20th

Shiflett, George and Hazel Garrison, Oct. 31st

Stargall, Arthur and Estelle Claiborne, Nov. 9th

Smith, Walter R. and Beatrice E. Leake, Dec. 25th

1918

Soule, Edwin E. and Rhoda L. Wood, Feb. 20th

Sandridge, William T. and Ethel L. Harris, May 1st

Stevens, Donald G. and Kathryn Loving, May 8th

Sleeth, Robert and Minnie S. Diggs, May 14th

Schnabel, Arthur and Mattie Marsh, May 30th

Shiflett, Willie and Martha Lewis, June 3rd

Sprouse, Wesley and Leah Rute, Sept. 1st

Sinler, Norman F. and Jessie G. Pierce, Oct. 5th

Simpson, Charlie and Myrtle Eubank, Dec. 20th

Showalter, Parke M. and Gladys P. Hamilton, Dec. 24th

1919

Spradlin, Willie M. and Sallie Robinson, Jan. 18th

Sandridge, James Thomas and Marie J. Gentry, Feb. 1st

Snead, Aubrey and Flora Lee Powell, Feb. 6th

Stringfellow, Frank and Ruth F. Lichliter, Feb. 20th

Shiflett, Arthur and Lily Mowbray, Mar. 1st

Snow, William Thomas and Susie B. Gibson, June 4th

Shiflett, Thomas and Barbara Fraizer, June 7th

Sam, Henry E. and Myrtle Rogers, June 11th

Sanger, Paul B. and Sophie E. Via, June 25th

Shiflett, George H. and Eva Lonie Niceby, June 30th

Sprouse, Joseph and Goldie C. Belew, July 3rd

Sprouse, James F. and Virginia L. Gibson, July 3rd

Shiflett, George F. and Ada Powell, July 26th

Sprouse, Rhodes E. and Mary E. Morris, Aug. 23rd

Sacre, Richard and Laura Gibson, Aug. 28th

Shadacle, Dr. William G. and Bessie T. Smith, Nov. 3rd

Seiler, George W. and Gladys Kourse, Nov. 27th

Short, Clark and Maidie Hensley, Nov. 26th

Sprouse, Albert J. H. and Susie Frazier, Dec. 20th

Salmon, William B. and Sarah E. Wood, Dec. 30th

1920

Shiflett, Robert E. and Jennie M. Hall, Jan. 16th

Snead, Grant and Carrie Thomas, Jan. 21st

Shiflett, Thomas and Lois Maupin, Jan. 23rd

Salmon, Reuben M. and Katie G. O. Brun, May 3rd

Scruggs, Dewey and Edith Thompson, July 10th

Spears, Lee H. and Bessie V. Critzer, Sept. 15th

Shiflett, William Dewey and Mary M. Wood, Sept. 27th

Smith, Willie E. and Ethel L. Mitchell, Oct. 6th

Stanford, Frank and Anna Colesberry Williamson, Nov. 1st

Shipp, Bernard A. and Lenora Webb, Nov. 9th

Sacre, John Lewis and Lucy Minter, Dec. 8th

1921

Shiflett, Joseph R. and Carrie E. Fisher, Jan. 21st

Shiflett, Emory and Ella Shiflett, Feb. 1st

Shiflett, Charles Howard and Bessie Davis, Feb. 8th

Spears, William Henry and Ida Drumheller, Mar. 26th

Shiflett, James H. and Lou A. Shiflett, Apr. 4th

Sheffer, John Edward and Ella Merle Rea, Apr. 4th

Staton, Benjamin W. and Jurushie Banton, May 24th

Sprouse, Joe Frank and Ida Hoover, June 20th

Shiflett, James C. and Grace Morris, Sept. 6th

Smith, Robert W. and Lillie G. Ferneyhough, Nov. 19th

Snow, William C. and Mary Frances ?

Sprouse, Samuel and Virgie M. Sprouse, Dec. 22nd

Scantling, Norman L. and Virginia A. Thurston, Dec. 29th

1922

Shiflett, Arthur and Thresa Shiflett, Mar. 10th

Stepherson, Alexandria S. and Nannie W. Gill, Mar. 30th

Scott, Mike and Myrtle Harris, Apr. 27th

Sacre, Roy and Searetha Gibson, May 6th

Smith, Louie E. and Beulah P. Marshall, May 20th

Shiflett, George and Bertha Shiflett, July 6th

Spradlin, Ollie H. and Lilly Robinson, July 11th

Smith, Samuel S. and Evelyn E. Gianning, July 26th

Stevens, Milton C. and Mary L. Leake, Aug. 12th

Sutherland, Boyd C. and Mary J. White, Aug. 18th

Stargell, Walter J. and Lucy S. Cleveland, Sept. 5th

Sprouse, Fred and Ruby Gibson, Sept. 13th

Sprouse, Roy and Gracie Sprouse, Sept. 24th

Sprouse, Perly and Mary S. Woodson, Oct. 9th

Shiflett, Jr., Edward L. and Ora Edna Wood, Dec. 2nd

Sipe, Charlie and May Mahanes, Dec. 2nd

Shiflett, Robert B. and Clara Bruce, Dec. 26th

Saltoff, Dan and Emily Sprouse, Dec. 18th

Sims, Mark M. and Viola Gibson, Dec. 27th

Sprouse, Alexandria and Essie M. Gibson, Dec. 22nd

1923

Sandridge, Luther R. and Virginia Thurston, Jan. 2nd

Shiflett, William David and Matilda Morris, Feb. 2nd

Sherrell, Charlie L. and Mary L. Marrs, Feb. 21st

Shaver, Nick and Lilian Shiflett, Feb. 27th

Simpson, Hurbert S. and Mable D. Gough, Mar. 31st

Smith, Emory B. and Gladys P. Leake, May 15th

Shiflett, Broadus and Katherine Walton, May 25th

Shepherd, Richard Lee and Susie Kent Hughes, May 25th

Sutton, Howard M. and Willie Mitchell, May 29th

Spanker, Stephen M. and Cynthia P. Cook, July 28th

Sprouse, Randolph and Maggie Falwell, Aug. 23rd

Scott, Elmore and Bertha Bryant, August 26th

Saunders, Roy and Evie Morris, September 8th

Seiler, Roy A. and Alice A. Quinn, September 12th

Sofley, George E. and Lucy S. Branham, September, 15th

Shiflett, Roy J. and Ula Jordan, September 24th

Shiflett, Oscar and Pearl Shiflett, September 28th

Sears, Archie A. and Virgie B. Marshall, October 27th

Stargell, John H. and Euniter M. Hawkins, November 6th

Shiflett, Clarence and Nellie Shiflett, December 3rd

Shiflett, Warner and Nellie Shiflett, December 16th

Shiflett, Elmer L. and Ethel Shiflett, December 24th

1924

Scott, Joseph and Ada V. Bryant, Feb. 14th

Shiflett, Allie B. and Alice R. Herring, Mar. 13th

Shiflett, Luther W. and Grace V. Shiflett, May 5th

Scruggs, Joseph and Annie Sipe, May 10th

Smith, Sidney W. and Viola M. Saunders, May 31st

Shiflett, Kys and Maggie Roberts, Aug. 26th

Sharpe, Edwin F. and Virginia M. Farley, Aug. 30th

Smith, Dewey and Mary Dudley, Sept. 22nd

Shiflett, Albert and Bessie Mawyer, Sept. 25th

Sprouse, Wesley and Ruby Gibson, Oct. 2nd

Sprouse, Walter and Grace Clements, Oct. 11th

Shiflett, Prentis and Vessie Shiflett, Oct. 30th

Snead, Lawson and Ruby Carter, Nov. 14th

Shiflett, Ashby and Myrtle Harlow, Nov. 17th

Siple, Charlie and Annie Robertson, Nov. 26th

1925

Sullivan, Newman and Mary Herring, Jan. 15th

Sandridge, Bernie and Bessie Payne, Mar. 17th

Squire, George H. and Margaret Peters, Apr. 1st

Stephens, Joseph W. and Maude Farish, Apr. 11th

Shaver, Henry and Nora Lamb, May 6th

Snead, Robert and Bessie Gardner, June 3rd

Shiflett, Chancellor and Bertha Lamb, Aug. 6th

Sprouse, Richard W. and Lillie Dunwan, Aug. 8th

Shiflett, Robert and Margaret Craig, Oct. 5th

Smith, Herman G. and Mary Ellen Hilt, Oct. 6th

Shotwell, Stanley and Dorothy Virginia Albest, Oct. 23rd

Suddarth, Joseph B. and Fannie B. Bishop, Oct. 31st

Saunders, Lewis and Grace Drumheller, Nov. 14th

Stump, John E. and Irene B. Jones, Nov. 12th

Sacre, Jack and Gertie Gibson, Dec. 11th

Seigfield, Lindsey D. and Stella E. Earhart, Dec. 26th

Sandridge, Zetter and Ida Belle Vess, Dec. 24th

1926

Sievra, Julio Jimener and Lucile O. Payne, February, 3rd

Smith, Charles H. and Mabel E. Johnson, February 19th

Shiflett, Emitt and Tritty Mae Morris, May 14th

Sprouse, Fred and Mannie Stepp, May 24th

Sandridge, Guy D. and Gladys Madison, May 28th

Shiflett, James and Cora Shiflett, June 12th

Shelton, James L. and Pauline Wright, June 14th

Smith, George D. and Bessie Maupin, June 26th

Shackelford, Clarence A. and Cora Maupin, June 29th

Sandridge, John A. and Bonnie F. Dudley, July 7th

Smith, John H. and Edna E. Clayton, September 1st

Shiflett, Carl and Mary Wood, September 24th

Shiflett, Dewey and Cordelia Morris, October 23rd

Shiflett, Ellis and Annie Marrs, November 17th

Spencer, Edward W. and Myrtle Manuel, November 27th

Shiflett, Floyd E. and Pricy Sandridge, December 23rd

Shiflett, Herbert C. and Ruby L. Mundy, December 24th

1927

Shiflett, Jack L. and Sarah Barnett, March 26th

Smith, Roland A. and Arnette Thomas, April 16th

Shiflett, Lucian Y. and Virginia L. Shiflett, May 17th

Smith, James R. and Dorothy Whitten, June 27th

Sandridge, Malcolm W. and Davidson E. Hildebrand, July 30th

Shiflett, John F. and Bessie Lamb, August 1st

Sandridge, Carl W. and Gertie W. Toombs, August 29th

Spencer, Kirkwood, A. and Louise P. Pitts, September 20th

Snead, Jr., Nash P. and Janie M. Vermillon, October 10th

Solomon, McCauley and Tressie Mallow, October 20th

Sullivan, Weldon annd Isabel Morris, November 11th

Shiflett, Ernest and Emma G. Davis, December 20th

Sharpe, Lewis and Carrie Black, December 24th

1928

Shiflett, David and Elsie Bennett, January 14th

Smith, Paul and Nella Clarke, February 11th

Shiflett, Willie S. and Minnie B. Morris, February 24th

Shiflett, William H. and Laura M. Payne, February 29th

Sprouse, Lewis and Ruth Barnett, March 13th

Stinespring, William F. and Mary F. Albright, April 4th

Snow, Clarence and Mamie Garrison, April 23rd

Shiflett, Eunice and Lonie Shiflett, April 26th

Sandridge, Dabney W. and Josephine Coleman, May 2nd

Sprouse, Roland M. and Grace L. Critzer, June 13th

Scott, Thomas O. and Phyllis G. Rea, June 16th

Schofield, Edwin J. Jr., and Nannie S. Harris, June 17th

Shiflett, Cleveland and Elva R. Shiflett, June 17th

Surgant, George W. and Ida M. Hiles, June 16th

Sandridge, Charles J. and Eula M. Wyant, June 27th

Sandridge, Obra F. and Millie Louise Glass, July 9th

Shelton, Jr., Berkley W. and Alberta C. Rhodes, August 28th

Stargall, Thomas H. and Flossie M. Drumheller, September 22nd

Saunders, William A. and Pearl R. Bailey, November 17th

Sipe, Arthur G. and Elnora Ladd, November 23rd

Staton, Dabney R. and Eva M. Hunt, December 1st

Shiflett, Albert M. and Frances C. Shiflett, December 13th

Sacre, Everett and Gertrude Shiflett, December 29th

Shiflett, Joseph and B. Frances Sprouse, December 31st

1929

Seaes, Milton B. and Virginia D. Toms, January, 19th

Sprouse, William N. and Annie Virginia Banks, March 31st

Sprouse, Lewis W. and Mary E. Clements, May 18th

Sutton, Clifford L. and Laura A. Hurtt, May 18th

Schultz, Harry F. and Mary E. Murray, June 3rd

Seiler, Samuel L. and Evelyn H. Smith, June 6th

Smith, Willie M. and Mary C. Fincham, July 3rd

Shiflett, Kemper, and Cora Frazier, July 19th

Staton, Edwood and Fannie Breeden, July 23rd

Shiflett, George E. and Carrie P. Shiflett, July 30th

Smith, Cary W. and Virginia R. Kent, August 10th

Shiflett, Martin and Mary Birckhead, August 21st

Spencer, Howard and Susie Short, August 24th

Sprouse, James M. and Martha A. Woodson, August 27th

Shiflett, Emanuel and Fannie Shiflett, September 30th

Sprouse, Rubin and Nora Birckhead, October 12th

Shaver, Frederick and Janie Dovel, November 7th

Smith, Wilber Scott and Grace E. Mahanes, November 8th

Starcher, Harry W. and Eleanor F. Buchahan, November 9th

Scott, John and Nellie Brown, December 31st

T

1782

Tapp, Vincent and Susannah Gambell, June 22nd

1783

Terrell, Chiles and Margarett Meriwether, February 10th

1784

Timberlake, Joseph and Ann Douglass, December 11th

1785

Thurman, Richard and Mary Gardner, March 22nd

Tindall, John and Elizabeth Shelton, May 30th

1786

Thompson, John and Martha Langford, September 5th

Thomson, William and Frances Hoomes, September 16th

Tyra, Jonathan and Usly Gowing, October 21st

Tulley, Richard and Elizabeth Ballard, April 26th

1787

Thurmond, William and Mary Dickerson, January 10th

Thurmond, William and Martha Gooch, December 4th

Travillian, Thomas and Mary Carr, December 11th

Tylor, Thomas and Rosanah Terrell, January 31st

1788

Taylor, John and Anna Alford, December 14th

Tool, John and Sarah Moran, December 23rd

1791

Tinsley, John and Ann Washington, August 19th

Turner, George and Annay Maupin, February 14th

1792

Thomas, Michael and Elizabeth Staiton, December 1st

Thompson, William and Anna Mullins, November 8th

Tombs, John and Sally Graves, April 23rd

1793

Trower, John and Nancy Robinson, December 19th

Turner, Reuben and Nancy Jones, October 1st

1794

Thacker, Ezekiel and Anne Wood, March 20th

Tennell, Joseph and Mary P. Hicks, August 15th

Thomas, James and Lucy Glasby, September 20th

Travillian, Edmond and Susannah Carr, January 27th

Twyman, Joseph and Lucy Rodes, September 26th

1795

Terry, Nathaniel and Franky Watts, November 24th

Thomas, Lewis and Elizabeth Lane, August 28th

Thompson, Nathaniel and Lucy Brown, December 14th

1796

Tinnall, John and Elizabeth Meeks, August 2nd

Turner, Jerisha and Polly Dalton, March 16th

1798

Tilman, Jacob and Sally P. Lewis, December 8th

Toms, Alexander and Nancy Graves, November 9th

1799

Taylor, Joseph and Nancy T. Groom, December 31st

Terrell, Robert and Polly Lacy, April 30th

Tinnel, Hancock Lee and Susannah F. Hitchcock, May 29th

1801

Tennall, Robert and Susanna Pace, April 25th

Thomas, John and Jennett Haner, June 13th

1802

Thomas, Charles L. and Margaret M. Lewis, August 31st

Twyman, William and Lucy Crenshaw, November 1st

1803

Thorpe, George and Sarah Walker, May 13th

Tuggle, John and Elizabeth Gianniny, November 14th

Turner, William and Susannah Naylor, October 26th

1804

Thomas, Reuben and Polly Eubank, December 3rd

Tisdale, Robert and Mary Henderson, January 31st

1805

Thomas, Kemp and Nancy Baber, December 14th

Thomas, Ralph and Spicey Thomas, July 23rd

Thomason, John and Betsey Munday, February 18th

Thompson, Nelson and Hannah Blane, September 30th

Thurmond, Thomas and Patsey Norvell, January 25th

Tracy, Perry B. and Elizabeth Norvell, March 6th

1806

Townly, ? and Elizabeth Foster, November 26th

1807

Taylor, Brockman and Sally Herring, January 3rd

Thomas, Carver and Susan Watts, August 3rd

Tilman, Thomas and Patsy Morris, October 16th

Tyree, James and Caty Gowen, December 21st

1808

Thacker, Martin and Sally Barnett, January 11th

Tully, William and Liddy Jarrol, January ?

1809

Thomas, ? and Nancy Maupin, October 18th

Tilman, Paul and Jane Fitch, February 7th

Tomblin, William and Mary Leigh, December 22nd

1810

Thomas, James and Nancy Gaston, November 5th

Thomas, William and Jerusha Topling, March 27th

Thompson, Richard and Mary Rogers, May 29th

Thurmond, Thomas and Elizabeth Thomas, June 4th

Turner, Garfield and Ann Buck, January 15th

1811

Thomas, John H. and Nancy Gillum, September 30th

Thurmond, Thomas and Polly Johnson, January 8th

Turner, Joseph and Elizabeth Hestand, October 15th

Turner, ? and Isabella Hopkins, December 16th

1812

Taliaferro, Fletcher and Marie Lewis, February 13th

Taylor, William and Susannah Ashly, September 2nd

Thacker, Eli and Susannah Moore, August 1st

Thacker, Joseph and Nancy Moore, January 25th

Thomas, Edward and Mary Hamner November 16th

Thomas, John and Nancy Garton, January 30th

Tomblin, John and Nancy Tomblin, March 30th

Tomblin, John and Lucy Burton, December 22nd

Trevillian, Hundley and Patsy Fitch, January 6th

Triall, John G. and Elizabeth Binum, December 28th

Turhe, William W. and Sarah Harris, December 14th

1813

Teel, Lewis and Malerida W. Martin, November 15th

Thomas, Rhodes and Betsy Robertson, September 7th

Thompson, William S. and Eaves C. Bowen, March 1st

1814

Thomas, James and Mildred Hopkins, November 22nd

Travillian, James and Mildred Carr, December 15th

1815

Thacker, ? and Celia Sprouce, April 22nd

Thurmond, John T. and Alley Johnson, December 11th

Tooley, John and Polly Gilmore, May 4th

1816

Taylor, William and Darcus McCord, June 18th

Thomas, William and Peggy Carver, December 25th

Thompson, William and Mary Ballard, September 4th

Thurmond, Elisha and Lettice Hall, November 4th

Thurmond, Elisha H. and Mary D. Dickinson, December 18th

Tompkins, William and Ann Hudson, August 6th

Truslow, Thomas B. and Susan Bettys, January 24th

1817

Thacker, John and Sarah Key, December 17th

Thomas, Fountaine and Anna Hall, December 1st

Thompson, Nathaniel and Temperance Crenshaw, September 2nd

Triall, Stephen S. and Jane Maxwell, September 23rd

Twyman, Charles M. and E. A. H. Harring, December 11th

1818

Tate, John and Susanna Bowles, February 12th

Terrill, Lewis W. and Martha Loving, November 4th

Thacker, David and Sally Powell, April 6th

Thomas, John and Sarah Hill, August 6th

Travillian, Gordon C. and Hendley Carr, September 17th

1819

Thacker, Isom and Abby Thacker, November 4th

Thomas, James W. and Eliza Johnson, June 7th

Tomes, William and Susan Tomes, November 13th

Toms, Smithson and Nancy Jackson, May 11th

1820

Taylor, Benjamine and Mary McDaniel, September 4th

Thomas, Achilles and Rachel Baber, January 25th

Tilman, Zachariah and Patsy Moon, December 20th

1821

Thacker, Benjamin and Elerr Thacker, June 13th

Thomason, Richard and Sally Carden, March 20th

Thompson, Nelson and Malinda Lively, October 18th

Tomblin, James and Eliz. Tomblin, April 24th

1822

Tapp, Henry J. and Frances Gaimbell, December 12th

Tapscott, William H. and Eliza C. Chilores, May 27th

Thacker, Ezekial and Abby Dove, December 8th

Thomas, Samuel and Patsy Munday, August 8th

Tomes, Robert and Mary Ellerton, November 21st

Turner, Alex and Sarah Toms, December 27th

1823

Taylor, Benjamin T. and Sarah W. Coles, September 24th

Tooley, James and Susannah Pettett, October 21st

Turner, Samuel and Charlone Eades, February 25th

1824

Tate, Wills and Mary Gowing, November 4th

Thacker, Wilson and Mary B. Wingfield, December 23rd

Tompkins, Samuel W. and Sarah E. Gieme, April 22nd

Toms, Washington and Eliz. Toms, February 21st

Tyler, Joseph and Polly Pace, August 24th

1825

Taylor, William and Mary Bishop, April 27th,

Terrell, Richard, Jr., and Lucretia Lacey, August 11th

Thurston, Thomas and Eliz. Watson, December 25th

Thomas, Jessee and Mahala Correll, October 18th

Tompkins, James and Sarah E. Minor, December 19th

1826

Taylor, James and Lucy Jane Bailey, December 23rd

Tomblin, James and Mary Strange, April 11th

1827

Thurmond, William and G. A. Norvell, March 20th

True, James and Elizabeth Eastin, February ?

1828

Taylor, William and Susannah Bailey, March 26th

Thompson, William and Eliz. Ward, October 9th

Thurmond, Benjamin and Nancy W. Baber, April 10th

Tomblin, Thomas and Ann Jackson, June 21st

True, James and Ann Turner, October 12th

1829

Taylor, James and Mary Grooms, January 5th

Thacker, John R. and Jane Thorp, November 19th

Thomas, John and Frances C. Sullivan, January 6th

Thomas, Robert W. and Araminta Harden, April 6th

Thompson, David and Dorathor Crenshaw, July 6th

Tompkins, Albert G. and Sarah S. Robertson, October 22nd

Tompkins, Hiram A. and Sarah Ann Estes, October 27th

Tyree, Garrett and Mary Barnett, August 11th

1830

Thomas, Edward and Cally Man, December 21st

Thomas, Hudson and Sarah Clear, November 18th

Thomas, Thomas and Frances L. Silvey, December 15th

Thorp, Peter and Elizabeth Middlebrook, July 27th

Trower, John W. and Jane Breedlove, September 7th

1831

Taylor, George and Elizabeth F. Taylor, November 7th

Taylor, Simpson F. and Virginia Dowell, April 9th

Thacker, Henry and June Reynolds, November 7th

Truehart, Charles S. and Mildred H. Rose, November 9th

Turpin, George W. and M. B. Dickerson, January 5th

1832

Tate, Noah and Jensy Gowing, October 23rd

Taylor, John Jr. and Elizabeth S. Patterson, February 14th

Thomas, Garland and Aley Ann Kerby, December 6th

Thomas, Gipe and Nancy Gowing, October 23rd

Thurmond, John and Martha A. Y. Thomas, August 6th

Thurston, John W. and Mary E. Morris, November 22nd

1833

Thomas, Ralph and Lucy Brown, December 3rd

Tyler, John and Emily Susan Grove, April 9th

1834

Taylor, John C. K. and Patsy J. Randolph, December 22nd

Terrell, Albert C. and Eliza M. Barksdale, October 8th

Thomas, John L. and Nancy Thomas, March 3rd

Thurmond, David H. and Elizabeth B. Napier, March 31st

Trice, Benjamin F. and Sarah E. Phillips, January 16th

Twyman, Joseph W. and Elizabeth L. Crank, December 12th

1835

Taylor, John W. and Anna A. Taylor, March 6th

Terrell, William S. and R. Roberts, October 1st

Thacker, William and Eliza Curry, October 14th

Thomas, Albert and Catharine Norvell, August, 29th

Thurmond, George W. and Eliza Catterton, September 21st

1836

Taylor, Zachariah and Fran Pritchett, January 1st

Thomas, William A. and Eliza J. Collins, December 1st

Thurmond, Jorden and Sophia Thurmond, November 3rd

1837

Taylor, A. and Martha Foster, November 13th

Taylor, Charles W. and Martha R. Duke, February 14th

Terrell, Lewis K. and Mary E. Whitemurst, February 9th

Thomas, Alsen and Mary Martin, February 20th

Thomas, James and Emily Wood, January 10th

Thomas, John B. and M. A. Mann, July 15th

Thompson, Alfred and Sarah E. Sneed, October 24th

Thurmond, John W. and Mary Ann Simms, December 20th

Tompkins, W. W. and Frances S. Pendleton, May 24th

1838

Thomas, R. B. and Mildred Ann Sadler, December 4th

Townsend, William and Mary Winebarger, December 4th

1839

Thacker, John and Eliz. Britt, February 27th

Thomas, Joseph and Virginia Wood, December 17th

Turner, William H. and Mary P. Moon, January 7th

1840

Taxada, Lewis E. and Ann Lyon, August 3rd

Taylor, William P. W. and M. A. Fadley, December 30th

Thurmond, Benjamin and Mary A. Yancey, January 6th

Timberlake, E. J. and A. M. Bibb, December 29th

1841

Taylor, William and Ann A. Norris, May 17th

Teele, Samuel M. and Agness E. Johnson, April 3rd

Thacker, Lindsay and Polly Barnett, December 21st

Thompson, James and Agness A. White, January 22nd

Tunstall, Stokes and Elizabeth R. Mills, September 2nd

1842

Teel, John A. and Jane E. Teel, March 24th

Terrell, George H. M. and Virginia A. Brown, February 7th

Thurston, James A. and Mary Jane Clarke, October 13th

Todd, James H. and Mary E. Henderson, November 17th

Trice, Thomas M. and Mary M. Moon, September 6th

1843

Terrell, George and Frances A. Smith, April 3rd

Thacker, Benjamin and Adaminto Sarah Thacker, November 6th

Thacker, Nelson and Mary Sprouse, March 2nd

Thomas, David W. and Susan F. Garton, November 7th

Tilman, Overton G. and Susan Fretwel, November 28th

Timberlake, Gideon H. and Lucy M. Goodman, June 15th

Toms, Chastian and Eliza Ann Baber, January 20th

1844

Taylor, Valentine and M. A. Brockman, April 23rd

1845

Thacker, S. W. and Lucy Ann Dawson, January 8th

Thompson, William Rassel and Tomalia, V. Woodson, October 1st

Tilman, Paul Jr., and M. A. Fretwell, July 28th

Tucker, James and E. A. Foster, November 25th

1846

Taylor, Randolph and Emily Cooke, December 1st

Thomas, David and Frances Wood, May 25th

Tilman, Paul and Lucy Gillum, September 21st

Tomblin, Horace P. and Mildred Baber, December 23rd

Tyler, John W. and Caroline A. Branham, July 20th

1847

Thomas, James R. and M. J. Smith, February 17th

Timberlake, Horatio J. and G. Ann Sneed, October 27th

Tomblin, David J. and M. E. Martin, May 5th

Tooley, Joshua and Eliz. Gilmore, November 26th

1848

Tate, Hudson and M. S. Sneed, February 17th

Thurmond, Edward and A. R. Rogers, August 3rd

Tilman, William D. and N. F. Maupin, April 20th

Turner, William A. and Dollie Johnson, October 24th

1849

Taylor, Francis M. and Nancy Glass, March 24th

Tucker, George and E. A. Gilmer, September 19th

1850

Tate, Francis W. and Martha P. Norris, November 10th

Thomas, John and Eliz. Barnett, September 1st

Thomas, William and Susan Davis, August 8th

Thomley, James and Catharine C. White, April 16th

Townly, John B. and Susan L. Moore, December 24th

True, Robert N. and Lucy J. Minor, January 31st

1851

Thacker, Elias and Ruth A. Thacker, December 10th

Thomas, Thomas and Anna A. Gardner, September 14th

Thomeson, Samuel and Jane Woodson, May 6th

Thompson, Andrew J. and Aliena Virginia, February 23rd

Thompson, William N. and Nancy E. Ward, September 18th

Toms, Wilton and Angelina Field, February 13th

1852

Taylor, James F. and Martha Flannagin, December 1st

1853

Thacker, Elias A. and Mary M. Beddow, January 10th

Thacker, William and Sarah Robertson, November 7th

Thomas, Lewis R. and Martha F. Graves, September 1st

Thomas, William and Sarah Woody, January 13th

Thornton, Robert H. and M. L. Wingfield, January 26th

Tomblin, James C. and Auly Tomblin, August 2nd

Turner, Henry and Agnes C. Childress, October 1st

1854

Taylor, David M. and Lucy J. Collins, September 5th

Taylor, David M. and L. J. Collins, Sept. 5th

Thacker, John and Pelepa Beddon, August 6th

Thacker, William C. and Ann E. Wingfield, November 27th

Thornhill, George N. and Cornelia L. Bibb, November 16th

Thurmond, Newborn B. and Joseph H. Dawson, May 25th

Thurmond, N. B. and J. H. Dawson, May 25th

Thurston, James W. and Cynthia L. Clarke, February 16th

Thurston, Jas. W. and Cynthia F. Clarke, Feb. 16th

Travellian, James N. and Mary A. Shackelford, February 23rd

Travillian, Jas. M. and M. A. Shackelford, Feb. 23rd

1855

Taylor, Jno. B. and Mary L. Sneed, Dec. 6th

Taylor, J. B. and Mary L. Sneed, December 5th

Thacker, John and Pelisa Beddon, Aug. 6th

Thornhill, Geo. W. and Cornelia A. Bibb, Nov. 16th

Travillian, Geo. A. and Mary A. Martin, Dec. 3rd

Thurston, George R. and Amanda M. Toombs, July 4th

Thurston, Geo. R. and A. W. Toombs, July 4th

Tomblin, Garland G. and Frances Herron, January 11th

Toms, Moarman and Jinett Field, August 2nd

Toms, Naaman and Jineth Field, Aug. 2nd

Tomblin, Garland G. and Frances J. Herron, Jan. 14th

Travellian, George A. and Mary A. Martin, December 3rd

Turner, Peter P. and Agnes C. Dawson, November 8th

Turner, Peter P. and Agnes C. Turner, Nov. 8th

1856

Thurston, George F. and Susan J. Thurston, May 28th

Thurston, Geo. T. and Jane S. Thurston, May 28th

Tomblin, Horace L. and Rebecca Graves, September 11th

Tomblin, William O. and Malinda Tombs, September 10th

Tompkins, Samuel W. and Sarah J. Jarman, Jan. 8th

Tompkins, Samuel W. and Sarah E. Jarman, January 8th

Thomas, Wm. D. and Ella H. Jones, Oct. 15th

Travillian, G. C. and Mary D. Thurman, Nov. 14th

Timberlake, W. C. and S. A. Goodman, Feb. 3rd

Talifero, Edw. F. and Liza Dickinson, Oct. 26th

Tompkins, Wm. W. and Mary J. Ballard, July 15th

Thompson, Jno. P. and Sallie A. Payne, May 5th

1857

Taliaferro, Edward F. and Eliza P. Dickinson, October 19th

Thomas, William D. and Ella H. Jones, October 14th

Thompson, John P. and Sallie A. Payne, March 4th

Timberlake, W. Clark and Lettie A. Goodman, February 2nd

Tompkins, William W. and Mary J. Ballard, January 5th

Travellian, G. C. and Mary D. Thurman, August 31st

1858

Tate, Addison and Eliz. Shelton, September 1st

Taylor, James and Pirena Rea, May 17th

Tayler, James and Perena Rea, May 20th

Teazle, Theo. F. and Sarah F. Houchens, Nov. 15th

Terrell, William O. and Margaret M. Rogers, February 20th

Terrall, Wm. O. and Margaret M. Rogers, Feb. 23rd

Tompkins, James E. and Fannie E. Coleman, December 6th

1859

Tate, William and Catharine M. McCauley, September 26th

Tate,, Wm. and Catherine McCauley, Oct. 2nd

Thacker, Holman S. and Frances E. Thomas, November 28th

Thurmond, William H. and Sarah J. Mundy, October 10th

Timberlake, Jas. W. and Sallie A. Patrick, Feb. 22nd

Timberlake, James W. and Sallie A. Patrick, February 21st

Tomblin, Thomas W. and Eliza Ann Pugh, November 21st

Tomblin, Tho. W. and Eliza Ann Pugh, Nov. 23rd

1860

Tate, John N. and Sarah E. Holbert, February 6th

Tate, Jno. N. and Sarah E. Holbut, Feb. 9th

Thacker, Lewis and Mary F. Thacker, December 3rd

Thacker, Lewis, Jr. and Mary F. Thacker, Dec. 6th

Thomas, Jesse S. and Sarah A. Wade, January 30th

Thompson, Joseph R. and Mary C. Brown, December 27th

Tyree, David A. and Eliz. A. Chick, October 15th

1861

Tellier, William B. S. and Mary S. Martin, February 13th

Thomas, John R. and Sarah A. Saunders, March 1st

Thomas, John and Sarah A. Sandridge, Mar. 5th

Thompson, J. O. and Mary C. Brown, Jan. 2nd

Trotter, George and Amanda Bowers, April 4th

Tyler, Thos. R. and Sarah E. H. Layne, Jan. 10th

Tyler, Thomas R. and Sarah E. H. Layne, January 15th

Tyree, David A. and Eliz. Ann Cheek, Oct. 28th

Trooter, Geo. and Amanda Bowers, Apr. 4th

1862

Tompkins, Chas. G. and Augustena Poore, Apr. 12th

Thacker, Jas. A. and Selma H. Jones, May 15th

Thacker, Lewis and Rebecca Drumheller, Oct. 30th

Tyler, Geo. and Julia V. Magruder, Feb. 5th

1863

Terrell, Geo. W. and Mary E. Cash, Jan. 1st

Tamany, Phillip and Alice C. Wingfield, May 7th

1864

Turner, Wm. H. and Virginia Sandridge, May 15th

Tate, Jos. and Mary S. Cowen, Nov. 13th

Twyman, Theo. A. and Sally J. Wilhoit, May 5th

1865

Tapscott, W. S. and Sallie E. Nowell, Oct. 31

Toms, Garland and Minerva A. Kent, June 27th

Tuder, James R. and Ethaline N. Phillips, Feb. 1st

Thacker, Samuel D. and H. W. Drumheller, Sept. 19th

Thacker, Wm. M. and Sarah Jane Price, Nov. 28th

Tapscott, W. L. and Sallie E. Norvell, October 28th

Thacker, Samuel D. and Holly W. Drumheller, September 19th

Thacker, William M. and Sarah J. Price, November 28th

Toms, Garland and M. A. Kent, June 18th

Tudor, James R. and Etheline N. Phillips, February 1st

Tynan, Christopher B. and Helen A. Gibbs, October 23rd

1866

Thacker, David and Susan Ann Dudley, April 2nd

Thacker, Daniel and Susan D. Dudley, Apr. 12th

Thomas, Miles W. and Sarah A. Wood, Feb. 6th

Thomas, Miles W. and Sarah Ann Wade, January 30th

Thomas, Jesse N. and Mary E. Johnson, Dec. 20th

Thornton, John and Amanda M. Marshall, October 11th

Thorton, John and A. M. Marshall, Oct. 14th

Toombs, R. A. and Sidney M. Clark, Aug. 30th

Thurmond, Findel and Cornelia F. Dowell, February 12th

Thurston, Ben L. and Mary E. Thurston, January 20th

Thurston, Ben. L. and Mary E. Thurston, Jan. 24th

Thurston, John T. and Lucilla W. Clarke, January 17th

Thurston, Jno. T. and Lucilla W. Clarke, Jan. 23rd

Thurmond, Fendal and Cornelia F. Dowell, Feb. 13th

Thrift, James E. and Sally A. Bowcock, April 24th

Thrift, Jas. E. and Sally A. Bowcock, April 26th

Todd, George S. and Mary Ann Hutcheson, May 30th

Toler, Abram and Eliz. Tinsley, October 23rd

Toler, Abram and Betsy Tinsley, Oct. 27th

Toombs, Ryland A. and Sidney M. Clark, August 27th

Tuckett, William F. and Mary E. Wheeler, March 16th

Taylor, Geo. W. and Selina M. Lain, Dec. 24th

1867

Terrill, N. A. and Emma J. Dodd, Sept. 18th

Turner, Jno. T. E. and Ann E. Cocke, Oct. 3rd

Thomas, James A. and Caroline V. Humphreys, Nov. 7th

Thomas, Jas. A. and Caroline V. Humphreys, Nov 7th.

Thomas, James and Cornelia F. Garrison, Mar. 20th

Thomas, James and Cornelia F. Gardner, Mar. 20th

Thomas, Nelson and Eliza. Burks, Nov. 28th

Thomas, Wilson and Eliza Burks, Nov. 27th

Tucker, Mark and Isabella Waytts, Jan. 27th

1868

Tomblin, Benj. F. and Sallie J. Pugh, Dec. 17th

Thompson, Thos. W. and Pattie A. Dunn, Dec. 16th

Thurston, Chas. and Eliz. W. Pugh, May 20th

Thurston, Chas. and Eliz. W. Pugh, May 18th

Taylor, Martin S. and Julia W. Omohundro, Feb. 3rd

1870

Taylor, A. J. and C. Gooch, May 19th

Tallman, John S. and Sallie B. Edmonds, Dec. 28th

Tyree, Saml. and Mahala Edmund, July 24th

Taylor, F. A. and N. M. Purvis, Aug. 31st

Thomas, Jeremiah and Cor. E. Sandridge, Sept. 22nd

Thomas, Reuben and L. Derico, Nov. 20th

Thomas, Jno. J. and Mollie Goodwin, Dec. 15th

Templeman, Jas. A. and Lucy Dunkum, Nov. 29th

Tunstill, Stokes and Mary G. White, Dec. 22nd

Twyman, T. J. and K. A. Douglass, Dec. 18th

1871

Tate, Addison L. and Annie M. Hawes, March 14th

Thomas, Alex and Martha Brown, Sept. 23rd

Thompson, Jno. R. and Catharine L. Bryan, Oct. 17th

1872

Thomas, John N. and Corelia F. Sandridge, Feb. 11th

Thomas, Wm. Ralph and Mary E. Collins, Jan. 11th

Taylor, Wm. Andrew and Frances Hutchinson, Apr. 1st

Thompson, Sam. H. and Sallie P. Johnson, Sept. 10th

Turner, Lawson C. and Mary P. Wayland, Oct. 30th

1873

Thomas, Benj. and Eliza A. Flynt, Dec. 4th

Tomapson, J. H. and Mary F. Gleason, June 10th

1874

Timberlake, C. W. and Sallie J. Garland, Feb. 2nd

Thoms, Thos. and Victoria Norvill, May 23rd

Thomas, David A. and Louisa E. Batten, Jan. 16th

Tomlin, Jas. C. and Virginia A. Thacker, Nov. 24th

Tate, Franklin N. and Martha B. Smith, Dec. 15th

Toman, Aska and Kate Seay, Dec. 24th

Timberlake, J. E. and S. E. Fansler, Mar. 21st

1875

Tracey, Martin and Jane O. Toole, Jan. 8th

Tate, Jno. R. and Mary J. Durnella, Oct. 19th

1876

Tomlin, James C. and Eliza June Hicks, Feb. 14th

Tincler, Quntius and Georgianna Geonami, Mar. 23rd

Tyler, Joseph L. and Sallie C. Atkins, June 5th

Thomas, Benj. H. and V. Alice Gianning, Dec. 19th

Tillman, Jacob and Ellen E. Robertson, Dec. 26th

1877

Tinsley, Frank S. and Lucy J. Harding, Feb. 12th

Tate, Tyree H. and Lizzie J. Walton, Apr. 18th

Tutwiler, Thos. P. and Josephine L. Wright, June 4th

Thacker, Geo. P. and Mary F. Pleasants, Aug. 27th

Thompson, Henry Smith and Mary Davis, Oct. 16th

1878

Tyson, Wm. James and Lottie K. Parrott, Jan. 9th

Thacker, John N. and Mattie J. Johnson, Jan. 29th

Taylor, Jno. H. and C. L. Birckhead, May 13th

Taylor, John and Virginia B. Smith, Nov. 20th

Toms, William and Nancy B. Toms, Feb. 25th

Thomas, Geo. N. and Jemina Dickson, Oct. 8th

Tunstall, Chas. C. and Emmella J. Mason, Oct. 28th

1879

Tibbs, James T. Adelade H. Johnson, Apr. 2nd

Trice, Thomas A. and Bettie H. Bates, June 18th

Towles, William B. and Mary E. Thompson, June 30th

Thomas, Wm. H. and BeHyle Wheeler, Oct. 20th

Thacker, Caleb and Ann C. Fisher, Jan. 10th

Timberlake, Jas. E. and Annie M. Mayo, Nov. 3rd

Taylor, John F. P. and Sally R. Childress, Dec. 1st

1880

Tinsley, Frank and Nettie B. Johnson, May 14th

Taylor, C. P. and W. J. Cornell, July 8th

Thompson, H. S. and Harriett Fletcher, Aug. 12th

Taliferro, Jno. W. and Annie C. Champion, Sept. 29th

Tomlin, John H. and Bettie A. Thomas, Oct. 7th

Taylor, John Wm. and Willie A. Critzer, Nov. 15th

Topping, Nathan B. and Sarah A. Daniel, Dec. 4th

Thomas, John O. and Emma L. Brown, Dec. 17th

Taylor, Wm. W. and Ara J. Jones, Dec. 20th

Tyler, James F. and Mrs. Sally H. Patterson, Dec. 22nd

1881

Toms, Smith and Martha Ann Toms, Jan. 19th

Tyler, Geo. Wm. and Fanny G. Gianiny, Feb. 17th

Thomas, James E. and Willie Ann Jackson, Feb. 22nd

Tomblin, Wm. and Mary E. Bryant, Oct. 15th

Thurston, Elmore P. and Dora D. Wood, Oct. 26th

Tomlin, John H. and Lettie C. Reynolds, Nov. 21st

1882

Toombs, Charles and Anne S. Gibson, July 30th

Turner, Peter P. and Lucy T. Childress, Dec. 13th

Thurston, Wesley P. and Mary W. Wood, Dec. 20th

Thomasson, David W. and Willie Hicks, Dec. 28th

Thurston, James Marion and Mary Fanny Abell, Jan. 30th

Thomas, Luther Francis and Lucy Shelton Fortune, Mar. 22nd

1883

Taylor, George D. and Frances V. Jones, June 17th

Tooley, Marcellius D. and Mollie Louise Wood, May 23rd

Thomas, Lewis J. and Jenny A. Bingham, July 9th

1884

Thurston, Thos. W. and Susie A. Garrison, Oct. 2nd

Tilman, Rives and Ella Bragg, Sept. 10th

Toms, Chas. S. and Lucy Jane Wade, Nov. 13th

Tibbs, Jas. and Rebecca Johnson, Nov. 26th

1885

Thomas, Robt. Edward and Willie J. Thomas, Feb. 3rd

Toms, John and Fannie A. Mowyer, Mar. 19th

Tryall, Benj. P. and Molly I. Criddle, Dec. 20th

Thacker, Bernard F. and Lula H. Britt, Dec. 23rd

1886

Tomlin, Geo. Samuel and Eliza E. Reynolds, Jan. 1st

Thompson, Andrew J. and Harriet Thompson, Mar. 21st

Tyler, Lewis B. and Sallie E. Wash, Dec. 1st

Tucker, Claudine L. and Mary A. Carter, Dec. 7th

Thomson, Jas. L. and Mollie C. Lunesden, Dec. 8th

Thompson, R. N. Lee and Mary E. Fry, Dec. 16th

Tate, Jas. Wm. and Bettie E. Tate, Dec. 13th

1887

Terry, John and Willie A. Wilkinson, Sept. 25th

Taylor, Jas. Walter and Eliz. F. Melton, Nov. 28th

Thacker, Wm. M. Jr. and Lucy Jane Shackleford, Jan. 5th

Trevillian, Linwood and Gelley M. Dowell, Jan. 24th

Tyler, Willie Walker and Callie P. Black, May 22nd

Tallafero, H. A. and Sallie H. Ashlin, Nov. 16th

1888

Tomlin, Jno. E. and Sarah E. Parr, Feb. 27th

Thacker, Thos. J. and Fannie V. Graves, Feb. 27th

Taylor, T. U. and M. M. Moon, July 14th

Thomas, F. M. and Ida B. Spicer, Dec. 10th

Tompkins, W. A. and F. M. Durrett, Dec. 24th

1889

Tate, Jo. H. and Nannie B. Martin, Sept. 24th

Taylor, G. B. and L. G. Magruder, Oct. 30th

Tomlin, R. B. and K. L. Parr, Nov. 15th

1890

Thomas, J. B. and Armiminta Rhodes, Jan. 9th

Tucker, Horace and Julia E. Harrison, Mar. 20th

Timberman, C. M. and Maggie L. Bingler, May 27th

Turpin, J. B. and R. B. Smith, Sept. 3rd

Tomlin, J. S. and S. A. McAlerer, Sept. 4th

Toms, Alex and Ama A. Critzer, Oct. 20th

Toombs, Wm. L. and Geo. W. Thurston, Oct. 20th

Tyler, Robt. B. and Sallie F. Mayo, Oct. 20th

Toms, R. W. and J. C. Drumheller, Dec. 22nd

Thacker, H. H. and Maria J. Kirtey, Dec. 24th

1891

Thomas, J. L. and Virginia Durham, Jan. 14th

Thomas, L. F. and Emily Hays, Aug. 31st

1892

Taylor, W. J. and Alice E. Tate, Sept. 1st

Thurston, J. O. and E. D. Graves, Mar. 30th

Tisdale, Lewis and Mary S. Gray, Jan. 5th

Trevillian, Geo. E. and Lurene S. Austin, Oct. 5th

Tonemin, P. and G. D. Chewning, Oct. 11th

Tompkins, Stonewall, and J. H. Vanter, Oct. 12th

Tate, O. Q. and Sally Burrus, Oct. 29th

Thomas, H. S. and F. M. Hatcher, Nov. 23rd

Thacker, Chas. H. and Mattie V. Hunt, Dec. 27th

1893

Tisdale, G. B. and Maude Davis, July 3rd

Thurston, Jno. W. and M. A. L. Cash, July 6th

Tompkins, S. W. and Sarah N. Tompkins, Nov. 27th

1894

Tomlin, Jno. and Mattie A. Currier, Jan. 15th

Tillman, Jno. T. and F. L. Herndon, Feb. 10th

Thacker, Victor, and Evelena Wood, Mar. 10th

Timberlake, C. G. and May O. Martin, Dec. 8th

1895

Thacker, E. L. and B. A. Eatson, Feb. 21st

Thacker, Wm. M. and Mrs. M. E. Gay, Oct. 24th

Tomlin, Thos. and Daisy Lanum, May 3rd

Thomas, P. P. and Laurie L. Johnson, Aug. 17th

Toms, Jos. and Roberta Mawyer, Oct. 9th

Toombs, Robt. A. and Rebecca B. Gay, Dec. 24th

1896

Thacker, Victor E. and Martha Graves, Oct. 31st

Thacker, W. C. and A. L. Huffman, Jan. 30th

Troubetzkoy, P. P. and Amelia Rives, Feb. 18th

Taylor, J. W. and W. B. Kent, Apr. 2nd

Tillman, W. B. and S. W. Rea, Oct. 5th

Terrell, J. C. and M. J. Gate, Nov. 2nd

Tyree, Jasper and Ada Sneed, Nov. 14th

Taylor, R. C. and H. L. Tillman, Dec. 10th

Thomas, J. N. and Mary C. Thomas, Dec. 16th

1897

Thurston, W. L. and B. J. Graves, Apr. 15th

Tomlin, Garland and Hester L. Kirby, Aug. 14th

1898

Thomas, C. M. and A. C. Garland, Jan. 12th

Taylor, E. L. and Gertrude Sneed, Apr. 26th

Thomas, E. C. and A. E. Thomas, July 2nd

Thurman, Jas. W. and Ada F. Ragland, July 8th

Teasley, W. H. and Martha E. Clark, July 19th

Tomlin, Edgar and Bertie A. Kirby, Aug. 22nd

Tate, Oney and Mattie Thomas, Dec. 29th

1899

Toms, Stephen and Eva Davis, Apr. 3rd

Tomlin, John A. and S. B. Barksdale, May 13th

Tomlin, W. W. and Anna L. Gay, Apr. 25th

Taylor, Wm. R. and M. C. Edwards, May 9th

Tyler, W. W. and B. J. Dusenbury, Oct. 28th

Thomas, P. E. and M. W. Cocke, June 27th

Thomas, Jeff. and Maggie L. Bolden, Nov. 4th

Thacker, E. T. and E. J. Ward, Aug. 8th

Thompson, J. L. and Pearl Stickleyman, Aug. 11th

Toms, Andrew and Nora Kirby, Sept. 13th

Teel, S. S. and Mary L. Howard, Sept. 14th

Tombs, J. T. and Mary S. Clarke, Oct. 4th

1900

Tomlin, R. H. and M. I. Mawyer, Aug. 16th

Toombs, Geo. W. and Edna B. Wilkerson, Sept. 27th

Thompson, Elmore W. and Cora E. Douglas, Oct. 5th

Talley, J. E. and Alice Payne, Nov. 13th

Tomlin, G. S. and M. B. Suddarth, Nov. 19th

Taylor, O. O. and Willie K. Failes, June 21st

Thacker, S. D. and Anne Gibson, Feb. 20th

Thacker, Chas. T. and T. E. Dudley, May 14th

Thornton, Thos. D. and M. Jessie Wingfield, Apr. 19th

Thornton, John T. and Louisa L. Disney, Oct. 9th

1901

Tate, E. and L. Bishop, Jan. 23rd

Thomas, Michael and Mollie Wilkerson, Apr. 3rd

Thomas, D. W. and Rosa Kennedy, May 6th
Thomas, M. H. and E. L. Wheeler, July 2nd
Thurston, J. W. and B. C. Thurston, Apr. 23rd
Tilman, J. W. and L. L. Lannan, July 22nd
Thacker, J. M. and Gertrude D. Graves, Sept. 12th
Thomas, J. L. and Ethel Rhodes, Sept. 17th

1902

Thacker, S. M. and S. J. Tooley, Dec. 22nd
Thacker, E. L. and W. J. Thacker, Apr. 30th
Timberlake, M. and Elne B. Ellison, June 24th
Thomas, M. A. and E. G. Sutherland, July 16th

1903

Todd, H. T. and G. E. Chapman, Mar. 10th
Taylor, Selden C. and Bessie G. Broadhead, Apr. 21
Thomas, Wilber and Mary Clements, June 10th
Thomas, J. R. and Annie G. Via, Dec. 16th
Tilman, J. D. and M. W. Turner, Aug. 5th
Thomas, J. R. and F. L. Brown, Oct. 13th
Thurston, V. C. and Sallie H. Wood, Dec. 12th
Thompson, E. H. and L. A. Morris, Jan. 5th
Thomas, J. R. and Nannie G. Via, Dec. 16th

1905

Tayler, G. W. M. and F. E. Watson, June 5th
Taylor, G. W. M. and F. E. Watson, June 5th
Tomlin, E. S. and Susie Suddarth, Aug. 26th
Toms, Harry L. and Lottie Baber, Oct. 16th
Tate, Burleigh and Bettie L. Payne, Oct. 31st

1906

Thomas, Charles Benj. and Mary Frances Clark, Jan. 4th
Thurston, John W. and Mittie E. Snead, March 28th
Tomlin, John Nicholas and Dollie L. Tomlin, May 8th
Thacker, G. W. and Lillie Spherse, June 11th
Tomlin, George T. and Sarah E. Alexander, July 7th
Tisdale, John L. and Lelia C. Cannody, Sept. 17th
Thacker, Charles Thomas and Donnie Jones, Sept. 26th
Toms, Herbert L. and Susie J. Toms, Oct. 29th
Thomas, David S. and Lillian Busie, Oct. 31st
Talman, D. T. and B. L. Maupin, Nov. 21st

1907

Thomas, Franklin H. and Mary J. Smith, Feb. 11th
Tomlin, James and Lucy Moore, July 11th
Thurman, Charles R. and Eliza C. Thornton, Aug. 27th
Tooley, J. W. and Ellen L. Graves, Sept. 16th
Thornton, David and Josie Graves, Sept. 11th
Thomas, D. A. and Mary A. Ralston, Oct. 16th
Thacker, G. P. and Ada A. Bryant, Oct. 17th

Thurston, Joseph S. and Lelia Payne, Nov. 27th
Thomas, Robert and Henrietta Dowell, Dec. 30th

1908

Tate, Edward A. and Bertha Guerring, April 7th
Thomas, Willie H. and Luna B. Estes, Sept. 8th
Thompson, William T. and Florence E. Pugh, Nov. 25th
Tomlin, Tom and Georgia Harlow, Dec. 9th
Tyler, Floyd M. and Mary M. Weast, Dec. 8th

1909

Thomas, Charlie W. and Sallie Bishop, June 9th
Thompson, Charles E. and Bessie M. Kirby, Sept. 12th
Tranham, Cecil and Lillie Farrar, Sept. 28th
Thomas, Edward and Lottie Graves, Oct. 27th
Toms, Ernest and Martha Toms, Nov. 3rd

1910

Tate, Frank N. and Anna Wood, April 26th
Thomas, Massie and Mabel Thomas,, May 28th
Toms, George and Carrie Douglas, June 9th
Thomas, Thomas E. and Susie F. Hughes, June 14th
Tice, Fred L. and Judith Maury, June 27th
Thraves, Oscar R. and Ann Fontaine Maury, June 28th
Thurston, Claude and Mary Via, Oct. 19th

1911

Thomas, David and Rosa Watson, April 6th
Taylor, Walker L. and Sallie Zinnerman, June 1st
Turjman, Lovich P. and Willie Durrett, July 25th
Tabor, George William and Alinia Virginia Winn, Nov. 27th

1912

Thompson, Volney S. and Carrie B. Perry, Jan. 30th
Taylor, Jr., Dr. Richard V. and Anne R. Sampson, June 11th
Thacker, Samuel A. and Maggie L. Thacker, June 27th
Thurston, William L. and Matilda Gibson, Aug. 11th
Thompson, J. B. and E. M. Temple, Oct. 9th
Tomlin, David S. and Nannie M. Faris, Nov. 18th
Thacker, H. Aubrey and Gertrude A. Elliott, Nov. 21st
Thompson, Bernard N. and Alice M. Hawkins, Dec. 18th

1913

Thurston, John W. and Lillian Gooch, Jan. 15th

Toms, Wesley and Carrie Baber, April 23rd

Tomlin, D. S. and Mattie P. Cox, June 8th

Tyler, Floyd M. and Hattie L. Wood, June 25th

Thurston, Cole Y. and Alice B. Davis, July 2nd

Tillman, Albert J. and Bertie Carter, Aug. 20th

Tate, Louis and Fannie Woodson, Oct. 20th

Thornton, Hubert and Lillie Bracey, Nov. 10th

Thompson, Meel and Mary Sullivain, Dec. 31st

1914

Tate, Thomas M. and Addie Sprouse, Feb. 4th

Taylor, Edward L. and Edith Souers, Sept. 18th

Tindsall, James B. and Mary A. Tapscott, Oct. 27th

Thomas, Chesley and Bertha Harlow, Nov. 1st

Taylor, John W. and Lillie C. Pace, Nov. 6th

Thacker, Clarence and Mary E. Stone, Nov. 14th

Thurston, Waverly and Ludie Hicks, Dec. 23rd

1915

Taylor, Walter J. and Ethel McCary, Apr. 15th

Tomlin, Marcus E. and Nora M. Critzer, Apr. 17th

Tucker, Jr., Beverly D. and Eleanor Lile, Apr. 20th

Thomas, George W. and Georgia Carr, Apr. 20th

Thomas, Henry and Edna Rea, May 10th

Taylor, Warner L. and Blanchie M. Bruffey, May 29th

Taylor, Willie C. and Mammie W. Harlow, June 8th

Thacker, Lawrence E. and Lena Elsie Bledsoe, Oct. 13th

1916

Timberlake, Journey F. and Eva Goodwin, Jan. 11th

Thurston, Everett T. and Carrie L. Payne, Jan. 21st

Toms, Howell and Cora Mawyer, Jan. 24th

Thacker, Samuel E. and Eva Via, Feb. 23rd

Thomas, Robert and Mabel Lee Wood, May 17th

Toombs, Percy and Mary Powell, July 12th

Taylor, Thomas Leslie and Rosa Elizabeth Carver, Aug. 12th

Tomlin, Ernest S. and Phyllis L. Anderson, Oct. 1st

Thomas, Morris and Mary Lou Pritchett, Oct. 7th

Thompson, Henry N. and Gabie E. Via, Oct. 10th

Toms, Hilton H. and Annie G. Moyer, Dec. 27th

1917

Toms, Caspie and Cora Toms, June 10th

Timbus, Phillip and Sue Lockett, June 28th

Toms, S. P. and Blanche Baber, July 22nd

Thomasson, William Overton and Beatrice Payne, Sept. 2nd

Toombs, Amos and Lena Carter, Sept. 24th

Thurston, Everett A. and Julia G. Thurston, Oct. 10th

Thomas, William and Myrtle Munday, Nov. 28th

Tilman, Frederick G. and Gladys M. Houchens, Dec. 11th

1918

Treane, Maxenaliaw and Odetta C. Clements, Jan. 8th

Tate, Otis and Dolie A. Carter, April 11th

Taylor, Philip F. and Katherine O. Rossman, May 30th

Thurston, Roy C. and Mary Jane McAllister, Sept. 9th

Toms, Joseph W. and Nannie E. Baber, Oct. 26th

Thurman, Jas. Oscar and Maria S. Magruder, Nov. 16th

Thurston, Chas. E. and Annie S. Maupin, Nov. 27th

Toms, Daniel B. and Ada G. Baber, Dec. 22nd

Thurston, Guy and Virgilia Thurston, Dec. 23rd

Thompson, Walter G. and Fannie M. Bryan, Dec. 24th

1919

Thurman, Francis Lee and Nancy Dike Hancock, Feb. 15th

Tooley, Marshall and Carrie L. Moon, June 22nd

Toombs, Oliver E. and Lillian E. Mawyer, July 15th

Thomas, Everett E. and Ola S. Scruggs, Aug. 6th

Thomas, Jas. Monroe and Gracie May Sprouse, Sept. 27th

Turrell, Howard F. and Grace D. Baber, Nov. 4th

Taylor, Walter J. and Grace E. Brown, Nov. 15th

Thomas, Jas. G. and Annabelle Dudley, Nov. 19th

Thompson, Boyd W. and Nora F. Dunn, Nov. 26th

Turner, Allen J. and Violette M. Shisler, Dec. 8th

Thomas, David and Lucy Thomas, Dec. 22nd

Tooley, James B. and Annie D. Cobbs, Dec. 29th

1920

Toms, Jerry M. and Bannie Wood, Feb. 5th

Treslow, Montague and Sophie Ann Key, Feb. 14th

Tinsley, Luther R. and Mary Humphries, March 24th

Tomlin, James Wm. and Mary E. Bailes, April 18th

Thompson, Cleveland H. and Mary E. Douglas, April 21st

Thorne, Wm. D. and Oda May Lilly, May 29th

Toms, Marshall L. and Annie L. Toms, June 10th

Tooley, Charlie E. and Mamie Burgess, July 31st

Thompson, Eaton F. and Ettie R. Shiflett, Oct. 21st

Tunstall, Cuthbert and Mary Amis Moore, Dec. 23rd

1921

Turner, James E. P. and Della Stump, Jan. 25th

Toms, Bland John and Dultry D. Mawyer, Apr. 2nd

Townsend, Daniel S. and Maude Helen Critzer, Apr. 14th

Thompson, Walter Jackson and Rossie Howdyshell, May 4th

Tomlin, Ernest F. and Maude E. Dudley, May 7th

Topping, John Edward and Janie Arline Wilhoit, June 16th

Thompson, John H. and Mollie C. Moore, July 6th

Tompkins, Francis W. and Catherine T. Kennedy, Aug. 15th

Toombs, Harry and Glinna Maupin, Sept. 2nd

Thomas, Elisha J. and Louise A. Mahanes, Dec. 6th

1922

Tomlin, Grayeore W. and Elizabeth L. Perry, Jan. 2nd

Toms, Roy N. and Myrtle G. Powedd, Jan. 18th

Thomas, Elbert and Lula P. Roston, Jan. 19th

Thomas, John and Thelma Davis, May 22nd

Toms, Norman M. and Lillie O. Wood, May 30th

Tyree, Lonnie and Maude Hollow, July 18th

Tate, Elgin G. and Violet Birckhead, Sept. 16th

Thompson, J. B. and Olia R. Jamison, Dec. 4th

Terry, Hartwell and Lucy V. Morris, Dec. 16th

1923

Thacker, Tandy and Lula Gardner, Jan. 7th

Thomasson, Lawrence L. and Eva F. Herndon, Apr. 29th

Tomlin, Forrest E. and Mattie H. Collins, July 3rd

1924

Tramb, Harry and Maude Dowell, Jan. 19th

Thomas, Asbury W. and Emma D. Fry, Feb. 28th

Tapscott, Walter N. and Marie Tapscott, Mar. 15th

Tapscott, Joseph R. and Mary E. Guthrie, Mar. 15th

Thacker, Walter and Mamie Hunt

Tinnell, James M. and Madeline M. Johnson, May 8th

Taylor, Grover C. and Maggie Morris

Taylor, Sidney A. and Mathew J. Downer, Sept. 16th

Thomas, Paul W. and Sallie E. Wood, Sept. 23rd

Tomlin, Massie and Lilly H. Toms, Nov. 8th

Turner, Raymond F. and Mary R. Daughtry, Dec. 24th

Tinsley, Daniel A. and Nellie J. Goolsby, Dec. 24th

1925

Tobey, Jr., Clarence C. and Hattie F. Ladd, Jan. 3rd

Thacker, Sam A. and Rosa Bryant, Apr. 1st

Tomlin, Gordon and Mazie Mowyer, June 10th

Trumble, Joseph B. and Julia L. Abell, June 25th

Toms, George H. and Mildred S. Mawyer, Aug. 29th

Thomas, William D. and Susan M. Flint, Oct. 10th

Toms, William A. and Mary W. Johnson, Nov. 17th

1926

Toms, Phillip F. and Annie R. Kent, Feb. 24th

Tilman, Paul Bland and Susie L. Gann, Aug. 30th

Thomas, Clarence M. and Nannie Hilderbrand, Sept. 13th

Thurston, Finx and Jannie Thurston, Oct. 20th

Taylor, Francis William and Mae Van Wagner, Oct. 29th

Thacker, Corrie G. and Virginia Bryant, Dec. 24th

1927

Taylor, Edward and Nora E. Napier, Jan. 10th

Tomlin, Lewis H. and Florence Tomlin, Feb. 15th

Toms, John P. and Bessie B. Toms, Aug. 19th

Tomlin, Forrest L. and Nora F. Grenstead, Dec. 2nd

Toms, Emmett W. and Ora L. Pinchbeck, Dec. 24th

1928

Tant, Orbie W. and Gladys V. Clements, May 5th

Taylor, John William and Georgie B. Tomlin, June 11th

Tompkins, Charles W. and Kathleen P. Rogers, Aug. 15th

Thurston, Charlie F. and Ruth W. Belew, Nov. 20th

1929

Tomlin, James H. and Lee Ellen Fisher, Jan. 10th

Turner, Grover and Mary W. Staton, Jan. 26th

Terel, Stuart J. and Bessie Lee Holley, Feb. 25th

Thurston, Marshall and Sylvia M. Moses, May 18th

Tomlin, Virgil S. and Lola B. Kent, May 29th

Tate, Frank J. and Edna F. Gibson, June 25th

Trainham, Stuart T. and Vallie M. Deavers, July 1st

Tomlin, Marshall F. and Alma J. Marshall, Aug. 21st

Taylor, Guy N. and Ruby M. Holloway, Oct. 5th

Trainham, Elwood and Lelia McDaniel, Nov. 20th

U

1803

Uptergrove, Jessie and Milly Eubank, April 9th

1835

Underwood, Robert F. and Charlotte Boothe, May 27th

1847

Upp, Samuel and Mary J. Golding, May 22nd

1868

Utz, John J. and Mary F. Willes, Oct. 5th

1877

Urguhart, Whitnel H. and Ira Jordan, Nov. 6th

1879

Uppleby, John and Norah M. Betts, Dec. 12th

1885

Underwood, Oscar W. and Eugenia Massie, Oct. 8th

1886

Updike, Robt. L. and Annie E. Mimmo, July 27th

1889

Updike, Ab. and M. J. Walters, Feb. 25th

1898

Updike, Jas. E. and Rosa B. Updike, Dec. 21

1906

Uppleby, John and Jessie S. Harris, Nov. 15th

1924

Underwood, Lloyd and Madge Morris, Oct. 15th

1925

Updike, Jr., William E. and Gladys Mowbray, June 6th

V

1788

Vanstavern, Nicholas and Catey Howard, Mar. 31st

1789

Via, Micajah and Mary Mills, Jan. 14th 30th

1791

Via, Wade and Fanny Maupin, April 27th

1801

Via, Jonathan and Catharine O. Buck, Aug. 11th

Vines, John and Polly Hodge, Sept. 21st

1804

Varnon, Isaac and Nancy Patterson, Sept. 1st

1805

Via, Hezekiah and Elizabeth Jones, April 13th

1806

Via, Obediah and Ann Rogers, Sept. 8th

18?? ....

Via, Thomas and Sally Griggin, Jan. 1st

1814

Via, Daniel M. and Susannah Maupin, Aug. 16th

1815

Via, David and Elizabeth Bishop, July 17th

1816

Via, Clifton and Judy Sandridge, Feb. 5th

1818

Vermillion, James and Matilda Rippeto, Dec. 4th

Via, William and Nancy R. Maupin, Dec. 14th

1820

Vandergriff, David and Ann Wertenbaker, June 21st

1821

Via, Jonathan Jr. and M. E. Via, Dec. 15th

Via, Reubin and Sevina Garrison, Dec. 5th

1822

Via, Winstow and Malinda Via, March 28th

1823

Vowles, John and Lucy Ann Pendleton, Sept. 10th

1827

Venable, William L. and Sarah W. Eades, Jan. 30th

1828

Vermillion, James and Elizabeth Priddy, Nov. 6th

Via, Tarlton and Sarah Lane, Dec. 3rd

1829

Via, Henry and Polly Gentry, May 18th

Via, Tompson and Jane M. Via, Aug. 3rd

1830

Vest, William and Dorothy Fenwick, April 20th

1831

Via, Adam S. and Mary Elizabeth Via, Nov. 24th

Via, William W. and Elizabeth Clarke, Dec. 6th

1832

Via, Merewether and M. A. W. Watson, Jan. 3rd

1833

Vest, Gabriel and Mary Price, April 1st

Via, John A. and Mary Maupin, March 13th

1836

Via, Hiram and H. A. Nales, March 7th

Via, Thoams M. and Nancy J. Dunn, Nov. 7th

1837

Via, Archy and Eliza Nailor, Dec. 6th

Via, Samuel and Sarah A. Walton, Oct. 31st

Via, William W. and Sarah Baird, Dec. 19th

1838

Via, Nimrod F. and Maria P. Via, Dec. 13th

1839

Via, George A. and Elizabeth Lane, Dec. 2nd

1840

Via, Ira H. and Sarah Sandridge, May 5th

Via, Thomas D. and Elizabeth A. Norris, Sept. 1st

Vockrodl, John C. and M. J. Gillaspy, Sept. 24th

1841

Via, William A. and Mary A. Thurston, June 19th

Via, William W. and Susan Ballard, Nov. 15th

1842

Vasseur, Francis and Jane Carver, Dec. 22nd

Via, Brightberry and Susan Cox, Aug. 13th

1843

Via, David G. and Malinda J. Scantling, Feb. 14th

1844

Via, Brightberry and Judah Hall, Feb. 21st

1846

Via, James H. and A. Toole, Dec. 7th

1847

Vandergrift, David and Maria Halls, Feb. 25th

Via, Wade F. and Mary Ann Bailey, April 5th

1850

Valentine, Thomas J. and Virginia G. Poore, Aug. 6th

1851

Via, Thomas and Elizabeth M. Walton, Jan. 9th

1855

Venable, George S. and Sally M. Pullium, Feb. 14th

Venable, Geo. P. and Sally W. Pulliam, Feb. 14th

1856

Via, Thompson and Edney Patterson, Nov. 11th

Vest, Chas. R. and Eliz. Dudley, Nov. 24th

Vest, John R. and Lucy A. Burnley, July 28th

1857

Vandergrift, Ro. C. F. and Catherine E. Jokinson, Jan. 12th

Vest, Charles R. and Elizabeth Dudley, Nov. 24th

Vest, John R. and Lucy A. Burnley, July 11th

Via, James H. and Mary A. Keller, Oct. 21st

Via, James H. and Mary Ann Keller, Oct. 22nd

1858

Via, Charles F. and Lucinda E. Crenshaw, Oct. 11th

Via, Chas. F. and Susan E. Crenshaw, Oct. 14th

Vinson, Powhatan and Maria Smith, Feb. 24th

Vinson, Powhatan and Maria Smith, Feb. 28th

1859

Vandergrift, R. C. and Catharine C. Johnson, Jan. 11th

1860

Via, Charles E. and Mary J. Norris, Dec. 11th

1862

Voight, Lewis and Susan Seiler, Dec. 23rd

1863

Via, Wade R. and Lizzie A. Pace, Apr. 14th

1865

Via, George M. and Mary J. Wood, Dec. 4th

Via, Chas. E. and Mary Jane Norris, Dec. 20th

Via, Samuel and A. F. Herron, Dec. 12th

Vest, Wm. and Eliz. Marsh, Apr. 27th

1866

Vaughan, William H. and Eva T. Carter, July 25th

Via, Tho. D. and Sarah E. Thomas, Nov. 15th

Via, Pleasant M. and Martha S. Norris, Dec. 20th

1867

Via, Jno. W. and Mary E. Crenshaw, Feb. 20th

1868

Vaughan, Asa W. and Margaret Dowell, July 19th

1870

Via, John R. and Lucy A. Jones, Jan. 1st

1871

Via, Rhodes Johnson and Mary Eliz. Keaton, Dec. 12th

1872

Vest, Wm. Hiram and Eliz. S. Macauley, Jan. 4th

Via, George M. Elphas and Emma G. Johnson, Sept. 10th

Via, B. L. and Lucy E. Maupin, Dec. 5th

Via, Nicholas W. and Julia F. Harris, Dec. 3rd

Via, Horace W. and Lucibla Slayter, Oct. 20th

Via, Ira H. and Amanda Shifflet, Oct. 20th

1874

Via, Tyree, T. and Sallie L. Dunn, Sept. 17th

1875

Vear, Wm. A. and Fanny R. Fortune, Oct. 6th

1876

Via, Franklin H. and Sally A. Herndon, Apr. 4th

Venable, Chas. S. and Mary S. Brown, July 5th

Via, Hyram, K. and Fanny E. Coleman, Dec. 15th

1877

Via, Aldrekis R. and Martha F. Wood, Aug. 13th

1878

Varis, Octavius B. and Haldenia L. Patterson, Jan. 3rd

Villeneuve, Celestin and Jeannie W. Price, Aug. 23rd

Via, Mathew F. and Mrs. M. A. Ballard, Dec. 13th

1879

Via, David W. and Malinda Sipe, Dec. 5th

1880

Via, Archibald T. and A. V. Parrott, Apr. 8th

1882

Vermilion, Wm. H. and Mary G. Toombs, Apr. 25th

Via, Charles H. and Estelle M. Cox, Oct. 31st

Via, Albert F. and Alice A. Coleman, Nov. 2nd

1883

Via, James D. and Celeste Jane Hall, Nov. 29th

1885

Via, Wm. E. and Ida J. Bruce, ...

1888

Via, T. G. and Athaline Shiflett, Apr. 11th

1889

Via, J. R. and F. N. Walton, Mar. 27th

Vannosdall, J. and Eliz. Nolorn, Mar. 6th

Via, A. A. and L. M. Harris, Dec. 2nd

1891

Valentine, W. R. and M. C. Reynolds, Feb. 18th

Via, A. W. and M. C. Birckhead, Mar. 4th

Via, Wm. A. and Susie Carver, July 27th

1892

Via, H. P. and A. C. Berry, May 10th

Via, W. M. A. and M. A. Sandridge, Dec. 5th

1893

Vess, Chas. and V. B. McDaniel, Nov. 1st

1895

Vest, Geo. W. and Florence E. Nuttycombe, Mar. 14th

Via, Wm. M. and L. A. Shiflett, Sept. 25th

1896

Vest, Jas. H. and Susan Clemans, Feb. 3rd

1897

Vincent, C. W. and M. L. Pettit, June 2nd

Via, J. T. and M. T. Maupin, Oct. 9th

1898

Via, Jacob W. and Carrie F. Crenshaw, Feb. 22nd

Via, B. A. and Mary E. Elliott, Oct. 24th

Viele, Jas. M. and M. S. Hathersly, May 30th

1899

Via, C. H. and Carrie B. Lupton, Apr. 24th

Via, Chas. W. and Elnora P. Daughtry, Dec. 18th

Vess, S. K. and Lucy McDaniel, Aug. 23rd

1900

Via, A. Turk and Emily J. James, Nov. 16th

1901

Via, C. E. and M. Chisholm, May 1st

Vest, J. W. and Ella Johnson, Sept. 12th

Via, John A. and Beulah M. Maupin, Dec. 10th

1903

Vaughn, R. S. and M. E. Walker, Oct. 3rd

1906

Via, Daniel Rogers and Mary Clara Garrison, April 19th

Valentine, Robert L. and Clara C. Garnett, Nov. 29th

1907

Via, B. F. and Angie Isabella Ward, Dec. 25th

Vermillion, James H. and Emma D. Watts, Aug. 28th

1908

Via, Walker J. and Mary M. Elliott, April 1st

Via, Preston J. and Edna C. Ward, Aug. 19th

Via, William F. and Lois A. Munday, Nov. 21st

Vandoren, Mathew M. and Daisy M. Howard, Dec. 1st

Vaughn, John Wesley and Ada Belle Payne, Dec. 23rd

1909

Viers, James H. and Annie L. Walters, June 30th

Via, Oscar W. and Attela E. Wood, Nov. 17th

1910

Via, Roy L. and Ethel Craig, March 16th

1911

Via, Junius and Nannie Garrison, Feb. 15th

Via, James M. and Lena V. Crickenberger, Sept. 28th

1912

Vaiden, Henry K. and Eliza Faris, June 25th

1913

Vest, Charles C. and Grace C. Rhodes, Feb. 5th

Via, Thomas D. and Mrs. N. E. Detamore, March 11th

Via, James F. and Mary C. Sandridge, Dec. 10th

1914

Via, Clarence and Eveline Maupin, June 17th

Via, Rodes J. and Alice A. Proffit, Jan. 1st

Via, Floyd and Dora Francis Batten, December 21st

1915

Via, Robert and Fannie Hunt, January 3rd

Via, Willie L. Jr. and Janie Vess, May 3rd

Via, Lewis and Millie F. Lawson, June 1st

1916

Via, William K. and Cora B. Harris, November 8th

1917

Via, Gilbert L. and Mary Garrison, April 21st

Via, James M. and Blanche Harlow, June 20th

Via, Walter and Katie Maupin, October 20th

1918

Van Dyke, Henry P. and Eula B. Dowell, October 30th

Via, Clarence Edward and Mary Elsie Duncan, December 8th

1919

Via, David and Bessie Via, May 17th

Via, Hiram T. and Bertha V. Bryan, August 3rd

Via, William C. and Fannie Gardner, October 27th

Via, Charlie F. and Eva Virginia Garrison, December 24th

Via, Claude Lee and Carrie Lee Carter, April 3rd

Via, Percy and Clara E. Hunt, April 30th

1921

Via, Walter Samuel and Lottie L. Sandridge, November 1st

1922

Via, James, N. and Mary E. Dudley, November 28th

1923

Vest, Howard and Lelia V. Meeks, April 30th

Vesser, Robert W. and Mary Maud Foxx, October 22nd

1924

Vess, Forest K. and Bertha E. McDonald, April 26th

Via, Marvin and Lottie Garrison, June 7th

1927

Van Doel, Joseph W. and Nora Lee Hicks, January 12th

Via, William A. and Harriet Strickler, May 7th

Via, William and Lorraine Coleman, June 22nd

1928

Via, Dewey I. and Elizabeth J. Batten, November 5th

W

1782

Winston, James and Sally Marks, December 25th

1783

Warwick, William and Sarah Barksdale, January 17th

Wingfield, Charles and Mary Lewis, January 8th

1784

Watson, David and Nancey Eubanks, August 17th

White, Jeremiah and Jane Shelton, March 11th

1785

Washington, Henry and Ann Quarles, April 18th

Watson, Evan and Lucy Coleman, January 4th

Watts, David and Ruth Ivyman, April 14th

Wells, Thomas and Ann Taylor, January 10th

1786

Wheeler, Micajah and Mary Emerson, November 24th

1787

Ware, Robert and Mary Massie, January 2nd

Willis, William and Polly Ballard, May 22nd

Wood, Josiah and Patience Weatheread, May 8th

Wood, Samuel and Elizabeth Willis Watkins, May 8th

1788

Wilson, Alexander and Rachel Arnal, November 3rd

Wood, John and Elizabeth Yancy, February 3rd

Wood, John and Mary Terrell, October 9th

Woodfork, Thomas and Mary Cole, October 27th

1789

Watts, Charles and Elizabeth Buckner, November 7th

White, John Jr. and Mourning Shelton, August 19th

Wingfield, Joseph and Mary Tool, August 28th

Wood, Thomas and Mary Pulliam, March 3rd

1790

Wells, Humphrey and Molly Uptegraves, December 14th

Wingfield, Charles and Elizabeth Day, January 28th

Wingfield, Edward and Nancy Hazlerig, December 27th

1791

Wash, Nathan and Mercey Wood, January 13th

Williams, Joseph and Rosamond Simms, December 10th

Wood, John and Jean Shirley, April 19th

Wood, Thomas and Lucy Geehee, July 14th

1792

Waddel, James and Mildred T. Lindsay, April 16th

Williams, Hugh and Mary Brown, October 4th

Wood, Harrison and Mary Simmonds, August 7th

Wood, James and Elizabeth Carr, October 11th

Wood, William and Mary Martin, January 24th

1793

Walker, William and Elizabeth Jones, December 16th

Watts, James and Elizabeth Durrett, March 7th

1794

Wamsley, Nathan and Susanna Watts, March 1st

West, James H. and Susannah Harlow, August 29th

Wheeler, Robert and Fanny Bailey, June 13th

Willis, John and Mary Binge, May 19th

Wood, Drury and Caroline Matilda Carr, February 12th

Wood, Zachariah and Lucy Seamonds, April 23rd

1795

Walden, William and Milly Rodes, July 2nd

Wardlaw, William and Sally Minor, March 11th

Watkins, William and Elizabeth Clarkson, February 6th

Watson, James and Ann Key, December 22nd

Watson, John and Mary Gillum, January 8th

Watson, John and Jane Price, December 31st

Weathered, John and Elizabeth Gilmore, April 13th

Wingfield, Benjamin and Susannah Wingfield, February 2nd

Wirt, William and Mildred Gilmer, May 23rd

Wood, Henry and Elizabeth Bailey, February 6th

Wood, William J. and Betty Twyman, September 15th

1796

Walton, Ison and Franky Watson, January 4th

Wertrnbaker, Christian and Polly Grady, June 6th

White, James and Lucy Martin, April 2nd

White, John and Martha Key, January 1st

Wilderson, John and Jenny Hall, January 30th

Williams, Charles and Elizabeth Boyd, January 16th

1797

Walton, Rice and Rebecca Fraley, December 10th

Wingfield, John and Ann Buster, December 28th

1798

Watts, Nathan and Betsy P. Goodridge, December 13th

Wood, William and Milly Wheeler, December 18th

Woods, Parmenas and Nancy Musick, March 5th

1799

Walton, Francis and Nancy Spears, December 24th

Watson, Isaac and Susannah Roberts, April 3rd

Watts, David Jr. and Betsy Crenshaw, October 7th

Wheeler, John and Betsey Emmerson, December 20th

White, Chapman and Milly Maupin, March 23rd

White, Hugh and Nancy Cocke, October 7th

Wims, William and Pinney Brown, March 23rd

Wood, Hezekiah and Patsy Gentry, July 1st

Wood, James and Nancy Trice, October 7th

Woods, William and Polley Jarman, January 18th

Woodson, Tucker M. and Martha E. Hudson, March 11th

1801

Ward, Joseph and Ann Jopling, July 4th

Watts, William and Polly Ashley, August 1st

Wharton, Samuel and Lucinda Farrar, November 2nd

Wood, Edward and Elizabeth Stone, May 11th

1802

Weatherhead, William and Patience Gunter, September 1st

Wilkinson, Anthony and Lucy Priddy, January 2nd

Wingfield, Matthew and Martha Buster, November 20th

Wood, Isaac and Mildred Shelton, March 30th

Wood, James and Sally Martin, October 2nd

Wood, William and Nancy Field, April 15th

1803

Walton, Edmond P. and Elizabeth Maupin, November 19th

Watson, James and Catherine Watson, December 24th

Wetherred, Thomas and Nancy Gillaspy, December 22nd

Willis, Thomas and Sally Hamner, November 16th

1804

Walker, James and Martha Hamner, December 19th

Watson, James and Nancy Mabe, May 30th

1805

Waller, Absalom and Ciceley A. Shelton, November 8th

Watts, Phillip and Mary Barksdale, October 21st

West, Peter and Betsy Bartley, January 15th

Whaley, James and Mrs. Ann Cannel, July 27th

White, William and Judith Tompkins, October 19th

Woods, William and Nancy Jones, December 18th

Woodson, John and Susannah Wheeler, January 15th

1806

Wells, Sevy and Charlott Marshall, January 1st

Wetherhead, Francis and Nancy Dowell, December 5th

Windbarger, John and Lucy Ropson, December 23rd

Wren, William and Polly Huckstep, January 27th

Walton, ? and Sarah ?, January 27th

1807

W?, and Elizabeth Barksdale, February 23rd

Watson, ? and Sally Cleaveland, October 5th

Watson, John C. and Patsy Wood, December 10th

Wood, ? and Nancy Key, January 15th

Wood, Robert and Elizabeth Limnond, December 22nd

1808

Walls, Thomas and ? Thomas, ——

Walton, John and Agness, Snow January 26th

Wells, William and Mary Howard, December 15th

White, Crenshaw and Sally Austin, October 26th

Woods, Micajah and Sally Davenport, September 22nd

1809

Watson, Joseph and Nancy Wood, March 13th

Watson, Richard P. and Ann Anderson, June 5th

Wegate, Paul and Polly Johnson, February 10th

Wood, Henry and Elizabeth Collins, August 5th

Woody, Sam and Jemimah Gardner, August 8th

1810

Watson, Joab and Elizabeth Ward, January 29th

Warton, Joseph and Elizabeth Coleman, November 20th

Watson, James B. and Milley Rodes, February 8th

Wells, Levy and Nelly Summons, January 4th

Wood, James and Sarah Britt, October 7th

Wood, John and Sally Woody, September 24th

Wood, John and Sally Wheeler, October ?

1811

Wheat, ? and Polly Eubanks, April 30th

1812

Walton, John and Rholly Davis, November 25th

Watson, John F. and Polly Barnett, September 5th

Wayman, John and Nancy Newcomb, November 17th

Wheeler, Zachariah and Martha Britt, September 7th

Wingfield, Charles and Margaret Rossin, February 15th

Wood, Rice and Elizabeth Burges, October 5th

Wood, Samuel and Sarah Thompson, December 7th

1813

Wood, Gipe and Sarah Grayson, September 6th

Wood, John and Sally Jones, January 10th

Woodson, Fallon Jr. and Ann Davis, December 6th

1814

Webb, Benajah and Franky Scaminds, August 11th

Wood, Thomas and Susanna Irvin, May 23rd

Wright, John G. and Ann C. Wells, June 23rd

1815

Warren, Thomas and Malinda Roberts, August 13th

West, James and Sally Carrell, October 11th

White, Peter and Elizabeth Tompkins, February 18th

Wills, John and Mary R. Rodes, November 28th

Wingfield, Charles and Cary Ann Nicholas, February 9th

Wood, ? Jr. and Nancy Kinsolving, February 6th

Wood, Samuel and Elizabeth Dollins, September 20th

1816

Walker, John and Elizabeth Wertenbaker, June 21st

Walker, Meriweather L. and Maria Lindsay, May 16th

Walton, Edmund F. and Lettice Watson, February 13th

Walton, Jepe and Nancy Gentry, May 9th

Whiteham, Arthur and Lucretia Carver, May 28th

Woodson, Augustine and Nancy Martin, February 5th

Woodson, Pryor and Posey Smith Abell, November 13th

Wren, Nicholas and Polly A. Trevillion, December 21st

1817

Wheeler, George C. and Ann B. Childares, September 11th

Wheeler, John and Ann Woodson, October 14th

Wilson, John and Martha T. Woods, June 23rd

Wood, James and Rebecca Marshall, December 23rd

Wood, William and Martha Kinsolving, December 22nd

Woodson, John and Frances Garland, December 1st

Wyant, Abraham and Catharine Jarman, December 11th

1818

Ward, William and Susannah Corr Thompson, August 6th

Watts, Garrett and Martha T. Twyman, November 4th

Wells, John C. and Elizabeth Lewis, February 26th

Wood, Benjamin and Nancy W. Catterton, August 3rd

Wood, David and Lucy Gay, December 22nd

Wood, John and Artmipsie Walton, January 4th

Wood, John and Elizabeth G. Spencer, June 23rd

Woody, Hawkins and Jane S. Hughes, July 11th

1819

Watts, David W. and Mary T. Brown, February 10th

Wayland, Jeremiah and Mary Ramsey, January 14th

Williams, Joseph and Mary Catterton, November 15th

Winn, Joseph and Sarah Fox Brown, February 24th

Wood, Benjamin and Jane S. Anderson, October 4th

Wright, Bennett and Nancy I. White, December 6th

1820

Ward Samuel and Mildred Norris, February 8th

Wheeler, Benjamin and Sarah Ann Harp, April 10th

Wiant, David and Nancy T. Maupin, December 14th

Williams, Eli and Judah Carver, June 19th

1821

Wash, Henry and Martha McQuary, January 29th

White, John and Caroline Moore, October 23rd

Wingfield, Richard and Susie Gillum, November 15th

Wood, John and Frances Gay, September 4th

Wood, John and Sarah Thomson, November 19th

Woody, Benjamin and Susannah Hughes, April 23rd

Woollard, Samuel and Elizabeth Rogers, December 24th

1822

Walters, James O. and Malinda Perry, November 19th

Ward, John and Sarah Ward, October 2nd

Wheeler, Bennett and Elizabeth Moore, March 7th

Wood, John B. and Mary Newcom, February 28th

Wood, William and Mildred Austin, December 2nd

1823

Walker, Joseph and Nancy Noel, May 6th

Wingfield, John and Mary Ann Wingfield, October 2nd

Wingfield, Joseph F. and Ann P. Olds, October 6th

Wood, Ephraim and Polly Luck, February 3rd

Wood, James and Frances Allen, May 25th

Wood, Milton and Janet Field, March 20th

1824

Waltman, Jacob and Martha H. Heimer, July 20th

Watson, James R. and Ann M. Clarke, October 21st

Watson, Samuel and Polly A. Reynolds, October 21st

White, Garlsnd C. and Sarah R. Marrs, February 12th

Wilkerson, William P. and Nancy P. Sandridge, January 6th

Williams, George and Anna Via, December 13th

Wood, Achillis and Polly L. Via, November 28th

Wood, Jesse Jr. and Lucy Moore, May 13th

Wood, Reuben and Frances Wood, February 10th

Woods John and Margaretta Harris, November 6th

1825

Walters, William and Mary H. Perry, August 29th

Walton, John and Frances Fisher, August 17th

Walton, Warning H. and Lucyinda Sandridge, October 21st

Wills, Elias I. and Emily Eubank, August 2nd

Wilson, Elisha and Louisa Butler, December 22nd

Wingfield, Anderson and Spice L. Perry, ——

Wyborn, James S. and Angelina Gooch, September 5th

1826

Walker, Robin and Matilda A. Watson, April 20th

West, Nicholas B. and Harriot Jopling, January 25th

Wolfe, Ezra M. and Lucy J. P. Bishop, January 5th

Wood, George and Mary Ann Kidd, November 29th

1827

Wade, David and Louisa Toms, May 9th

Wade, James and Louisa Spradling, October 26th

Ware, William and Eliza White, November 5th

Wertenbaker, Edward and Ann Pettitt, December 27th

Wheat, Elisha and Susan Hughes, December 27th

Wheeler, Robert and Elizabeth Woodson, December 17th

Wood, Hillory and Bertha Snow, October 24th

Wood, William F. and Calsey Maupin, December 17th

Wood, William L. and Pamelia Dickerson, October 4th

Woodson, Tucker and Elizabeth G. Tillman, November 24th

1828

White, Thomas J. and June Frances Perry, July 3rd

Williams, John A. and Mary P. Mayo, March 27th

Wingfield, Anderson and Sally Hudson, January 2nd

Wingfield, Edward and Malinda Strange, October ?

Wingfield, James F. and Susan Wingfield, December 19th

Wingfield, Joseph and Sarah Wingfield, July 28th

Wood, David and Sarah A. Webb, November 3rd

Wood, Isaac and Rosanna R. Maupin, March 3rd

Wood, John T. and Mary M. Burnley, December 8th

Woodson, Stephen and Martha A. Anderson, November ?

1829

Watson, James A. and Mary J. Brown, March 24th

Watson, William and Elizabeth Coffman, September 18th

Wheeler, George and Paulina Bragg, June 6th

White, Garnett and Dicey Gemms, March 19th

Wolfe, George and Margaret Rea, November 2nd

Wolfe, Henry M. and S. F. M. Day, March 9th

Wood, David W. and Lucy Ann Duke, October 12th

1830

Wash, William and Martha Moore, November 27th

Watts, Crenshaw and Patsy Robinson, February 18th

Wingfield, John M. and Julia Thacker, December 20th

Wingfield, Robert C. and Eliza Elsom, February 1st

Wingfield, Thomas and Kitty Lowell, November 20th

Woods, William and Nancy R. Jones, September 23rd

1831

Walton, Gustavus A. and M. A. Wydown, August 20th

Ware, Peter M. and Elizabeth Mayo, May 27th

Watson, John M. C and Catharine F. Davis, September 8th

Werdmeyer, John F. and Lucinda Draffen, January 3rd

Wheat, John F. and Patsy Sims, July 28th

Wheeler, Micajah and J. A. Martin, February 7th

Wilkerson, Ambrose H. and Sarah Sandridge, January 30th

Williams, Abner and Julia A. Shickler, August 18th

Wingfield, Anderson and Mary E. Bailey, September 6th

Wingfield, John and A. D. G. Eubank, December 26th

Wood, Reuben and Patsey M. Wood, November 10th

Wood, Willis and Emily Walton, March 1st

Woodson, Thomas A. and Elizabeth Mills, June 27th

Wright, Charles and Agness P. Terrell, June 1st

1832

Walton, James B. and Eliza Jane Via, November 22nd

Warwick, William L. and Elizabeth F. Goodman, May 20th

Wayt, John G. and Cynthia K. Watson, August 4th

West, Nathan H. and Jane Isaac, March 27th

Wilkerson, Nicholas and Nancy Luck, November 9th

Wood, John and Anna Collins, August 8th

1833

Walks, Lawrence and Susan C. Mayo, April 4th

Walton, Alamond and Charlotte F. Dowell, December 12th

Walton, Campbell A. and and Jane Gilmore, March 14th

Watson, Elbert R. and Mary K. Norris, September 3rd

Watts, James D. and Eliza H. Goodman, December 19th

Wheeler, Joel A. and Martha Hobday, November 6th

White, James E. and Matilda Rosenbarogs, March 4th

White, John and Eliza M. Simms, December 19th

Widderfield, James and Eliza Jane Branham, March 17th

Willis, William S. and Eliza G. Barksdale, July 27th

Wood, Eli and Susan F. White, December 2nd

Wood, Ezekiel and Patsy Thomas, March 14th

Wood, William and Frances Wood, January 17th

1834

Watson, Daniel E. and Mary E. Harris, May 8th

Wood, James B. and Nancy A. Lloyd, December 9th

Wood, Samuel C. and Sarah E. Rodes, August 30th

1835

Walton, Edward and Ag. H. Walton, December 30th

Watson, John R. and Catharine Watson, December 22nd

Walton, Joseph W. and Ann Dickerson, August 3rd

Wharton, James and Mary Davenport, April 20th

White, Chapman and Virginia Powers, November 24th

Williams, James N. and Martha Johnson, October 31st

Wingfield, Edward and Frances Gilmore, November 12th

Wingfield, Richard and Mildred S. Early, November 23rd

Winn, James and Susan Lacey, October 3rd

Wolfe, George and Ellie Ferguson, February 18th

Wood, Harrison and Polly Thomas, December 7th

Wood, John and Eliza Jane Harper, February 4th

Wood, Nicholas and Susan Thomas, December 14th

Wood, Zachariah Jr. and Mary A. Wood, December 14th

Wright, James and Persilla Cosby, January 28th

1836

Wade, Peter B. and Christian Noel, September 28th

Watson, Benjamin and Eliza Hines, September 5th

White, John D. and Eliz. Gilmore, March 5th

Willis, William D. and Susan T. Perry, July 5th

Winebarger, John and Lucinda Winebarger, November 2nd

Wingfield, John B. and Elizabeth Carr, November 26th

Wren, James A. and Mary F. Gillum, January 5th

1837

Walker, James B. and Maria Burgess, February 23rd

Watson, Walter Jr., and Eliz. Maury, November 6th

Winebarger, Charles and Jane M. Bailey, March 20th

Winn, Benjamin B. and Mary Jane Garrett, November 20th

Woods, William M. and Louisa E. Dabney, September 28th

Woodson, William D. and Lucy Jane Ammonett, December 19th

1838

Wallace, William and Amanda Lobbin, January 20th

Walton, Tipton P. and Sally Dowell, October 1st

Watson, Benjamin N. and Lucy J. Maury, August 27th

Winebarger, John and Martha Garner, September 11th

Winslow, George N. and Martha E. Cockerill, December 3rd

Witt, David H. and Jane M. Bates, February 15th

Wolfe, Ezra M. and Ann Terrell, January 11th

Woodson, Lindsay and Amdia W. Garland, October 1st

1839

Watts, James D. and Lucy Ann Sims, April 6th

Wood, Amenson and Veranda Cox, October 11th

Wood, Meredith and Judy M. Thomas, December 19th

Wood, Richard P. and Eliza A. Tomblin, November 12th

Wood, Winston and Sarah Ward, December 23rd

Wright, William B. and Lucy R. Johnson, June 28th

1840

Wheeler, James D. and A. E. Thurmond, December 7th

Wheeler, Joshua and Rebecca Pollack, March 5th

Winn, John J. and Ann C. Wood, September 30th

Wood, Henry and Frances Thomas, December 8th

Wood, Solomon and Nancy Splice, September 17th

Woods, Peter A. and Twymonia L. Wayt, January 30th

1841

Welch, Charles G. and Lucy M. Bellew, September 11th

Willims, George L. and Eliza Huckstep, January 21st

Wilson, James and Sarah Ann Moon, September 23rd

Woods, Samuel S. and Abby D. Bates, August 30th

1842

Watson, Matthew P. and Eliza R. Norris, May 26th

Wayland, William H. and Mary Crank, January 4th

Wilmore, J. F. B. and Helen Skipwith, March 29th

Wood, David H. and M. A. Lewis, January 3rd

Wood, Elijah and Lucinda Wood, November 13th

Woods, John G. and Ellen Strange, December 18th

1843

Walker, Thomas B. and Susan T. Saunders, December 20th

Wheat, John and Martha N. Rosson, July 6th

Wilkinson, Thomas M. and Abby Ann Goolsby, February 21st

Willis, Edward J. and Virginia A. Sneed, April 12th

Wood, Alfred C. and Martha W. Rogers, December 18th

Wood, Drury and Laura T. Poore, October 12th

Wood, Jerome B. and Catharine E. Brown, October 31st

Wood, William P. and Sarah Rodes, August 1st

Woods, William A. and Mary Jane Harper, January 24th

Woodward, John P. S. and Mary M. Minor, October 26th

Wright, James and Eliza King, January 11th

1844

Walters, James O. and Mildred Thurmond, October 8th

Wingfield, John F. and M. W. Gibson, December 11th

1845

Ward, Thompson and Amanda M. Head, February 27th

Weeks, Alfred C. and N. S. Hunter, July 3rd

Wheeler, Benjamin W. and Demaria P. Brown, January 9th

Wheeler, John N. and M. A. Thompson, February 6th

White, James G. and Rebecca M. Byrd, October 7th

White, John S. and Nancy Martin, July 31st

Wind, William and Maramnith Greely, April 18th

Wingfield, Edward C. and Eliza M. White, January 29th

Wood, Edward S. and Amonia Shelton, February 19th

Wood, Simeon and Louisa C. Cobbs, January 30th

1846

Walker, William T. and Mary E. Travillian, March 10th

Watson, Benjamin and Sarah E. Jones, February 12th

Wilkerson, Lindsay and Eliza A. Thomas, December 24th

Wood, William T. and Norris Fielding, June 19th

Wood, William H. and Sarah M. Wood, December 20th

Woodson, Benjamin and Mary M. Powell, November 19th

1847

Wilmer, George T. and Mary P. Gilmore, April 20th

Wings, Charles S. and C. J. Phillips, October 19th

1848

Wade, Harden and M. McAlexander, February 23rd

Ward, Richard F. and M. F. Head, March 9th

Watson, William and S. H. Clarke, August 8th

Watts, R. M. and C. A. Simms, June 27th

Weeks, George A. and V. C. Blackwell, September 19th

Wood, John H. and S. A. Via, October 10th

Widderfield, William and E. Branham, June 8th

Wood, William H. and M. E. Robertson, May 29th

Woodson, Aug. S. and E. S. Pretty, February 7th

Workman, William H. R. and Maria A. Minor, October 18th

1849

Walker, Benjamin J. and O. A. Bailey, February 15th

Wade, Samuel C. and Lucy Toms, March 22nd

Walton, William F. and Ann E. Sandridge, May 23rd

Ward, Joseph and Marion J. F. Maupin, November 23rd

Wood, James and Dicy J. Sprouce, February 6th

Wood, William L. and C. J. Walton, June 21st

Woody, Austin and Mary J. Graley, August 7th

1850

Ward, John and Cynthia A. B. Smith, August 7th

Ward, William and Elvira Norris, July 4th

Webb, Henry J. and Mary Ann Faris, December 23rd

West, Nelson J. and Mary Martin, December 20th

White, Samuel G. and Sally C. White, March 12th

Wilkerson, John A. and Mary Ann Brock, December 2nd

Woody, James and Eliz. F. Tooley, June 12th

Wood, Sysander S. and Sarah Ann Maupin, February 26th

1851

Walstrum, C. and Eliza Wingfield, February 4th

Walters, Wyatt and Sarah J. Widderfield, January 13th

Ward, Samuel and Mary I. Catterton, July 21st

Wilkerson, John A. and M. A. Brockman, December 30th

Winn, Tavner and Lucy Ann White, April 11th

Wood, Richard N. and Sarah M. P. Moon, October 23rd

Wood, Robert and Sarah J. Campbell, September 18th

Wood, Zachariah T. and Sarah M. Phelps, December 3rd

Woodson, Shepherd and Mary Montgomery, July 20th

Wright, Leander and Sarah Cloak, October 29th

Wright, Robert and Eliza Shultz, September 10th

1852

Walker, Lawrence and S. V. Baily, October 27th

Ward, Henry and Sally A. Salmon, March 1st

Wayland, A. G. and Lucy A. Early, January 21st

Wheeler, George W. and N. M. Burch, April 11th

Wiant, James C. and S. A. Maupin, December 6th

Wiant, William I. and B. P. Kiblinger, April 1st

Williams, Andrew S. and Mildred F. Flannagan, December 11th

Wilson, James M. and C. B. Rogers, October 27th

Wingfield, Richard and Sarah Stout, May 11th

Woodson, Thomas and E. C. Carr, June 22nd

1853

Wallace, Michael and Susan A. Wayland, August 7th

Ward, John and Christina J. Wood, February 10th

Wash, William I. and Martha J. Houchens, November 7th

Weyland, James and I. I. Woodson, February 16th

White, John P. and Ann S. Lewis, September 7th

White, N. L. and Mary S. Harris, February 22nd

Wingfield, Henry C. and Frances E. Nicholas, November 29th

Wood, John and C. I. Wood, February 5th

Woodson, James G. and Bettie A. Bullock, September 7th

1854

Wade, William M. and Martha A. Mathews, June 21st

Walton, Alfred and Sarah E. Walton, May 11th

Walton, George E. T. and Eliz. A. Davis, October 16th

Walton, Jesse R. Jr., and Mary J. Lane, July 22nd

Walton, Geo. E. and Eliz. A. Davis, Oct. 11th

Walton, Perry R. and Mary S. Payne, July 22nd

Weeks, Henry and M. A. Mahanes, Dec. 21st

Wheeler, Robert S. and Bettie M. Woodson, September 27th

Whitborger, George W. and E. P. Drumheller, August 31st

White, William A. and Susan P. Rothwell, March 5th

Willoughby, Walker A. and Mary Eubank, March 30th

Wilson, John A. Jr., and Margaret S. Strange, November 28th

Wilson, John A. Jr. and Mary S. Strange, Nov. 28th

Wingfield, Charles M. and Rebecca T. Wingfield, January 11th

Wingfield, Chas. M. and Reb. L. Wingfield, Jan. 11th

Willoughby, W. S. and Mary Eubank, Mar. 30th

Winston, Oliver P. and Ann Watts, Sept. 20th

Winston, William A. and F. M. Rittenhouse, May 22nd

Winston, Wm. A. and F. M. Rittenhouse, May 30th

Wood, Clifton R. and Eliza A. Sandridge, December 21st

1855

Wade, James and Sarah A. Field, March 31st

Ward, Henry and Isabella M. Via, July 18th

Wells, John H. and Ann E. Summerson, February 28th

Woods, Andrew J. and M. A. Gibson, November 27th

Wood, Thomas W. and Lydia G. Leained, September 20th

Wood, Thos. W. and G. G. Seatned, Sept. 20th

Wood, Clif. R. and E. A. Sandridge, Dec. 21st

Wheeler, Robert S. and Bettie M. Woodson, Sept. 27th

White, Wm. A. and Susan P. Rothwell, Mar. 1st

1856

Walker, Marshall and Callie Garth, November 27th

Walker, Marshall and Cellia Garth, Nov. 27th

Wallace, John P. and Mary L. Carr, January 21st

Walters, Wyatt and Clarissa J. McAlister, July 7th

Watson, Egbert R. and Jane L. Creigh, April 29th

Wheeler, Robert S. and Lucy J. Goodwin, November 4th

White, Newton V. and Lucy J. Rothwell, October 19th

Wiant, David H. and Sarah C. Wiant, February 12th

Wallace, John P. and Mary L. Carr, Jan. 21st

Wise, E. S. H. and Virginia A. Dodd, Mar. 25th

Wood, Henry J. and Eliz. M. Cox, Nov. 15th

Wood, James H. and Columbia A. Wood,

Wood, Jno. M. and Julia A. E. Estes, Dec. 4th

Wood, Jno. M. and Marg. A. Bailes, Oct. 22nd

Wood, Albert and Sidney J. Dunn, Jan. 7th

Wood, Hillary and Mary W. Wood, June 12th Mar. 20th

Wilkerson, Wm. P. and Harriet Flynt, July 13th

White, Newton V. and Lucy J. Rothwell, Oct. 19th

Williams, Jas. W. and Mary A. Perrow, Oct. 28th

Wingfield, Jno. E. and Martha E. Roberts, May 21st

Wood, C. M. and Samantha S. Wood, Feb. 14th

Wiant, David H. and Sarah C. Wiant, Feb. 12th

Woods, Wm. R. and S. Ellen Woods, Sept. 3rd

Woodhouse, Wm. K. and Virg. P. Terrell, Aug. 4th

Wingfield Jno. W. and Maria L. Wingfield, Feb. 10th

Wheeler, Robt. S. and Lucy J. Goodwin, Nov. 6th

Wright, Wm. B. and (Cunoulellegeble), Dec. 25th

Wilkinson, William P. and Harriet Flynt, July 13th

Williams, James W. and Mary A. Perrow, October 28th

Willis, David and Jane Haislip, May 12th

Wingfield, John E. O. and Martha E. Roberts, May 21st

Wise, E. S. H. and Virginia A. Dodd, March 25th

Wood, Albert and Sydney J. Dunn, January 7th

Wood, Chapman M. and Samantha S. Wood, February 14th

Wood, Henry J. and Eliz. M. Cox, May 15th

Wood, Hillary and Lotty Thomas, June 10th

Wood, James H. and Columbia A. Wood, May 20th

Wood, John M. and Margaret A. Bailes, October 22nd

Wood, John M. and Ann E. Estes, December 4th

Woodward, William and Virginia H. Totty, August 18th

Wright, William B. and Mary B. McLain, December 25th

1857

Walton, Richard T. and Lucy Ann Madison, November 9th

Wash, Charles C. and Mandarin Eubank, May 14th

Whitehead, Paul and V. M. Timberlake, December 7th

Whitehead, Paul and Virgelia M. Timberlake, Dec. 8th

Wingfield, Charles L. and Ann E. Johnson, December 14th

Wingfield, John W. and Maria L. Wingfield, February 2nd

Wingfield, Robert L. and Euphema White, May 27th

Woodhouse, William K. and Virginia P. Terrell, Aug. 3rd

Woods, William P. and Ellen Woods, Aug. 13th

1858

Walton, Newell J. and Amanda E. Dornan, Feb. 17th

Walton, Newell J. and Amanda Dunn, Feb. 24th

Wayland, Abram and Martha T. Woodson, May 3rd

Wayland, Abram and Martha T. Woodson, May 12th

Wertenbaker, Charles C. and Mary E. Poindexter, Sept. 21st

Wertenbaker, Chas. C. and Mary E. Poindexter, Sept. 23rd

White, John S. and Martha O. Moon, March 8th

White, Jno. S. and Martha O. Moon, Mar. 9th

Wilkerson, Ambrose H. and Mary Ann Wood, July 26th

Wilkerson, Amb. H. and Mary Ann Wood, July 28th

Williams, Thomas J. and Anna Harmon, July 6th

Williams, Tho. J. and Anna Hanmor, July 7th

Wood, Edward and Etta C. Morris, May 24th

Wood, Richard R. and Lucinda H. Bryan, April 10th

Wood, Richard R. and Lucinda H. Bryan, May 2nd

Wood, Edward and Ella C. Morris, June 3rd

Wood, Wilson D. and Susan F. Brown, Nov. 26th

Wood, Wilson D. and Susan F. Brown, Dec. 2nd

Woods, John J. and Martha L. McGehee, Feb. 3rd

Woods, Jno. J. and Martha S. McGehee, Feb. 4th

Woods, Sampson L. and Martha Durrett, Nov. 10th

Woods, Sampson S. and Mattie Durrett, Nov. 16th

1859

Walton, Boyd H. and Virginia A. Marshall, Feb. 7th

Walton, Boyd H. and Va. Ann Marshall, Feb. 9th

Watson, James R. and Jane E. Scott, April 6th

Wills, Thomas and Maria S. Craven, Dec. 19th

Wingfield, Benjamin F. and Betty Perly, May 9th

Wingfield, Benj. F. and Betty Perley, May 10th

Wooling, Joseph and Letticus F. Tollin, Nov. 15th

Woolling, Jos. Jr., and Lettia F. S. Tellier, Nov. 16th

1860

Wade, John and Everline Toms, Oct. 15th

Wade, John and Eveline Toms, Nov. 1st

Watkins, T. F. and Catharine Bowles, Aug. 25th

Watkins, Tuylur F. and Cath. A. Bowles, Aug. 30th

Wills, Thos. and Maria L. Craven, Nov. 1st

Wingfield, Thomas F. and Susan F. Dudly, Dec. 3rd

Wingfield, Thos. F. and Susan F. Dudley, Dec. 6th

Wood, John T. and Virginia E. Via, Oct. 22nd

Wood, John T. and Virginia E. Via, Nov. 1st

Wyant, Jesse and Martha J. Garrison, Oct. 10th

Wyant, Jesse and Martha J. Garrison, Oct. 25th

1861

Widderfield, M. V. and Matilda L. Dudly, April 2nd

Williams, William S. and Susan Patrick, June 17th

Wells, Fred M. and Sallie H. Burnley, Feb. 28th

Wills, Fred M. and Sallie H. Burnley, Feb. 13th

Wingfield, William O. and Dorotha M. Childress, Feb. 25th

Wingfield, Wm. O. and Doratha M. Childress, Feb. 26th

Woodward, John W. and Maria M. Quinn, Nov. 30th

Woodward, John H. and Maria M. Quinn, Dec. 5th

1862

Washington, B. B. and Anna D. Buckhaman, Mar. 20th

Watkins, Wm. T. and Ellen Belle Garrett, Feb. 18th

Worth, Wm. J. and Sarah E. Johnson, Dec. 31st

1863

Wood, Alfred T. and Molly E. Wood, Dec. 22nd

Wood, Elijah A. and Ardenia J. Wood, October 15th

Wood, Henry N. B. and Martha A. Wood, Feb. 3rd

Witkins, Geo. W. and Nannie Johnson, May 6th

Wheeler, Joel J. and Mary F. Garland, April 30th

Whitehead, Wm. Reddick and E. F. Beaton, December 24th

Walters, James W. and Eliza J. Herron, Dec. 24th

Wiant, Isaac and Mary F. Gibson, Dec. 7th

Woolford, Henry and Sarah Martin, Oct. 22nd

Worthington, Jno. C. and Susan M. White, Sept. 14th

Weems, Octa T. and Janney E. Huffman, Sept. 24th

Willis, Henry D. and Jane Holbert, Mar. 24th

Wingfield, Ro. S. and Ann A. White, Apr. 1st

Wheeler, Alex S. C. and Martha A. Harden, Mar. 24th

1864

Wood, Jno. C. and Mary W. Digges, Mar. 1st

Wash. Henry and Mary Wood, Jan. 17th

Wine, Robert E. and Mary E. Spradling, Feb. 4th

Wallace, Jno. S. and Mary S. Black, Jan. 19th

Watts, David C. and Cynthia J. Herndon, Feb. 3rd

Wilson, Thos. J. and Margaret D. Ross, Aug. 9th

Willis, Ro. W. and Frances Madison, Aug. 11th

Watts, Geo. W. and Maria Kerby, Sept. 7th

Wood, Columbus S. and Mary S. Edwards, Oct. 3rd

1865

Walton, Nath P. and Mary S. Tellier, Sept. 27th

Walton, Matt. T. and Mary S. Tellier, Sept. 28th

West, William and Elizabeth Marsh, April 25th

White, Samuel H. and Sallie C. Sheats, Oct. 11th

Wingfield, S. C. and Mary W. Bunch, Apr. 27th

Wingfield, Samuel C. and Mary W. Bunch, June 25th

Winn, William H. and Eliza C. Herron, Dec. 21st

Winn, Wm. H. and Eliza A. Herron, Dec. 21st

Wood, Parks E. and Emily A. Wood, Dec. 16th

Woods, Robert H. and Georgia E. Maupin, March 25th

Woods, Ro. H. and Georgia E. Maupin, Mar. 28th

Woodward, W. F. and Mary E. Sandredge, June 22nd

1866

Wallace, Alex and Fanny Quarles, Oct. 1st

Wood, Wm. R. and Sallie M. Harris, Dec. 11th

Wood, Jacob R. and Lucilla M. Wood, Dec. 10th

Woodward, Tho. H. and Matty A. Wyatt, Dec. 24th

Wicks, Randall and Rachel Cobb, Dec. 28th

Wood, George H. S. and Susan Jane Wood, Nov. 10th

Wood, E. M. and Sidney Dowell, Dec. 3rd

Wingfield, Matthews W. and America J. Gianniny, Dec. 3rd

Wood, Wm. Rice and Sallie M. Harris, Dec. 8th

Wood, Alexander and Cornelia Tunstall, Dec. 25th

Wood, Peter and Augusta Wood, Dec. 19th

Wood, Parks E. and Emily A. Wood, Dec. 21st

Walker, Cuter and Mary Smith, May 6th

Wood, William R. and Drucilla E. Wood, Jan. 16th

Wood, Wm. R. and Druicella E. Wood, Jan. 18th

Wood, William D. and Vienna F. Howard, Feb. 13th

Wood, Wm. D. and V. F. Howard, Feb. 15th

Wolfe, Thomas B. and Eliza A. Lane, Jan. 20th

Wolfe, Thos. B. and Eliza A. Lane, Feb. 25th

Wayland, Abra and Evelina Wayland, Mar. 8th

Wayland, Al and Eveline Wayland, March 5th

Williams, Wm. H. and Rose Lindsay, June 7th

Williams, William H. and Rose Lindsay, June 1st

Wilt, George W. and Virginia C. Hubard, July 18th

Wilt, Geo. W. and Va. C. Hoband, July 19th

Wingfield, Chas. H. and M. J. Sutter, Oct. 9th

Wingfield, Charles H. and Maida J. Suller, Oct. 4th

Wingfield, John F. and Caroline E. Smith, March 7th

Wright, Thos. W. and Maria C. Wheeler, Oct. 23rd

Wright, W. T. and M. C. Wheeler, Oct. 22nd

Wood, Silas W. and Susan H. Dulaney, Nov. 10th

Wood, Geo. H. S. and Susan J. Wood, Nov. 13th

Wingfield, John F. and C. E. Smith, Mar. 14th

1867

Wood, Horace W. and Sarah E. Wood, Jan. 7th

Wood, Eli J. and Mary E. Ward, Jan. 8th

Woodson, J. S. and Susan J. Day, Oct. 9th

Whitescarver, Geo. H. and Sarah A. Wood, Sept. 5th

Wingfield, Geo. W. and O. Nana White, Feb. 16th

Watts, J. S. and Sally E. Clements, Mar. 9th

Wirlington, Chas. A. and Mary A. Terrell, Apr. 16th

Wicks, Peter and Siscely A. Douglass, July 27th

Ware, Felix H. and Kate W. Purvis, Sept. 16th

Whitecarver, Geo. H. and Sarah A. Wood, Sept. 5th

Williams, John and Tacy Coleman, Oct. 17th

Winn, Thos. J. and Mary Jane Beck, Dec. 7th

Watson, Calvin G. and Lavinia Spears, Dec. 9th

Watson, J. C. and Lavinia Spears, Dec. 12th

Walton, Edgar R. and Mary E. Jones, Dec. 10th

Ward, John R. and Louisia N. Henbook, July 11th

Ward, John R. and Felice Key, July 11th

Wright, Wm. W. and Rebecca R. Estes, July 1st

1868

Ward, Robert and Coletda A. F. Wood, Jan. 16th

Watson, John D. and Susan H. Smythe, Dec. 30th

Wallace, Alex and Milly Brown, July 18th

Wallace, Alex and Milly Brown, July 19th

Webb, Wm. F. and L. V. Shepherd, Jan. 25th

Westley, John and Eliza Burwell, August 24th

Wood, Chris C. and Mary S. Ballard, Jan. 6th

Wood, Enoch and Mary M. Beacon, Oct. 5th

Wood, Enoch, and Mary M. Brown, Oct. 6th

Wood, Joseph F. and Sarah E. Gooch, Dec. 24th

Wood, Wm. F. and Eliz. McClarmock, Dec. 10th

Wolfe, Adolphus and Ann Watson, March 27th

Worledge, Webster W. and S. D. Goodman, Apr. 9th

White, John M. and Gay P. Leake, Mar. 5th

Worledge, Webster W. and Sarah D. Goodman, Apr. 9th

Watkins, Wilson and Martha Turner, May 18th

Winn, Miles and Martha Coles, June 3rd

Williamson, Tho. and Sallie B. Nelson, Aug. 25th

Williamson, Thos. and Sallie B. Nelson, Aug. 26th

Wilkerson, E. W. and Mollie A. McCauley, Oct. 16th

Willoughby, Alfred and Eliz. Martin, Oct. 8th

Willoughby, Alfred and Eliz. Martin, Oct. 3rd

Wheeler, W. W. and Lavinia Rea, Jan. 4th

Wheeler, David H. and Mary F. Foster, Jan. 26th

Wheat, John N. and Marg. Garland, Dec. 24th

1869

Wingfield, L. R. and M. R. Wingfield, Mar. 25th

Wood, Wm. R. and Martha Calvertz, Mar. 29th

Wells, James and July Anna Johnson, Apr. 11th

Webb, Geo. S. and M. E. Taylor, May 18th

Walker, Chas. and G. Washington, July 3rd

Wiscott, Richard E. and V. P. Gaulding, Sept. 2nd

Woodfox, Matt. and Susan Fanxs, Sept. 29th

Walker, Chs. and Mana Johnson, Nov. 13th

Wallace, Geo. W. and Sally W. Chewings, Oct. 27th

Washington, James and Agnes Carry, Nov. 18th

1870

Wells, James and Naney Armstead, Feb. 20th

Wyatt, Jas. M. and Ida M. Wyatt, Mar. 9th

Wallace, C. J. and M. L. Sclater, Nov. 17th

Webb, Wm. C. and Sallie E. Hall, Dec. 20th

Williams, Robt. O. and Sallie W. Bibb, Nov. 30th

1871

Wood, Eli Y. and Fanny M. Morris, Mar. 28th

Winebarger, Wm. A. and Margaret E. Johnson, Mar. 13th

Wallis, John C. and Christian H. Oliver, Apr. 27th

Watkins, Mat. and Louisa Wood, July 23rd

Willis, Joseph N. and B. Alice Sneed, Nov. 21st

Wood, Winston T. and G. B. Clark, Nov. 24th

Wood, Robert Anderson and Sally Thomas Rothwell, Dec. 11th

Weeks, John James and Laura Esteline Bowen, Dec. 12th

Wiseman, Wm. Henry B. and Luella A. Sandridge, Dec. 25th

Wood, Jacob N. and Frances E. Garrison, Dec. 19th

Wood, George V. and Ellen Herndon, Dec. 21st

1872

Williams, Quntins and Virginia E. Fritz, Jan. 16th

Woodpin, Samuel E. and Molly S. Alexander, Feb. 1st

Wright, Wm. Henry and Ann C. Wood, Jan. 10th

Wood, Robert B. and Harriet A. Marsh, Sept. 22nd

Wood, Edward S. and Martha F. Crenshaw, January 16th

Wallace, George T. and Julia M. Chewning, Oct. 16th

1873

Wiseman, C. H. and Ann J. Maury, Apr. 16th

Walker, J. S. and Mary C. Clarke, Aug. 30th

Wilson, Daniel R. and L. V. Branham, Sept. 1st

Wood, Jas. T. and Susan F. Ballard, Dec. 1st

Walters Wm. and Jane Scruggs, Dec. 12th

Wood, Cornelius and Emma Jane Rothwell, Dec. 8th

Wertenbaker, Chas. C. and Fannie T. Leptwich, June 23rd

Walker, Jno. F. and Nannie V. Flannagan, Dec. 18th

1874

Williams, John and Sarah Dunham, Jan. 1st

Williams, Abner C. and Margaret Carroll, Jan. 20th

Walton, Wm. F. and Mary L. Hoy, Feb. 5th

Winchester, Thos. P. and Nanna Thurman, Feb. 11th

Woodson, Jno. T. and Sallie F. Shelton, Mar. 18th

Wood, David E. and Nanny E. Munday, Apr. 6th

Williams, Thos. E. and Jacintha J. Lawson, June 24th

Walton, G. W. and Bettie Whitlock, Aug. 18th

Wade, Jas. and Emma Martin, Dec. 7th

Wood, Davis E. and Eliza M. McCauley, Dec. 22nd

1875

Woodson, Wm. L. and Betty J. Sutherland, Jan. 11th

Woody, Mayo C. and Willey J. Miller, Feb. 25th

Ward, Jno. R. and Lucy A. Herndon, Mar. 24th

Ward, Elgin H. and Eliz. E. Dunn, Mar. 31st

Wood, Chas. S. and Sarah A. Brown, Sept. 13th

Wood, Geo. N. and Lucy F. Jones, Nov. 1st

Weaver, Wm. F. and Sally E. Creel, Nov. 9th

Wood, Richard M. and Sally S. Clarke, Nov. 12th

Wilkerson, Wm. P. and Emily E. Leake, Nov. 23rd

1876

Wood, Willis H. and Fannie P. Wood, Jan. 31st

Wood, Henry B. and Martha F. Ward, Feb. 7th

Wells, Alexander B. and Willie B. Chapman, Apr. 11th

Walker, Jno- H. and Willie E. Bellomy, May 30th

Williamson, Tho,. L. and Bettie K. Burnley, June 6th

Wright, Robt. G. and Sallie G. Johnson, June 24th

Wells, Jos. and Susan A. Thacker, Oct. 21st

Ward, Avington, S. and Susan M. Harris, Nov. 21st

Wright, Thos. R. B. and Margaret D. Preston, Nov. 28th

1877

Wood, Jas. Wm. and Susan M. Craig, Jan. 1st

Wood, Jas. B. and Angeline V. Powell, Jan. 17th

Wood, Jno. W. and Lucy V. Rhodes, Sept. 7th

Wood, Nicholas T. and Nancy E. Rhodes, January 22nd

White, Jerry M. and Nannie Sutherland, Oct. 18th

Walton, Virgil L. and Willie B. Bass, Nov. 5th

West, Joseph M. and Olivia N. Hawkins, Nov. 5th

Williams, Jas. F. and Emma J. Garrison, Dec. 19th

Wood, John and Isabel Marsh, Dec. 21st

1878

Walton, David F. and Va. Garrison, Feb. 18th

Watson, J. I. and Nancy E. Jones, Apr. 10th

Woodson, Jno. T. and Sally B. Early, June 27th

Wingfield, James and Mary Addie Gay, Nov. 12th

Wayland, Jas. T. and Naney L. Michie, Dec. 2nd

Warwick, Abram R. and Sarah E. Goodwin, Apr. 11th

1879

Wade, John and Jane J. Baber, Aug. 15th

Wade, Jerry F. and Martha J. Suddarth, Nov. 24th

Ward, Wm. P. and Alice G. Croberger, Feb. 17th

Walker, Thos. J. and Nannie A. Fretwell, Feb. 25th

Wilkinson, Henry J. and Matilda E. Davis, Apr. 14th

White, Geo. W. and Anne M. Wayland, May 26th

Wright, Samuel A. and Mary E. Wood, June 3rd

Wilkinson, Ira T. and Mrs. R. A. Wright, Aug. 12th

Winn, Jerry and Farence D. Dollins, Sept. 8th

Watson, Egbert R. and Nannie H. Cocke, Sept. 17th

Wood, Zacheriah D. and Julia C. Garrison, Sept. 22nd

Walton, Samuel H. and Minnie F. Thomas, Sept. 29th

Woodson, James T. and Ritter Dollins, Oct. 23rd

Wood, Theophelius D. and Sussie Gilbert, Nov. 10th

Wilhoit, Ezekiel T. and Georgia A. Gentry, Nov. 14th

Wood, Millard F. and Annie P. Hudson, Nov. 18th

Wranek, Joseph and Letitia A. Hill, Oct. 16th

Walker, Wm. W. and Eliza L. C. Smith, Dec. 3rd

1880

Wright, Thos. W. and Mollie P. Johnson, Aug. 2nd

Wood, Geo. W. and Bettie C. Abell, Oct. 19th

Wayland, Robert F. and Dora C. Herndon, Sept. 29th

Winn, John T. and Jennie B. Smith, Dec. 4th

Ward, William A. and Susan A. Newell, Dec. 24th

Walton, John Fountain and Ann Eliza Garrison, Dec. 23rd

1881

Williams, William D. and Lilly H. Kirby, Mar. 1st

Ward, Alderlus W. and Ella Jane Mayo, Sept. 7th

Wood, William L. and Mary S. Wayland, Nov. 6th

White, John Lee and Sally W. Modena, Nov. 10th

Walton, William F. and Mattie V. Ballew, Dec. 14th

1882

Walker, James and Lon Hill, Sept. 13th

Ward, Theodore Corndius and Drusella Agney Estes, December 24th

Washington, Fielding and Lula Ann Ward, Jan. 18th

Wood, Edgar E. and Louisa Farrer, Feb. 7th

Wood, James R. and Ella R. Rogers, Jan. 2nd

Williams, John and Clementia Marshall, May 9th

Wood, John J. and Laura A. Eubank, Sept. 30th

Woodson, Samuel A. and Sarah E. Leake, Oct. 25th

Wood, William H. and Annie Gibson, Nov. 19th

Wilson, David W. and Rachel T. Bramham, Dec. 13th

Woodson, Franklin and Martha A. Spencer, Dec. 14th

1883

Womack, John and Kitty Garland, Mar. 15th

Wood, Chas. P. and Eliza E. Wood, July 21st

Walton, Jesse R. and Lucy Jane Bailey, Sept. 27th

Walker, Lindsay and Susan Vashte Wood, Oct. 11th

Walker, Charles C. and Lucy Shackelford, Oct. 18th

Wallace, Wm. H. and Lucy Burch, Nov. 11th

Wells, James and Georgianna Porter, Nov. 18th

Webb, William C. and Jennie Scott Walker, Nov. 29th

1884

Wash, Chas. Henry and Lucy Ann Simpson, Sept. 7th

Walcott, Thoe. G. and Louisa E. Aloise, Sept. 10th

Wine, Christian J. and Rosaline A. Hawkins, Apr. 4th

Williams, Frank W. and Nannie A. Watson, Oct. 8th

Wood, Robert L. and Ella Florence Hall, September 4th

Wood, Virgil B. and Mattie E. Gay, Feb. 7th

Wood, Sunderland W. and Marion S. Wood, Apr. 16th

Wood, T. T. and Emma G. Douglass, May 8th

Wood, Wm. R. and Rosa Bell Sandridge, Sept. 11th

Wood, James Burnley and Lucy D. Waddell, Sept. 3rd

Wood, James F. and Mary F. Thomas, Oct. 19th

Wright, Jas. H. Mollie L. Rittenhouse, Oct. 9th

Woods, Robt. H. and Annie E. Rothwell, Nov. 12th

Woodson, Wilhoit and Bell Adeline Shelton, Nov. 19th

Woodward, Chalmers L. and Emma J. Gardner, Dec. 28th

1885

Webb, James M. and Kate S. Novell, May 7th

Woodson, Benj. F. and Mary F. Gibson, Aug. 4th

Whitmore, Clarence W. and Mattie E. Jones, Sept. 17th

Wade, Wm. and Martha J. Moyer, Nov. 5th

Ward, Joseph E. and Lucy V. Davis, Dec. 20th

Walton, Samuel H. and Elmore Walton, Dec. 21

1886

Walters, Jno. L. and Mollie G. Bailey, Feb. 23rd

Webb, Octavius H. and Sallie H. Mahanes, Mar. 9th

Wheeler, Bernard and Anna Cora Fitz, Mar. 11th

Walker, Jas. Lewis and Wille Bellomy, Mar. 30th

Wingfield, Henry C. and Rosa E. Stevens, July 18th

Ward, Aaron and Bettie Clifton, Sept. 1st

Walker, Geo. N. and Annie L. Dmen, Sept. 8th

Warnick, Jm. H. and Mattie R. Mann, September 14th

Wood, Robt. H. and Isabella P. Hedges, September 16th

Witt, Lafayette W. and Nannie W. Witshire, September 28th

Wood, Wm. and Eliza Jane Rogers, December 25th

1887

Wood, Warren and Maggie L. Woods, January 5th

Wildshire, Montgomery and Cassie J. Sheeler, April 28th

Walton, Joseph J. and Bertie A. Melton, November 22nd

Wilson, Stanyame and Lucy G. Burnet, December 12th

Wayland, A. C. and Mary E. Humphrey, December 29th

1888

Woodson, O. A. and Bettie Wilkerson, January 8th

Wood, Wm. J. and Emma Birckhead, February 6th

Wood, Eugene L. and Emma E. Via, November 8th

Ward, Richard F. and Clarissa A. E. Jordon, March 13th

Will, D. K. and A. C. Bailey, April 25th

Wood, E. N. and N. E. Browning, July 19th

Woodson, Wm. H. and Eliza N. Sprouse, September 29th

Woilford Jas. R. and Mary S. Hoy, September 29th

Wade, R. S. and Mary E. Suddarth, October 29th

Walker, Wm. and Anna Ayee, November 13th

Walker, Simon and Lutie Burnley, November 17th

1889

Wood, C. H. and F. C. Sullivan, January 3rd

Wood, F. T. and J. A. Porter, January 31st

Ward, Davie T. and Lavinia H. Wood, April 18th

Wilson, Robt. D. and Ellen C. Conway, June 24th

Wash, Geo. T. and Willie E. Lanes, July 1st

Wilkins, S. S. and Estelle Wood, September 19th

Wade, J. D. and M. E. Toms, October 28th

Wingfield, J. H. and L. E. Dudley, October 24th

Woodson, J. L. and C. R. Ellinger, October 29th

Wood, Jno. R. and E. D. Ford, December 23rd

Woolfrod, W. H. and M. M. Davis, December 23rd

Woodson, Buck and Mary L. Gibson, December 23rd

Wood, A. C. and M. S. Newton, December 24th

1890

Walton, Chas. T. and Mary J. F. Sullivan, March 26th

Windsor, E. E. and B. O. Price, April 2nd

Whitaker, T. W. and M. H. Worthington, April 22nd

Wood, Geo. W. and Lucy V. Via, September 29th

Winn, H. R. and C. J. Winn, October 14th

Wood, James W. and Susan M. Wood, December 23rd

1891

Woody, H. B. and M. J. Bowers, June 9th

Wilson, J. M. and Nellie Michie, August 4th

Walton, S. F. and S. H. Wostham, December 11th

1892

Wheeler, J. W. and B. E. Price, January 1st

Ward, J. R. and M. E. Laundree, January 19th

Wood, J. W. and Lavina Rhodes, January 20th

Worthy, Albert and Bettie E. Perkins, April 6th

Walton, J. E. T. and E. D. Patterson, September 28th

Walters, Lilburn and Jimmie Galdeling, November 14th

Willis, D. B. and Mollie E. Brooks, November 21st

1893

Walters, R. B. and M. F. Thomas, August 23rd

Webb, Geo. W. and Ada F. Wood, September 1st

Wood, Jas. N. and S. L. Humphrey, October 23rd

Wood, Sylvester and M. P. Wood, October 27th

Wiers, Thos. J. and Berdie Townley, October 30th

Wright, Jno. W. and R. E. Harlow, November 29th

1894

Wood, Jno. C. and H. L. Eddens, January 16th

Walker, L. M. and Maud Waddell, April 2nd

Wood, Wm. G. and Ella J. Batton, April 3rd

Williams, Daniel J. annd M. H. Sneed, June 2nd

Woodson, Peyton and Ella Gibson, June 11th

Woodson, D. P. and Mosy J. Rogers August 30th

Wilkerson, E. M. and K. C. Childress, September 23rd

Wood, Wm. E. and Nellie M. Mullins, September 17th

Woods, R. S. and Willie A. Jones, November 28th

Wood, E. Y. and J. B. Harlow, November 29th

Wade, Jno. and M. E. Toms, December 14th

Watts, J. B. and M. F. Clatterbuck, December 17th

Walfer, Jno. W. and Cornelia Layne, November 5th

Wood, Liv. E. and Luenn Lupton, November 10th

Wright, H. H. and Carrie O. Hawkins, November 20th

Wilson, Jno. and S. C. Minor, November 21st

Wade, Henry and Lily Norvell, November 21st

1895

Williams, Jas. M. and Lillie E. Garland, February 7th

Wayland, Benj. A. and H. L. Kirby, June 13th

Wood, Jas. C. and Maud I. Brubeck, June 14th

Wood, B. I. and E. A. Elliott, September 19th

Wade, S. E. and Maggie Campbell, October 19th

West, Jno. E. and M. B. Stachlin, October 22nd

White, J. H. and M. B. Whitmore, November 22nd

Walton, B. E. and M. L. Humphrey, December 12th

1896

White, J. C. and S. M. Dettor, April 15th

Wood, Eze. B. and M. S. Wood, June 8th

Wash, Henry and Carrie Wash, September 7th

Wingfield, E. A. and M. L. Daucin, October 27th

Woodson, L. L. and M. G. Brown, November 4th

1897

Walker, Sam'l M. and Ella Johnson, October 25th

Walton, G. W. and Lou Walton, January 10th

Wood, F. J. and B. Blanche Munday, February 20th

Woods, Jno. H. and Helen A. Durrett, February 23rd

Wiant, E. A. and M. F. Head, March 6th

White, Thos. L. and Rita C. Rodes, March 20th

Wood, Jno. O. and Annie L. Newman, March 31st

Waddell, H. G. and M. K. Rodes, September 2nd

Whitehead, W. W. and Mildred W. Nelson, October 6th

Wolfe, Chas. H. and Leone J. White, October 25th

Walker, Geo. E. and Annie Watson, November 9th

Wood, D. G. and S. E. Wood, November 16th

Wright, Jno. D. and Lottie Warren, December 22nd

Wade, Ardie L. and Rosa Lee Kirby, December 22nd

1898

Wisely, W. L. and Alice Martin, January 4th

Wood, Walter D. and Blanche E. Flint, February 22nd

Wood, Paul W. and Martha Wood, February 28th

Wineberger, C. and E. L. Critzer, May 10th

Wilson, Jas. A. B. and Ella K. Clark, August 22nd

Walters, G. W. and Annie L. Rhodes, December 20th

Wheeler, S. S. and L. K. Payne, December 21st

1899

Ward, Wm. S. and S. E. Wood, January 9th

Wheat, C. C. and Sally L. Burgess, October 25th

Wingfield, J. A. and V. F. Carter, January 3rd

Willis, W. D. and C. M. Coleman, December 23rd

Wingfield, A. L. and Kate L. Munday, January 9th

Wood, Philys and Annie N. Walton, November 15th

Wood, H. L. and M. L. Marsh, March 23rd

Wood, W. E. and Myrtie C. Via, September 4th

Wingfield, A. M. and M. F. Snead, May 22nd

Wood, Wiley and V. F. Daughtry, June 14th

Walker, Jas. A. and Irie R. Poindexter, August 30th

1900

Walton, E. B. and Dicey C. Lane, December 19th

Ward, D. T. and Emily C. Hall, February 5th

Walden, Wm. H. and Minta Marshall, April 23rd

Watson, Geo. N. and Mary M. Burnette, September 24th

Webb, James J. and Susan J. Campbell, April 11th

Wilkes, Louis D. and Susanna C. Nelson, March 1st

Wingfield, Samuel and Susie V. Snead, November 27th

Wilkerson, Thos. E. and Carrie B. Fisher, December 22nd

Willis, M. L. and Cora E. Evans, April 9th

Willis, Callie and Roberta Marshall, April 16th

Wrenn, Wm. J. and Etta V. Johnson, July 16th

Wood, B. S. and N. H. Giles, March 5th

Wood, Algourney, and Druscilla E. Wood, April 23rd

Wood, G. B. and J. Creasy, November 30th

Wood, Geo. G. and Virginia Railey, January 20th

Wood, E. H. and Lola E. Haney, September 16th

Wood, S. A. and Eva C. Twyman, September 24th

Wood, Wm. E. and Mollie E. Weber, September 25th

Wood, Ellis and Ella Wood, December 17th

Wood, E. A. and C. D. Phillips, December 18th

Wood, J. R. and Lucy Milton, December 24th

1901

Wood, E. E. and L. A. Douglass, January 15th

Wood, Willie A. and M. B. Deane, April 3rd

Wood, L. L. and C. E. Thurston, April 23rd

Wingfield, Jas. J. and Carrie Birckhead, May 16th

Witsel, G. G. and Ida I. Wood, May 29th

Walker, R. E. and S. F. Breeden, June 12th

Wood, F. L. and M. E. Cox, October 10th

Wood, Hunter and Mary Mundy, November 28th

Wilkerson, Ted D. and Rosa L. Pace, December, 16th

Woods, J. H. and Annie Rhodes, December 26th

1902

Wood, Oscar and Grace Marrs, April 29th

Webber, Robt. D. and Bessie Buoic, June 11th

Walters, J. A. and Ora P. Douglass, June 18th

Winn, Chas. W. and Lelia V. Kidd, July 9th

Woody, Wm. T. and Rosa Lee Martin, August 9th

Wise, John F. and Nita Jones, August 11th

Walfert, Geo. and Sally E. Ray, September 10th

Wash, A. N. and M. J. Baber, September 15th

Wood, W. L. and E. H. Sale, September 16th

Worthington, R. B. and E. K. Barlow, September 23rd

Wisley, John M. and May B. Stachlin, October 13th

Whittington, Geo. P. and Susan B. D. Bubank, November 19th

Wood, R. W. and I. B. Melton, December 13th

Woodford, J. S. and C. L. Langhorne, December 17th

1903

Wagner, G. E. and C. M. Wheeler, August 3rd

Walton, Fountain and Manda Hensley, December 2nd

Weadel, H. D. and L. B. Ballow, November 2nd

Wyant, J. A. and A. K. Lynch, August 3rd

Winfield, A. L. and H. W. Rea, September 16th

Wood, E. O. and M. F. Cox, October 29th

1904

Wash, John Walla and Lucy Eliz. Phillips, January 18th

Wheeler, W. J. and Julia E. Goin, March 23rd

Weitzel, Harry E. and Annie L. Bush, May 25th

Wright, E. J. and H. E. Parsons, May 30th

Wilkerson, I. E. and E. I. Herndon, August 15th

Whittington, Chas. A. and Susan C. McCauley, August 31st

White, Chas. D. and Nellie Marshall, September 30th

Ward, J. W. and B. V. Maupin, October 4th

Woodward, M. F. and Nellie J. Shipp, October 12th

Wright, Walter Spencer and Lelie Overton Chambers, October 15th

Wade, Captain A. and J. V. Tomlin, October 18th

White, Wm. C. and Marie C. Nicholas, October 25th

Wharam, Charlie and Nellie B. Mayo, November 7th

Walters, Richard L. and Virgie L. Lang, November 7th

Waybright, C. J. and S. I. Sensibaugh, November 30th

1905

Walton, Jas. Thos. and Lucy Bettie Ruburch, January 5th

Walton, Geo. and Rosa Keyton, July 18th

Walton, Maurice and Maggie Morris, October 19th

Walton, Mannice and Maggie Morris, October 19th

Ward, Lewis Avington and Annie Lee Haney, September 26th

Ward, Lewis Airington and Annie Lee Haney, September 26th

Wills, Roy B. and Emma J. Reer, June 21st

Wells, John Calvin and Julettie McClure, July 14th

Wood, Richard and Anna Edwards, September 14th

Wood, A. and Carrie Marsh, October 7th

Wood, Wilson Purvis and Betty Frances Maupin, November 17th

Wood, Stephen Grayson, and Lillian Electra McAllister, December 19th

Wood, Richard and Anna Edwards, September 14th

Wood, A. and Carrie Marsh, October 7th

Woodson, Jas. Lewis and Ossie Burks, November 28th

Wood, Wilson Purvis and Betty Frances Maupin, November 17th

Woodson, James Lewis and Ossie Burks, November 28th

Wood, Stephen Grayson and Lillian Electra McAllister, December 19th

1906

Wheeler, Joseph and Mattie Young Wood, May 23rd

Ward, William Wyant and Ella Grayson Ponts, June 14th

Watson, Norton and Janie Willis Nairne, June 27th

West, Charles A. and Watt Mars, August 21st

Worsham, Robert Franklin and Ollie Turpin, September 20th

Wilbourn, R. W. and Eva Mae Gibson, October 17th

Whitten, George H. and Georgie Purvis, October 17th

Wheeler, William E. and Cynthia A. Burton, October 31st

Wright, William P. and Annie E. Simpson, December 4th

West, William R. and Nora Munday, December 19th

Wade, Cal. Clark and Sallie M. Tomlin, December 27th

1907

Wood, Thomas W. and Mary E. Morris, January 24th

Wood, Edward and Hattie Vaughan, February 7th

Wood, Howard B. and Nannie B. Berry, June 5th

Williams, Jonathan and Gertie Via, July 13th

Ward, L. A. and E. M. Phillips, August 7th

Wood, W. L. and Ora C. Gibson, August 14th

Wood, R. E. and Carrie Rothwell, September 4th

Witt, J. J. and Lenney Elsom, September 17th

Wood, Otie A. and Sallie B. Norford, October 30th

Wood, V. C. and Alma T. Cobbs, December 18th

Walton, Nueal and Linda Jane Roston, December 25th

1908

Ward, William S. and Luella Wood, January 15th

Whitlock, Alfred and Alice Fox, January 16th

Walters, Major and Annie Barkel, January 26th

Wood, William S. and Virginia E. Michie, February 5th

Walton, Stonewall J. and Ethel C. Coleman, February 17th

Woodson, Hamilton Browning and Sallie C. Phillips, March 29th

Winn, James E. and Bessie E. Spencer, April 19th

Warren, William T. and Willie N. Patterson, April 21st

Wood, Theodore I. and Ethel May Moore, July 8th

Walker, Charlie D. and Emma J. Davis, July 28th

Watson, Daniel E. and Elizabeth F. Garnett, October 28th

Wade, Henry M. and Susanna Parr, November 4th

Wood, Littleton H. and Myrtie B. Walker, December 27th

1909

Ward, Luther E. and Linney C. Pitman, February 24th

Wood, Mann L. and Dora C. Kirby, February 24th

Walton, Charlie F. and Mittie L. Shiflett, February 28th

Wood, Percy E. and Mabel A. Via, March 15th

Woods, George W. and Daisy F. Morris, May 14th

Warren, William R. and Margaret W. White, June 2nd

Ware, Samuel D. and Charlotte T. Marshall, June 19th

Wilkerson, Chester W. and Lula D. Kirtley, August 25th

Whitlock, Lawrence and Carrie E. Seiler, September 29th

White, James S. and Mary A. Shepherd, November 23rd

Wood, James E. and Grace L. Dowell, November 25th

Woodson, George and Annie Birckhead, December 12th

1910

Wood, J. J. and Rachael E. Tomlin, February 20th

Weaver, E. M. and L. B. Gallahs, June 4th

Woodson, Oscar and Ethel Moses, June 22nd

Weislrod, Walter and Ida W. Watts, July 20th

Wood, Joseph E. and Mary E. Payne, August 1st

Woodson, William E. and Lucy H. Miller, August 3rd

Walton, Ephram and Nettie H. Chisholm, September 27th

Wood, Monte T. and Lucy L. Ware, September 20th

Ward, Robert N. and Carrie J. Sandridge, November 16th

Wright, Thomas W. and Annie M. Adams, November 27th

Wingfield, Emmett L. and Janie E. Johnson, December 16th

Woods, Oscar B. and Fannie B. Powell, December 28th

Waddell, Don E. and Mary Lou Wilhoit, December 28th

Wood, Bennie F. and Lottie E. Thompson, December 28th

1911

Walton, Rice E. and Maud V. Shepent, February 10th

Ward, Cornelius and Bettie M. Fry, May 2nd

Ward, Orestes V. and Margaret R. Harlow, May 20th

Wilberger, Wallace W. and Frances I. Via, June 29th

Walton George Edward and Bessie Mauk, July 3rd

Whitner, Ira W. and Jennie V. Beazley, July 12th

Wood, Theodore C. and Isabel Thomas, July 18th

Walton, Charlie E. and Lizzie M. Coleman, July 19th

Williams, Charles F. and Mary E. Thurston, August, 20th

Wood, Cincinnati A. and Leona C. Mawyer, October 11th

Wheeler, Richard J. and Myra B. Morris, October 18th

Wood, Wilmer W. and Fannie S. Alexander, November 18th

Wood, Dillard and Emily Lancaster, November 23rd

Walton, Eddie B. and Lucy P. Lamb, November 25th

Weast, James Gordon and Lillian Mabel Watson, December 21st

1912

Wheeler, John W. and Mattie W. Faris, January 1st

Wooley, S. Tredwell and Carolene McIrney, April 10th

Williams, Jim and Mabelle Easton, April 15th

Wood, Rollie and Peachy Eubank, April 20th

Wood, W. F. and A. M. Wood, May 28th

Wooding, Charles E. and Marie H. Earley, June 19th

Walker, Charles B. and Sarah F. Walker, June 19th

Williams, Samuel H. and Mattie S. Gentry, June 26th

Walton, John W. and Virtie L. Walton, June 26th

Wilson, George and Eliza Woodson, September 7th

Woolsley, Ernest and Virgie Reburn, September 19th

Wodstsie, Edward and Nellie Baber, October 16th

Witt, Sam A. and Annie E. Leonard, November 21st

Willis, William D. and Pearl V. Centris, November 30th

Wood, Joseph A. and Lizzie Detamore, December 8th

Woody, Letcher and Effie Baber, December 18th

Wood, John and Sadie Thurston, December 27th

1913

Wells, Austin and Alberta Barksdale, January 13th

Wood, Arthur C. and Margaret C. Wood, March 5th

Willis, Turner A. and Mrs. Julia Carroll Walton, March 25th

White, Everett V. and Gracie P. ?, March 23rd

Wood, Ray O. and Mattie A. Stribling, March 26th

Wood, John S. and Eva Carter, April 1st

Wilford, Ernest A. and Morrell A. Houchens, April 16th

Wood, Willie and Nealie Morris, April 22nd

Wood, Monroe and Mollie Bowen, May 1st

Ward, B. E. and L. B. Anderson, June 10th

Wood, Ellis W. and Victoria V. Shiflett, September 10th

Walton, Ben and Nora Lee Hensley, December 17th

1914

Wood, Lawson and Daisy G. Foster, April 8th

Wilbourne, Littleton Thurston and Rosa Gibson, April 13th

Wood, Stuart G. and Anna McAllister, May 13th

Ward, G. N. and Margie L. James, June 24th

Wood, Ollie A. and Nettie L. Hackett, July 6th

Ward, Pleasant T. and Nettie F. James, July 8th

Walton, John F. and Lucy McAllister, July 16th

Wood, Massie W. and Jane M. Harlow, September 7th

Wheeler, John W. and Maggie V. Wolfe, September 7th

Wood, George L. and Elinor B. Cox, September 21st

Winn, James M. and Ruth White Anderson, November 8th

Walton, Samuel and Myrtle McAlister, November 25th

Woodson, John O. and Elizabeth Kathleen Jones, December 2nd

Walton, Mace and Mittie Garrison, December 19th

1915

Wood, Ernest H. and Pearl M. Wood, January 4th

Willis, Hugh H. and Cornelia C. Morris, January 12th

Wood, Sellis and Deanie Dunn, March 7th

Weiss, William and Myrta L. Harris, April 5th

Wilkerson, Frank D. and Virginia K. Norris, May 26th

Wade, Nathaniel S. and Ada C. Tomlin, June 3rd

Wood, George F. and Mary L. Williams, June 27th

Watson, Dallas and Friddie M. Gibson, August 11th

Warwick, Edward C. and Ethel V. Hamner, August 31st

White, Hunter E. and Annie N. Omohundra, September 8th

West, Luther and Lee McFarley, November 5th

Ward, Allen and Arkie Thompson, November 25th

Woody, Thomas H. and Myrtle R. Pleasants, December 21st

1916

White, James G. and Mary Turner, January 4th

Wood, Carl C. and Fannie R. Houchens, January 12th

White, Allen N. and Pauline M. Nre. January 26th

Wood, Emmett and Pearl Dickerson, February 16th

Wayland, Edwin M. and Eleanor H. Sayler, February 17th

Whilbetch, Marshall and Elsie Lee Bell, April 11th

Walker, Eli W. and Sallie M. Birckhead, April 19th

Woodson, Albert S. and Ethel B. Lee, April 22nd

Woods, Nebb Androw and Maggie Lee Cox, June 10th

Walters, Bernie L. and Mary A. Robertson, July 19th

Walton, James A. and Mary Via, September 11th

Wormick, Clyde and Mary Kennedy, September 26th

Wray, Joe and Ella C. Robertson, October 20th

Walker, Percy F. and Delia V. Closley, November 14th

Weller, Walton T. and Arinenia P. Rea, November 29th

1917

Wilkerson, Beverly N. and Belle M. Ross, April 9th

Ward, H. F. and Rochel Harlow, April 23rd

Wiley, Hugh T. and Mabel G. Patterson, June 23rd

West, Layton Paul and Mattie F. Harvey, July 28th

Whitacker, Floyd and Bertha M. Wood, August 2nd

Wilkins, Herbert C. and Bessie L. Jarrell, August 8th

Woodson, James M. and Dorothy Turner, April 23rd

Walsh, George A. and Eunice M. Carter, September 16th

Woody, John E. and Lelia May Eubank, November 23rd

Washington, W. Warren and M. Margaret Hughes, December 26th

Wood, Broadus Lee and Thelma Via, December 28th

1918

Walsh, Vernon T. and Margareth Showalter, January 16th

West, Walter and Rhoda Breeden, March 4th

Wade, Bledsoe and Evelyn Parr, May 27th

Wayland, Roy and Lillian S. Miller, August 16th

Watson, Alex. and Lucy Williams, August 29th

Wood, Elliott G. and Irleane Marshall, September 21st

Woods, Charlie and Dora Haney, September 26th

Walton, Ellis and Mannie Walton, January 1st

Wade, Grover and Blanche Martin, October 2nd

West, Allen T. and B. B. Lively, October 14th

Wood, Samuel G. and Clara A. Roberts, December 24th

Wheeler, Roy S. and Emily R. Smith, January 18th

1919

Wilson, Lewis T. and Lizzie Sprouse, January 25th

Wood, Lysander Thomas and Lula A. Dickerson, February 6th

Wood, Leonard and Annie S. Marshall, February 20th

Wood, Leroy T. and Nellie Virginia Wood, March 5th

Walsh, Thomas G. and Beulah Bessie Bryant, March 20th

Wood, Lawrence U. and Anna L. Jones, April 14th

Walker, James W. and Virginia S. Keaster, June 4th

Wyant, Andrew K. and Irene M. Clark, June 10th

Wright, Johnnie S. and Flrence C. Hall, June 10th

Wickline, Simpson A. and Mary B. Rothwell, July 12th

Wharm, John L. and Nora Damron, July 20th

Wood, George C. and Essie L. Wood, August 2nd

Woodson, Henry and Florence Gibson, August 25th

Williams, James and Dora Dawson, November 15th

1920

Weller, Joseph I. and Margaret V. Barringer, May 8th

Wingfielld, Charles Vest and Willie M. Garth, June 26th

Woodson, Ben and Annie Kirby, July 17th

Wyant, Thomas R. and Emma L. Dollins, July 21st

Wisleard, Bernard D. and Minnie M. Hamm, August 18th

Workman, Paul W. and Violet C. Snow, September 1st

Ward, Wallace J. and Fannie B. Alderman, September 18th

Walton, Frank and Cora Rogers, September 25th

Wood, Anderson, and Mary Lee Word, October 20th

Wood, Manis M. and Minnie Frances Harris, November 2nd

Walton, Thomas and Sarah L. Shiflett, November 11th

Woolford, William H. and Bessie C. Gentry, December 7th

Walker, Moffett M. R. and Lottie Blanch Crenshaw, December 21st

Woody, Charles F. and Lilly M. Marshall, December 30th

1921

Wood, Roy F. and Victoria E. Hilderbrand, January 15th

Wood, George M. and Minnie K. Batten, February 12th

Wilkerson, John N. and Janet Ida Harris, February 19th

West, George W. and Nettie Richardson, April 30th

Walker, Bennie C. and Ethel Blanche Gibson, May 1st

Wood, Noel and Annie Lively, May 19th

Watts, Lucian L. and Martha Cantant, June 10th

Wilson, Edward Ross and Fannie B. Hadley, June 20th

Wood, Clyde A. and Bettie L. Bolton, July 2nd

Wood, James N. and Evelyn Lee Thurston, July 11th

White, Sam T. and Elizabeth Pannel, July 30th

Wood, Frank L. and Bertha A. Wood, August 31st

Wingfield, Emmett E. and Margaret L. Craddock, September 10th

Weatherly, Henry M. and Marian W. Lewis, September 13th

Wells, Oliver M. and Janie M. Via, November 12th

Wood, Clarence T. and Mildred Brown, November 24th

Walker, Paris C. and Mary E. Layne, December 24th

1922

Walton, Carroll and Lucy Hazel Lang, March 18th

Webb, Walter and Addie Morris, April 17th

Walton, Samuel H. and Mrs. Ells Breeden, April 20th

Wayland, George B. and Alfred N. Adams, May 2nd

Wood, R. Warren and Matbilde W. Lewis, January 28th

Ward, Hugh and Pearl A. Sprouse, August 23rd

Walton, Edward H. and Mary W. Dexter, November 2nd

Wood, George E. and Mary B. Baker, November 11th

Watson, Robert L. and Hattie L. Gibson, December 27th

1923

Weymouthe, William P. and Ada Gear Rosser, March 5th

White, William Rhodes and Frances B. Smith, March 31st

Wilber, Charles R. and Rachel E. Allamony, April 6th

Wheeler, John H. and Eula B. Goolsby, May 24th

Walton, William J. and Carrie B. Batten, June 14th

Wright, John T. and Ella M. Fielding, June 28th

Wood, James E. and Katie Perry Carr, July 11th

Willis, Richard L. and Elizabeth Harris, August 2nd

Wayland, Roy J. and Herreitta G. Walsh, September 19th

Wood, Willie L. and Nealie Morris, ? ?

Walsh, Cary W. and Mary Wheeler, November 3rd

Wright, Wingate L. and Maude Payne, November 20th

Walker, Maurice D. and Mary L. Wood, November 28th

Wood, Rubin and Lizzie Wyant, November 29th

Woodson, Andrew A. and Ruby M. Critzer, December 24th

Ward, Milton and Edna Kurtz, December 15th

Woodson, James and Jennie Carr, December 19th

Walker, Jeff R. and Edna T. Amiss, December 20th

White, Will A. and Mary B. Harding, December 24th

1924

Ward, Robert and Ruby Hunt, January 6th

Woodson, Andrew and Edith V. Gibson, January 22nd

Wilson, Jerry M. and Rosa G. Harlow, February 9th

Wood, Claude A. and Mary E. Marshall, April 24th

Wood, Oscar B. and Charity W. Davis, May 2nd

Wood, Cuyler D. and Cora A. Keller, May 5th

White, John S. and Mary E. Fenurck, July 2nd

White, Francis S. and Lottie I. Norvell, July 16th

Wood, Lawrence N. and Linney Watson, August 13th

Whitted, Clarence A. and Mary W. Gardner, August 12th

Wheeler, John H. and Ruby E. Banton, September 25th

Walker, Robert and Mattie Dolman, October 18th

Wood, Robert N. and Viola Earl Mundie, November 26th

Wheeler, Lee and Pearl Gibson, November 29th

1925

Wilkerson, Emmett S. and Mabel J. Dowell, March 21st

Wood, Linwood L. and Mary L. Wood, June 20th

Wilson, Willie J. and Gershon B. Allen, November 17th

Wood, William M. and Minnie Berckhead, November 20th

Wolfe, Thomas W. and Cora Lee Abell, November 25th

Wilson, Elwwod Lee and Gladys J. Gibson, December 19th

Werner, Edward A. and Ethel M. Cook, June 8th

Wood, Vander E. and Daisy Davis, July 31st

Wood, Herbert R. and Edna P. Marion, August 17th

Walters, William D. and Mabel B. Glass, September 24th

Walker, James M. and Lottie B. Beck, October 20th

Walton, George and Mary Garrison, November 3rd

Wade, Ethelburst and Ruby Mawyer, November 8th

Walsh, William R. and Inez T. Jones, December 4th

Wright, Linwood E. and Minnie P. Lamb, December 30th

1927

Wade, Jacob E. and Annie M. Bailes, January 3rd

Wallace, John W. and Irena T. Robinson, February 8th

Wilkerson, Clarence W. and Jessie Dowell, February 19th

Wharam, James O. and Mattie E. Price, July 16th

Woodson, Edward G. and Vernon L. Newton, August 6th

Wells, Clyde V. and Mary E. Critzer, September 4th

Walton, Melvin N. and Ellie P. Shiflett, September 19th

Wood, Noah and Marie Crawford, September 28th

White, Rufus D. and Helen A. Alwood, October 15th

Walton, Norman W. and Carrie M. Harlow, October 15th

Woodson, James M. and Elsie Mae Cook, October 25th

Woodson, Lewis and Louisa Sprouse, November 4th

Wood, George Chapman and Madie M. Wood, November 21st

Westervelt, George C. and Rieta B. Langhorne, December 20th

Wayland, Frederic G. and Sarah C. Meredith, December 6th

Woodward, Melton and Louise Sprouse, December 6th

Wood, Lawrence and Alice Johnson, December 21st

Woodson, Zeke and Carrie Gibson, December 24th

1928

Woodson, Edgar O. and Thelma M. Pugh, January 14th

Wingfield, Joseph O. and Arbutus Kidd, March 30th

Wright, Peicie M. and Ethel Burkley, April 6th

Wood, Clarence E. and Roney P. Marshall, July 4th

Walsh, Walter H. and Elsie V. Thomas, July 17th

Wood, Warner W. and Elva L. Watson, July 30th

Watkins, Robert C. and Florence M. Wiley, September 24th

Wood, Richard L. and Thelma V. Gardner, November 5th

1929

Ward, David S. and Susan A. Carr, February 20th

Whitman, Paul W. and Mary R. Bowen, February 5th

Williams, George and Eliner A. Gibson, March 27th

Woodson, John M. and Elsie M. Humphreys, June 22nd

Wood, Lacy H. and Virginia E. Wood, July 3rd

Wheeler, Willie Ira and Mabel J. Powell, July 20th

Wood, J. R. and Sadie E. Thurston, August 17th

Walton, George and Nellie Shiflett, October 25th

Williams, Homer G. and Hazel E. Lambert, December 10th

Y

1786

Yancey, Charles and Sarah Field, June 8th

1790

Yarley, Richard and Hannah Jameson, January 12th

1793

Yancey, Jechonias and Mildred Wood, October 14th

1795

Yancey, Robert and Phebe Rasel, December 9th

1804

Yancey, Charles and Jane Alexander, January 2nd

1805

Yancey, David and Ann Minor, July 20th

1809

Yancy, Jeremiah and Sarah Roathwell, November 10th

Young, David and Mary Hurt, April 25th

1812

Yancy, Ralph H. and Patsy H. Garrison, September 7th

1815

Yancey, David and Milley W. Fields, March 27th

1818

Yancey, Muriah and Celia Martin, September 7th

1820

Yancey, William and Mildred White, April 12th

1823

Yancey, Joel and Elizabeth Brown, December 12th

1826

Young, William and Mary W. Bishop, August 31st

1828

Yancey, Robert and A. G. A. Norvell, January 12th

1833

Yancey, Jechonias and Julia L. Winn, June 28th

Yates, Thomas C. and Mrs. Martha Gilmore, November 26th

1835

Yancey, Alex K. and S. S. Farrar, October 13th

1836

Yancey, Wiliam and Mary E. Crank, July 11th

1846

Yager, Joseph H. and Martha A. B. Fray, February 3rd

Young, William and Sarah Pace, January 3rd

1847

Young, Sowin and M. E. Wheeler, January 12th

1851

Young, George A. and Sarah Smith, April 24th

1854

Yampurt, A. H. D. and C. H. Turpin, October 26th

1855

Yateman, Rich. H. and Ann H. Bishop, April 12th

1865

Young, Theo and M. Walker, September 27th

1866

Young, George H. and Mary E. Tomblin, September 14th

Young, Geo. H. and Mary E. Tombelin, September 16th

1868

Young, Geo. H. and Mil. M. Fields, December 3rd

1882

Yowell, Henry Y. and Laura M. Thomas, April 18th

1890

Yancey, Chas. and Belle W. Hall, January 1st

1896

Young, A. A. and Ida C. Layne, November 30th

1897

Yancey, John F. and Alberta B. Robertson, November 27th

Young, Benj. S. and Johanna Carver, December 21st

1899

Young, Jas. L. and Carry L. Davis, June 28th

1900

Yancey, R. A. and Annie Durrett, February 13th

Yude, Alfred M. and Mary B. Patterson, April 2nd

Young, B. R. and Sallie E. Mawyer, December 22nd

1901

Yancey, C. R. and L. E. Parr, October 26th

1903

Young, John and Hannah Stuart Nicholson, December 1st

Yowell, Chas. Herbert and Carrie Virgie Mccauley, December 26th

1904

Yeomans, Clifton and Nellie G. Dawson, August 15th

1906

Yancy, Thomas H. and Elsie M. Hasher, August 15th

1908

Yowell, J. L. and Lelia G. Chisholm, January 15th

Yowell, Madeus M. and Esther Allen, December 23rd

1914
Yates, Benjamin F. and Sarah A. Taylor, April 24th

1919
Yowell, Roscoe M. and Elsie Payne, May 19th

1923
Yoe, Thomas H. and Clara G. Robertson, March 30th

1925
Yancey, Charles H. and Rosa Lee Critzer, December 30th

1926
Young, Harry B. and Virginia Lee Beverly, October 1st

Z

1855
Zatiman, Robert and Ann H. Bishop, April 12th

1876
Zinmerman, Wm. and Harriett E. Spradling, December 14th

1877
Zimmerman, Chas. R. and Amanda Spradling, February 12th

Zimmerman, Samuel M. and Amanda J. Robinson, August 16th

1878
Zettee, Geo. W. and Alice S. Marshall, March 18th

1888
Zerkel, B. N. and N. F. Horton, December 11th

1898
Zbonil, F. D. and M. E. Estes, May 18th

1915
Zitzer, Charles F. and Vernie Esther Brown, August 4th

City of Charlottesville Virginia

Marriages of 1888 - 1929

A - Z

A

1890

Anderson, C. R. and R. S. Loflennd, Oct. 22nd

1891

Allen, W. E. and S. C. Sterling, Nov. 18th

1892

Atkins, Jas. M. and Annie M. Dupre, Feb. 9th

1893

Abell, Benj. Franklin and Maggie M. Moon, Oct. 27th

1894

Anderson, John K. and Mary S. Hurdum, Jan. 25th

1896

Allen, W. W. and Nellie R. Harris, Nov. 17th

1897

Armstrong, Lee B. and Henrietta M. Hoge, Feb. 8th

1907

Anastasi, Antonia and Hamnud Cocivera, March 20th

1908

Ayers, Tyler J. and Gladys L. Hughes, Mar. 3rd

Alwood, H. J. and Fannie J. Herrman, Dec. 27th

Allen, John C. and Allie C. Carter, Dec. 28th

1909

Ashford, M. S. and Orah M. Rogers, Jan. 26th

1910

Adams, James E. and Daisy V. F. Mays, Feb. 11th

Adams, John R. and Margaret D. Irene, July 31st

1912

Allegree, Aubrey N. and B. Corinne Edwards, Oct. 2nd

1914

Alderson, Grover and Alice C. Wingfield, Dec. 3rd

1916

Austin, Harvey W. and Sadie E. Ballard, May 27th

Atkins, James M. and Edna W. Webb, Nov. 2nd

1917

Amonette, Clarence O. and Lena Webb Adams, May 26th

1918

Atkins, G. W. and Eva B. Thomas, Aug. 27th

Anderson, Rob't Eastwood and Margaret Buchanan, Sept. 6th

1919

Anthony, John B. and Ruth B. Burnley, Feb. 5th

Adams, Wm. Bryan and Ethel M. Holsinger, May 17th

1920

Ackles, Frank O. and Emma T. Canfield, Jan. 6th

Adams, Robert O. and Annie E. Ballard, Aug. 21st

1921

Anderson, Theron Bruce and Alice Shrum, Feb. 23rd

Aery, George C. and Ella L. Brown, Oct. 5th

Anderson, John L. and Anna H. McCampbell, Nov. 1st

1922

Arey, Marshall L. and Lydia M. Dudley, May 30th

Amos, Leonard J. and Virginia Spencer, July 22nd

Acree, Linwood R. and Lennie Pearl Trainum, Aug. 5th

1923

Ashby, Rob't L. and Blanche D. Brown, Feb. 15th

Alcock, Robert W. and Maude E. Jones, April 16th

Adams, Wm. L. and Gertrude M. Williams, July 2nd

1924

Arbogast, Frank and May Bailey, May 1st

Alexander, Abraham S. and Elizabeth L. R. Goodyear, June 7th

1926

Atwood, Geo. Willard and Peggy Virginia Brown, July 28th

Aiken, Jno. Porter and Mable Boland, July 30th

1928

Allen, Murray B. and Irene C. Alcock, Aug. 1st

Allen, Thos. D. and Willie Maude Branham, Sept. 8th

Allen, Thos. Jackson and Evelyn Derinda Watson, Sept. 30th

Armstrong, Thos. Clerims and Viola Margaret Hooper, Dec. 23rd

Anderson, Joseph Walker and Florence Adosia Martin, April 20th

1929

Adolph, Walter Edward and Mary Virginia Gill, June 26th

B

1888

Bishop, Jonathan A. and Florence H. Collier, Nov. 13th

Brown, Elisha A. and M. E. —— ——

1890

Bennett, Fred C. and Sarah Tolbert, Aug. 7th

Burgess, Rob't N. and Fannie H. Marshal, Sept. 22nd

Brown, Ch. L. and Lucy E. Chisholm, Nov. 18th

1891

Busenger, Jno. Lee and Susie C. Via, Aug. 9th

Burnley, Wm. S. and Lula Payne, Aug. 14th

Baker, Jno. W. and Mary E. Dudley, Dec. 23rd

1892

Becker, Jas. J. and Leonnie Moses, May 31st

Baber, James G. and Bettie B. Bryant, Sept. 27th

Bunch, Edward Jackson and Martha Jane Bonds, Dec. 21st

1893

Balser, Z. R. and Dora L. Harris, Mar. 1st

Brown, Rob Alex and V. T. Long, Nov. 8th

1895

Broadhead, Wm. F. and Ella Rasche, Oct. 26th

Blakley, A. R. and Mary E. Walker, Nov. 16th

1896

Bidgood, Charles West and Minnie M. Young, Jan. 15th

Brown, Roy and Mary Annie Scruggs, Jan. 29th

Bradley, Lee C. and Eleanor Lyns, June 29th

Butler, Linwood and Lou Wood, Aug. 20th

Buck, F. W. and Emma A. Harlow, Sept. 23rd

Blake, John Lewis and Pauline Steptoe Thomas, Nov. 4th

1897

Bowman, R. M. and Jimmie C. Houchens, July 28th

1898

Bowers, Forest R. and Ada F. Gilbert, Sept. 15th

1899

Baber, Jas. Hall, and Lillian M. Williams, June 15th

Bryant, Vernon P. and Lizzie P. Harris, July 4th

Boland, Chas. and Annie Hall, July 21st

Brown, G. M. and M. A. Chambers, Oct. 18th

1900

Barksdale, H. L. and Minnie O. Sandridge, Oct. 17th

1901

Bullitt, Jas. B. and Evelyn Bryan, May 30th

Bacon, Richard and Lucinda E. Nickell, July 5th

Burgess, Jas. W. and Mrs. Ida Seal, Oct. 16th

Bane, Chas. L. and May Talbott, Nov. 28th

1902

Baird, Turney W. and Clara L. Brown, Jan. 23rd

Burgess, Rob't. J. and Lizzie M. Pratt, Feb. 19th

Buck, Geo. W. and Annie Bayles, Mar. 27th

Boland, John and Martha Farish, June, 21st

Branham, L. C. and M. H. Marshall, Dec. 30th

1903

Branzell, Jno. H. and Lizzie Kennedy, Feb. 24th

Barrs, Gustaine and Ruth Davis, Aug. 4th

Bibb, Ward E. and Fannie McAllister, Aug. 19th

Birch, S. A. and A. B. McKnight, Dec. 23rd

1904

Brown, Chas. Lewis and Mary L. Snow, Jan. 19th

Bennet, Wm. E. and Julia A. Bridgewater, Jan. 19th

Ballon, J. C. and T. V. Lang, Feb. 3rd

Birch, Frank H. and Mrs. Ida L. Sneed, Feb. 19th

Blakey, Smith G. and Lillie T. Woods Oct. 31st

1905

Bullard, Henry Clay and Gertrude L. Irvine, Aug. 16th

Bradley, Walter J. and Athea L. Hester, Dec. 12th

1906

Blue, Willie P. and Lillie May Murray, Jan. 4th

Barnes, Lawton H. and Valeria S. Norris, Mar. 23rd

1907

Birch, Charles H. and Anna P. Hudson, Apr. 1st

Barnett, Roy E. and Daisy E. Dove, Apr. 2nd

Bryant, James E. and Elizabeth F. Payne, June 3rd

Baum, Louis and Lillian V. Newman, Nov. 6th

1908

Burgess, Alfred L. and Nannie L. Critzer, June 25th

Baker, Rob't. B. and Mrs. B. F. Goff, July 4th

Blake, Charles S. and Bertha Settle, Aug. 12th

Bragg, Wm. S. and Lillie E. Tyler, Sept. 17th

1909

Bell, Andrew and Virginia A. Witt, June 23rd

Badham, Vernon C. and Lelia Johnston, Aug. 3rd

1911

Bailey, Henry M. and Nellie V. Melton, Feb. 5th

Brockman, Oliver P. and Lillie S. Dudley, Sept. 10th

Bashaw, Wm. L. and May L. Johnson, Oct. 24th

1912

Bailey, Cabell P. and Lynda R. Carter, Apr. 24th

Brown, Thomas and Mary E. Cox, June 26th

Brown, Wm. J. and Mrs. Irene Shelton, July 25th

Barnett, Wirgil L. and Mannie S. Diggs, Nov. 25th

Bailey, Wm. M. and Clara E. Sandridge, Nov. 26th

Beck, Charles N. and Virginia H. Carver, Dec. 31st

1913

Bowles, Harry T. and Ida Louise M. Hanckle, Feb. 11th

Brooks, John C. and Evelyn V. Patten, Mar. 6th

Beach, Claude H. and Mabel G. Ladd, June 25th

Byers, E. Thomas and Lena May Taylor, Aug. 8th

Booker, Lewis and Kathleen M. Flannagan, Sept. 3rd

Bragg, Robert L. and Lucy M. Birckhead, Sept. 8th

Bourne, James D. and Marion L. Thurston, Sept. 8th

Bishop, Elma G. and Carlisle Keller, Sept. 14th

Bishop, Melvin R. and Pearl J. Bragg, Oct. 6th

Bragg, R. L. and Olivia L. Pratt, Oct. 8th

Barnet, Thomas J. and Essie O. Graves, Nov. 5th

Bernard, Frank W. and Margery A. Evans, Dec. 22nd

1914

Buchanan, William J. and Bessie G. Dinwiddie, Jan. 14th

Bishop, Herbert T. and Frances E. Kirtley, May 11th

Barton, Geo. Lloyd, Jr. and Joan M. White, June 11th

Betts, William V. and Bessie A. Cannon, Sept. 11th

Braddock, A. R. and L. C. Fitzpatrick, Dec. 12th

Blankenship, Robert E. and Martha A. Wooley, Dec. 16th

Brown, Herman and Malind Stratton, Dec. 23rd

1915

Bardin, James C. and Sally N. Nelson, June 19th

Blanton, Grover C. and Cora Campbell, July 15th

Black, Sam'l. C. and Jennie B. Hantzman, Sept. 2nd

Barnes, Bennett H. and Mary Isabell Robertson, Oct. 27th

Beaver, Moses L. and Laura M. Maupin, Dec. 11th

Bagby, Floyd N. and Rosa May Wingfield, Dec. 26th

1916

Blue, Charlie L. and Gracie Clements, Jan. 1st

Biddinger, Guy B. and Virgilia H. King, Mar. 9th

Bunch, Melvin T. and Henrietta J. Smith, June 3rd

Butler, Henry D. and Etty L. Bourne, June 28th

Boothe, George R. and Lunna A. Smith, Aug. 19th

1917

Birckhead, Willie and Lillie Lee Houchens, Feb. 12th

Batchelder, Ralph T. and Nora B. Maupin, Mar. 28th

Betts, Thos. Jeffries and Elizabeth Mc. J. Randolph, Aug. 22nd

Bailey, W. L. and Blanch Beach, Dec. 12th

1918

Benson, Theodore B. and Rebecca Dean Albin, January 26th

Burruss, J. Henry and Bernice D. Bangher, Feb. 5th

Battilles, Russell and Gertrude Shiflett, Feb. 11th

Bibb, Rob't. E. and Josephine Powell, Mar. 30th

Baltwood, Jas. Walter and Mamie Lang, May 13th

Bailey, C. Bernard and Laura Poore Wood, Aug. 8th

Burthe, Eustice E. and Lucile E. Enloe, Oct. 21st

Battle, Jno. S. and Mary Jane Lipscomb, June 12th

Bellomy, Sam'l J. and Mary Hitt, Nov. 2nd

1919

Bolling, Albert S. and Susan Gordon Dabney, Apr. 30th

Brown, Frank W. and Florence A. Goode, May 13th

Back, Aldine M. and Violet Va. Marshall, June 3rd

Beauchamp, Chas. W. and Eliz. Stewart White, June 7th

Byrd, Mason Selby and Ida Mary Dillard, June 17th

Branham, Alexander V. and Ruby M. Gay, Oct. 14th

Bush, Jno. G. and Jane Robertson, Nov. 15th

Belew, Alex and Fannie Moore, Dec. 22nd

1920

Butt, Fairlie and Fredreka Harris, Jan. 3rd

Blakey, Grover C. and Daisy L. Smith Jan. 22nd

Black, Oscar W. and Rachel King Feb. 20th

Brown, Clarence Cecil and Bessie Lee Staples, Mar. 15th

Blanton, Geo. S. and Melvinia L. Walsh, May 8th

Belew, Russell J. and Doris O. Reynolds, July 1st

Burgess, Jno. Jeff and Ruby Bingler, Oct. 1st

Bryant, P. G. and Lillian M. Amiss, Oct. 3rd

Banks, Jno. Bankhead and Jeannie Dewees Loury, Dec. 6th

Brooks, Henry M. and Lottie Shiflett, Dec. 26th

1921

Bishop, Bernard O. and Mannie D. Ray, March 7th

Barnett, Dewey S. and Stella N. Day, Apr. 24th

Burnet, Hugh G. and Margaret A. Bryan, June 2nd

Bishop, Vernon E. and Bonnie Gianniny, June 14th

Bingler, Willie R. and Florence Alverta Dobbs, July 10th

Bowyer, J. Fred and Mary Yancey Clifton, July 22nd

Bell, Eugene and Julia Dysart, Sept. 14th

Brooks, Cecil E. and Clara M. Cummings, Oct. 3rd

Bryson, Samuel Z. and Katharine L. Fitzpatrick, Oct. 28th

Brown, Joseph Kent and Gladys Gertrude Gentry, Dec. 20th

1922

Barksdale, Ernest E. and Dora B. Landes, Jan. 11th

Brown, H. L. Thomas and Blanch V. Wilmer, Feb. 18th

Butler, Soloman R. and Carrie L. Huckstep, Mar. 14th

Burgess, Wilmer R. and Mary L. Hawkins, Apr. 30th

Ballentine, Harper and Margaret W. Wagaman, May 3rd

Brown, Wm. F. and Edna McDonnell, May 18th

Biggers, Dr. Isaac A. and Beatrice E. Haslam, Sept. 9th

1923

Baker, James E. and Julia M. Humphreys, Jan. 6th

Blakey, Rob't. Silvey and Natalie Louise Bourne, Jan. 8th

Bunch, Roy S. and Mrs. Annie Smith, Mar. 12th

Burnett, Ric'd. Edw. and Margaret M. Wood, Mar. 24th

Ball, Wm. David and Mary Ann Burnley, Apr. 21st

Beguiristian, Gustava M. and Clara Geneviene Higgins, June 21st

Brown, Ralph A. and Annie Tomlin, Aug. 12th

Becker, Harry W. and Mabel E. Bartlett, Oct. 13th

Berryman, Sam'l. Edw. and Nora Pearl Perry, Oct. 24th

Baycalari, John and Alma H. Webb, Oct. 10th

Belew, Everett Lee and Lula J. Moore Dec. 29th

1924

Bishop, Bernard O. and Hazel M. Norford, Jan. 12th

Blackman, Arthur V. and Edith E. Marsh, May 3rd

Brown, Lawrence H. and Lillie Mabel Staples, June 2nd

Blackman, Leonard J. and Rose L. Jacobson, June 11th

Bainbridge, Frederick F. and Cornelia W. Burnley July 7th

Breeden, Hansford C. and Elizabeth C. Wade, Sept. 7th

Barnett, Percy Elliott and Agnes Hortence Townsend, Sept. 24th

Boger, Jno. Clarence and Viola Sensibaugh, Oct. 1st

1925

Baker, Linwood E. and Hattie B. Slaughter, Jan. 12th

Broome, Lemuel R. and Dorothy D. Houchens, Jan. 17th

Brooks, Lucian Overton and Josie Annie Wade, Sept. 29th

Brown, Virgil K. and Evelyn M. Calles, Nov. 14th

Bridgewater, Frank M. and Alice C. Norford, Nov. 25th

Breeden, Carl James and Anna Lee Partlow, Dec. 24th

Brown, Wade H. and Bessie Bishop, Dec. 23rd

1926

Beale, Rob't. Cecil and Frances G. Dunnington, Aug. 7th

Bruce, Rob't. F. and Susie M. Hurt, Aug. 9th

Blincoe, Jas. Wm. and Mary Lewis Burnley, Aug. 19th

Brannon, Clarncee and Mary Elizabeth Cloud, Sept. 7th

Brookman, Melvin Perry and Lottie Frances Updike, Sept. 7th

Bagby, Floyd Nicholas and Annie Lee Davis, Dec. 28th

1927

Brithain, Rufus and Elizabeth Spotts Roberts, Jan. 29th

Battilles, Russell Munday and Mattie Va. Sharp, Mar. 24th

Bunch, Floyd Oren and Fanny Grace Kelley, Apr. 2nd

Belew, Curtis W. and Mable Clair Wood Apr. 30th

Barlow, Geo. Worthington and Sarah McCartley George, June 11th

Belber, Milton Henry and Amelia Bennet Oberdofer, June 28th

Bragg, Clyde Irving and Mary Lee Thompson, Sept. 4th

Brochtrup, Nicholas Joseph and Helen Marie Bamer, Oct. 17th

Butler, James Perry and Gladys Wooding Sandridge, Oct. 1st

Barnett, Irvin Holstead and Josephine Gibson, Dec. 24th

1928

Bailey, Harry Franklin and Ethel M. Wood, Jan 1st

Benson, Russell Morris and Mary Anna Johnson, Mar. 20th

Butler, Ernest Frederick and Lucy Pearl Dudley, Mar. 30th

Blue, Julian Bledsoe and Ollie Rith Marsh, May 3rd

Barr, Claude Shelton and Norma Lena Via, Aug. 25th

Bryant, Geo. Marshall and Ruby Maxine Marshall, Nov. 27th

Bunch, Rob't. Harry and Mary Lewis Collins, Dec. 15th

Bethel, Elbert Geo. and Geneva Peyton, Dec. 22nd

1929

Bingler, Ernest Hughson and Mabel Irving Ray, June 24th

Barnett, Ernest and Carrie E. Durham, Aug. 17th

Barger, Otis Edw. and Gertrude Lee Woodson, Aug. 30th

Boyd, Thomas Munford and Dorothy Leigh Pilkington Sept. 10th

Bullock, Franklin Wallis and Gladys Williams Dove, Sept. 16th

Blue, Chas. Edwin, Jr. and Marion Sterling Daniel, Oct. 18th

Blackwell, Charles Randolph and Rubie Katharine Smith, Nov. 2nd

Brown, Jury Nelson and Lois Wilson, Nov. 6th

Brown, Robert and Bessie Lewis, Dec. 28th

C

1888

Clarke, Fred W. and Setutra Conway, Dec. 10th

Craft, Jacob N. and S. R. Craig, Dec. 22nd

1892

Cohen, Alfred E. and Frances E. Annhime, April 5th

Craven, Geo. B. and Nora E. Moses, June, 2nd

Craven, Harry E. and Lula A. Bryant, June 2nd

Carr, David and V. V. Tompkins, June 6th

Connel, Geo, E. and C. M. Jett, Sept. 7th

1894

Colomb, B. A. and Margaret S. Gilman, Oct. 23rd

Canada, J. J. and Lottie Henry, Dec. 29th

1895

Craghan, Daniel and Maggie R. Ingersoll, Sept. 9th

Carter, Roy H. and May E. Brand, Oct. 26th

Cramwell, Jas. and Ida Haislip, Dec. 17th

Carter, C. E. and E. E. McKnight, Dec. 24th

1896

Cox, Jas. Reuben and Annie N. Gatch, Jun. 24th

1897

Cage, R. R. and Minnie C. Dobbins, May 17th

1898

Cleaton, Jas. B. and Willie T. Tate, Mar. 28th

Coyner, Edgar T. and Emma C. Hentman, Aug. 16th

Cowhig, Wm. M. and Annie E. Kelley, Sept. 19th

1899

Cochrane, Dr. J. I. and Mary R. Jones, Aug. 14th

1900

Carter, Jno. P. and Mrs. E. Whitten Pratt, Feb. 25th

Chamberlain, William and K. T. Nelson, April 25th

Clark, Edward J. and Ella Broadhead, Aug. 8th

Cutcherson, Jas. D. and Jennie A. Saunders, Dec. 21st

Condrey, Wm. R. and Ruth R. Murrell, Dec. 24th

1902

Crockett, Samuel M. and Orra E. Brown, June 26th

Carmon, Francis L. and Mary H. Hove, July 3rd

Carver, Jas. E. and Sadie L. Pratt, Jul. 14th

1903

Cook, Rich'd. L. and Helen M. Finniley, June 24th

1904

Conder, E. P. and Clara E. McGhee, Jan 9th

Cameron, Thomas and Eva Sacree, Jan. 14th

Callie, J. P. M. and H. R. Bibb, Mar. 29th

Cowles, Peter T. and Anbtnitte M. DuPre, May 11th

Clarke, Geo. E. and Mrs. Alice Goosby- May 10th

Correll, Frank M. and Virgie I. Bethel, July 4th

Carter, Ivy D. and Nettie E. Deffenbaugh, Sept. 21st

1905

Chanceller, S. C. and C. R. Rodes, June 27th

Cornell, Jos. M. and Eliza H. Riggs, Aug. 2nd

1906

Cash, Walter L. and Eliz. Scantling, June, 27th

1907

Chisman, W. G. and R. E. Eastham, Jan. 30th

Conchie, Byrd, P. M. and Annie E. Wilkins, Aug. 12th

Chewning, M. S. and Mrs. M. E. Brown, Sept. 17th

1908

Coley, Luther B. and Hattie L. Perry, Feb. 26th

Curry Isaac and Annie L. Owens, May 27th

Campbell, William H. and M. E. Jones, June 29th

1909

Carter, Francis M. C. and Ada F. Harbottle, Feb. 23rd

Cooke, James E. and Margaret C. Gibbs, Mar. 9th

Corbin, Claude D. and Mae M. Ward, Apr. 3rd

Coulter, Jay C. and Carrie L. Clarke, June 28th

Creasy, Awe B. and Clara E. Wood, Dec. 6th

1910

Clark, Jesse E. and Allie F. Mayo, Oct. 19tb

Carr, Bernard J. and Beatrice B. Booth. Nov. 18th

Chambers, Abner A. and Ola M. Robinson, Nov. 23rd

1911

Clifton, Hilleary V. and Nora E. Powers, May 24th

Cole, Roy S. and Isla Hudson, May 31st

Clark, Harry L. and Gertrude C. Martin, Nov. 30th

1912

Cash, Robert B. and Troye C. Edwards, June 12th

Clements, John W. and Maggie L. Long, June 17th

Costan, James G. and Leona Brown, June 29th

———, ——— — and Hattie A. Jones, Dec. 26th

Charlie, E. M. and Ida Azar, Dec. 31st

1913

Cook, Wm. A. and Lilly G. George, June 18th

Clements, John W. and Mrs. Bertha Dunn, June 28th

Crow, Gus B. and Evelyn L. Holbrook, Oct. 25th

Cooke, Edward W. and Nannie W. Triplett, Dec. 3rd

Conmer, Zeph G. and Italy Grippa, Dec 11th

1914

Carter, Kemp L. and Gracie L. Shepherd, Dec. 23rd

Clements, Wesley S. and Grace V. Lunsden, Dec. 25th

Costen, Rufus J. and Mary Elizabeth Carter, Apr. 2nd

1915

Cobbs, Tilgham L. and Beulah V. Carter, June 10th

Claibourne, Frank W. and Pauline B. Townsend, Sept. 29th

Clements, Walter Lee and Georgia A. Hamilton, Dec. 6th

Campbell, Thomas C. and Kate H. Duke, Mar. 24th

1916

Chisholm, John M. and Annie B. Averill, Apr. 19th

Cox, Lynn T. and Mary E. Kline, May 22nd

Clements, Jesse and Lutie Easton, Aug. 23rd

Childress, T. J. and Sadie L. Wright, Nov. 30th

1917

Cason, W. T. and Vera Wickline, Feb. 7th

Cash, Lonnie M. and Irene Craddock, Mar. 19th

Clarke, Rob't. L. and Annie M. Wiseman, Apr. 2nd

Craven, Watson E. and Sarah G. Eheart, Apr. 11th

Cox, Clifford N. and Nellie F. Smith, Apr. 17th

Comra, Stephen and Hettie Marple, Apr. 25th

Cooke, Ernie and Eva Breeden, June 2nd

Clarke, Henry J. and Maggie M. Ware, Aug 11th

Cobb, Wallie F. and Flossie Myers, Sept, 8th

Chisholm, V. C. and Lillie C. Lang, Oct. 29th

Cundiff, Posey L. and Florence Dudley, Dec. 1st

Coleman, Jno. W. and Hannah M. Robinson, Dec. 15th

Carter, Gardner L. and Fannie M. Harmon, Dec. 26th

1918

Coleman, Francis A. Jr. and Catherine G. Robertson, March 1st

Coiner, Preston B. and Virginia Moran, June 3rd

Colcock, Dan'l. S. Jr. and Lucy W. Dinwiddie, June 29th

1919

Childress, Marvin T. and Mary Viola Ross, May 20th

Cash, Luther and Sallie Ellen Mallory, June 4th

Cummings, Allan T. and Frances M. Thomas, Nov. 17th

Cornnett, Milton J. and Bansford B. Lang, Dec. 10th

Chewning, Wm. T. and Emma D. Markwood, Dec. 10th

1920

Crawford, L. S. and Emma J. Grady, Apr. 3rd

Collins, Wylie H. and Ella S. Hickey, Aug. 27th

Cameron, Brodmox and Julia D. Spngg, Oct. 20th

Crickenberger, Herbert L. and Gladys Craft, Dec. 1st

Cook, George Jr. and Virginia E. Wood, Dec. 10th

Cason, Manace H. and Myrtle R. Houchens, Dec. 11th

Crickenberger, Everet C. and M. Ruth Craft, Dec. 21st

1921

Clarke, Jas. E. and Virginia Shiflett, Jan. 31st

Conley, Carl C. and Bessie May Luke, July 6th

Clements, Edward and Lucy A. Shiflett, Aug. 12th

Clements, Thomas L. Jr. and Julia Morris, Nov. 19th

Cleveland, Gordon Steele and Esther Dobson, Dec. 3rd

Carson, Sanford J. and Margaret E. Erwin, Dec. 14th

Carruth, Emmett L. and Florence Mae Spenver, Dec. 22nd

Carver, Thos Cornelius and Adelaide Whittemore Dec. 24th

1922

Creasy, Luther and Mary Deane, Mar. 4th

Carr, Stewart S. and Pina McClung, Mar. 10th

Carter, Harry L. and Bettie L. Garrison, May 10th

Carter, Jas. H. and Allie Pearl Estes, Aug. 22nd

Cranwell, James E. and Garnett Busch, Oct. 31st

Cooper, Dewey and Mary Clark, Nov. 25th

Carey, Jesse A. and Sadie N. Burns, Dec. 24th

Craig, Harvey W. and Fannie E. Marshall, Dec. 23rd

1923

Craddock, Henry W. and Alice May Hall, Apr. 3rd

Chambers, Emmett C. and Virgie M. Weakley, May 30th

Cassity, Asa Marion and Louise Butler, July 4th

Cummings, Percie E. and Hazel Eva Reed, Sept. 15th

1924

Cardwell, John C. and Eleanor N. Harlow, Jan. 10th

Creasy, Lloyd E. and Reva M. Black, May 13th

Carpenter, Jas. S. and May R. Childs, May 17th

Christian, Wesley W. and Ruth Lindsay Holcombe, July 23rd

Cornwell, Thornton and Frace J. Marshall, July 29th

Connell, Wm. Curtis and Helen Lee Hardwick, Sept. 6th

Campbell, Lonnie Preston and Elizabeth Mae Oliver, Oct. 1st

Conley, Claude S. and Marion Ward, Nov. 26th

Cason, Elmer F. and Virginia M. Matten, Dec. 27th

Cannon, F. S. and Margaret S. Mohler, Dec. 27th

1925

Culbertson, Leo Hart, and Nell Maxwell Ketner, Jan. 17th

Craig, Frank H. and Mary A. Fisher, Dec. 31st

1926

Catlett, Fred and Annie May Gardner, Jan 1st

Clarke, Carroll and Lucy Gertrude Gilbert, Jan. 9th

Clements, Henry Jackson and Nauoff Roberts, Feb. 4th

Carter, Jno. C. Jr. and Dorothy F. Norford, Feb. 20th

Craven, Carl F. and Minnie O. Morris, May 15th

Coleman, Wirt Henry and Mary Moore Burwell, June 5th

Clary Walter F. and L. Catherine Johnson, July 8th

Collins, Jno. Z. Jr. and Christine Palmer Duffey, Aug. 2nd

Critzer, Monroe W. and Lena Elizabeth Hudson, Aug. 3rd

Crimes, Thomas Neblette and Margaret Glenna Case, Aug. 4th

Craddock, Jas. Emmett and Lillie May Brown, Dec. 27th

1927

Cash, Wallace Bryan, and Matilda Ann Powell, Feb. 21st

Campbell, Jno. Wesley and Frances Alma Tyler, Apr. 19th

Cassell, George Wm. and Marion Weaver, June 18th

Crews, Randolph Edward and Kathleen M. Gentry, August 2nd

Cooper, Phalander Morton, Jr. and Bessie Temple Reese, Dec. 18th

Craven, Watson Elliott and Lila Ola Maddex, Dec. 31st

1928

Cary, Jas. Miles and Lou Margaret Jarman, Apr. 18th

1929

Carr, Paul Lewis and Lucille Mason Gianniny, Feb. 14th

Carter, Eds. Baskerville and Viola Mildred Barfield, April 15th

Chisholm, Roy Lewis and Agness Rebecca Payne, June 8th

Carter, Claude Marion and Anne Blair Johns, June 11th

Cox, Everett Benj. and Iris Margaret Amiss, Sept. 21st

Cox, Edwin Gaines, and Lula Etta Williams, Nov. 3rd

D

1888

Dowdy, Wm. C. and Hester L. Hicks, Oct. 2nd

Donahoe, C. P. and L. J. Fitch, Dec. 6th

Dettor, Geo. M. and Maggie V. Atkinson, Jan. 22nd

1889

Dettor, Joseph L. and Mary L. Brown, Oct. 1st

Duffell, Jas. L. and Mary E. Page, Dec. 23rd

1891

Dillard, Chas. R. and Mollie F. Purvis, Sept. 21st

Davis, Chas. and Sarah Bruffey, Oct. 21st

1892

Davis, Jno. L. and Sallie K. Clarke, Jan. 30th

Douglass, H. B. and Bettie B. Johns, May 12th

1893

Dawson, B. B. and M. Adelicia Jones, Feb. 23rd

Doman, B. and Sallie E. Johnson, May 10th

Dillins, Jno. N. and Myrtle L. Hull, June 8th

Draper, J. E. and Sarah E. Bunch, Oct. 25th

1895

Dudley, Chas. L. and Lene Wingfield, Oct. 26th

Dunn, Joseph B. and Martha C. Southall, Nov. 26th

1896

Dunn, Wm. M. and V. E. Hunter, Jan. 9th

Devine, W. L. and Mattie B. Thompson, July 23rd

1897

Davis, Joseph and Sadie A. Eiserman, July 6th

1899

Douglas, Chas. H. and Mary M. Phillips, July 27th

Duffey, H. J. and A. P. Hawkins, Nov. 1st

1900

Duggan, Frank Joseph and Cora B. Thomasson, Apr. 6th

1901

Doyle, Timothy J. and Mollie E. Bibb, Oct. 8th

Davis, S. F. and Manvellion Dickerson, Nov. 14th

1902

Dickinson, Chas. H. and Nella M. Payne, Aug. 19th

Dudley, Emmet T. and Ada M. Bethel, Oct. 16th

Davis, L. T. and G. E. Bishop, Oct. 28th

1903

Davis, Mathews J. and Minnie Dean, Feb. 12th

Dean, Mauliff Hayes and Lillian Gay, June 18th

DeCross, Wm. E. and Blanch P. Thomas, Dec. 23rd

1904

Dabney, A. D. and L. W. Funkhouser, Apr. 20th

1906

Davis, John L. and Susie B. Thomas, May 30th

1908

Davis, Herbert S. and Susan M. Moore, Dec. 26th

1910

Derr, John S. and Jeannette Humphreys, Apr. 20th

Dodson, Wm. J. and Mrs. Mary F. Law, Apr. 12th

Dudley, Carter T. and Rebecca Raines, May 23rd

Davis, Hugh W. and Ange D. Walpole, Nov. 2nd

Denton, Lewis E. and Margaret R. Greaver, Nov. 21st

Dudley, John W. and Mary H. Carr, Dec. 19th

1911

Dyemond, Bart and Olive F. Triplett, July 1st

Douglass, John W. and Anna V. Levern, Nov. 27th

1912

Draper, Taverun W. and Bettie C. Webber, July 16th

Dean, Elbert M. and Louisa G. Wagner, Sept. 25th

Davis, George E. and Lillie M. Payne, Sept. 28th

1913

Duke, Raleigh A. and Margarette K. Early, Jan. 16th

Dudley, Wm. A. and Verttie V. Johnson, Feb. 8th

Davis, Floyd M. and Mary F. Raines, Mar. 24th

Davis, Lucian E. and Mary A. Dudley, May 10th

Dettor, Charles L. and Cora L. Oehlrick June 16th

Dowda, Fred W. J. and Florence H. Black, July 5th

Durbin, George N. and Margaret J. Mooney, Sept. 2nd

1914

Dunville, Samuel L. and Nettie B. Hall, Dec. 9th

1915

Doome, John D. and Jessie E. Bailey, May 29th

Dixon, William L. and Jane C. McKennie, Nov. 17th

Dickerson, Broadus C. and Ada M. Davis, Dec. 1st

1916

Dettor, Norman M. and Eva M. Hannagan, Nov. 1st

Daniel, R. C. and Mollie Dowell, Dec. 26th

Davis, T. L. and Alice R. Fatwell, Jan. 2nd

1917

Durrer, Geo. V. and Marguerite M. Goodwin, June 2nd

Drumm, Jno. R. and Lillian B. Johnson, July 14th

Dutar, Joseph J. and Grace W. Mitchell, Aug. 20th

Dobbs, Waverly T. and Florence A. Maupin, Aug. 29th

1918

Dudley, Hunter S. and Lelia L. Ladd, Feb. 23rd

Dunlop, David and Mary J. Massie, Aug. 31st

1919

Durham, Wm. A. and Ludie Payne, Mar. 5th

Dudley, Geor. W. and Doris Earle Sullivan, Apr. 30th

Dean, George E. and Gertrude Lamb, June 7th

Dull, Emmett P. and Edith M. Greaver, Jun. 14th

Durham, Jno. W. and Grace S. Carter, July 18th

Durham, Tucker Stricker and Emma Marie Masenheimer, Aug. 8th

Davis, Chester M. and Nora L. Sacre, Dec. 17th

Davis, J. Frank and Susan M. Dunn, Dec. 24th

1920

Durrett, Sam'l. R. and Elizabeth D. Rice, Jan. 6th

Dickson, Alex E. and Madge A. Edwards, Sept 3rd

Dudley Laurence T. and Ruth Edith Brown, April 18th

1921

Darroch, William J. and Dorothy B. Downer, June 7th

Dice, Joseph and Mary D. Townhill, Oct. 5th

Dudley, Jas. E. and Mable Nash, Nov. 10th

1922

Durham, Geo. L. and Irene Bowen, Jan. 23rd

Disselbutt, Barney and Edna Richardson, Oct. 3rd

Davis, Foyd F. and Ethel E. Wade, Dec. 23rd

1923

Deane, Scott M. and Carrie May Baker, Apr. 3rd

Druin, Marvin W. and W. Jaunita Mundy, May 7th

Dudley, Wm. H. and Carroll Powell, Sept. 1st

Davis, J. F. and Lillian L. Dowell, Sept. 19th

1924

Dudley, Early F. and O. Frances Elliton, Jan. 5th

Dudley E. Carroll and Ruby Bruce, Mar. 31st

Dill, Harry A. and Mary Pearl Craft, July 5th

Dameron, Jetie J. and Hannah J. McFarland, July, 7th

Dougherty, Jas. Purnell, Jr. and Dorothy Lee Gibson, Aug. 20th

Dixon, Joseph B. and Lee Anna Chambers, Sept. 3rd

Dyer, Ernest Linwood and Martha Elvin Behrendt, Sept. 6th

1925

Dettor, Jas. L. and Gertrude S. Thomas, Jan. 15th

Desler, Roy Tuttle and Edna May Ponton, Jan. 17th

Davis, Berleigh Carl and Bertie Lee Ray, Dec. 7th

Dettor, Jas. Alvin and Ruth Hatcher Thomas, Dec. 17th

1926

Davis, Jno. Andrew and Hattie Virginia Clemons, Apr. 29th

Douglass, Jno. Magill and Nannie Whitaker Cawthorne Aug. 2nd

Davis, Terry Hunter and Mattie May Parsons, Oct. 3rd

Diedrich, Carl B. and Doris Elizabeth Hall, Oct. 26th

Dillon, Luther C. and Hazel Va. Conley, Nov. 22nd

1927

Dudley, Walter E. and Anne Cleveland Spencer, Jan. 12th

Doom, Erenst Floyd and Martha Wingfield Garth, May 14th

Dove, Charles Hinks, and Elizabeth Hitt, Aug. 24th

Detamore, David Jacob and Viola Elizabeth Diggs, Sept. 13th

Dudley, Richard D. and Grace Edan Norcross, Sept. 14th

Davis, Clarence M. and Edith Catherine Marrs, Oct. 1st

Davis, Wm. McKinley and Virginia E. Bishop, Oct. 22nd

1928

Diggs, Jno. Thurman and Sarah Virginia Nicklin, Jan. 28th

Douglass, Eugene Elbert and Mary Lucie Hamner, Apr. 26th

DuPont, Ernest, Jr. and Virginia Lewellyn Darling, June 28th

Desper, Robert Lyman and Minerva Dorothy Marshall, Oct. 27th

Davis, Lyle McDonald and Maggie Florence Lawson, Dec. 22nd

1929

Dudley, Chas. Ashly and Beulah Irene Good, Jan. 14th

DeShazo, John King and Doris Elizabeth Mallory, Mar. 30th

Dull, Roskwell and Pauline Boyle Sturgis, Apr. 6th

Davis, Ellis Jackson and Va. Elizabeth Dickerson, Aug 3rd

Dowell, Willie and Annie Lee Fincham, Aug. 31st

Day, William Means and Elizabeth Leibert Hartman, Sept. 12th

Davis, LeRoy Edward and Evelyn Ernestine King, Oct. 12th

deVyver, Wayne Joshua and Ethel Elizabeth Stickler, Nov. 23rd

E

1889

Ellinger, Andrew W. and Winnie G. McClair, May 29th

1898

Edwards, A. L. and M. Mary C. Blakey, May 4th

Ellis, R. F. and Martha F. Martin, Nov. 23rd

1899

Ellis, Jas. and Mattie Johnson, June 28th

1901

Ellis, Robt. F. and Emma J. Harris, Nov. 26th

1906

Edgaw, Edwin E. and Marie L. Keller, June 20th

Edgar, Geo. P. and E. L. Robertson, Nov. 29th

Estes, Essie G. and Laura E. Carr, Dec. 25th

1912

Estes, Geo. L. and Clara W. Martin, Oct. 26th

Elliott, Wm. R. and Blanch E. Morris, Dec. 30th

1913

Early, Theo. W. and Bertha May Dollins, Feb. 18th

1914

Elliott, Howard and Ida B. Wiseman, Jan. 7th

1916

Ellis, G. N. and Elizabeth Joseph, Feb. 4th

1917

Ellington, Sam'l. and Ruby Elizabeth Harris, Dec. 14th

1918

Echols, Angus, B. and Helen James Page, Apr. 27th

Eckford, Jamson I. and Elizabeth U. Dettor, June 23rd

Estes, Walter C. and Laura L. Lewis, Dec. 24th

1920

Estes, Jas. M. and Edna E. Lewis, Jan. 19th

Etheridge, James Edw. and Mary Stuart Gooch, Apr. 24th

Estes, Thos. and Mildred Shiflett, Dec 1st

1921

Estes, Walter Lee and Mollie L. Brown, Mar. 24th

Edmunds, Jno. Reade, Jr. and Norvine B. Thomas, May 14th

Edwards, Dudley P. and Maggie M. Dameron, Nov. 15th

1922

Estes, Eugene E. and Julia Marsh, Apr. 29th

1923

Eager, Geo. B. Jr. and Emily C. Walton, June 15th

Eksteen, Ernest Z. and Gertrude Payne, Dec. 25th

1924

Early, John Levering and Maebelle Clair Brooks, June 2nd

Eary, George W. and Catherine A. Boland, Sept. 22nd

Elmore, Jno. Jefferson and Hilda A. Pace, Dec. 23rd

1925

Eary, Lawrence and Clara Wingfield, Oct. 5th

1924

Edwards, Cornelius M. and Lula K. Houghton, July 20th

1926

Easton, Jno. W. and Laura Mildred Smith, July 4th

Easton, Lewis H. and Estelle Gibson, July 3rd

Estes, Zirkle J. and Virginia Adelaide Martin, July 6th

Eisenbrandt, Frederick H. and Veronica C. Ralston, Nov. 24th

1927

East, Cecil Barriett Payne and Harriett Douglas Macon, Feb. 19th

Estelle, Weldon Wayne and Caroleen Amelia Garrison, May 20th

Estes, Douglas Russell and Frances Allen Townsend, June 15th

1928

Ellis, Guy Paul and Mary Ann Charlie, July 3rd

1929

Easton, Linwood Wells and Ruby Estelle Melton, Aug. 26th

F

1890

Florence, S. H. and M. B. Baxter, Feb. 9th

1892

Farish, R. J. and Mattie F. Roberts, Oct. 1st

1894

Falconer, W. A. and Nannie L. Gilmore, Oct. 23rd

1895

Flannagan, L. E. and Lizzie G. Sinclair, Apr. 16th

1896

Franks, John Henry and Sarah Daniel Purvis, Dec. 15th

1897

Ferguson, H. G. and M. Ella Wertenbaker, Dec. 21st

1898

Fishburne, Jno. W., and Mary N. Lyons, Sept. 15th

1902

Failes, J. R. and Bertie L. Tate, Feb. 18th

Fletcher, C. B. and Jennie M. Denton, Apr: 16th

1905

Fleet, Jno. S. and Ludie L. Bibb, Sept. 2nd

Fant, James O. and Linda R. Allen, Sept. 2nd

1907

Fewell, Wilmer and Mabel Martin, Oct. 9th

Franklin, Wm. E. and Susie M. Millert, Nov. 7th

Fauber, Jas. E. and Alma E. Carter, Nov. 27th

1908

Ferguson, Herbert W. and Carrie E. McVeigh, June 19th

Fry, John W. Jr. and Virginia C. Steele, Nov. 4th

Faville, Mark R. and Norma C. Lindsay, Dec. 24th

1909

Fitch, Chas. H. and Elizabeth M. Vandegrit, Nov. 17th

1910

Francis, James D. and Pernele C. Elliott, June 14th

1911

Fry, S. Gross and Josephine E. Cassaday, Apr. 13th

1912

Flippo, Robert T. and Blurna W. Harris, Feb. 19th

Franke, Kurt W. and Mildred L. Bruffy, July 1st

Ferguson, Walter S. and Nannie T. Twyman, Oct. 22nd

1913

Furmiss, Howard H. and Mattie L. Flannagan, July 12th

1914

Fewner, George A. and Betty V. Townsend, Aug. 11th

1916

Feisea, Wm. J. and Anna M. Russow, Mar. 15th

Fitch, Wm. W. and Mary A. Marshall, Sept. 25th

1918

Franks, John H. and Mrs. Gertrude McCall, Jan. 10th

Fisher, Alex M. and Eva B. Beck, Feb. 2nd

Fisher, Geo. J. and Nettie L. Johnson, Feb. 27th

Foster, Frank Lloyd and Mabel M. McKinnie, Mar. 28th

Faber, Everette Franklin, and Lois Ann Beck, Nov. 27th

Frierson, David E. and Florence H. Sinclair, Dec. 21st

1920

Painter, Francis F. and Gladys B. McNair, Apr. 6th

Fleet, Wm. Otis and Edna G. Young, May 29th

Forloines, Jno. B. and Mary S. Davis, May 29th

Floyd, Francis P. and Eva R. McClure, June 1st

1921

Fultz, Robt. P. and Mabel C. Sullivan, May 23rd

1922

Flewellyn, Conway Barbour and Hilda Helina Harrison, Oct. 7th

Faw, Jas. Clarence and Alice Sims Jones, Dec. 26th

1923

Frazier, William V. and Clara B. Yoe, Dec. 22nd

1924

Fite, Edward H. and Elizabeth C. Williams, June 12th

1925

Farrar, Jas. Elvin and Katherine L. Throckmorton, Dec. 26th

1926

Flagg, Thos. G. Jr. and Alma Stella Brown, Jan. 16th

Fisher, Ralph and Esterline Knight, Jan. 22nd

Frendenbert, Earhart R. and Ella K. Fife, Aug. 12th

Furman, Robert Eugene and Anna Virginia Watts, Jan. 2nd

1927

Fry, Sam'l. Gross and Mrs. Sadie L. Carver, Mar. 31st

Fischer, Laurence Ziegler and Mary Eugene Peyton, Mar. 14th

Farnhan, Harry Lathron and Grace Packard Gildden, Nov. 14th

1928

Ferguson, Wilson Robert and Ruth Elizabeth Norris, Jan. 12th

Fitzhugh, Francis Wilbur and Hester Virginia Johnson, June 16th

Fox, Hiram Heaton and Evamae Braswell, Aug. 8th

Fitzgerald, Wallace Vernon and Annie Lee Durham, Oct. 20th

G

1889

Graves, John W. and Bettie Wells, Dec. 17th

1890

Griffon, John Henry and Mary Eliza Garland, July 25th

1892

Gardner, Theo. W. and Annie O. Wert, April 11th

1893

Garison, R. D. and M. E. Jackson, Oct. 11th

Gentry, Albert B. and Linda Goodman, Nov. 1st

1897

Garland, Chas. H. and Va. Snead, July 11th

Gayhart, Jacob Henry and E. Foster, Apr. 13th

Gibbon, Jno. Ed. and Helen M. Durrett, Oct. 1st

Gooch, C. J. and M. Histelow, Oct. 26th

Gleason, M. S. and L. F. Dillard, Oct. 28th

1898

Grady, H. P. and Addie T. Mays, Apr. 12th

Gibson, Jno. R. and Lucile Jones, Dec. 28th

1900

German, Rich'd and Evie R. Rogers, Aug. 29th

1901

Gregory, Edwards W. and Katie W. Cleveland, Feb. 20th

1903

Greaver, Henry Walker and Alice A. Dunn, Feb. 25th

1904

Gutermuth, H. E. and M. L. Wood, Oct. 20th

1905

Geff, Jno. R. H. and Mrs. Bettie F. Johnson, Mar. 22nd

1906

Gleason, Wm. P. and Bulah B. Burgess, Jan. 23rd

Goodyear, John V. and Edith V. Balthis, Mar. 13th

Gianniny, J. O. and Esthel V. Mason, Apr. 24th

1907

Gillespie, Willard W. and Emma E. Gooch, Mar. 4th

Giles, R. P. and L. S. Hale, Apr. 21st

1908

Goldstein, Joseph and Rebecca S. Shapero, Jan. 21st

Greaver, Howard F. and Ella Sneed, May 12th

Grady, Wm. J. and Emma T. Garrison, Sept. 18th

1909

Giles, Thos. W. and Mattie E. Green, June 16th

Gardner, Russell E. and Bessie N. Estes, June 21st

Gay, Ernest C. and Sarah E. Dudley, Aug. 30th

1910

Good, David A. and Lizzie L. Stringfellow, Jan. 5th

1911

Golding, Robert D. and Lottie L. Phillips, June 28th

Givens, Darwin G. and Clara B. Pugh, Nov. 15th

1912

Gibson, Albert M. and Lelia M. Reynolds, July 12th

Gibson, Marion and Florence Melton, Dec. 11th

1913

Guyer, Arthur L. and Nannie L. Dowell, Apr. 30th

Gamble, Frank A. and Sally N. Nelson, Sept. 11th

Gillespie, John L. and Virgie Sanghorne, Dec. 30th

1914

Gillespie, Arthur H. and Gracie M. Bunch, Jan. 9th

Gitchell, Frank L. and Laura Mae Miller, May 2nd

Gravitt, Charles M. and Elizabeth Blanton, Aug. 13th

1915

Graf, John and Lily Mae Towsend, Jan. 20th

Glenham, Marvin T. and Aluse C. Howard, Jan. 25th

Golladay, Edward G. and Rosalie L. Mooney, July 28th

1916

Giles, Rader B. and Edna E. King, Apr. 26th

Giles, John H. and Leona B. Updike, Dec. 12th

Greaver, Maurice F. and Celeste B. Ballard, Nov. 15th

1917

Glascock, Barr R. and Susan W. Harman, Apr. 18th

Grimes, Philip H. and Christie A. Lilly, May 5th

1918

Gooch, Laurence and Bertha A. Jameson, July 27th

Germany, Geo. M. and Flora Stuart, Aug. 22nd

Gordon, Junior D. and Daisy B. Melton, Mar. 20th

1919

Gannaway, Albert C. and Annie Yancey, Mar. 22nd

Graves, L. Prescott and Jo Phillips Stuart, Apr. 26th

Garth, Egbert Tyler and Gladys Ola Triplett, June 25th

Gwinn, Geo. Emerson and Margaret A. Mitchell, Aug. 27th

Graves, Linndeus C. and Mabel C. Munday, Oct. 1st

Greaver, Chas. E. and Bertha May Powell, Nov. 3rd

Giles, Jno. H. and Louise L. Ladd, Nov. 17th

Guiff, Gerry F. and Pearl Crawford, Nov. 18th

Gibson, Sam'l. L. and Martha Quick, Dec. 2nd

1920

Gianniny, Preston L. and Lula B. Fitzgerald, Jan. 31st

Gilmer, George and M. Ruth Dettor, Feb. 17th

Gardner, Wm. J. and Rosebud Johnson, Aug. 16th

Garrison, Jos. B. and Mary F. Sacre, Oct. 16th

1921

Gibson, Walter E. and Virginia D. Pitzer, Jan. 5th

Graves, Leroy W. and Charlotte V. Dofflenyer, Feb. 1th

Gibson, Ernest Gordon and Lottie Lee Culpeper, July 18th

Glass, Asa and Maggie J. Durbin, Oct. 1st

Green, George W. and Eva Mae Berrey, Oct. 31st

Gay, William M. and Dora L. Diggs, Nov. 21st

Gabler, Denton B. and Nora Lee Draper, Dec. 20th

Gibson, Ernest C. and Lillian F. Cummings, Dec. 26th

1922

George, Harry Alex and Virginia S. Fleetcher, May 10th

Gordon, Armistead C. and Cornelia D. Waddell, Aug 29th

Goodman, Thos. M. and Alice May Divine, Nov. 19th

1923

Gay, Earle W. and Helen E. Rutledge, Feb. 19th

Gardner, Sam'l. E. and Mazie Gibson, Apr. 1st

Graham, Roland W. and Ruby C. Smith, Sept. 9th

Gooch, Landon C. and Hattie May Bragg, Oct. 2nd

1924

Garrison, Bennie and Millie L. Via, May 17th

Gay, Harry Gilmore and Frances Selma Hall, Dec. 25th

1925

Grigg, Montie Lee and Eunice E. Jarrell, Oct. 14th

Graves, Charles Alfred and Catherine Rebecca Lipop, Dec. 26th

1926

Godwin, Henry D. and Mary Elizabeth Hall, Feb. 9th

Grinstead, Herbert C. and Lottie M. Patterson Mar. 18th

Gibson, Clyde and Rosa Lee Mitchell, Apr. 2nd

Gibson, Wm. E. and Catherine Louise Beaton, May 16th

Groves, Herbert F. and Daisy M. Poe, May 20th

Gentry, W. Bryan and Mable Virginia Foster, Sept. 2nd

Gentry, Jno. E. and Elizabeth Hodges, Sept. 16th

Gentry, Jno. Sam'l. Jr. and Mary Jane Scott, Dec. 25th

Gordon, Thos. Harrington and Rosa Lee Herndon, Dec. 26th

1927

Gianniny, James Vernon and Edith Marie Clemons, Apr. 9th

Griffith, Wilton Aloises and Ardilla Parker Maupin, Apr. 19th

Golding, Albert Frank and Mary Louise Richardson, May 24th

Gentry, Minor Stuart and Lucy Anna Knight, July 4th

Gardner, Marden Orth and Eva Mae Cash, Aug. 1st

Gentry, Walter Nicholas and Thelma Gladys Reese, Sept. 1st

Gooch, Berkeley M. and Ruth Charlotte McCauley, Sept. 15th

Glass, Bernard Lee and Pauline Shiflett, Oct. 20th

Graves, Claude W. and Thelma G. Amiss, Nov. 5th

Gitchell, Frank Leigh and Mary Hopkins Omohundro, Nov. 19th

Gibson, Arthur Cover and Isabel Zora Lang, Dec. 24th

1928

Griffin, Robt. Handsel and Ruth Ruckman, Apr. 24th

George, Harry Alexander and Josephine Culin, June 9th

Gay, Geo. Woods and Emma Aline Taylor, June 30th

Graham, Jas. Montrose and Alice Winifred Garner, July 6th

Gooch, Robert Kent and Florine Kinney Holt, July 21st

Gwathmey, Geo. Tayloe and Anne Connelly Ashurst, Aug 9th

Gayhart, Wilbur K. and Evelyn Va. Waywright, Dec. 12th

1929

Grant, Carroll Dulin and May Ruth Kunz, Jan 1st

Greaver, Lawrence and Norma Brown Allan, June 10th

Grigg, Milton LaTour and Grace Vestal Thomas, Aug. 31st

Garrison Fred Larus and Agens Mabel Owen, Sept. 17th

Glass, Booker Franklin and Dorothy Sherman Farrish, Sept. 14th

Goolsby, Robt. Marshall and Myrtle May Mawyer, Sept. 14th

Guy, Benj. Harrison and Helen Amanda Wood, Nov. 30th

H

1888

Hall, Edward and Ida R. Walstrom, Nov. 15th

1889

Hoy, Robt. and M. P. Frazier, Aug. 26th

Hudson, C. N. P. and F. M. Spencer, Nov. 6th

Huse, Everett A. and Ella E. Bingham, Dec. 23rd

1890

Hilterbrand, H. T. and R. H. Williams, Jan. 1st

Hull, J. H. and F. B. Morris, Nov. 31st

Hanckel, A. R. and A. W. Robertson, Dec. 11th

1891

Humphrey, Jno. Doss and Julia B. Hutcheson, Sept. 7th

Howard, Chas. Ed. and Minnie F. Via, Dec. 25th

1892

Huitt, Dr. R. M. and S. H. Michie, Feb. 6th

Howell, Obed Canert and Nettie Dull, July 15th

Head, Thos. M. and M. Lucy A. Wright, Dec. 21st

1893

Homan, B. and Sallie Johnson, May 10th

Hancock, D. W. and M. B. Moon, Oct. 24th

1894

Howe, Rockwood M. and Minnie O. Harris, Apr. 26th

1895

Humphrey, L. M. and Lula R. Diggs, Jan. 23rd

Hodgkins, D. F. E. and Lois G. Bowman, Oct. 16th

1896

Humphrey, J. E. and Lucy Newton, July 31st

Hecht, Joseph and Holtze A. Leterman, Oct. 21st

Harris, Wm. D. and Etta A. McGehee, Dec. 9th

Hall, Peyton and Florence E. Tranium, Dec. 16th

Heinemann, Sydnor I. and Lilyan L. Antrium, May 28th

1897

Hawkins, Hugh Russell and May Morris Gleason, July 20th

Hogan, Sam'l. F. and Lula George Harris, July 31st

Harlow, Wm. M. and Minnie Lee Hall, June 29th

Huffman, Chas. W. and Margaret C. Harris, Nov. 15th

1899

Hodge, F. A. and Roberta Mullan, Sept. 7th
Harlow, Horace I. and Minnie E. Woodward, Sept. 21st
Hawkins, Oscar E. and Bertie C. Thomasson, Nov. 29th

1901

Hawkins, B. Lee and Lilian L. Balthis, Feb. 19th

1902

Hart, Jno. N. and Lena S. Spotts, Feb. 12th
Hida, Whirley E. and Etta R. Wagner, Feb. 21st
Hayes, Edgar and Anna Louise Quackenback, Aug. 6th
Hudgins, John M. and Arabella A. Moran, Sept. 18th
Harris, Frank and Ada B. Townsend, Oct. 29th
Harris, Arthur B. and Caroline B. Lyons, Dec. 23rd

1903

Humphries, French Pasco and Cornelia Ellen Morris, Apr. 29th
Hemnies, C. F. and Mrs. L. S. Whitlock, Sept. 12th
Harloe, Walter Weldon and Effie Lenora Merritt, Oct. 14th
Henze, Albin H. and Anner J. Hartsook, Nov. 24th

1904

Hoy, James, Jr. and Lindsay H. Walker, May 4th
Holladay, Jeter Z and Eliz. C. Nicholas, May 29th
Huff, H. B. and C. B. Bagby, Oct. 10th
Hale, Jno. J. and Annie Bruffey, Nov. 28th

1905

Harlow, Wm. I. and S. Olive Gay, Mar. 18th
Harmon, D. W. and Vertie M. Irvine, Mar. 20th
Herndon, A. E. and L. J. Johnson, July 10th
Gulnace, Robert E. and Lucile E. Harris, Aug. 17th
Harris, Samuel J. and Bettie A. Drumheller, Dec. 27th

1906

Hancock, Jno. T. and Nan L. McGee, Nov. 19th

1907

Hughson, Sam'l. R. and Lillie Dudley, Nov. 28th
Hooker, Richards and Lucy J. David, Oct. 16th

1908

Humphreys, Wm. J. and Margaret G. Antrium, Jan. 11th
Hill, Jas. D. and Clara Madison, Nov. 5th

1910

Hancock, Chas. Nathan and Margariet Marshall, Feb. 24th
Higgins, Chas. H. and Emma Higgins, July 20th

1911

Hill, Dr. Emory and Julia D. Hawes, Apr. 18th
Haxall, Wm. N. and Nannie G. Shelkett, June 19th
Hicks, J. Elmer and Mary G. Marsh, Oct. 29th

1912

Hawkins, Clarence B. and Lizzie S. Gleason, Feb. 14th
Harrison, John H. and Berta S. Watson, June 3rd
Hawkins, Edward H. and Mattie E. Cannon, July 24th
Harlow, Robert S. and Etta M. Carter, Oct. 21st

1913

Hinshaw, Charles H. and Lizzie C. Flannagan, Feb. 26th
Hill, Thomas R. and Mildred C. Fitzhugh, Apr. 6th
Harden, Kennedy W. and Susie A. Shelton, May 26th
Huffman, Henry C. and Nellie Woodward, Aug. 7th
Hamm, Strother F. and Ruby F. Barksdale, Dec. 25th

1914

Harlow, Wm. Norman and Mearle Manley, Feb. 29th
Hall, Harvey Edward and Cora Louise Brand, Aug. 26th
Harlow, Eddie and Zunnie Gibson, Dec. 27th

1915

Herndon, Booton and Bertie S. Wood, Jan. 20th
Hill, Joe F. and Eva C. Moore, Sept. 21st
Hurtt, Stephen and Mattie I. Dudley, Sept. 23rd
Hase, Edward W. and Mima E. Russow, Nov. 10th
Houchens, Floyd E. and Myrtle R. Hughes, June 14th

1916

Hensley, Harvey and Nora Brown, Sept. 30th
Hall, Jenny M. and Carrie M. Wingfield, Nov. 10th
Harris, W. H. and Blanche Payne, Dec. 29th

1917

Hutter, Chris S. Jr. and Eleanor F. Butman, Apr. 23rd
Harris, John Woods, Jr. and Eugenia Davis, June 14th

Hendrickson, Dean W. and Mary M. Humphreys, Nov. 13th

1918

Hawley, Geo. W. and Mrs. Rosa Britton, June 12th

Haglin, Chas. F. Jr. and Isabel Blackburn, Oct. 27th

Hastings, Elijah, Wm. and Gladys Goss Brenham, Nov. 16th

Helgoth, Charles A. and Susie W. Marsh, Dec. 18th

Herron, Austin Flint and Virginia Lunsford Craven, Mar. 20th

1919

Harris, Charlie P. and Belle Crowe, Apr. 21st

Harrison, Wm. B. Jr. and Eva M. Detamore, July 10th

Herndon, Chas. T. Jr. and Olga A. Wheatley, Sept. 15th

Humphreys, Wm. H. and Carrie Lee Robinson, Oct. 22nd

1920

Hipp, Edward and Catherine E. Smith, Mar. 10th

Hurdle, Seth Hunter and Bluma Mae Creasey, June 26th

Hibler, Harry G. and Leona Gentry, Oct. 16th

Hilderbrand, Leonard G. and Anna Eliz. Burgess, Nov. 22nd

Humphrey, Jas. A. and Georgia Basick, Dec. 22nd

Halstead, Lester and Nannie Jane Cash, Dec. 27th

1921

Herndon, Chas. E. and Bessie May Wingfield, Jan. 26th

Hartigan, Jesse J. and Blanch Wood, Sept. 26th

1922

Harlowe, Harry N. and Fontella F. Goodman, Jan. 25th

Hall, Edmund Laurence and Ocey Camon Lenoir, Feb. 6th

Huckstep, Ennis C. and Madeline W. Lang, Mar. 8th

Hurtt, Stephen and Eleanor S. Dollins, Mar. 9th

Horton, Bayard T. and Jane Heyle, May 13th

Hatton, Jacob Homer, and Ruth E. Wiant, Oct. 1st

Ham, Russell A. Jr. and Viola V. Haynes, Nov. 13th

Hampton, Harry L. Jr. and Margaret A. Woods, Dec. 16th

Head, Wilton A. and Florence E. Purvis, Dec. 26th

1923

Ham, Clayton E. and Addie May Haynes, Feb. 4th

Harler, Robt. J. and Ruth Inez Estes, May 9th

Huffman, Guy W. and Leone Vest Cook, June 15th

Holladay, Lewis L. and Elizabeth McM. Dinwiddie, July 16th

Hurtt, Kenneth P. and Pearl Farrish, Sept. 12th

Harlow, Porter and Blanch D. Sullivan, Sept. 16th

Hand, G. Curtis and Nancy P. Craft, Sept. 21st

Hamilton, Olon A. and Alice D. Harlow, Dec. 15th

1924

Hildreth Wm. S. and Elizabeth W. Michie, Mar. 29th

Holt, Homer Adams and Isabel Hedges Wood, Mar. 22nd

Howard, Harry M. and Constance L. Martin, Mar. 20th

Harris, Marion E. and Alta C. Blake, Apr. 3rd

Hoddinott, Hugh K. and Jessie W. Druin, Apr. 26th

Harlow, Percy Gordon and Mary Louise Elgert, May 3rd

Harlowe, Edgar Ross and Estelle Gay, May 4th

Haley, Patrick, J. and Helen Pace, June 23rd

Hall, Robert E. Jr. and Adele T. Schultz, July 26th

Harris, Ernest Gordon and Lillian C. Wheat, Aug. 14th

Harlow, Leslie Burton and Pauline Sara Harlow, Aug. 14th

Hewson, Thomas T. and Cecile B. Bolton, Sept. 18th

Hughson, Edward Thimothy and Dorothy L. Mooney, Nov. 16th

Hord, J. D. and Lillian Claire Burrage, Dec. 29th

1925

Hurt, Edward L. and Susie V. Cason, Jan 1st

Harlan, John Frederick and Myrtle Mildred Clarke, Jan. 10th

Hamlet, Frederick P. and Annie Eliz. Wiseman, Feb. 2nd

Housley, Wm. R. and I. Pauline Smith, Oct. 16th

Ham, Elwood M. and Ruby Elizabeth Herring Nov. 12th

1926

Henwood, Albert F. and Emma Gladys Newton, May 15th

Humphreys, Hardin D. and Beatrice B. Carr, Sept. 8th

Houchens, Lewis Dillard and Alice Va. Pearce, Dec. 22nd

1927

Hawkins, Jas. Leigh and Virginia Valentine Stinson, Jan. 6th

Harris, Wm. C. and Emma Louise Herndon, Jan. 19th

Hill, Luther Thomas and Grace V. Bonninwell, Apr. 17th

Headley, Robert T. French and Barbara Vance Allen, Apr. 24th

Harlow, Lloyd, E. and Helen F. Hawley, June 11th

Herring, Alfred Darrell and Mabel Christine Phillips, June 25th

Harlow, Harvey Lee and Lottie May Atkins, July 2nd

Howard, George Wilson and Nellie Ruth Lamb, July 30th

Herring, Ralph Krider and Matilda Rebecca Richards, Aug. 7th

Heyward, John Taff and Haidee Watson Michie, Aug. 15th

Holmes, Edwin R. Jr. and Ellen Bland Massie, Nov. 2nd

Hines, Lonnie Mike and Violet Cecila Payne, Oct. 31st

Holt, Frederick Wm. and Edna Lucile Clements, Dec. 24th

1928

Harlow, John and Alice Wilton Gentry, Feb. 11th

Hall, Joseph L. and Frances Ellen Wood, Apr. 7th

Hughes, Jesse Bowles and Edith Violet Walton, May 12th

Hawkins, Roy Wm. and Norma Northington Thomas, May 21st

Harlow, Sidney Coleman and Mary Rebecca Woodson, May 22nd

Hughes, James Wm. and Pearl Rebecca Chishol, May 31st

Hurtt, Cecil Manley, and Eunice Viola Watson, June 18th

Hurtt, Morris, Jr. and Sarah Eliz. Morris, July 21st

Henderson, Hoseta R. and Helen May Bussinger, Aug. 15th

Harlow, Wm. Cardian and Virginia Brown, Sept 1st

Himmelsback, Clifton Keck, and Virginia Thurmond Martin, Apr. 28th

Hughes, Wm. Lanch and Zella Homs Harris, Dec. 7th

1929

Holsapple, Lacy and Jessie Goode, January 12th

Hall, Cedric Ival- and Dorothy Mae Walton, Mar. 3rd

Humphrey, Jas. Edward and Violet Brown, Mar. 20th

Harvey, Ezra Edwd. and Ruby Elizabeth Marsh, Apr. 12th

Hall, Henry Grant and Evelyn Mae Harris, May 30th

Hughes, Walter Howard and Ruby Belle McCauley, Aug. 17th

Harlowe, Geo. Wm. and Edna Mae Toms, Aug. 24th

Hawkins, Delmar Harrison and Margie Ann Walton, Oct. 14th

Hodges, Jas. Barnett, and Frances Hartwell Long, Oct. 19th

Hensley, Geo. Conrad and Merle Ella Harlow, Nov. 28th

I

1911

Ivey, Eugune C. and Annie C. Vasseur, Oct. 25

1922

Irving, Jas. Robt. and Elnora Melton, July 3rd

J

1889

Jackson, Addison and Susie Dudley, Oct. 21st

1892

Jarman, M. F. and M. L. Fretwell, Jan. 26th

Jordan, C. T. and M. J. Moses, Aug. 17th

1893

Johnston, Jas. Houstoun and Delia Bryant Page, Sept. 6th

1895

James, Wm. R. and Lizzie B. Marsh, Jan. 10th

1899

Jessup, Wm. H. and Dora B. Wood, July 4th

Jones, Jesse P. and Eliz. C. Wise, Sept. 21st

1900

Jones, Thos. M. and Mary A. Luckett, Sept. 4th

1902

Jarman, Marvin B. and Lucy S. Berley, July 8th

1905

Jarman, R. H. and M. L. Jameson, July 19th

Jacobs, I. T. and Reva M. Eastham, Oct. 17th

1907

Johnson, Frank, E. and Vera A. Norvell, Feb. 6th

Joyner, Edward R. and Eleanora K. Taylor, Oct. 9th

1911

Jaeger, Jacob and Geraline Seaman, June 6th

Johnson, Elmer L. and Kathleen F. Wheeler, Oct. 18th

Johnson, Thomas R. and Grace Taylor, Nov. 24th

1912

Johnson, Rupert and Emma Perry, July 23rd

Johns, Ira W. and Lucy W. Parrish, Aug 12th

1914

Jones, Samuel M. and Lillian E. Black, Nov. 25th

1916

Jefferies, B. E. Jr. and Lucy W. Cox, June 21st

1917

Johnson, Wm. S. and Elizabeth Williams, Apr. 28th

Jones, Robt. S. and Gertrude V. Allegree, June 27th

1918

Johnson, Rich'd. F. and Muriel W. Saltonstall, Mar. 5th

Johnson, Ralph W. and Lula Alberta Marsh, Sept. 9th

1919

Jones, Montie N. and Blanche Purvis, Dec. 27th

1920

James, Benj. R. and Julia M. Neal, Sept. 1st

Jones, Griffith G. and Nannie Blake, Oct. 9th

Julian, Leo Sease and Dorothy J. Woods, Nov. 11th

James, Allen C. and Maude Blanche Mason, Nov. 18th

Johnson, Walter W. and F. Bertha Druin, Dec. 29th

1922

Johnson, Thos. Elsom and Angie Rosa McCauley, May 15th

Johnson, Wallace S. and Hilda E. Desper, May 7th

Jarvis, David Henry and Mary Webb Pilkington, May 17th

Johnson, Roy M. and C. Virginia Thompson, May 26th

Johnson, Chas. Early and Lutie Estelle Southard, Oct. 14th

1923

Jenkins, Albert M. and Margaret M. McPeak, July 18th

Jones, James L. and Mrs. Eliz. D. Magruder, Aug. 6th

Jarrell, Wm. M. and Virginia I. Collins, Sept. 8th

Johnson, Russell Aubrey and Helen Marie Mason, Sept. 15th

1924

Johnson, Harry W. and Mary McDaniel, June 21st

1925

Johnson, Wm. E. and Mary Virginia Wood, Dec. 30th

1926

Johnson, Floyd Elwood and Ida May Pugh, May 17th

Johnson, Jas. Thomas and Pearl Dowell, June 10th

Jennings, Wm. Rufus and Ruby Lucille Heatwole, June 24th

Johnson, Junius J. and Emma R. Hawkins, Aug. 30th

1927

Jones, Jas. Burnett and Pauline Inez Edwards, Jan. 14th

Johnson, Paul Stuart and Virginia Gertrude Jackson, July 3rd

Jones, Eldred P. and Lottie C. Jones, July 23rd

Jackson, Sam'l. Longstreet and Alice Kramer, Oct. 3rd

Johnson, John Minor and Ruby Scott Thomas, Nov. 10th

1928

Jennings, Moses S. and Julia McCleary, Feb. 3rd

Jordan, Horace Marcellus and Emma Elizabeth Coniner, Dec. 30th

1929

Jervey, Jas. Wilkinson and Laura Aetta Wood, Apr. 20th

Johnson, Alfred Edw. and Lillian McAlister, Apr. 27th

Johnson, Chas. Christain and Va. May Hilderbrand, Sept. 28th

K

1889

Kirby, John M. and Annie L. Hughes, Dec. 23rd

1890

Kassel, Jacob and Lola Katzoff, Feb. 2nd

Kohen, Sam and Martha Wolf, Mar. 11th

1893

Kemper, H. Mc. and Verelia Trice, ——?

1895

King, L. Marshall and Virgilia M. Hanckel, Jan. 17th

1896

Kent, Jno. C. and Sallie B. Holland, Feb. 6th

1899

Kiener, Chas. and A. L. Yager, May 20th

1900

King, Jas. M. and Bertha L. Failes, Mar. 1st

1902

Kelley, J. E. and S. F. Hawthorne, Jan. 15th

1904

Kaufmann, Samuel and Gertrude B. Leter-
mann, Aug. 10th

Kirby, Thomas L. and Lucinda F. Dickerson,
Dec. 21st

Keeler, Thos. L. and Mary E. Farmer, Dec. 5th

1905

Kelley, J. F. and Annie E. Valentine, Dec. 13th

Kennedy, A. Louis and Mattie A. Gianniny,
Mar. 16th

1910

Kateen, Meyer and Pearl Shapero, Apr. 20th

1911

Knoblock, Jacob and M. Murriel Jarman, July
31st

1912

King, Geo. D. and Gracie M. Dillard, June
26th

1914

Kassel, Max and Frances Bland Shapero, Oct.
27th

Kirby, Herbert G. and Agnes Lee Mitchell,
Nov. 10th

1916

Killby, Harold O. and Mable A. Cook, Aug.
21st

1917

Keyser, Herbert F. and Mamie Emma Johnson,
June 6th

Kay, Robt. Elwood and Blanche Myers, July
16th

Kauduros, G. B. and Ollo Maudros, Sept. 9th

Kerry, C. E. and Lucille Porter, Oct. 22nd

1918

Kennan, Jack and Arline Claire Thomas, Aug.
3rd

1919

Koiner, Junius S. and Mary M. Herrmann,
May 20th

Kines, Robert and Catherine Hughes, Dec. 21st

1920

Keith, Arthur M. and Ellie Wood Page, Sept.
9th

Kennedy, Jno. Henry and Flo Nell Price, Nov.
1st

Kirby, Edw'd F. and Viola Gibson Dec. 25th

1921

Kennedy, Herbert F. and Eva May Cummings,
March 29th

King, Charles Leslie Jr. and Mildred Jane
Burnley, July 23rd

1922

Kessler, Andrew A. and Chloe C. Caldwell,
Aug. 11th

Kelly, Hubert Bagard and Virginia Alice Goddin, Dec. 25th

1923

Kelley, Joseph Edgar and Julia Anderson Tyler,
July 2nd

Kelley, Emmett L. and Elva M. Moore, July
21st

King, Gordon and Dora Thorne Bell, Oct.
13th

1925

Kirby, Gerald L. and Annette C. Hale, Jan.
3rd

1926

King, Kenneth C. and Anneta Brown, Apr.
12th

Kassakatis, Herman A. and Nettie May Rohde,
Nov. 24th

1927

Kidd, Jas. Henry and Helen V. Lawter, Sept
5th

1928

Kirby, Teby Lewis and Virginia Florence Carver, May 16th

Kells, Paul and Beatrice Bertha Easton, June
15th

Kellogg, Rufus Gardner and Kathryn Arnold,
June 5th

1929

Kelsey, Denham Arthur Oswald and Herberta
Nancy, ——?

——, —— and Anne Moore, Nov. 6th

Kidd, Ernest Lee and Myrtle Lewey, Nov. 26th

Keller, Marvin Pierce and Florence Hoy, Dec.
2nd

L

1888

Loving, Orville W. and Annie E. Brand, Oct.
20th

1889

Lambert, Charles R. and Pocahontas Smith,
Jan. 29th

Lynn, Mathew P. and Ida J. Melton, Nov. 21st

1891

Leftwich, R. H. and V. H. Davis, Jan. 21st

Leftwich, D. L. and R. L. Wertenbaker, June
30th

1892

Leitch, Felix C. and Lucy H. Martin, March
22nd

Lumden, Wm. C. and Emma Gardner, Mar.
29th

Lowenberg, H. L. and L. S. Leterman, Nov. 11th

1893

Lewis, Jas. H. and E. R. Littleton, Jan. 10th

Loving, Jo and Delia Clark, Feb. 2nd

Leachman, T. R. and M. C. Carroll, ——?

Lenahan, J. S. and S. A. Burch, Aug. 23rd

1894

Lewis, Robert D. and Minnie E. Bruffey, July 12th

Lifof, John J. and Annie D. Sinclair, Sept. 10th

1895

Lanier, J. E. and F. M. Stephenson, Jan. 2nd

Lindsay, James G. and Evelyn B. Hill, Nov. 27th

1898

Lindsay, Jas. M. and Susie Lowe, March 23rd

Lacy, W. B. and Maggie C. Bolser, Apr. 27th

Lipscomb, A. C. and M. M. Payne, Dec. 6th

1899

Leake, Wm. Jas. and Annie M. Thomas, Jan. 1st

Livick, Geo. H. and Nelie B. Smith, Feb. 22nd

1900

Lynn, Jas. A. and Eliz. W. Antrium, Aug. 29th

Lovejoy, Wm. E. and Mamie T. Anderson, Oct. 16th

1901

Langhorne, Harry and Genevie Peyton, Nov. 25th

1902

Leake, Harry W. and Adalie Harris, Sept. 17th

Long, Thomas and Ellen Alexander, Sept. 17th

Lea, Langdon and Lavilla B. Lyons, Nov. 12th

1903

Langhorne, Henry and Genevie G. Peyton, Nov. 19th

1905

Lydiatt, Jno. and Mabel B. Ward, Apr. 18th

Lamsdale, Dr. P. S. and Annie E. Pyle, Nov. 29th

Latham, Rowland H. and Mamie Brown, Dec. 1st

1906

Lumsden, Oscar L. and Anna B. Morris, Nov. 29th

1907

Leake, Herbert F. and Lizzie Payne, Feb. 5th

1908

Lupton, Frank A. and Mary Watts Woods, Feb. 12th

1909

Loving, Wm. E. and Susie A. Flannagan, Apr. 29th

Levi, Harold H. and Viola M. Leterman, May 20th

Lyons, Julius J. and Evelyn G. Steven, June 30th

Lyries, Jackson C. and Murriel E. Wilson, July 31st

1910

Lee, Edwin G. and E. M. Behrendt, June 29th

Leake, Samuel C. and Florrie M. Wood, Oct. 3rd

Lane, James W. and Anna L. Elliton, Nov. 22nd

1911

Lyons, Thomas F. and Mary A. Rodgers, Oct. 6th

Lazarus, Martin L. and Louise Newman, Oct. 18th

1912

Littrell, Arthur W. and Sue E. Nolen, Apr. 23rd

Latane, James A. and Mary D. Dabney, Sept. 14th

1913

Ligon, Bosher H. and Edith M. Woody, Aug. 22nd

1914

Livingston, Clarence and Leona V. Reynolds, Nov. 2nd

1915

Lee, Alonza and Nora Sacree, Jan. 2nd

Layton, John L. and Lillie M. Withers, Aug. 3rd

1917

Lawson, Roy T. and Mary Louise Pace, Jan. 24th

1918

Lushbaugh, Clyde E. and Flossie M. Johnson, May 8th

Lowmaster, Frank L. and Faith Thompson, June 8th

1919

Layman, Jno. Thos. and Bertha Smythe Marsh, Feb. 20th

Lamb, Edward W. and Willie M. Bowen, Apr. 15th

1920

Lowe, Harry and Mattie Eleanor Smith, Feb. 19th

Lucado, Allen C. and Mary Maxie, June 5th

1921

Lamb, W. Ellis, and Frances B. Marshall- Feb. 1st

Lambert, Wm. and Bessie L. Madison, May 6th

Layne, Roy Edw. and Bertha Hawley, July 7th

Lee, Benjamin and Mannie Hartley, Sept. 3rd

Ledford, W. B. and Fannie Elliott, Nov. 23rd

1922

Lake, Ludwell, Jr. and Mary A. Grover, Mar. 15th

Lang, Wm. Shirley and Clara Spencer, July 22nd

Lawter, Raymond W. and Helen Boland, Aug. 12th

Light, Lawrence L. and Audrey V. Edwards, Sept. 18th

Love, J. Leo and Lillian D. Chewning, Dec. 28th

1923

Lewter, Otis E. and Bertha F. Mittleman, Feb. 26th

Latham, Kenneth and Mary J. Keeton, Apr. 1st

Lupton, Olyn J. and Meryle T. Pugh, June 20th

Leftwich, Charles W. and Kaleistia Maguire, Dec. 15th

Lewis, William T. and Julis B. Street, Dec. 24th

1924

Lancaster, Saml. V. and Lucille V. Patterson, Jan. 9th

Lewis, Richard S. and Bessie F. Owen, Mar. 1st

Laternean, Joseph and Nellie Woerz, Sept. 6th

Lindsay, Jas. Gordon and Elsie Marie Maphis, Oct. 15th

1925

Lindsay, Robt. S. and Sidney Allen Sloan, Oct. 14th

1926

Leffler, Arlie Vernis and Marcella Childress, Aug. 7th

Lupton, Semple Via and Norma Orfa Walker, Oct. 16th

Lejeune, Andre Pierce and Marie Louise Thomas, Nov. 20th

1928

Lang, Frank Nathan and Ruby Elizabeth Pugh, Dec. 24th

1929

Lowe, Clifton Wills and Annie Lee Marshall, Mar. 30th

Lathrop, Willis and Josie F. Day, Apr. 18th

M

1888

Muir, Upton W. and Hebe Harrison, Nov. 21st

1890

Morris, Sylvannus and R. L. Lewis, January 28th

1891

Marshall, Wm. F. and Carrie M. Harris, Sept. 30th

Martin, Jas. Ellis and Mary P. Bailey, Oct. 21st

Melton, C. D. and L. A. R. Davis, Nov. 19th

Meeks, W. L. and F. F. Martin, Nov. 19th

Marshall, Eugene B. and Hester E. Kennady, Dec. 27th

1893

Marsh, Wm. H. and Mary L. Smith, Jan. 10th

Maynard, Jas. H. and Pattie E. Bailey, May 10th

1894

Maintcastle, A. L. and Alice Maintcastle, Feb. 8th

Maupin, Asa W. and Pearl M. Ward, May 1st

Manly, Henry and Susie E. Tisdale, Dec. 20th

1895

Maphis, L. W. and Lula L. Conway, Apr. 16th

Mitz, J. W. and Maggie B. Farrar, Apr. 24th

1896

Moore, Saml. and S. C. Roberts, Sept. 8th

1897

Melton, Geo. and Fannie Hall, July 13th

Michie, G. R. B. and Hoy Watson Perkins, May 18th

1898

Maury, Henry Lowndes and Annie H. Perkins, Nov. 22nd

1899

Matthews, J. C. and Mattie Gleason, Apr. 26th

Morgan, Frank and Bertie L. Hilderbrand, July 3rd

1900

Marshall, Lester Lee and Hattie D. Pratt, July 14th

1901

Moore, John Alan and Ethel Daniel, Feb. 5th

Martin, John Harry and Florence Adosia Johnson, Sept 17th

Mills, Thos. and Bettie Jenkins, Oct. 30th

Marcus, H. D. and Yetta Kaufman, Nov. 5th

1902

Macon, Wm. D. and Mary E. Johnson, Apr. 8th

Martin, Willard and Ida M. Farish, June 16th

Miller, Wm. and Minnie Suthers, Sept. 30th

Meeks, Thos. Walter and Sallie R. Chambers, Dec. 10th

Mayo, Ernest L. and Lutie E. Tate, Dec. 25th

1903

Morris, Jesse and Dora Thomas, Mar. 26th

Maupin, Claude Victor and Leita May Carter, June 10th

Miller, William Jackson and Lillian Katie Digges, June 25th

Mays, Dan'l. W. and Luler Wingfield, Aug. 26th

1904

Moore, M. Van B. Jr. and Sallie M. Noell, Jan. 4th

Macht, Henry E. and Jennie F. Rubin, Mar. 15th

Munday, Lynn and Blanch D. Sullivan, Oct. 3rd

Morris, E. M. and M. M. Kline, Dec. 28th

1905

Moffett, Wm. S. and Frances A. Bailie, May 18th

Mars, Thomas and Lillie Thompson, Sept. 12th

Murray, M. L. and Hattie H. Thomas, Dec. 12th

1906

Minor, James F. and Lillian F. Lyman, Oct. 18th

1907

Mitchell, Junius W. and Bessie A. Wood, June 3rd

Moore, Joseph L. and Fanny B. Gray, July 22nd

Miller, Ernest W. and Blanch E. Sullivan, Nov. 27th

1908

Maupin, Bayard S. and Ethel M. Wingfield, June 8th

Moon, John S. and Ada B. Edwards, Oct. 10th

Marshall, Henry Rice and Eliz, A. Cartriell, Nov. 8th

Maupin, Alonzo R. and Elsie M. Johns, Dec. 8th

Monroe, Jas. Henry and Lelia Dickerson, Dec. 28th

1909

Morrison, Sidney R. and Lillian E. Eversale, Mar. 8th

Moon, Alex B. and Caroline B. Watson, June 19th

Michie, Jas. H. and Ida May Early, Aug. 7th

Maupin, Robert H. and Pattie D. Cash, Oct. 5th

1910

Marshall, Robert and Sarah G. Gardner, Apr. 25th

Maddux, H. Cabell, and Katherine R. Oliver, May 26th

Morris, Eldridge S. and Lillie B. Newton, Dee. 25th

1911

May, James H. and Mattie B. Jones, June 21st

Marable, Geo. F. and Anne M. Wheeler, June 24th

Montgomery, Paul M. and Lula M. Vasseur, Oct. 25th

1912

Mayo, Landy and Clarice R. Lacy, Oct. 9th

Morris, Sam O. and Jane M. Robinson, Oct. 27th

Masino, Bernard and Rosa E. Dameron, Dec. 26th

1913

Marshall, Walter N. and Virgie H. Taylor, Apr. 2nd

Myers, Walter and Katherine Lyons, June 4th

Martin, Sampson H. and Ruth J. McVeigh, Sept. 24th

Mickle, Samuel R. and Gertrude Mayhew, Nov. 26th

1914

Mitchell, Charles S. and Lena E. Houchens, Feb. 17th

Mooney, Charles N. and Evie Lu Wilkerson, Feb. 19th

Mitchell, Geo. W. and Susie Gibson, Apr. 28th

Merz, Albert R. and Florence E. Hartman, Sept. 23rd

1915

Mundy, Lee and Virginia M. Snead, Aug. 24th

Minter, Charlie and Willie Ann Martin, Sept. 4th

1916

Marshall, Albert H. and Vera Adell Hall, Apr. 23rd

Moore, Joseph F. and Edith P. Rixey, June 17th

Masincup, John W. and Lizzie M. Bolen, July 5th

Morris, John E. and Lena B. Williams, July 20th

Marsh, W. T. and Lucy Bishop, Nov. 25th

Mutherspar, Chas. and Sarah F. Mouroe, Nov. 29th

1917

Marsh, Raymond and Julia B. Street, May 7th

Maupin, Melvin N. and Irene Vollner, June 2nd

Mitchell, Robt. J. and Alma D. Beede, June 2nd

Myers, Daisey G. and Ino Unity Milliken, Aug. 18th

Mays, Charlie Jackson- and Daisy Ella Dowell, Sept. 5th

Marshall, Wesly L. and Mary B. Estes, Nov. 3rd

Martin, James Willford and Martha H. Carroll, Nov. 20th

Mays, Charile Jackson, and Elnora Holt, Dec. 27th

1918

Michael, James H. and Ruby C. Shelton, Jan. 1st

Mann, Hunter R. and Constance A. Vandergrift, Apr. 27th

Moore, Walter F. and Jennie W. Draper, Apr. 27th

Morris, James S. and Ruberter L. Steele, June 12th

Massey, Jas. T. and Annie Spicer, Sept. 17th

Marshall, Robt. Linwood and Evie May Dudley, Sept. 7th

Meyer, Jos. Francis and Inez Va. Dettor, Nov. 5th

Mowbray, Ernest and Queenie N. Daniel, Nov. 25th

1919

Mason, John Blair and Helen H. Washabaugh, Apr. 21st

Munday, Herbert L. and Lois B. Baber, Nov. 26th

Morton, Richard L. and L. Estelle Dinwiddie, Dec. 20th

1920

Mann, A. Wendell, and Caroline Gianniny, Jan. 6th

Morris, Jas. Emmett, and Alma D. Thompson, Mar. 23rd

Manley, Add Woody and Sadie M. Bowen, Apr. 2nd

Mackellar, Wm. and Jean Gault Kinney, June 17th

Miller, Walter C. and Flossie B. Mundy, Aug. 16th

Marshall, Richard T. and Alma E. Eheart, Aug. 31st

Morgan, Chas. L. and Olive R. Anderson, Sept. 2nd

Majer, Edwin F. and Caroline Burnley, Sept. 20th

Martin, Jas. Harold and Algra Alverta Deiter, Nov. 1st

Miller, Guy L. and Hazel H. Heatwole, Nov. 26th

Morris, Frederick and Lena Fitzgerald, Dec. 28th

1921

Morris, Henry Jas. and Queenie Harlow, Mar. 15th

Meeks, Luther Geo. and Mattie Nora Campbell, Mar. 27th

Mangum, Ernest L. and Marg. Taylor, May 16th

Mooney, Leslie J. and Sarah Gentry, May 30th

Moorefield, John A. and Johnie Verna Burgess, June 7th

Mahanes, Hugh Elliott and Elizabeth Frances Walsle, June 11th

Melton, Geo. W. and Ellen Johnson, June 15th

Mount, Morris Blake, and Elizabeth Fairfax Lindsay, June 29th

Morrissette, Chas. Jefferies and Lottie Marie Duncan, June 30th

Melton, Harvey L. and Mrs. Willie M. Hope, Sept. 29th

Maupin, J. Irving and Rosalie Bruffey, Oct. 5th

Maddox, Lacy L. and Charlotte Louise Johnson, Oct. 26th

Marion, Frank M. and Sarah R. Childress, Oct. 29th

Mays, Charlie Preston and May Leona Wingfield, Dec. 24th

Morris, Charlie Eugene and Carrie Sacre, Dec. 26th

1922

Miller, W. Allan and Forrest L. Proffitt, Jan. 18th

Miller, Robt. Wayt and Lottie Ruth Baker, Feb. 16th

Martin, W. Herbert and Rose Lillian Roberts, May 24th

Massey, Joseph C. and Evelyn Maupin, Aug. 26th

Morrisette, Saml. Carlisle and Mary Evelyan Roadcup, Sept 1st

Morris, John and Olive Saunders, Sept. 2nd

Marsh, C. R. and Annie E. Nimmo, Dec. 13th

Morris, Clarence L. and May L. Scruggs, Dec. 27th

1923

Moon, Irvine E. and Nellie Thomas Wood, Jan. 15th

Moss, James M. and Irene L. Payne, Mar. 21st

Marsh, Russell A. and Iola McDonald, Apr. 1st

Marsh, Earl H. and Grace B. Wood, Apr. 26th

Mahone, Wm. L. and Inez K. Moore, May 10th

Miller, Hampton K. and Rita A. Austin, June 1st

Moore, Frank S. and Lottie M. Jones, July 4th

Morris, Charlie W. and Fannie Helen Seay, Aug. 4th

Martin, Lewis A. and Lillian B. Detamore, Oct. 4th

1924

Marsh, Charlie R. and Eunice Marsh, Apr. 5th

Miller, Chas. Albert and Apsie Meredith Bransford, June 10th

Martin, Chas. Harrison and S. Marguerite Kent, June 20th

Moore, Wm. L. and Mary J. Lamb, July 3rd

Melton, Hunter M. and Alice C. Mayo, Aug. 5th

Michie, A. Hewson and Katharine B. Fishburne, Oct. 14th

Mawyer, Ned Marshall and Katie Marie Puckett, Dec. 23rd

1925

Moore, Dewey E. and Effie May Morris, Nov. 25th

Moore, Ernest Jas. and Winifred Irene Wilkerson, Dec. 24th

1926

Morse, Frederick Tracy and Mary Geneviene Forbes, Jan 1st

Minter, Edward C. and Irene J. Leonard, Jan. 16th

Morris, Henry Herron and Ora Vistiser Johnson, Feb. 20th

Moore, Massie S. and Nellie Wilson Jones, Mar. 6th

Miller, Emmett W. and Helen Batis, May 23rd

Martin, Jas. Richard and Zadie Archer Deane, Aug. 12th

Michie, Robert D. and Victoria E. Herndon, Sept. 7th

Michael, Olaff and Myrtle Garrison, Nov. 17th

Moore, James Lawrence and Frances Melissa Purvis, Dec. 23rd

1927

Meeteer, Elwood Jackson and Agnes Lee Huyett, Jan. 1st

Mundie, Joseph Edward and Marel Scott Bybee, Mar. 18th

Martin, Edward Franklin and Nannie Raymond Fitzgerald, Apr. 11th

Mann, Auburn Page and Aylor Mildred Ellinger, Apr. 16th

Mawyer, Everett Early and Gretchen Fisher, May 7th

Mancine, Quindo M. and Virginia Louise Pace, May 30th

Marshall, Virgil L. and Mabel Lawson, July 2nd

Munn, Earl Randolph and Catharine E. Forloines, Sept. 3rd

Mahanes, Maxwell C. and Stella Frances Rudacille, Sept. 12th

Melton, Geo. Washington and Bronnie M. Chewning, Oct. 1st

Markham, Talmadge T. and Lillian Geraldine Dillard Oct. 31st

Mitchell, Wm. Clarence and Hazel Florine Stokes, Dec. 24th

1928

Mallory, Luther Stinson and Effie Kathleen Hooper, Feb. 25th

May, Landon Cutler and Doris Dodd Maddox, Mar. 17th

Melton, Robt. E. and Fannie Tweedy, Apr. 16th

Markham, Edwin Carlyle and Anne Janet Whitlock, May 27th

Mickley, John Hoke and Ruth Irene Hoar, July 28th

Morgan, Marion Hewitt, Jr. and Elizabeth Jury Brown, Sept 1st

Mayo, Geo. Richard and Eliz. Edmonia Glass, Oct. 13th

1929

Miller, Llewellyn and Sarah Peel Watts, May 4th

Merrill, Randolph Searing and Annie Hill Revercomb, June 8th

Martin, William Edw. and Margaret Estelle Morris, June 22nd

Martin, Chas. P. and Dorothy L. Purvis, July 3rd

Maupin, Vivian Franklin and Mary Va. Shipp, Nov. 2nd

Morris, Milford Dudley and Alma Dessle Armstrong, Nov. 30th

Matacia, Louis J. and Anna Margaret Perry, Dec. 28th

Mc

1889

McCreasy, Jas. Lewis and Bonnie Belle Hall, Jan. 30th

1891

McKnight, William L. and H. G. Bensley, Apr. 14th

1900

McCue, Ed. O. and Mary P. Michie, Apr. 18th

1905

McAllister, Wm. F. and Onie T. Granzell, Apr. 22nd

1907

McClure, Wm. N. and Mary J. Moon, Apr. 1st

McBride, M. D. M. and Nellie C. Watson, Oct. 3rd

1908

McAllister, James F. and Mollie Wilson, Aug. 31st

1910

McCarty, Sherman and Hazel K. Fletcher, Oct. 25th

McPherson, Edgar H. and A. Josephine Cox, Apr. 8th

McElroy, John H. and M. Mae Prine, Oct. 16th

1917

McNamara, Frank V. and Margaret E. Grinder, Nov. 3rd

1918

McCormich, Cutter Orliffe and Virginia Allen Vest, Sept. 30th

1919

McMillian, Leslie P. and Maggie P. Huffman, Oct. 8th

1922

McCann, James and Ada Jordan, Oct. 17th

1924

McCauley, Emmett M. and Anna Walter Brown, Apr. 19th

McDearmon, Geo. C. and Mary Jane Roberts, June 9th

1926

McGahey, Randolph and Winiwaindah Elaine King, July 6th

McCauley, Vivian Linwood, Va. Ella Payne, Dec. 27th

1928

McBride, Jerome N. and Marg M. Post, Dec. 29th

1929

McCarrell, John Poindexter and Florence Angeline Warmick, Jan. 9th

McDonald, William S. and Annie Gertrude Payne, March 4th

McMullen, Francis Bruce and Portia Virginia Lynham, Mar. 29th

N

1892

Noel, Henry S. and Maude A. Wingfield, Dec. 28th

1900

Nimmo, Jesse W. and Emma J. Farish, Jan. 1st

1905

Nichols, Herbert and Martha M. Byran, Nov. 7th

1906

Neil, M. B. and Nellie P. Carney, Sept. 6th

1908

Nolley, Lawton and Rena H. Bailey, June 16th

1910

Nayler, Herbert and Lydid Hudson, May 8th

Nimmo, Geo. F. and Anna E. Thomasson, June 22nd

Nix, R. A. and Evelyn G. Alexander, July 30th

1912

Norvell, Wm. W. and Sarah G. Alexander, July 27th

Northey, Thos Jas and Clara S. Smith, Dec. 18th

1914

Norman, Jesse Lee and Helen Irene Painter, Aug. 12th

1918

Nicholas, John S. and Mary Du P. Holladay, June 9th

Nicholas, Andrew L. and Nora Bussenger, Sept. 7th

Nicholson, Lemuel B. and Virginia Louise Williams, Dec. 2nd

1919

Nicholson, Berlin B. and Mabel T. Jefferies, Aug. 16th

1920

Nickell, Henry K. and Laura T. Wood, Jan. 13th

Nicholas, Wm. E. and Elsie A. Holler, Mar. 17th

Naylor, Tommie and Viola Shifflette, Apr. 29th

Nofsinger, Warner W. and Grace H. Page, Oct. 30th

1921

Norcross, Jno. E. and Mannie C. Giles, Aug. 27th

1922

Nimmo, Walter J. and Mary M. Bishop, Feb. 28th

1923

Nutter, Willis J. C. and Bertha Ellen Houser, July 20th

Neal, Lewis W. and Malinda Wheatley, Sept. 8th

1925

Nicklos, Daniel Oscar and Nellie Grace Wingfield, Sept. 16th

1926

Norris, Eugene F. and Pauline V. Amiss, July 3rd

Norford, Wm. Clyde and Zylah Virginia Carpenter, Aug. 12th

1927

Norris, Hunter Wellington and Ruth Walker Ford, July 14th

1928

Norcross, Geo. Milton and Lucy May Goodwin, Mar. 8th

1929

Nielson, Geo. Rbt. and Elizabeth Sinclair, Aug. 10th

Nicholas, Eugene Motley and Mary Cornelia Dixkinson, Aug. 10th

Newcomb, Lewis Henry and Edith Claudin Fout, Aug. 17th

Nichols, Ransom Bingham and Gladys Halsey Wilkes, Oct. 26th

Nokes, Jno. McIntire and Anna Macon Fawcus, Nov. 14th

O

1906

O'Brien, Edwin and Ruby E. Wingfield, July 7th

1910

O'Brien, Isaac K. and Frances E. Morrow, Oct. 18th

1911

Owne, William A. and Ruth H. Via, Jan. 30th

1912

Oliver, Roland B. and Elizabeth C. Irving, Jan. 17th

1913

Omohundro, Samuel and Lelia Belle Coleman, Dec. 3rd

1919

Oakey, Hugh E. and May Vandevender, Feb. 26th

1921

Omohundro, Carl B. and Mary Eliz. Wingfield, June 22nd

Oakey, Wm. Hamsted and Daisy Louise Woods, July 15th

1924

Odell, Earl and Bonnie B. Simmons, Feb. 11th

Orr, Harry Allen, Jr. and Alice Walton Jones, Oct. 20th

Owens, Wm. E. Jr. and Anna Cecelia Gradcok, Dec. 11th

1928

Omohundro, Miles Parker and Nancy Lee Yates, Jan. 5th

Overman, Carl Martin and Carrie Katherine Harouff, Sept. 15th

1929

Oldenburg, Chas. Henry and Katheryn Fithian, Feb. 23rd

P

1889

Prince, Edwin O. and E. S. Brennon, Apr. 29th

Purvis, Duncan and Eliz. J. Dudley, Dec. 23rd

1891

Payne, Everett Lee and Alice A. Newman, Sept. 12th

Porterfield, Wm. and Julia Randolph, Sept. 26th

1892

Pace, R. B. and M. E. Bowen, Oct. 21st

1893

Page, Chas. G. and Lena F. Norvell, Jan. 10th

1894

Patterson, M. C. and Juainta Massie, Feb. 19th

Pettie, Charles A. and Annie P. Wingfield, June 5th

Peyton, Thos. P. and Annie Buck Hill, Sept. 4th

1895

Peet, Wm. S. and Ellen Hill, Aug. 26th

Phelps, Charles and Lucy James Bailey, Dec. 24th

1896

Powell, Wm. Albert and Lillian Jones, July 8th

Pendleton, Louis and Ellar May Glass, Oct. 31st

1898

Parkinson, Wm. U. and Caroline P. Wood, Aug. 8th

Powell, Rufus W. and Rosa A. Carter, Nov. 22nd

1900

Porter, Dr. Carry W. and Josephine T. Morris, June 16th

Payne, James L. and Lillie L. Bunch, Aug. 29th

1901

Petrnan, Alex W. and Lillie L. Huyett, Apr. 25th

1903

Pryor, Edward Marshall and Mary Ellen Jackson, June 24th

Peaco, Chas. D. and Bessie Lee Wingfield, Aug. 26th

Poole, Walter F. and Muita H. Durrer, Oct. 22nd

1904

Perkins, Fred A. and Nellie S. Johns, Dec. 22nd

Porter, Jno. L. and M. A. Ward, Dec. 28th

1905

Phillips, Thos. J. and Lillie Johnson, May 30th

Phillips, James H. E. and Jenny M. Johnson, Aug. 7th

1906

Payne, Henry J. and Lulu E. Smith, Apr. 30th

Parker, Henry S. and Margareth Jenkins, June 4th

Purvis, Willie Lee and Mary Ann Bolond, June 6th

Pugh, Earnest L. and Mable M. Payne, Sept. 3rd

Parker, S. H. and Florence C. Jones, Nov. 19th

Payne, Jas. F. and Nannie E. George, Nov. 20th

1908

Payne, Leonard C. and Bessie M. Hughson, Apr. 20th

1909

Peaco, Saml. W. and Alice R. Wingfield, Jan. 25th

Pleasants, Cameron E. and Annie McL. Whittey, Nov. 3rd

Parrott, John B. and Julia Holstine, Dec. 27th

1910

Peele, Joseph S. and Thelma B. Mayo, Feb. 14th

Pyle, T. Myron and Ruth Hidy, Apr. 27th

1911

Pinck, Guy W. and Marie M. McKennie, Apr. 8th

Potts, Edward C. and Willye T. Rothwell, Aug. 21st

1912

Packard, Wzell D. and Hattie L. Rambo, July 12th

Pugh, Nicholas W. and Mary N. Payne, Sept. 10th

Profitt, Carl D. and Bertha E. Bethel, Sept. 25th

Payne, Fountain and Bergie J. Edwards, Oct. 9th

Pace, Dona B. and Bertha E. Dudley, Oct. 30th

1913

Ponton, Samuel H. and Nannie E. Purvis, Sept. 26th

1915

Payne, Lauris R. and Mary Catherine Jarman, June 4th

1916

Page, Walter H. and L. Maude Greaver, Apr. 29th

Phillips, Levit L. and Adeline S. Davis, Oct. 6th

1917

Peterson, Wm. C. and Mary Stella Laterneau, Feb. 2nd

Pace, Loranzo D. and Eliza Jones, Apr. 9th

Payne, Harold A. and Bertha C. Jones, June 4th

Poindexter, Seldon L. and Ruby Pearl Mundy, Nov. 14th

Pace, Jeller and Lillie Keister, Nov. 18th

1918

Payne, Wm. E. and Emma C. Barksdale, Dec. 10th

Parrott, Jas. N. and Bessie Lee Allegree, Dec. 21st

1919

Puckett, Nicholas and Ruth L. Bethel, Mar. 22nd

Pirozok, Stephen and Elizabeth Semmelock, Apr. 22nd

Pitt, Wm. F. and Elizabeth F. Staley, Nov. 15th

1920

Powell, Roy and Cora Morris, Feb. 29th

Poe, Keithen and Ida Belle Davis, Oct. 28th

1921

Payne, James A. and Elizabeth Harlow, Jan. 18th

Peyton, Thos. D. Jr. and Eliz. Churchill Cooke, June 4th

Perley, Jno. W. and Tulliola Howe Yoe, Nov. 22nd

1922

Pole, Edgar A. and Mary Alice Clarke, Jan. 2nd

Pace, Frank H. and Mamie Jarrell, Jan. 28th

Payne, Alfred J. and Mrs. Willie Dunn, Feb. 5th

Patton, Henry Wilds, and Ossie Price Morris, Apr. 1st

Patterson, Harry M. and Madie W. O'rork, May 7th

1923

Parrott, George H. and Annie L. Bolton, Jan. 6th

Payne, Roy F. and Elizabeth E. Minter, May 22nd

Pitzer, Chas. Wm. and Leah E. Garner, June 7th

Perry, Randolph Hope and Clarissa Buchannon Canfield, July 7th

Pierce, Dr. Patton K. and Helen F. Hamner, July 16th

Patterson, Earl Grayson and Myrtle Ruth Jackson, Sept. 11th

Purvis, Jas. Nelson and Mattie Eliz. Stevens, Sept 12th

1924

Powell, Rev. Noble C. and Mary Wilkins Rustin, Apr. 21st

Powers, Raymond B. and Edna Ruth Burks, Apr. 26th

Pugh, Lucian F. and Eva Mawyer, Oct. 12th

1925

Parrack, Vasco Roosevelt and Edna Roselle Wingfield, Sept. 19th

1926

Pendleton, Edmund Cole and Johanna Maria Hedwig Kramer, Apr. 7th

Price, Robert Blair and Kathleen McCarthy Carroll, June 24th

Payne, Lloyd Nicholas and Lillie Lewis Davis, July 3rd

Palmer, Chas. W. and M. Lucille Saunders, Aug. 7th

Poland, Samuel and Ethel Lyon, Aug. 30th

Poss, Robert Henry and Bernice Mathilda Johnson, Oct. 23rd

1927

Pegan, Dr. Arthur August and Susie Byrd Wills, June 29th

Panell, Herbert E. and Beulah H. Thomas, Sept. 10th

1928

Pittman, Charles Calvin and Willie Margaret Gentry, Apr. 4th

Phillips, Forrest A. and Clara Lee Patterson, May 12th

Parker, Winfrey Royal and Lucy Hatcher Jessup, May 30th

Powell, Daniel and Maggie Lee Sprouse, Aug. 11th

Powell, H. Clay, Jr. and Elizabeth Shanklin, Aug. 24th

Parker, Lawrence Benj. Franklin and Carrie Frances Marsh, Sept. 8th

Ponton, Edwd. Avon and Linnie A. Farrish Hurtt, Oct. 6th

Parrott, Ernest Rosser and Gracie Eva Wood, Nov. 27th

Ponton, Geo. Leland and Lyla Florence White, Dec. 12th

1929

Perry, Manuel Elliott and Annie Lee Cook, Mar. 2nd

Pritchett, Rufus Gordon and Marg. Frances Sprouse, Mar. 16th

Paylor, Frank Woods and Margie Lee Shirlen, May 17th

Page, Robert M. and Della P. Johnson, Oct. 5th

Payne, Grafton Danl., Jr. and Minnie Annette Freese, Sept. 26th

Q

1909

Quaintance, Jas. O. and Rosa L. Gleason, June 16th

1910

Quarles, Wirt and Emma V. Wingfield, June

1916

Quarles, James C. and Lucy Sinclair, Oct. 4th

Quinn, Emory B. and Cynthia K. Woods, Dec. 20th

Quinn, Brice P. and Ruby Gordon Flood, Dec. 5th

1928

Quick, Jas. Benj. and Lizzie Gertrude Mawyer, Oct. 13th

R

1888

Robinson, Geo. Marshall and Ora Bailey, Oct. 25th

1889

Rohr, Phillip T. and Rosa D. Birch, Jan. 14th

1891

Randolph, W. C. N. and M. W. McIntire, June 10th

1892

Rosson, R. Lee and Mary Ella Bibb, Apr. 11th

1895

Robertson, J. M. and Jane D. Forbes, Dec. 4th

1897

Rhodes, Thomas F. and Lou M. Gentry, Dec. 28th

1898

Ruffuer, W. D. and Lula F. Kidd, Jan. 4th

1900

Rawlings, Rich'd. H. and Sallie T. Templeton, Feb. 28th

1901

Rothwell, T. C. and Lilliane Mills, Dec. 18th

Randolph, Thos. F. and Edith Durrett, Dec. 31st

1902

Rolley, Jas. W. and Lucy P. McAllister, Oct. 29th

1903

Rhodes, Solomon S. and Lelia F. Davis, Jan. 17th

1904

Runkle, A. M. E. and Mrs. C. B. Rippon, Dec. 8th

1905

Rhea, John Wilson and Bessie J. Lewis, Apr. 26th

1907

Royal, F. Adams and Lee Price, Jan. 18th

Ritchie, Jas. E. and Maggie Lee Embrey, June 26th

Rea, Montie L. and Pearl Watson, Dec. 18th

1908

Rhodes, Eugene C. and Elizabeth C. Garner, Mar. 16th

Robothorn, Arthur and Sally M. Smith, June 17th

1909

Rock, Elmer T. and Mary E. Witt, Aug. 16th

Rhodes, Robt. A. and Annie C. Jarman, Nov. 17th

1910

Rucker, Wm. J. and Sallie S. Woods, Apr. 28th

1911

Rothwell, Henry M. and Jessie M. Brubeck, June 8th

Robinson, Richard M. and Nellie J. Heremann, Nov. 22nd

1913
Rosson, John Carl and Elner C. Wingfield, Nov. 1st

Rozwankaski, Raymond and Dora B. Jessup, Dec. 22nd

1914
Renewu, Charles S. and Jettie F. Early, Dec. 26th

1915
Rhea, William Francis and Rosa Smith Turpin, Jan. 20th

Robertson, Judson and Mary C. Brown, Aug. 31st

Richards, George A. and Alice C. Maupin, Oct. 16th

Rusher, George E. and Ethel W. Vasseur, Oct. 28th

1916
Redd, J. Kay and Roberta W. Flanagan, Dec. 6th

1917
Ramsey, Ervine R. and Duane E. White, June 6th

Rucker, Tommie D. and Pearl Coulter, Dec. 20th

Richardson, Raymond, R. and Carrie L. Worrell, Dec. 22nd

1918
Riley, Robert D. and Lillie Mae King, April 2nd

Reynolds, Clifton J. and Jane Elizabeth Via, June 9th

Robertson, Wm. Hilton and Armond Reedy, Oct. 22nd

1919
Rhodes, Hoy L. and Nettie H. Smith, Mar. 19th

Roberts, Frank E. and Elletie B. Snead, Dec. 24th

1920
Robinson, Wm. M. and Eddie Cash, May 29th

Rogers, Wm. Hudson and Mary Thornton Wood, June 24th

Ricks, Erenst and Mattie Devine, Nov. 2nd

Ross, Abraham G. and Virginia M. Mundy, Dec. 16th

1922
Richardson, Jno. Crobett and Cora Jackson Thomas, Jan 2nd

Rhodes, Arnold S. and Annie Louise Cox, Jan. 16th

Reynolds, Jno. B. and Ethel H. Reynolds, July 3rd

1923
Robertson, Tyler and Ruth Hicks, Feb. 8th

Rife, Eugene F. and Carrie B. Gisiner, Apr. 18th

1924
Rigby, George Lawrence and Harriet Gilbert Grodon, Sept. 20th

1925
Reese, Jno. Thomas Sinion and Beatrice Olive Tomlin, Jan. 1st

1926
Rogers, Chas. Wm. and Bertha Lucy Branham, Jan. 28th

Roudabush, Carrol D. and Maggie E. Richardson, Mar. 15th

Roberts, Jas. D. and Mabel F. King, July 3rd

Roupas, Christ G. and Olga X. Markri, Aug. 29th

Rutledge, Lawrence M. and Hallie R. Young, Sept. 18th

Ragland, Edwin Hughes and Eleanor Eliz. Barnsley, Oct. 30th

Reed, Claude Adam and Daisy Irene McCauley, Nov. 4th

1927
Ripley, James Vincent and Myrtle Lee Hurt, May 3rd

1928
Reed, Arthur Love and Corinnie Desiree Bryant, Apr. 26th

Reed, John and Emaline MacHoward, Sept. 21st

Rodes, Thomas Layton and Carolyn Josephine Smith, Oct. 13th

Rothwell, Walter Ernest and Velma Sawyer Haden, Oct. 28th

Reese, Ernest Franklin and Mabel Odessa Hooper, Nov. 12th

Roberts, Jean Morris, and Bessie Belle Detamore, Dec. 23rd

1929
Rankin, Crayton Wilber and Beatrice Anderson Harlow, Jan. 30th

Raney, George Pettus and Louise Stuart Williams, Feb. 20th

Roebling, Donald and Florence Spotswood Parker, June 6th

Ramsey, Robt,. Burrus and Ernestine Feuchtenberger, June 8th

Robertson, Chas. E. and Ruth Lucas Twyman, Oct. 7th

S

1888
Schneider, Chas. F. and Mary E. Murrary, Oct. 3rd

Saunders, Geo. M. and Lula H. Wertenbaker, Oct. 3rd

1889

Sessons, Julius O. and Virginia Kent, April 22nd

Scheaper, John E. and Nodie F. Turner, Dec. 11th

1890

Spangler, H. P. and Ida M. Ferron, Apr. 15th

Skinner, Wm. A. and G. P. Johnston, June 24th

Shepherd, O. W. and M. B. Bingham, June 26th

Steel, T. A. and R. C. Larrie, June 28th

Schriver, F. H. and S. E. Moore, Nov. 26th

1891

Spencer, Jno. A. and Virgie L. Chiles, Sept. 29th

Smith, Willie P. and Susan M. Brown, Dec. 15th

1892

Stevens, Chas. B. and Lulah Linox, July 14th

1893

Shipman, Edmund and Sophie Brooks, Feb. 22nd

1895

Story, Robt. B. and Kathie Lee Wranek, Jan. 5th

1896

Scott, Robt. E. and Justine Jones, Feb. 4th

Sweeney, Rich'd. F. and Octavia E. Lester, Feb. 19th

Sneller, Wm. R. and Mary A. Hall, Apr. 15th

Sinclair, John W. and Blanche J. Stevens, Dec. 16th

1897

Smith, J. P. and M. A. Montculls, Aug. 2nd

Sneed, N. K. and L. R. Wood, Nov. 3rd

Snead, Daniel and M. Mattie Walton, Nov. 11th

1899

Saunders, Jno. and Bettie Saunders, May 31st

1900

Snead, Wm. B. and Lizzie Fox, Oct. 29th

1901

Sheetz, F. P. and Nellie Cummings, Jan. 10th

Simes, Thos. W. and Catharine M. Taylor, June 3rd

Smith, R. P. and M. N. Perry, June 18th

Smith, C. T. Jr. and E. N. Wingfield, Oct. 29th

1902

Southes, John K. and Marg. L. Taylor, Jan. 15th

Schellion, Chas. H. and Lelier Thomas, Mar. 31st

Scott, William C. Jr. and Mary Tyler, Nov. 26th

1903

Skinner, Benj. F. and Jennie Skinner, June 1st

Shafer, Saml. W. and Josie Sullivand, Aug. 12th

Shaffer, E. M. and Sallie R. Wolfe, Oct. 26th

1904

Steed, Chas. C. and Hattie R. Benley, Apr. 20th

Sutherland, Richard and Hannah Harbottle, Oct. 4th

1905

Sprouse, Carey R. and Cornelia Y. Gulbar, Jan. 1st

Sneed, Ed. Benj. and Emma G. Peers, Jan. 14th

Shipp, Joseph R. and Bessie M. Manley, May 3rd

Symmons, James K. and Agens L. Shirly, Sept. 7th

Shultes, Lammat and Daisy W. Davis, Oct. 18th

Schriver, Fred J. and Eva D. Jacobs, Dec. 20th

1906

Sneed, John P. and Ellen Fitzhugh, June 20th

Smith, Jas. R. and Rosa E. Wood, Oct. 15th

Steele, Hampton and Katherine Housey, Oct. 31st

1907

Snapp, James P. and Sadie M. Clifton, Sept. 16th

Swink, Robt. N. and Va. E. Thomas, Sept. 18th

Somerville, C. B. and Eva R. Harris, Oct. 22nd

Swortzel, Ezra H. and Sallie Ann Jarman, Nov. 27th

1906

Stone, Samuel and Hortense P. Leterman, Oct. 31st

1908

Sprouse, Alfred C. and Maggie Boland, Mar. 24th

Sparrow, Jas. L. M. and Gracia M. Walker, May 25th

Shepherd, James W. and Mary Ella Gibson, Oct. 18th

1909

Short, Alex A. and Nancy L. Evans, May 27th

1910

Sneed, Robt. L. and Sadie A. Chambers, June 21st

Sprouse, Tho. H. and Jossie M. Dudley, June 23rd

Sappington, Geo. R. and M. D. Cox, Sept. 29th

Souder, Wm. F. and Stella R. Carroll, Nov. 25th

Snyder, Ernest Lee and Sallie A. Womack, Nov. 14th

Sprouse, G. C. and Ruth Mitchell, Dec. 26th

Steinhauer, Ernest P. and M. Florence Rodes, Dec. 28th

1911

Snyder, Wm. H. and Mattie V. Trice, Jan. 4th

Sprouse, George A. and Mrs. Grace Nicely, May 15th

Stewart, Zeno C. and Mavis W. Harris, June 14th

Snow, Leroy H. and Maggie S. White, Aug. 6th

Siler, Joseph T. and Kate D. McNeill, Dec. 28th

1912

Saunders, Newton L. and Mable Bair, Feb. 7th

Stulling, Claude F. and Sadie B. Norris, Sept. 10th

Smith, Russell W. and Julia G. Dudley, Sept. 25th

Sandridge, John T. and Mimmie Lee Smith, Dec. 24th

1913

Smith, Emmett C. and Margaret C. Moran, Apr. 26th

Shilling, Eric K. and Claire L. Branden, June 15th

Snoddy, John L. and Hannah Martin, Aug. 6th

1914

Smith, Herman and Rosa A. Smith, Jan. 15th

Scruggs, Benj. J. and Anna A. Haden, Mar. 4th

Sacre, George and Bessie L. Gentry, July 21st

Snead, Robert L. and Elizabeth Walton, Sept. 2nd

Smith, Howard W. and Hallie M. James, Dec. 16th

1915

Snidow, Conley T. and Maybelle C. Chestnutt, June 30th

Snyder, Ira D. and Ora L. Guthrie, July 1st

Sutherland, Edward S. and Maggie S. Mooney, Sept. 22nd

Sensibaugh, John P. and Sallie J. Harris, Oct. 6th

Shaw, Joseph C. and Willie M. Walden, Dec. 11th

1916

Saunders, Roland L. and Maggie L. Bishop, Apr. 27th

Sims, Jessie L. and Eva H. White, June 7th

Schnabeb, Henry M. and Beatrice M. Cummings, June 24th

Satterfield, Wm. L. and Nellie B. Hale, Aug. 22nd

Smith, Chas. H. and Addie V. Kenney, Sept. 8th

1917

Snead, Robt. L. and Alice M. Smith, Jan. 27th

Sandridge, Roy P. and Jane P. Gleason, Mar. 8th

Shepherd, S. W. and May B. Wood, Apr. 25th

Sands, Geo. Dewey and Nelle Evelyn Bathis, June 28th

Sacre, Alfred and Addie Mays, Aug. 20th

Shaver, Duke Lee and E. Louise Houchens, Sept. 8th

1918

Smith, Everett Monroe and Bettine McK. Pratt, Feb. 25th

Saltsman, Saml. A. and Elizabeth W. Wood, May 3rd

Scribner, DeMolay and Annie Evelyn Jones, June 9th

Shiflett, Dewey H. and Mary Connell, Dec. 24th

1919

Sanford, Walter Erving and Cora Elsie Morris, Mar. 13th

Smith, Shirley H. and Margaret P. Rothwell, June 28th

Smith, Everett Earley and Alberta Virginia Price, June 29th

Smith, Walter L. and Ola Bell Powell, Aug. 30th

Sumner, Chas. F. and Pickett A. Holmquest, Oct. 4th

Smith, Benj. L. and Lucille Hackney, Oct. 27th

Spencer, Chas. F. and Florence E. Dragoo, Nov. 9th

Snoddy, Laurence F. and Beatrice M. Huffman, Nov. 15th

1920

Seiler, Stuart S. and Ruth Pearl Geer, Feb. 14th

Saksen, Louis Jr. and Mattie Payne Hughes, June 2nd

Sneed, Benj. Nobel and Lona Belle Calhoun, June 12th

Smith, Jas. Robert Jr. and Elizabeth C. Baumgartner, Aug. 25th

Setzler, Geo. B. and Jane C. Gaiyot, Oct. 20th

Stewart, Chas. W. and Lucy Newton, Dec. 23rd

Stanfield, Harold E. and Jane B. Wingfield, Dec. 30th

1921

Sisk, H. Lester and Lena E. Wade, June 7th

Stratton, Vernon Newton and Alice Gertrude Eutwisle, June 7th

Sandridge, Allen L. and Amanda C. Davis, July 23rd

Stultz, Wm. Lewis and Gladys Dean Valentine, Dec. 20th

Sterling, Carl Soloman and Ida Adelaide Rubin, Dec. 27th

1922

Sheppe, Dr. Wm. Marco and Olive Row Harris, Feb. 16th

Spencer, Luther S. and Joycelyn L. Clarke, Feb. 22nd

Sullivan, Dennis L. and Dorothy K. Harton, Feb. 25th

Snyder, Leo and Mabel E. Sprouse, Mar. 18th

Sour, Henry Albert and Kathryn Chalmers Minson, July 17th

Sizmore, Freeman and Annie Bingler, Aug. 24th

Shaw, John Pierson and Treeby Coleman Michie, Sept. 9th

Smith, Jeffries M. and Virgie Bunch, Nov. 26th

Staley, Jas. Henry G. and Mattie Fielding, Dec. 24th

Spencer, Clarence Edwd. and Irene Goolsby, Dec. 23rd

1923

Shepherd, Guy Howard and Willie Lee Moore, Feb. 25th

Sillett, Benj. H. and Effie Pearle Pritchett, Apr. 14th

Street, Alan T. and Madeline C. Blakey, Aug. 18th

Scott, Stoner Minter and Catherine Peyton, Sept. 19th

1924

Sprouse, Jesse Maury and Mamie Gibson, Apr. 19th

Standish, Granville S. and Sarah Mildred Pettitte, July 8th

Stewart, Harry E. and Inez E. Drumheller, Aug. 30th

Simms, Wm. M. and Virginia Mildred Austin, Aug. 28th

Shanks, Geo. Andrew and Laura Belle Jarrell, Sept. 20th

Shisler, Robt. H. and Kathleen V. Petitt, Oct. 15th

Schiveickert, Louie C. and Alia Carroll, Nov. 8th

Smith, Joseph O. and Margaret L. Safley, Oct. 29th

1925

Simms, Roy Ashly and Jo Simms, Nov. 20th

1926

Staples, Albert A. and Elizabeth M. King, Feb. 16th

Stearns, Palmer N. and Lucile K. Williams, Apr. 10th

Smith, Irvin Miller and Lois Agathea Hodge, May 7th

Sibrell, Wm. Henry and Margaret S. Bruffey, June 16th

Staley, Joseph Patrick and Elizabeth Jane Clarity, June 23rd

Sandridge, Dabney W. and Clara Amelia Shiflett, July 10th

Stone, James A. and Mabel Desler, Aug. 3rd

Smith, Geo. Thomas and Helen Gould Johnson, Sept. 1st

Sumner, Emmett A. and Eller Gertrude Rea, Sept. 3rd

Seay, Walter D. and Margarette L. Snyder, Oct. 9th

Sprouse, Charlie Alfred and Lula Y. Birckhead, Oct. 6th

Sawyer, Sim and Nora Sprouse, Oct. 25th

Swecker, John Preston and Emma Va. Wilkins, Oct. 27th

Snoddy, John Lee and Bessie Rebecca Hilderbrand, Nov. 6th

Spencer, George Clyde and Louise Katharine Muse, Dec. 25th

1927

Sprague, George Ellsworth and Josephine Sprague, Mar. 29th

Smith, William and Elizabeth Gertrude Rhodes, May 9th

Snead, J. Melvin and Nella Marill Young, Aug. 20th

Sprouse, Herman A. and Irma Edna Martin, Sept. 14th

Short, Raymond Don and Ollie Ellen Marsh, Oct. 12th

Suchting, Henry, Jr. and Marita Rose Carroll, Oct. 21st

Stenrud, Earl Roy and Florence Bertha Figgat, Oct. 29th

Shumate, Wm. Bailey and Sarah Louise Petitt, Nov. 5th

Shackelford, Neil Henry and Pauline Elizabeth Breeden, Dec. 24th

1928

Sacre, Robert Lee and Julia Childs, Jan. 3rd

Smith, John Edward and Elizabeth Winston Elliott, Feb. 25th

Scruggs, Claude Houston and Tiny Bernice Garrison, Mar. 30th

Spicer, Murray Stacy and Margueritte Browning Head, Apr. 28th

Shiflett, Edw. Thurman and Pauline Elizabeth Cash, May 16th

Snead, Littleton Carroll and Virginia Martha Belew, June 9th

Stubbs, Perry Roderick and Susie Evelyn Coleman, July 1st

Scruggs, John Wesley and Lillian Hope Ford, July 25th

Smith, Ernle Vivian and Isabell Cropp, Aug. 24th

Shelton, Oits Norcross and Ruth Blackwell, Sept. 26th

Sacres, Mott Murray and Erby Della Morris, Oct. 20th

Smith, Edward Asa and Edna Marie Lang, Dec. 4th

1929

Sullivan, Emmett and Agens Cecelia Purvis, Jan. 19th

Savin, Garnett West, III and Winifred Davis Toombs, Feb. 1st

Stokes, Bennie Wallace and May Jane Sprigg, May 28th

Snow, Elmer James and Constance Camilla Kidd, June 3rd

Sandridge, Albert Lewis and Eula Mae Davis, June 23rd

Saunders, Jas. Bernard and Pauline Mae Alexander, Aug. 17th

Shearon, Wm. Anthony and Dorothy England Carter, Aug. 31st

Smith, Robert Archie and Ruth Strickler Hern, Dec. 21st

T

1888
Thomas, M. C. and Lula T. Snead, Dec. 5th
1889
Tompkins, Jas. Henry and Ida Easton, Jan. 30th

1890
Tate, Henry Rich'd. and Georgia A. Shackelford, July 17th

Tilman, H. N. and S. J. Jarman, Sept. 2nd

1893
Tatum, B. H. and Rosa E. Carper, Nov. 28th

1894
Thurman, Albert Lee and Mary M. Cochran, Apr. 23rd

Tompkins, Leslie H. and Laru Adalaide Carver, June 27th

1895
Tucker, G. Pinckerny and Florence W. Roush, June 9th

Thomas, James E. and Daisy D. Spencer, June 26th

1896
Turner, S. H. and C. F. Cleveland, July 7th

Thomas, A. L. and Birdie L. Bailey, Aug. 20th

1897
Thomas, Edwin J. and Eva V. Kirby, Sept. 25th

1898
Tobias, David A. and Tilly Kinlwieth, Mar. 21st

1899
Thomas, Ned and Sophie Brooks, Nov. 1st

1901
Tate, John H. and Elsie G. Gardner, July 10th

Tate, Armonde D. and Rosa Bell Maynard, Sept. 18th

Turner, Chas. W. and Rosalie C. Harris, Dec. 18th

1902
Thomas, D. P. and J. L. Madison, Jan. 15th

1903
Tyler, Henry B. and Laura E. Wood, Jan. 19th

Turner, Mark and Mrs. Angie Hase, May 18th

Taylor, Linwood C. and Nannie G. Wright, Dec. 15th

1904
Triplett, R. and Lelia Jackson, June 1st

1905
Thimal, Charles J. and Eva Lee Davis, Jan. 17th

Trevillian, Robt. C. and Mamie A. Perry, Sept. 6th

Tinder, C. F. and J. M. Woodson, Oct. 31st

1906
Tennant, Chas. C. and Adelaide J. Fletcher, Mar. 5th

Thomas, Martin L. and Virgie Dentin, July 3rd

1907
Thomas, Grover C. and Dicie E. Lanum, Aug. 11th

1909
Truslow, Joseph R. and Martha Marsh, Feb. 10th

Thomasson, David W. and Minnie G. Walten, May 18th

Todd, Gordon L. and Adeline P. Rixey, Oct. 25th

Taylor, Wm. R. and Sarah E. Draper, Dec. 30th

1910
Twyman, Fred W. and Sallie W. Baker, July 6th

1911
Thompson, Charles H. and Mary H. Tatum, June 7th

Thomas, Joseph and Lucy A. Healey, July 5th

Turner, Fancher L. and Gladys L. Terrell, Nov. 29th

1912
Taylor, Charles C. and Lizzie Carvin, Apr. 10th

1913
Tatum, Jesse C. and Catharine Touring, Apr. 24th

1914
Thomas, Clarence R. and Annie M. C. Godwin, Feb. 18th

1915

Thomas, Wilbur W. and Cora L. Wine, Jan. 21st

Trevillian, Wallace D. and Sadie E. Davis, Mar. 6th

1916

Towsey, Elliott W. and Alma E. Gooch, July 24th

Taylor, Earle H. and Carrie E. Bussenger, Dec. 21st

1917

Thurston, Austin Dan'l. and Dennis Scott Pratt, May 31st

Todd, Thos. H. and Sallie Stuart Bolling, Aug. 15th

1918

Taylor, Daniel Carlton and Dorthy W. Jacobs, Jan. 9th

Tilman, Thos. Howard and Virginia Floyd Walsh, Sept. 28th

Taylor, Manson and Addie Payne, Dec. 24th

Tyler, Chas. F. and Mary M. Mortimer, Dec. 24th

1919

Tucker, Wm. C. and Margaret Fife, Apr. 3rd

Thompson, Jas. E. and Marion E. Ballard, June 16th

Thomas, Walker W. and Mary A. Thurston, July 8th

Taylor, Clarence M. and Grace Eliz. Willis, Aug. 17th

Tilman, Leonard L. and Pearl S. Lang, Aug. 23rd

Thomas, Delaware P. and Maude M. Graves, Sept. 13th

Thomas, Robert and Emily Southall Waters, Sept. 20th

Thomas, Oscar L. and Sarah Margarette Wilmer, Dec. 27th

1920

Thomas, Roy S. and Ethel May Wheat, May 5th

1921

Tankersly, Jas. R. and Madge Ward, Feb. 16th

Thrasher, Herbert F. and Crystal S. Johnson, March 16th

Thornton, Watkins L. and Kansas Bartley, June 2nd

1922

Thacker, Everett Thos. and Catherine Eliz. Estes, February 14th

1923

Thompson, Douglas and Gertrude Harlow, Feb. 10th

Thomas, Albert B. and Grace D. Webber, March 31st

Tranium, Thos. J. and Lois P. Crawford, Sept. 8th

Tate, Russell and Lizzie Harlowe, Sept. 8th

Triptapoe, Harry G. and Mary Lucille Wilson, Oct. 10th

1924

Tessmann, Arthur M. and Ida T. Sieburg, Apr. 12th

Terry, Alonza E. and Cedora E. Bunch, July 10th

Taylor, Wm. Riley and Alice May Bourne, July 16th

1925

Trainum, Jno. L. Jr. and Gladys Ione Buck, Jan. 15th

Tompkins, Edwin Harrison and Doris Maude Driscoll, Sept. 19th

Thomas, Otis and Margie Shiflett, Oct. 27th

Turner, Wm. L. and Pearl Powell, June 24th

1926

Tyler, James R. and Mary Katherine Bruce, Sept. 1st

Thomas, Harvey Lee and Ruby Dunn Herndon, Dec. 11th

Taylor, Randolph William and Jean Falconer Grant, Dec. 18th

1927

Terrell, Thos. Alexander and Margerette A. Lang, Apr. 2nd

Thomas, Hugh Taylor and Mary Campbell Kirby, Apr. 2nd

Thorne, St. Clair Laurence and Nina Reed Stout, Apr. 4th

Taylor, Hugh Jackson and Sallie Mae Beck, Nov. 5th

Thomas, Allen F. and Virginia West, Nov. 25th

1929

Turner, Edwin Lewis and Dorothy Louise Hughes, Feb. 23rd

Turner, Phil Clarkson Sargeant and Marian Anne Dabney, June 15th

Taylor, Aubrey Maphis and Evelyn Va. Newton, Aug. 3rd

Tighe, Matthew G. and Helen Ann Watkins, Oct. 6th

U

1894

Uoyes, Bradford and Repie K. Young, Feb. 27th

1911

Updike, Leslie and Lula May Thomasson, Apr. 17th

Uedemann, Rollants and Blanche H. Jarman, Sept. 5th

1917

Updike, Gilbert S. and Alma J. Humphrey, Oct. 27th

1922

Upchurch, Wade H. and Sarah B. Florence, January 19th

1927

Updike, Robert Lee and Mrs. Agens Craft, May 24th

V

1890

Voigt, Louis, Jr. and S. P. Moses, Nov. 31st

1898

Via, Harold C. and Annie E. W. Brown, Aug. 9th

1908

Venable, Ernest H. and Elizabeth R. Dabney, Sept. 8th

1912

Via, Herbert A. and Hallie T. Lovegrove, Feb. 14th

1913

VanDwen, Melberell B. and Betty H. Johnson, Apr. 17th
Via, James H. and Flora M. Mansfield, June 25th
Valenzuela, John and Jane Marion Robertson, Dec. 15th
Via, Guy F. and Mary E. Carter, Jan. 9th

1916

Via, Bernard Starr and Gladys Armen Hawkins, Dec. 28th

1917

Valentine, Cecil L. and Bessie Conway Hughes, Nov. 10th

1918

Via, Dan Otto and Josephine G. Carter, July 10th

1920

Via, David M. and Madge Lee Bruffey, March 30th
Vasseur, H. Franklin and Nettie F. Ward, May 12th
Via, Edgar and Guila Estes, Oct. 5th

1921

Via, Henry and Ola L. Craig, Jan. 17th
Viar, Thomas Ivan and Carrie Walton Harlowe, Apr. 23rd

1922

Via, Roy J. and Mattie Va. Ferneyhough, Sept. 30th

1923

Voorhess, Louise F. and Elizabeth A. Peyton, June 2nd
Vest, J. Austin and Bessie L. Campbell, July 3rd
Via, Earl Hampton and Adelaide C. Watson, Dec. 27th

1924

Vaughan, Earl H. and Amy T. Young, Oct. 16th

1926

Via, Harold A. and Louise A. Leachman, Feb. 25th

1927

Van de Kamp, Peter and Emma M. B. Basenan, May 24th

1928

Van Nosdoll, Leslie and Pearl Carter Helmandollar, Dec. 10th

1929

Van Fossen, Cecil King and Sadie Bezril Maupin, Aug. 24th
Via, Roy Jake and Shela Vivinda Estes, Oct. 16th

W

1888

Webb, Saml. N. and Alice Walker, Oct. 18th
Ware, John H. Jr. and Lula S. Covington, Oct. 24th
Ward, Arron and Mildred A. Brown, Jan. 30th

1889

Williamson, H. M. and Maud G. Mallory, Feb. 25th

1890

Wilkinson, Walter and N. O. Garrison, Apr. 4th
Waddell, W. W. and M. T. Payne, Dec. 10th

1891

Witkins, Wm. L. and Katie R. Bromhomer, Jan. 21st
Whitlock, Wm. T. and Annie P. Purvis, Jan. 28th
Williams, Jas. F. and Emmie W. Edwards, June 1st
Wood, Ed. P. and Cebrta A. Scruggs, June 17th
Wise, S. A. annd S. J. Estes, July 29th
Wills, F. C. and M. M. Terrill, Nov. 25th

1892

Walsh, Robt. E. and Mary E. Huffman, Oct. 12th

1893

Wright, Jas. W. and Maud E. Suler, June 14th

1894

Whittington, C. A. and Susan Booth, July 14th
Waters, Thos. L. and Emily V. Southall, Oct. 10th

1895

Ward, Harry K. and Mattie J. Beasley, Dec. 17th

1897

Waddell, J. N. and M. B. Daniel, May 25th
Wheeler, James B. and Annie R. Clarke, Oct. 26th

1898

Wood, J. H. and R. L. Newman, Dec. 28th

1900

Wood, Oscar and Blanch Sullivan, Feb. 13th
Wood, O. M. and F. M. Johns, Nov. 17th

1901

Williston, Robt. L. and M. R. Bryan, June 22nd
Wingfield, W. T. and S. Roberta Fitch, Dec. 10th

1902

Wade, Percy F. and Lucy L. Toms, Dec. 24th

1903

Waters, Herbert Dorsey and Frances T. Bland Walker, Feb. 14th
Whaite, Jno. S. and Hettie M. Wolfe, Dec. 7th

1904

Wood, Hayes W. and Annie L. Harris, May 18th
Wallace, E. M. and Daisy A. Jones, Aug. 10th
Wisemein, Thos. H. and Birdye F. Purvis, Dec. 8th

1905

Wilkins, Jno. E. and Cary H. Embrey, Feb. 28th
Weeks, Jno. H. and Dora Mays, March 29th
Wagner, Isaac R. and Bessie L. Conway, June 15th
Woodson, Eugene T. and Mary S. Morgan, Oct. 21st
White, Dr. C. C. and Emma Lee Smith, Oct. 25th
Wagner, Albert L. and Virgie Hudson, Dec. 29th

1906

Wilson, Alexander and Sallie R. Meeks, March 8th

1907

West, Richard and Ada E. Pearce, June 15th

Wilkerson, Albert W. and Mattie H. Goode, Nov. 12th
Walker, Albert E. and Bessie C. Valentine, Dec. 31st

1909

Wunder, C. Richard and Anna M. Russow, Jan. 1st
Westcott, Bernard E. and Annie E. Willis, Aug. 24th
Williams, Henry H. and Frances C. Berkeley, Aug. 28th

1910

Walker, Robt. C. and Etta L. Tyler, July 1st

1911

Weaver, Jno. W. and Mary B. Wingfield, April 25th
Wright, Chas. L. and Mary L. Wingfield, July 4th

1912

Walden, Lonnie C. and I. Zetta D. Lamb, Apr. 22nd
Wolfe, Roy E. and Gladys V. Alexander, Apr. 27th
Woods, Charles S. and Kate P. Daniel, Oct. 29th
Walker, Charles H. and Mrs. Mary M. Wills, Dec 10th

1913

Woodward, George A. and Lutie Hall Rea, Jan. 7th
Woodie, Wm. H. and Thalma B. Mayo, Sept. 9th

1914

Witt, John W. and Sallie F. Morris, Feb. 27th
Walters, Jesse C. and Bertha G. Landon, Oct. 14th
Wilson, J. A. and Frances Reynolds, Oct. 14th
Wilson, Monroe O. and Mary S. Goss, Dec. 9th
Wood, Carroll M. and Ada L. Mann, Dec. 22nd

1915

Williams, George P. and Emma S. Young, Jan. 4th
Wiebel, R. A. and Katie E. Purvis, Dec. 21st
Wyne, Robert M. and Loula M. Southard, Dec. 27th

1916

Watson, Oscar and Lucinda F. Kirby, Apr. 22nd
Willis, Berry D. and Helene V. Martin, Oct. 28th

1917

Woodson, Hunter D. and Robinett Pace, Feb. 24th
Wolford, J. H. and Lester G. Keuzer, March 20th

Wilkins, Alfred R. and Annie Lee Birckhead, April 16th

Wood, Harrison and Blanche D. Sullivan, May 5th

Woods, Frank W. and Daisy L. Dettor, June 20th

Woodson, Shepherd and Libby L. Chewning, July 21st

Wells, Geo. H. and Mary Barbour Powers, Dec. 12th

1918

Ward, Chas. C. and Estelle V. Davis, Feb. 9th

Walker, Edw. V. and M. Evelyn Irving, April 6th

Woodberry, Dr. H. S. and Ruby F. Davis, April 7th

Wells, John A. and Bertha Cammie Dameron, April 27th

Walker, Jno. E. and Annie E. Goodyear, June 3rd

Watson, Herbert Berger and Mary Elizabeth Whisemant, June 20th

White, Jno. Shelton and Alice Chancellor Davis, June 27th

Watson, J. F. and Laura E. Grady, June 29th

Wood, Walter T. and Maude Agnes Lang, Aug. 12th

Wilkerson, Ira Davis and Daisy Lee Purvis, Sept. 26th

Walker, Chas. C. and Helen McCall, Nov. 12th

1919

Wilkins, Jno. W. and Evelyn M. Wheeler, Sept. 18th

Waltrip, Thos. L. and Daisy Hooker, Sept. 27th

Wood, Howard and Eunice Alexander, Oct. 23rd

Williams, Jas. S. and Lillian B. Kirby, Nov. 15th

Wade, Jas. B. and Wilvie Va. Robinson, Nov. 20th

Whitlock, Claudius E. and Mary C. Howard, Nov. 29th

1920

Wingfield, Vernon Edw. and Mary Jane Clements, April 23rd

Wheeler, Luther L. and Elizabeth R. Thomas, April 26th

Wendt, Jno. Scott and Mary V. Peyton, June 7th

Weast, Frank P. and Juanita M. Aobogast, Aug. 19th

Wells, Benjamin J. and Katheryn R. Howard, Aug. 23rd

Weaver, Havard F. and Daisy E. Wingfield, Sept. 21st

Wilson, Wm. Ronald and Annie T. Nookes, Oct. 19th

Wood, Jno. R. and Catherine L. Gibson, Dec. 14th

Wilmer, Williams and Garnett Norvell, Dec. 18th

Watson, Elijah D. and Minnie E. Slaughter, Dec. 22nd

1921

Wood, Charlie E. and Mollie May Wood, Jan. 4th

Whitlock, W. Carl and Sara E. Hamilton, Jan. 5th

Watkins, Thomas J. and Edith E. Vassur, May 1st

Wood, Bernard A. and Bessie M. Jones, June 4th

Wilson, Eldon D. and Kate Williamson Burnley, June 8th

Wingfield, Roy L. and Evelyn Bingler, Oct. 22nd

Wade, Harry E. and Mrs. Lizzie Lamm, Dec. 26th

1922

Watson, Frederick L. and Marg. W. Waddell, Jan. 14th

Wilson, James S. and Bertha Shiflett, Jan. 21st

Woodward, Raymond W. and Lella L. Huckstep, April 11th

Wright, Robt. L. and Julia C. Wingfield, April 26th

Weaver, John Chas. and Magie R. Hewitt, July 17th

Wilson, Harry Minor and Catherine E. Vasseur, Oct. 4th

Wright, James M. and Gidie M. Walters, Oct. 24th

Wright, Jas. B. and Lottie B. Dudley, Dec. 15th

1923

Wade, Guy Eric and Fern Hester Craven, June 2nd

Wood, James Edwin and Emily Mildred Battle, June 27th

Ward, Rogers E. and Mattie L. Purvis, July 21st

Watts, Robt. E. and L. Elsie Thacker, Dec. 18th

Wishon, Everett F. and Bertha E. Thomas, Dec. 26th

1924

Weaver, Walter C. and Earcel M. O'Brien, Feb. 9th

Woodson, Hunter D. and Ruth Schultz, March 15th

Woods, Stanley Early and Emmie Estelle Dudley, April 17th

Walker, Geo. Edw. and Julia F. Sinclair, May 31st

Weinberg, Sol B. and Florence G. Buckelew, June 29th

Wood, Algerman A. and Gertrude E. Jones, Aug. 9th

Watson, Marion Howell and Alma Anne Mays, Aug. 23rd

Walker, Charlie and Nellie Wood, Oct. 17th

Walton, Claude Miller and Maude Marie Hicks, Dec. 24th

1925

Watkins, Howard S. and Martha Lois Coiner, Jan. 17th

Walker, John N. Jr. and Lois B. Driscoll, Oct. 15th

Wingfield, Jno. Wilbert and Bertha May Bingler, Nov. 25th

1926

Wood, George W. and Nellie A. Coleman, Jan. 30th

Wallace, Wm. Earl and Louise Lambert, Feb. 19th

Womack, Herbert C. and Corinne E. Carter, March 8th

Walker, George Edw. Jr. and Mary Elizabeth Ashhurst, April 9th

White, Jno. Henry and Ruby Salome Alban, Apr. 29th

Walp, Paul Knott and Edna Wilma McNolly, June 17th

Worley, Flynn O. and Bessie F. Hurley, Sept. 8th

Woodson, John Talton and Mrs. Mary E. Cason, Oct. 31st

1927

Williams, Clayton D. and Norma D. Brand, Jan. 22nd

Watson, Corlton Egbert and Helen Gregory Breeden, Feb. 14th

Wiley, Gordon Eldridge and Mildred Louise Mays, May 20th

Wood, James Price and Lelia Byrd Gilkerson, May 25th

Wilson, Hube Bluch and Emma Marie Lyon, July 2nd

Weber, Edward H. and Hallie L. Thomas, Dec. 31st

1928

William, Gray and Eleanor Snowden Fishburne, Feb. 18th

Wilson, Theodore and Helen May Bethel, May 7th

Wentz, Harry Phillips and Navora Katherine Roberts, Aug. 4th

Williams, Frederick and Carrie Bell Thompson, Sept. 13th

Wood, Russell E. and Ada M. Johnson, Oct. 13th

1929

Woods, William S. D. and Page Bird, April 17th

Williston, Wm. Wardlow and Sally Roane McMurdo, June 6th

Webb, Joseph Wildare and Myrtle Irene Wood, June 25th

Woods, John Rodes and Polydora Eugenia Goss, Sept. 4th

Worrall, James Mohr Douglass and Isabel Anderson Flippin, Nov. 17th

Y

1909

Yowell, Guy D. and Zelma L. King, Feb. 16th

Young, Rosser C. and Cynthia Craig, Dec. 23rd

1913

Yarbough, Henry C. and Blanch Ramsey, May 30th

1921

Yowell, Roy McK. and Louise R. Chisholm, May 3rd

1923

Young, Tyler L. and Mildred L. Mitchell, Oct. 31st

1924

Young, Jno. Coleman, Jr. and Evie Jewel Rivercomb, Sept. 12th

1926

Young, Walter C. and Eunice E. Harlowe, Jan. 16th

Youden, Harry and Gertrude West, Aug. 24th

1927

Yancey, Albert Shipp and Charlotte Elizabeth Jennings, Dec. 26th

1928

Yoe, Harry Howard and Portia Marie Higgins, Sept. 2nd

1929

York, Levi Dee and Sue Gee Smith, June 22nd

www.ingramcontent.com/pod-product-compliance
Lightning Source LLC
Chambersburg PA
CBHW020454030426
42337CB00011B/117